Houghton
Mifflin
Harcourt

CALIFORNIA
JOURNEYS

2

D0904712

CALIFORNIA
JOURNEYS

Program Consultants

Shervaughnna Anderson · Marty Hougen
Carol Jago · Erik Palmer · Shane Templeton
Sheila Valencia · MaryEllen Vogt

Consulting Author · Irene Fountas

2

● ● ● ● ● ● **TEACHER**

Program Consultants

Teach with confidence. Journeys is a research-based, comprehensive English Language Arts program developed by literacy experts and backed by proven results.

Shervaughnna Anderson Director of the California Reading and Literature Project at UCLA. Ms. Anderson brings an extensive knowledge of coaching and has experience in establishing and nurturing professional learning communities. She is a former teacher, coach, and site- and district-level administrator. In addition, she has served on state committees addressing English Language Arts instruction, English Learners, and instructional practices for African American students.

Martha Hougen National consultant, presenter, researcher, and author. Areas of expertise include differentiating instruction for students with learning difficulties, including those with learning disabilities and dyslexia. Recently her focus has been on working with teacher educators to enhance teacher and leader preparation to better meet the needs of all students.

Carol Jago Teacher of English for 32 years and director of the California Reading and Literature Project at UCLA. Past president of the National Council of Teachers of English, Ms. Jago edits the journal of the California Association of Teachers of English, *California English*. Ms. Jago has served on the planning committee for the 2009 NAEP Reading Framework and the 2011 NAEP Writing Framework.

Erik Palmer Veteran teacher and education consultant based in Denver, Colorado. Dr. Palmer's areas of focus include improving oral communication, promoting technology in classroom presentations, and updating instruction through the use of digital tools. He has worked with school districts in the United States and Mexico in the area of teaching speaking skills to 21st century learners. He has also worked with private and public schools as a consultant on two topics: teaching oral communication and showing non-tech-savvy teachers practical ways to use technology in the classroom. He is a frequent presenter and keynote speaker at state, regional, and national conferences of education professionals.

Shane Templeton Foundation Professor Emeritus of Literacy Studies at the University of Nevada, Reno. A former classroom teacher at the primary and secondary levels, Dr. Templeton's research has focused on developmental word knowledge in elementary, middle, and high school students. He is co-author of *Words Their Way; Vocabulary Their Way: Word Study for Middle and Secondary Students; Words Their Way with Struggling Readers, Grades 4–12; and Words Their Way with English Learners.* His other books include *Teaching the Integrated Language Arts and Children's Literacy: Contexts for Meaningful Learning.*

MaryEllen Vogt Distinguished Professor Emerita of Education at California State University, Long Beach. Dr. Vogt has been a classroom teacher, reading specialist, special education specialist, curriculum coordinator, and university teacher educator, and served as president of the International Reading Association. Her research interests include improving comprehension in the content areas, teacher change and development, and content literacy and language acquisition for English learners. Dr. Vogt was inducted into the California Reading Hall of Fame and received her university's Distinguished Faculty Teaching Award.

Sheila Valencia Professor of Language, Literacy, and Culture at the University of Washington, where she teaches and conducts research in the areas of literacy assessment, instruction, policy, and teacher development. Dr. Valencia began her career as a 6th grade teacher in an urban district in New York City, followed by several years as a teacher in a rural district, and then as director of a reading clinic for students with reading difficulties. She went back into public education for six years before returning to academia as a teacher educator and researcher. In 2008, Dr. Valencia was inducted into the International Reading Association Reading Hall of Fame.

SPECIAL CONSULTANT

Irene Fountas Former classroom teacher, language arts specialist, and consultant in school districts across the nation and abroad. Ms. Fountas works extensively in the literacy education field and directs the Literacy Collaborative in the School of Education at Lesley University. She spends her time providing training to literacy coaches and key administrators who play roles in teacher development and school improvement. Along with her co-author, Gay Su Pinnell, she has developed the country's most widely used standard for leveling text for small group instruction. Dr. Fountas is the recipient of the Greater Boston Council and the International Reading Association's Celebrate Literacy Awards.

Unit 4

Heroes and Helpers

Student Book Table of Contents

Read and Comprehend
Every week in the Student Book, children prepare to read and discuss the Anchor Text through the lens of the lesson topic.

Where Do Polar Bears Live?
INFORMATIONAL TEXT
by Sarah L. Thomson • illustrated by Jason Chin

2

3

Grammar
Interactive grammar lessons, which children apply to speaking and writing, also feature a connection to the lesson's writing task.

Exemplar Texts
Exemplar texts in the *Student Book* and in Extended Reading lessons ensure that children are consistently engaging with appropriately complex and high-quality text.

Heroes and Helpers

ENGLISH LANGUAGE SUPPORT

Cognate Wall/Pared de Cognados

All Proficiencies Begin an English-Spanish cognate wall for this unit, focusing on general academic vocabulary and domain-specific vocabulary. Start with words useful for the activities on this page. Add simple sketches or pictures to help children remember the words. Guide them to use the words in their everyday speech and writing. **ELD** ELD.PI.2.12b

English	Spanish
special	especial
community	comunidad
extraordinary	extraordinario/a
problem	problema

Use Visuals Use online Picture Cards ⤢ as a discussion aid and to help children think of words about the topic of heroes and helping. Suggested images: *badge, crossing guard, doctor, dog, family, firefighter, hammer, hands, hospital, lifeguard, map, mechanic, medicine, money, police officer, smile, teacher*

Motivate and Engage

Have children open to **Student Book** p. 9, and tell them that today they will begin a unit called Heroes and Helpers. Play the Stream to Start media ⤢ to spark children's curiosity about the unit topic and discuss it. Ask questions such as these: **ELA** SL.2.2 **ELD** ELD.PI.2.1, ELD.PI.2.6

- What is a hero?

- Who are some helpers you know at school or in your community?

Access Prior Knowledge

Write *People Who Help* on chart paper or on the board, read it with children, and circle the phrase to become the center of a web. Then ask this question: *Who are people who help others?* Have children recall information from the video or from their own experience as you add their ideas to the web. Throughout the unit, add new information to the web when children mention something new about people who help others. **ELA** W.2.8 **ELD** ELD.PI.2.1, ELD.PI.2.12a

ENGLISH LANGUAGE SUPPORT Encourage children to express their knowledge about heroes in various ways, such as in their first language or by drawing a picture and sharing it with the class. Say the English words as you add each to the web, use each word in a sentence, and have the group repeat. **ELD** ELD.PI.2.1, ELD.PI.2.12a

Analyze an Image

Ask children to look closely at the photograph on **Student Book** p. 9 and to think about what it means to be a hero or a helper.

Think Allow some quiet time for children to think about the image. Ask them what words they would use to describe a hero or a helper.

Pair Have partners discuss these questions:

- How can you tell the boy is a superhero? What clues in the photo help you know?

- How are heroes and helpers different from other people? Why do you think this?

Share Call on pairs to share their responses and evidence from the photograph that supports their insights. Encourage children to ask questions as needed for clarification. Guide children to follow discussion rules, such as listening carefully to speakers, taking turns speaking, and staying on topic.
ELA SL.2.1a **ELD** ELD.PI.2.1, ELD.PI.2.3, ELD.PI.2.5, ELD.PI.2.6

Heroes and Helpers

Stream to Start

 To be afraid and to be brave is the best kind of courage of all.

— Alice Dalgliesh

Performance Task Preview

At the end of this unit, you will think about two of the texts you have read. Then you will use information from the texts to write a story about an adventure you take!

fyi
hmhfyi.com

1

Channel One News®

9

BACKGROUND

The quotation for this unit comes from "a pioneer in the field of children's historical fiction", Alice Dalgliesh, born in 1893. Growing up, Alice loved reading and hearing her grandfather's stories. She began writing when she was only six years old and won her first writing contest when she was just 14. In 1912, she moved to America to go to college for teaching. After she received her master's degree from Teachers' College at Columbia University, Alice taught college courses on children's literature and taught grade school as well.

Alice was hired at Charles Scribner's and Sons as their first female editor. In 1924, she published her first children's book, *A Happy School Year*. She went on to write, and even illustrate, over 40 fiction and nonfiction books, most of which were children's books.

Her works are recognized for their historical accuracy and detail with believable characters and dramatic plots. Ms. Dalgliesh won Newbery Honors for three of her books, including *The Courage of Sarah Noble* and *The Bears of Hemlock Mountain*. She died at the age of 86 in 1979 in Woodbury, Connecticut.

Discuss the Quotation

Read aloud the quotation on **Student Book** p. 9 to children, and then reread it with them. Ask them to tell what they think the quotation means and discuss what courage is. Explain that when we have courage, we believe that we can be brave and face something even if we are afraid. Have children use words from the web to tell how people help. For example: *A police officer helps by catching criminals. A doctor helps by making you feel better.*
ELA SL.2.1 **ELD** ELD.PI.2.1

ENGLISH LANGUAGE SUPPORT Tell children that the word *brave* means "possessing courage." When we are brave, we have the courage to face our fears. Ask children to think of things brave people do. Then ask how heroes and helpers have courage.
ELD ELD.PII.2.4

Preview Unit Texts

Have children page through the selections in the unit. Have them describe a few of the people and things they see and what is happening in various illustrations and photographs. Discuss what the selections might be about and which show people who help others. **ELA** SL.2.1 **ELD** ELD.PI.2.1

Performance Task Review

Read the information on **Student Book** p. 9 to children. Explain that at the end of the unit, they will use what they have read to help them write a story about an imaginary adventure they could take. The unit texts and the lessons below will prepare children for this culminating task.

Lesson	Grammar	Writing
16	Pronouns	Story Paragraph
17	Subject-Verb Agreement	Story Paragraph
18	The Verb *be*	Descriptive Paragraph
19	Commas in Dates and Places	Fictional Story
20	Commas in a Series	Fictional Story

Digital Resources

Encourage children to research the unit topic on their own.

fyi
hmhfyi.com

Channel One News®

		Lesson 16	**Lesson 17**	**Lesson 18**
	ESSENTIAL QUESTION	*How can helping others make you feel good?*	*Why is it important to keep trying even if something is difficult to do?*	*Why are reading and writing important?*
Whole Group	**Oral Language**	**Teacher Read Aloud** "A Better Way to Save"	**Teacher Read Aloud** "The Crowd Roared!"	**Teacher Read Aloud** "Doctor Salk's Treasure"
	Vocabulary	Oral Vocabulary Homographs	Oral Vocabulary Antonyms	Oral Vocabulary Suffixes -y, -ful
	Text-Based Comprehension • Skills and Strategies • Craft and Structure	**Target Skill** Story Structure **Target Strategy** Infer/Predict **Anchor Text** *Mr. Tanen's Tie Trouble* **Connect to the Topic** *The Jefferson Daily News*	**Target Skill** Sequence of Events **Target Strategy** Visualize **Anchor Text** *Luke Goes to Bat* **Connect to the Topic** *Jackie Robinson*	**Target Skill** Understanding Characters **Target Strategy** Analyze/Evaluate **Anchor Text** *My Name Is Gabriela* **Connect to the Topic** *Poems About Reading and Writing*
	Research and Media Literacy Speaking/ Listening	Create Audio Recordings	Compare and Contrast Media Messages	Recount an Experience
	Foundational Skills • Fluency • Phonics	**Fluency** Rate **Phonics** Base Words and Endings -ed, -ing	**Fluency** Stress **Phonics** Long *i* (*i, igh, y*); Cumulative Review	**Fluency** Expression **Phonics** The Long *e* Sound for *y*; Changing *y* to *i*
Whole Group Language Arts	**Spelling Grammar Writing**	**Spelling** Base Words with Endings -ed, -ing **Grammar** Pronouns **Writing** Narrative: Story Paragraph	**Spelling** Long *i* (*i, igh, y*) **Grammar** Subject-Verb Agreement **Writing** Narrative: Story Paragraph	**Spelling** Long *e* Spelled *y* **Grammar** The Verb *Be* **Writing** Narrative: Descriptive Paragraph
Small Group	**Vocabulary Reader**	Differentiate *Raising Funds*	Differentiate *The Brooklyn Dodgers*	Differentiate *All About Chile*
	Leveled Readers	○ *Our Library* ▲ *The Bake Sale* ■ *The Town Auction* ◆ *Ms. Hawkins and the Bake Sale*	○ *The Winning Hit* ▲ *Take Me Out to the Ballpark* ■ *The New Field* ◆ *The Summer of Baseball Parks*	○ *Beatrix Potter* ▲ *The Life of Jack Prelutsky* ■ *The Life of Langston Hughes* ◆ *Jack Prelutsky*
	Differentiate Instruction	Differentiate Phonics, Comprehension, Fluency, and Vocabulary Strategies	Differentiate Phonics, Comprehension, Fluency, and Vocabulary Strategies	Differentiate Phonics, Comprehension, Fluency, and Vocabulary Strategies

Key ○ Struggling Readers ▲ On-Level Readers ■ Advanced Readers ◆ English Learners

Multimedia Profiles

Children will research an American hero and create a visual display about the hero.

Checkpoints

☐ Brainstorm a list of heroes and discuss traits that make someone a hero.

☐ Research one hero and write about that person.

☐ Use images and other items to create a visual display.

☐ Give an oral presentation about the hero and show the visual display.

Lesson 19

How are signs helpful?

Teacher Read Aloud
"Wild Friends, Wow!"

Oral Vocabulary
Shades of Meaning

Target Skill Text and Graphic Features
Target Strategy Question
Anchor Text *The Signmaker's Assistant*
Connect to the Topic *The Trouble with Signs*

Matching Game: Synonyms

Fluency Phrasing: Punctuation
Phonics Words with *ar*

Spelling Words with *ar*
Grammar Commas in Dates and Places
Writing Narrative: Fictional Story

Differentiate *Signs Are Everywhere*

⚪ *Aldo and Abby*
🔺 *Finding the Party*
◼ *Too Many Signs!*
◆ *Sam Finds the Party*

Differentiate Phonics, Comprehension, Fluency, and Vocabulary Strategies

Lesson 20

What makes someone a hero?

Teacher Read Aloud
"Ordinary Heroes"

Oral Vocabulary
Prefix *over-*

Target Skill Compare and Contrast
Target Strategy Monitor/Clarify
Anchor Text *Dex: The Heart of a Hero*
Connect to the Topic *Heroes Then and Now*

Compare and Contrast

Fluency Intonation
Phonics Words with *or, ore*

Spelling Words with *or, ore*
Grammar Commas in a Series
Writing Narrative: Fictional Story

Differentiate *Everyday Hero*

⚪ *Two Heroes*
🔺 *Superheroes to the Rescue*
◼ *The Mysterious Superhero*
◆ *Superheroes Save the Day*

Differentiate Phonics, Comprehension, Fluency, and Vocabulary Strategies

Performance Tasks
• Write About Reading
• Write a Story

EXTENDED READING

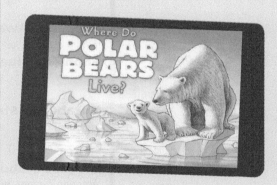

Two weeks of this unit are dedicated to the Extended Reading Trade Book lesson for *Where Do Polar Bears Live?* by Sarah L. Thomson. Use the instructional plan on pp. T505–T536 to guide a **close reading and analysis** of this **informational text**. The trade book lesson also features:

• Teacher Read Aloud
• Build Background with Media
• Content-Area Vocabulary
• Integrated Language Arts: Grammar, Spelling, and Writing
• Collaborative Project

For daily **Intervention** lessons, see the tab at the back of this *Teacher's Edition*.

Unit 4
Planning for English Language Development

	Lesson 16 *Mr. Tanen's Tie Trouble*	**Lesson 17** *Luke Goes to Bat*	**Lesson 18** *My Name is Gabriela*
Begin with High-Utility Words **Tier 1 Words** * = Spanish cognates	**High-Utility Words** *fixed, proud, selling, signs, together, clothes, money* • Language Support Card 16 • Oral Language Chant • Online Picture Card Bank	**High-Utility Words** *chance, crowd, missed, strike, swing, field, players, stands* • Language Support Card 17 • Oral Language Chant • Online Picture Card Bank	**High-Utility Words** *important*, learn, noticed, sounds, traveled, students, teachers, words* • Language Support Card 18 • Oral Language Chant • Online Picture Card Bank
Develop Foundational Literacy Skills • Phonological Awareness • Fluency • Linguistic Transfer	**Phonemic Awareness** • Syllables in Spoken Words **Phonics & Fluency** • Base Words and Endings *-ed, -ing* • Rate **Vocabulary Strategies** • Homographs	**Phonemic Awareness** • Segment Phonemes **Phonics & Fluency** • Long *i* • Stress **Vocabulary Strategies** • Antonyms	**Phonemic Awareness** • Identify Sound Placement; Blend Phonemes **Phonics & Fluency** • Long *e* Sound for *y*; Changing *y* to *i* • Expression **Vocabulary Strategies** • Suffixes *-y, -ful*
Develop Academic Language **Tier 2 & 3 Words** * = Spanish cognates	**Target Vocabulary** *received*, account, budget, disappointed, chuckled, staring, repeated*, fund* • Vocabulary in Context cards • Oral Language Chant • Decodable Readers • Anchor Text **Reading/Language Arts Terms** *vowel*, consonant*, base word*, realistic fiction*, character, setting, plot, problem*, infer*, predict*, homograph*, informational text*, pronoun*, subject*, story paragraph, details** **How English Works** • Language Support Card 16 • Text X-Ray • Language Detective	**Target Vocabulary** *practice*, hurried, position*, roared, extra, curb, cheered, final* • Vocabulary in Context cards • Oral Language Chant • Decodable Readers • Anchor Text **Reading/Language Arts Terms** *vowel*, realistic fiction*, sequence of events*, visualize*, antonym*, infer*, informational text*, pronoun*, verb*, story paragraph, dialogue** **How English Works** • Language Support Card 17 • Text X-Ray • Language Detective	**Target Vocabulary** *accepted*, express*, taught, grand, pretend, prize*, wonder, fluttering* • Vocabulary in Context cards • Oral Language Chant • Decodable Readers • Anchor Text **Reading/Language Arts Terms** *syllables*, vowel*, biography*, character, analyze*, evaluate*, suffix*, base word*, trait, infer*, poetry*, plural*, verb*, descriptive paragraph*, description*, sense words* **How English Works** • Language Support Card 18 • Text X-Ray • Language Detective
Scaffold Comprehension	**Build Background** • Language Support Card 16 • Unit 4 Stream to Start Video **Comprehension** • Anchor Text Support • Paired Selection Support **Story Structure** • Language Support	**Build Background** • Language Support Card 17 **Comprehension** • Anchor Text Support • Paired Selection Support **Sequence of Events** • Language Support	**Build Background** • Language Support Card 18 **Comprehension** • Anchor Text Support • Paired Selection Support **Understanding Characters** • Language Support
Scaffold Language Production	**Narrative Writing:** Story Paragraph • Common Core Writing Handbook: Story Paragraph **Write About Reading** **Grammar:** Pronouns • *Linguistic Transfer:* Subject Pronoun Omission • Language Support Card 16: Verbs and Verb Phrases in Questions; *Because of* **Collaboration**	**Narrative Writing:** Story Paragraph • Common Core Writing Handbook: Story Paragraph **Write About Reading** **Grammar:** Subject-Verb Agreement • *Linguistic Transfer:* Subject-Verb Agreement • Language Support Card 17: Statements; Complex Sentences **Collaboration**	**Narrative Writing** Descriptive Paragraph • Common Core Writing Handbook: Descriptive Paragraph **Write About Reading** **Grammar:** The Verb *Be* • *Linguistic Transfer:* The Verb *Be* • Language Support Card 18: Past-Tense Verbs **Collaboration**

Journeys Language Workshop and Integrated ELD ensure that English learners build literacy skills while meeting the language demands of complex texts and rigorous content standards. This chart provides an overview of the skills, materials, and scaffolds in this unit that support instruction for English learners.

Lesson 19
The Signmaker's Assistant

High-Utility Words *angry, confused*, danger, lost, mistakes, road, signs*
- Language Support Card 19
- Oral Language Chant
- Online Picture Card Bank

Phonemic Awareness
- Substitute Phonemes

Phonics & Fluency
- Words with *ar*
- Phrasing: Punctuation

Vocabulary Strategies
- Shades of Meaning

Target Vocabulary *assistant*, agreed, polite, failed, tearing, wisdom, cleared, trouble*
- Vocabulary in Context cards
- Oral Language Chant
- Decodable Readers
- Anchor Text

Reading/Language Arts Terms
vowel*, humorous fiction*, text feature*, graphic feature*, prediction*, question, synonym*, interpret*, graphic, play, date, comma*, fictional narrative*, story*, beginning, middle, end, character, setting, problem*

How English Works
- Language Support Card 19
- Text X-Ray
- Language Detective

Build Background
- Language Support Card 19

Comprehension
- Anchor Text Support
- Paired Selection Support

Text and Graphic Features
- Language Support

Narrative Writing: Fictional Story
- Common Core Writing Handbook: Fictional Story

Write About Reading

Grammar: Commas in Dates and Places
- *Linguistic Transfer:* Using Capital Letters
- Language Support Card 19: Present-Progressive; Adverbs

Collaboration

Lesson 20
Dex: The Heart of a Hero

High-Utility Words *busy, courage, save, strong, training, bird, cape, cloud*
- Language Support Card 20
- Oral Language Chant
- Online Picture Card Bank

Phonemic Awareness
- Substitute Phonemes

Phonics & Fluency
- Words with *or, ore*
- Intonation

Vocabulary Strategies
- Prefix *over-*

Target Vocabulary *depended*, sore, sprang, studied*, gazing, hero*, exercise*, overlooked*
- Vocabulary in Context cards
- Oral Language Chant
- Decodable Readers
- Anchor Text

Reading/Language Arts Terms
vowel*, fantasy*, compare*, contrast*, monitor, clarify*, prefix*, base word*, connect*, informational text*, comma*, fictional narrative*, story*

How English Works
- Language Support Card 20
- Text X-Ray
- Language Detective

Build Background
- Language Support Card 20

Comprehension
- Anchor Text Support
- Paired Selection Support

Compare and Contrast
- Language Support

Narrative Writing: Fictional Story
- Common Core Writing Handbook: Fictional Story

Write About Reading

Grammar: Commas in a Series
- *Linguistic Transfer:* Overuse of Articles
- Language Support Card 20: Conjunctions; Adverbs *anymore*

Collaboration

LANGUAGE WORKSHOP

Language Workshop lessons provide skill and strategy instruction targeted to individual proficiency levels.

Lesson 16: Language Skills/Strategies
- **Collaborate:** Apologize; Build on Responses
- **Interpret:** Evaluate Language Choices
- **Produce:** Give Presentations; Support Opinions
- **How English Works:** Use Prepositional Phrases; Adverbs
- **Vocabulary Network**

Lesson 17: Language Skills/Strategies
- **Collaborate:** Ask and Answer *wh* Questions; Listen
- **Interpret:** Analyze Language Choices
- **Produce:** Write Collaboratively; Recount Experiences
- **How English Works:** Conjunctions
- **Vocabulary Network**

Lesson 18: Language Skills/Strategies
- **Collaborate:** Offer Opinions with Learned Phrases
- **Interpret:** Analyze Language Choices
- **Produce:** Give Presentations; Recount Experiences
- **How English Works:** Condense Clauses
- **Vocabulary Network**

Lesson 19: Language Skills/Strategies
- **Collaborate:** Gain and Hold the Floor
- **Interpret:** Describe Ideas
- **Produce:** Write Collaboratively; Retell Texts
- **How English Works:** Comprehend/ Compose Texts
- **Vocabulary Network**

Lesson 20: Language Skills/Strategies
- **Collaborate:** Negotiate with Others
- **Interpret:** Ask and Answer Questions
- **Produce:** Use Technology; Give Presentations
- **How English Works:** Possessive Pronouns
- **Vocabulary Network**

American Heroes Hall of Fame Display

Some selections in this unit deal with heroes. Children will research an American hero and create a visual display presenting the hero to the class.

▶ SHARE OBJECTIVES

- Write informational articles. LANGUAGE
- Improve writing through revision and editing.
- Work with others on research and writing projects. LANGUAGE

DEVELOP BACKGROUND

- Explain to children that a hero is someone we look up to. A hero is often brave and honest. We admire what heroes do or say and the things they create.
- Explain that there are many famous heroes throughout history. Some heroes are leaders, presidents, athletes, musicians, actors, writers, or scientists. All have made big contributions to society.

Materials

- reference books and informational text about famous Americans
- poster paper and cardboard or two-fold display boards
- scissors, glue, and tape

Step 1   ELA SL.2.1a ELD ELD.PI.2.1, ELD.PI.2.3

Plan and Organize Help children brainstorm heroes for their visual display.

a Begin brainstorming by asking questions: *What famous heroes do we study in school? Name a person who has changed the world and done good things for others.* As necessary, offer examples such as Eleanor Roosevelt, Martin Luther King Jr., and Abraham Lincoln.

b Write children's ideas on the board, adding your own as necessary. Guide them in discussing why each person is a hero. Help them discuss the traits each of these people have in common and how these traits make them more than just average good citizens.

ENGLISH LANGUAGE SUPPORT Write these frames on the board to guide children's discussion: *(Name) was a hero because ____; (Name) was a ____ person; (Name) helped others by ____.*

Step 2

ELA W.2.1, W.2.4, W.2.5, W.2.7, W.2.10 **ELD** ELD.PI.2.1, ELD.PI.2.2, ELD.PI.2.10

Research and Create Guide children as they work on their displays.

a Have small groups work together to choose a hero and then research and write an article. Each display should answer the question *What makes this person a hero?* The completed articles will be part of displays that will also contain graphics such as photos, drawings, and charts, all with captions.

b Tell children to use multiple sources, such as encyclopedias and other nonfiction books, to do their research. Remind them to use features such as tables of contents, headings, photos, and indexes to help them gather the information they need.

c Instruct groups to write first drafts of the written portions of the display and then revise and edit them before creating a final draft. Remind children to use the language skills they are learning in the unit.

Step 3

ELA W.2.4, W.2.6, W.2.10, SL.2.6 **ELD** ELD.PI.2.1, ELD.PI.2.9

Present Have children create and present their finished product.

a Tell the groups to create a visual display using poster board mounted on cardboard, or a two-fold display board.

b Instruct each group to present their hero to the class using their visual display. Remind children to stay focused on their topic as they speak clearly and audibly in complete sentences.

c Ask children what they have learned about heroes from the presentations: *Which heroes did you find the most inspiring? Do the heroes give you ideas or goals for your own lives?*

ENGLISH LANGUAGE SUPPORT Provide the following sentence frames for children to use as they respond to classmates' presentations: *(Name) is a good example of a hero. I like that (Name) was so _____. I like that (Name) helped others by _____.*

ENGLISH LANGUAGE SUPPORT

Comprehensible Input

Emerging Have children complete the sentence frame: *A hero is someone who _____.* **ELD** ELD.PI.2.1

Expanding As children progress through the unit, have them discuss what it means to be a hero, using characters from the selections as examples. **ELD** ELD.PI.2.1

Bridging As children progress through the unit, have them pick a character and write reasons why he or she is a hero. **ELD** ELD.PI.2.1

Research Skills

For instruction in the following applicable skills, see the lessons in the **Resources** section, pp. R2–R5.

Unit 4 Research Skills

p. R2	• Alphabetical Order
p. R2	• Choose Appropriate Sources
p. R3	• Use an Encyclopedia
p. R3	• Use an Atlas
p. R4	• Read a Chart
p. R4	• Distinguish Fact from Fantasy
p. R5	• Interview
p. R5	• Use Multiple Sources

PROJECT ASSESSMENT

Assess children's work on the project by reviewing multiple factors:

☑ **Speaking and Listening:** Do children listen to each other and follow rules for discussion when working together? Do they speak clearly and audibly in complete sentences when giving their presentations?

☑ **Writing:** Do children write articles that are clear and easy to understand?

☑ **Language:** Do children use correct punctuation and capitalization? Has their work been revised to correct spelling and grammatical errors?

See **Giving Presentations Rubric and Writing Rubric** on pp. R17–R23.

 Have children record progress of their **Research and Media Performance Task** in *my*WriteSmart.

Correlations

California Common Core State Standards for English Language Arts

Standard	Standard Language	Key Citations	Additional Practice and Application
LITERATURE			
Key Ideas and Details			
RL.2.1	Ask and answer such questions as *who*, *what*, *where*, *when*, *why*, and *how* to demonstrate understanding of key details in a text.	**2-1:** T348, T448 **2-3:** T411 **2-4:** T19, T219, T323, T332, T419 **2-5:** T123, T130, T319, T352 **2-6:** T119	**2-1:** T14, T25, T26–T30, T39, T50, T88, T89, T90, T317, T318, T320–T322, T324–T327, T332, T338, T386, T387, T388, T393, T419, T420, T422, T424–T428, T430, T486, T487, T490, T491, T492, T497, S5, S7, S11, S12, S15, S17, S20, S22, S35, S37, S39, S45, S47, S49 **2-2:** T117, T123, T124, T125, T126, T129, T130, T131, T154, T189, T192, T193, T194, T323, T352, T354, T388, T389, T392, T393, T394, T399, T442, T508, T514, T516, T524, T526, T532, S15, S17, S19, S21, S35, S37, S39, S45, S47, S49 **2-3:** T25, T26–T28, T30, T32–T33, T44, T52, T63, T86, T87, T90, T91, T92, T414, T417, T418, T421, T422, T423, T424, T433, T444, T482, T483, T486, T487, T488, T493, S5, S7, S11, S45, S47 **2-4:** T23, T24, T26, T31, T34, T35, T37, T46, T54, T92, T93, T94, T125, T127, T128, T131, T132, T134, T154, T192, T193, T194, T326, T328, T329, T334, T335, T336, T354, T388, T389, T392, T393, T394, T413, T425, T426, T428, T429, T431, T432, T433, T434, T436, T446, T454, T496, T497, T498, T510, S5, S7, S15, S17, S35, S37, S45, S47 **2-5:** T126, T128, T129, T131, T144, T154, T188, T189, T192, T193, T194, T254, T288, T289, T322, T327, T328, T329, T330, T331, T332, T333, T344, T354, T388, T389, T392, T393, T394, T399, S4, S5, S7, S9, S15, S17, S19, S24, S25, S27, S29, S31, S37, S39 **2-6:** T26, T27, T28, T29, T30, T32, T33, T34, T35, T45, T54, T92, T93, T94, T144, T226, T227, T240, T248, T259, T288, T289, T290, T324, T325, T326, T329, T340, T350, T388, T389, T390, S5, S7, S11, S25, S27, S31, S35, S37
RL.2.2	Recount stories, including fables and folktales from diverse cultures, and determine their central message, lesson, or moral.	**2-1:** T22, T27, T38–T39, T358, T359 **2-2:** T364, T365 **2-4:** T122, T135, T144–T145 **2-6:** T222, T229, T238–T239	**2-1:** T31, T50, T84, T85, T95, T328, T329, T339, T348, T386, T387, T388, T431, S4, S31, S44 **2-2:** T134, T135, T154, T323, T325, T330, T332, T354, T516 **2-3:** T35, T52, T425, T444, T455 **2-4:** T54, T136, T146, T188, T189, T199, T325, T337, T346, T354, T425, T437, T454, S51 **2-5:** T134, T154, T230, T254, T323, T333, T344, T354, T364, T365 **2-6:** T36, T54, T240, T241, T248, T260, T284, T285, T288, T289, T290, T295, T328, T331, T340, T350, T360, T361, S24, S31
RL.2.3	Describe how characters in a story respond to major events and challenges.	**2-1:** T321 **2-2:** T320, T325, T342–T343 **2-4:** T19, T29, T44–T45, T419 **2-5:** T122, T142–T143, T219 **2-6:** T19, T318, T325, T338–T339	**2-1:** T318, S11 **2-2:** T128, T130, T189, T324, T326, T327, T328, T329, T331, T333, T388, T389, T392, T393, T394, T399, T419, T511, T516, T524, T526, T532, S34 **2-3:** T26, T28, T30, T46, T86, T87, T90, T91, T92, T211, T309, T410, T421, T433, T434, T482, T483, S47 **2-4:** T28, T30, T31, T32, T33, T34, T126, T127, T128, T129, T132, T135, T327, T328, T332, T333, T334, T335, T336, T422, T430, T434, T435, T445, T446, T473, T496, T497, T498, T510, S15, S21, S45, S51 **2-5:** T127, T145, T188, T189, T192, T193, T194, T199, T364, T365, S11, S14, S17, S19 **2-6:** T27, T29, T30, T32, T34, T92, T93, T94, T226, T227, T239, T240, T260, T326, T327, T329, T340, T361, T384, T385, T388, T389, T390, T395, S34
Craft and Structure			
RL.2.4	Describe how words and phrases (e.g., regular beats, alliteration, rhymes, repeated lines) supply rhythm and meaning in a story, poem, or song. **(See grade 2 Language standards 4–6 for additional expectations.) CA**	**2-1:** T158, T423, T438–T439 **2-2:** T262, T263, T327, T342–T343 **2-3:** T31, T42–T43, T156, T157 **2-4:** T264 **2-5:** T131, T142–T143	**2-1:** T39, T48, T95, T321, T323, T327, T328, T337 **2-2:** T129, T514 **2-3:** T86, T255, T420 **2-4:** T130, T422, T429, T430, T432, T445, T492, T493, T503 **2-5:** T330, T332, S33
RL.2.5	Describe the overall structure of a story, including describing how the beginning introduces the story and the ending concludes the action.	**2-1:** T22, T38–T39, T146, T416, T430, T438–T439 **2-4:** T35 **2-5:** T52, T252 **2-6:** T22, T35, T448	**2-1:** T25, T30, T84, T85, T88, T89, T90, T95, T317, T323, T420, T440, T448, T486, T487, T490, T491, T492, T497, S4, S41, S44 **2-2:** T123, T134, T143, T188, T199, T250 **2-3:** T442, S14, S15, S51 **2-4:** T22, T26, T45, T88, T89, T92, T93, T94, T99, T192, T193, T194, T429, T510, S4, S11, S17 **2-5:** T132 **2-6:** T45, T88, T89, T99, T229, T288, T289, T290, T322, T329
RL.2.6	Acknowledge differences in the points of view of characters, including by speaking in a different voice for each character when reading dialogue aloud.	**2-4:** T329, T344–T345, T364 **2-5:** T342–T343 **2-6:** T327	**2-2:** T128, T365 **2-3:** S15 **2-4:** T333, T336, T347 **2-5:** T331 **2-6:** T31, T228, T339

Standard	Standard Language	Key Citations	Additional Practice and Application
Integration of Knowledge and Ideas			
RL.2.7	Use information gained from the illustrations and words in a print or digital text to demonstrate understanding of its characters, setting, or plot.	**2-1:** T441, T459 **2-2:** T142–T143 **2-3:** T32, T42–T43 **2-4:** T344–T345 **2-5:** T122, T342–T343 **2-6:** T35, T44–T45	**2-1:** T26, T27, T28, T29, T30, T50, T318, T320, T321, T322, T323, T324, T325, T326, T327, T328, T348, T382, T383, T420, T421, T424, T425, T427, T428, T429, T440, T448 **2-2:** T121, T125, T127, T128, T129, T132, T133, T134, T144, T154, T188, T199, T344, T511, T514, T516, T521, T524, T526, T532, S11, S21, S51 **2-3:** T22, T23, T27, T29, T30, T33, T34, T44, T52, T63, T97, T410, T414, T415, T417, T418, T419, T420, T421, T422, T423, T424, T433, T434, T444, T493, S5, S7, S11, S14, S15, S45 **2-4:** T27, T28, T29, T35, T65, T129, T131, T132, T133, T135, T147, T154, T322, T326, T331, T346, T354, T365, T388, T389, T392, T393, T394, T399, T422, T426, T428, T431, T433, T435, T445, T454, T465, T510, S5, S45 **2-5:** T126, T127, T130, T142–T143, T144, T145, T154, T254, T322, T326, T329, T330, T331, T333, T344, T354, T399, S11, S14, S21, S31, S51 **2-6:** T26, T28, T29, T31, T33, T54, T248, T258, T259, T260, T261, T318, T322, T324, T325, T328
RL.2.8	(Not applicable to literature)		
RL.2.9	Compare and contrast two or more versions of the same story (e.g., Cinderella stories) by different authors or from different cultures.	**2-5:** T373 **2-6:** T261, T269, T361	**2-6:** T258
Range of Reading and Level of Text Complexity			
RL.2.10	By the end of the year, read and comprehend literature, including stories and poetry, in the grades 2–3 text complexity band proficiently, with scaffolding as needed at the high end of the range.	**2-1:** T24–T30, T316–T328, T418–T430 **2-2:** T122–T134, T262, T322–T333 **2-3:** T24–T34, T156, T412–T424 **2-4:** T264–T265, T324–T336, T424–T436 **2-5:** T124–T133, T324–T333 **2-6:** T24–T35, T320–T329	**2-1:** T7, T51, T103, T149, T158, T201, T247, T299, T349, T358, T401, T449, S5, S7, S15, S17, S35, S37, S45, S47 **2-2:** T7, T51, T105, T155, T207, T253, T305, T355, T364, T407, T453, T508, T516, T524, T526, S15, S17, S35, S37, S51 **2-3:** T7, T53, T105, T147, T199, T245, T297, T395, T445, S5, S45 **2-4:** T7, T24, T55, T107, T155, T207, T255, T307, T355, T364, T407, T455, S7, S35, S37, S47, R4 **2-5:** T7, T55, T107, T155, T207, T255, T307, T355, T364–T365, T407, T451, S5, S7, S15, S17, S25, S27, S37 **2-6:** T7, T55, T107, T155, T207, T249, T258–T261, T303, T351, T360–T361, T403, S5, S7, S11, S25, S27, S35, S37
INFORMATIONAL TEXT			
Key Ideas and Details			
RI.2.1	Ask and answer such questions as who, what, where, when, why, and how to demonstrate understanding of key details in a text.	**2-1:** T123 **2-2:** T23, T27 **2-3:** T121, T125, R4 **2-4:** T119, T252 **2-5:** T152 **2-6:** T123, T127, T152	**2-1:** T121, T122, T124, T126–T128, T137, T138, T148, T159, T182, T183, T186, T187, T188, T193, T219, T220, T222, T223, T226, T235, T246, T280, T281, T284, T285, T286, T287, T291, S25, S27 **2-2:** T25, T26, T28, T30, T31, T32, T50, T90, T91, T92, T97, T225, T226, T227, T228, T230, T231, T232, T252, T271, T425, T426, T430, T431, T432, T433, T452, T494, T495, T496, T501, T520, T532, S5, S7, S25, S27, S29 **2-3:** T117, T123, T126, T128, T138, T146, T184, T185, T186, T217, T218, T220, T222, T223, T224, T225, T244, T282, T283, T284, T315, T316, T318, T322, T334, T342, T353, T376, T377, T380, T381, T382, T407, S17, S21, S25, S27, S35, S37, S39, S41 **2-4:** T173, T225, T227, T229, T232, T234, T244, T254, T265, T292, T293, T294, T513, T516, T518, T520, T522, T528, T530, T532, S25, S27 **2-5:** T26, T27, T29, T30, T32, T44, T54, T88, T89, T92, T93, T94, T99, T165, T222, T226, T228, T229, T230, T231, T232, T233, T234, T243, T244, T292, T293, T294, T295, T426, T429, T432, T442, T450, T488, T489, T492, T493, T494, S41, S45, S47, S49 **2-6:** T46, T126, T128, T129, T130, T131, T133, T144, T154, T192, T193, T194, T369, T422, T424, T426, T427, T440, T450, T492, T493, T494, T506, T508, T509, T510, T512, T514, T516, T517, T518, T522, T524, S15, S17, S45, S47
RI.2.2	Identify the main topic of a multiparagraph text as well as the focus of specific paragraphs within the text.	**2-2:** T222, T232, T240–T241, T242 **2-3:** T214, T225, T234–T235 **2-4:** T252 **2-5:** T22, T29, T42–T43	**2-1:** T60, T129, T148, T227, T256 **2-2:** T33, T50, T226, T228, T286, T287, T290, T291, T292, T297, T317, T428, T437, T444, T452, S24, S31 **2-3:** T146, T223, T226, T236, T244, T278, T279, T282, T283, T284, T289, T319, T321, T322, T323, T325, T334, S21 **2-4:** T122, T229, T235, T254, T265 **2-5:** T31, T34, T54, T88, T89, T92, T93, T94, T99, T235, T450 **2-6:** T134, T154, T426, T450, T506, T512, T514, T518, T524

Standard	Standard Language	Key Citations	Additional Practice and Application
RI.2.3	Describe the connection between a series of historical events, scientific ideas or concepts, or steps in technical procedures in a text.	**2-2:** T227, T240–T241 **2-3:** T321, T332–T333 **2-5:** T27, T42–T43, T164, T229, T242–T243, T423, T469 **2-6:** T418, T425, T438–T439	**2-1:** T182, T183, T186, T187, T188, T280 **2-2:** T26, T50, T230, T231, T286, T287 **2-3:** T316, T319, T376, S41 **2-4:** T516, T518, T528, T530 **2-5:** T22, T31, T33, T44, T228, T230, T233, T244, T245, T264, T292, T293, T294, T295, T429, T430, T431, T432, T441, T443 **2-6:** T126, T145, T164, T165, T192, T193, T194, T261, T422, T428, T429, T430, T440, T461, T488, T489, T492, T493, T494, T499, T516, T522, T524, T526

Craft and Structure

Standard	Standard Language	Key Citations	Additional Practice and Application
RI.2.4	Determine the meaning of words and phrases in a text relevant to a *grade 2 topic or subject area.* **(See grade 2 Language standards 4–6 for additional expectations.) CA**	**2-2:** T27, T40–T41, T62 **2-5:** T226 **2-6:** T128, T438–T439	**2-2:** T86, T87, T425, T427, S13, S23, S33, S43 **2-5:** S3, S13, S23, S43 **2-6:** T423, T506, T510, T512, T524
RI.2.5	Know and use various text features (e.g., captions, bold print, subheadings, glossaries, indexes, electronic menus, icons) to locate key facts or information in a text efficiently.	**2-2:** T22, T31, T40–T41, T62 **2-3:** T120, T125, T136–T137, T352 **2-4:** T64, T164 **2-5:** T64, T422, T427, T440–T441 **2-6:** T422	**2-1:** T60, T223, T224, T226, T256, T458, R3 **2-2:** T28, T42, T43, T60, T61, T86, T87, T90, T91, T92, T97, T462, S4, R2–R5 **2-3:** xxxvii, T62, T127, T128, T138, T157, T180, T181, T184, T185, T186, T191, T221, T224, T235, T236, T278, T279, T322, S17, R2–R5 **2-4:** T265, T464, T513, T528, S31, R4 **2-5:** T443, T460, T461, T488, T489, T492, T493, T494 **2-6:** T509, T512, T514, T522, T524, T526
RI.2.6	Identify the main purpose of a text, including what the author wants to answer, explain, or describe.	**2-1:** T217, T225, T234–T235 **2-3:** T312, T323, T332–T333 **2-4:** T165 **2-5:** T431 **2-6:** T65, T133, T142–T143, T426	**2-1:** T221, T280, T281, T284, T285, T286, T287, T291, S24 **2-2:** T29, T31, T252, T443, T490, T491, T520, T532 **2-3:** T124, T126, T127, T128, T138, T219, T225, T231, T236, T244, T316, T376, T377, T387, S31, S37, S39 **2-4:** T222, T229, T233, T243, T288, T289, T299, T323, T513, T530 **2-5:** T26, T32, T33, T429 **2-6:** T64, T518, T522

Integration of Knowledge and Ideas

Standard	Standard Language	Key Citations	Additional Practice and Application
RI.2.7	Explain how specific images (e.g., a diagram showing how a machine works) contribute to and clarify a text.	**2-3:** T120, T125, T136–T137, T352, T361 **2-4:** T464 **2-5:** T231, T273, T422, T427, T440–T441 **2-6:** T164	**2-1:** T60, T121, T124, T125, T137, T193, T220, T222, T225, T467 **2-2:** T32, T60, T71, T90, T91, T92, T97, T225, T227, T229, T242, T426, T430, T433, T444, T462, S4 **2-3:** T45, T124, T127, T138, T139, T180, T181, T215, T221, T235 **2-4:** T226, T230, T231, T233, T516, T520, T526, T528, S31, R4 **2-5:** T28, T30, T33, T128, T222, T243, T244, T245, T299, T442, T460, T492, T493, T494, T499, S41, S44 **2-6:** T46, T132, T460, T512, T516, T522, T524, T526
RI.2.8	Describe how reasons support specific points the author makes in a text.	**2-2:** T431, T442–T443 **2-3:** T127, T136–T137 **2-6:** T122, T129, T130, T142–T143, T429	**2-1:** T225, T433 **2-2:** T50, T165, T230, T427, T429, T430, T490, T491 **2-3:** T180, T181, T223, T244 **2-4:** T482, T520, T528, T530 **2-5:** T54, T450 **2-6:** T154, T188, T189, T199, T422, T425
RI.2.9	Compare and contrast the most important points presented by two texts on the same topic.	**2-1:** T61 **2-2:** T63, T165 **2-4:** T534 **2-5:** T65 **2-6:** T461, T530	**2-2:** T271, T463, T532 **2-3:** T353 **2-4:** T465, T522 **2-5:** T265 **2-6:** T369, T518, T531

Range of Reading and Level of Text Complexity

Standard	Standard Language	Key Citations	Additional Practice and Application
RI.2.10	By the end of year, read and comprehend informational texts, including history/social studies, science, and technical texts, in the grades 2–3 text complexity band proficiently, with scaffolding as needed at the high end of the range.	**2-1:** T120–T128, T218–T226 **2-2:** T224–T232, T424–T433 **2-3:** T122–T128, T314–T323 **2-4:** T224–T234 **2-5:** T164–T165, T424–T433 **2-6:** T420–T430	**2-1:** T7, T51, T60, T103, T149, T201, T247, T256, T299, T349, T401, T449, T458, S25, S27 **2-2:** T7, T24–T33, T51, T60–T63, T105, T155, T207, T253, T305, T355, T407, T453, T462, S25, S27 **2-3:** T7, T53, T62, T105, T147, T199, T216, T245, T297, T343, T395, T445, S25, S27, R2, R5 **2-4:** T7, T55, T107, T155, T207, T255, T307, T355, T407, T455, T465, T522, T526, T532, S25, S27, R4 **2-5:** T7, T24, T25, T55, T64–T65, T107, T155, T207, T255, T264–T265, T307, T355, T407, T451, T460–T461, S45, S47 **2-6:** T7, T55, T64–T65, T107, T155, T164–T165, T207, T249, T303, T351, T403, T451, T460–T461, T512, T514, T518, T524, T526, T530, S15, S17, S45, S47

Correlations

Standard	Standard Language	Key Citations	Additional Practice and Application
FOUNDATIONAL SKILLS			
Phonics and Word Recognition			
RF.2.3a	Know and apply grade-level phonics and word analysis skills in decoding words **both in isolation and in text.** CA Distinguish long and short vowels when reading regularly spelled one-syllable words.	**2-1:** T17, T37, T113, T135, T157, T211, T212, T233, T309, T335, T446, T457 **2-3:** T340, T351 **2-4:** T117	**2-1:** T18, T47, T59, T67, T80, T86, T114, T115, T145, T165, T178, T192, T263, T276, T290, T310, T345, T378, T392, T482, T488, T496, S2, S5, S6, S12, S15, S16, S25, S32 **2-2:** T39, T141 **2-3:** T111, T133, T143, T144, T153, T163, T210, T233, T261, T288, T307, T350, T359, T372, T453, T484, T492, S36 **2-4:** T52, T98, T141, T142, T143, T151, T161, T163, T171, T263, S12, S16 **2-5:** T437, T447, T467 **2-6:** T139, T171, T345
RF.2.3b	Know and apply grade-level phonics and word analysis skills in decoding words **both in isolation and in text.** CA Know spelling-sound correspondences for additional common vowel teams.	**2-3:** T115, T135, T209, T242, T253, T331 **2-4:** T117, T143, T162, T163, T263 **2-6:** T116, T117, T141, T313, T337, T346, T347, T413	**2-3:** T116, T124, T144, T154, T163, T176, T190, T210, T222, T233, T252, T261, T274, T275, T280, T288, T307, T308, T321, T340, T350, T351, T359, T372, T378, T386, T453, S12, S16, S22, S26, S32 **2-4:** T63, T90, T118, T171, T184, T198, T284, T290, T352, T363, T384, T398, T452, T488 **2-5:** T117, T141, T163, T190 **2-6:** T30, T118, T132, T359, T367, T394, T437, T459, T467, T498, S32, S42
RF.2.3c	Know and apply grade-level phonics and word analysis skills in decoding words **both in isolation and in text.** CA Decode regularly spelled two-syllable words with long vowels.	**2-2:** T351 **2-3:** T50, T115, T209, T453 **2-4:** T117, T217, T241 **2-6:** T313, T337, T413	**2-1:** T50, T325 **2-2:** T349, T361, T371, T390, T398, S36 **2-3:** T135, T154, T163, T176, T242, T252, T253, T261, T340, T351, T359 **2-4:** T52, T163, T263, T352, T390 **2-5:** T341 **2-6:** T335, T359, T367, T437, T445, T459, T467, T498, S32, S42
RF.2.3d	Know and apply grade-level phonics and word analysis skills in decoding words **both in isolation and in text.** CA Decode words with common prefixes and suffixes.	**2-5:** T151, T217, T241, T263, T317, T448 **2-6:** T52, T63	**2-1:** T494, T495 **2-2:** T94, T95, T97, T498, T499, T501, S26, S32 **2-3:** T88, T94, T95, T182, T280, T358, T384, T385, S2, S3, S5, S6 **2-4:** T84, T296, T297, T500, T501, S2, S3, S6 **2-5:** T231, T271, T298, T318, T328, T341, T363, T371, T398, T498, S16, S22, S32 **2-6:** T98, S13
RF.2.3e	Know and apply grade-level phonics and word analysis skills in decoding words **both in isolation and in text.** CA Identify words with inconsistent but common spelling-sound correspondences.	**2-1:** T243, T345, T346, T356 **2-2:** T315, T341 **2-3:** T17, T60, T350 **2-4:** T217 **2-6:** T17, T117, T163, T217, T218	**2-1:** T263, T282, T384, S22, S26, S36 **2-2:** T236, T269, T288, T363, T371, T384, T492, S26, S32 **2-3:** T18, T41, T50, T69, T82, T96, T340, T351, T359, S46 **2-4:** T17, T43, T62, T63, T71, T171, T241, T263, T271, T290, T298, T352, T363, T415, S12, S22 **2-5:** T17, T18, T41, T51, T52, T90, T98, T198, T251, T318, T351, T362, T371, T390, T417, T418, T439, T458, T467, S2, S6, S42, S46 **2-6:** T18, T43, T62, T118, T141, T171, T198, T213, T235, T237, T245, T246, T255, T256, T257, T266, T267, T294, S2, S6, S12, S22, S26, S36
RF.2.3f	Know and apply grade-level phonics and word analysis skills in decoding words **both in isolation and in text.** CA Recognize and read grade-appropriate irregularly spelled words.	**2-1:** T13, T35, T45, T57, T109, T143, T155, T165 **2-2:** T13, T37, T47, T69, T111, T149, T161, T171, T213, T231, T247, T259, T269 **2-3:** T13, T39, T49, T59, T69, T111, T143, T153, T163 **2-4:** T13, T41, T51, T61, T71, T113, T141, T151, T161, T171 **2-5:** T13, T39, T49, T61, T71, T112, T139, T149, T161, T171 **2-6:** T13, T41, T51, T61, T71, T113, T139, T149, T161, T171	**2-1:** T20, T67, T116, T133, T207, T214, T231, T253, T263, T305, T312, T333, T339, T343, T355, T361, T365, T371, T407, T412, T414, T435, T445, T455, T465, T496, S3, S4, S8, S13, S14, S23, S24, S28, S33, S34, S38, S43, S44, S48 **2-2:** T18, T20, T96, T116, T118, T133, T184, T198, T220, T237, T311, T316, T318, T349, T413, T418, T420, T439, T449, T459, T469, S3, S4, S8, S14, S18, S24, S28, S33, S34, S38, S44, S48 **2-3:** T17, T18, T116, T205, T210, T231, T241, T251, T261, T303, T308, T329, T339, T349, T359, T401, T429, T439, T441, T451, T461, T492, S4, S8, S14, S18, S24, S28, S34, S44, S48, S50 **2-4:** T213, T239, T249, T261, T271, T313, T341, T351, T371, T413, T441, T451, T461, T471, S4, S8, S14, S18, S23, S24, S28, S34, S38, S44, S48 **2-5:** T20, T52, T120, T213, T220, T239, T249, T261, T271, T313, T339, T349, T361, T371, T413, T437, T447, T457, T467, S3, S4, S8, S13, S14, S18, S23, S24, S28, S33, S34, S38, S43, S44, S48 **2-6:** T20, T120, T213, T220, T235, T245, T255, T267, T309, T316, T320, T335, T345, T357, T367, T409, T416, T420, T445, T457, T467, S3, S4, S8, S13, S14, S18, S24, S28, S33, S34, S38, S43, S44

Standard	Standard Language	Key Citations	Additional Practice and Application

Fluency

Standard	Standard Language	Key Citations	Additional Practice and Application
RF.2.4a	Read with sufficient accuracy and fluency to support comprehension. Read on-level text with purpose and understanding.	**2-1:** T25 **2-2:** T25, T123 **2-3:** T25, T145 **2-4:** T25, T125, T225, T325, T425 **2-5:** T25, T125, T219, T225, T325, T425 **2-6:** T25, T125, T225, T321, T421, T449	**2-1:** T80, T82, T83, T88, T89, T90, T94, T115, T121, T146, T149, T180, T181, T186, T187, T188, T244, T278, T279, T280, T281, T284, T285, T286, T287, T317, T346, T380, T381, T385, T386, T387, T388, T419, T484, T485, T486, T487, T490, T491, T492, T497 **2-2:** T51, T84, T85, T88, T152, T189, T192, T193, T194, T225, T250, T253, T290, T291, T292, T323, T352, T392, T393, T394, T425, T494, T495, T496 **2-3:** T84, T85, T86, T87, T90, T91, T92, T123, T147, T178, T179, T217, T245, T276, T277, T315, T376, T377, T380, T407, T413, T442, T480, T481, T482, T483, T486, T487, T488 **2-4:** T55, T153, T286, T287, T292, T293, T294, T386, T387, T388, T389, T455, T490, T491, S19 **2-5:** T52, T53, T55, T86, T87, T88, T89, T90, T92, T93, T94, T152, T186, T187, T188, T189, T252, T253, T255, T286, T287, T288, T289, T319, T352, T355, T386, T387, T388, T389, T392, T393, T394, T419, T488, T489, S29, S49 **2-6:** T19, T92, T93, T94, T119, T152, T192, T193, T194, T348, T382, T383, T388, T389, T390, T415, T448, T492, T493, T494, S29, S49
RF.2.4b	Read with sufficient accuracy and fluency to support comprehension. Read on-level text orally with accuracy, appropriate rate, and expression on successive readings.	**2-1:** T48, T49, T146, T147 **2-2:** T49, T251 **2-3:** T51, T145, T243, T443 **2-4:** T53, T153, T253 **2-5:** T252, T253, T353 **2-6:** T53, T349, T449	**2-1:** T14, T19, T86, T87, T115, T149, T184, T185, T192, T226, T306, T311, T346, T347, T385, T392, T408, T489, S9, S19, S39, S49 **2-2:** T14, T19, T51, T82, T89, T90, T91, T92, T112, T117, T152, T153, T184, T185, T190, T191, T198, T219, T250, T253, T282, T289, T296, T312, T353, T391, T392, T393, T394, T414, T493, T494, T495, T496, T528, S9, S19, S29, S39, S49 **2-3:** T14, T19, T82, T89, T90, T91, T92, T117, T176, T183, T184, T185, T186, T309, T341, T379, T380, T381, T382, T407, T485, T486, T487, T488, S9, S19, S39, S49 **2-4:** T14, T19, T55, T91, T92, T93, T94, T119, T152, T191, T192, T193, T194, T219, T255, T291, T292, T293, T294, T314, T319, T353, T391, T392, T393, T394, T414, T419, T453, T455, T495, T496, T497, T498, T522, S9, S29, S39, S49 **2-5:** T19, T52, T53, T91, T92, T93, T94, T153, T191, T192, T193, T194, T219, T255, T291, T292, T293, T294, T295, T319, T352, T355, T391, T392, T393, T394, T419, T449, T451, T491, S9, S29, S39 **2-6:** T14, T19, T91, T119, T153, T191, T219, T247, T287, T310, T348, T351, T387, T448, T491, T518, S9, S19, S39, S49
RF.2.4c	Read with sufficient accuracy and fluency to support comprehension. Use context to confirm or self-correct word recognition and understanding, rereading as necessary.	**2-1:** T213, T244, T245, T247, T349, T449 **2-2:** T155, T355, T453 **2-3:** T211, T243, T245 **2-4:** T155 **2-5:** T153	**2-1:** T88, T89, T90, T149, T282, T283, T288, T289, T390, T391, S29, S33 **2-2:** T112, T414, T508, T518, T520, T528 **2-3:** T53, T281, T282, T283, T284, T416, T418, T445, S29 **2-4:** T55, T196, T197, T355 **2-5:** T96, T97, T119, T152, T155, T191, T196, T197, T396, T397, T496, T497, S19 **2-6:** T55, T249, T451, S23

WRITING

Text Types and Purposes

Standard	Standard Language	Key Citations	Additional Practice and Application
W.2.1	Write opinion pieces in which they introduce the topic or book they are writing about, state an opinion, supply reasons that support the opinion, use linking words (e.g., *because*, *and*, *also*) to connect opinion and reasons, and provide a concluding statement or section.	**2-3:** T131, T141, T151, T161, T168–T169, T327, T337, T347, T357, T364–T365, T427, T437, T449, T459, T466–T467 **2-4:** T173 **2-6:** T137, T147, T159, T169, T176–T177, T233, T243, T253, T265, T272–T273, T433, T443, T455, T465, T472–T473	**2-1:** T41, T139, T339, T441 **2-2:** T243, T345, T445, T511 **2-3:** xxxvi–xxxvii, T37, T45, T47, T57, T63, T67, T74, T139, T229, T239, T249, T259, T266–T267, T335, T472, T473, T474 **2-4:** xxxvi–xxxvii, T47, T147, T265, T447, T532 **2-5:** T145, T245 **2-6:** T69, T76, T173, T333, T341, T343, T359, T365, T372–T373, T441, T478, T479, T480
W.2.2	Write informative/explanatory texts in which they introduce a topic, use facts and definitions to develop points, and provide a concluding statement or section.	**2-2:** T55, T67, T74, T159, T169, T176, T235, T245, T257, T267, T275, T437, T447, T457, T467, T474 **2-5:** T269, T276–T277, T337, T347, T359, T369, T376–T377, T435, T445, T455, T465, T472–T473	**2-1:** xxxvi–xxxvii **2-2:** xxxvi–xxxvii, T35, T43, T45, T137, T145, T147, T480, T481, T482, T526 **2-3:** T237 **2-4:** T245, T513, T518, T525, T526, T527, T530, T535, T536 **2-5:** T37, T47, T59, T69, T76–T77, T137, T147, T159, T169, T176–T177, T237, T247, T259, T443, T478, T479 **2-6:** T47, T145, T241, T510, T511, T513, T514, T517, T521, T522, T523, T526, T531, R2
W.2.3	Write narratives in which they recount a well-elaborated event or short sequence of events, include details to describe actions, thoughts, and feelings, use temporal words to signal event order, and provide a sense of closure.	**2-1:** T43, T55, T65, T72, T331, T341, T353, T363, T370, T433, T443, T453, T463, T470 **2-4:** T39, T49, T59, T69, T76–T77, T139, T149, T159, T169, T176–T177, T339, T349, T359, T369, T376–T377, T439, T449, T459, T469, T476–T477	**2-1:** T33, T131, T141, T153, T163, T170, T229, T239, T251, T257, T261, T268, T476, T477, T478 **2-2:** T516, T530 **2-3:** T358 **2-4:** T237, T247, T259, T269, T276, T347, T482, T483, T484, T515 **2-5:** T165 **2-6:** T528

Correlations

Standard	Standard Language	Key Citations	Additional Practice and Application
Production and Distribution of Writing			
W.2.4	With guidance and support from adults, produce writing in which the development and organization are appropriate to task and purpose. (Grade-specific expectations for writing types are defined in standards 1–3 above.) CA	**2-1:** T65, T153, T170, T251, T353, T433, T443, T453, T463 **2-2:** T55, T159, T176–T177, T257, T267, T275, T369, T376–T377, T437, T447, T457, T467, T474–T475 **2-3:** T57, T67, T74–T75, T151, T161, T168–T169, T249, T259, T266–T267, T347, T357, T364–T365, T449, T459, T466–T467 **2-4:** T59, T69, T76–T77, T159, T169, T176–T177, T259, T269, T276–T277, T359, T369, T376–T377, T439, T449, T459, T469, T476–T477 **2-5:** T59, T69, T76–T77, T159, T169, T176–T177, T259, T269, T276–T277, T359, T369, T376–T377, T455, T465, T472–T473 **2-6:** T59, T69, T76–T77, T159, T169, T176–T177, T253, T265, T272–T273, T359, T365, T372–T373, T455, T465, T472–T473	**2-1:** xxxvi–xxxvii, T33, T41, T43, T55, T61, T72, T131, T137, T141, T147, T163, T229, T239, T257, T261, T268, T331, T341, T359, T363, T370, T459, T470, T476, T480 **2-2:** xxxvi–xxxvii, T35, T43, T45, T63, T67, T74, T145, T169, T235, T243, T245, T337, T345, T347, T359, T365, T445, T463, T481, T513, T519, T523, T526, T533 **2-3:** xxxvi–xxxvii, T37, T47, T63, T131, T139, T141, T229, T237, T239, T255, T327, T335, T337, T427, T437 **2-4:** xxxvi–xxxvii, T39, T45, T47, T49, T65, T139, T147, T149, T165, T237, T245, T247, T265, T339, T347, T349, T447, T523 **2-5:** xxxvi–xxxvii, T37, T45, T47, T65, T137, T145, T147, T237, T245, T247, T265, T337, T347, T365, T435, T443, T445, T461, T478, T479 **2-6:** xxxvi–xxxvii, T39, T47, T49, T65, T137, T145, T147, T165, T233, T243, T261, T333, T341, T343, T361, T433, T441, T443, T461, T478, T518
W.2.5	With guidance and support from adults and peers, focus on a topic and strengthen writing as needed by revising and editing.	**2-1:** T72, T170, T268–T269, T463, T470–T471 **2-2:** T74–T75, T176–T177, T274–T275, T467, T474–T475 **2-3:** T74–T75, T168–T169, T266–T267, T459 **2-4:** T76–T77, T176–T177, T276–T277, T469, T476–T477 **2-5:** T76–T77, T176–T177, T276–T277, T465, T472–T473 **2-6:** T76–T77, T176–T177, T272–T273, T465, T472–T473	**2-1:** xxxvi–xxxvii, T70, T168, T266, T370, T468, T477, T478 **2-2:** T72, T374, T474, T480, T482, T513, T523, T533 **2-3:** xxxvi–xxxvii, T72, T166, T168, T255, T264, T266, T362, T464, T466, T473 **2-4:** T74, T274, T374, T472, T473, T474, T482, T483, T484, T515, T525, T527, T535 **2-5:** T74, T165, T174, T274, T374, T470, T480 **2-6:** T59, T74, T165, T174, T270, T370, T372, T470, T479, T480
W.2.6	With guidance and support from adults, use a variety of digital tools to produce and publish writing, including in collaboration with peers.	**2-1:** T433, T443, T453, T463, T470 **2-2:** T447, T457, T467, T474 **2-4:** T439, T449, T459, T469, T476 **2-5:** T435, T445, T455, T465, T472 **2-6:** T173	**2-1:** T331, T478 **2-2:** T437, T482, T512, T525 **2-3:** T437, T449, T459, T466 **2-4:** xxxvi–xxxvii, T484 **2-5:** T359, T480 **2-6:** xxxvi–xxxvii, T176, T433, T443, T455, T465, T472, T480, T517, T523, R2
Research to Build and Present Knowledge			
W.2.7	Participate in shared research and writing projects (e.g., read a number of books on a single topic to produce a report; record science observations).	**2-2:** T271 **2-5:** T73 **2-6:** T159, T169, T173, T176–T177	**2-1:** xxxvi–xxxvii, T44, T230, T364, T434, R3 **2-2:** xxxvi–xxxvii, T36, T63, T170, T365, T438, T463, T468, T512, T519, T525, R2–R4 **2-3:** xxxvi–xxxvii, T38, T58, T152, T165, T241, T250, T255, T329, T450, R2–R3 **2-4:** T40, T60, T140, T270, T360, T370, T521, T527, T531, R2–R5 **2-5:** xxxvi–xxxvii, T38, T45, T65, T70, T160, T248, T370, T461, R3 **2-6:** xxxvi–xxxvii, T65, T137, T147, T261, T366, T510, T513, T515, T517, T520, T523, R2, R3
W.2.8	Recall information from experiences or gather information from provided sources to answer a question.	**2-1:** T61, T265, T353, T453 **2-2:** T71, T271 **2-3:** T165 **2-5:** T73 **2-6:** T173, T369	**2-1:** xxx, T359, T367, T467, T476 **2-2:** vi, xxxvi–xxxvii, T447, T457, T480, T526, T530 **2-3:** vi, xxxvi–xxxvii, T361, T472 **2-4:** vi, T65, T73, T173, T465, T482, T512, T521, T527, T531, T532, T534 **2-5:** vi, xxxvi–xxxvii, T265, T273, T365, T479, T480 **2-6:** vi, xxxvi–xxxvii, T47, T511, T514, T517, T519, T521, T522, T523, T528, T531, R2
W.2.9	(Begins in grade 4)		

Standard	Standard Language	Key Citations	Additional Practice and Application

Range of Writing

Standard	Standard Language	Key Citations	Additional Practice and Application
W.2.10	Write routinely over extended time frames (time for research, reflection, and revision) and shorter time frames (a single sitting or a day or two) for a range of discipline-specific tasks, purposes, and audiences. CA	**2-1:** T55, T65, T72, T153, T163, T170, T251, T261, T268, T353, T370, T433, T443, T453, T463, T470 **2-2:** T55, T67, T74, T159, T169, T176, T257, T267, T275, T369, T376, T437, T447, T457, T467, T474 **2-3:** T57, T67, T74, T151, T161, T168–T169, T249, T259, T266–T267, T347, T357, T364–T365, T449, T459, T466–T467 **2-4:** T59, T69, T76–T77, T159, T169, T176–T177, T237, T247, T259, T269, T276–T277, T359, T369, T376, T439, T449, T459, T469, T476–T477 **2-5:** T59, T69, T76–T77, T159, T169, T176–T177, T259, T269, T276–T277, T359, T369, T376–T377, T455, T465, T472–T473 **2-6:** T59, T69, T76, T159, T169, T176–T177, T359, T365, T372–T373, T455, T465, T472–T473	**2-1:** xxxvi–xxxvii, T33, T41, T43, T61, T131, T137, T139, T141, T147, T229, T239, T257, T331, T339, T341, T347, T359, T363, T441, T459, T476 **2-2:** xxxvi–xxxvii, T35, T43, T45, T63, T145, T235, T243, T245, T337, T345, T359, T365, T445, T463, T480 **2-3:** xxxvi–xxxvii, T37, T45, T47, T63, T131, T138, T141, T229, T237, T239, T255, T327, T335, T337, T427, T437 **2-4:** xxxvi–xxxvii, T39, T47, T49, T65, T139, T147, T149, T245, T265, T339, T347, T349, T447 **2-5:** xxxvi–xxxvii, T37, T45, T47, T65, T137, T145, T147, T237, T245, T247, T265, T337, T347, T365, T435, T443, T445, T461, T480 **2-6:** xxxvi–xxxvii, T39, T47, T49, T65, T137, T145, T147, T165, T241, T261, T333, T341, T343, T361, T433, T441, T443, T461, T479, T480, T514, T521, T523, T526, T528, T531

SPEAKING AND LISTENING

Comprehension and Collaboration

Standard	Standard Language	Key Citations	Additional Practice and Application
SL.2.1a	Participate in collaborative conversations with diverse partners about *grade 2 topics and texts* with peers and adults in small and larger groups. Follow agreed-upon rules for discussions (e.g., gaining the floor in respectful ways, listening to others with care, speaking one at a time about the topics and texts under discussion).	**2-1:** T50, T69, T119 **2-2:** T50, T223, T321, T471 **2-3:** T23, T71, T466 **2-4:** T223, T476 **2-5:** T223, T323, T469 **2-6:** T73	**2-1:** xxx, xxxi, xxxvi–xxxvii, T12, T23, T30, T40, T45, T53, T56, T57, T61, T108, T138, T143, T148, T151, T155, T206, T214, T246, T252, T253, T304, T315, T328, T338, T343, T348, T355, T361, T366–T367, T406, T430, T440, T445, T448, T453, S9, S13, S19, S21, S23, S29, S33, S43 **2-2:** vi, xxxvi–xxxvii, T12, T23, T32, T42, T46, T47, T53, T57, T63, T134, T144, T157, T161, T173, T212, T226, T242, T246, T247, T252, T255, T259, T263, T268, T310, T338, T344, T348, T349, T354, T412, T414, T423, T433, T438, T444, T449, T452, T459, T463, T515, T519, T527, T529, T530, T534, S3, S9, S13, S19, S20, S23, S27, S29, S33, S37, S43, S47 **2-3:** vi, xxxvi, T12, T34, T44, T49, T52, T55, T59, T68, T110, T121, T128, T132, T138, T146, T149, T153, T165, T204, T215, T225, T236, T241, T244, T247, T251, T302, T313, T323, T334, T342, T345, T349, T353, T401, T424, T434, T439, T444, T447, T451, S3, S9, S13, S19, S23, S29, S30, S33, S43, S49 **2-4:** vi, xxxvi, T12, T23, T35, T46, T54, T57, T61, T112, T123, T135, T146, T151, T154, T157, T161, T234, T244, T249, T254, T257, T261, T312, T322, T336, T341, T346, T351, T354, T357, T361, T373, T412, T423, T436, T446, T451, T454, T457, T461, T465, T512, T514, T517, T519, T521, T524, T527, T529, T531, T532, T535, T536, S3, S9, S13, S19, S23, S24, S29, S33, S34, S39, S41, S43, S44, S49 **2-5:** vi, xxxvi, T12, T21, T23, T33, T49, T54, T57, T61, T65, T112, T123, T133, T144, T149, T154, T157, T161, T234, T244, T249, T254, T257, T261, T265, T344, T349, T354, T357, T361, T373, T412, T423, T442, T447, T450, T453, T457, T461, T472, T478, S3, S13, S23, S33, S37, S43 **2-6:** vi, T12, T23, T35, T46, T51, T54, T57, T61, T76, T112, T133, T144, T149, T154, T157, T161, T165, T212, T223, T229, T240, T245, T248, T251, T255, T308, T319, T329, T340, T345, T350, T353, T357, T365, T408, T419, T434, T440, T445, T450, T453, T457, T469, T472, T478, T513, T520, T521, T523, T525, T527, T528, T532, S3, S4, S9, S13, S14, S19, S21, S23, S29, S33, S39, S41, S43, S44, S49, S51, R3
SL.2.1b	Participate in collaborative conversations with diverse partners about *grade 2 topics and texts* with peers and adults in small and larger groups. Build on others' talk in conversations by linking their comments to the remarks of others.	**2-1:** T50, T69 **2-2:** T223, T423, T471 **2-3:** T71 **2-4:** T323 **2-5:** T23, T333 **2-6:** T35, T73, T223	**2-1:** T40, T61, T66, T128, T142, T154, T214, T354, T366–T367, T448, T454, S10, S20, S30, S40 **2-2:** T50, T56, T63, T148, T154, T258, T333, T344, T349, T354, T365, T370, T452, T459, T481, T519, T522, T527, T534, S7 **2-3:** T34, T146, T162, T165, T230, T236, T244, T334, T342, T361, T424, T434, T438, T444, S10, S20, S50 **2-4:** T54, T170, T173, T234, T346, T354, T436, T446, T450, T454, T512, T514, T517, T519, T521, T524, T527, T529, T531, T532, T535, T536 **2-5:** T48, T54, T154, T165, T170, T244, T254, T265, T273, T344, T354, T450 **2-6:** T144, T154, T171, T229, T248, T261, T350, T440, T450, T467, T469, T510, T513, T520, T523, T525, T527, T528, T532

Standard	Standard Language	Key Citations	Additional Practice and Application
SL.2.1c	Participate in collaborative conversations with diverse partners about *grade 2 topics and texts* with peers and adults in small and larger groups. Ask for clarification and further explanation as needed about the topics and texts under discussion.	**2-1:** T219, T265, T306, T408 **2-2:** T50, T173 **2-3:** T361 **2-5:** T73, T469 **2-6:** T35	**2-1:** T14, T50, T61, T119, T246, T315, T348, T353, T366–T367, T453, T455, T478, S51 **2-2:** T23, T32, T144, T154, T252, T312, T333, T344, T354, T414, T452, T463, T467, T482, T522, T524, T527 **2-3:** T14, T112, T146, T206, T244, T304, T315, T342, T353, T402, T413, T444 **2-4:** T23, T135, T146, T173, T244, T314, T425, T454, T473, T484, T512, T514, T517, T519, T521, T524, T527, T529, T531, T532, T535, T536 **2-5:** xxxvii, T14, T54, T114, T173, T254, T273, T333, T414, T450, T480 **2-6:** xxxvii, T248, T329, T369, T410, T450, T469, T480, T508, T513, T516, T520, T523, T525, T527, T528
SL.2.2	Recount or describe key ideas or details from a text read aloud or information presented orally or through other media. a. Give and follow three- and four-step oral directions. CA	**2-1:** T14, T208, T306, T408 **2-2:** T373, T457, T467, T474 **2-3:** T70, T263, T463 **2-4:** T72, T273 **2-5:** T72, T123, T165, T173, T469 **2-6:** T72, T269	**2-1:** xxx, T69, T110, T358 **2-2:** T14, T112, T173, T312, T414 **2-3:** T14, T112, T206, T304, T402 **2-4:** T14, T114, T214, T314, T414, T473, T510, R5 **2-5:** T14, T33, T114, T133, T214, T314, T414, T478, R2 **2-6:** T14, T114, T133, T214, T269, T310, T410, T430
SL.2.3	Ask and answer questions about what a speaker says in order to clarify comprehension, gather additional information, or deepen understanding of a topic or issue.	**2-1:** T265, T467 **2-3:** T361 **2-4:** T273 **2-5:** T73, T469	**2-1:** T69, T110, T119, T167, T353, T453 **2-2:** T14, T63, T71, T144, T263, T463, T471, T522, T527, T529 **2-3:** T14, T23, T63, T112, T123, T206, T263, T353, T402, T474 **2-4:** T223, T244, T473, T484, T524, T529, T531, T532 **2-5:** xxxvii, T14, T114, T165, T173, T265, T273, T314, T344, T432 **2-6:** xxxvii, T114, T123, T173, T214, T269, T369, T410, T480, T510, T518, T520, T525

Presentation of Knowledge and Ideas

Standard	Standard Language	Key Citations	Additional Practice and Application
SL.2.4	Tell a story or recount an experience with appropriate facts and relevant, descriptive details, speaking audibly in coherent sentences. a. Plan and deliver a narrative presentation that: recounts a well-elaborated event, includes details, reflects a logical sequence, and provides a conclusion. CA	**2-1:** T470 **2-2:** T457, T467, T474 **2-3:** T463 **2-4:** T265, T273 **2-5:** T73, T173	**2-1:** T23, T25, T40, T119, T217, T257, T265, T315, T331, T338, T440, T459, T478 **2-2:** T63, T71, T121, T223, T242, T263, T271, T313, T344, T364, T423, T444, T512, T515, T522, T525, T527, T529 **2-3:** xxxvi–xxxvii, T23, T121, T434 **2-4:** T25, T46, T125, T146, T225, T244, T325, T465, T484, R5 **2-5:** xxxvii, T265, T273, T365, T472, T478, T480, S10, R2 **2-6:** xxxvii, T73, T76, T369, T469, T472, T479, T480, T525, T527
SL.2.5	Create audio recordings of stories or poems; add drawings or other visual displays to stories or recounts of experiences when appropriate to clarify ideas, thoughts, and feelings.	**2-1:** T158, T470 **2-2:** T457, T467, T474 **2-3:** T361 **2-4:** T73 **2-5:** T273 **2-6:** T73, T241, T461, T469	**2-1:** T23, T359, T478 **2-3:** T474 **2-4:** T536 **2-5:** T73, T165, T173, T265, T365, R3 **2-6:** T240, T261, T369, T519, T523, T527
SL.2.6	Produce complete sentences when appropriate to task and situation in order to provide requested detail or clarification. (See grade 2 Language standards 1 and 3 for specific expectations.)	**2-1:** T40, T116, T145, T243, T459, T467 **2-2:** T20, T112, T151, T321, T351 **2-3:** T361, T463 **2-4:** R5 **2-5:** T73, T251	**2-1:** T50, T167, T214, T246, T257, T312, T348, T414, T430, T448, S30, S40, S50, R2 **2-2:** T50, T63, T71, T134, T144, T164, T249, T263, T271, T354, T365, T370, T373, T452, T458, T468, T513, T523, T530, T533, S10, S20, S30, S40, S50 **2-3:** xxxvii, T23, T146, T215, T231, T233, T244, T342, T444 **2-4:** xxxvii, T25, T35, T54, T114, T125, T187, T225, T325, T336, T454, T473, T532, S40, S50 **2-5:** T20, T25, T54, T120, T144, T151, T154, T165, T173, T220, T254, T273, T320, T333, T354, T420, T442, T450, S20, S30, S40, S50 **2-6:** T20, T120, T220, T248, T316, T369, T416, T466, T519, T531, S10, S20, S30, S40, S50

LANGUAGE

Conventions of Standard English

Standard	Standard Language	Key Citations	Additional Practice and Application
L.2.1a	Demonstrate command of the conventions of standard English grammar and usage when writing or speaking. Use collective nouns (e.g., *group*).	**2-2:** T54, T67, T72–T73, T368 **2-5:** T47	**2-2:** T96, T398, S8, S10
L.2.1b	Demonstrate command of the conventions of standard English grammar and usage when writing or speaking. Form and use frequently occurring irregular plural nouns (e.g., *feet, children, teeth, mice, fish*).	**2-2:** T44, T72–T73 **2-3:** T66, T67 **2-6:** T355	**2-2:** T34, T96, T482, S8, S10

Standard	Standard Language	Key Citations	Additional Practice and Application
L.2.1c	Demonstrate command of the conventions of standard English grammar and usage when writing or speaking. Use reflexive pronouns (e.g., *myself, ourselves*).	**2-4:** T58, T69, T74–T75 **2-5:** T68, T159	**2-3:** T490, T491 **2-4:** T98, T483, T484, S8 **2-5:** T69
L.2.1d	Demonstrate command of the conventions of standard English grammar and usage when writing or speaking. Form and use the past tense of frequently occurring irregular verbs (e.g., *sat, hid, told*).	**2-5:** T236, T246, T258, T268, T336, T346, T358, T374, T434, T444, T470 **2-6:** T464	**2-1:** T478 **2-4:** T246, T258, T298, T483, T484, S28, S30 **2-5:** T274, T298, T398, T498, S28, S30, S38, S40, S48, S50 **2-6:** T264, T364
L.2.1e	Demonstrate command of the conventions of standard English grammar and usage when writing or speaking. Use adjectives and adverbs, and choose between them depending on what is to be modified.	**2-5:** T36, T46, T58, T74, T136, T146, T158, T174 **2-6:** T68, T136, T146, T158, T168, T174, T432, T442, T454, T470	**2-1:** T43, T64, T65, T239, T261, T463 **2-2:** T359, T498, T499, T501 **2-3:** T384, T385 **2-4:** T515 **2-5:** T98, T198, T479, T480, S8, S10, S18, S20 **2-6:** T198, T244, T498, T511, T521, S48, S50
L.2.1f	Demonstrate command of the conventions of standard English grammar and usage when writing or speaking. Produce, expand, and rearrange complete simple and compound sentences (e.g., *The boy watched the movie; The little boy watched the movie; The action movie was watched by the little boy*).	**2-1:** T54, T70, T152, T168, T266 **2-2:** T374 **2-3:** T46, T56, T72, T130, T140, T150, T166 **2-5:** T158, T374 **2-6:** T174	**2-1:** T42, T94, T130, T140, T162, T192, T260, T290, T362, T392, T443, T462, T477, T496, S8, S18, S20 **2-2:** T20, S28, S48 **2-3:** T36, T45, T96, T139, T190, T237, T335, T473, T474, S8, S10, S18, S20 **2-4:** T147, T245, T347, T447, T483, T484, T515, T535 **2-5:** T20, T45, T145, T245, T443 **2-6:** T47, T48, T145, T241, T341, T441
L.2.1g	Demonstrate command of the conventions of standard English grammar and usage when writing or speaking. **Create readable documents with legible print. CA**	**2-1:** T32, T42, T64, T72, T140, T170, T238, T260, T268, T340, T362, T442, T470, R22–R23 **2-2:** T44, T66, T74, T146, T168, T176, T244, T266, T274, T346, T446, T474 **2-3:** T46, T140, T160, T168, T238, T266, T336, T356, T436, T466, R24–R25 **2-4:** T48, T76, T148, T168, T176, T246, T268, T276, T348, T368, T448, T468, T476, R24–R25 **2-5:** T46, T68, T76, T146, T168, T176, T276, T346, T444, T472, R22–R23 **2-6:** T48, T68, T76, T146, T176, T242, T264, T342, T364, T442, T464, T472, R22–R23	**2-1:** T61, T257, T359, T459, T476, T478 **2-2:** T365, T480, T482 **2-3:** T63, T255, T258 **2-4:** T365
L.2.2a	Demonstrate command of the conventions of standard English capitalization, punctuation, and spelling when writing. Capitalize holidays, product names, and geographic names.	**2-2:** T136, T158, T174–T175 **2-3:** T160, T336, T362 **2-4:** T368	**2-2:** T198, S18, S20 **2-3:** T386, S38, S40 **2-4:** T398
L.2.2b	Demonstrate command of the conventions of standard English capitalization, punctuation, and spelling when writing. Use commas in greetings and closings of letters.	**2-1:** T163, T170 **2-3:** T37, T67, T74 **2-4:** T358	**2-1:** T131 **2-3:** T63
L.2.2c	Demonstrate command of the conventions of standard English capitalization, punctuation, and spelling when writing. Use an apostrophe to form contractions and frequently occurring possessives.	**2-2:** T441, T460 **2-3:** T50, T61, T155 **2-6:** T38, T48, T58, T74, T232, T242, T252, T270, T441	**2-2:** T417, T418, T436, T446, T466, T472, T486, T500, S42, S46 **2-6:** T98, T151, T190, T294, T479, S10

Correlations

Standard	Standard Language	Key Citations	Additional Practice and Application
L.2.2d	Demonstrate command of the conventions of standard English capitalization, punctuation, and spelling when writing. Generalize learned spelling patterns when writing words (e.g., cage -> badge; boy -> boil).	**2-1:** T345, T356 **2-3:** T336 **2-4:** T148, T363, T448 **2-5:** T46, T218, T444 **2-6:** T48, T347	**2-1:** T32, T42, T54, T64, T70, T130, T140, T152, T162, T165, T168, T178, T192, T228, T238, T250, T260, T263, T266, T276, T290, T330, T340, T352, T362, T368, T432, T442, T452, T462, T468 **2-2:** T34, T44, T54, T66, T72, T136, T146, T158, T168, T174, T184, T198, T234, T244, T256, T266, T269, T272, T282, T288, T296, T336, T346, T358, T368, T374, T436, T456, T466, T472, T492 **2-3:** T36, T46, T56, T66, T72, T130, T140, T150, T160, T163, T166, T228, T238, T248, T258, T264, T326, T336, T346, T356, T362, T426, T436, T448, T458, T464 **2-4:** T38, T48, T58, T68, T71, T74, T138, T158, T168, T174, T236, T246, T258, T268, T274, T338, T348, T358, T368, T374, T438, T458, T468, T471, T494, T502 **2-5:** T36, T58, T68, T71, T74, T84, T136, T146, T158, T168, T174, T236, T246, T258, T268, T271, T274, T284, T336, T346, T358, T368, T371, T374, T434, T455, T464, T467, T470, T484 **2-6:** T38, T58, T68, T74, T84, T136, T146, T158, T168, T174, T184, T232, T242, T264, T267, T270, T280, T332, T342, T354, T364, T370, T380, T432, T442, T454, T464, T470, T484
L.2.2e	Demonstrate command of the conventions of standard English capitalization, punctuation, and spelling when writing. Consult reference materials, including beginning dictionaries, as needed to check and correct spellings.	**2-1:** T463, T470 **2-2:** T467, T474 **2-3:** T466 **2-4:** T476 **2-5:** T472	**2-5:** T446 **2-6:** T272, T472

Knowledge of Language

Standard	Standard Language	Key Citations	Additional Practice and Application
L.2.3a	Use knowledge of language and its conventions when writing, speaking, reading, or listening. Compare formal and informal uses of English.	**2-1:** T141, T167 **2-2:** T471 **2-3:** T67, T74, T263 **2-4:** T129, T144–T145	**2-2:** T245, T267 **2-4:** T515 **2-5:** T480 **2-6:** T58, T460

Vocabulary Acquisition and Use

Standard	Standard Language	Key Citations	Additional Practice and Application
L.2.4a	Determine or clarify the meaning of unknown and multiple-meaning words and phrases based on *grade 2 reading and content*, choosing flexibly from an array of strategies. Use sentence-level context as a clue to the meaning of a word or phrase.	**2-1:** T259, T361 **2-2:** T40–T41, T167 **2-3:** T159 **2-4:** T167 **2-5:** T167, T367, T463 **2-6:** T67, T423, T438–T439	**2-1:** T82, T83, T180, T181, T224, T278, T279, T288, T289, T380, T381, T390, T391, T393, T484, T485 **2-2:** T27, T84, T85, T86, T87, T186, T187, T196, T197, T199, T284, T285, T367, T396, T397, T399, T466, T488, T489, T521 **2-3:** T84, T85, T188, T189, T191, T480, T481, S13, S23, S33, S43 **2-4:** T27, T29, T67, T86, T87, T96, T97, T99, T126, T186, T187, T196, T197, T199, T267, T286, T287, T386, T387, T490, T491, S3, S13, S23, S33, S43 **2-5:** T86, T87, T96, T97, T186, T187, T196, T197, T199, T286, T287, T386, T387, T396, T397, T496, T497, T499 **2-6:** T86, T87, T96, T97, T99, T186, T187, T282, T283, T363, T382, T383, T395, T463, T486, T487, T496, T497, T506, T512, T519, S3, S13, S27, S33, S43
L.2.4b	Determine or clarify the meaning of unknown and multiple-meaning words and phrases based on *grade 2 reading and content*, choosing flexibly from an array of strategies. Determine the meaning of the new word formed when a known prefix is added to a known word (e.g., *happy/unhappy; tell/retell*).	**2-2:** T64–T65 **2-3:** T64–T65 **2-4:** T466–T467 **2-5:** T316–T317, T340–T341	**2-2:** T94, T95, T97 **2-3:** T94, T95, T97 **2-4:** T500, T501, T503 **2-5:** T384, T398
L.2.4c	Determine or clarify the meaning of unknown and multiple-meaning words and phrases based on *grade 2 reading and content*, choosing flexibly from an array of strategies. Use a known root word as a clue to the meaning of an unknown word with the same root (e.g., *addition, additional*).	**2-1:** T460–T461 **2-2:** T464–T465 **2-3:** T456–T457 **2-5:** T212 **2-6:** T462–T463	**2-1:** T494, T497 **2-2:** T13, T498 **2-3:** T493 **2-4:** T296, T297, T500, T501 **2-6:** T496, T497, T499

Standard	Standard Language	Key Citations	Additional Practice and Application
L.2.4d	Determine or clarify the meaning of unknown and multiple-meaning words and phrases based on *grade 2 reading and content*, choosing flexibly from an array of strategies. Use knowledge of the meaning of individual words to predict the meaning of compound words (e.g., *birdhouse, lighthouse, housefly; bookshelf, notebook, bookmark*).	**2-2:** T264–T265 **2-3:** T404–T405 **2-5:** T266–T267, T270 **2-6:** T131	**2-2:** T294, T295, T297 **2-3:** T428, T492 **2-5:** T296, T297, T299
L.2.4e	Determine or clarify the meaning of unknown and multiple-meaning words and phrases based on *grade 2 reading and content*, choosing flexibly from an array of strategies. Use glossaries and beginning dictionaries, both print and digital, to determine or clarify the meaning of words and phrases **in all content areas. CA**	**2-1:** T53, T160–T161, T249, T351, T451 **2-2:** T255, T357 **2-3:** T159, T345 **2-4:** T357, R2 **2-5:** T117, T167 **2-6:** T67	**2-1:** T63, T92, T93, T95, T151, T190, T191, T193, T259, T288, T289 **2-2:** T53, T157, T455, R4 **2-3:** T55, T65, T149, T188, T189, T247, T257, T286, T287, T289, T355, T384, T387 **2-4:** T57, T157, T257, T447, T457 **2-5:** T57, T67, T96, T97, T99, T157, T198, T257, T357, T453 **2-6:** T57, T96, T97, T157, T251, T353, T363, T392, T393, T395, T453
L.2.5a	Demonstrate understanding of word relationships and nuances in word meanings. Identify real-life connections between words and their use (e.g., describe foods that are *spicy* or *juicy*).	**2-1:** T150, T248, T350, T450 **2-2:** T52, T156, T254, T356, T454 **2-6:** T263	**2-1:** T52, T68, T109, T166, T264, T305, T435, T451 **2-2:** T47, T57, T70, T138, T149, T161, T172, T259, T270, T339, T349, T360, T372, T439, T449, T455, T459, T466, T470, T513, T523 **2-3:** T54, T70, T148, T164, T246, T262, T344, T360, T446, T462 **2-4:** T56, T72, T130, T156, T160, T172, T248, T256, T272, T356, T360, T372, T456–T457, T460, T472, S20, S30 **2-5:** T56, T60, T72, T156, T160, T172, T256, T260, T272, T338, T356, T360, T372, T452–T453, T456, T468 **2-6:** T56, T60, T72, T156, T160, T172, T250, T268, T352, T368, T452–T453, T468
L.2.5b	Demonstrate understanding of word relationships and nuances in word meanings. Distinguish shades of meaning among closely related verbs (e.g., *toss, throw, hurl*) and closely related adjectives (e.g., *thin, slender, skinny, scrawny*).	**2-2:** T367 **2-4:** T366–T367, T373 **2-5:** T247 **2-6:** T166–T167	**2-2:** T396, T397, T399 **2-4:** T396, T397, T399 **2-5:** T156, T276 **2-6:** T196, T197, T199
L.2.6	Use words and phrases acquired through conversations, reading and being read to, and responding to texts, including using adjectives and adverbs to describe (e.g., *When other kids are happy that makes me happy*).	**2-1:** T20, T23, T53, T306, T333, R2 **2-2:** T20, T53, T70, T255 **2-3:** T55, T70, T247 **2-4:** T57, T72, T141 **2-5:** T20, T57, T120, T220, T320, T420 **2-6:** T20, T57, T120, T220, T316, T416	**2-1:** xxxi, T13, T35, T45, T57, T66, T67, T68, T82, T83, T116, T132, T133, T143, T151, T154, T155, T165, T166, T180, T181, T214, T231, T249, T253, T263, T264, T278, T279, T288, T291, T312, T339, T342, T351, T365, T366, T380, T381, T414, T426, T430, T435, T444, T451, T455, T465, T466, T484, T485 **2-2:** T32, T37, T56, T68, T69, T84, T85, T118, T134, T157, T160, T171, T172, T186, T187, T220, T232, T237, T246, T247, T258, T269, T270, T284, T285, T318, T349, T357, T371, T372, T386, T387, T420, T439, T448, T455, T458, T469, T470, T488, T489 **2-3:** T25, T39, T49, T59, T69, T84, T85, T123, T128, T133, T142, T143, T149, T153, T163, T164, T178, T179, T217, T231, T241, T251, T260, T261, T262, T276, T277, T304, T315, T329, T338, T345, T348, T349, T359, T360, T374, T375, T413, T429, T438, T439, T447, T451, T461, T462, T480, T481, S10, S20, S30, S40, S50 **2-4:** T35, T41, T50, T51, T61, T71, T86, T87, T135, T150, T151, T157, T161, T171, T172, T186, T187, T239, T248, T249, T257, T260–T261, T271, T272, T286, T287, T336, T341, T351, T357, T360, T361, T371, T372, T386, T387, T440, T441, T451, T457, T461, T471, T472, T490, T491, T523, T532, S10 **2-5:** T39, T49, T60, T61, T71, T72, T86, T87, T138, T139, T149, T157, T160, T171, T172, T184, T186, T187, T239, T249, T257, T260, T261, T271, T272, T286, T287, T333, T338, T339, T349, T357, T360, T361, T371, T372, T386, T387, T414, T437, T446, T447, T453, T456, T457, T467, T468, T486, T487, S30 **2-6:** T39, T41, T49, T51, T59, T60, T69, T70, T71, T72, T76, T139, T149, T157, T160, T171, T172, T174, T235, T244, T245, T251, T254, T255, T267, T268, T329, T335, T345, T353, T356, T367, T368, T382, T383, T435, T444, T445, T453, T456, T457, T467, T468, S40

Correlations

California English Language Development Standards

Standard	Standard Language	Key Citations

PART I: INTERACTING IN MEANINGFUL WAYS

A. COLLABORATIVE

1. Exchanging information and ideas

ELD.PI.2.1

Emerging Contribute to conversations and express ideas by asking and answering *yes-no* and *wh-* questions and responding using gestures, words, and learned phrases.

Expanding Contribute to class, group, and partner discussions, including sustained dialogue, by listening attentively, following turn-taking rules, asking relevant questions, affirming others, and adding relevant information.

Bridging Contribute to class, group, and partner discussions, including sustained dialogue, by listening attentively, following turn-taking rules, asking relevant questions, affirming others, adding pertinent information, building on responses, and providing useful feedback.

2-1: xxx, xxxi, xxxvi–xxxvii, T12, T20, T21, T23, T25, T30, T45, T50, T53, T56, T57, T60, T62–T63, T66, T68–T69, T80, T81, T82, T83, T85, T86, T88, T89, T90, T91, T94, T95, T110, T116, T117, T118, T119, T121, T128, T138, T142, T143, T151, T154, T155, T159, T160, T166–T167, T178, T179, T180, T181, T182, T183, T184, T186, T187, T188, T189, T190, T191, T192, T193, T206, T214, T215, T216, T217, T219, T226, T246, T252, T253, T257, T258, T264–T265, T276, T277, T278, T279, T280, T281, T282, T284, T285, T286, T287, T288, T289, T290, T291, T304, T306, T312, T313, T315, T317, T328, T336, T343, T348, T351, T354, T355, T359, T360, T366–T367, T378, T379, T380, T381, T383, T384, T386, T387, T388, T389, T390, T391, T392, T393, T406, T408, T414, T415, T416, T417, T419, T430, T438, T440, T445, T448, T454, T455, T460–T461, T464, T466–T467, T476, T478, T482, T483, T484, T485, T486, T487, T488, T490, T491, T492, T493, T494, T495, T496, T497, S2, S3, S4, S6, S7, S8, S9, S11, S13, S14, S16, S17, S18, S19, S21, S24, S26, S27, S28, S29, S30, S32, S34, S35, S36, S37, S38, S39, S40, S42, S43, S44, S45, S46, S47, S48, S49, S50, S51

2-2: vi, vii, xxxvi–xxxvii, T12, T14, T20, T21, T22, T23, T32, T40, T42, T46, T47, T50, T53, T56, T57, T64, T70–T71, T82, T83, T84, T85, T86, T87, T90, T91, T92, T93, T94, T95, T96, T97, T118, T119, T120, T121, T134, T142, T144, T148, T149, T154, T156, T157, T161, T165, T166–T167, T168, T172–T173, T174, T184, T185, T186, T187, T189, T192, T193, T194, T195, T196, T197, T198, T199, T212, T220, T221, T222, T223, T232, T240, T242, T246, T247, T248, T249, T252, T254, T255, T258, T259, T262, T263, T264–T265, T268, T270–T271, T273, T282, T283, T284, T285, T286, T287, T290, T291, T292, T293, T294, T295, T310, T312, T318, T319, T320, T321, T323, T333, T338, T342, T344, T345, T348, T354, T361, T365, T366–T367, T370, T372, T374, T384, T385, T386, T387, T388, T389, T392, T393, T394, T395, T396, T397, T412, T414, T420, T421, T422, T423, T425, T433, T442, T444, T445, T449, T452, T454, T456, T459, T463, T464, T466, T470–T471, T480, T482, T486, T487, T488, T489, T494, T495, T496, T497, T498, T499, T508, T510, T515, T516, T517, T519, T522, T524, T525, T526, T527, T529, T530, T533, T534, S3, S4, S6, S8, S9, S10, S12, S13, S14, S15, S16, S18, S19, S20, S22, S23, S24, S25, S26, S27, S28, S29, S30, S32, S33, S38, S39, S40, S42, S43, S44, S45, S46, S47, S49, S50

2-3: vi, vii, xxxvi–xxxvii, T12, T14, T23, T25, T34, T44, T49, T52, T54–T55, T59, T62, T63, T64–T65, T68, T70–T71, T72, T73, T82, T83, T84, T85, T86, T87, T90, T91, T92, T93, T94, T95, T96, T97, T110, T112, T120, T121, T123, T128, T132, T138, T143, T146, T148–T149, T153, T157, T158, T162, T164–T165, T167, T176, T177, T178, T179, T180, T181, T184, T185, T186, T187, T188, T189, T190, T191, T204, T206, T212, T214, T215, T217, T225, T230, T236, T241, T244, T246, T247, T251, T255, T256, T262–T263, T264, T274, T275, T276, T277, T278, T279, T282, T283, T284, T285, T286, T287, T288, T289, T302, T312, T313, T315, T323, T332, T334, T339, T342, T344–T345, T349, T353, T354–T355, T360–T361, T372, T373, T374, T375, T376, T377, T380, T381, T382, T383, T384, T385, T386, T387, T401, T410, T411, T413, T424, T429, T434, T438, T439, T444, T446–T447, T451, T455, T456–T457, T462–T463, T472, T474, T478, T479, T480, T481, T482, T483, T486, T487, T488, T489, T490, T491, T492, T493, S3, S4, S6, S7, S8, S9, S10, S11, S13, S14, S16, S17, S18, S19, S21, S22, S23, S24, S25, S26, S27, S28, S29, S30, S31, S32, S33, S34, S35, S36, S37, S38, S40, S41, S42, S43, S44, S45, S46, S47, S48, S49

2-4: vi, vii, xxxvi–xxxvii, T12, T14, T23, T25, T35, T44, T50, T51, T54, T56, T57, T61, T65, T66–T67, T71, T72–T73, T84, T85, T86, T87, T88, T89, T92, T93, T94, T95, T96, T97, T98, T99, T112, T114, T122, T123, T125, T135, T144, T146, T154, T156–T157, T161, T165, T166, T170, T172–T173, T184, T185, T186, T187, T188, T189, T192, T193, T194, T195, T196, T197, T198, T199, T214, T222, T223, T225, T234, T242, T244, T254, T256–T257, T261, T265, T266, T268, T272–T273, T284, T285, T286, T287, T288, T289, T292, T293, T294, T295, T296, T297, T298, T299, T304, T312, T314, T322, T323, T325, T336, T340, T346, T351, T354, T357, T365, T366–T367, T372–T373, T384, T385, T386, T387, T388, T389, T392, T393, T394, T395, T396, T397, T398, T399, T402, T412, T414, T422, T423, T425, T436, T446, T451, T454, T456–T457, T461, T465, T466, T472–T473, T482, T484, T488, T489, T490, T491, T492, T493, T496, T497, T498, T499, T500, T501, T502, T503, T510, T512, T513, T514, T515, T516, T517, T518, T519, T521, T522, T523, T524, T525, T526, T527, T528, T529, T530, T531, T532, T534, T536, S2, S3, S4, S5, S6, S7, S8, S9, S12, S13, S14, S15, S16, S17, S18, S19, S20, S21, S22, S23, S24, S25, S26, S27, S28, S29, S30, S31, S32, S33, S34, S35, S36, S37, S38, S39, S40, S41, S42, S43, S44, S45, S46, S47, S48, S49, S50, S51

Standard	Standard Language	Key Citations
		2-5: vi, vii, xxi, xxxvi–xxxvii, T12, T14, T20, T21, T22, T23, T25, T33, T42, T44, T48, T49, T54, T57, T61, T66–T67, T72–T73, T86, T87, T88, T89, T92, T93, T94, T95, T96, T97, T98, T99, T112, T120, T121, T122, T123, T133, T142, T144, T149, T154, T156–T157, T161, T166–T167, T170, T172–T173, T186, T187, T188, T189, T192, T193, T194, T195, T196, T197, T198, T199, T214, T220, T221, T222, T223, T234, T242, T244, T249, T254, T257, T261, T266–T267, T272–T273, T286, T287, T288, T289, T292, T293, T294, T295, T296, T297, T298, T299, T314, T320, T321, T322, T323, T333, T344, T349, T354, T356–T357, T366–T367, T372–T373, T386, T387, T388, T389, T392, T393, T394, T395, T396, T397, T398, T399, T412, T414, T420, T421, T422, T423, T432, T440, T442, T450, T452–T453, T457, T462–T463, T468–T469, T478, T479, T486, T487, T488, T489, T492, T493, T494, T495, T496, T497, T498, T499, S2, S3, S4, S5, S6, S7, S8, S9, S10, S11, S12, S13, S14, S15, S16, S17, S18, S20, S22, S23, S24, S25, S26, S27, S28, S29, S31, S32, S33, S34, S35, S36, S37, S38, S39, S40, S41, S42, S44, S45, S46, S48, S50 **2-6:** vi, vii, xxxvi–xxxvii, T12, T14, T20, T21, T22, T23, T35, T44, T46, T51, T54, T56–T57, T61, T64, T65, T66–T67, T72–T73, T86, T87, T88, T89, T92, T93, T94, T95, T96, T97, T98, T99, T112, T120, T121, T122, T123, T133, T142, T144, T149, T154, T156–T157, T164, T165, T166–T167, T170, T172–T173, T186, T187, T188, T189, T192, T193, T194, T195, T196, T197, T198, T199, T212, T214, T220, T221, T222, T223, T229, T238, T240, T245, T248, T250–T251, T255, T262, T264, T265, T268–T269, T282, T283, T284, T285, T288, T289, T290, T291, T292, T293, T294, T295, T308, T310, T316, T317, T318, T319, T329, T340, T345, T350, T352–T353, T357, T362–T363, T364, T365, T368–T369, T382, T383, T384, T385, T388, T389, T390, T391, T392, T393, T394, T395, T408, T410, T416, T417, T418, T419, T430, T434, T440, T445, T450, T452–T453, T457, T460, T461, T462–T463, T466, T468–T469, T478, T486, T487, T488, T489, T492, T493, T494, T495, T496, T497, T498, T499, T506, T508, T509, T510, T511, T512, T513, T514, T515, T516, T517, T518, T519, T520, T521, T522, T523, T524, T525, T526, T527, T528, T531, T532, S2, S3, S4, S5, S6, S7, S8, S9, S10, S11, S12, S13, S14, S15, S16, S17, S18, S19, S20, S21, S22, S23, S24, S25, S26, S27, S28, S29, S30, S32, S33, S34, S35, S36, S37, S38, S39, S40, S41, S42, S43, S44, S45, S46, S47, S48, S49, S50, S51

2. Interacting via written English

Standard	Standard Language	Key Citations
ELD.PI.2.2	**Emerging** Collaborate with peers on joint writing projects of short informational and literary texts, using technology where appropriate for publishing, graphics, etc. **Expanding** Collaborate with peers on joint writing projects of longer informational and literary texts, using technology where appropriate for publishing, graphics, etc. **Bridging** Collaborate with peers on joint writing projects of a variety of longer informational and literary texts, using technology where appropriate for publishing, graphics, etc.	**2-1:** xxxvi–xxxvii, T44, T230, T257, T332, T362, T364, T434, S4, S14, S24, S34, S44 **2-2:** xxxvi–xxxvii, T36, T54, T63, T167, T170, T226, T236, T265, T375, T438, T442, T456, T463, T465, T468, T473, T480, T512, T525 **2-3:** xxxvi–xxxvii, T38, T58, T73, T150, T165, T167, T240, T255, T264, T329, T450, T474, S4, S14, S24, S34 **2-4:** xxxvi–xxxvii, T40, T60, T66–T67, T140, T242, T270, T360, T370, T466, T515, T527, T530, T534, T536, S4, S14, S24, S34, S44 **2-5:** xxxvi–xxxvii, T21, T38, T65, T70, T160, T248, T273, T370, T440, T461, T480 **2-6:** xxxvi–xxxvii, T65, T137, T147, T148, T159, T169, T173, T176, T366, T480, T510, T511, T515, T517, T523, T530, S4, S14, S24, S34, S44

3. Offering opinions

Standard	Standard Language	Key Citations
ELD.PI.2.3	**Emerging** Offer opinions and negotiate with others in conversations using learned phrases (e.g., *I think X.*), as well as open responses, in order to gain and/or hold the floor. **Expanding** Offer opinions and negotiate with others in conversations using an expanded set of learned phrases (e.g., *I agree with X, but X.*), as well as open responses, in order to gain and/or hold the floor, provide counterarguments, etc. **Bridging** Offer opinions and negotiate with others in conversations using a variety of learned phrases (e.g., *That's a good idea, but X.*), as well as open responses, in order to gain and/or hold the floor, provide counter-arguments, elaborate on an idea, etc.	**2-1:** xxx, T21, T23, T40, T61, T63, T69, T117, T119, T121, T125, T138, T144, T148, T159, T217, T248, T257, T265, T315, T317, T326, T328, T358, T359, T367, T417, T428, T429, T430, T459, T463, T467, T472, S6, S16, S20, S26, S36, S46 **2-2:** vi, xxxvi, T22, T63, T65, T71, T120, T132, T133, T165, T175, T215, T222, T225, T232, T242, T255, T263, T265, T319, T320, T323, T344, T345, T365, T368, T422, T433, T442, T444, T445, T454, T471, T473, T490, T491, T494, T495, T496, T497, T501, T510, T530, S4, S34, S49 **2-3:** vi, xxxvi, T23, T27, T34, T44, T62, T63, T71, T121, T138, T148, T157, T159, T236, T246, T250, T262–T263, T334, T347, T353, T424, T434, T455, T460, T474, S6, S16, S20, S26, S36, S46 **2-4:** vi, xxxvi, T26, T65, T73, T123, T135, T165, T173, T222, T223, T231, T233, T265, T322, T323, T329, T330, T336, T346, T356, T365, T422, T423, T436, T446, T465, T473, T517, T524, T525, T529, T530, T531, T532, T536, S6, S16, S26, S36, S46 **2-5:** vi, T23, T25, T72, T121, T129, T131, T144, T233, T234, T244, T323, T333, T344, T373, T422, T423, T461, T469 **2-6:** vi, T35, T44, T65, T122, T132, T156, T165, T169, T223, T261, T262–T263, T265, T318, T319, T328, T333, T343, T345, T352, T353, T359, T361, T363, T369, T418, T419, T430, T438, T441, T443, T452, T463, T465, T469, T478, T510, T513, T514, T515, T520, T521, T522, T523, T526, S6, S16, S26, S36, S46

Correlations

Standard	Standard Language	Key Citations
4. Adapting language choices		
ELD.PI.2.4	**Emerging** Recognize that language choices (e.g., vocabulary) vary according to social setting (e.g., playground versus classroom) with substantial support from peers or adults. **Expanding** Adjust language choices (e.g., vocabulary, use of dialogue, etc.) according to purpose (e.g., persuading, entertaining), task, and audience (e.g., peers versus adults) with moderate support from peers or adults. **Bridging** Adjust language choices according to purpose (e.g., persuading, entertaining), task, and audience (e.g., peer-to-peer versus peer-to-teacher) with light support from peers or adults.	**2-1:** T110, T141, T163, T167 **2-2:** T245, T267, T275, T359, T376, T471, T516, S10 **2-3:** T63, T255, T263, T426 **2-4:** T145 **2-5:** T167, T463, S20, S50 **2-6:** T38, T58, T68, T74
B. INTERPRETIVE		
5. Listening actively		
ELD.PI.2.5	**Emerging** Demonstrate active listening to read-alouds and oral presentations by asking and answering basic questions with oral sentence frames and substantial prompting and support. **Expanding** Demonstrate active listening to read-alouds and oral presentations by asking and answering detailed questions with oral sentence frames and occasional prompting and support. **Bridging** Demonstrate active listening to read-alouds and oral presentations by asking and answering detailed questions with minimal prompting and light support.	**2-1:** xxx, T14, T67, T82, T83, T84, T85, T110, T119, T165, T180, T181, T208, T216, T217, T263, T278, T279, T306, T315, T365, T367, T380, T381, T408, T465, T478, T484, T485, T486, S2, S8, S10, S12, S14, S18, S22, S24, S28, S32, S38, S42, S48, S50 **2-2:** vi, T14, T69, T84, T85, T86, T87, T112, T171, T173, T186, T187, T269, T284, T285, T312, T371, T386, T387, T414, T469, T471, T482, T488, T489, T508, T527, T530, T532, S2, S4, S5, S6, S8, S12, S14, S15, S16, S17, S18, S20, S22, S24, S26, S34, S35, S36, S37, S40, S42, S44, S50 **2-3:** vi, T14, T69, T71, T84, T85, T112, T163, T191, T206, T261, T263, T276, T277, T304, T359, T361, T374, T375, T402, T461, T480, T481, S2, S8, S10, S12, S14, S18, S22, S24, S28, S32, S38, S42, S48, S50 **2-4:** vi, T14, T71, T73, T86, T87, T114, T171, T186, T187, T214, T271, T286, T287, T314, T371, T386, T387, T414, T471, T474, T484, T490, T491, T510, T512, T519, T524, T527, T529, T531, T532, S5, S8, S10, S12, S14, S18, S22, S24, S28, S30, S32, S38, S42, S44 **2-5:** vi, T14, T71, T86, T87, T114, T164, T171, T186, T187, T214, T286, T287, T314, T371, T386, T387, T414, T467, S2, S5, S6, S8, S12, S14, S16, S18, S22, S24, S26, S32, S34, S36, S40, S42, S44, S46 **2-6:** vi, T14, T71, T73, T114, T171, T186, T187, T214, T267, T282, T283, T310, T367, T382, T383, T410, T467, T506, T508, T510, T511, T513, T514, T516, T517, T519, T520, T521, T522, T528, S2, S8, S10, S12, S14, S18, S22, S24, S28, S30, S32, S38, S42, S44, S48, S50
6. Reading/viewing closely		
ELD.PI.2.6	**Emerging** Describe ideas, phenomena (e.g., plant life cycle), and text elements (e.g., main idea, characters, events) based on understanding of a select set of grade-level texts and viewing of multimedia with substantial support. **Expanding** Describe ideas, phenomena (e.g., how earthworms eat), and text elements (e.g., setting, events) in greater detail based on understanding of a variety of grade-level texts and viewing of multimedia with moderate support. **Bridging** Describe ideas, phenomena (e.g., erosion), and text elements (e.g., central message, character traits) using key details based on understanding of a variety of grade-level texts and viewing of multimedia with light support.	**2-1:** xxx, T21, T22, T25–T31, T39, T40, T50, T61, T91, T95, T121–T129, T137, T138, T144, T145, T148, T167, T182, T183, T186, T187, T188, T189, T193, T219–T227, T235, T246, T256, T257, T280, T281, T284, T285, T286, T287, T291, T317–T329, T337, T338, T348, T358, T359, T382, T383, T393, T417, T419, T439, T440, T448, T459 **2-2:** vi, T23, T26–T33, T40–T41, T42, T50, T63, T90, T91, T92, T93, T97, T121, T124–T135, T142–T143, T154, T165, T188, T189, T192, T193, T194, T195, T199, T223, T225, T226–T233, T240–T241, T242, T243, T252, T263, T290, T291, T292, T293, T297, T321, T323–T335, T342–T343, T344, T345, T354, T365, T373, T392, T393, T394, T395, T399, T423, T424–T437, T442–T443, T444, T445, T452, T463, T486, T487, T490, T491, T492, T493, T494, T495, T496, T497, T501, T508, T510, T514, T516, T519, T520, T521, T524, T526, T530, T532, S21, S34, S51 **2-3:** vi, T22, T23, T24, T26–T35, T42–T43, T44, T52, T62, T63, T86, T87, T90, T91, T92, T93, T121, T122, T124–T129, T137, T138, T146, T180, T181, T214, T215, T216, T218–T226, T235, T236, T244, T263, T265, T278, T279, T282, T283, T284, T285, T312, T314, T315, T316–T325, T333, T334, T342, T353, T365, T376, T377, T411, T410, T412, T413, T414–T425, T432–T433, T434, T444, T455, T482, T483, T486, T487, T488, T489 **2-4:** vi, T22, T23, T25, T26–T37, T44–T45, T46, T54, T65, T88, T89, T92, T93, T94, T95, T99, T122, T125, T126–T137, T144–T145, T146, T154, T165, T192, T193, T194, T195, T199, T222, T225, T226–T235, T242, T244, T254, T288, T289, T292, T293, T294, T295, T299, T322, T323, T325, T326–T337, T345, T346, T354, T388, T389, T392, T393, T394, T395, T399, T422, T425, T426–T437, T444, T445, T446, T454, T492, T493, T496, T497, T498, T499, T503, T510, T512, T513, T515, T516, T518, T520, T522, T523, T526, T528, T530, T531, T532, T534 **2-5:** vi, T21, T22, T26–T35, T43, T44, T54, T65, T73, T88, T89, T92, T93, T94, T95, T99, T122, T126–T135, T142, T143, T144, T154, T165, T188, T189, T192, T193, T194, T195, T199, T221, T222, T226–T235, T242, T243, T244, T254, T265, T273, T288, T289, T292, T293, T294, T295, T299, T321, T322, T326–T335, T342, T343, T344, T354, T373, T388, T389, T392, T393, T394, T395, T399, T422, T426–T433, T441, T442, T450, T478, T488, T489, T492, T493, T494, T495, T499, S4, S14, S19, S21, S51 **2-6:** vi, T22, T26–T37, T45, T46, T54, T73, T92, T93, T94, T95, T99, T121, T122, T126–T135, T143, T144, T154, T192, T193, T194, T195, T199, T222, T226–T231, T238, T239, T240, T248, T259, T260, T269, T284, T285, T288, T289, T290, T291, T295, T317, T318, T322–T331, T338, T339, T340, T350, T388, T389, T390, T391, T395, T418, T422–T431, T439, T440, T450, T460, T488, T489, T492, T493, T494, T495, T499, T506, T509, T510, T512, T514, T516, T517, T518, T518, T522, T524, T526, T528, T530

Standard	Standard Language	Key Citations

7. Evaluating language choices

Standard	Standard Language	Key Citations
ELD.PI.2.7	**Emerging** Describe the language writers or speakers use to present an idea (e.g., the words and phrases used to describe a character) with prompting and substantial support. **Expanding** Describe the language writers or speakers use to present or support an idea (e.g., the author's choice of vocabulary or phrasing to portray characters, places, or real people) with prompting and moderate support. **Bridging** Describe how well writers or speakers use specific language resources to support an opinion or present an idea (e.g., whether the vocabulary used to present evidence is strong enough) with light support.	**2-1:** T29, T39, T125, T137, T141, T167, T222, T223, T235, T337, T423, T438–T439 **2-2:** T129, T228, T231, T343, T427, T431, T432, T513, T514, T521, T523, T526, S11 **2-3:** T30, T43, T63, T127, T255, T317, T417, T420 **2-4:** T27, T45, T128, T129, T130, T145, T167, T228, T242, T345, T430, T432, T445, T523, T528, T530 **2-5:** T142, T143, T226, T242, T328, T332 **2-6:** T28, T38, T68, T74, T226, T326, T425, T426, T429, T439, T460, T511, T512, T519, T532

8. Analyzing language choices

Standard	Standard Language	Key Citations
ELD.PI.2.8	**Emerging** Distinguish how two different frequently-used words (e.g., describing a character as *happy* versus *angry*) produce a different effect on the audience. **Expanding** Distinguish how two different words with similar meaning (e.g., describing a character as *happy* versus *ecstatic*) produce shades of meaning and different effects on the audience. **Bridging** Distinguish how multiple different words with similar meaning (e.g., *pleased* versus *happy* versus *ecstatic*, *heard* or *knew* versus *believed*) produce shades of meaning and different effects on the audience.	**2-1:** T312 **2-2:** T272–T273, T456 **2-4:** T145, T166, T366–T367, T373, T396, T397, T399 **2-5:** T57, T67, T122, T320 **2-6:** T166–T167, T199, T316, T363, T463

C. PRODUCTIVE

9. Presenting

Standard	Standard Language	Key Citations
ELD.PI.2.9	**Emerging** Plan and deliver very brief oral presentations (e.g., recounting an experience, retelling a story, describing a picture). **Expanding** Plan and deliver brief oral presentations on a variety of topics (e.g., retelling a story, describing an animal). **Bridging** Plan and deliver longer oral presentations on a variety of topics and content areas (e.g., retelling a story, recounting a science experiment, describing how to solve a mathematics problem).	**2-1:** T338, T364, T366, T470, T478 **2-2:** T70, T470–T471, T457, T467, T474, T482, T512, T515, T527, T529 **2-3:** xxxvi–xxxvii, T136, T255, T361, T450, T463, T466, T474 **2-4:** xxxvi–xxxvii, T273, T360, T476, T484, T529, T531 **2-5:** xxxvi–xxxvii, T70, T73, T161, T165, T172, T273, T373, T472, T480, S10, S43, S50 **2-6:** xxxvi–xxxvii, T73, T76, T173, T369, T469, T472, T480, T520, T523, T525, T527, T532, S4

10. Writing

Standard	Standard Language	Key Citations
ELD.PI.2.10	**Emerging** Write very short literary texts (e.g., story) and informational texts (e.g., a description of a volcano) using familiar vocabulary collaboratively with an adult (e.g., joint construction of texts), with peers, and sometimes independently. **Expanding** Write short literary texts (e.g., a story) and informational texts (e.g., an explanatory text explaining how a volcano erupts) collaboratively with an adult (e.g., joint construction of texts), with peers, and with increasing independence. **Bridging** Write longer literary texts (e.g., a story) and informational texts (e.g., an explanatory text explaining how a volcano erupts) collaboratively with an adult (e.g., joint construction), with peers and independently.	**2-1:** xxxvi–xxxvii, T33, T43, T53, T55, T65, T73, T131, T141, T153, T163, T170, T229, T249, T251, T257, T261, T265, T268, T318, T331, T341, T351, T353, T363, T370, T433, T451, T453, T463, T467, T470, T476, T477, T481, S8, S18, S28, S38, S48 **2-2:** xxxvi–xxxvii, T35, T41, T43, T45, T53, T55, T67, T71, T74, T137, T145, T147, T157, T159, T169, T176, T235, T239, T243, T245, T255, T257, T267, T275, T337, T345, T347, T357, T359, T369, T376, T437, T443, T445, T447, T455, T456, T457, T459,T464, T467, T474, T480, T482, T511, T512, T513, T516, T519, T523, T525, T526, T530, T533 **2-3:** xxxvi–xxxvii, T37, T45, T47, T55, T57, T67, T74, T139, T141, T149, T151, T161, T167, T168, T237, T239, T247, T249, T259, T266, T327, T332, T335, T337, T345, T347, T357, T358, T364, T427, T435, T437, T447, T449, T459, T466, T472, T473, T474, S8, S18, S28, S38, S48 **2-4:** xxxvi–xxxvii, T39, T47, T49, T57, T59, T69, T76–T77, T139, T147, T149, T154, T157, T159, T165, T169, T176–T177, T237, T245, T247, T257, T259, T269, T276–T277, T339, T347, T349, T357, T359, T369, T376–T377, T439, T447, T449, T457, T459, T469, T476–T477, T482, T483, T484, T513, T514, T515, T518, T521, T523, T525, T526, T527, T530, T532, T534, T535, S8, S18, S28, S38, S48 **2-5:** xxxvi–xxxvii, T37, T45, T47, T57, T59, T65, T66, T69, T76–T77, T137, T145, T147, T157, T159, T169, T173, T176–T177, T237, T245, T247, T257, T259, T265, T269, T276–T277, T337, T345, T347, T357, T359, T365, T369, T376–T377, T435, T443, T445, T453, T455, T461, T465, T472–T473, T479, T480 **2-6:** xxxvi–xxxvii, T39, T47, T49, T57, T59, T65, T69, T73, T76–T77, T137, T145, T147, T157, T159, T165, T169, T176–T177, T233, T241, T243, T251, T256, T261, T265, T272–T273, T333, T341, T343, T353, T359, T361, T365, T369, T372–T373, T433, T441, T443, T453, T455, T461, T465, T472–T473, T479, T480, T509, T511, T514, T515, T517, T518, T519, T521, T522, T523, T526, T528, T531, S8, S18, S28, S38, S48

Correlations

Standard	Standard Language	Key Citations
11. Supporting opinions		
ELD.PI.2.11	**Emerging** Support opinions by providing good reasons and some textual evidence or relevant background knowledge (e.g., referring to textual evidence or knowledge of content). **Expanding** Support opinions by providing good reasons and increasingly detailed textual evidence (e.g., providing examples from the text) or relevant background knowledge about the content. **Bridging** Support opinions or persuade others by providing good reasons and detailed textual evidence (e.g., specific events or graphics from text) or relevant background knowledge about the content.	**2-1:** T21, T40, T41, T42, T63, T69, T119, T138, T139, T159, T217, T220, T248, T263, T265, T314, T326, T328, T338, T339, T359, T367, T428, T429, T430, T440, T441, T454, T459, T467 **2-2:** T60, T65, T71, T132, T144, T145, T164, T165, T175, T232, T242, T265, T266, T321, T344, T365, T368, T442, T444, T471, T473, T511, T532, S7, S14, S48 **2-3:** T34, T44, T45, T57, T62, T71, T138, T139, T141, T148, T151, T157, T159, T161, T168, T236, T237, T239, T249, T262–T263, T265, T323, T334, T335, T353, T357, T364, T424, T434, T435, T455, T459, T466, T472, T474 **2-4:** T26, T47, T65, T73, T147, T165, T173, T222, T231, T329, T330, T346, T356, T365, T422, T436, T446, T465, T472, T473, T524, T530, T532, T535 **2-5:** T72, T122, T129, T144, T167, T233, T234, T244, T344, T373, T462, T469, T478, T479, T480, S16 **2-6:** T35, T159, T165, T169, T176, T253, T262–T263, T265, T272, T318, T328, T333, T343, T345, T359, T361, T363, T369, T372, T430, T433, T438, T441, T455, T463, T469, T472, T478, T479, T480, T523, T531
12. Selecting language resources		
ELD.PI.2.12a	**Emerging** Retell texts and recount experiences, using key words. **Expanding** Retell texts and recount experiences, using complete sentences and key words. **Bridging** Retell texts and recount experiences, using increasingly detailed complete sentences and key words.	**2-1:** xxx, T22, T23, T25, T26, T27, T31, T39, T40, T41, T50, T63, T119, T129, T138, T139, T144, T145, T148, T166–T167, T208, T217, T219, T227, T234, T246, T265, T306, T315, T317, T329, T338, T339, T348, T366, T382, T383, T386, T387, T388, T389, T408, T417, T419, T440, T441, T448, T467, S4, S6, S16, S26, S31, S34, S36, S44, S46, S50 **2-2:** vi, T23, T25, T33, T42, T43, T50, T70–T71, T121, T123, T135, T154, T172, T174, T223, T225, T233, T240, T242, T243, T245, T252, T263, T267, T271, T275, T312, T320, T321, T323, T335, T342, T344, T345, T354, T356, T364, T365, T374, T414, T422, T423, T425, T431, T442, T444, T445, T452, T470–T471, T480, T481, T508, T513, T516, T523, T533, S6, S16, S24, S26, S31, S36, S43, S46 **2-3:** vi, T14, T23, T25, T35, T44, T45, T52, T54, T62, T71, T72, T112, T121, T123, T128, T129, T136, T138, T139, T146, T148, T165, T167, T206, T215, T217, T226, T236, T237, T244, T246, T263, T265, T313, T315, T324–T325, T332, T334, T335, T342, T344, T353, T362, T411, T425, T434, T435, T444, T446, T463, S4, S6, S16, S26, S34, S36, S44, S46, S51 **2-4:** vi, T23, T25, T27, T37, T44, T46, T47, T56, T65, T123, T125, T136–T137, T146, T147, T156, T214, T223, T225, T234, T235, T244, T245, T246, T256, T273, T323, T325, T337, T346, T347, T354, T356, T414, T423, T425, T437, T446, T447, T454, T456, T465, T473, S16, S26, S34, S36, S46 **2-5:** vi, T14, T23, T33, T34, T35, T44, T45, T54, T73, T114, T123, T134, T135, T144, T145, T154, T156, T165, T173, T223, T235, T244, T245, T254, T256, T265, T273, T314, T323, T334–T335, T342, T344, T345, T354, T365, T414, T423, T432, T433, T442, T443, T450, T461, T469, T479, S6, S14, S24, S34, S44, S49 **2-6:** vi, T14, T23, T37, T46, T47, T54, T56, T87, T88, T89, T123, T133, T134, T135, T144, T145, T154, T156, T172, T223, T226, T230, T231, T240, T241, T248, T250, T269, T310, T318, T319, T330, T331, T338, T340, T341, T350, T352, T361, T369, T410, T419, T431, T440, T441, T450, T452, T461, T462, T479, T512, T514, T522, T524, T526, S6, S16, S24, S26, S31, S34, S36, S46
ELD.PI.2.12b	**Emerging** Use a select number of general academic and domain-specific words to add detail (e.g., adding the word *generous* to describe a character, using the word *lava* to explain volcanic eruptions) while speaking and writing. **Expanding** Use a growing number of general academic and domain-specific words in order to add detail, create an effect (e.g., using the word *suddenly* to signal a change), or create shades of meaning (e.g., *scurry* versus *dash*) while speaking and writing. **Bridging** Use a wide variety of general academic and domain-specific words, synonyms, antonyms, and non-literal language (e.g., He was *as quick as a cricket.*) to create an effect, precision, and shades of meaning while speaking and writing.	**2-1:** xxx, xxxi, T20, T21, T66, T68, T116, T117, T214, T215, T220, T257, T259, T265, T312, T313, T358, T368, T414, T415, T461, T477, S10, S20, S30, S33, S40, S41 **2-2:** vi, T20, T21, T60, T118, T119, T145, T164, T174, T220, T221, T222, T242, T243, T246, T273, T318, T319, T344, T345, T366–T367, T420, T421, T438, T444, T445, T458, T513, T523, T533 **2-3:** vi, T54, T148, T246, T344, T355, T367, T446, S13, S18, S20, S23, S30, S33, S40, S43, S50 **2-4:** vi, T65, T156, T166, T167, T256, T356, T456, S10, S11, S13, S20, S30, S33, S40, S43, S50 **2-5:** vi, T20, T21, T56, T67, T120, T121, T220, T221, T320, T321, T359, T367, T369, T414, T420, T421, T465, T483, T479, S40, S47, S50 **2-6:** vi, T20, T21, T39, T44, T49, T56, T59, T67, T69, T76, T120, T121, T156, T220, T221, T316, T317, T352, T416, T417, T452, T463, T512, T519, T522, T528, S10, S20, S30, S40, S50

Standard	Standard Language	Key Citations

PART II: LEARNING ABOUT HOW ENGLISH WORKS

A. STRUCTURING COHESIVE TEXTS

1. Understanding text structure

Standard	Standard Language	Key Citations
ELD.PII.2.1	**Emerging** Apply understanding of how different text types are organized to express ideas (e.g., how a story is organized sequentially) to comprehending and composing texts in shared language activities guided by the teacher, with peers, and sometimes independently. **Expanding** Apply understanding of how different text types are organized to express ideas (e.g., how a story is organized sequentially with predictable stages versus how an information report is organized by topic and details) to comprehending texts and composing texts with increasing independence. **Bridging** Apply understanding of how different text types are organized predictably to express ideas (e.g., a narrative versus an informative/explanatory text versus an opinion text) to comprehending and writing texts independently.	**2-1:** T14, T24, T26, T33, T39, T55, T65, T84, T85, T88, T89, T90, T91, T95, T120, T131, T137, T153, T158, T163, T208, T221, T223, T251, T256, T358, T363, T408, T416, T422, T433, T439, T476, T477, T486, T487, T490, T491, T492, T493, T497, S4 **2-2:** T24, T31, T41, T55, T67, T143, T159, T169, T176, T257, T267, T369, T376, T437, T444, T463, T480, T481 **2-3:** T22, T57, T67, T151, T161, T216, T235, T259, T333, T357, T402, T421, T427, T434, T459, T466, T472, T473, T474, T482, T530, T532 **2-4:** T22, T23, T39, T45, T59, T69, T76, T99, T139, T159, T169, T176, T188, T189, T192, T193, T194, T195, T199, T237, T259, T269, T276, T339, T349, T358, T359, T369, T376, T439, T449, T476, T483, T484 **2-5:** T22, T24, T73, T137, T214, T237, T244, T259, T269, T276, T337, T347, T365, T369, T376, T435, T445, T455, T472 **2-6:** T45, T222, T284, T285, T288, T289, T290, T291, T295, T455, T530, S4

2. Understanding cohesion

Standard	Standard Language	Key Citations
ELD.PII.2.2	**Emerging** Apply basic understanding of how ideas, events, or reasons are linked throughout a text using more everyday connecting words or phrases (e.g., *today*, *then*) to comprehending and composing texts in shared language activities guided by the teacher, with peers, and sometimes independently. **Expanding** Apply understanding of how ideas, events, or reasons are linked throughout a text using a growing number of connecting words or phrases (e.g., *after a long time*, *first/next*) to comprehending texts and writing texts with increasing independence. **Bridging** Apply understanding of how ideas, events, or reasons are linked throughout a text using a variety of connecting words or phrases (e.g., *for example*, *after that*, *suddenly*) to comprehending and writing texts independently.	**2-1:** T22, T38–T39, T55, T110, T126, T138, T153, T163, T363, T443, T477, T478 **2-2:** T26, T112, T127, T144, T159, T241, T337, T369, T424, T437, T467, T481, T514 **2-3:** T22, T24, T112, T151, T333, T433, T473, T474, S8, S10 **2-4:** T122, T144–T145, T332, T424, T439, T469, T476, T482, T483 **2-5:** T45, T127, T129, T133, T173, T243, T259, T269, T430, T443 **2-6:** T73, T114, T144, T145, T159, T238, T323, T530

B. EXPANDING & ENRICHING IDEAS

3. Using verbs and verb phrases

Standard	Standard Language	Key Citations
ELD.PII.2.3a	**Emerging** Use frequently used verbs (e.g., *walk*, *run*) and verb types (e.g., doing, saying, being/having, thinking/feeling) in shared language activities guided by the teacher and sometimes independently. **Expanding** Use a growing number of verb types (e.g., doing, saying, being/having, thinking/feeling) with increasing independence. **Bridging** Use a variety of verb types (e.g., doing, saying, being/having, thinking/feeling) independently.	**2-1:** T20, T24, T42, T54, T70, T71, T116, T120, T168, T214, T259, T260, T312, T329, T414, T464 **2-2:** vi, vii, T20, T118, T125, T220, T234, T244, T256, T272–T273, T296, T312, T318, T344, T374–T375, T420, T446, T456, T472, T533, S28 **2-3:** vii, T30, T138, T216, T258, T264, T356 **2-4:** T24, T30, T138, T158, T174, T175, T214, T233, T244, T258, T259, T275, T298, T346, T474, T475, T483 **2-5:** vi, vii, T20, T44, T120, T220, T298, T320, T374, T398, T414, T420, T498, S26, S28 **2-6:** vii, T20, T120, T220, T264, T316, T364, T417, T464, T521
ELD.PII.2.3b	**Emerging** Use simple verb tenses appropriate for the text type and discipline to convey time (e.g., simple past for recounting an experience) in shared language activities guided by the teacher and sometimes independently. **Expanding** Use a growing number of verb tenses appropriate for the text type and discipline to convey time (e.g., simple past tense for retelling, simple present for a science description) with increasing independence. **Bridging** Use a wide variety of verb tenses appropriate for the text type and discipline to convey time (e.g., simple present for a science description, simple future to predict) independently.	**2-1:** T460–T461, T477, T494, T495, T497 **2-2:** T244, T268, T269, T273, T371, T374, T384, T385, T398, T436, T446, T456, T472, T473, T500, S28, S38, S48 **2-3:** T264, T314, T356, T458 **2-4:** T14, T27, T30, T46, T59, T71, T72, T224, T236, T246, T258, T274, T324, T429, T483, S28, S30 **2-5:** T14, T24, T31, T236, T246, T258, T268, T274, T275, T336, T346, T358, T374, T375, T434, T442, T444, T455, T470, T471, S28, S30, S38, S40, S48, S50 **2-6:** T214, T226, T253, T264, T364, T464

4. Using nouns and noun phrases

Standard	Standard Language	Key Citations
ELD.PII.2.4	**Emerging** Expand noun phrases in simple ways (e.g., adding a familiar adjective to describe a noun) in order to enrich the meaning of sentences and to add details about ideas, people, things, etc., in shared language activities guided by the teacher and sometimes independently. **Expanding** Expand noun phrases in a growing number of ways (e.g., adding a newly learned adjective to a noun) in order to enrich the meaning of sentences and to add details about ideas, people, things, etc., with increasing independence. **Bridging** Expand noun phrases in a variety of ways (e.g., adding comparative/superlative adjectives to nouns) in order to enrich the meaning of phrases/sentences and to add details about ideas, people, things, etc., independently.	**2-1:** xxxi, T20, T21, T33, T43, T65, T72, T120, T168–T169, T215, T220, T222, T229, T239, T251, T257, T259, T261, T320, T408, T414, T422, T463, T468, T477, T478 **2-2:** T28, T145, T168, T174, T368, T375, T423, T440, T456, T457, T466, T473, T481, T482, T498, T499, T501, T533, S44 **2-3:** T67, T130, T140, T150, T166–T167, T304, T317, T334 **2-4:** vii, T49, T76, T237, T247, T259, T269, T276, T434, T444, T483, T515 **2-5:** vi, T31, T36, T46, T58, T74, T98, T114, T129, T144, T159, T198, T220, T347, S8, S10, S18, S20, S36 **2-6:** T126, T168, T220, T240, T322, T410, T429, T432, T440, T442, T454, T470, T471, T531, S48

Correlations

Standard	Standard Language	Key Citations
5. Modifying to add details		
ELD.PII.2.5	**Emerging** Expand sentences with frequently used adverbials (e.g., prepositional phrases, such as *at school, with my friend*) to provide details (e.g., time, manner, place, cause) about a familiar activity or process in shared language activities guided by the teacher and sometimes independently. **Expanding** Expand sentences with a growing number of adverbials (e.g., adverbs, prepositional phrases) to provide details (e.g., time, manner, place, cause) about a familiar or new activity or process with increasing independence. **Bridging** Expand sentences with a variety of adverbials (e.g., adverbs, adverb phrases, prepositional phrases) to provide details (e.g., time, manner, place, cause) independently.	**2-1:** T33, T43, T65, T72, T218 **2-2:** T14, T28, T55 **2-3:** T73, T122, T166, T206, T224, T236, T249, T384, T385, T387 **2-4:** T49, T59, T76, T114, T131, T146, T159, T247, T259, T269, T276, T324, T362, T363, T375, T439, T476, T484 **2-5:** T347, T479, T480 **2-6:** T14, T31, T46, T146, T174, T175, T324, T470, T471, T511
C. CONNECTING & CONDENSING IDEAS		
6. Connecting ideas		
ELD.PII.2.6	**Emerging** Combine clauses in a few basic ways to make connections between and to join ideas (e.g., creating compound sentences using *and, but, so*) in shared language activities guided by the teacher and sometimes independently. **Expanding** Combine clauses in an increasing variety of ways to make connections between and to join ideas, for example, to express cause/effect (e.g., *She jumped because the dog barked.*) with increasing independence. **Bridging** Combine clauses in a wide variety of ways (e.g., rearranging complete, simple-to-form compound sentences) to make connections between and to join ideas (e.g., *The boy was hungry. The boy ate a sandwich. -> The boy was hungry so he ate a sandwich.*) independently.	**2-1:** T70, T220, T339, S18 **2-2:** T72, T242, T257, T267, T374, T414, T427, T444 **2-3:** T36, T44, T46, T56, T72–T73, T126, T150, T151, T161, T166–T167, T168, T259, T266, T327, T459, T473, T474, T493 **2-4:** T124, T274, T414, T433, T446, T474, T532 **2-5:** T169, T176, T431 **2-6:** T32, T169, T176, T228, T265, T272, T310, T329, T340, T341, T427, T433, T441, T472, T479, T480
7. Condensing ideas		
ELD.PII.2.7	**Emerging** Condense clauses in simple ways (e.g., changing: *It's green. It's red. -> It's green and red.*) to create precise and detailed sentences in shared language activities guided by the teacher and sometimes independently. **Expanding** Condense clauses in a growing number of ways (e.g., through embedded clauses as in, *It's a plant. It's found in the rainforest. -> It's a green and red plant that's found in the rainforest.*) to create precise and detailed sentences with increasing independence. **Bridging** Condense clauses in a variety of ways (e.g., through embedded clauses and other condensing as in, *It's a plant. It's green and red. It's found in the tropical rainforest. -> It's a green and red plant that's found in the tropical rainforest.*) to create precise and detailed sentences independently.	**2-1:** T306, T324, T338 **2-3:** T14, T33, T57, T263 **2-4:** T273, T314, T333 **2-5:** T74, T75, T314, T327, T344 **2-6:** T73, T174, T369
Part III: USING FOUNDATIONAL LITERACY SKILLS		
Foundational Literacy Skills (See Appendix A-Grade Two)		
ELD.PIII.2	Literacy in an Alphabetic Writing System • Print concepts • Phonological awareness • Phonics & word recognition • Fluency	**2-1:** T16, T19, T32, T36, T46, T49, T80, T81, T86, T87, T92, T93, T112, T115, T130, T134, T144, T178, T179, T185, T210, T213, T228, T242, T244, T282, T283, T308, T311, T330, T334, T344, T410, T413, T432, T488, S2, S3, S4, S5, S6, S9, S12, S13, S14, S15, S16, S19, S22, S23, S24, S25, S26, S28, S29, S32, S33, S34, S36, S38, S39, S43, S44, S48, S49 **2-2:** T16, T19, T34, T88, T89, T96, T114, T117, T150, T190, T198, T216, T219, T234, T238, T248, T282, T288, T289, T296, T297, T314, T317, T336, T350, T390, T391, T398, T416, T419, T436, T440, T456, T460, T486, T492, T493, T500, T508, T518, T520, T528, S4, S8, S9, S10, S14, S18, S19, S24, S26, S28, S29, S30, S32, S34, S36, S38, S39, S42, S44, S46, S48, S49 **2-3:** T16, T19, T36, T40, T88, T114, T117, T130, T182, T208, T211, T228, T280, T306, T309, T326, T373, T378, T404, T407, T426, T440, T484, T492, S2, S3, S4, S5, S6, S8, S9, S12, S14, S15, S16, S18, S19, S22, S24, S26, S28, S29, S32, S34, S36, S39, S44, S46, S48, S49, S50 **2-4:** T16, T19, T38, T58, T90, T119, T138, T190, T216, T219, T236, T250, T258, T290, T316, T319, T338, T358, T390, T416, T419, T438, T458, T494, T522, S2, S3, S4, S6, S8, S9, S12, S14, S16, S18, S19, S22, S23, S24, S28, S29, S34, S38, S39, S44, S48, S49 **2-5:** T16, T19, T36, T40, T50, T53, T58, T84, T85, T90, T116, T119, T150, T153, T184, T185, T190, T198, T216, T219, T250, T253, T284, T290, T316, T340, T350, T384, T385, T390, T416, T419, T434, T454, T459, T484, T485, T490, S2, S3, S4, S6, S8, S9, S13, S14, S16, S18, S19, S20, S22, S24, S28, S29, S30, S32, S34, S38, S39, S42, S43, S44, S46, S48, S49 **2-6:** T16, T19, T53, T58, T84, T85, T90, T116, T150, T184, T185, T190, T213, T216, T219, T252, T280, T281, T286, T315, T346, T354, T380, T381, T386, T412, T415, T446, T484, T485, T490, T518, S2, S3, S4, S6, S8, S9, S12, S13, S14, S18, S19, S22, S23, S24, S26, S28, S29, S32, S33, S34, S36, S38, S39, S42, S43, S44, S49

Anchor Text

Paired Selection

JOURNEYS

Teacher Dashboard

Log onto the Teacher Dashboard and *my*SmartPlanner. Use these searchable tools to customize lessons that achieve your instructional goals.

Interactive Whiteboard Lessons

- Vocabulary Strategies: Homographs
- Phonics: Base Words and Endings -*ed*, -*ing*

- Write About Reading
- Narrative Writing: Story Paragraph

 **Assess It Online!**

- Weekly Tests
- Assessment-driven instruction with prescriptive feedback

Student eBook

✎ 🗂 Annotate it! **Strategies for Annotation**

Guide children to use digital tools for close reading.

Children may also use the interactive features in their Student eBooks to respond to prompts in a variety of ways, including:

- short-answer response
- spoken response
- fill-in-the-blank
- drag-and-drop
- multiple choice
- drawing

 High-Interest Informational Texts and Multimedia

Have children explore the FYI website for additional information about topics of study.

Culturally Responsive Teaching

Helping Hands Tell children that this week, they will be reading and thinking about helping others.

- Lead a group discussion about ways people can work together to solve a problem or accomplish a goal, such as holding a used-book sale to raise money for new library books or working in teams to clean up a playground or a park.

- Create a word bank as children give examples of how people can work together to help others. Help English learners use the word bank to participate in the discussion.

- Create a "Helping Hands" display. Have children use hand-shaped papers to write a sentence about how they helped a classmate, a younger child, a family member, or a neighbor. Have them add their notes to the display. Review the notes together daily or at the end of the week.

Use Dialogue Journals To monitor and assess the progress of your English learners, use print or electronic dialogue journals on a regular basis. For example, teacher entries could ask questions about why they helped someone. Children can write a short reply to respond.

Language Support Card

Use the Lesson 16 Language Support Card to activate prior knowledge, frontload vocabulary, and teach academic English.

Use the Text X-Ray on page T9 to review the language demands of *Mr. Tanen's Tie Trouble* with the needs of English learners in mind.

Language Workshop for Designated ELD

- Connection to Essential Question
- Vocabulary Network
- Focus on Interacting in Meaningful Ways
- Discussion Frames
- How English Works
- Word Learning Strategies

You may wish to use the following suggestions to modify instruction according to children's needs.

Classroom Routines and Access

For children who do well with a predictable structure, continue to provide a classroom schedule in writing, as well as visually and orally. In addition, you may want to use some or all of the following strategies to improve access:

- Meet with each child who has special needs, and find out which parts of the school day are most rewarding and which are most stressful or challenging, and make appropriate adjustments.
- Consider allowing some children to skip a particular responsibility to gain more activity or transition time.
- Allow more breaks as needed to avoid discomfort.
- For a child who uses large-print materials, provide a large reading surface.
- For a child who uses a wheelchair, ensure clear access to his or her seating area.
- A child who uses American Sign Language may benefit from an interpreter to help him or her fully access instruction and discussion.
- Assess whether seating arrangements and routines are successfully minimizing distractions for all children.

Flexible Learning Environment

The following modifications may be used to meet the needs of children.

- **Incorporate Movement** into daily activities, for example, by having children stand and sit as they review the week's spelling words.
- **Provide Extra Time** for completing seatwork or transitioning, for example by having some children begin to clear work areas before others.
- **Break Down Directions and Tasks** into smaller chunks. Provide visuals when possible. Ask children to restate directions or steps.

Student eBook

- **Audio** can be activated to support fluency, decoding, and comprehension.
- **Alternative Text** provides spoken information that can be used in place of the information provided in the book's images.
- **Vocabulary Pop-Ups** contain point-of-use definitions for selection vocabulary.

Math

Solve Money Word Problems Have children solve word problems involving dollar bills and coins.

- Remind children that the Helping Hands club held a bake sale in "The Jefferson Daily News." Tell them that they will solve word problems about using money at a bake sale.
- Display a set of prices for a bake sale, such as the following:
  Muffins: 75¢   Cookies: 25¢   Cupcakes: 50¢
- Present word problems similar to the following. Solve the first problem together, and then have children solve the rest independently or with a partner.

  1. Maria has 1 quarter, 2 dimes, and 2 nickels. How much money does she have? Does she have enough money to buy a cupcake at the bake sale? *(55¢; yes)*

  2. Keiko has 1 dime, 2 nickels, and 3 pennies. How much money does she have? Does she have enough money to buy a cookie? *(23¢; no)*

  3. Zack has 1 quarter, 2 dimes, 1 nickel, and 8 pennies. How much money does he have? If he and Keiko put their money together, can they buy a muffin to share? *(58¢; yes)*

  4. Ora has a dollar bill, a quarter, a nickel, and 5 pennies. How much money does she have? Does she have enough money to buy a muffin and a cupcake? *($1.35; yes)*

LESSON **16**

Our Focus Wall

ANCHOR TEXT

Mr. Tanen's Tie Trouble
Realistic Fiction

Paired Selection

The Jefferson Daily News
Informational Text

ESSENTIAL QUESTION

How can helping others make you feel good?

FOUNDATIONAL SKILLS

☑ High-Frequency Words

also	look
fly	river
gone	said
have	saw
horse	something

Phonics

Base Words and Endings
-ed, -ing

Fluency

Rate

READING LITERATURE & INFORMATIONAL TEXT

Comprehension Skills and Strategies

☑ TARGET SKILL
• Story Structure
• Understanding Characters

☑ TARGET STRATEGY
• Infer/Predict

LANGUAGE

☑ Target Vocabulary

received	chuckled
account	staring
budget	repeated
disappointed	fund

Vocabulary Strategies

Homographs

Grammar

Pronouns

Spelling

**Base Words and Endings
*-ed, -ing***

running	pinned
clapped	cutting
stopped	sitting
hopping	rubbed
batted	missed
selling	grabbed

WRITING

Writing

Narrative Writing:
Story Paragraph
Focus Trait: Elaboration

ANCHOR TEXT

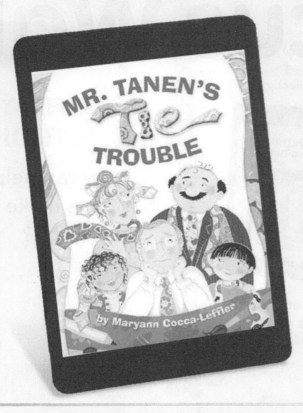

Mr. Tanen's Tie Trouble
GENRE: Realistic Fiction

21st Century Theme: Financial, Business, and Entrepreneurial Literacy

Prepare for Complex Texts For a comprehensive overview and analysis of key ideas and academic language features of this lesson's Anchor Text, see pages T8–T9.

The Jefferson Daily News
GENRE: Informational Text

Digital Resources

- ▶ eBook: Annotate it!
- ▶ Interactive Whiteboard Lessons
  - Vocabulary Strategies: Homographs
  - Phonics: Base Words and Endings -ed, -ing
- ▶ GrammarSnap Videos
  - Pronouns

- ▶ Multimedia Grammar Glossary
- ▶ mySmartPlanner
- ▶ Parent Resource

Additional Resources

- Vocabulary in Context Cards 121–128
- Reader's Notebook, pp. 1–15
- Independent Reading
- Lesson 16 Blackline Masters
- Decodable Readers
- Blend-It Books 109–112

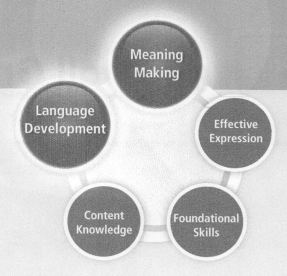

LINGUISTICALLY DIVERSE LEARNERS

⌄ Integrated English Language Support

● **Interacting in Meaningful Ways**

Classroom Conversations
- Think-Pair-Share, p. T23
- Collaborative Conversation, pp. T14, T35, T46, T72
- Turn and Talk, p. T46

Interactive and Collaborative Writing
- Story Paragraph, p. T49
- Write About Reading, p. T47

● **Learning About How English Works**

Scaffold the Texts
- Text X-Ray: Focus on Academic Language, p. T9
- Verb Tenses, p. T27

Communicative Modes
- Interpretive, pp. T14, T27
- Collaborative, pp. T20, T46
- Productive, p. T59

● **Using Foundational Literacy Skills**

Support Linguistic Transfer
- Base Words and Endings *-ed, -ing,* pp. T16, T38
- Subject Pronouns, p. T58

Fluency: Rate, p. T53

Phonics, pp. T16–T17, T18, T42–T43, T52, T62–T63, T84–T85, T90–T91

Apply Language Skills
- Pronouns, pp. T74–T75

⌄ Standard English Learners

- *-ed* Ending of Verbs, p. T30

ASSESSMENT

● **Formative Assessment**
- Phonics: Base Words and Endings *-ed, -ing,* pp. T17, T63
- Target Vocabulary, p. T21
- Decodable Reader, p. T19
- Target Skill: Story Structure, p. T45
- Vocabulary Strategies: Homographs, p. T67
- Using Data to Adjust Instruction, p. T79

● ✓ **Assess It Online!**
- Weekly Test

Performance Tasks
- Write About Reading, p. T47
- Story Paragraph, p. T39

⌄ Vocabulary Reader

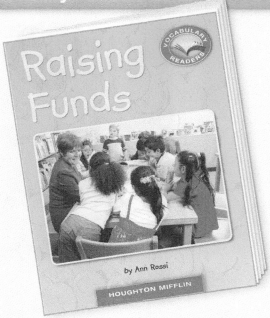

Raising Funds

by Ann Rossi

HOUGHTON MIFFLIN

● **Vocabulary Reader**
for all levels

Provide strategic scaffolding to support all students in reading on-level text and in acquiring general academic and domain-specific vocabulary. Use the instructional supports on pp. T86–T87 or the Leveled Reader Teacher's Guide.

Guided Reading Level: J

Lexile: 610

DRA: 18

Leveled Reader Teacher's Guide ↗

⌄ Weekly Leveled Readers

Guide children to read and comprehend additional texts about the lesson topic. Use the instructional supports on pp. T92–T95 or the Leveled Reader Teacher's Guides.

Struggling Readers	**On Level**	**Advanced**	**English Language Learners**
Guided Reading Level: I	**Guided Reading Level: K**	**Guided Reading Level: M**	**Guided Reading Level: K**
Lexile: 300	Lexile: 580	Lexile: 650	Lexile: 530
DRA: 16	DRA: 20	DRA: 28	DRA: 20
Leveled Reader Teacher's Guide ↗	Leveled Reader Teacher's Guide ↗	Leveled Reader Teacher's Guide ↗	Leveled Reader Teacher's Guide ↗

Our Library

by Alvin Court
Illustrated by Ann Iosa

HOUGHTON MIFFLIN

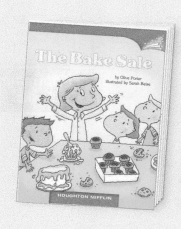

The Bake Sale

by Olive Porter
Illustrated by Sarah Beise

HOUGHTON MIFFLIN

The Town Auction

by Sharon Richards
Illustrated by Holli Conger

HOUGHTON MIFFLIN

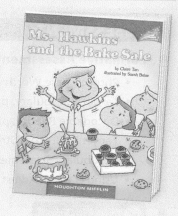

Ms. Hawkins and the Bake Sale

by Claire Tan
Illustrated by Sarah Beise

HOUGHTON MIFFLIN

Meaning
Making

Language
Development

Effective
Expression

Content
Knowledge

Foundational
Skills

Language Workshop for Designated ELD

- Provides an additional hour of daily instruction for targeted language support.

- **Supports English learners** at three different proficiency levels as they dig deeper into the language of the lesson texts.

- Guides students in collaboration, interpretation, and production of English.

Lesson 16 Focus

Collaborate: Apologize; Build on Responses

Interpret: Evaluate Language Choices

Produce: Give Presentations; Support Opinions

How English Works: Use Prepositional Phrases; Adverbs

Vocabulary Network

Intervention

 Strategic Intervention Tier II

Write-In Reader: *Kate's Helping Day*

- Interactive worktext with selection that connects to the lesson topic

- Reinforces the lesson's vocabulary and comprehension

- Builds skills for reading increasingly complex texts

- Online version with dual-speed audio and follow-text

Daily Lessons See this week's daily Strategic Intervention Lesson on pp. S2–S11.

- Preteach and reteach daily instruction
- Oral Grammar
- Words to Know
- Decoding
- Comprehension
- Fluency
- Grammar
- Written Response
- Unpack Meaning

Curious About Words Provides oral vocabulary instruction for children with limited vocabularies.

 HMH Decoding Power: Intensive Reading Instruction

- **Provides reteaching and practice in the key foundational skills** for reading: print concepts, phonological/phonemic awareness, phonics and word recognition, and fluency.

- **Explicit, sequential, and systematic instruction** designed to bring students up to grade level.

✓ *Assess It Online!*

Intervention Assessments place individual students within the system, ensure students are making satisfactory progress, and provide a measure of student readiness to exit the system.

What My Other Students Are Doing

Digital Resources

Literacy Centers: Word Study, Think and Write, Comprehension and Fluency

iRead

my WriteSmart   fyi hmhfyi.com   1 Channel One News

 Additional Resources

- Vocabulary in Context Cards 121–128

- Reader's Notebook, pp. 1–15

- Independent Reading

- Lesson 16 Blackline Masters

- Decodable Readers

- Blend-It Books 109–112

Literacy Centers

Comprehension and Fluency

Materials
- Student Book
- Decodable Reader: *We Helped*
- Audio
- Paper and pencil

A Fine Helper

You Will Need
Student Book, paper, pencil

Get Started!

Entry Level

1. Listen to the story *Mr. Tanen's Tie Trouble*. Look at the pictures.

2. Tell your partner why Mr. Tanen is a helper. Listen to your partner tell you why.

3. Write how you helped someone. Tell what you did that made you a helper.

Lesson 16

You Will Need
We Helped, paper, pencil

Reach Higher!

On Level

Read aloud two pages in *We Helped*. Then listen to your partner read. Read again a little faster.

Challenge Yourself!

Challenge

- Think about a friend.
- Write how you and a friend help each other.

Lesson 16

Word Study

Materials
- Paper and pencil

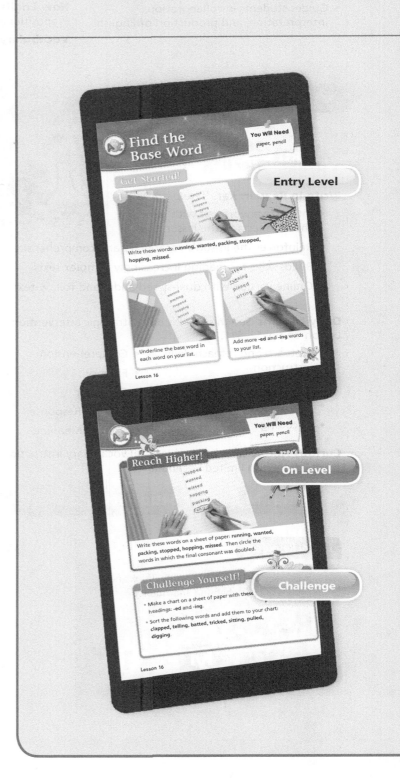

Find the Base Word

You Will Need
paper, pencil

Get Started!

Entry Level

1. Write these words: running, wanted, packing, stopped, hopping, missed.

2. Underline the base word in each word on your list.

3. Add more -ed and -ing words to your list.

Lesson 16

You Will Need
paper, pencil

Reach Higher!

On Level

Write these words on a sheet of paper: running, wanted, packing, stopped, hopping, missed. Then circle the words in which the final consonant was doubled.

Challenge Yourself!

Challenge

- Make a chart on a sheet of paper with these headings: -ed and -ing.
- Sort the following words and add them to your chart: clapped, telling, batted, tricked, sitting, pulled, digging.

Lesson 16

Meaning
Making

Language
Development

Effective
Expression

Content
Knowledge

Foundational
Skills

Assign Literacy Center activities during small group time. Each center contains three activities. Children who experience success with the entry-level activity move on to the on-level and challenge activities, as time permits.

Think and Write

Materials

- Student Book
- Paper, pencil, crayons
- Construction paper

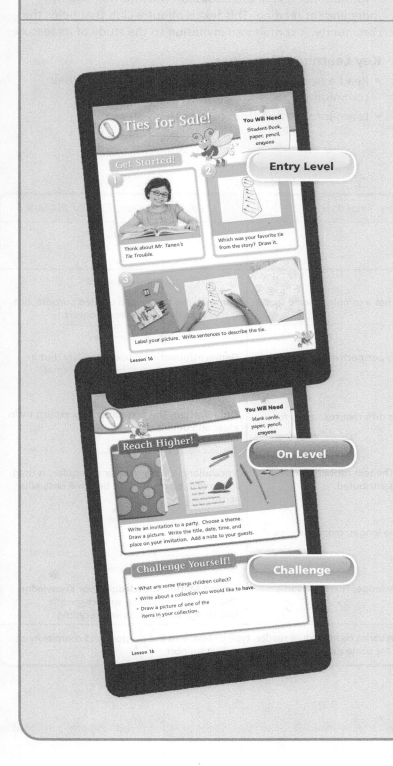

Independent Reading

Student Choice Children who choose their own books will be more actively involved in the reading process.

- In a group discussion, ask children how they choose books. Record their responses on a chart, and display it in the classroom library.

- Then suggest questions children can ask themselves when selecting a book, such as these:

  - Do I want to read a make-believe story (fiction) or something with true facts (informational text)?

  - Have I already read this book? If I have, should I read it again?

  - Have I read other books by this author? Did I like them enough to read another one?

  - Am I interested in this topic?

  - Did someone else recommend this book? If so, am I usually happy when I take their recommendations?

See pp. T54–T55 for additional independent reading support.

ELA RL.2.10, RI.2.10

Prepare for Complex Texts

Mr. Tanen's Tie Trouble
by Maryann Cocca-Leffler

GENRE: Realistic Fiction

Why This Text?

Realistic fiction stories are popular reading choices for children. This text about a school that needs to raise money to build a new playground contains a clear problem and solution for children to identify and analyze.

Key Learning Objectives

• Analyze the characters, setting, and plot of a story.
• Understand characters through their actions.

The Jefferson Daily News
by Ben Watts

GENRE: Informational Text

Why This Text?

Children will regularly encounter informational text in textbooks, on the Internet, and in independent reading. This text is about a club that helps the community; it contains an invitation to the study of its features.

Key Learning Objectives

• Read a newspaper article about children helping their community.
• Learn information from captions.

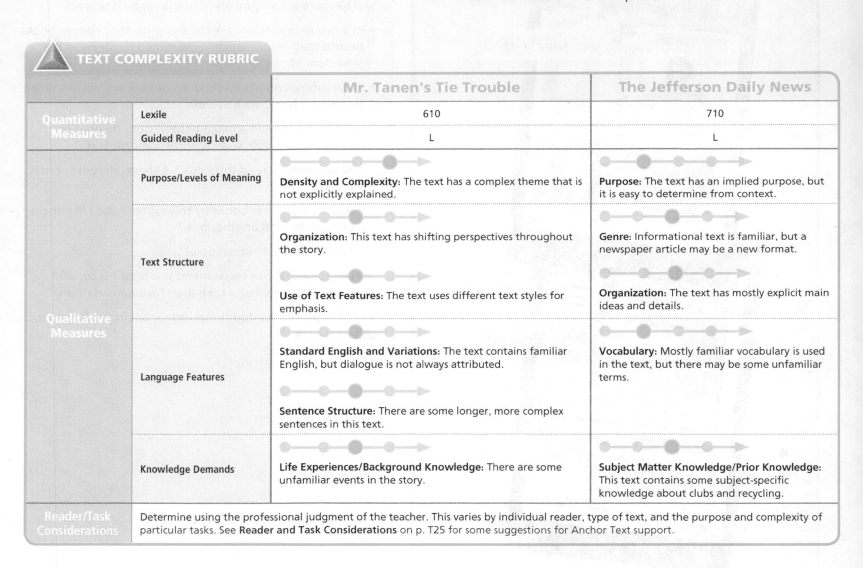

TEXT COMPLEXITY RUBRIC		Mr. Tanen's Tie Trouble	The Jefferson Daily News
Quantitative Measures	Lexile	610	710
	Guided Reading Level	L	L
Qualitative Measures	Purpose/Levels of Meaning	**Density and Complexity:** The text has a complex theme that is not explicitly explained.	**Purpose:** The text has an implied purpose, but it is easy to determine from context.
	Text Structure	**Organization:** This text has shifting perspectives throughout the story.	**Genre:** Informational text is familiar, but a newspaper article may be a new format.
		Use of Text Features: The text uses different text styles for emphasis.	**Organization:** The text has mostly explicit main ideas and details.
	Language Features	**Standard English and Variations:** The text contains familiar English, but dialogue is not always attributed.	**Vocabulary:** Mostly familiar vocabulary is used in the text, but there may be some unfamiliar terms.
		Sentence Structure: There are some longer, more complex sentences in this text.	
	Knowledge Demands	**Life Experiences/Background Knowledge:** There are some unfamiliar events in the story.	**Subject Matter Knowledge/Prior Knowledge:** This text contains some subject-specific knowledge about clubs and recycling.
Reader/Task Considerations		Determine using the professional judgment of the teacher. This varies by individual reader, type of text, and the purpose and complexity of particular tasks. See **Reader and Task Considerations** on p. T25 for some suggestions for Anchor Text support.	

 ENGLISH LANGUAGE SUPPORT Use the Text X-Ray below to prepare for teaching the Anchor Text *Mr. Tanen's Tie Trouble*. Use it to plan, support, and scaffold instruction in order to help children understand the text's **key ideas** and **academic language features**.

Zoom In on Key Ideas
Children should understand these **key ideas** after reading *Mr. Tanen's Tie Trouble*.

Key Idea | pp. 16–19

Mr. Tanen, the school principal, loves to collect and wear unusual ties. When he learns there is not enough money to build a new playground, he decides to sell his ties. He will use the money to help build a new playground.

Have children use the pictures to tell how they know Mr. Tanen has many different kinds of ties.

Key Idea | pp. 20–23

People in the town find out about the tie sale. Everyone wants to help the school.

Ask children to tell how they know the people in the town all like Mr. Tanen.

Key Idea | pp. 24–29

At the sale, the townspeople pay a lot of money for the ties. The sale is a big success. Mr. Tanen says, "The more you give, the more you get." Mr. Tanen feels sad after the auction. He misses his ties. He also feels happy that the playground is being built at last.

Ask children to tell how the townspeople feel about having Mr. Tanen's ties.

Key Idea | pp. 30–35

When opening day of the new playground arrives, the townspeople have a big surprise for Mr. Tanen.

Have children use the picture on p. 31 to tell how they think Mr. Tanen feels when he sees the playground.

Zoom In on Academic Language
Guide children at different proficiencies and skill levels to understand the structure and language of this text.

Focus: Word Level | p. 18

Point out the sentence: *Now I'm in a real pickle!* Tell children that this is **figurative language**; Mr. Tanen is not in an actual pickle, but he has a problem. Restate the sentence using literal language: *Now I really have a problem!* Ask children to tell which sentence they like more.

Focus: Sentence Level | p. 18

Point out the wavy lines of text. Tell children that authors use special **text features** to give words more meaning to the reader. Explain that the wavy lines of text are to make the words Mr. Apple said appear to be floating above Mr. Tanen's head. If necessary, assign parts and have different children read Mr. Tanen's words and Mr. Apple's words.

Focus: Text Level | pp. 24–27

The story contains a clear **problem and solution** in the **plot**. Guide children to identify Mr. Tanen's problem and what he did to solve his problem.

Focus: Text Level | p. 32

Point out the common saying: *The more you give, the more you get.* Ask children what Mr. Tanen gave up during the story. Then guide them to see that giving up his ties helped him raise money to build the playground. Reread the text on p. 32 with children, and have them tell how they know the townspeople also understood Mr. Tanen's words.

Content and Language Instruction

Make note of additional **content knowledge** and **language features** children may find challenging in this text.

mySmartPlanner

Auto-populates the suggested five-day lesson plan and offers flexibility to create and save customized plans from year to year.

See **Standards Correlations** on p. C1. In your eBook, click the Standards button in the left panel to view descriptions of the standards on the page.

	DAY 1	**DAY 2**
	Materials	**Materials**
	• Blend-It Books: Books 109–112	• Decodable Reader: *Beep! Beep!*
	• Common Core Writing Handbook, Lesson 16	• GrammarSnap Video: Pronouns
	• Decodable Reader: *Beep! Beep!*	• Graphic Organizer 10
	• GrammarSnap Video: Pronouns	• High-Frequency Word Cards 151–160
	• High-Frequency Word Cards 151–160	• Instructional Routine 15
	• Instructional Routines 3, 7, 11, 12	• Letter Cards
	• Language Support Card, Lesson 16	• Literacy and Language Guide, pp. 86–87
	• Letter Cards; Picture Cards; Word Cards	• Picture Card: hop
	• Literacy and Language Guide, pp. 86–87	• Projectables S1, 16.4, 16.5
	• Projectables S1, 16.1, 16.2, 16.3	• Reader's Notebook Vol 2 pp. 3–6
	• Reader's Notebook Vol 2 pp. 1–2	• Student Book pp. 14–39
	• Retelling Cards 61–64	• Vocabulary in Context Cards 121–128
	• Student Book pp. 10–35	• Word Card: hop
	• Vocabulary in Context Cards 121–128	

Whole Group	**Daily Language** • Oral Vocabulary • Phonemic Awareness • Speaking and Listening	**Opening Routines,** T12–T13 **Read Aloud** "A Better Way to Save," T14–T15 **Phonemic Awareness,** T16	**Opening Routines,** T40–T41 **Phonemic Awareness,** T42
	Vocabulary **Text-Based Comprehension** • Skills and Strategies • Craft and Structure	☑ **Introduce Target Vocabulary** T20–T21 ☑ **Read and Comprehend** T22–T23 **FIRST READ** **Think Through the Text** Read the Anchor Text: *Mr. Tanen's Tie Trouble,* T24–T37 **Research/Media Literacy,** T73	☑ **Dig Deeper, T44–T45** • Story Structure • Understanding Characters **SECOND READ** **Analyze the Text** Reread the Anchor Text: *Mr. Tanen's Tie Trouble,* T24–T35 **Your Turn,** T46–T47 **Research/Media Literacy,** T73
	Foundational Skills • Phonics and Word Recognition • Fluency	☑ **Fluency** Rate, T14 ☑ **Phonics** • Base Words and Endings *-ed, -ing,* T16–T18 **Read** *Beep Beep!,* T19	☑ **Fluency** Rate, T43 ☑ **Phonics** • Base Words and Endings *-ed, -ing,* T42–T43
Whole Group Language Arts	**Spelling** **Grammar** **Writing**	☑ **Spelling** Base Words with Endings *-ed, -ing;* Pretest, T38 ☑ **Grammar** Pronouns, T38 Daily Proofreading Practice, T39 ☑ **Narrative Writing:** Story Paragraph Introduce the Model, T39	☑ **Spelling** Base Words with Endings *-ed, -ing,* T48 ☑ **Grammar** Pronouns, T48 Daily Proofreading Practice, T49 ☑ **Narrative Writing:** Story Paragraph Focus Trait: Elaboration, T49
Small Group		Suggestions for Small Groups (See pp. T81–T99.)	
Language Workshop	**Designated English Language Support**	**Connect to Text:** *Mr. Tanen's Tie Trouble* **Introduce Vocabulary Network:** Words About Helping Friends	**Expand Vocabulary Network** **Collaborate:** Apologize; Add Relevant Information; Build on Responses

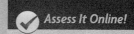

iRead Use *iRead*, an adaptive digital foundational reading skills program, to personalize learning for students.

Integrated English Language Support
See page T3 for instructional support activities for Diverse Linguistic Learners.

✓ **Assess It Online!**
▶ Lesson 16 Assessment

DAY 3

Materials
- Cold Reads
- Decodable Reader: *We Helped*
- GrammarSnap Video: Pronouns
- Graphic Organizer 4
- High-Frequency Word Cards 151–160
- Instructional Routine 13
- Letter Cards; Picture Cards; Word Cards
- Literacy and Language Guide, pp. 86–87, 146–147
- Projectables 16.6, 16.7
- Reader's Notebook Vol 2 pp. 7–11
- Sound Spelling Card: ocean
- Student Book pp. 14–35
- Vocabulary in Context Cards 121–128

Opening Routines, T50–T51
Phonemic Awareness, T52

Independent Reading, T54–T55
- Reader's Guide: *Mr. Tanen's Tie Trouble,*
- Self-Selected Reading
- Self-Correction Strategies
Apply Vocabulary Knowledge, T56–T57
Research/Media Literacy, T73

☑ **Fluency**
Rate, T53
☑ **Phonics**
- Review, T52

☑ **Spelling**
Base Words with Endings -ed, -ing, T58
☑ **Grammar**
Pronouns, T58
Daily Proofreading Practice, T59
☑ **Narrative Writing:**
Story Paragraph
Prewrite, T59

DAY 4

Materials
- Decodable Reader: *We Helped*
- High-Frequency Word Cards 151–160
- Instructional Routine 14
- Interactive Whiteboard Lesson: Homographs
- Literacy and Language Guide, pp. 86–87
- Projectables 16.8, 16.9
- Reader's Notebook Vol 2 pp. 12–14
- Sound/Spelling Card: eagle
- Student Book pp. 40–43
- Vocabulary in Context Cards 121–128

Opening Routines, T60–T61
Phonemic Awareness, T62

Connect to the Topic
- Read Informational Text: *The Jefferson Daily News,* T64
- Introduce Genre and Text Focus, T64
☑ **Compare Texts,** T65
☑ **Vocabulary Strategies,**
Homographs, T66–T67
Research/Media Literacy, T73

☑ **Fluency**
Rate, T63
☑ **Phonics**
- Phonics Review, T62–T63

☑ **Spelling**
Base Words with Endings -ed, -ing, T68
☑ **Grammar**
Spiral Review, T68
Daily Proofreading Practice, T69
☑ **Narrative Writing:**
Story Paragraph
Draft, T69

DAY 5

Materials
- Blackline Masters: Writing Rubric, Proofreading Checklist
- Graphic Organizer 6
- High-Frequency Word Cards 151–160
- Interactive Whiteboard Lesson: Phonics: Base Words and Endings -ed, -ing
- Projectable 16.10
- Reader's Notebook Vol 2 p. 15
- Student Book pp. 44–47
- Vocabulary in Context Cards 121–128
- Close Reader, Lesson 16

Opening Routines, T70–T71
Speaking and Listening, T73

Close Reader
- Lesson 16
Extend the Topic
- Domain-Specific Vocabulary, T72
- Research/Media Literacy: Create Audio Recordings, T73
- Optional Second Read: *The Jefferson Daily News,* T64

☑ **Fluency**
Accuracy, T79
☑ **Phonics**
- Phonics Review, T71

☑ **Spelling**
Base Words with Endings -ed, -ing, T74
☑ **Grammar**
Pronouns, T74–T75
Daily Proofreading Practice, T76
☑ **Narrative Writing:**
Story Paragraph
Revise and Edit, T76–T77

Tier II Intervention provides 30 minutes of additional daily practice with key parts of the core instruction. (See pp. S2–S11.)

Interpret: Evaluate Language Choices
Unpack a Sentence

Produce: Plan a Speech
Focus on How English Works: Modify Sentences to Provide Detail

Share and Reflect

DAY 1

Today's Goals

Vocabulary & Oral Language
- **Teacher Read Aloud:**
  "A Better Way to Save"
- **Oral Vocabulary**
- **Listening Comprehension**
- **Introduce Vocabulary**

TARGET VOCABULARY

received	chuckled
account	staring
budget	repeated
disappointed	fund

Phonemic Awareness
- **Syllables in Spoken Words**

Phonics & Fluency
- **Listening Comprehension**
- **Base Words and Endings** *-ed, -ing*
- **Read Decodable Reader:**
  Beep! Beep!
- **Fluency:** Rate
- **High-Frequency Words**

Text-Based Comprehension
- **Listening Comprehension**
- **Read and Comprehend**
- **Read the Anchor Text:**
  Mr. Tannen's Tie Trouble

Grammar & Writing
- **Pronouns**
- **Narrative Writing:** Story Paragraph

Spelling
- **Base Words with Endings** *-ed, -ing*

Opening Routines

Warm Up with Wordplay

Share a Riddle

Display and read aloud the following riddle:

> ## What did the man's tie say to his hat?

Tell children the answer: *"You go on ahead! I'll hang around for a while."*

Have children turn and talk to a partner about why the riddle is funny. Remind them to use discussion rules. Discuss the meanings of the expressions *go on ahead (you go on a head)* and *hang around*. Tell children that expressions are usually not meant to be taken word-for-word.

Tell children that this week, they will read a story about a man who has a thousand neckties. **ELA** SL.2.1a **ELD** ELD.PI.2.1

Daily Phonemic Awareness

Syllables in Spoken Words

- *Listen to these action words that tell about something that happened in the past:* wanted, picked. Explain that a word with an *-ed* ending means the action happened before what is happening now.

- *I will say a word and clap to count the syllables. Listen to the word:* wanted. *Now clap and say each part of the word.* want-ed *How many syllables do you hear?* two

- Continue with these words: *picked*, *jumped*, *mixed*, *waited*, *clapped*, *parked*, *parted*.

Corrective Feedback

- If a child struggles with counting syllables, say the word, give correction, and model the task. Example; *Listen to this word:* tricked. *Try it with me.* Clap the syllable as you say *tricked*. *Now you try it on your own.*

- Tell children to put their hands under their chins and count how many times their chin touches their hand as they say the word.

Daily High-Frequency Words

- Say: *This week, our new High-Frequency Words are* horse, river, *and* something. *Our review words are* also, fly, gone, have, look, said, *and* saw.

- Use Instructional Routine 11 and **High-Frequency Word Card 153** to introduce the word *something*.

- Repeat the routine with **High-Frequency Word Cards 158** and **159** for new words *horse* and *river*, and with **High-Frequency Word Cards 151, 152, 154–157,** and **160** for review words *gone, said, fly, also, saw, look,* and *have*. **ELA** RF.2.3f

Corrective Feedback

- If a child does not recognize the word *something*, say the correct word and have children repeat it. Something. *What is the word?* something

- Have children spell the word. *s-o-m-e-t-h-i-n-g How do we say this word?* something

- Have children reread all of the cards in random order.

Daily Vocabulary Boost

- Preview the Target Vocabulary by displaying the **Vocabulary in Context Cards** and discussing the words. For example, use sentences such as these to discuss the words *account* and *budget*.

  Having an account at the bank gives you a place to put the money you save.

  Many families are on a budget to help them keep track of money.

- Tell children that they will find these and other Vocabulary Words when they read *Mr. Tannen's Tie Trouble.*

account
The girl opened a bank account with the money from her allowance.

Vocabulary in Context Cards 121–128

☑ **Target Vocabulary**

received
account
budget
disappointed
chuckled
staring
repeated
fund

Teacher Read Aloud

▶ **SHARE OBJECTIVES**

- Listen to fluent reading.
- Read at an appropriate rate.
- Retell key details from a story. LANGUAGE
- Identify and use verbs in the past tense in sentences. LANGUAGE

PREVIEW

☑ **TARGET VOCABULARY**

staring looking hard at something

disappointed filled with a sad feeling

repeated did something again

received got, was given

fund an amount of money saved for a special purpose

account something people keep their money in at the bank

chuckled laughed gently

budget a list of ways you plan to spend money

ENGLISH LANGUAGE SUPPORT

Comprehensible Input

All Proficiencies To assist children with accessing the content and topic of the Teacher Read Aloud, complete the Build Background activities on Lesson 16 **Language Support Card**.

Model Fluency

Rate Explain that when good readers read aloud, their rate should be at a speed that still allows them to understand what they are reading.

- Display Projectable 16.1 ⌐. As you read the story, read the first paragraph very slowly, the second paragraph very quickly, and the third paragraph at the appropriate speed. Discuss how the rate could affect your comprehension.

- Explain to children that reading for different purposes affects the rate at which they should read. If they are reading a story for fun, they might read a little faster than if they're reading nonfiction to learn new facts.

- Reread the paragraphs together with children at a rate that is appropriate for the text. Then read the remainder of the story aloud. **ELA** RF.2.4b

Listening Comprehension

Read aloud the story. Pause at the numbered stopping points to ask children the questions below. Discuss the meanings of the highlighted words, as needed, to support the discussion. Tell children they will learn more about the words later in the lesson. **ELA** SL.2.2 **ELD** ELD.PI.2.5

1 *What questions do you have after reading the first paragraph? Sample answer: Why is the money in a wet wad? Who broke the piggy bank? Why did they break the piggy bank?* ANALYZE STORY STRUCTURE

2 *What problem does Timmy have? Sample answer: Timmy's dog chewed on money Timmy was saving to buy a uniform.* ANALYZE STORY STRUCTURE

3 *What does Dad do when Timmy shares his problem? Sample answer: He shows Timmy how to dry his money on the ironing board; he makes a plan to open a bank account for Timmy, and he adds some money to buy toys for Bruno to the family budget.* UNDERSTANDING CHARACTERS

💬 **Classroom Collaboration**

Begin a discussion by asking a child to describe what Timmy saw in his bedroom. *His piggy bank was smashed, and the dollars he had saved were in a soggy wad.* Continue by asking other children what happened next until the entire story has been shared. **ELA** SL.2.2 **ELD** ELD.PI.2.1, ELD.PI.2.5, ELD.PI.2.12a

🔍 Language Detective

How English Works: Verb Tenses Remind children that verbs are action words that describe what someone or something does. Explain to children that verb tenses show when things happen—for example, *right now (in the present)* or *yesterday (in the past)*. Reread the first paragraph, emphasizing the past-tense verbs as you read them. As you write each verb on the board, explain that past tense verbs show that the action happened in the past. Then reread the sixth paragraph, and have children give a thumbs up when they hear a verb in the past tense. Guide children to practice writing sentences that contain verbs in the past tense. **ELD** ELD.PII.2.3b

A Better Way to Save

1 Timmy was **staring** with disbelief at the mess on the floor of his bedroom. His piggy bank was smashed in pieces. The dollars he had worked so hard to save lay in a soggy wad in the corner.

Just then, Dad passed by Timmy's room. "What's wrong, Tim?" he asked. "You look so **disappointed**."

2 Timmy answered sadly, "Remember last month when Bruno chewed up my soccer uniform? Well, he **repeated** that stunt, only this time he broke my piggy bank. Then he chewed up the dollars I **received** from Grandpa for my birthday. I was starting a **fund** to buy a new uniform!"

When Timmy first got Bruno, Dad had said Timmy needed to be responsible for him. No matter what Timmy did, it seemed that Bruno was always getting into trouble, mostly by chewing on things he shouldn't.

"Let's dry out your wet dollars," Dad said. "Then we'll need to come up with a plan. We need a better way to save!"

Timmy pulled apart the soggy wad of money. Dad showed him how to iron the dollars on the ironing board so they dried quickly and lay flat once again. Fortunately, Bruno hadn't actually chewed holes in the dollar bills or swallowed any of them!

3 "All right, Tim," said Dad. "Now we need to take your money to the bank and open an **account** where it will be safe from Bruno!" he **chuckled**.

Timmy's father continued, "All this talk about bank accounts and saving and spending money makes me realize something.

"I forgot to include an important item in our monthly **budget**. Bruno needs to have some toys that he can chew so he doesn't go borrowing money from you. If we spend a little on toys for Bruno, we may just end up saving money in the end!"

DAY 1

Phonics

▶ **SHARE OBJECTIVES**

- Identify and count syllables in base words with endings -ed, -ing.
- Learn the spelling-sound correspondences for endings -ed, -ing.
- Blend and decode regularly spelled base words with endings -ed, -ing.

▶ **SKILLS TRACE**

Base Words and Endings -ed, -ing	
Introduce	pp. T16–T17, T42–T43
Differentiate	pp. T84–T85
Reteach	p. T98
Review	p. T62
Assess	Weekly Tests, Lesson 16

ENGLISH LANGUAGE SUPPORT

Comprehensible Input

Emerging Use gestures and demonstrations to reinforce the meanings of verbs in the lesson, such as *bat*, *drop*, *nap*, and *fix*. Demonstrate an action as you say the corresponding word. Have children copy your movements and repeat the word.

Expanding Help children recognize that the pronunciation of the ending -ed is not always /ĕd/. Provide additional practice reading words such as *wagged*, *picked*, *grabbed*, and *clapped*, in which the -ed ending is pronounced /d/ or /t/. **ELD** ELD.PIII.2

Bridging Write two base words. Have children choose a word and say one sentence with the base word and one with an -ing ending.

Base Words and Endings -ed, -ing

ENGLISH LANGUAGE SUPPORT English learners (including speakers of Spanish, Hmong, Haitian Creole, and Korean) may have trouble with the /ng/ sound at the end of many English words, including words ending in -ing. Model pronouncing the sound, and have children practice pronouncing words such as these: *digging*, *running*, and *sitting*. Use each word in a brief sentence to reinforce meaning. **ELD** ELD.PIII.2

Phonemic Awareness Warm-Up *Let's clap to count the syllables in words. I'll do it first. Listen:* wanted. **(two claps)** *I hear two syllables in the word* wanted: want, ed. *Now you try one with me. Repeat the word and clap to count the syllables. Listen:* pack. *How many syllables do you hear?* **one** *Listen to this word:* packing. *How many syllables do you hear in* packing? **two**

Let's do some more. Repeat the word and clap the syllables: trick **one**, tricked **one**, fanned **one**, cutting **two**, drop **one**, dropped **one**, trot **one**, trotted **two**, nod **one**, nodded **two**, tip **one**, tipping **two**.

If children count two syllables for words such as *tricked*, tell them to put their hands under their chins and count how many times their chin hits their hand to count vowel sounds/syllables.

1 Teach/Model

Word Card and Picture Card Display the cards for *dig*. Read the word that names the picture and have children repeat after you. *Listen:* dig. *Now you say it.*

- Point out that *dig* has one vowel followed by a single consonant. Explain that when a word has one vowel followed by a single consonant, we usually double the consonant before adding the ending -ed or -ing.

- Write and read *digging*. Underline the base word, or root word, *dig* and circle the ending -ing. *This is the word* digging. *I see the base word* dig *and the ending* -ing. *I doubled the final consonant* g *in* dig *before adding* -ing. **Read the word together:** digging. *How many syllables do you hear in* digging? **two**

- Write and read *batted*. Follow a similar process to point out the base word *bat* and the ending -ed. Guide children to recognize that -ed stands for the /ĕd/ sound in *batted*.

- Repeat the procedure with the words *fixed* and *picked*. Point out that the ending -ed can also stand for the sounds /d/ and /t/.

2 Guided Practice

Continuous Blending Routine Use Instructional Routine 3 to blend *dropped*.

- Display **Letter Cards** *d, r, o, p, p, e, d.* Name the letters.

- Blend the sounds. *Listen: /d/ /r/ /ŏ/ /p/ /t/.* Then have children blend with you and say the word.

Blending Lines

Blend Words Have children read the following words chorally; provide Corrective Feedback as needed. Help children compare the sounds and spellings in each line.

1. run	running	nod	nodded	sit	sitting
2. wag	wagged	rip	ripping	hum	hummed
3. napping	fitted	batting	dotted	cutting	popped

Related Words Have children read the following words chorally. Help them compare the word parts and spellings in each set of related words.

4. pot	potted	potting	stop	stopped	stopping
5. grab	grabbed	grabbing	clap	clapping	clapped
6. drop	dropped	dropping	trap	trapped	trapping

Challenge Call on above-level children to read the words in Line 7 and discuss the elements. Then have the class read the sentences chorally.

> 7. wrapped recapping unplanned forgetting submitted traveling
> 8. Joan <u>said something</u> about being <u>gone</u> all week.
> 9. While Lin was <u>gone</u>, Jack wrapped the pot he painted. **ELA** RF.2.3e, RF.2.3f

3 Apply

Have partners take turns rereading Blending Lines 1–3 and 4–6. Then tell each partner to sort the words. Children might sort words according to their *-ed* or *-ing* ending, or by words with and without endings. Have partners read each other's lists and identify the criteria used for sorting. **ELA** RF.2.3e, L.2.2d

Distribute Reader's Notebook Volume 2 page 1 or leveled practice in Grab-and-Go™ Resources to children to complete independently.

Corrective Feedback When a child mispronounces a letter-sound, highlight that letter, restate its sound, have children repeat the sound, and then guide them to blend the word. See the example below.

Decoding Error:
A child reads *hummed* in Line 2 as a two-syllable word.

Correct the error. Say the word and the sound. *The word is* hummed; *the letters* e, d *stand for the sound /d/.*

Model as you touch the letters. *I'll blend: /h/ /ŭ/ /m/ /d/. What is the word?* hummed

Guide *Let's blend together: /h/ /ŭ/ /m/ /d/. What is the word?* hummed

Check *You blend: /h/ /ŭ/ /m/ /d/ What is the word?* hummed

Reinforce Go back two or three words and have children continue reading. Make note of errors and review those words during the next lesson.

 Go to pp. T84–T85 for additional phonics support.

Phonics

▶ SHARE OBJECTIVES

- Write words with endings -ed, -ing.
- Read on-level text with base words with endings -ed, -ing and High-Frequency Words.
- Practice reading fluently at an appropriate rate.

▶ DICTATION SENTENCES

- **wagged** The dog *wagged* its tail.
- **trotted** The horse *trotted* along the trail.
- **grinning** Jan was *grinning* from ear to ear.
- **mopped** Ted *mopped* the dirty floor.
- **fixing** Nate is *fixing* the car.
- **patted** Kay *patted* her cat on the head.

ENGLISH LANGUAGE SUPPORT

Use Visuals and Gestures

All Proficiencies Use pantomime and visuals to reinforce the meanings of the dictation words and sentences. For example, pantomime the actions for *grinning*, *mopped*, and *patted* as you use the word to describe what you are doing. Have children repeat the words as they pantomime the actions. Show photographs or illustrations to represent *wagged*, *trotted*, and *fixing*. Have children say the words after you. Finally, say the words at random and ask children to pantomime the appropriate action or point to the corresponding image.

Blend-It Books

To provide reading practice with new sound/spellings in decodable texts, see **Blend-It Books** 109–112.

Write Words with Endings *-ed, -ing*

1 Teach/Model

Connect Sounds to Spelling Display the **Word Card** and **Picture Card** for *hop*. Remind children that when a word has one vowel followed by a single consonant, we usually double the final consonant before adding the ending -ed or -ing. Write *hopped* and read it aloud. Tell children they will now write words with endings -ed and -ing.

Use Instructional Routine 7 ⤴ to dictate the first sentence at left. *Listen as I say a word and use it in a sentence.*

- Model how to spell the word *wagged*. *The word* wagged *begins with the sound /w/. The /w/ sound is spelled w, so I'll write w. The next sound in* wagged *is /ă/, spelled a. I'll write a next. The next sound is /g/. I know that g stands for /g/, so I'll write g. The final sound I hear in* wagged *is /d/. I know that the ending -ed can stand for /d/. But first, I remember that I need to double the g before I add -ed. I'll reread to check the whole word:* wagged.

2 Guided Practice

Connect Sounds to Writing Continue the dictation, using the sentences at left.

- Have children say each dictation word aloud after you. Then have them identify the sounds they hear at the beginning, middle, and end and write the letters that spell each sound. **ELA** L.2.2d

- Remind children to write only the dictation word.

3 Apply

Read aloud the following decodable sentence for children to write. Remind children to look at the Focus Wall if they need help spelling *said*, *something*, or *gone*. **ELA** RF.2.3f, L.2.2d

> Jake <u>said</u> he dropped <u>something</u> when he was running, and now his key is <u>gone</u>.

Print the dictation words and decodable sentence for children to check their work.

Decodable Reader

Read *Beep! Beep!*

Review Base Words with Endings *-ed*, *-ing* and High-Frequency Words Review adding endings *-ed* and *-ing* to base words. Then review the High-Frequency Words *also*, *fly*, *gone*, *have*, *horse*, *look*, *river*, *said*, *saw*, and *something*.

Preview Have children read the title, browse beginning pages, and discuss what they think the story is about.

Use Projectable S1 to review the **Phonics/Decoding Strategy**. Model the strategy using the title.

Have children read the first page silently. Then ask a child to read the page aloud while others follow, tracking the print. Repeat for each page.

Decodable Reader

ENGLISH LANGUAGE SUPPORT Point out that *beep* is an English word that names a sound. Explain that the word itself sounds like the noise that certain machines make. Have children repeat the word several times. If possible, allow children to listen to a recording of the "beep" sound that a toy robot might make to compare the sound and the word. **ELD** ELD.PIII.2

If children make more than six total errors, use the **Corrective Feedback** steps to help them reread aloud with accuracy. If they make fewer than six errors, have them reread and retell the story.

Fluency: Rate

Remind children that when good readers read aloud, their reading sounds as if they are telling a story or talking to a friend. Good readers read at a speed that is just right—it is neither too fast nor too slow. Display and read aloud these sentences:

> Dan and his mom went shopping on Main Street.
> Dan was jogging along.

Model Fluency and Rate Read each sentence slowly, pausing after each word. Then ask children whether your reading is easy to follow and understand. Repeat the sentences, reading very rapidly. Again, have children respond to your reading. Then model using appropriate rate. *Notice the speed at which I'm reading. It is neither too fast nor too slow. The words are easy to listen to and understand.* Reread the sentences fluently and have children repeat them. *Let's read the sentences together. Read at a comfortable rate that sounds natural.*

ENGLISH LANGUAGE SUPPORT As children read, monitor their pronunciation of base words with endings *-ed*, or *-ing*. Provide modeling and support as needed. **ELD** ELD.PIII.2

Responding Ask children to read aloud sections of the text that tell what the robots could do. Then have them write one sentence that tells something the robots could do that surprised Dan and his mom. **ELA** RL.2.1, RL.2.3

Reread for Fluency Use Instructional Routine 12 to reread *Beep! Beep!* chorally. Remind children to read at a steady and natural rate. **ELA** RF.2.4b

Corrective Feedback When a child mispronounces a word, point to the word and say it. Call attention to the element that was mispronounced, say the sound, and then guide children to read the word. See the example below.

Decoding Error:
A child reads *beeped* on page 2 as *beep*.

Correct the error. Say the word. *That word is beeped.*

Guide Have children repeat the word. *What is the word?* beeped

Check *Go back to the beginning of the sentence and read it again.*

Reinforce Record the error and review the word again before children reread the story.

 Go to pp. T84–T85 for additional phonics support.

DAY 1

Introduce Vocabulary

▷ **SHARE OBJECTIVES**
- Acquire and use vocabulary. LANGUAGE
- Use a variety of vocabulary in shared language activities. LANGUAGE
- Create complete sentences using Vocabulary words. LANGUAGE

Teach

Display and discuss the **Vocabulary in Context Cards,** using the routine below.

1 Read and pronounce the word. Read the word once alone and then together.

2 Explain the word. Read aloud the explanation under *What Does It Mean?*

ENGLISH LANGUAGE SUPPORT Review these cognates with Spanish-speaking students.
- recibió (received)
- repitió (repeated)

3 Discuss vocabulary in context. Together, read aloud the sentence on the front of the card. Help children explain and use the word in new sentences.

4 Engage with the word. Ask and discuss the *Think About It* question with children.

Practice/Apply

Give partners or small groups one or two **Vocabulary in Context Cards.** Help children complete the *Talk It Over* activities for each card.
ELA RF.2.3f **ELD** ELD.PII.2.3a

Read aloud and have children complete the activity at the top of **Student Book** p. 10.

Then guide children to complete the Language Detective activity. Work with them to create sentences using Vocabulary words. Have children share the sentences with the class.
ELA RF.2.3f, SL.2.6, L.2.6 **ELD** ELD.PI.2.1, ELD.PI.2.12b

Lesson 16

Q LANGUAGE DETECTIVE

Talk About Words
Work with a partner. Use the Vocabulary words in new sentences that tell about the photos. Write the sentences.

 myNotebook

Add new words to **myWordList.** Use them in your speaking and writing.

10   **ELA** L.2.1f, L.2.6 **ELD** ELD.PI.2.12b

Vocabulary in Context

▶ **Read each** Context Card.

▶ **Use a Vocabulary word to tell about something you did.**

1   received
The boys received some money for raking leaves in the yard.

2   account
The girl opened a bank account with the money from her allowance.

ENGLISH LANGUAGE SUPPORT
Comprehensible Input

Emerging Point out cognates *received/recibido* and *repeated/repetido.* Use gestures to demonstrate the meanings. Have children repeat the gestures after you.
ELD ELD.PI.2.12b

Expanding Ask children questions to confirm their understanding. Example: *What makes you disappointed?*
ELD ELD.PI.2.12b

Bridging Have partners write questions and answers using Vocabulary words. Example: *Why was Marta staring out her window?*
ELD ELD.PI.2.12b

③ budget

A budget is a plan for how you should spend your money.

My budget for the Field Trip
I have $11.
I will spend $4 on lunch.
I will spend $5 on souvenirs.
I will spend $2 on a snack.

④ disappointed

He was disappointed, or sad, that he would not be able to buy the book.

⑤ chuckled

Her dad chuckled when he saw her tiny piggy bank.

⑥ staring

The girl was staring at the money. Should she save it or spend it?

⑦ repeated

The car wash was such a big success that the class repeated it in May.

⑧ fund

The players got new shirts by raising money for the team fund.

11

FORMATIVE ASSESSMENT   RtI

Are children able to understand and use Target Vocabulary words?

IF...	THEN...
children struggle,	▶ use **Vocabulary in Context Cards** and differentiate **Vocabulary Reader,** *Raising Funds,* for Struggling Readers, p. T86. *See also Intervention Lesson 16, pp. S2–S11.*
children are on track,	▶ use **Vocabulary in Context Cards** and differentiate **Vocabulary Reader,** *Raising Funds,* for On-Level Readers, p. T86.
children excel,	▶ differentiate **Vocabulary Reader,** *Raising Funds,* for Advanced Readers, p. T87.

SMALL GROUP Options

Vocabulary Reader, pp. T86–T87
Scaffold instruction to the English learner's proficiency level.

ENGLISH LANGUAGE SUPPORT

More Vocabulary Practice

Emerging/Expanding Distribute Dialogue, EL16.5 🔲. Read the title aloud and have children repeat. Have children look at the title, images, and other information on the page. Then have them predict what they think the dialogue will be about.

• As you read the dialogue aloud, display the Context Cards for *received, fund, chuckled,* and *disappointed.* After you read the dialogue, reread the part of Rami and have the class choral read the part of Rosita. Then switch roles.

• Have children listen as you describe a clothing sale, rummage sale, or other community effort to raise money.

• Have children ask questions about your story. Help them phrase their questions appropriately.

• Allow children to include language from the dialogue. Encourage them to use high-utility words. Answer their questions or have them guess the answers. **ELD** ELD.PI.2.1, ELD.PI.2.12b

DAY 1

Read and Comprehend

Read and Comprehend

▶ **SHARE OBJECTIVES**
- Identify and describe setting, characters, and plot.
- Make inferences and predictions.
- Access prior knowledge to exchange information about a topic. LANGUAGE

☑ **TARGET SKILL**

Story Structure

- Read the top section of **Student Book** p. 12 with children.

- Tell children that fictional stories have a plot, characters, and a setting. Explain that in many realistic fiction stories, the plot will involve a problem that the characters must solve.

- Explain that readers should try to select the most important events of the story. To do this, they might ask themselves, *what is the story's problem? How might the characters solve the problem?*

- Draw children's attention to the graphic organizer on **Student Book** p. 12. Tell them that, as they read, they can use this story map to record information about the characters, setting, and the major events of the plot.

- Review how to fill in the graphic organizer with children using a simple story they have read recently. **ELA** RL.2.1, RL.2.5 **ELD** ELD.PI.2.6

ENGLISH LANGUAGE SUPPORT Draw a story map on the board. Have children name a movie that they are all familiar with. Use the movie to complete a story map together, discussing each of the elements as you write them in the chart. **ELD** ELD.PII.2.1

☑ **TARGET SKILL**

Story Structure The characters, setting, and plot of a story make up the **story structure**. The **setting** is where and when the story takes place. The **characters** are the people in the story. The **plot** is what happens in the story.

As you read *Mr. Tanen's Tie Trouble*, think about what the important events are. You can use a story map like the one below to show the main parts of the story.

Characters	Setting
Plot	

☑ **TARGET STRATEGY**

Infer/Predict Use clues, or text evidence, to figure out more about story parts.

ELA RL.2.5, SL.2.1a **ELD** ELD.PI.2.1, ELD.PI.2.3, ELD.PII.2.1

ENGLISH LANGUAGE SUPPORT

Comprehensible Input

Emerging Guide children to complete sentence frames. Say: *The people and animals in a story are the _____.* characters *The events in a story make up the _____.* plot *Where the story takes place is the _____.* setting **ELD** ELD.PII.2.1

Expanding Ask children to think about their favorite cartoon. Ask them to write a sentence describing one of the characters. Then have them write a sentence describing the setting. **ELD** ELD.PII.2.1

Bridging Have children complete the Expanding activity by thinking about a story they have read. Then have children write a third sentence describing the plot of that story. **ELD** ELD.PII.2.1

There are many ways to help other people. Holding the door for someone is one small way to help a person. Visiting someone who is sick can help make him or her feel better. Taking care of family pets or doing chores can help out at home. Helping others makes them feel good, and it can make you feel good, too!

You will read about a principal who helps his school in *Mr. Tanen's Tie Trouble*.

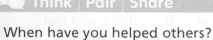

Think | Pair | Share

When have you helped others? Talk about it with a partner.

▸ Who did you help and why?

▸ Has anyone ever helped you?

Share your answers with the class. Listen carefully to others.

13

COMPREHENSION STRATEGIES

Use the following strategies flexibly as you read with children by modeling how they can be used to improve comprehension and understanding of a text. See scaffolded support for the strategy shown in boldface during this week's reading.

- **Monitor/Clarify**
- Visualize
- **Summarize**
- Analyze/Evaluate
- **Infer/Predict**
- Question

Use Strategy Projectables 🔗, S1–S8, for additional support.

DOMAIN: Civics

LESSON TOPIC: Helping Others

✓ TARGET STRATEGY

Infer/Predict

- Read the bottom of **Student Book** p. 12 with children. Tell them that they can use story clues to make inferences and predictions about story events. Remind them that making inferences and predictions go together because they are guessing things the author does not tell them.

- Tell children that as they read, they can check to see if their predictions are correct. As they monitor their predictions, they can make new predictions based on new story clues.

- Explain that they can use their story maps to record story structure and form predictions.

- Then explain that you will guide them to use this strategy when you read *Mr. Tanen's Tie Trouble* together. **ELA** RL.2.1 **ELD** ELD.PI.2.6

PREVIEW THE TOPIC

Helping Others

- Tell children that today they will begin to read *Mr. Tanen's Tie Trouble*. Read the information at the top of **Student Book** p. 13 with children.

- Lead a discussion about the ways that they help each other in the classroom, at home, or in their town. Record their ideas in a three-column chart.

- Read the last sentence on **Student Book** p. 13. Ask children to predict what kind of story they will be reading.

Think-Pair-Share

- Read the collaborative discussion prompt with children. Remind them to ask and answer questions if something isn't understood.

- Before children share their sentences, model what it means to listen when others speak, and discuss what might happen when this rule is not followed. Tell them to think about and practice listening when others speak. After, have children share examples of how they were good listeners. **ELA** SL.2.1a, SL.2.1c, SL.2.3 **ELD** ELD.PI.2.1

ENGLISH LANGUAGE SUPPORT Use the image on Lesson 16 **Language Support Card** to review the lesson topic with children. Guide children to share and summarize what they have learned. **ELD** ELD.PI.2.1, ELD.PI.2.12a

DAY 1

Read the Anchor Text

 GENRE

Realistic Fiction

- Read the genre information on **Student Book** p. 14 with children.

- Preview the story with children, and model identifying the characteristics of realistic fiction.

 Think Aloud *I read the title and looked at the illustrations. All the people look like real people I might know, and the events look as if they could happen in real life. This is a type of story called realistic fiction.*

- As you preview, ask children to identify other features of realistic fiction. **ELA** RL.2.10 **ELD** ELD.PI.2.6

ENGLISH LANGUAGE SUPPORT Guide children at the emerging and expanding levels to complete the Academic English activities on Lesson 16 **Language Support Card**. **ELD** ELD.PII.2.3a

Lesson 16
ANCHOR TEXT

 **MEET THE AUTHOR AND ILLUSTRATOR**

Maryann Cocca-Leffler

Many of Maryann Cocca-Leffler's books are based on her own life. *Clams All Year* is about the time she went clam digging with her grandpa following a big storm. She wrote *Jack's Talent* after a boy said during a school visit that he had no talent for anything. The tie-loving Mr. Tanen was the principal at an elementary school that the author's two daughters attended.

GENRE

Realistic fiction is a story that could happen in real life. As you read, look for:
▶ characters who act like real people
▶ a setting that could be a real place

14

ELA RL.2.3, RL.2.5, RL.2.10
ELD ELD.PI.2.6, ELD.PII.2.1

Scaffold Close Reading

Strategies for Annotation

✏️ 🖥️ *Annotate it!*

As you read the selection with children, look for this icon ✏️🖥️ *Annotate it!* for opportunities to annotate the text collaboratively as a class.

Think Through the Text
FIRST READ

Develop comprehension through
- Guided Questioning
- Target Strategy: Infer/Predict
- Vocabulary in Context

Analyze the Text
SECOND READ

Support analyzing short sections of text:
- Story Structure
- Understanding Characters
Use directed note-taking by working with children to complete a graphic organizer during reading. Distribute copies of Graphic Organizer 10 🗗.

Independent Reading

- Children analyze the text independently, using the Reader's Guide on Reader's Notebook Volume 2 pp. 8–9 🗗. (See p. T54–T55 for instructional support.)
- Children read independently in a self-selected trade book.

Mr. Tanen's Tie Trouble

by Maryann Cocca-Leffler

ESSENTIAL QUESTION

How can helping others make you feel good?

15

READER AND TASK CONSIDERATIONS

ELA RL.2.1, SL.2.4, SL.2.6
ELD ELD.PI.2.1, ELD.PI.2.6, ELD.PI.2.12a

Determine the level of additional support your children will need to read and comprehend *Mr. Tanen's Tie Trouble* successfully.

READERS

- **Motivate** Ask children to tell about a time they saved money for something.

- **Access Knowledge and Experience** Review with children the chart you completed as part of the Talk It Over activity on the back of Lesson 16 **Language Support Card**. Ask children to share with a partner experiences they've had with one or more of the fundraising activities on the chart. Encourage them to use complete sentences as they share.

TASKS

- **Increase Scaffolding** Stop periodically as you read to help children visualize what they are reading.

- **Foster Independence** Have children read the story in small groups. Have children stop periodically to ask and answer questions they have about the story.

ESSENTIAL QUESTION

- Read aloud the Essential Question on **Student Book** p. 15: *How can helping others make you feel good?* Then tell children to think about this question as they read *Mr. Tanen's Tie Trouble*.

Predictive Writing

- Tell children to write the Essential Question.

- Explain that they will write about what they expect *Mr. Tanen's Tie Trouble* to be about. Ask them to think about how the Essential Question relates to what they noticed while previewing the selection or what they already know about the Essential Question from their own experiences or past readings.

- Guide children to think about the genre of the selection as they write.

Set Purpose

- Explain that good readers set a purpose for reading based on their preview of the selection and what they know about the genre.

- Model setting a reading purpose.

> **Think Aloud** *As I preview the illustrations, I see ties everywhere, and the title is Mr. Tanen's Tie Trouble. One purpose for reading might be to find out what Mr. Tanen's problem is and what ties have to do with it.*

- Have children page through the story and set their own purpose for reading. Ask several children to share their purpose for reading.
ELA RF.2.4a, RL.2.10

FOR STUDENTS WITH DISABILITIES To help make the text accessible to all children, consider modifications such as these:

- Allow children to record the text discussion and listen to it later as needed.

- Seat children in a position in the classroom that is most beneficial to the child's learning style.

Mr. Tanen loves being the principal of the Lynnhurst School. He also loves ties. In fact, he has almost one thousand crazy ties!

When Mr. Tanen returned from winter vacation, he received a call from Mr. Apple at the School Department. Mr. Apple told him that because many things at the school had to be fixed, there wasn't enough money left for a new playground. **1**

Mr. Tanen sadly hung up the phone and gazed out at the broken-down playground. He heard a *clink-clank*. He looked up to see Kaylee and Alex lugging in a big jar filled with money.

"Here it is! $148.29 for the playground fund!" said Kaylee proudly.

"New playground, here we come!" cheered Alex.

Mr. Tanen didn't know what to say. **2**

16

17

ENGLISH LANGUAGE SUPPORT

Use Visuals

Emerging Show the **Online Picture Card** for *playground*. Ask, *What things do you find on a playground?*

Expanding Show the **Online Picture Card** for *playground*. Have children complete sentence frames: *A seesaw is _____. A slide is _____. Swings are _____.*

Bridging Have children use the illustrations on pp. 16–17 to predict what might happen.

FIRST READ

Cite
Text Evidence

Think Through the Text

1 *What problem does Mr. Tanen have?* There isn't enough money to build the playground. *Why isn't there enough money?* All of the money was spent fixing other things at the school. **ELA** RL.2.1, RL.2.5 **ELD** ELD.PI.2.6

ENGLISH LANGUAGE SUPPORT Tell children that the word *received* has a cognate in Spanish: *recibió*. Remind children to look for cognates as they read to help them figure out the meanings of key words.

2 *What kind of fund might you like to start at your school? Explain why.* Sample answer: *I would like to start a new library fund because we need new books.* **ELD** ELD.PI.2.6

ENGLISH LANGUAGE SUPPORT Provide a sentence frame to encourage participation. *I would like to start a _____ fund because _____.* **ELD** ELD.PI.2.3, ELD.PI.2.11

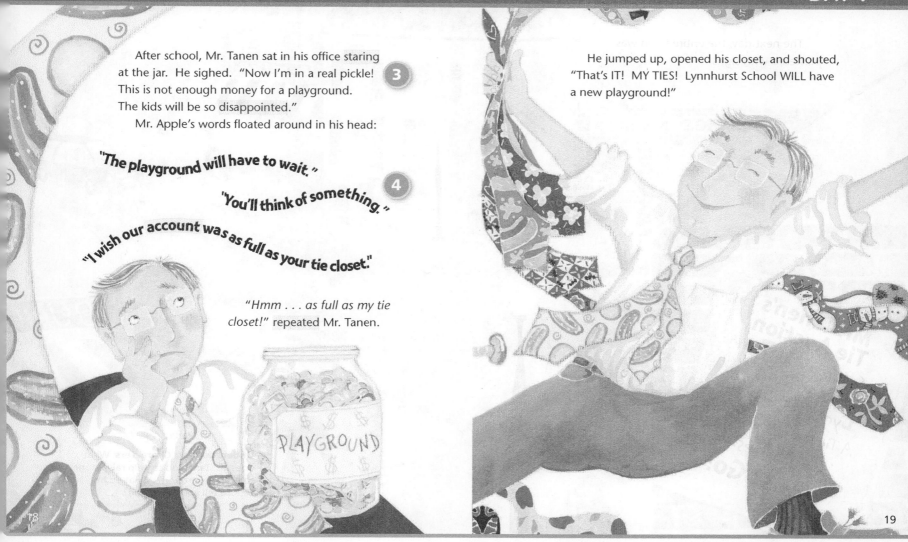

After school, Mr. Tanen sat in his office staring at the jar. He sighed. "Now I'm in a real pickle! This is not enough money for a playground. The kids will be so disappointed."

Mr. Apple's words floated around in his head:

"The playground will have to wait."

"You'll think of something."

"I wish our account was as full as your tie closet."

"Hmm . . . as full as my tie closet!" repeated Mr. Tanen.

PLAYGROUND

18

He jumped up, opened his closet, and shouted, "That's IT! MY TIES! Lynnhurst School WILL have a new playground!"

19

---

3 *What do you think Mr. Tanen means by being "in a real pickle"?* having a problem. **ELA** L.2.4a **ELD** ELD.PI.2.6

ENGLISH LANGUAGE SUPPORT Explain to children that the phrase *in a pickle* is a funny way of saying that someone is in some kind of trouble. The author uses the phrase here to show that Mr. Tanen is in trouble. **ELD** ELD.PI.2.7

4 *How does the illustration of words above Mr. Tanen's head relate to what is going on in the story?* Mr. Tanen is remembering Mr. Apple's words, so they are "floating around in his head." **ELA** RL.2.7 **ELD** ELD.PI.2.6

☑ **TARGET STRATEGY** | Infer/Predict

Use the Infer/Predict strategy to help children use text clues to predict what will happen next in the story. Model the strategy:

> **Think Aloud** *Mr. Tanen remembers what Mr. Apple says about his ties, and this gives him an idea. I think he will sell his ties to raise money for the playground fund.*

ENGLISH LANGUAGE SUPPORT

How English Works: Interpretive

Verb Tenses Remind children that verb tenses show when things happen—for example, they can show that something is happening right now or they can show that something has happened in the past. Read page 19 aloud, emphasizing the following past-tense verbs as you read them: *jumped, opened, shouted.* Explain that these past-tense verbs let the reader know that the action happened in the past. Guide children to retell the story events so far using past-tense verbs. **ELD** ELD.PI.2.6, ELD.PI.2.12a, ELD.PII.2.3b

The next day, the entire town was plastered with signs.

Mr. Tanen's Tie Auction Saturday at 7pm at the Lynnhurst School A Tie For Any Occasion! All Ties **Must Go!**

ANALYZE THE TEXT

Understanding Characters What does Mr. Tanen do to help raise money for the playground? What do his actions tell you about him?

ENGLISH LANGUAGE SUPPORT

Comprehensible Input

Emerging Name the job done by each worker on pp. 22–23. Have children point to each person and name the job.

Expanding Have children make a list of all the workers on pp. 22–23 and add other workers' names to the list.

Bridging Have partners brainstorm different workers, starting with those on pp. 22–23. Discuss the jobs they might want.

FIRST READ

Cite Text Evidence

Think Through the Text

5 *What is Mr. Tanen's plan for the playground fund? He plans to sell his ties to raise money for the new playground. How can you tell? I can read the sign that says "Mr. Tanen's tie auction."* **ELA** RL.2.3, RL.2.7

ENGLISH LANGUAGE SUPPORT Point out that the sign tells people about an auction, which is a special kind of sale. Read the sign to children, emphasizing the last sentence: *All Ties Must Go!* Explain to children that this sentence is another way of saying that all of Mr. Tanen's ties will be for sale. Mr. Tanen wanted to let people know that if they come to the auction, they will be able to buy any one of his ties. **ELD** ELD.PI.2.6

Mrs. Sweet Apple noticed the sign on the grocery store window. She called her husband, Mr. Apple.

"Why is Mr. Tanen selling all his ties? Has he gone crazy?"

Mr. Apple told her about the school budget and the playground money. The town was buzzing all day . . .

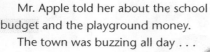

6

Mrs. Sweet Apple called Monsieur Bijou at the bakery,

who called Cleo at the cleaners,

who called Dr. Demi the dentist . . .

It went on and on, until even Zack, the night watchman at the zoo, got the word:

"Mr. Tanen is selling his ties!" **7**

22   23

6 *What clues in the text help you understand the meaning of the word* budget? *The sentence mentions playground money for the school, so a budget must be a plan for how the school spends money.* **ELA** L.2.4a **ELD** ELD.PI.2.6

7 *How do the characters react when they hear about the tie auction? Why? They are surprised that Mr. Tanen is selling all of his ties because they know how important the ties are to him. What do you think the characters will do? They will probably go to the auction and buy the ties.* **ELA** RL.2.3

ENGLISH LANGUAGE SUPPORT Provide this sentence frame to encourage participation. *The people in the town feel _____ when they find out about the auction.* surprised **ELD** ELD.PI.2.6

SECOND READ   DAY 2   Analyze the Text

Understanding Characters

Read the Analyze the Text box on **Student Book** p. 21 with children. Tell children they should make smart guesses about what Mr. Tanen is like based on how he responds to the challenge of the playground. Remind children that they can use words and pictures to help them. Then have children discuss their answers to the questions. Children should recognize that Mr. Tanen cares about his students so much that he'll give up his ties to help them raise money for a playground. **ELA** RL.2.3, RL.2.7 **ELD** ELD.PI.2.6

✏️ 🖥 *Annotate it!* Work with children to highlight sentences that show that Mr. Tanen cares about his students.

On Saturday, the whole town showed up for the auction. Monsieur Bijou started the bidding. "I'll give you $50 for the Doughnut and Danish Tie!"

Lolly the librarian bought the Book Tie.

Dr. Demi was the proud owner of the Toothbrush Tie.

Kaylee handed over her entire piggy bank for the Hot Dog Tie.

Mrs. Sweet Apple just had to have the Wedding Bells Tie, and of course, Mr. Apple chuckled as he paid quite a bit of cash for the Crabapple Tie.

24

Emerging Have children complete: *Mr. Tanen _____ 1,000 ties. The townspeople _____ buying ties.* Provide linking verbs: *is, was, are, has* **ELD** ELD.PII.2.3a

Expanding Write the linking verbs *have* and *has*. Have pairs write a sentence that uses the correct tense of each verb. **ELD** ELD.PII.2.3b

Bridging Have children write two sentences that describe what one of the ties in the story looks like. **ELD** ELD.PI.2.6

FIRST READ

Think Through the Text

 Why do you think the townspeople pay so much for the ties? They want to help the school raise enough money for the playground. They like the ties because they are very unusual. **ELA** RL.2.3 **ELD** ELD.PI.2.6

STANDARD ENGLISH LEARNERS Children may drop the inflected *-ed* ending from words. Remind children that the *-ed* ending of a verb lets them know that the action took place in the past. Give examples such as: *People showed up for the auction, Mr. Apple chuckled about the tie.* Write additional familiar verbs with the *-ed* ending. Have children read them and use them in oral sentences.

☑ PHONICS/DECODING STRATEGY

Use Projectable S1 to help children apply the Phonics/Decoding strategy while reading **Student Book** pp. 24–25. Model analyzing the word's parts to read the word *bidding*. Guide children to identify that the final *d* in the word *bid* is doubled before adding the *–ing* ending. Call attention to the word *chuckled*. Guide children to identify that the word *chuckle* already ends in *e*, so you drop the *e* to add the *–ed* ending.

The auction was a huge success! Every tie was sold, except one. Mr. Tanen couldn't part with his beloved Blue Ribbon Tie. It was a present from Mr. Apple for being a great principal. He looked out at a sea of townspeople, all wearing his ties.

9

"Thank you all. I have always taught my students, 'The more you give, the more you get.' With this money, the Lynnhurst School will have a new playground!"

Mr. Tanen swallowed hard. "My ties now belong to the town. Wear them proudly."

10

And throughout the spring, that's just what everyone did.

26
27

9 *What does Mr. Tanen mean when he says, "The more you give, the more you get"?* **If you do good things, you will feel better about yourself and make your world a better place to live.**
ELA RL.2.1 **ELD** ELD.PI.2.6

10 *How do you think Mr. Tanen feels about selling his ties?* **Sample answer: I think he feels happy because now there is enough money to build a playground. He probably feels sad, too, because now he doesn't have any ties.** **ELA** RL.2.3

ENGLISH LANGUAGE SUPPORT Provide sentence frames to encourage participation. *I think Mr. Tanen feels ____ about having money to build a playground.* **happy** *I think Mr. Tanen feels ____ about not having any ties.* **sad** **ELD** ELD.PI.2.6

But sometimes Mr. Tanen would forget his closet was empty. He would open it to get a tie, and with a tinge of sadness, he would remember. He only had one tie—and he was wearing it. Then he'd look outside at the playground being built.

"You have to give to get," he thought.

Soon it was Opening Day at the new playground. Mr. Tanen had invited the whole town to the ribbon-cutting ceremony. He tucked his speech in his pocket, grabbed his special scissors, and adjusted his tie. He wished he had on his official Ribbon-Cutting Tie.

The schoolyard was overflowing with people. Mr. Tanen made his way through the crowd.

28

29

Infer/Predict IF children have difficulty applying the Infer/Predict strategy, **THEN** use this model:

Think Aloud *I know that the kind townspeople bought all of Mr. Tanen's ties to raise money for the playground. I also know that Mr. Tanen is a very generous and thoughtful person. I predict that the townspeople will do something nice for Mr. Tanen.*

FIRST READ

Cite
Text Evidence

Think Through the Text

11 *What does Mr. Tanen remind himself of when he looks out the window?* You have to give to get. *Why does he do this?* He is sad that his ties are gone, so he is trying to feel better by reminding himself that he gave them away for a good cause. **ELA** RL.2.3 **ELD** ELD.PI.2.6

12 *What clues in the text tell us that Mr. Tanen misses his ties?* Mr. Tanen opens his closet and is sad to remember he no longer has his many ties. He wishes he had his Ribbon-Cutting tie to wear to the ceremony. **ELA** RL.2.3 **ELD** ELD.PI.2.6

ENGLISH LANGUAGE SUPPORT Tell children that the words *ceremony* and *invite* have cognates in Spanish: *ceremonia* and *inviter*, respectively. Remind children to look for cognates as they read to help them figure out the meanings of key words.

Then he saw it!

Mr. Tanen's Playground

The playground was tied in a giant ribbon made from Mr. Tanen's ties! **13**

30

31

13 *Why did the townspeople use Mr. Tanen's ties to make a ribbon for the new playground?* **Sample answer:** *They want to show their appreciation to Mr. Tanen for the new playground. How does Mr. Tanen feel about it?* **Sample answer:** *He is happy and excited to see the new playground and his ties.* **ELA** RL.2.3

ENGLISH LANGUAGE SUPPORT Provide sentence frames to help children make an inference, or best guess, about Mr. Tanen's feelings. *The townspeople made a ribbon from _____. Mr. Tanen's ties In the picture, Mr. Tanen looks very _____. surprised I think Mr. Tanen feels _____ to see his ties at the playground. happy* **ELD** ELD.PI.2.6

☑ **TARGET STRATEGY | Infer/Predict**

Tell children to practice the Infer/Predict strategy as they read **Student Book** pp. 28–31 silently to themselves. Ask children what details from the text helped them to make their inferences and predictions. As children read through the end of the story, ask them to confirm if their predictions were correct or not. **ELD** ELD.PI.2.6

Mrs. Sweet Apple and Mr. Apple were at the microphone.

"Mr. Tanen, you have taught us all, 'The more you give, the more you get,'" said Mrs. Sweet Apple. "You have given us a playground. We are giving you back your ties."

With that, Mr. Apple untied the tie ribbon and announced: "Mr. Tanen's Playground is

NOW OPEN!"

14   15

32   33

○ **DOMAIN: Civics**

LESSON TOPIC: Helping Others

Cross-Curricular Connection Lead a discussion with children about how they can make a positive contribution to their town or community. Write their suggestions on the board. Then ask children to work in pairs to make a poster for a community project and to provide a plan for how a community might accomplish such a project. Ask children to share their posters.

FIRST READ

Cite Text Evidence

Think Through the Text

14 *Why do you think the author used bold, wavy words for the words "Now open!" at the bottom of p. 33?* Possibly to show how excited Mr. Apple was when he said those words. **ELA** RL.2.1 **ELD** ELD.PI.2.6

15 *Why do you think the townspeople decide to give back Mr. Tanen's ties?* They know the importance of giving. **ELA** RL.2.3 **ELD** ELD.PI.2.6

ENGLISH LANGUAGE SUPPORT Tell children that the word *announce* has a cognate in Spanish: *anunciar*. Remind children to look for cognates as they read to help them figure out the meanings of key words.

Mr. Tanen and his ties were together again!

He slipped on his Swing and Slide Tie and smiled. **16**

ANALYZE THE TEXT

Story Structure What problem does Mr. Tanen have after he sells his ties? How does the ending solve Mr. Tanen's problem?

34

35

---

16 *How does Mr. Tanen feel at the end of the story? How do you know? He is happy because he is smiling and wearing one of his ties. He has all of his ties back and a new playground for the school.* **ELA** RL.2.1, RL.2.7 **ELD** ELD.PI.2.6

Collaborative Conversation

Remind children they have been reading about a principal who has a problem to solve. Working in groups, have children discuss how Mr. Tanen feels about being principal of Lynnhurst School. Guide them to use text evidence to explain their answers. Before beginning their discussions, remind children what it means to ask questions to clarify information. Model the skill for children using the following examples: *Can you give an example?, Can you show me in the text?* Have children practice asking questions during their discussions. **ELA** SL.2.1, SL.2.6, L.2.6 **ELD** ELD.PI.2.1, ELD.PI.2.6

SECOND READ **DAY 2** *Analyze the Text*

Story Structure

Read the Analyze the Text box on **Student Book** p. 35 with children. Then display Projectable 16.4 and distribute Graphic Organizer 10. Tell children that you will work together to complete the graphic organizer.

Remind children that a story's structure is made up of a setting, characters, and a plot. Explain that the plot usually has a problem and a solution. Prompt children to complete the graphic organizer by looking back through the selection and providing information to complete it. Then use the completed graphic organizer to answer the questions in the box. **ELA** RL.2.5 **ELD** ELD.PI.2.6

✎ ▢ *Annotate it!* Work with children to highlight sentences that describe how the problem in the story was solved.

DAY 1

Guided Retelling

Oral Language

Use the prompts on the **Retelling Cards** to guide children to identify the main idea about the topic and retell key details as they summarize the selection. **ELA** RL.2.1 **ELD** ELD.PI.2.6, ELD.PI.2.12a

front

back

front

back

front

back

RETELLING RUBRIC

4	Highly Effective	The retelling names the characters, describes the setting and the problem, and tells important events in order. It includes several details and tells how the problem was solved.
3	Generally Effective	The retelling names the characters and tells most of the important events in order, including how the problem was solved. It includes some details.
2	Somewhat Effective	The retelling includes a few elements of the story, but omits important characters or events and provides few details.
1	Ineffective	The reader is unable to provide any accurate elements of *Mr. Tanen's Tie Trouble*.

ENGLISH LANGUAGE SUPPORT

Review Key Ideas

All Proficiencies Pronounce and explain *retell*, reminding children that when they retell a story they are describing the main events in the order they happened. Page through *Mr. Tanen's Tie Trouble* with children and share the following sentence frames to help them retell the selection.

Mr. Tanen needs _____ to build the playground. **money** *He decides to _____ his ties.* **sell** *After the auction, Mr. Tanen misses his _____ .* **ties** *The townspeople give back the ties when _____ . the playground is built* **ELD** ELD.PI.2.6, ELD.PI.2.12a

Grammar Pronouns

▶ SHARE OBJECTIVES

- **Grammar** Use pronouns *I, he, she, it, we,* and *they.* LANGUAGE
- **Spelling** Spell words with endings *-ed* and *-ing.*
- **Writing** Identify the characteristics of a good narrative paragraph. LANGUAGE

ENGLISH LANGUAGE SUPPORT

Comprehensible Input

All Proficiencies Remind children that certain pronouns take the place of nouns doing actions. Write *I, he, she, it, we,* and *they* on the board. Write these sentence frames on the board: *Sarah ran fast. ___ ran fast. Tom and Jen ran, too. ___ ran, too.* Have children identify the correct pronouns to use.

Linguistic Transfer English learners may have difficulty with the different sounds of the ending *-ed* in words. Help children read the spelling words with *-ed* endings and sort them into three categories for the sound of *-ed:* /t/, /d/, /ed/. Then provide other words for children to read and sort, such as *popped, hugged,* and *patted.* **ELD** ELD.PIII.2

1 Teach/Model

Naming with Pronouns Display Projectable 16.2 ⬈. Remind children that a noun is a word that names a person, place, animal, or thing. Remind them that the naming part, or subject, of a sentence tells who or what does or did something. A noun can be replaced by a pronoun.

- Write the pronouns *I, he, she, it, we,* and *they. These pronouns can replace the subject of a sentence.* Model identifying the subject and replacing it with a pronoun. *Sam swings. He swings in the playground.*

Think Aloud *To identify the pronoun to use, I ask this Thinking Question: Which pronoun can take the place of the noun or nouns in the subject? Sam is the subject of the sentence. Sam is one boy, so I'll use the pronoun he because it names one boy. The pronoun he can replace the subject Sam.*

ENGLISH LANGUAGE SUPPORT Note that the Spanish cognates for *pronoun* and *noun* are *pronombre* and *nombre,* respectively.

2 Guided Practice/Apply

- Have children use the Thinking Question on **Projectable 16.2** to help them identify the pronoun that can replace each subject.
- Distribute Reader's Notebook Volume 2 page 2 ⬈ to children to complete independently.
- For additional support, have children view the GrammarSnap Video ⬈ that supports Lesson 16.

Spelling Base Words with Endings *-ed, -ing*

SPELLING WORDS AND SENTENCES

BASIC

1. *running* He was *running* fast.
2. *clapped* We *clapped* our hands.
3. *stopped* The car *stopped* at the light.
4. *hopping* He was *hopping* on one foot.
5. *batted* My brother *batted* the ball to me.
6. *selling** Our class is *selling* cookies to raise money.
7. *pinned* I *pinned* a flower on my dress.
8. *cutting** She is *cutting* the pie.
9. *sitting* He is *sitting* up straight.

10. *rubbed* I *rubbed* soap on it.
11. *missed* We *missed* the bus.
12. *grabbed** I *grabbed* the sled and took off.

REVIEW

13. *mixed* We *mixed* the batter.
14. *going* When are we *going*?

CHALLENGE

15. *wrapped* We *wrapped* the gifts.
16. *swelling* As the storm continued, the river kept *swelling.*

A form or forms of these words appear in the literature.

Administer the Pretest

Say each Spelling Word. Then say it in the sentence and repeat the word. Have children write the word. **ELA** L.2.2d

Teach the Principle

- Demonstrate when to double the consonant when the ending *-ed* or *-ing* is added to a base word. Write *run* and *running* on the board.
- Explain that if the base word ends in a double consonant, just the *-ed* or *-ing* is added. The spelling of the base word does not change. Write *sell* and *selling* on the board.

Model a Word Sort

Model sorting words based on word endings *-ed* and *-ing.* Present the Model the Sort lesson on page 86 of the **Literacy and Language Guide.**

Narrative Writing Introduce the Model

1 Teach/Model

Story Paragraph Tell children that this week they will be writing a story paragraph. Ask children to name stories they have read recently. Then display and read aloud Projectable 16.3 ⬀.

- Use the labels for paragraph 1 on the projectable to identify the beginning sentence, the details, and the action.

- Read and discuss the Writer's Checklist about story paragraphs.

Writer's Checklist

What Makes a Great Story Paragraph?

- It has an interesting **beginning sentence**.

- It has interesting **details**.

- There is **action**. Something interesting happens.

- The events are in an order that makes sense.

2 Guided Practice/Apply

- With children, label the beginning sentence, the details, and the action in paragraph 2 on **Projectable 16.3**.

Model Study Ask children to list the events from the paragraph in the order in which they happened. Have them explain why one sentence should be moved. *The sentence tells an event out of order. Rosa has to roll the dough flat before she can cut out shapes. The order must make sense.* Have children tell where the sentence should be placed. Mark the projectable to show the correct placement.

ELA W.2.3, W.2.4, W.2.10 **ELD** ELD.PI.2.10, ELD.PII.2.1

ENGLISH LANGUAGE SUPPORT Discuss what the word *action* means. Using the Read Aloud text as a guide, explain that the action in the story starts with Bruno chewing up Timmy's money. Ask children to tell what else happened in the Read Aloud that would be considered action events.

Daily Proofreading Practice

I see mrs. Green siting in the park.

She is waiting for the parade.

Performance Task

Children may prewrite, draft, revise, and publish their narrative writing task through *my*WriteSmart beginning on Day 3.

Common Core Writing Handbook

Additional support for Narrative Writing appears in the **Common Core Writing Handbook,** Lesson 16.

DAY 2

Today's Goals

Vocabulary & Oral Language

☑ **TARGET VOCABULARY**

received	chuckled
account	staring
budget	repeated
disappointed	fund

Phonemic Awareness
• **Syllables in Spoken Words**

Phonics & Fluency
• **Base Words and Endings** *-ed, -ing*
• **Fluency:** Rate
• **Read Decodable Reader:**
  Beep! Beep!
• **High-Frequency Words**

Text-Based Comprehension
• **Dig Deeper:** Use Clues to Analyze the Text
• **Story Structure**
• **Understanding Characters**
• **Reread the Anchor Text:**
  Mr. Tanen's Tie Trouble

Grammar & Writing
• **Pronouns**
• **Narrative Writing:** Story Paragraph
• **Trait:** Elaboration

Spelling
• **Base Words with Endings** *-ed, -ing*

Opening Routines

Warm Up with Wordplay

Make a Rhyme

Display and read aloud the following word: *tie.*

Have children work with partners to list as many words that rhyme with *tie* as they can. Remind children that the long *i* sound can have different spellings.

When children are ready, compile their words on the board. Depending on the words that children suggest, you may want to add others.

lie	my	try
buy	high	fly
why	cry	guy
die	sigh	pie

Have children make up an opening line for a poem, ending with one of the rhyming words. Let children choose their favorite opening line, and then, as a class, write a short poem using rhyming words in the list.

ELA W.2.7 **ELD** ELD.PI.2.2

Daily Phonemic Awareness

Syllables in Spoken Words

- Have children listen for syllables and clap them out with you. *Listen to this word:* helped. *How many syllables do you hear in* helped? *Let's clap it out:* helped. *one*

- *Let's do the same with this word:* walking. *How many syllables do you hear in* walking? *Let's clap it out:* walking. *two*

- Continue with the following words: *hopping, singing, slotted, boating, stranded, selling, ended, shopped, cutting, going.*

Corrective Feedback

- If a child struggles with counting syllables, give correction and model the task. Example: *Listen to this word: rowing. Clap the syllables. How many syllables do you hear? two*

- Have children repeat once with you before doing it on their own. Continue with the list at left.

Daily High-Frequency Words

- Point to **High-Frequency Word Card 158,** *horse.*

- *Say the word.* horse *Spell the word.* h-o-r-s-e *Write the word. Check the word.*

- Repeat the routine with new words *river* and *something,* and with review words *gone, said, fly, also, saw, look,* and *have.* **ELA** RF.2.3f

Snap and Clap

- Have children look at the words *horse, something,* and *river.* Tell them they will read each word and listen for syllables.

- Explain that children should clap their hands when they say the first syllable and snap their fingers when they say the second syllable, if there is a second syllable.

Corrective Feedback

- If a child does not recognize the word *said,* say the correct word and have children repeat it. Said. *What is the word? said*

- Have children spell the word. s-a-i-d *How do we say it? said*

- Have children reread all of the cards in random order.

Daily Vocabulary Boost

- Review Target Vocabulary and definitions with children. (See p. T14.) Remind children that they heard these words in the Read Aloud, "A Better Way to Save."

- Recall with children the story events they heard. Guide them to interact with each word's meaning.

  Timmy was staring *at the mess in his bedroom. What is something you are* staring *at right now?*

  Bruno chewed up the dollars I received *from Grandpa for my birthday. Can you name something you have* received?

  You look so disappointed. *Why might a person look* disappointed?

- Continue together, in the same manner, with *fund, account,* and *budget.* **ELA** L.2.6

staring
The girl was staring at the money. Should she save it or spend it?

Vocabulary in Context Cards 121–128

☑ **Target Vocabulary**

received
account
budget
disappointed
chuckled
staring
repeated
fund

DAY 2

Phonics

▶ **SHARE OBJECTIVES**

- Identify and count syllables in base words with endings *-ed, -ing*.
- Blend, build, decode, and write base words with endings *-ed, -ing*.
- Reread on-level text with base words with endings *-ed, -ing* and High-Frequency Words for fluency practice.

▶ **SKILLS TRACE**

Base Words and Endings *-ed, -ing*	
Introduce	pp. T16–T17, T42–T43
Differentiate	pp. T84–T85
Reteach	p. T98
Review	p. T62
Assess	Weekly Tests, Lesson 16

ENGLISH LANGUAGE SUPPORT

Comprehensible Input

All Proficiencies Continue to reinforce the meanings and pronunciations of the words children decode in Blending Lines. Use a word in a simple sentence, such as "I can **hum** a song." Have children repeat your sentence. Then have them say the sentence again, completing it with a word(s) that they choose: *I can* **hum** *[a tune]*. Repeat with other words in Blending Lines, for example: *Shhh!* _____ *is* **napping**. *The children* **clapped** *after* _____. *My friend* **dropped** _____.

Base Words and Endings *-ed, -ing*

Phonemic Awareness Warm-Up *Let's clap to count the syllables in words. I'll do it first. Listen:* wanted. **(two claps)** *I hear two syllables in* wanted. *Now you do it with me. Repeat the word and clap to count the syllables. Listen:* clapping. *How many syllables do you hear in the word* clapping? *two*

Let's do some more. Listen: clapped *one,* getting *two,* mixed *one,* folded *two,* bagged *one,* selling *two,* dripped *one,* started *two,* popped *one,* melted *two*

1 Teach/Model

Review base words and endings *-ed, -ing*. Display the **Picture Card** and the **Word Card** for *hop*. Read the word that names the picture and have children repeat after you.

- Point out that *hop* has one short vowel followed by a single consonant. Remind children that when we add endings to words with this spelling pattern, we usually double the final consonant before adding the ending.

Continuous Blending Routine
Display **Letter Cards** *h, o, p, p, e, d*. Name each letter.

h	o	p	p	e	d

Then use the routine to model blending *hopped*.

2 Guided Practice

Blending Lines

Blend Words Repeat the blending routine with the first two words in Line 1 below; help children compare the words. Point to each word as children read the entire line chorally. Continue with the remaining lines. Then call on volunteers to reread selected words until children can identify the words quickly.

1. run	running	nod	nodded	sit	sitting
2. wag	wagged	rip	ripping	hum	hummed
3. napping	fitted	batting	dotted	cutting	popped

Related Words Use a similar process to have children read Lines 4–6.

4. pot	potted	potting	stop	stopped	stopping
5. grab	grabbed	grabbing	clap	clapping	clapped
6. drop	dropped	dropping	trap	trapped	trapping

Challenge Call on above-level children to read the words in Line 7. Then have the class read the sentences chorally.

7. wrapped recapping unplanned forgetting submitted traveling
8. Joan <u>said</u> <u>something</u> about being <u>gone</u> all week.
9. While Lin was <u>gone</u>, Jack wrapped the pot he painted. **ELA** RF.2.3e, RF.2.3f

Build Words Model how to spell *skipped. The letters s and k stand for the first sounds in skip. The next sound is /ĭ/. The letter i stands for /ĭ/. The next sound is /p/. The letter p stands for /p/. The ending ed stands for the final sound /t/ in skipped. Skip has one short vowel followed by a single consonant, so I need to double the final consonant, p, before I add ed. Now I'll read the whole word: skipped.*

s	k	i	p	p	e	d

• Guide children to identify sounds and spell *jogging, pinned, jumping, slipping,* and *melted.* Children can spell with **Letter Cards** while others check their work. **ELA** L.2.2d

3   Apply

Have partners take turns rereading Blending Lines 1–3 and 4–6. Tell each partner to choose and sort any ten words according to their *-ed* and *-ing* endings. Have them write the sorted words in two columns. Tell partners to read aloud each other's lists.

Distribute <u>Reader's Notebook Volume 2 page 3</u> or <u>leveled practice</u> in Grab-and-Go™ Resources for children to complete independently.

Practice Fluency

Use <u>Instructional Routine 15</u> to have partners read the **Decodable Reader** *Beep! Beep!* Remind them that their reading should sound natural, as if they are talking to a friend.

Decodable Reader

Corrective Feedback When a child mispronounces a letter-sound, highlight that letter, restate its sound, have children repeat the sound, and then guide them to blend the word. See the example below.

Decoding Error:
A child reads *nodded* in Line 1 as *nod.*

Correct the error. Say the word and the sound. *The word is* nodded; nodded *has two syllables. The letters e, d stand for the sound /ĕd/.*

Model as you touch the letters. *I'll blend: /n/ /ŏ/ /d/, /ĕd/. What is the word?* nodded

Guide *Let's blend together: /n/ /ŏ/ /d/, /ĕd/. What is the word?* nodded

Check *You blend. /n/ /ŏ/ /d/, /ĕd/ What is the word?* nodded

Reinforce Go back two or three words and have children continue reading. Make note of errors and review those words during the next lesson.

Go to pp. T84–T85 for additional phonics support.

Dig Deeper: Use Clues to Analyze the Text

▶ SHARE OBJECTIVES
- Describe setting, characters, and plot.
- Make inferences and predictions.
- Use complete sentences to increase language production. LANGUAGE

ENGLISH LANGUAGE SUPPORT

Expand Language Production

Emerging Reread **Student Book** pp. 24–25. Ask questions with one-word answers: *What does Mr. Tanen sell?* ties Expand the response: *Mr. Tanen sells his ties.* **ELD** ELD.PI.2.6

Expanding Have children look back at **Student Book** pp. 22–23. Ask questions about how the townspeople react when they find out about the tie auction. Challenge children to answer using complete sentences. **ELD** ELD.PI.2.6, ELD.PI.2.12a

Bridging Have partners look at **Student Book** p. 24 and write in their own words what they predict will happen. Encourage them to use complete sentences. Have them discuss story clues that led to their predictions. **ELD** ELD.PI.2.1, ELD.PI.2.6, ELD.PI.2.12a

---

Text-Based Comprehension

1	**Teach/Model**

Terms About Literature

characters the people and animals in a story

plot the order of story events, including the problem and how it is solved

setting when and where the story takes place

Remind children that they have just read *Mr. Tanen's Tie Trouble,* a realistic fiction story about a school principal who sells his ties to raise money. Read **Student Book** p. 36 with children.

- Review the terms *character* and *setting.* Remind children that the plot is the story's events. Most plots will involve a problem that the characters must solve. The story problem usually appears at the beginning of a story.

ENGLISH LANGUAGE SUPPORT Tell children that the word *problem* has a cognate in Spanish: *problema.*

- Point out that children can use a story map like the one shown on **Student Book** p. 36 to record and describe the story's overall structure. Then discuss the story map using this model.

> **Think Aloud**
>
> *First, I will write the characters and the setting. Mr. Tanen is the main character, and the setting is the school. Then I will add the first event that takes place in the story—Mr. Tanen finds out there is not enough money to repair the school playground. As I read, I will fill in the important plot events to complete the story map.*

Next, read the top of **Student Book** p. 37 with children.

- Have children discuss how the people in the town show that they want to help. Have them recall a character's words or actions to explain.

- Remind children that they should focus on how the characters solve problems in the story. What characters do to solve problems and challenges tells you more about them.

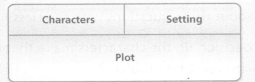

🔍 BE A READING DETECTIVE

Dig Deeper

Use Clues to Analyze the Text

Use these pages to learn about Story Structure and Understanding Characters. Then read *Mr. Tanen's Tie Trouble* again. Use what you learn to understand it better.

Story Structure

In *Mr. Tanen's Tie Trouble*, you read a story about a principal who has to solve a problem. Who are the characters? Where does the story take place?

Think about how the beginning of the story tells the problem that the characters have. How is the problem solved at the end? Use a story map to help you describe the **characters, setting,** and **plot** of *Mr. Tanen's Tie Trouble*.

Characters	Setting
Plot	

Understanding Characters

The way that **characters** act when they have a problem tells you more about them. Think about how the people in the town try to help Mr. Tanen and the school. Many people come to the auction and buy Mr. Tanen's ties. This text evidence shows that they want to help raise money for the playground. Understanding how characters think, act, and feel helps you to better understand why things happen in the story.

---

2 Guided Practice/Apply

Analyze the Text

Begin a second read of *Mr. Tanen's Tie Trouble* with children. Use the stopping points and instructional support to guide them to think more deeply about the text.

- Story Structure, p. T35 ELA RL.2.5 ELD ELD.PI.2.6, ELD.PII.2.1

- Understanding Characters, p. T29 ELA RL.2.3 ELD ELD.PI.2.6, ELD.PI.2.7

Directed Note Taking The graphic organizer will be completed with children during a second read on p. T35. ELA RL.2.5 ELD ELD.PI.2.6, ELD.PII.2.1

FORMATIVE ASSESSMENT   🔺 RtI

Are children able to identify story structure as they read a story?

IF...	THEN...
children struggle,	use **Differentiate Comprehension** for Struggling Readers, p. T88. See also Intervention Lesson 16, pp. S2–S11.
children are on track,	use **Differentiate Comprehension** for On-Level Readers, p. T88.
children excel,	use **Differentiate Comprehension** Advanced Readers, p. T89.

Differentiate Comprehension, pp. T88–T89
Scaffold instruction to the English learner's proficiency level.

Your Turn

Cite Text Evidence

▶ **SHARE OBJECTIVES**

- Demonstrate understanding of characters, setting, and plot.
- Write an opinion piece about a topic or book under discussion.
- Use verbs in the past tense in sentences. LANGUAGE

RETURN TO THE ESSENTIAL QUESTION

As partners discuss the Essential Question, have them use text evidence to support their thinking. Ask children to discuss ways that Mr. Tanen and the townspeople worked together to help each other in the story. Then have children work with a partner to talk about ways that real people can help each other. Have children share experiences of how they have helped others and how helping others made them feel. Remind children to follow discussion rules and speak clearly as they share their experiences.

ELA SL.2.1a, SL.2.4 **ELD** ELD.PI.2.1, ELD.PI.2.6, ELD.PI.2.12a

Classroom Conversation Have children continue their discussion of *Mr. Tanen's Tie Trouble* by reminding them that we can tell a lot about a character by what they say, think, and do. Ask children if they think it is necessary to receive a reward for helping others. Guide them to see that the benefit of helping others should be reward enough. Have all children participate in the discussion and follow rules for discussion.

ELA RL.2.1, RL.2.3, RL.2.7, SL.2.1a **ELD** ELD.PI.2.1, ELD.PI.2.6

ENGLISH LANGUAGE SUPPORT Use sentence frames such as the following to support discussion.

The characters help Mr. Tanen solve his problem by ____.

The people gave the ties back to Mr. Tanen because ____.

Mr. Tanen feels ____ when the people give him back his ties. I know this because ____.

As children share their ideas, have them use gestures and refer to the story for help completing the sentence frames. **ELD** ELD.PI.2.6, ELD.PI.2.12a

---

Your Turn

RETURN TO THE ESSENTIAL QUESTION

Turn and Talk **How can helping others make you feel good?** Talk with a partner. Use text evidence from *Mr. Tanen's Tie Trouble* to tell your ideas. Also talk about times that you have helped others. Take turns listening and speaking. Use respectful ways to take your turn speaking.

Classroom Conversation

Now talk about these questions with the class.

1 What decision do the characters make that helps Mr. Tanen solve his problem?

2 Why do the people in the town give Mr. Tanen his ties back?

3 How does Mr. Tanen feel when the people in the town give him back his ties? How do you know?

38   **ELA** RL.2.1, RL.2.3, W.2.1, W.2.4, W.2.10, SL.2.1a, SL.2.4 **ELD** ELD.PI.2.1, ELD.PI.2.6, ELD.PI.2.10, ELD.PI.2.11, ELD.PI.2.12a

ENGLISH LANGUAGE SUPPORT

How English Works: Collaborative

Verb Tenses Before children begin discussing the Essential Question, have them think about the verb tense that they will use while sharing. Review the verb tenses and purposes with children. Help children realize that telling about how they have helped people will require them to use verbs in the past tense. Guide children at different proficiency levels to make short lists of verbs in the past tense to use during their discussions. **ELD** ELD.PII.2.3b

WRITE ABOUT READING

Response How do you think the people in the town feel about Mr. Tanen? Write a few sentences to explain your ideas. Use the words and pictures in the story as text evidence to support your opinion.

Writing Tip

Remember to start each proper noun with a capital letter.

39

Tell children they will write a response to the story that gives an opinion about how the people in town feel about Mr. Tanen.

- Remind children that an opinion is the way a person feels about something. There are no right or wrong answers.

- Help children get started by telling them to put themselves in Mr. Tanen's place. Have them think about how they would feel if they worked out a problem by giving up something they really love.

- Ask children to look back through the story and use any words or pictures to help them write a few sentences explaining their opinion.

Writing Tip Make sure children read the Writing Tip before they begin writing. Remind them that sentences also always begin with a capital letter. **ELA** W.2.1, W.2.4, W.2.10, L.2.1f **ELD** ELD.PI.2.11

See **Analytic Writing Rubric** on p. R17.

Have children complete the Write About Reading activity through *my*WriteSmart. Children will read the prompt within *my*WriteSmart and have access to multiple writing resources, including the Student eBook, Writing Rubrics, and Graphic Organizers.

ENGLISH LANGUAGE SUPPORT

Comprehensible Input

All Proficiencies Ask children to remember what the townspeople did to help Mr. Tanen. Guide them to realize how generous the townspeople were in purchasing ties and then giving them all back to Mr. Tanen. Ask children to think of people they would help out like that. Then help them understand that the townspeople must have really liked and supported Mr. Tanen to give so much to help him. For children who need the support, provide the sentence frame *The people in the town (like/don't like) Mr. Tanen. I know this because in the story, _____.* **ELD** ELD.PI.2.10, ELD.PI.2.11, ELD.PI.2.12a

Grammar Pronouns

- **Grammar** Use pronouns *me, him, her, it, us,* and *them.* LANGUAGE
- **Spelling** Spell words with endings *-ed* and *-ing.*
- **Handwriting** Write Spelling Words.
- **Writing** Use details in a narrative paragraph to help readers picture what is happening. LANGUAGE

ENGLISH LANGUAGE SUPPORT
Comprehensible Input

All Proficiencies Write in a box: *I, he, she, it, we, they.* Write in a circle: *me, him, her, it, us, them.* Read the words chorally. Have a child tap his or her desk. Write: *(Name) taps the desk.* Replace *(Name)* with *he* or *she.* Explain that you used a pronoun from the box. Then replace *the desk* with *it.* Explain that you used a pronoun from the circle. Repeat with another child and action.

Primary-Language Support First-language partners can review what they have learned about pronouns using their primary language. They can also point out words in their first language that have the same function or ask each other questions about nouns to clarify.

1 Teach/Model

Object Pronouns Display Projectable 16.5. Remind children that a pronoun can take the place of a noun in a sentence.

- Write *me, him, her, it, us,* and *them. Some nouns come after the verb. These pronouns can take the place of nouns that come after the verb.* Use the example sentences on the projectable. Model how to use pronouns to replace a noun that is not the subject.

Think Aloud *To identify the correct pronoun to use, I ask this Thinking Question: Which pronoun can take the place of the noun or nouns after the verb? Since the noun* book *comes after the verb, I can replace it with one of these pronouns:* me, him, her, it, us, *or* them. Book *names one thing, so I will use the pronoun* it.

ENGLISH LANGUAGE SUPPORT Write sentence frames such as *Music makes Keith happy. Music makes _____ happy.* Have children complete the frames with the correct pronoun.

2 Guided Practice/Apply

- Have children use the Thinking Question on **Projectable 16.5** to correctly identify the pronoun that replaces the underlined noun.
- To reinforce concepts as needed play the GrammarSnap Video that supports this lesson.
- Distribute Reader's Notebook Volume 2 page 5 to children to complete independently.

Spelling Base Words with Endings *-ed, -ing*

SPELLING WORDS

BASIC

running	rubbed
clapped	missed
stopped	grabbed*
hopping	**REVIEW**
batted	mixed
selling*	going
pinned	**CHALLENGE**
cutting*	wrapped
sitting	swelling

A form or forms of these words appear in the literature.

Teach/Word Sort
- Review *-ed* and *-ing* endings. Have children practice doubling the final consonant.
- Draw a two-column chart. Write the base words in one column. Have children add an *-ed* or *-ing* ending to each word and write the Spelling Word in the second column.

Base Word	-ed, -ing
clap	clapped
stop	stopped

- Distribute Reader's Notebook Volume 2 p. 4 to children to complete independently. **ELA** L.2.2d

Word Hunt
For additional practice with the Spelling Words, guide children to complete the Word Hunt activity on page 86 of the **Literacy and Language Guide.**

Handwriting
Model how to form the Basic Words *running, clapped, stopped, hopping, batted,* and *selling.* Handwriting models are available on pp. R24–R29 and on the Handwriting Models Blackline Masters. Remind children to write legibly and stay within the margins. **ELA** L.2.1g

Narrative Writing Focus Trait: Elaboration

1 Teach/Model

Details Explain that including interesting details about characters and settings is one way authors help readers to picture what is happening. The details in a story can make the events in it seem realistic.

Connect to *Mr. Tanen's Tie Trouble*	
Instead of this...	**...the author wrote this.**
He heard a noise. He saw Kaylee and Alex with a jar.	"He heard a *clink-clank*. He **looked up** to see Kaylee and Alex **lugging in a big** jar **filled with money**." (p. 17)

- *Why are the author's sentences better?* The details help the reader imagine what is happening. They help the reader picture the sights and hear the sounds.

2 Guided Practice/Apply

- Write: *The town had signs.*

- Look at the picture on **Student Book** pp. 20–21 of *Mr. Tanen's Tie Trouble*. Ask children to suggest details to make the sentence above more interesting. Possible response: *The <u>entire</u> town had <u>yellow</u> signs on <u>walls and windows</u> about <u>Mr. Tanen's Tie Auction</u>.*

- Write: *Mr. Tanen has ties.*

- Ask children to look at the pictures in the story and add details to the sentence. Possible response: *Mr. Tanen loves crazy, colorful, funny ties.*

- Distribute <u>Reader's Notebook Volume 2 page 6</u> to children to complete independently. **ELA** W.2.3, W.2.4, W.2.10 **ELD** ELD.PI.2.10, ELD.PII.2.4, ELD.PII.2.5

ENGLISH LANGUAGE SUPPORT

Comprehensible Input

All Proficiencies Have children practice adding details to nouns by using their senses. Write a few nouns on the board, such as *apple, playground,* and *crowd.* Draw a word web on the board for each noun, each with six circles. Write the noun in the middle circle and the five senses in the other circles. Work with children to complete the webs.

myWriteSmart Children may prewrite, draft, revise, and publish their narrative writing task through *my*WriteSmart beginning on Day 3.

DAY 3

Today's Goals

Vocabulary & Oral Language
- Apply Vocabulary Knowledge

☑ TARGET VOCABULARY

received	chuckled
account	staring
budget	repeated
disappointed	fund

Phonemic Awareness
- Syllables in Spoken Words

Phonics & Fluency
- Words with Long
  o (o, oa, ow)
- Read Decodable Reader:
  We Helped
- Fluency: Rate
- High-Frequency Words

Text-Based Comprehension
- Independent Reading
- Reader's Guide
- Self-Selected Reading

Grammar & Writing
- Pronouns
- Narrative Writing:
  Story Paragraph

Spelling
- Base Words with Endings
  -ed, -ing

Opening Routines

Warm Up with Wordplay

Descriptive Words

Have children turn to a partner and share thoughts about what an ideal playground would be like. Partners should think of two words or phrases that describe how the playground would look or what features it would contain. Ask them to write their ideas on a sheet of paper. Then collect the responses and write them on the board.

sports	colorful	swings
parallel bars	slides	climbing
lots of room	trees	fountains

Have children discuss the importance of each feature. Then have them vote on the two most important features. **ELA** L.2.6 **ELD** ELD.PI.2.1

Daily Phonemic Awareness

Syllables in Spoken Words

- *Let's say some words and listen for the syllables. We'll stomp our feet as we say each syllable of the word. Listen to the word: stomping. Now stomp one foot as you say each syllable:* stomp-ing. *How many syllables do you hear?* two

- Have children continue with the following words: *played, playing, tasted, tasting, rubbed, rubbing.*

Corrective Feedback

- If a child struggles with counting syllables, say the word, give correction, and model the task. Example: *Listen to this word: pinned. Clap the syllables. How many syllables do you hear?* one

- *Say* pinned *with me:* pinned. *Now you clap the syllables.* Then have children continue with the rest of the words.

Daily High-Frequency Words

- Point to **High-Frequency Word Card 159,** *river.*

- *Say the word.* river *Spell the word.* r-i-v-e-r *Write the word. Check the word.*

- Repeat the routine with the words *gone, something,* and *said.* **ELA** RF.2.3f

Guess the Word

- Tell children you are going to give them clues to a word on the Focus Wall.

- Give them these clues: *The word has five letters. It begins with the letter r. The first vowel is i.*

- Repeat the activity for the words *horse* and *something.*

Corrective Feedback

- If a child does not recognize the word *gone,* say the correct word and have children repeat it. *Gone. What is the word?* gone

- Have children spell the word. *g-o-n-e How do we say it?* gone

- Have children reread all of the cards in random order.

Daily Vocabulary Boost

- Guide children to interact with Target Vocabulary by asking the following questions. Remind them to speak clearly when participating in the discussion.

  Why would it be a good idea to make a budget?·

  If you received *some money, how might you use it? Would you start a* fund? *If so, what kind of* fund?

- Have children work together to explain *budget, received,* and *fund* in their own words. Make sure children follow appropriate rules for discussion, such as listening to speakers, taking turns, and staying on topic.
ELA SL.2.1a, L.2.6, **ELD** ELD.PI.2.1

budget
A budget is a plan for how you should spend your money.

My budget for the field Trip
I have $11.
I will spend $4 on lunch.
I will spend $5 on souvenirs.
I will spend $2 on a snack.

Vocabulary in Context Cards 121–128

☑ **Target Vocabulary**

received
account
budget
disappointed
chuckled
staring
repeated
fund

Phonics

▶ **SHARE OBJECTIVES**

- Segment and name sounds in words.
- Blend and decode regularly spelled words with the long o sound spelled o, oa, ow.
- Read on-level text fluently with base words with endings -ed and -ing and High-Frequency Words.

FORMATIVE ASSESSMENT **RtI**

Corrective Feedback When a child mispronounces a letter-sound, highlight that letter, restate its sound, have children repeat the sound, and then guide them to blend the word. See the example below.

Decoding Error:
A child reads *soaking* as *socking*.

Correct the error. Say the word. *That word is* soaking. *The letters* oa *together stand for* /ō/.	
Guide Have children repeat the word. *What is the word?* soaking	
Check *You read the word.* soaking	
Reinforce Have children continue reading the word list. Record the errors and review those words during the next lesson.	

 Go to p. T90 for additional phonics support.

Cumulative Review

Phonemic Awareness Warm-Up *I'll say a word. You tell the sounds you hear and name the vowel sound. I'll do it first. Listen:* float. *The sounds are /f/ /l/ /ō/ /t/. The vowel sound in* float *is /ō/. Now you do it. Listen to each word, say the sounds, and name the vowel sound. Listen:* cold, */k/ /ō/ /l/ /d/, /ō/;* soak, */s/ /ō/ /k/, /ō/;* grow, */g/ /r/ /ō/, /ō/;* coach, */k/ /ō/ /ch/, /ō/.*

Sound/Spelling Card Display **Sound/Spelling Card** *ocean*. Review the *o, oa,* and *ow* spellings for long *o*.

Word Sort Write the words below on the board. Then introduce the **Picture Cards** and **Word Cards** for *yo-yo, boat,* and *snow*. Create a three-column chart on the board. Use each **Picture Card** and its matching **Word Card** as a column head.

- Have children take turns reading the words aloud. Then call on individuals to write each word beneath the picture whose name has the same spelling for long *o*.

- Have children read the word groups aloud as they listen for the long *o* sound /ō/. Guide children to conclude that the long *o* sound /ō/ can be spelled *oa* at the beginning or in the middle of a word. It can be spelled *o* or *ow* at the beginning, middle, or end of a word. **ELA** RF.2.3a, RF.2.3c

float	own	fold	oak	oatmeal
moment	toad	bowl	solo	borrow
coach	most	open	flow	owner
throw	soaking	pillow	gold	toasted

We Helped
by Suzanne Martinucci

I help Nell kick. Nell is learning to kick. She must not bend her leg when she is striking this bag. I help Nell until her kicking is just right. She kicked and kicked. Nell likes kicking and striking.

Decodable Reader

Practice Fluency

Use Instructional Routine 13 to read the **Decodable Reader** *We Helped* with children.

Fluency

Rate

1 Teach/Model

Explain to children that when good readers read aloud, they read at a rate, or speed, that is neither too fast nor too slow. This helps listeners follow along and understand the meaning of the text.

Display Projectable 16.6. Read aloud the first paragraph. Model how to read at an appropriate rate. Then organize the class into two groups. Have one group read aloud the paragraphs about school fundraising with you, and ask the other group to listen to the rate on two repeated readings. Then have groups switch roles. Note how the reading rate changes as readers get more familiar with the words and sentences they are reading.

2 Guided Practice

Have children return to p. 22 of *Mr. Tanen's Tie Trouble* in the **Student Book**. Reread the first few sentences in a slow, laboring fashion. Ask children how the reading sounded, leading them to conclude that it was too slow. Ask them to join you as you read the page at the appropriate rate. Repeat. Help children conclude that the reading gets smoother with repeated readings.

3 Apply

Have pairs take turns reading the page to each other two or three times. Ask them to help each other read the text smoothly and with the appropriate rate. **ELA** RF.2.4b

Have partners use a signal to alert one another of an issue with their reading rate. For example, one child might raise a hand if his or her partner's reading is too slow, and tap a finger to show that it is too fast. Point out that reading at an appropriate rate helps listeners to focus on the meaning of a text.

Distribute Reader's Notebook Volume 2 page 7 or leveled practice in Grab-and-Go™ Resources for children to complete independently.

▶ **SHARE OBJECTIVE**

- Read on-level text fluently at an appropriate rate.

> **Go to p. T91 for additional fluency support**

ENGLISH LANGUAGE SUPPORT

Checking Comprehension

Some English learners can demonstrate all the components of fluency and yet, they do not comprehend what they are reading. This is especially true with children who are fluent in a Latin-based language. It is important for teachers to pair fluency instruction with periodic comprehension checks. This practice helps children understand that both oral reading fluency and meaning-making are important.

HOUGHTON MIFFLIN HARCOURT

JOURNEYS

Cold Reads

GRADE 2

Cold Reads: Support for fluent reading and comprehension

Independent Reading

- Read and comprehend literature.
- Ask and answer questions about what you read.
- Use evidence from the text to answer questions and support opinions. LANGUAGE
- Read independently from a "just right" book.

ENGLISH LANGUAGE SUPPORT

Review Key Ideas

Emerging Ask children *yes/no* questions about the selection. **ELD** ELD.PI.2.6

Expanding Ask children some details about the story, such as *How many ties does Mr. Tanen have?* and *Why did Mr. Tanen sell his ties?* **ELD** ELD.PI.2.6

Bridging Have children summarize the selection, discussing the lesson that they learned. **ELD** ELD.PI.2.6

Reader's Guide

Revisit the Anchor Text Lead children in a brief discussion about *Mr. Tanen's Tie Trouble.* Have them retell important events in the order they happened and summarize the story. Remind children to listen with care when others are speaking and to speak one at a time. **ELA** RL.2.2, SL.2.1a **ELD** ELD.PI.2.1, ELD.PI.2.6, ELD.PI.2.12a

Have children read *Mr. Tanen's Tie Trouble* on their own. Then distribute 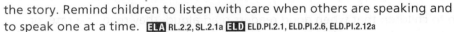 Reader's Notebook Volume 2 pages 8–9 ⬚ and have children complete them independently. **ELA** RL.2.1 **ELD** ELD.PI.2.6

Model Questioning Demonstrate generating a question about *Mr. Tanen's Tie Trouble.* For example: *What kind of person is Mr. Tanen?* Reread **Student Book** p. 16 with children, and look at the illustrations together to respond to the question. **ELA** RL.2.1 **ELD** ELD.PI.2.6

Generate Questions Have children generate questions about *Mr. Tanen's Tie Trouble.* Ask children to share their questions. Begin a class discussion of questions that children have in common or that are most significant to their understanding of the story. Guide children to build on others' talk by linking their comments and to use complete sentences when providing detail or clarification. **ELA** RL.2.1, SL.2.1a, SL.2.1b, SL.2.6 **ELD** ELD.PI.2.1, ELD.PI.2.6

Self-Selected Reading

What is a "Just Right" Book? Remind children that when they select books for reading, they should choose something that interests them. They should also choose a book that is neither too easy, nor too difficult. Discuss the following points with children:

- Why is it important to choose a book that interests you?
- Why is it important to choose a book that is not too easy?
- Why is it important to choose a book that is not too difficult?

Make sure children understand that reading should be fun as well as useful. An interesting book will be more fun to read. When they learn new words, they become better readers, so it is a good idea for them to challenge themselves with books that are not too easy. However, if a book is too difficult, they won't understand what they are reading; they might get frustrated and reading it won't be fun. **ELA** RL.2.10, RI.2.10

Self-Correction Strategies

Read for Fluency and Appropriate Rate Remind children that good readers do not read too fast, and they do not read too slowly. Reading at an appropriate rate will help them understand what they are reading when they read quietly to themselves. It will also help listeners understand what they are reading and hearing when they read aloud.

Tell children that rereading difficult pages is good practice for learning to read at an appropriate rate. Model reading difficult text in *Mr. Tanen's Tie Trouble*, and then model rereading to improve your reading rate. Have children join in a choral reading of the text with you.

Have partners practice reading and rereading aloud to each other from their self-selected books. When one child has finished reading, his or her partner should provide feedback about rate. Then have the partner read aloud from his or her book and receive feedback. **ELA** RF.2.4a, RF.2.4b, RF.2.4c

Apply Vocabulary Knowledge

- Use words and phrases acquired through conversations, reading and being read to, and responding to texts. LANGUAGE
- Identify real-life connections between words and their use. LANGUAGE
- Use an online dictionary. LANGUAGE

ENGLISH LANGUAGE SUPPORT

Access Prior Knowledge

Emerging Write *generosity* on the board. Have children answer yes/no questions about different ways to show generosity.

Expanding Have children talk about a time they felt disappointed. Have them use the sentence frame *Once I felt disappointed with _____ because _____.* **ELD** ELD.PI.2.12a

Bridging Have children talk about a time they received exciting news. **ELD** ELD.PI.2.12a

---

☑ Review Target Vocabulary

Review with children the Vocabulary in Context Cards on **Student Book** pp. 10–11. Call on children to read the context sentences and explain how the photograph demonstrates the meaning of the word.

Enrich Vocabulary Write the following Related Words on the board. Read each word aloud, and have children repeat after you. Then read the child-friendly explanation for each word. Connect each word's meaning to the story *Mr. Tanen's Tie Trouble* by writing the context sentences on the board and reading them aloud. **ELA** L.2.5a

generosity: Being ready to give what you have is generosity. *Mr. Tanen showed generosity by giving his ties to raise money for the school.*

cooperative: People who are willing to work together to get something done are cooperative. *The people in Mr. Tanen's community were very cooperative.*

bid: A bid is an offer to pay a certain price for something at an auction. *Monsieur Bijou bid $50 for the Doughnut and Danish Tie.*

Make Connections Discuss all of the words using the items below to help children make connections between vocabulary words and their use. **ELA** L.2.5a **ELD** ELD.PI.2.1, ELD.PI.2.12a, ELD.PI.2.12b

- How can **generosity** be helpful?
- What do you think a school includes in their **budget**?
- Tell something that you have **chuckled** at.
- How much would you **bid** for a chance to meet the President of the United States?
- Tell about a time you were **disappointed** and what made you feel better.
- Tell one thing you have given and another you have **received**.
- How is it useful to have a bank **account**?
- What is a creative way that you could start a **fund** and raise money for a project?
- Is there a song you would like to hear **repeated** every day?
- Tell about a time your family, neighbors, or friends were **cooperative**.

Dictionary Skills

Discuss Using a Digital Dictionary Log onto the Internet to discuss with children how to look up words in a digital dictionary. Remind children never to go online without an adult's permission and only to use websites that they are familiar with.

Ask children to show you how to locate the search box. Ask a child to enter *bid*. As a class, discuss the different meanings of *bid* and how to tell which meaning would be best for *Mr. Tanen's Tie Trouble*. Point out that the most helpful definition for this selection is the one that relates to an auction. Ask children to look up definitions for *cooperative* and *generosity*. **ELA** SL.2.1a, L.2.4e **ELD** ELD.PI.2.1

QUICKWRITE Read aloud each question below. Pause a few minutes between each item to allow children to write a response. **ELA** L.2.6

1. What would you like to **bid** on at an auction?

2. Whom do you know who shows **generosity**?

3. How does being **cooperative** help people get things done?

ENGLISH LANGUAGE SUPPORT Write the following sentence frames on the board to support children in writing: *I would like to bid on _____ at an auction. My _____ shows generosity. Being cooperative helps people get things done because _____.* Read the sentence frames aloud with children. Ask them to write to complete the sentences. **ELD** ELD.PI.2.10

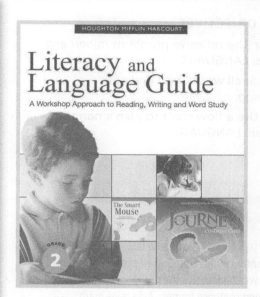

HOUGHTON MIFFLIN HARCOURT

Literacy and Language Guide

A Workshop Approach to Reading, Writing and Word Study

GRADE 2

For additional practice with the lesson's Target Vocabulary words, use the activities on pages 146–147 of the **Literacy and Language Guide**.

- Introduce Target Vocabulary; Base Words and Ending *-ing*
- Guess My Category
- I Spy Clues
- Relating Words Questions
- Four-Square Map

Grammar Pronouns

▶ SHARE OBJECTIVES

- **Grammar** Use reflexive pronouns *myself* and *ourselves*. LANGUAGE
- **Spelling** Spell words with endings *-ed* and *-ing*.
- **Writing** Use a flow chart to plan a narrative paragraph. LANGUAGE

ENGLISH LANGUAGE SUPPORT

Comprehensible Input

All Proficiencies Write in a box: *I, he, she, it, we, they*. Organize children into mixed-proficiency small groups. Have children use the pronouns to complete the following sentence frames: *Julia does math. ___ does math. Tim studies hard. ___ studies hard. The children eat lunch. ___ eat lunch*. Write in a circle: *me, him, her, us, it, them*. Use pronouns to complete the frames: *Frank eats an apple. Frank eats ___. Sam gave it to Ana. Sam gave it to ___. Reese went with his parents. Reese went with ___.*

Linguistic Transfer The subject pronoun can be omitted from a sentence in many languages. Children who speak Cantonese, Hmong, Spanish, Vietnamese, or Haitian Creole may say, *Is good* instead of *It is good*. Give extra practice with subject pronouns, for example, *It is ready. She is tired.* **ELD** ELD.PIII.2

1 Teach/Model

Reflexive Pronouns Remind children that *I* is the pronoun we use when we talk about ourselves doing an action.

- Point to yourself. Say and write: *I walked home.* Then tell children that you walked home with a friend. Say and write: *My friend and I walked home.* Explain that you named the other person first and yourself last.

- Next to the first sentence write: *I walked home by myself.* Next to the second sentence write: *My friend and I walked home by ourselves.* Explain that *myself* and *ourselves* are reflexive pronouns. They have *self* at the end, and they refer back to the subject of the sentence. *Myself* refers to the singular subject *I*, and *ourselves* refers to the plural subject, *my friend and I.*

2 Guided Practice/Apply

- Write these incomplete sentences on the board and work with children to complete them: *I make my bed by _____. My mother and I fixed the bike by _____.*

- Write these sentences and have partners complete them: *I can _____ by _____. My friend and I _____ by _____.* Call on children to read their sentences.

- To reinforce concepts as needed, play the GrammarSnap Video ⧉ that supports this lesson.

- Distribute Reader's Notebook Volume 2 page 11 ⧉ to children to complete independently. **ELA** L.2.1c

Spelling Base Words with Endings *-ed, -ing*

SPELLING WORDS

BASIC

running	rubbed
clapped	missed
stopped	grabbed*
hopping	REVIEW
batted	mixed
selling*	going
pinned	CHALLENGE
cutting*	wrapped
sitting	swelling

A form or forms of these words appear in the literature.

Segment Sounds

- Model segmenting sounds. *Listen to me as I say the word* running: rrruunning. *Listen for the /ng/ sound in the word* running. *Now you say it with me:* rrruunning.

- Repeat with *selling* and *clapped*. Tell children that saying sounds slowly will help them spell words.

Build Words with *-ed* and *-ing*

- Use **Letter Cards** to model building *pinned* and *sitting*. Have children read the words with you and begin to list the Spelling Words.

- Have partners use **Letter Cards** to build words with *-ed* and *-ing* and add them to their lists.

- Have partners read and spell one word they built using **Letter Cards**.

- Distribute Reader's Notebook Volume 2 page 10 ⧉ to children to complete independently. **ELA** L.2.2d

Blind Writing Sort

For additional practice with the Spelling Words, have children complete the Blind Writing Sort activity on page 87 of the **Literacy and Language Guide.**

Narrative Writing Prewrite

1 Teach/Model

Setting Explain that the setting of a story tells where and when the story happens. Tell children that it is important for the setting to be clear to readers.

Unclear Setting	Clear Setting
It was a long day.	It was a long summer day at the playground.

- *Which word in the second sentence tells when the story takes place?* summer
  Which words in the sentence tell where the story takes place? at the playground

2 Guided Practice/Apply

Story Paragraph Display Projectable 16.7 ⬀. Read the prompt aloud.

- Work with children to complete the flow chart.
- Save the completed Flow Chart for Day 4.

Think Aloud *I will write a story about a mother and daughter who went flower shopping. What happened first? They went to the garden center. What did they see there? They saw pretty flowers. They saw sunflowers.*

Prewriting Read together the prompt on **Projectable 16.7**. Have children list things they have done to help their parents. Suggest that they choose one of those ideas for their character to do. Distribute Graphic Organizer 4: Flow Chart ⬀. Then have children complete their own flow charts. Have children plan a conclusion for their story paragraphs in their flow charts. Remind them to add details about when and where their story takes place. Have children save their completed flow charts for use on Day 4. **ELA** W.2.3, W.2.4, W.2.10 **ELD** ELD.PI.2.10, ELD.PII.2.1, ELD.PII.2.5

Daily Proofreading Practice

The cookies sue made were seling fast. Jack
                                              ed
count how much money we made to fix the
          y
plaground.

ENGLISH LANGUAGE SUPPORT

How English Works: Productive

Verb Tenses Before children begin drafting their story paragraph, have them think about the verb tense that they will use in their writing. Review the verb tenses and purposes with children (*past: to tell about things that have already happened; present: to tell about things that happen now; future: to tell about things that will happen tomorrow or later*). Help children decide which verb tense will be a good fit for their topics. Guide children at different proficiency levels to make short lists of verbs in the tense they choose to use while drafting. **ELD** ELD.PII.2.3b

myWriteSmart Have children prewrite their narrative writing task through *my*WriteSmart.

DAY 4

Today's Goals

Vocabulary & Oral Language
- **Vocabulary Strategies:** Homographs

 TARGET VOCABULARY

received	chuckled
account	staring
budget	repeated
disappointed	fund

Phonemic Awareness
- **Syllables in Spoken Words**

Phonics & Fluency
- **Base Words and Endings** *-ed, -ing*
- **Fluency:** Rate
- **Read Decodable Reader:** *We Helped*
- **High-Frequency Words**

Text-Based Comprehension
- **Connect to the Topic**
- **Read Informational Text:** *The Jefferson Daily News*
- **Compare Texts**

Grammar & Writing
- **Spiral Review:** Kinds of Sentences
- **Narrative Writing:** Story Paragraph

Spelling
- **Base Words with Endings** *-ed, -ing*

Opening Routines

Warm Up with Wordplay

Using Vocabulary

Write the following Related Words from p. T56 on the board: *generosity, cooperative, bid*. Have children read them with you and explain the definitions.

Display the sentence frames below and underline the vocabulary words. Read the sentence frames with children.

> Ella showed such <u>generosity</u> when she
> _____.
>
> My parents made a <u>bid</u> at the auction and bought a big _____.
>
> Ronald is always <u>cooperative</u> when he is asked to _____.

Have partners work together to complete the sentence frames. Then have them write a second sentence to elaborate on the event. Have children share and compare their responses with the class.

ELA W.2.7 **ELD** ELD.PI.2.2

Daily Phonemic Awareness

Syllables in Spoken Words

- *Let's say some words that end in -ed. As we say the words, we'll clap our hands to show how many syllables are in each word. Listen:* warmed. *How many syllables do you hear?* one Repeat with the words *created* three and *settled* two.

- Continue with these words: *snacked, rested, wished, batted, repeated, disappointed.*

Corrective Feedback

- If a child struggles with counting syllables, say the word, give correction, and model the task. Example: *Listen to this word:* snacked. *I clap once for one syllable.*

- *Now you do it. Clap the syllables. How many syllables do you hear in* snacked? *one*

- Have children repeat with you and then continue on their own.

Daily High-Frequency Words

- Point to **High-Frequency Word Card 155,** *also.*

- *Say the word.* also *Spell the word* a-l-s-o *Write the word. Check the word.*

- Repeat the routine with the new words *something, river,* and *horse,* and with review words *fly, gone, have, look, said,* and *saw.*
  ELA RF.2.3f

Fill in the Blanks

- Draw four blanks. Tell children they will guess letters to spell a High-Frequency Word.

- Invite children to take turns guessing a letter. If the letter is correct, write it in the blank.

- Repeat with other high-frequency words.

Corrective Feedback

- If a child does not recognize the word *river,* say the correct word and have children repeat it. *River. What is the word?* river

- Have children spell the word. *r-i-v-e-r How do we say this word?* river

- Have children reread all of the cards in random order.

Daily Vocabulary Boost

- Guide children to interact with the Target Vocabulary by asking the following questions. Remind them to speak clearly when participating in the discussion.

  When have you chuckled *out loud?*

  Show me the face you might make if you feel disappointed. *What might make a child feel* disappointed?

  Describe a time when I repeated *something.*

- Have children work together to explain *chuckled, disappointed,* and *repeated* in their own words. Make sure children follow appropriate rules for discussion, such as listening to speakers and taking turns. **ELA** SL.2.1a, L.2.6 **ELD** ELD.PI.2.1

chuckled
Her dad chuckled when he saw her tiny piggy bank.

Vocabulary in Context Cards 121–128

☑ **Target Vocabulary**

received
account
budget
disappointed
chuckled
staring
repeated
fund

Phonics

Review Base Words and Endings -ed, -ing

▶ **SHARE OBJECTIVES**

- Identify and count syllables in base words with endings -ed, -ing.
- Write words with endings -ed, -ing.
- Review words with vowel teams ee, ea.
- Read on-level text fluently at an appropriate rate.

▶ **SKILLS TRACE**

Base Words and Endings -ed, -ing	
Introduce	pp. T16–T17, T42–T43
Differentiate	pp. T84–T85
Reteach	p. T98
▶ Review	**p. T62**
Assess	Weekly Tests, Lesson 16

ENGLISH LANGUAGE SUPPORT

Use Visuals and Gestures

All Proficiencies Use visuals and gestures to reinforce or develop the meanings of words in the Spell Words to Solve Riddles activity. Display photographs or illustrations that show ice or ice cream melting. Say the word *melt* and have children echo you. Repeat with an image that shows someone slipping to teach the word *slip*. Pantomime the relevant actions as you say the following words: *grin, help, tug, wrap, nap,* and *dot*. Have children repeat each word as they mimic your action. Then say a target word at random and ask volunteers to identify an image or perform the action.

Phonemic Awareness Warm-Up *Let's clap to count the syllables in words. I'll do it first. Listen:* jogging. (two claps) *How many syllables do you hear?* two *Now you do it with me. Say:* tapped. (one clap) *How many syllables do you hear?* one *Now you do it. Repeat the word and clap the syllables:* nodded, *two;* tugged, *one;* wrapped, *one;* mopping, *two;* skipped, *one;* potted, *two;* tagged, *one;* dotted, *two;* cutting, *two.*

Spell Words to Solve Riddles Display the base words shown below and ask children to read them aloud. Then read aloud each of the following riddles. Have children add the ending -ed or -ing to a base word to solve each riddle. Have them write the words on a sheet of paper. Remind children that for base words with a short vowel sound followed by a single consonant, they should double the final consonant before adding the ending. Then have a volunteer write the answer on the board.

1. What is the opposite of freezing? *melting*

2. What did you do if you pulled on a rope? *tugged*

3. What did you do before you gave a gift? *wrapped*

4. What is another word for sleeping? *napping*

5. What did you do to the *i*'s you made on your paper? *dotted*

6. What word means about the same as the word *smiling*? *grinning*

7. What could you have done on the ice? *slipped*

8. What did you do if you set the table? *helped*

Call on children to read aloud the pairs of words on the board. Use the **Corrective Feedback** steps if they need additional help. **ELA** RF.2.3e, L.2.2d

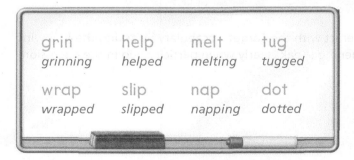

grin	help	melt	tug
grinning	*helped*	*melting*	*tugged*
wrap	slip	nap	dot
wrapped	*slipped*	*napping*	*dotted*

Cumulative Review

Phonemic Awareness Warm-Up *Listen to the words and tell which two words have the same vowel sound. I'll do it first. Listen: free, tray, tree. The words free and tree both have the same long vowel sound. Now you try it. Listen: sheep, steam, shine. Which two words have the same vowel sound?* sheep, steam

Let's do some more. Listen to the words and tell which two words have the same vowel sound: beach, wave, **weave**, **beach**, weave; throw, **teeth**, please, **teeth**, please.

Listen for the Same Sound Write on the board each set of three words below. Have children read aloud each set of words and name the two words with the same vowel sound.

feed	fed	cheek	snake	sneak	team
wheel	weak	wet	leaf	least	loaf

Sort Words Display the **Sound/Spelling Card** *eagle*. Review the ee and ea spellings for long e. List these words on the board: *sweep, heat, weekend, dream, season, agree, peanut, meet, team, fifteen, seashore, least, eager, need, indeed, sweeten.* Have children read the words aloud.

Have partners work together to write each word on an index card. Tell them to shuffle their cards and place them on a desk, face-down. Explain that partners should take turns turning over two cards and reading the words. If the long e spellings in the two words match, that child keeps the cards. Play continues until all cards are gone. **ELA** RF.2.3b, RF.2.3e

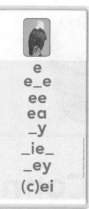

e
e_e
ee
ea
_y
_ie_
_ey
(c)ei

Corrective Feedback When a child mispronounces a word, point to the word and say it. Call attention to the element that was mispronounced, say the sound, and then guide children to read the word. See the example below.

Decoding Error:
A child reads *tugged* in the Riddles activity as *tug-ged.*

Correct the error. *The word is* tugged. *The letters -ed were added to the base word,* tug. *The letters -ed stand for the sound* /d/.

Model Write the word *tugged* on the board; underline *tug* and circle *-ed. The base word is* tug. *The ending -ed stands for the sound* /d/. *What is the word?* tugged

Guide *The base word is* tug. *Let's say the ending together:* /d/. *Let's say the word:* tugged.

Check *What is the base word?* tug *What is the ending?* -ed *Say the word.* tugged

Reinforce Make note of the error and review the word again during the next Opening Routines.

Practice Fluency

Use Instructional Routine 14 to reread the **Decodable Reader** *We Helped* with children. Have them practice reading fluently at a natural rate.

We Helped
by Suzanne Martinucci

I help Nell kick. Nell is learning to kick. She must not bend her leg when she is striking this bag. I help Nell until her kicking is just right. She kicked and kicked. Nell likes kicking and striking.

Decodable Reader

✅ **GENRE**

Informational text gives facts about a topic.

✅ **TEXT FOCUS**

A **caption** tells more about a photo.

The Jefferson Daily News

November 5

Club Helps in Many Ways

by Ben Watts

The Helping Hands Club is one of the best clubs at Jefferson Elementary School. The children in this club volunteer their time to help other people and the community. Last month they gathered items to recycle from home and school. Many items, such as water bottles and juice containers, were placed in recycle bins. Some other items were used in the art classroom.

The club's sponsor, Mrs. Waters, was proud of all who helped. "Students created beautiful artwork from cloth and paper scraps. The club's hard work gave these items a new purpose," she said.

Art made from scraps

The Helping Hands Club has done many more things to help the community. They cleaned up the park and playground and collected food for the food bank. They had a bake sale to raise money for the animal shelter. Club members even decorated posters for bike safety week.

Malik is one of the members of the club. He told how the club helped someone he knew. "The Helping Hands Club helped my neighbor, Mrs. Dodge," he said. "She is 80 years old and lives alone. Our parents brought her hot food, and we pulled weeds in her yard. She was so happy and thankful, and she gave us all lemonade. Helping her made me feel happy, too!"

The club holds a bake sale to help animals.

The club helps to clean up the park.

40 ᴱᴸᴬ RI.2.5, RI.2.10 ᴱᴸᴰ ELD.PI.2.1, ELD.PI.2.6, ELD.PI.2.10, ELD.PI.2.11, ELD.PI.2.12a

41

LESSON TOPIC: Helping Others

Cross-Curricular Connection Write the word *volunteer* on the board and discuss its meaning with students. Ask children ways that they might volunteer around their school and their town to help others. Make a list of their suggestions on the board. Have them add to the list as they read the selection.

FOR STUDENTS WITH DISABILITIES

Students may have difficulty comprehending informational text. Divide reading assignments into short, manageable sections. Have students write down key words and phrases and include drawings or simple charts to help them recall information.

Connect to the Topic: Informational Text

Introduce Genre and Text Focus

- Read with children the genre and text focus information on **Student Book** p. 40. Tell them that they will read an informational text that is a newspaper article.

- Point out the characteristics of a newspaper article: a headline, dateline, byline, photos with captions, and text in narrow columns. Explain that the headline is like a title of any story or informational text and tells what the article will be about. Ask them to tell how the dateline and byline also give information.

ENGLISH LANGUAGE SUPPORT Write the words *headline*, *dateline*, and *byline* on the board and read them aloud with children. Have children point out the different features on the page as you explain the purpose of each.

- Ask children to preview the photos and captions in the article. Have children tell how using text and graphic features can help them find information. ᴱᴸᴬ RI.2.5

The Helping Hands Club would like to invite you to a meeting. You can find out what the club is all about and how you can participate. You can even share your own ideas! "This club helps in many ways," said Principal Ramirez. "It is a great club to join!"

Principal Ramirez tells about the club.

What:

Helping Hands Club Meeting

When:

December 1

Time:

3:30 p.m.

Where:

Mrs. Waters's classroom, Room 107

42

Compare Texts

TEXT TO TEXT

Compare and Contrast Imagine that Mr. Tanen is the principal at Jefferson Elementary School. Would he think that the Helping Hands Club is a good club to join? Explain your thoughts to a partner. Use text evidence from both selections to help you answer.

TEXT TO SELF

Write a Description Which of Mr. Tanen's ties do you like the best? Write a few sentences describing the tie you like. Then tell when a person might wear the tie.

TEXT TO WORLD

Connect to Science Think about what you might see, hear, or feel at Mr. Tanen's playground. Write a poem about it. Use describing words.

ELA RL.2.1, RL.2.7, W.2.4, W.2.8, W.2.10 **ELD** ELD.PI.2.1, ELD.PI.2.6, ELP.PI.2.12b

43

Compare Texts

TEXT TO TEXT

Compare and Contrast
Have children point out facts as they review *The Jefferson Daily News*. Then have them list reasons why Mr. Tanen would think Helping Hands is a good club with examples from the story.
ELA RL.2.7

ENGLISH LANGUAGE SUPPORT
Provide sentence frames for children, such as *Mr. Tanen (would/would not) think the Helping Hands Club is a good club because ____.* Ask children to share their sentences with the class.
ELD ELD.PI.2.1, ELD.PI.2.3, ELD.PI.2.6, ELD.PI.2.11

TEXT TO SELF

Write a Description Model filling in a web graphic organizer to help children get started. Have them write their favorite tie in the center of the web. Then help them fill in the outer parts of the web with descriptive details such as color, shapes, patterns, and styles. Then have them use the web to construct their descriptive sentences.

TEXT TO WORLD

Connect to Science Have children look at the picture of Mr. Tanen's playground. Ask them to visualize examples of what they imagine seeing, hearing, and feeling. Write the responses on the board, dividing them by sense. Children may refer to the board as they write. **ELA** W.2.4, W.2.8, W.2.10

ENGLISH LANGUAGE SUPPORT Have children go outside and make a list of things they see, hear, smell, and touch on the playground. Provide assistance with unknown vocabulary. Then have them use this list to complete the activity. **ELD** ELD.PI.2.1, ELD.PI.2.3, ELD.PI.2.11, ELD.PI.2.12a, ELD.PI.2.12b

Vocabulary Strategies

- Use sentence-level context as a clue to the meaning of a word or phrase. LANGUAGE

▶ SKILLS TRACE

Homographs	
Introduce	**T66–T67**
Differentiate	T96–T97
Reteach	T99
Assess	Weekly Tests, Lesson 16

ENGLISH LANGUAGE SUPPORT
Build Background

Emerging Use gestures and simplified language to explain both meanings of *kind*. Say, *I don't like this kind of juice.* Ask which meaning of *kind* was used in the sentence.

Expanding Write several sentences that contain homographs, such as *kind* and *store*. Help children locate the homograph in each sentence and use context clues to tell the meaning.

Bridging Have partners write sentences to show different meanings of homograph pairs.
ELD ELD.PI.2.2

Homographs

1 Teach/Model

Terms About Language

homographs words that have the same spelling but different meanings. Some homographs have different pronunciations.

Spanish cognate: homógrafo

ENGLISH LANGUAGE SUPPORT Preteach homographs. Write and pronounce *light*. *The word* light *can mean "brightness." *Light *can also mean "not heavy." *Light *is a homograph.* Write *rose*. Have children think of one meaning for it. Then have partners look up the words in a dictionary to find all the meanings. **ELD** ELD.PI.2.1

- Explain that homographs are words that have the same spelling but different meanings. Some homographs are pronounced the same; others have different pronunciations.

- Point out that homographs have separate entries in a dictionary because they are different words even though they are spelled the same. Tell children that using context clues around the word will help them identify the correct meaning of a homograph.

- Model using context clues to identify the meaning of the homograph *store* on **Student Book** p. 22 of *Mr. Tanen's Tie Trouble*.

Think Aloud *The story says, "Mrs. Sweet Apple noticed the sign on the grocery* store *window." My mom always wants to* store *things for the winter, so I know that* store *can mean "to put something away to use later." She always goes to the store for groceries, so I know* store *can also mean "a shop where you buy things." I'll use the context clues to help me choose the right meaning. The words "grocery* store *window" help me understand that this* store *is a place, not something someone does. This sentence uses the "shop" meaning of the homograph* store.

2 Guided Practice

- Display the sentences at the top of Projectable 16.8 . Read the first sentence aloud.

- Have children identify the homograph *kind* in the first two sentences. Circle *kind* in each sentence.

- Display the chart at the bottom of the projectable. Have children read the two meanings of *kind*.

- Help children identify context clues in the first two sentences to help them figure out which is the correct meaning of *kind* in each sentence.

- Write the correct meaning for *kind* next to each sentence. Then have children choral-read the two sentences aloud.

3 Apply

- Read the remaining sentences on Projectable 16.8 aloud with children.

- Have children identify the homograph pair in each sentence and use context clues to determine the correct meaning of the homograph in each sentence. Write the definitions of each homograph next to the corresponding sentences. **ELA** L.2.4a

ENGLISH LANGUAGE SUPPORT Write these frames on the board, and help children use them to participate: *The word ____ means ____ in this sentence. The words that help me know this are ____.*

- Have children check dictionary meanings of any homographs that remain unclear.

FOR STUDENTS WITH DISABILITIES Some children may need assistance to understand the meanings of the homographs. Model using context clues to figure out the meaning of each. Work with children to highlight or underline the clue words in the sentence. Then create a class notebook with examples of homographs, their definitions, example sentences, and illustrations.

- Distribute Reader's Notebook Volume 2 page 12 or leveled practice in Grab-and-Go™ Resources to children to complete independently.

Interactive Whiteboard Lesson Use **Vocabulary Strategies: Homographs** to use context clues to determine the meanings of homographs.

Can children understand and distinguish the meaning of homographs?

IF...	THEN...
children struggle,	▶ use **Differentiate Vocabulary Strategies** for Struggling Readers, p. T96.
children are on track,	▶ use **Differentiate Vocabulary Strategies** for On Level Readers, p. T96.
children excel,	▶ use **Differentiate Vocabulary Strategies** for Advanced Readers, p. T97.

SMALL GROUP Options

Differentiate Vocabulary Strategies: pp. T96–T97 *Scaffold instruction to the English learner's proficiency level.*

ENGLISH LANGUAGE SUPPORT

Peer-Supported Learning

All Proficiencies Organize children into mixed-proficiency small groups to create sentences that contain the homographs they learned in this lesson: *kind/kind, store/store, pound/pound, ball/ball,* and *rose/rose.* Have group members take turns saying sentences that use two of these homographs. Provide these sentence frames and help children use them if they need support: *The ____ is on the playground. My grandparents went dancing at the ____.* Have each group choral-read its sentences a few times. When children are finished with their sentences, call on groups to share them with the class. Then have the group decide which sentences they like best for each homograph pair and write them. Tell children that they can use the homographs they learned when they speak and write. **ELD** ELD.PI.2.1, ELD.PI.2.2

Grammar Spiral Review: Kinds of Sentences

▶ SHARE OBJECTIVES

- **Grammar** Review kinds of sentences. LANGUAGE
- **Spelling** Spell words with endings -ed and -ing.
- **Handwriting** Write Spelling Words.
- **Writing** Draft a narrative paragraph. LANGUAGE

ENGLISH LANGUAGE SUPPORT

Access Prior Knowledge

All Proficiencies Point at a child. Say and write: *[Name] is listening to the lesson.* Explain that this is a statement. Circle the period. Point at another child. Say and write: *Is [Name] listening to the lesson?* Explain that this is a question. Circle the question mark. Point at a third child. Say and write: *Listen to the lesson.* Explain that this is a command. Circle the period. Use emphasis as you say each sentence.

---

1 Teach/Model

Kinds of Sentences Review with children that all sentences begin with a capital letter.

- A *statement* tells something. A statement sentence ends with a period.

- A *command* tells a person or animal to do something. A command usually begins with an action word and ends with a period.

- A *question* asks something. It ends with a question mark and often starts with question words such as *Can, What, Where, Who, How,* and *When.*

2 Guided Practice/Apply

- Write these sentences on the board without punctuation.

  1. I like math *statement: I like math.*

  2. What do you like *question: What do you like?*

  3. Tell me your favorite subject *command: Tell me your favorite subject.*

- Have children identify each kind of sentence and add the correct punctuation.

- Distribute Reader's Notebook Volume 2 page 14 ⬚ and have children complete it independently.

Spelling Base Words with Endings -ed, -ing

SPELLING WORDS

BASIC

running	rubbed
clapped	missed
stopped	grabbed*
hopping	**REVIEW**
batted	mixed
selling*	going
pinned	**CHALLENGE**
cutting*	wrapped
sitting	swelling

*A form or forms of these words appear in the literature.

Connect to Writing

- Ask children to use the Spelling Words to write sentences about how people in a community work together.

- Have them proofread their sentences. Then ask volunteers to read their sentences aloud.

- As a class, have children say each Spelling word and spell it aloud.

- Distribute Reader's Notebook Volume 2 p. 13 ⬚ to children to complete independently. **ELA** L.2.2d

Handwriting

Model how to form the Basic Words *pinned, cutting, sitting, rubbed, missed,* and *grabbed.* Handwriting models are available on pp. R24–R29 and on the Handwriting Models Blackline Masters ⬚. Remind children to write legibly and stay within the margins. **ELA** L.2.1g

Speed Sort

For additional practice with the Spelling Words, have children complete the Speed Sort activity on page 87 of the **Literacy and Language Guide. ELA** L.2.2d

Narrative Writing Draft

1 Teach/Model

Dialogue Explain that dialogue is the exact words characters say. Dialogue can show how a character thinks or feels. It brings the characters to life by letting the reader hear their voices. It can also tell what happens in a story.

Remind children to use quotation marks to show the exact words a character says. Write and discuss this model.

Without Dialogue	With Dialogue
Dad said he needed help.	"The garden is a mess! I won't be able to finish weeding without you," said Dad.

• *Why is the sentence with dialogue better?* *It shows how the character feels. It tells what is happening.*

• *What did the writer use to show you where the character's exact words begin and end?* *quotation marks*

2 Guided Practice/Apply

Story Paragraph Briefly review the Flow Chart on Projectable 16.7 . Then display Projectable 16.9 .

• Use the Think Aloud to model drafting a story paragraph including dialogue.

> **Think Aloud** *My story is about a mother and a daughter who went flower shopping. Maybe I can use dialogue to start my paragraph by writing:* "Let's go shopping for flowers," *Christa's mom said.*

Drafting Have children begin drafting their own story paragraphs using their flow charts from Day 3. Remind them to use dialogue to show how the characters think and feel and to help the reader hear their voices. Remind children that the reflexive pronouns *myself* or *ourselves* can be used when the subject in a sentence has been named. Have children find opportunities for their characters to use reflexive pronouns in the dialogue. Children should also create a strong conclusion that tells how the problem worked out. **ELA** W.2.3, W.2.4, W.2.10, L.2.1c **ELD** ELD.PI.2.10, ELD.PII.2.1

Daily Proofreading Practice

Juan asked, "What can we do outsid? e "

Rose said, "We can help clean the

town park."

ENGLISH LANGUAGE SUPPORT

Comprehensible Input

All Proficiencies Explain that dialogue in a story is the words that a character actually spoke. Ask a child to read a simple sentence, such as *I went to recess today.* Turn this sentence into written dialogue using quotation marks and attributing the quote to the child. Have other children volunteer to have their words turned into dialogue that you write on the board.

myWriteSmart Have children draft their narrative writing task through *my*WriteSmart.

DAY 5

Today's Goals

Vocabulary & Oral Language
- Domain-Specific Vocabulary
- Speaking & Listening

☑ TARGET VOCABULARY

received	chuckled
account	staring
budget	repeated
disappointed	fund

Phonemic Awareness
- Syllables in Spoken Words

Phonics & Fluency
- Interactive Whiteboard Lesson
- High-Frequency Words

Text-Based Comprehension
- Extend the Topic
- Research/Media Literacy:
  Create Audio Recordings

Assess & Reteach
- Assess Skills
- Respond to Assessment

Grammar & Writing
- Pronouns
- Narrative Writing:
  Story Paragraph

Spelling
- Base Words with Endings -ed, -ing

Opening Routines

Warm Up with Wordplay

The Never-Ending Story

Children have been reading a story about a man who sold his ties to help pay for a playground. Tell them that today they will tell a story about someone else who helps the community. Each child will make up a small part of the story.

Display and read aloud the following opening for the story.

> **Dora thought the park needed new trees for shade, but she didn't know how to get it done. And then . . .**

Pick one child to continue the story. When the child has finished the part, he or she says, "and then . . ." The next child then adds to the story.

ELA SL.2.1b **ELD** ELD.PI.2.1

Interactive Whiteboard Lesson

For cumulative review, use **Phonics: Base Words and Endings -ed, -ing** to reinforce blending, reading, and building decodable words with endings -ed and -ing. **ELA** RF.2.3e, L.2.2d **ELD** ELD.PII.2.3b

Daily Phonemic Awareness

Syllables in Spoken Words

- *Let's say some words that end in -ing. As we say the words, we'll clap our hands to show how many syllables are in each word. Listen:* sleeping. *How many syllables do you hear?* two Repeat for the words *snowing* two and *explaining.* three

- Continue with these words: *falling, camping, discussing, talking, singing, flapping.*

Corrective Feedback

- If a child struggles with counting syllables, say the word, give correction, and model the task. Example: *Listen to this word:* cooling. *I clap two syllables.*

- *Now you say* cooling *and clap the syllables. How many syllables do you clap?* two *Clap the syllables. How many syllables?* two

- Have children continue with the rest of the words.

Daily High-Frequency Words

- Point to **High-Frequency Word Card 152,** *said.*

- *Say the word.* said *Spell the word.* s-a-i-d *Write the word. Check the word.*

- Repeat the procedure with five words from this week (*also, fly, horse, look, river, saw*) and five words from last week (*care, ever, off, over, though*t). **ELA** RF.2.3f

Making Sentences

- Dictate sentences using both this week's High-Frequency Words and words from other weeks, such as *I saw the horse. It went over the river.*

- Give children time to find and write the words.

- Have children write sentences of their own.

Corrective Feedback

- If a child does not recognize the word *also,* say the correct word and have children repeat it. Also. *What is the word?* also

- Have children spell the word. a-l-s-o *How do we say this word?* also

- Have children reread all of the cards in random order.

Daily Vocabulary Boost

- Reread "A Better Way to Save" aloud to children. (See pp. T14–T15.)

- As you read each Target Vocabulary word in the selection, pause to have a child explain or describe its meaning.

- After reading, review the Target Vocabulary words and their definitions. (See p. T14.) Challenge children to use the words in their everyday speech. **ELA** L.2.6 **ELD** ELD.PI.2.5

fund
The players got new shirts by raising money for the team fund.

Vocabulary in Context Cards 121–128

☑ **Target Vocabulary**

received
account
budget
disappointed
chuckled
staring
repeated
fund

DAY 5

Extend the Topic

▶ **SHARE OBJECTIVES**

- Acquire and use domain-specific vocabulary. LANGUAGE
- Participate in conversations about a topic. LANGUAGE
- Create audio recordings of a story.

Words About the Topic:
Helping Others

- **duties** responsibilities, jobs
- **citizen** a legal resident of a country
- **responsibility** something you have to do

Domain-Specific Vocabulary

Introduce Words About the Topic Remind children that this week's topic is Helping Others. Display the words shown at left. Tell children that these are words that can help them learn more about the topic. Read aloud the meaning of each word, and have children respond to the following prompts. **ELA** L.2.5a, L.2.6

- *What are some duties of good citizens?* Accept reasonable responses.

- *What is one way that we benefit from being citizens of the United States?* Accept reasonable responses, including: going to school, the right to vote when we are old enough, to be free.

- *It is your _____ to clean your room.* responsibility

ENGLISH LANGUAGE SUPPORT Guide children to interact with the words by discussing as a class questions such as these: *What are some of your duties, or chores, around the house? What is one quality of a good citizen? When did you show responsibility, and what did you do?* **ELD** ELD.PI.2.1, ELD.PI.2.12a

Interact with the Words Have children work in small groups to create a Four-Square Map for each of the domain-specific words. For each of the domain-specific words, children should fold a blank sheet of paper into four equal sections. Work with them to follow the steps below for each word. As needed, display the meanings of the words on the board. Ask individual children to use the words in a sentence orally. Then write the sentence on the board for other children to copy.

1 In the first corner, draw a picture for the word.

2 In the second corner, write the meaning of the word.

3 In the third corner, write a sentence using the word.

4 In the fourth corner, write the word.

When groups have finished, have them share their Four-Square Maps with the class. **ELA** L.2.5a, L.2.6 **ELD** ELD.PI.2.1

Give, Restate, and Follow Directions Have small groups practice giving, restating, and following four-step directions to help them understand and complete the activity above. Display a set of simplified directions and read them with children, such as *1. Draw a picture of the word. 2. Write the meaning. 3. Write a sentence using the word. 4. Write the word.* One group member states directions 1 through 4. *1. In box 1, draw a picture of the word. 2. In box 2, write the meaning. 3. In box 3, write a sentence. 4. In box four, write the word.* Another group member restates the directions in his or her own words. The other group members follow the directions to create the Four-Square Map. **ELA** SL.2.2a **ELD** ELD.PI.2.1

Research and Media Literacy:

Create Audio Recordings

Model Reading Aloud Tell children that they are going to make audio recordings of *Mr. Tanen's Tie Trouble* using equipment in your classroom. Explain that when they read aloud, it is important to speak with expression. Tell them to listen carefully as you demonstrate.

Read the first two pages of the book, using a different voice for every character who speaks. Use tone and expression to show what each character is like and to convey a sense of the mood and feeling of the story. **ELD** ELD.PI.2.5

Demonstrate Equipment Demonstrate how to turn on the computer, video, or other recording equipment in your class. Record yourself as you read the first two pages aloud one more time. Then demonstrate how to play back the recording.

Replay and review the recording with the class. Ask them to point out things that you did well and things you could improve.

Practice Reading With Expression In groups of four, have children practice reading the first two pages of *Mr. Tanen's Tie Trouble* aloud, chorally.

Once they are comfortable reading aloud chorally, have each group member take a part: narrator, Kaylee, Alex, and Mr. Tanen. Remind them that the narrator reads everything except what is in quotation marks. Children will rotate parts. **ELD** ELD.PI.2.1

Make Audio Recording Have groups record themselves, first reading chorally, then with individual children taking parts. The group can decide who will take each role. If there is time, they can rotate and record several versions. **ELA** SL.2.5

Listen and Repeat Have groups replay and review their recordings. Have them discuss in their groups what went well and what could be done better. Allow groups to re-record in order to improve their performance. **ELA** SL.2.5 **ELD** ELD.PI.2.1

Skill Focus: Analyze Sources Explain to children that when they research information and write reports, they should look for good sources that fit the ideas in their reports. Then provide the following scenario:

- *You are writing a report about ways that everyday people contribute to their communities. You found two sources: a fiction story about a little boy and his community, and a magazine article about how people around the country have raised money for their schools. Which source would you use in your report? Why?* **ELA** RI.2.7, W.2.8

Day 1 Model Reading Aloud

Day 2 Demonstrate Equipment

Day 3 Practice Reading with Expression

Day 4 Make Audio Recording

Day 5 Listen and Repeat

ENGLISH LANGUAGE SUPPORT

Use Language Models

All Proficiencies After children replay and review their recordings, but before they begin their discussions, explain what it means to provide different opinions. Point out that one of the reasons we have conversations is to listen to many opinions. Explain that sometimes children will not agree with what they hear or will have different ideas. Model the following sentence starters for giving a different opinion, and encourage children to use them when they discuss their recordings.

I see your point, but _____.

I agree with you, but _____.

I understand, but _____.

You make a good point, but have you thought _____?

ELD ELD.PI.2.1, ELD.PI.2.3, ELD.PI.2.11

Grammar Weekly Review: Pronouns

▶ SHARE OBJECTIVES

- **Grammar** Replace nouns, including repeated nouns, with pronouns; use reflexive pronouns. LANGUAGE
- **Spelling** Assess words with endings *-ed* and *-ing*.

ENGLISH LANGUAGE SUPPORT

Review Key Ideas

All Proficiencies English learners will benefit from a review of pronouns. Read aloud a passage from the selection. As you read, have children point to the pronouns. Encourage them to tell what words the pronouns replace. Then have them reread the sentences using the words.

---

1 Review/Practice

Pronouns Read together the text on **Student Book** p. 44.

- *To replace nouns that tell who or what is doing something, use the pronouns* I, he, she, it, we, *or* they.

- *To replace nouns that come after verbs, use the pronouns* me, him, her, it, us, *or* them.

- Read and discuss the first two pairs of examples in the chart.

- Support children as they read the sentences with the correct pronouns in the Try This! activity.

- *Reflexive pronouns* myself *and* ourselves *can be used when the subject has already been named*. Review that *myself* refers to the singular subject *I. Ourselves* refers to a plural subject that includes the speaker and at least one other subject. Discuss examples.

2 Connect to Writing

- Read together **Student Book** p. 45. Point out that using pronouns to replace repeated nouns makes writing flow better.

- Read and discuss the examples in the chart.

- Together, read the directions for Connect Grammar to Writing ⬀ at the bottom of the page. Support children as they replace nouns with pronouns in their writing.

- Distribute Reader's Notebook Volume 2 page 15 ⬀ to children to complete independently. **ELA** W.2.5, L.2.1c

---

Spelling Base Words with Endings *-ed, -ing*

SPELLING WORDS AND SENTENCES

BASIC

1. *running* He was *running* fast.
2. *clapped* We *clapped* our hands.
3. *stopped* The car *stopped* at the light.
4. *hopping* He was *hopping* on one foot.
5. *batted* My brother *batted* the ball to me.
6. *selling** Our class is *selling* cookies to raise money.
7. *pinned* I *pinned* a flower on my dress.
8. *cutting** She is *cutting* the pie.
9. *sitting* He is *sitting* up straight.

10. *rubbed* I *rubbed* soap on it.
11. *missed* We *missed* the bus.
12. *grabbed** I *grabbed* the sled and took off.

REVIEW

13. *mixed* We *mixed* the batter.
14. *going* When are we *going*?

CHALLENGE

15. *wrapped* We *wrapped* the gifts.
16. *swelling* As the storm continued, the river kept *swelling*.

*A form or forms of these words appear in the literature.

Assess

Say each Spelling Word, read aloud its sentence, and then repeat the word. Have children write the word. **ELA** L.2.2d

Corrective Feedback

Review any words that children misspell. If children misspell two or more words, then revisit the Day 2 Word Hunt activity on page 86 of the **Literacy and Language Guide**.

Grammar

Pronouns A **pronoun** can take the place of a noun. To replace a **noun** that is the subject of a sentence, use the pronoun *I, he, she, it, we,* or *they.* To replace a noun that comes after a **verb,** use the pronoun *me, him, her, it, us,* or *them.* **Reflexive pronouns,** such as *myself, himself, herself, themselves,* and *ourselves,* are also used after verbs.

Nouns	Pronouns
The children want a new playground.	They want a new playground.
Mr. Tanen likes ties.	He likes ties.
My mother helped the principal.	My mother helped him.
Our family bought ties for our family.	Our family bought ties for ourselves.

Try This! **Name the pronouns that can replace the underlined words. Then rewrite the sentences using the pronouns.**

1. <u>Lou and Kim</u> sat on the swings.

2. I like <u>the slide</u>.

3. My brother plays by <u>my brother</u> in the sand.

When you write, try not to use the same nouns over and over again. Use pronouns or reflexive pronouns to take the place of repeated nouns. This will make your writing better.

Sentences with Repeated Subjects	Better Sentences
The two girls counted the money. The two girls hoped they had raised enough.	The two girls counted the money. They hoped they had raised enough.

Connect Grammar to Writing

When you revise your story paragraph, look for repeated nouns. Use pronouns to take their place.

44   ELA L.2.1c

45

1. They

2. it

3. him

ENGLISH LANGUAGE SUPPORT

Comprehensible Input

Emerging Model using different pronoun choices in the Try This! sentences and ask: *Should this pronoun take the place of this noun?* Have children respond with *yes/no* answers. Reveal the answer and explain why it is correct.

Expanding Provide children with index cards with a pronoun written on each one. Read the Try This! sentences aloud and have children hold up the pronoun that should take the place of the noun(s) in each sentence. Reveal the answer and explain why it is correct.

Bridging Remind children to think about whether the underlined word in each Try This! sentence comes before or after the verb. Then guide them to choose among the appropriate pronouns to complete the sentences.

Narrative Writing Revise and Edit

▶ SHARE OBJECTIVE

• **Writing** Revise, edit, and publish a narrative paragraph. LANGUAGE

ENGLISH LANGUAGE SUPPORT
Peer-Supported Learning

Emerging Write this sentence on the board, and guide children as they work with partners to add details. *Joe wears a shirt. Joe wears a red shirt with white stripes and short sleeves.* **ELD** ELD.PII.2.4

Expanding Have children complete the following sentence frames with partners using their classroom as the setting: *Ella sat in the warm classroom. She could hear quiet talking.* **ELD** ELD.PII.2.4

Bridging Write these sentences on the board: *Lisa is in her room. She wears a t-shirt and jeans. She is drawing.* Ask partners to rewrite the sentences with details. **ELD** ELD.PII.2.4

Daily Proofreading Practice

the clas plants a garden for the Kindergarten. Wil you help us

my WriteSmart Have children revise, proofread, and publish their narrative writing task through *my*WriteSmart.

---

1 Teach/Model

Story Paragraph: Elaboration Remind children that good writers make their ideas clear by using details to help readers see what is happening.

• Read the top of **Student Book** p. 46 with the class. Discuss the revisions made by the student writer, Ahmed.

• *How does each revision make Ahmed's ideas clearer?*

• To see and discuss revisions made by Ahmed, display Projectable 16.10 ⎘.

• Point out how Ahmed applied these revising skills: adding details, adding dialogue, and adding setting.

2 Guided Practice/Apply

Story Paragraph Read and discuss Ahmed's final copy on **Student Book** p. 47.

• Discuss the Reading as a Writer questions.

Revising Have children use the Writing Rubric Blackline Master ⎘ to evaluate their stories.

Proofreading Have children use the Proofreading Checklist Blackline Master ⎘ to proofread and edit a partner's paragraph. Have children check for a conclusion in each other's paragraphs.

Handwriting If you have children write their final pieces rather than use digital tools, tell them to focus on using their best handwriting. *See also pp. R24–R29 for handwriting support.*

Publishing Have children make a neat final copy and share their writing.

ELA W.2.3, W.2.4, W.2.5, W.2.10, L.2.1g **ELD** ELD.PI.2.10, ELD.PII.2.1, ELD.PII.2.4, ELD.PII.2.5

Narrative Writing ✔️WriteSmart

☑️ **Elaboration** Use details when you write a **story**.
Details help your reader picture what the story is about.

Ahmed drafted a one-paragraph story about a little boy who helped his mother. Later, he added some details to make his story more interesting.

Writing Checklist

☑️ **Organization**
Did I include a beginning, a middle, and an end?

☑️ **Development**
Do my words tell what the characters are feeling?

☑️ **Elaboration**
Did I add details to tell the reader more?

☑️ **Conventions**
Did I use spelling patterns to help me spell words?

Revised Draft

Omar wanted to help his
~~She had been sick for a week.~~
mother. ∧He came home early
playing with his friends in
one day from∧the park. His
 kitchen
mother was sitting at the ∧table.

He wanted to do something to

help. First, he began to rinse

the dishes.

46 ELA W.2.3, W.2.4, W.2.5, W.2.10, L.2.2d ELD ELD.PI.2.10, ELD.PI.2.12b

Final Copy

Omar's Gift
by Ahmed Hakin

Omar wanted to help his mother. She had been sick for a week. He came home early one day from playing with his friends in the park. His mother was sitting at the kitchen table. He wanted to do something to help. First, he began to rinse the dishes. After that, he put them in the dishwasher. His mother looked at him and said, "You are a good son, Omar." She smiled at him. Omar knew that he had just given his mother a gift. It was a gift that made them both happy.

Reading as a Writer

How do the details that Ahmed added tell his readers more? Where can you add details to your story?

I added details to my final paper to make it more interesting.

47

NARRATIVE WRITING RUBRIC
See also the Multipurpose Writing Rubric on p. R18.

Score	4	3	2	1	NS
Purpose /Organization	The narrative is clear and well organized. It is appropriately sequenced and has closure. • Plot contains a well-elaborated event or a short sequence of events • Setting and characters are included and well-maintained • Plot events follow a logical sequence • Includes an effective conclusion	The narrative is generally clear and organized. The sequence is adequately maintained, and the plot has closure. • Plot contains a well-elaborated event or a short sequence of events • Characters and setting are included and adequately maintained • Plot events follow an understandable sequence • Includes an adequate conclusion	The narrative is somewhat organized but may be unclear in parts. The sequence is weak. The plot lacks closure. • Minimal development of plot • Characters and setting are included but are minimally maintained • Sequence of events is poorly organized • Conclusion is inadequate or missing	The narrative's focus is unclear, and it is poorly organized. The narrative lacks sequence and has no closure. • Little or no plot • No attempt to maintain characters or setting • Sequence of events is not organized • Conclusion is missing	• not intelligible • not written in English • not on topic • contains text copied from another source • does not address the purpose for writing
Development/ Elaboration	The narrative includes effective elaboration, and details describing actions, thoughts, and feelings. • Clear effort to develop experiences, characters, setting, and events • Contains strong use of details • Writer uses temporal words to signal the order of events	The narrative includes adequate elaboration, and details describing actions, thoughts, and feelings. • Some attempt to develop experiences, characters, setting, and events • Contains adequate use of details • Contains adequate use of temporal words to signal the order of events	The narrative includes only partial or ineffective elaboration. The narrative includes some details. • Little attempt to develop experiences, characters, setting, and events • Contains weak use of details • Contains little use of temporal words. • Order of events is not clear	The narrative provides little or no elaboration and few details. • No attempt to develop experiences, characters, setting, and events • Few or no details • No use of temporal words • Order of events is confusing	• not intelligible • not written in English • not on topic • contains text copied from another source • does not develop the writing

Score	2	1	0	NS
Conventions	The narrative demonstrates adequate command of conventions. • Consistent use of complete sentences, correct sentence structures, punctuation, capitalization, grammar, spelling	The narrative demonstrates partial command of conventions. • Limited use of complete sentences, correct sentence structures, punctuation, capitalization, grammar, spelling	The narrative demonstrates little or no command of conventions. • Does not use complete sentences, correct sentence structures, punctuation, capitalization, grammar, spelling	• not intelligible • not written in English • not on topic • contains text copied from another source

Formative Assessment

Weekly Tests

At the end of the lesson, administer the Weekly Test. This will give you a **snapshot of how children are progressing** with the Reading and Language Arts skills in this lesson and can give you **guidance on grouping, reteaching, and intervention.** Suggestions for adjusting instruction based on these results can be found on the next page.

Access Through Accommodations

When you administer the Weekly Test, some children may have problems accessing all or parts of the assessment. The purpose of the Weekly Test is to determine children's ability to complete the Reading and Language Arts tasks they learned in this lesson. Any barriers to them accessing the tasks demanded of them should be lowered so they can focus on skill demonstration.

When choosing accommodations, you will want to avoid invalidating the test results if you are measuring a child's reading skill. For example, you will not want to read aloud the passage. The following accommodations, if needed, will not interfere with the Weekly Test's validity:

- Read aloud the assessment directions and item prompts. If children are English learners, read aloud the assessment directions and item prompts in the child's native language, if possible.

- Define any unknown words in the directions or item prompts that do not give away the answers to the items.

- Allow for a break during the assessment.

- Simplify the language of assessment directions and item prompts.

- Administer the assessment in a smaller group setting.

- Administer the assessment on a computer or other electronic device.

- Provide audio amplification equipment, colored overlays, or visual magnifying equipment to maintain visual/audio attention and access.

- Allow children to complete the assessment items orally or by having another person transcribe their responses.

Using Data to Adjust Instruction

Use children's scores on the Weekly Test to determine Small Group placement, reteaching, and potential for intervention.

☑ VOCABULARY AND COMPREHENSION

Story Structure; Understanding Characters; Anchor Text

Target Vocabulary; Homographs

IF STUDENT SCORES...	
...at acceptable,	**...below acceptable,**
THEN continue core instruction.	**THEN** use Reteach Comprehension Skill and Vocabulary Strategies lessons. For struggling students, administer the *Intervention Assessments* to determine if students would benefit from intervention.

☑ PHONICS

Base Words and Endings -ed, -ing

IF STUDENT SCORES...	
...at acceptable,	**...below acceptable,**
THEN continue core instruction.	**THEN** use Reteach Phonics lesson. Administer the *Intervention Assessments* to determine if students would benefit from intervention.

☑ LANGUAGE ARTS

Pronouns

IF STUDENT SCORES...	
...at acceptable,	**...below acceptable,**
THEN continue core instruction.	**THEN** use Reteach Language Arts lesson. Administer the *Intervention Assessments* to determine if students would benefit from intervention.

☑ FLUENCY

Fluency Plan

Assess one group per week using the <u>Fluency Tests</u> 🔗 in the *Grab-and-Go™* Resources. Use the suggested plan at the right.

● Struggling Readers	Weeks 1, 2, 3
▲ On Level	Week 2
■ Advanced	Week 5

IF...	
...students are reading on-level text fluently,	**...students are reading below level,**
THEN continue core instruction.	**THEN** provide additional fluency practice using the **Student Book,** the **Cold Reads,** and the Leveled Readers. For struggling students, administer the *Intervention Assessments* to determine if students would benefit from intervention.

JOURNEYS
Cold Reads
2

The **Cold Reads** passages increase gradually in Lexile® measures throughout the year, from below grade level to above grade level.

- Each passage is accompanied by several selected-response questions and one constructed-response prompt, requiring children to read closely, answer questions at substantial DOK levels, and cite text evidence.

- The **Cold Reads** may be used to provide practice in reading increasingly complex texts and to informally monitor children's progress.

- The **Cold Reads** may be used to estimate children's Lexile® levels in order to recommend appropriately challenging books for small-group instruction or independent reading.

→ Turn the page for more information about using **FORMATIVE ASSESSMENT** for **ELD AND INTERVENTION.**

Assess It Online!

▶ Language Workshop
Assessment Handbook

▶ Intervention
Assessments

Formative Assessment for ELD and Intervention

Formative Assessment for English Learners

English learners should engage in the same rigorous curriculum and formative assessment as other students. However, it is important to remember that English learners face a dual challenge: they are strengthening their abilities *to use* English at the same time that they are learning challenging content *through* English. Use the following strategies and resources for ongoing assessment of English language development, in addition to the assessments you use with all children:

- A combination of **observational measures,** such as listening in as children read aloud or participate in collaborative conversations. Be prepared to provide **"just-in-time" scaffolding** to support students. For example, if children are retelling a story, you could help them use sentence structures with past-tense verbs and time-order transition words.

- **Constructive feedback** that focuses on communication and meaning-making. Avoid overcorrecting in a way that makes English learners reluctant to speak up. You might try recasting a child's statement more correctly, making a note to address the target form more directly during Designated ELD time.

- **Student self-assessment,** through children's own notes in their vocabulary notebooks or other learning journals. If possible, meet with each child to review his or her self-assessments and provide encouragement and feedback.

- **Formative assessment** notes that are integrated into the Language Workshop Teacher's Guide for use during Designated ELD.

- **Language Workshop Assessment Handbook** for longer-cycle assessment to make sure students are progressing in their English development.

Response to Intervention  RtI

Use the Weekly Tests and Benchmark and Unit Tests, along with your own observations, to determine if individual students are not responding to primary instruction and need additional testing to identify specific needs for targeted intervention.

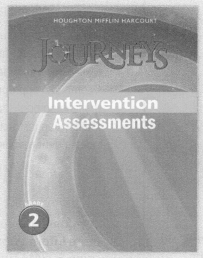

Intervention Assessments

Assessment for Intervention

Administer these assessments to

- children who are receiving supplemental intervention to gauge progress toward exit from the intervention program.

- children who demonstrate lack of success with Weekly Tests, Benchmark and Unit Tests, and core instruction to determine if they might benefit from additional practice or intervention.

DAY 1

Differentiate **Phonics**
- Base Words and Endings -ed, -ing

Vocabulary Reader
- *Raising Funds*

DAY 2

Differentiate **Comprehension**
- Story Structure
- Infer/Predict

DAY 3

Differentiate
Phonics & Fluency
- Cumulative Review
- Rate

Leveled Readers
- ⬤ *Our Library*
- ▲ *The Bake Sale*
- ■ *The Town Auction*
- ◆ *Ms. Hawkins and the Bake Sale*

DAY 4

Differentiate
Vocabulary Strategies
- Homographs

DAY 5

Options for Reteaching
- Phonics
- Language Arts
- Vocabulary Strategies
- Comprehension

Literacy Centers

Independent Practice
- Word Study, T6
- Think and Write, T7
- Comprehension and Fluency, T6

Teacher-Led

		DAY 1	DAY 2	DAY 3
	Struggling Readers	**Vocabulary Reader**, *Raising Funds*, Differentiated Instruction, p. T86 **Differentiate Phonics:** Base Words and Endings *-ed*, *-ing*, p. T84 **English Language Support**, pp. T85, T87	**Differentiate Comprehension:** Story Structure; Infer/Predict, p. T88 **Reread** *Beep! Beep!* **English Language Support**, p. T89	**Leveled Reader** *Our Library*, p. T92 **Differentiate Phonics:** Cumulative Review, p. T90 **English Language Support**, Leveled Reader Teacher's Guide, p. 5
	On Level	**Vocabulary Reader**, *Raising Funds*, Differentiated Instruction, p. T86 **English Language Support**, pp. T85, T87	**Differentiate Comprehension:** Story Structure; Infer/Predict, p. T88 **Reread** *Beep! Beep!* **English Language Support**, p. T89	**Leveled Reader** *The Bake Sale*, p. T93 *Ms. Hawkins and the Bake Sale*, p. T95 **Differentiate Fluency:** Rate, p. T91 **English Language Support**, Leveled Reader Teacher's Guide, p. 5
	Advanced	**Vocabulary Reader**, *Raising Funds*, Differentiated Instruction, p. T87 **English Language Support**, pp. T85, T87	**Differentiate Comprehension:** Story Structure; Infer/Predict, p. T89 **English Language Support**, p. T89	**Leveled Reader** *The Town Auction*, p. T94 **Differentiate Fluency:** Rate, p. T91 **English Language Support**, Leveled Reader Teacher's Guide, p. 5

What are my other children doing?

		DAY 1	DAY 2	DAY 3
	Struggling Readers	**Word Building:** Build and read Spelling Words • Leveled Practice, SR16.1	**Partners:** Vocabulary in Context Cards 121–128 **Partners:** Reread *Beep! Beep!* • Leveled Practice, SR16.2	**Partners:** Reread Leveled Reader *Our Library* • Leveled Practice, SR16.3
	On Level	**Word Building:** Build and read base words with endings *-ed* and *-ing* using Letter Cards **Complete** Reader's Notebook, pp. 1–2 or Leveled Practice, EL16.1	**Target Vocabulary:** Practice reading using Vocabulary in Context Cards 121–128 **Reread** *Beep! Beep!* **Complete** Reader's Notebook, pp. 3–6 or Leveled Practice, EL16.2	**Partners:** Reread Leveled Reader *The Bake Sale* or *Ms. Hawkins and the Bake Sale* **Complete** Reader's Notebook, pp. 7–11 or Leveled Practice, EL16.3
	Advanced	**Vocabulary in Context Cards** 121–128 *Talk It Over* activities • Leveled Practice, A16.1	**Reread** *Mr. Tanen's Tie Trouble* Student Book, pp. 14–35 • Leveled Practice, A16.2	**Partners:** Reread Leveled Reader *The Town Auction* • Leveled Practice, A16.3

For strategic intervention for this lesson, see pp. S2–S11.

DAY 4

Differentiate Vocabulary Strategies: Homographs, p. T96
Reread *We Helped*
English Language Support, p. T97

Differentiate Vocabulary Strategies: Homographs, p. T96
Reread *We Helped*
English Language Support, p. T97

Differentiate Vocabulary Strategies: Homographs, p. T97
English Language Support, p. T97

Partners: Reread *We Helped*
• Leveled Practice, SR16.4

Reread *We Helped*
Complete Reader's Notebook, pp. 12–14 or Leveled Practice, EL16.4

Partners: Reread
The Jefferson Daily News,
Student Book, pp. 40–43
• Leveled Practice, A16.4

DAY 5

Options for Reteaching, pp. T98–T99
Reread *Beep! Beep!* or *We Helped* or one of this week's Blend-It Books.

Options for Reteaching, pp. T98–T99
Reread *Beep! Beep!* or *We Helped* or one of this week's Blend-It Books.

Options for Reteaching, pp. T98–T99
Reread *Beep! Beep!* or *We Helped* or one of this week's Blend-It Books.

Partners: Choose among stories for this week to reread
• Complete and share Literacy Center activities

Partners: Reread Leveled Reader *The Bake Sale* or *Ms. Hawkins and the Bake Sale*
• Complete and share Literacy Center activities
• Self-Selected Reading
Complete Reader's Notebook, p. 15

Partners: Reread Leveled Reader *The Town Auction*
• Complete and share Literacy Center activities
• Self-Selected Reading

English Language Support

Use the Leveled Reader Teacher's Guide to support ELs during differentiated instruction.

• **Characteristics of the Text** (p. 1)

  Identify challenging language features, such as text structure, literary features, complex sentences, and vocabulary.

• **Cultural Support/Cognates/Vocabulary** (p. 5)

  Explain unfamiliar features of English and help ELs transfer first-language knowledge.

• **Oral Language Development** (p. 5)

  Check comprehension using dialogues that match children's proficiency levels.

Book Share

Use this routine at the end of the week to show children that they have become experts on their Leveled Readers.

Step 1:

Help each group write a presentation of their Leveled Reader **Responding** page. Use the following routine:

• Briefly tell what your book is about.

• Show your graphic organizer and explain what you added to complete it.

• Tell about your favorite part of the book.

Every child should have his or her own presentation to share with a new group.

Step 2:

Have children number off. Assign places in the classroom for 1s to gather, 2s, and so on. Help children find their new groups.

Step 3:

Have children take turns sharing their book presentations in the new groups. Continue until all children have finished sharing. Encourage children to ask questions. Give the following frames for support.

Can you tell me more about _____?

I wonder why _____?

What do you think about _____?

Differentiate Phonics
Base Words and Endings -ed, -ing

Struggling Readers

ELA RF.2.3d
ELD ELD.PI.2.1

I DO IT

- Display **Picture Card** *hug* and name the picture.

- Write *hugged*. Read the word aloud.

- Underline the base word *hug* and circle the *-ed* ending. Explain that when *-ed* is added to a base word that has a short vowel followed by a single consonant, the final consonant is doubled. Point out the consonants *gg* in *hugged*.

- Read the word again and clap the syllables. Point out the /d/ sound for *-ed*.

- Follow a similar procedure with *camped* and *waited*. Point out that the final consonant is not doubled when *-ed* is added to *camp* and *wait* because the base word *camp* has a short vowel followed by two consonants and the base word *wait* has two vowels together that make the long *a* sound. Then call attention to the /t/ and /ed/ sounds for *-ed*.

- Repeat with *hugging*, pointing out the ending, *-ing*. Remind children that adding an ending sometimes adds a syllable to a base word.

- Follow up with *camping* and *waiting*.

- Review base words with endings *-ed* and *-ing* in the **Decodable Reader** *Beep! Beep!*

WE DO IT

- Display **Letter Cards** *j, o, g, g, e, d*.

- Ask volunteers to write on the board the base word and the ending. Then ask another volunteer to tell which consonant was doubled and why.

- Together with children, blend the sounds and read the word.

- Repeat the procedure with the words below. Provide **Corrective Feedback** if children need additional help.

swimming	patted
wagging	tugged
winning	jumping
shopped	trotted

YOU DO IT

- Have partners take turns using **Letter Cards** to build words with endings *-ed* and *-ing*. If needed, start them off with these base words: *skip, dot, help, beg, drip, nod, want, lock*.

- Have children record the words they make and read the list to the group.

Corrective Feedback

When a child mispronounces a word, point to the word and say it. Call attention to the element that was mispronounced, say the sound, and then guide children to read the word. See the example below.

Phonics Error:

A child reads *tugged* as a two-syllable word.

Correct the error. Say the word. *The word is* tugged. *It has just one syllable.*

Model as you touch the letters. *I'll blend: /t/ /ŭ/ /g/ /d/. What is the word?* tugged

Guide *Let's blend together: /t/ /ŭ/ /g/ /d/. What is the word?* tugged

Check *You blend. /t/ /ŭ/ /g/ /d/ What is the word?* tugged

Reinforce Go back two or three words in the list and have children continue reading. Make note of errors and review those words during the next lesson.

English Language Support

ELD ELD.PI.2.1

Provide Struggling Readers, On Level, and Advanced ELs proficiency-level support during differentiated instruction. Give children in all groups extra practice identifying base words and endings -ed and -ing.

- Show **Picture Card** *hop* and name the picture. Write the word *hop* on the board and read it aloud. Point out that *hop* has one short vowel followed by a single consonant.

- Write *hopped*. Underline the base word *hop* and circle the *-ed* ending. Explain that when you add the ending *-ed* to the base word *hop*, you double the final consonant. Use Instructional Routine 3 ⤴ to model how to blend *hopped*.

- Repeat the procedure with *hopping* and the ending *-ing*.

Emerging

- Have children point to and say the final consonant in *hop*.

- Then have them say the vowel that comes before the final consonant.

- Finally, have them point to or say the consonant that is doubled in *hopped* and *hopping*.

Expanding

- Give children a list of base words, all of which require the doubling of the final consonant before adding an ending. Guide children to write the base words, adding *-ed* or *-ing*. Then have them read aloud the words.

Bridging

- Provide children with a list of base words. Have them first sort the words into those that require the final consonant to be doubled before adding an ending and those that do not. Have children write the base words, adding *-ed* or *-ing*. Have them read aloud the words.

On Level

See Literacy Centers—Unit 4 Lesson 16 Word Study

If children have time after completing the purple activity, have them try moving on to the blue activity.

Advanced

See Literacy Centers—Unit 4 Lesson 16 Word Study

If children have time after completing the blue activity, have them reread Decodable Reader *Beep! Beep!* or another book independently.

Vocabulary Reader
Raising Funds

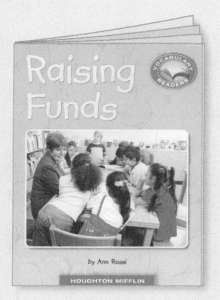

by Ann Rossi

HOUGHTON MIFFLIN

Summary

Some schools do not have enough money to pay for things like field trips. Children can work hard to have fundraisers to make more money for their school.

☑ TARGET VOCABULARY

received	chuckled
account	staring
budget	repeated
disappointed	fund

Struggling Readers

ELA L.2.4a, L.2.6
ELD ELD.PI.2.1, ELD.PI.2.5

- Explain to children that schools do not always have the funds necessary for children to do activities, such as going on field trips.
- Guide children to preview the selection. Ask them to tell what is happening in the photos, using Target Vocabulary when possible.
- Have children alternate reading pages of the selection aloud. Remind children that word and picture clues can help them determine the meaning of an unfamiliar word (or phrase). As necessary, use the **Vocabulary in Context Cards** to review how the Target Vocabulary words are used.
- Have partners work together to complete the Responding page. Then review the directions on Blackline Master 16.4 ⬚ and guide children to complete it.

On Level

ELA L.2.4a, L.2.6
ELD ELD.PI.2.1, ELD.PI.2.5

- Explain to children that students can help to raise funds for special school events.
- Guide children to preview the selection. Ask them to describe what they think the selection is about, using Target Vocabulary when possible.
- Have children alternate reading pages of the selection aloud. Guide them to use context clues to figure out the meanings of unfamiliar words (or phrases).
- If children cannot figure out the meaning of a word after looking for context clues, guide them to use a dictionary.
- Assign the Responding page and Blackline Master 16.4 ⬚. Review the directions with children.

Advanced

ELA L.2.4a, L.2.6
ELD ELD.PI.2.1, ELD.PI.2.5

- Have children preview the selection, using information from the preview and prior knowledge to make predictions about what they will read. Guide them to discuss their predictions with a partner, using Target Vocabulary when possible.

- Remind children to use context clues to help them determine the meanings of unknown words (or phrases), and encourage them to use a dictionary to confirm their understanding. Have children read the selection with their partners.

- Assign the Responding page and Blackline Master 16.4 ⌐. For the Write About It activity, remind children to include facts and details to support their ideas.

English Language Support

ELD ELD.PI.2.1

Provide Struggling Readers, On Level, and Advanced ELs proficiency-level support during differentiated instruction.

Emerging

- Give children sentence frames they can orally complete as they are called upon to tell what the selection is about. Display the following frames and help children complete them as needed: *I think this selection is about _____. The picture on this page shows _____.*

Expanding

- Use visuals, simplified language, and gestures to preteach the following selection vocabulary: *bake sale, car wash, talent show, craft fair.* Encourage children to use the terms as they describe to other children in their group what the selection is mostly about.

Bridging

- Help children prepare for the Write About It activity. Review examples of events that people hold to raise funds. Then give children sentence frames they can complete to respond to the writing prompt. For example: *I want to raise funds to _____. I am going to have a / hold a _____ to raise funds.*

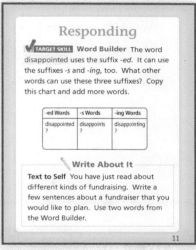

Raising Funds, p. 11

Differentiate Comprehension
Story Structure; Infer/Predict

Struggling Readers

ELA RL.2.5
ELD ELD.PI.2.1, ELD.PI.2.6

I DO IT

- Explain that readers infer and predict to figure out what will happen in a story.
- Read aloud **Student Book** p. 27 and model how to infer and predict.

> **Think Aloud** *Mr. Tanen swallows hard before saying that his ties belong to the town. Mr. Tanen must feel sad to have lost his ties. I predict that Mr. Tanen will feel sad when people wear his ties.*

WE DO IT

- Have children read **Student Book** p. 30.
- Help children infer what must have happened in order for the playground to be decorated with Mr. Tanen's ties.
- Help children predict Mr. Tanen's reaction to this gesture. Write their predictions on the board.

YOU DO IT

- Have children review the entire selection *Mr. Tanen's Tie Trouble*.
- Have children complete a Story Map of the story, including Characters and Setting in two boxes at the top, then Plot in the bottom box—with further subdivisions into Beginning, Middle, and End.
- Point out that the sentences on their Story Map form a summary of the story.

On Level

ELA RL.2.5
ELD ELD.PI.2.1, ELD.PI.2.6

I DO IT

- Read aloud **Student Book** p. 17.
- Remind children that readers infer unstated events and predict future events. Model predicting to figure out story structure.

> **Think Aloud** *I can infer that Kaylee and Alex feel proud when they bring in the jar of money. Why doesn't Mr. Tanen know what to say? I'll bet it's because he doesn't want to disappoint them. I predict that Mr. Tanen will try to find another way to raise money.*

WE DO IT

- Have children read aloud **Student Book** pp. 18–19.
- Have a volunteer make an inference about Mr. Tanen's feelings on both pages.
- Work together to infer why Mr. Tanen's feelings change and to predict how he will feel when the playground is built.

YOU DO IT

- Have children complete a Story Map for *Mr. Tanen's Tie Trouble*.
- Distribute index cards to children. Assign to each child one portion of a Story Map, including beginning, middle, and end of the plot. Have children complete the cards with information about the story. Then collect the cards and shuffle them.
- Have partners take turns putting the cards in order and retelling the story.

Advanced

ELA RL.2.5
ELD ELD.PI.2.1, ELD.PI.2.6

I DO IT

- Read aloud **Student Book** pp. 17–18.

- Point out that we can infer feelings and make predictions about different characters at different parts of the story. Model asking questions to help make inferences: *How do Kaylee and Alex feel when they bring the money jar to Mr. Tanen? How would they feel if they learned it is not enough?*

WE DO IT

- Have children read **Student Book** p. 22.

- *How does Mrs. Sweet Apple feel when she hears about the tie auction? How do her feelings change? How will the rest of the town feel after they hear the news?* Mrs. Sweet Apple says that she thinks Mr. Tanen might be crazy. When Mr. Apple says that Mr. Tanen is selling his ties for the playground, she probably admires Mr. Tanen. The rest of the town will also admire him for caring about the playground.

YOU DO IT

- Have children summarize the main events in *Mr. Tanen's Tie Trouble.*

- Have them explain the inferences they made about characters and events that helped them to better understand the story structure.

- Ask volunteers to share their thinking with the group.

English Language Support

ELD ELD.PI.2.1

Provide Struggling Readers, On Level, and Advanced ELs proficiency-level support during differentiated instruction.

Emerging

- Before children take part in discussions about the selection, check their understanding of terms used to talk about story structure.

- Model identifying the characters, setting, and plot in *Mr. Tanen's Tie Trouble*. Have children draw and label a picture of Mr. Tanen in one of the settings from the story.

Expanding

- Before children take part in discussions about the selection, review their understanding of key characters and events in the story.

- Page through *Mr. Tanen's Tie Trouble*, **Student Book** pp. 16–34, and ask children simple questions about story structure. For example, *Who is this story about? What happens to Mr. Tanen's ties?*

Bridging

- Give children frames they can use to express their understanding of story characters and events. *Who/Characters, Where/Setting,* and *What/Plot* on the board.

- Pair children with more fluent speakers in their group. Have partners page through *Mr. Tanen's Tie Trouble*, asking and answering *Who, Where,* and *What* questions about the story.

Differentiate Phonics and Fluency

Struggling Readers

ELA RF.2.3b
ELD ELD.PIII.2

Phonics

Cumulative Review

I DO IT

- Display **Picture Card** *goat*. Name the picture, emphasizing the long *o* vowel sound.

- Use Instructional Routine 3 to model blending *goat*, displaying **Letter Cards** *g*, *oa*, *t*. Point out the *oa* spelling for /ō/.

- Replace **Letter Card** *g* with *b*. Blend and read *boat*.

- Repeat the procedure with the following word sets, pointing out the *o* and *ow* spellings for /ō/: *fold/cold, slow/ glow*.

WE DO IT

- Write *float* on the board.

- Have children use **Letter Cards** to build *float*. Blend the sounds. *Listen: /f/ /l/ /ō/ /t/, float*. Have children blend with you. *Now you blend the sounds: /f/ /l/ /ō/ /t/, float*.

- Then have children replace the blend *fl* with the letter *c*. Together, blend and read *coat*.

- Repeat the procedure with the following word sets, working with children to build, blend, and read each word: *most/host; show/flow*. Provide **Corrective Feedback** if needed.

- Then write the following words on the board, and have children blend and read the words: *over, rowboat, pillow, oatmeal, solo, owner, soapsuds*.

YOU DO IT

- Have children build and read *sold, bold, toast, coast, grow,* and *crow*.

- Encourage children to build additional rhyming words with *o, oa,* and *ow* spellings for /ō/.

FORMATIVE ASSESSMENT

Corrective Feedback

When a child mispronounces a word, point to the word and say it. Call attention to the element that was mispronounced, say the sound, and then guide children to read the word. See the example below.

Phonics Error:

A child builds *sold* as *soald*.

Correct the error. *The /ō/ sound in* sold *is spelled with the letter* o.

Model using **Letter Cards** to build *sold*. *I'll build: s, o, l, d; sold*.

Guide *Let's build* sold *together: s, o, l, d. What is the word?* sold

---

Check *You build* sold. *s, o, l, d What is the word?* sold

Reinforce Have children continue building and reading rhyming words. Note any errors and review them during later lessons.

ELA RF.2.4b

All Levels

Fluency

Rate

I DO IT

- Write: *We helped out in the garden by digging holes.*

- Use a **Think Aloud** as you model reading the sentence twice. First, read too slowly. Next, read too quickly.

Think Aloud *I want listeners to understand my reading. If I read We • helped • out • in • the • garden • by • digging • holes, that is too slow! If I read We helped out in the garden by digging holes, that is too fast. So I pause only after groups of words that go together, and I do not rush any of the words.*

- Model reading the sentence at an appropriate rate, neither too fast nor too slow.

WE DO IT

- Write two sentences from *Our Library, The Bake Sale, The Town Auction,* and *Ms. Hawkins and the Bake Sale.*

- Have children first read the sentences silently. Then have them practice reading the sentences aloud.

- Work with children to identify readings that are too slow or too fast. Provide **Corrective Feedback.**

- Have children take turns reading the sentences at an appropriate rate.

YOU DO IT

- Have partners choose a page from a **Leveled Reader** and take turns reading aloud. Remind them to read at an appropriate rate.

- Monitor and provide **Corrective Feedback** as needed.

FORMATIVE ASSESSMENT — RtI

Corrective Feedback Work with children to correct errors, following the model below.

Fluency Error: A child reads the text too quickly.

Correct the error. Remind children to read at a rate that is neither too slow nor too fast.

Model Model reading a sentence at an appropriate rate. *If my reading sounds too slow, I'll speed up. If it sounds too fast, I'll slow down.*

Guide Have children echo your reading.

Check Have children read the sentence on their own.

Reinforce Have children go back a sentence or two and begin reading on their own again.

Leveled Readers

TARGET SKILL

Story Structure

TARGET STRATEGY

Infer/Predict

TARGET VOCABULARY

account	fund
budget	received
chuckled	repeated
disappointed	staring

ELA RL.2.1, RL.2.5, RF.2.4b
ELD ELD.PI.2.1, ELD.PI.2.6

Struggling Readers

 Our Library

Summary The children are excited to get a children's room at the library. But there is a problem: there aren't many books! The children know how to solve this problem.

Genre: Realistic Fiction

Introducing the Text

- Explain that the children are getting a new children's room at their town library. When it opens, they are disappointed because there are only a few books.

- Remind children that using a story map can help them organize information about the setting, characters, events, and story details.

Supporting the Reading

- **p. 6** *Which character takes care of the library, and what is the setting for this page?* Mr. Moore; the children's room in the library

- **p. 6** *What can you infer about how Mr. Moore feels? Which clues help you? He is upset. The clues: Mr. Moore tries to explain why there are so few books; he tries to solve the problem by telling the children to take turns with the books.*

Discussing and Revisiting the Text

Critical Thinking After they discuss the book, have children read the instructions on the top half of Responding p. 11 in *Our Library.*

- Have partners return to the text to review the story details.

- Have children complete Blackline Master 16.5.

FLUENCY: RATE Model reading p. 9 at a proper rate. Then have partners echo-read p. 9. Monitor their reading rate.

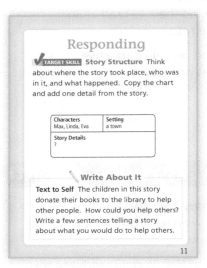

Responding

TARGET SKILL Story Structure Think about where the story took place, who was in it, and what happened. Copy the chart and add one detail from the story.

Characters	Setting
Max, Linda, Eva	a town
Story Details	
?	

Write About It

Text to Self The children in this story donate their books to the library to help other people. How could you help others? Write a few sentences telling a story about what you would do to help others.

11

Our Library, p. 11

On Level

ELA RL.2.1, RL.2.5, RF.2.4b
ELD ELD.PI.2.1, ELD.PI.2.6

 The Bake Sale

Summary Ms. Hawkins's class needs money for a field trip. They decide to have a bake sale, but their baking skills are terrible! After Ms. Wells gives the class a baking lesson, their bake sale is a success. Now they can go to the museum.

Genre: Realistic Fiction

Introducing the Text

• Explain that the children in Ms. Hawkins's class need money to go on a field trip. They want to have a bake sale, but their baking skills are terrible. After Ms. Wells gives them a baking lesson, their bake sale is a success.

• Remind children that using a Story Map can help them organize information about the characters, setting, events, and story details.

Supporting the Reading

• **p. 4** *What can you tell about the setting? Where and when does the story take place? The setting for this story is at school during winter.*

• **p. 14** *What can you infer about Ms. Wells's baking skills? Sample answer: I think that Ms. Wells's baking skills are good because after she gives the children their baking lesson, they are able to bake delicious things.*

Discussing and Revisiting the Text

Critical Thinking After they discuss the book, have children read the instructions on the top half of Responding p. 15 in *The Bake Sale.*

• Have children work individually or in pairs to complete Blackline Master 16.6 .

FLUENCY: RATE Have partners practice reading their favorite parts of *The Bake Sale,* using an appropriate rate.

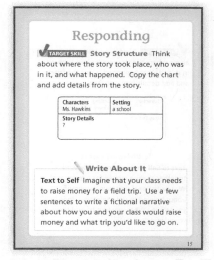

Responding

✓ TARGET SKILL **Story Structure** Think about where the story took place, who was in it, and what happened. Copy the chart and add details from the story.

Characters	Setting
Ms. Hawkins	a school
Story Details	
?	

✏ **Write About It**

Text to Self Imagine that your class needs to raise money for a field trip. Use a few sentences to write a fictional narrative about how you and your class would raise money and what trip you'd like to go on.

15

The Bake Sale, p. 15

TARGET SKILL
Story Structure

TARGET STRATEGY
Infer/Predict

TARGET VOCABULARY

account	fund
budget	received
chuckled	repeated
disappointed	staring

The Town Auction, p. 15

Leveled Readers

Advanced

ELA RL.2.1, RL.2.5, RF.2.4b
ELD ELD.PI.2.1, ELD.PI.2.6

▢ The Town Auction

Summary A town doesn't have the funds to build a town pool. The town decides to hold an auction to raise money. The children want to help, so they donate their personal collections.

Genre: Realistic Fiction

Introducing the Text

- Explain that a town needs to raise money to build a pool. People donate items for an auction so other people can buy them. The town will use money raised from the auction to pay for the pool.

- Remind children that as they are reading they should think about the story structure, including characters, setting, and events.

Supporting the Reading

- **p. 9** *Which two characters get an idea that will allow the children to help with the auction? What is their idea?* Lou and Carl get the idea; the idea is for the children to sell their collections at the auction.

- **p. 11** *What can you infer about how much Carl wants to have the town pool?* Sample answer: I can infer that Carl really wants the town pool because he donates his baseball card collection, which he really likes a lot.

Discussing and Revisiting the Text

Critical Thinking After they discuss the book, have children read the instructions on the top half of Responding p. 15 in *The Town Auction.*

- Have children look through the text to find story details and the names of characters.

- Have children add them to Blackline Master 16.7 [↗].

FLUENCY: RATE Have children practice reading their favorite parts of *The Town Auction* at an appropriate rate.

ELD ELD.PI.2.1, ELD.PI.2.6

English Language Support

 ## Ms. Hawkins and the Bake Sale

Summary Ms. Hawkins's class wants to sell baked goods to raise money for a field trip, but the children aren't very good at baking. After Ms. Wells gives them a baking lesson, their bake sale is a success!

Genre: Realistic Fiction

Introducing the Text

- Explain that the children in Ms. Hawkins's class need some help to make their bake sale a success.

- Remind children to look for information about the characters, setting, story events, and story details to help them understand what they read.

Supporting the Reading

- **pp. 6–7** *Who are the characters you have read about so far?* Some of the children are Tina, Celine, and Dustin.

- **pp. 6–7** *After the children taste the first things they baked, what can you infer about their baking skills?* Sample answer: *The children do not have very good baking skills and they probably need more practice.*

Discussing and Revisiting the Text

Critical Thinking After they discuss the book, have children read the instructions on the top half of Responding p. 15 in *Ms. Hawkins and the Bake Sale*.

- Have children work individually or in pairs to complete Blackline Master 16.8.

FLUENCY: RATE Model reading pp. 6–7 of *Ms. Hawkins and the Bake Sale* using appropriate rate. Then have children echo-read using an appropriate rate.

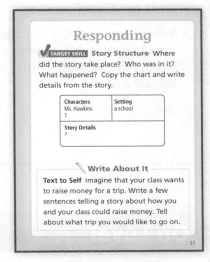

Ms. Hawkins and the Bake Sale, p. 15

Differentiate Vocabulary Strategies
Homographs

Struggling Readers

ELA L.2.4a
ELD ELD.PI.2.1

I DO IT

- Write on separate lines on the board *I can do it. I opened a can of beans.* Read the sentences aloud.

- Emphasize that although homographs are spelled the same way, they have different meanings.

- Circle *can* in each sentence.

- Tell children that the homographs *can* have two different meanings. The words have separate entries in the dictionary.

WE DO IT

- Write on the board two definitions of *can*: *to be able to* and a *metal container*.

- Help children identify context clues in each sentence to figure out which meaning goes with which homograph in the two sentences.

- Draw a line from each sentence to the correct meaning of *can*.

YOU DO IT

- Provide sentences for children to identify homographs, circle context clues, and determine the meanings of the homographs.

- Have children explain how they determined the meanings of the homographs.

On Level

ELA L.2.4a
ELD ELD.PI.2.1

I DO IT

- Write *ball* on the left side of the board. Write *ball* again on the right side of the board.

- Explain that homographs are words with the same spelling, but different meanings.

- Tell children that a homograph pair is made of two different words that have separate entries in a dictionary.

- Write the two meanings of ball. Write *fancy dance* on the left side and *round toy* on the right.

WE DO IT

- Write in the middle of the board, *I arrived at the* ball *carrying a rubber* ball *so I could play with the* ball *if I was bored at the* ball.

- Circle *ball* each time it appears in the sentence.

- Read the meanings of each homograph.

- Help children use context clues to determine which meaning *ball* has each time it appears in the sentence.

YOU DO IT

- Have children work with partners to write a sentence for each meaning of *ball*.

- Have partners read their sentences aloud while you write them on the left or right side of the board beneath the correct meaning.

Advanced

ELA L.2.4a
ELD ELD.PI.2.1

I DO IT

- Write *Hold the railing when you go down the stairs.* Then write *I can't sleep without my down pillow.*
- Point out context clues that can help readers figure out the meaning of each homograph.
- Help children define each homograph.
- Tell children that homographs have separate entries in the dictionary.

WE DO IT

- Write *bow*. Explain that this word has two different pronunciations. Pronounce *bow* /bō/ and /bou/. Repeat with children.
- Write two meanings of the homographs *bow*: *fancy ribbon* and *to bend low*.
- Have children say sentences using one of the meanings for *bow*. Make sure children are using the correct pronunciation. Write the children's sentences on the board under the correct meaning.

YOU DO IT

- Write *I can sing, A rock washed up on the river bank,* and *Feathers are very light.*
- Circle *can*, *bank*, and *light*. Tell children that they are homographs.
- Have children work with partners, and challenge them to identify homographs for each circled word and then write sentences using the the homographs they identified.

English Language Support

ELD ELD.PI.2.1

Provide Struggling Readers, On Level, and Advanced ELs proficiency-level support during differentiated instruction.

Emerging

- Use pictures to represent the homograph pairs they are presented with in their respective groups. (e.g. *can, ball, bank*)
- Hold up each picture and say the word both times. Then say the word in oral sentences while holding up the corresponding picture.
- To confirm children's understanding of the meaning of each homograph pair, say aloud a sentence containing the word and have children point to the correct picture.

Expanding

- Remind children they can use context clues, or other words and phrases that surround a word, to confirm a word's meaning.
- If appropriate, model with an example:
- Write *tie: cloth worn around the neck* and *tie: to make a knot.*
- Write *I have to* tie *my dog to the pole so she doesn't run away.*
- Guide children to use context clues to choose the correct meaning of *tie* in the sentence.

Bridging

- If children need help completing the You Do It activity in their group, encourage them to look up the homographs in a dictionary.
- Have them look up each word as they work and go through each definition to find the one that makes sense in each sentence.
- Have them explain why the other definitions listed do not make sense in context and why the definition they chose works.

Options for Reteaching

ELA RF.2.3a ELD ELD.PI.2.1

Reteach Phonics

Base Words and Endings -ed, -ing

I DO IT

- Write the word *clap* on the board. Read the word aloud and use it in a sentence. *Sometimes we clap the syllables in words.*

- Write *clapping* and read it aloud. Point out the base word, *clap,* and the ending, *-ing*. Explain that you doubled the final consonant *p* before adding the ending. Use *clapping* in a sentence.

- Repeat the procedure with the word *clapped*. Point out that *-ed* stands for /t/ in *clapped*.

WE DO IT

- Write *grab* on the board and read it aloud. Ask a volunteer to use the word in a sentence.

- Write *grabbing*. Have children blend the sounds and read the word. Ask a volunteer to use the word in a sentence.

- Repeat the procedure with *grabbed*. Point out that *-ed* stands for /d/ in *grabbed*.

- Repeat this process with *pack/packing/packed*.

YOU DO IT

- Have partners work together to read **Decodable Reader** *We Helped*.

Decodable Reader

ELA L.2.1c ELD ELD.PI.2.1

Reteach Language Arts

Pronouns

I DO IT

- Review pronouns with children.

- *I can replace nouns that tell who or what does something with the pronouns* I, he, she, it, we, *or* they. Write: *Ed writes books. He writes books.*

- *I can replace nouns that come after verbs with the pronouns* me, him, her, it, us, *or* them. Write: *Ed writes sentences. Ed writes them.*

- Then write: *Ed writes a chapter. Ed writes a chapter.* Model replacing each underlined noun.

WE DO IT

- Write this sentence on the board and tell children that it is the first sentence in a story. *My sister plays the piano.*

- Write this sentence as the next sentence in the story and underline the subject. *My sister plays my favorite song.* Ask children to choose a pronoun to replace the subject. *she*

- Then guide children as they write the next sentence and choose a pronoun to replace the object. *She plays my favorite song well. it*

YOU DO IT

- Write this sentence on the board: *Tony walks the dog.* Have children write a sentence with *Tony* as the subject. Then have them replace *Tony* with a subject pronoun. *he*

- Then write this sentence on the board: *I like Tony's sister.* Rewrite the sentence replacing *Tony's sister* with a pronoun. *her*

ELA L.2.4a ELD ELD.PI.2.1

Reteach Vocabulary Strategies

Homographs

I DO IT

- Review the **Vocabulary Strategies** with children.

- Emphasize that although homographs are spelled the same way, they have different meanings and sometimes different pronunciations.

- Remind children that they can look for context clues in a sentence to figure out which meaning of a homograph is being used.

WE DO IT

- Write on the board the sentence *The sun rose in the blue sky.* Have children read it aloud.

- Model Step 2 of the **Vocabulary Strategy** to determine the correct meaning of the homograph *rose* in the context of a specific sentence.

Think Aloud *I read the sentence* The sun rose in the blue sky. *I know the word* rose *can mean "climbed higher" or "a flower." I'll look for clues around the word* rose *to help me choose the correct meaning of the word in the sentence. I see the word* sun *and the phrase "in the sky." I know the sun moves up in the sky. I think the correct meaning of* rose *is "climbed higher."*

YOU DO IT

- Write these two sentences: *I had to pay a fine because my library book was late* and *John felt sick this morning, but now he feels fine.*

- Tell children that *fine* can mean *okay* or *money.* Have them work with partners to look for context clues to figure out which meaning of the homograph *fine* is used in each sentence.

ELA RL.2.5 ELD ELD.PI.2.1, ELD.PI.2.6, ELD.PII.2.1

Reteach Comprehension Skill

Story Structure

I DO IT

- Remind children that the *plot* tells the order of story events. At the beginning of the plot, the characters are faced with a *problem* and try to solve it. At the end of the story, the characters finally solve the problem. They find a *solution.*

WE DO IT

- Ask children to brainstorm what would happen if Mr. Tanen decided *not* to sell his ties.

- Model how to generate new plot details and a new story ending based on Mr. Tanen's decision not to sell his ties.

Think Aloud *I'm thinking about what Mr. Tanen is planning to do. It seems as if giving up his ties is a big deal for him! I wonder what would happen in the rest of this story if Mr. Tanen just couldn't sell his ties. How would the story end if this happened?*

YOU DO IT

- Distribute Graphic Organizer 10 : **Story Map.**

- Have children fill in the characters and setting of the story, as well as the story's beginning. Then, in the Middle and End portions of the Story Map, have them list the new possible plot details they have discussed, based on Mr. Tanen making a different decision on p. 19.

- Review and discuss their completed Story Maps.

Teacher Notes

Anchor Text

Paired Selection

LESSON 17

JOURNEYS

Teacher Dashboard

Log onto the Teacher Dashboard and *my*SmartPlanner. Use these searchable tools to customize lessons that achieve your instructional goals.

Interactive Whiteboard Lessons

• Vocabulary Strategies: Antonyms
• Phonics: Words with Long *i (i, igh, ie, y)*

• Write About Reading
• Narrative Writing: Story Paragraph

 **Assess It Online!**

• Weekly Tests
• Assessment-driven instruction with prescriptive feedback

Student eBook

Annotate it! Strategies for Annotation

Guide children to use digital tools for close reading.

Children may also use the interactive features in their Student eBooks to respond to prompts in a variety of ways, including:

• short-answer response
• spoken response
• fill-in-the-blank
• drag-and-drop
• multiple choice
• drawing

High-Interest Informational Texts and Multimedia

Have children explore the FYI website for additional information about topics of study.

Culturally Responsive Teaching

Readers' Theater Tell children that this week, they will be reading and thinking about why it is important to keep trying.

• Use *Luke Goes to Bat* for a Readers' Theater activity. Choose sections of the selection that include two or more characters and dialogue and assign each section to a small group.

• Choose roles for children or have them choose their own. Consider their levels of fluency, and ensure that they will be able to read their parts with ease.

• Allow children to practice reading aloud alone. Remind them to use their voices to show how a character feels. Then have small groups practice reading their section aloud together several times. Monitor groups to provide modeling and support.

• Invite each group to present their reading to another small group.

Build Language Awareness Point out examples of informal, everyday language that characters use in *Luke Goes to Bat,* and lead a discussion about why informal language is appropriate in those contexts. With English learners, discuss and explain common idioms and the use of nonstandard English in the selection, such as "'He better not mess up.'"

Language Support Card

Use the Lesson 17 Language Support Card to activate prior knowledge, frontload vocabulary, and teach academic English.

 Use the Text X-Ray on page T109 to review the language demands of *Luke Goes to Bat* with the needs of English learners in mind.

Language Workshop for Designated ELD

• Connection to Essential Question
• Vocabulary Network
• Focus on Interacting in Meaningful Ways
• Discussion Frames
• How English Works
• Word Learning Strategies

You may wish to use the following suggestions to modify instruction for some children, according to their needs.

Learner's Journal

Keeping a Learner's Journal can help children see themselves as successful, growing learners. Developing a sense of ownership in children can motivate them to reach their highest potential. Have children begin a Learner's Journal to help them keep track of their growing knowledge and skills. Depending on children's needs and skills, have them record information about what they are learning. Some examples:

- Day 1: Vocabulary: *practice, extra, hurried, curb, position, cheered, roared, final*
- Day 2: The title of the Anchor Text, *Luke Goes to Bat,* and words or pictures about the text
- Day 3: Write and draw about something new they learned about why it is important to keep trying. To help, you might want to discuss with children the Essential Question and their ideas about it.
- Day 4: Write one or more words they have learned to spell this week.
- Day 5: Write about how they are becoming better writers. For example, "I am learning to write a story paragraph."

Student eBook

- **Audio** can be activated to support fluency, decoding, and comprehension.
- **Alternative Text** provides spoken information that can be used in place of the information provided in the book's images.
- **Vocabulary Pop-Ups** contain point-of-use definitions for selection vocabulary.

History-Social Science

People Who Made a Difference: Civil Rights Even after Jackie Robinson's remarkable career in baseball, he continued to make a difference in the lives of African Americans. Have children explore and share biographies of other civil rights heroes.

- Collect print and digital biographical accounts of civil rights leaders, such as Rosa Parks, Martin Luther King Jr., Thurgood Marshall, César Chávez, Dolores Huerta, Roberto Clemente, Stuart Ishimaru, and Rose Ochi.
- Have children choose a biographical account of a civil rights leader to read. After, have them collect an image and write a short paragraph to describe how the person they read about stood up for others and helped bring about change.
- Invite partners or small groups to discuss the biographies they read and how the subject of the biography made others' lives better.
- Create a "People Who Made a Difference" class book or display, and have children add their summaries to it.

LESSON 17

Our Focus Wall

Paired Selection

Luke Goes to Bat
Realistic Fiction

Jackie Robinson
Informational Text (Biography)

ESSENTIAL QUESTION

Why is it important to keep trying even if something is difficult to do?

FOUNDATIONAL SKILLS

☑ High-Frequency Words

any	room
blue	studied
carry	sure
doing	teacher
else	turned

Phonics

Long *i* (*i, igh, ie, y*)

Fluency

Stress

READING LITERATURE & INFORMATIONAL TEXT

Comprehension Skills and Strategies

☑ **TARGET SKILL**
• Sequence of Events
• Formal and Informal Language

☑ **TARGET STRATEGY**
• Visualize

LANGUAGE

☑ Target Vocabulary

practice	extra
hurried	curb
position	cheered
roared	final

Vocabulary Strategies

Antonyms

Grammar

Subject-Verb Agreement

Spelling

Long *i* (*i, igh, y*)

night	right
kind	high
spy	wild
child	July
light	fry
find	sigh

WRITING

Writing

Narrative Writing:
Story Paragraph
Focus Trait: Development

Whole Group Resources

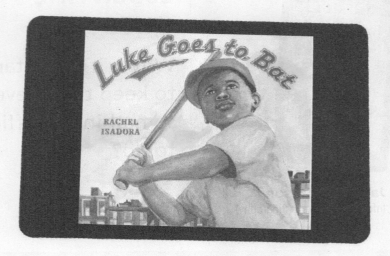

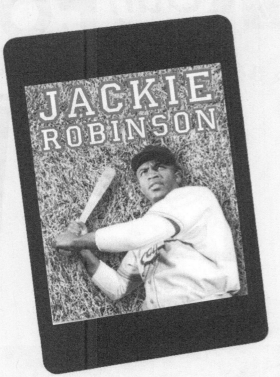

Luke Goes to Bat
GENRE: Realistic Fiction

21st Century Theme: Global Awareness

Prepare for Complex Texts For a comprehensive overview and analysis of key ideas and academic language features of this lesson's Anchor Text, see pages T108–T109.

Jackie Robinson
GENRE: Informational Text

Digital Resources

▶ **eBook: Annotate it!**

▶ **Interactive Whiteboard Lessons**
  • Vocabulary Strategies: Antonyms
  • Phonics: Words with Long *i (i, igh, ie, y)*

▶ **GrammarSnap Videos**
  • Subject-Verb Agreement

▶ **Multimedia Grammar Glossary**

▶ *my*SmartPlanner

▶ **Parent Resource**

Additional Resources

• Vocabulary in Context Cards 129–136
• Reader's Notebook, pp. 16–30
• Independent Reading

• Lesson 17 Blackline Masters
• Decodable Readers
• Blend-It Books 113–116

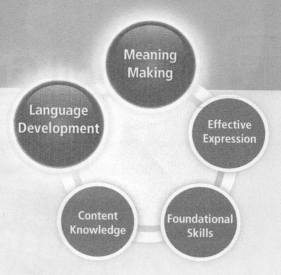

Meaning Making

Language Development

Effective Expression

Content Knowledge

Foundational Skills

LINGUISTICALLY DIVERSE LEARNERS

∨ Integrated English Language Support

Interacting in Meaningful Ways

Classroom Conversations
- Talk About It, p. T123
- Collaborative Conversation, pp. T114, T135, T146, T172
- Turn and Talk, p. T146

Interactive and Collaborative Writing
- Story Paragraph, p. T149
- Write About Reading, p. T147

Learning About How English Works

Scaffold the Texts
- Text X-Ray: Focus on Academic Language, p. T109
- Prepositional Phrases, p. T131

Communicative Modes
- Interpretive, p. T114
- Collaborative, pp. T120, T146
- Productive, p. T159

Using Foundational Literacy Skills

Support Linguistic Transfer
- Words with Long *i (i, igh, ie, y),* pp. T116, T138
- Singular-Subject Pronouns and Verbs, p. T158

Fluency: Stress, pp. T153, T191

Phonics, pp. T116–T117, T118, T142–T143, T152–T153, T162–T163, T184–T185, T190–T191

Apply Language Skills
- Subject-Verb Agreement, pp. T174–T175

∨ Standard English Learners

- Final *s* in Third-Person Present-Tense Regular Verbs, p. T148

ASSESSMENT

Formative Assessment
- Phonics: Long *i (i, igh, ie, y),* pp. T117, T152
- Target Vocabulary, p. T121
- Decodable Reader, p. T119
- Target Skill: Sequence of Events, p. T145
- Vocabulary Strategies: Antonyms, p. T167
- Using Data to Adjust Instruction, p. T179

Assess It Online!
- Weekly Test

Performance Tasks
- Write About Reading, p. T147
- Story Paragraph, p. T139

Vocabulary Reader

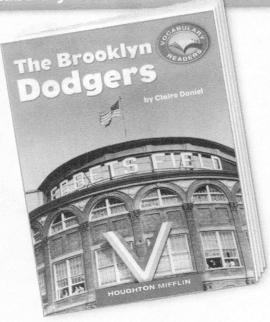

The Brooklyn Dodgers
by Claire Daniel

● Vocabulary Reader
for all levels

Provide strategic scaffolding to support all students in reading on-level text and in acquiring general academic and domain-specific vocabulary. Use the instructional supports on pp. T186–T187 or the Leveled Reader Teacher's Guide.

Guided Reading Level: J

Lexile: 570

DRA: 18

Leveled Reader Teacher's Guide

Weekly Leveled Readers

Guide children to read and comprehend additional texts about the lesson topic.
Use the instructional supports on pp. T192–T195 or the Leveled Reader Teacher's Guides.

Struggling Readers

Guided Reading Level: G

Lexile: 170

DRA: 12

Leveled Reader Teacher's Guide

On Level

Guided Reading Level: K

Lexile: 440

DRA: 20

Leveled Reader Teacher's Guide

Advanced

Guided Reading Level: M

Lexile: 660

DRA: 28

Leveled Reader Teacher's Guide

English Language Learners

Guided Reading Level: K

Lexile: 460

DRA: 20

Leveled Reader Teacher's Guide

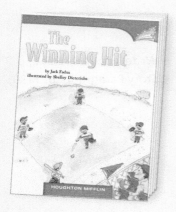

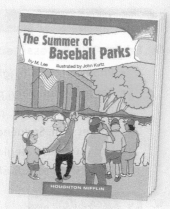

Language Workshop for Designated ELD

- Provides an additional hour of daily instruction for targeted language support.

- **Supports English learners** at three different proficiency levels as they dig deeper into the language of the lesson texts.

- Guides students in collaboration, interpretation, and production of English.

Lesson 17 Focus

Collaborate: Ask and Answer *wh* Questions; Listen

Interpret: Analyze Language Choices

Produce: Write Collaboratively; Recount Experiences

How English Works: Conjunctions

Vocabulary Network

Intervention

 Strategic Intervention Tier II

Write-In Reader: *True Heroes*

- Interactive worktext with selection that connects to the lesson topic
- Reinforces the lesson's vocabulary and comprehension
- Builds skills for reading increasingly complex texts
- Online version with dual-speed audio and follow-text

Daily Lessons See this week's daily Strategic Intervention Lesson on pp. S12–S21.

- Preteach and reteach daily instruction
- Oral Grammar
- Words to Know
- Decoding
- Comprehension
- Fluency
- Grammar
- Written Response
- Unpack Meaning

Curious About Words Provides oral vocabulary instruction for children with limited vocabularies.

 HMH Decoding Power: Intensive Reading Instruction

- **Provides reteaching and practice in the key foundational skills** for reading: print concepts, phonological/phonemic awareness, phonics and word recognition, and fluency.

- **Explicit, sequential, and systematic instruction** designed to bring students up to grade level.

 Assess It Online!

Intervention Assessments place individual students within the system, ensure students are making satisfactory progress, and provide a measure of student readiness to exit the system.

What My Other Students Are Doing

Digital Resources

Literacy Centers: Word Study, Think and Write, Comprehension and Fluency

Additional Resources

- Vocabulary in Context Cards 129–136
- Reader's Notebook, pp. 16–30
- Independent Reading
- Lesson 17 Blackline Masters
- Decodable Readers
- Blend-It Books 113–116

Literacy Centers

Comprehension and Fluency

Materials

- Student Book
- Decodable Reader: *Wild Cats*
- Audio
- Timer
- Paper and pencil

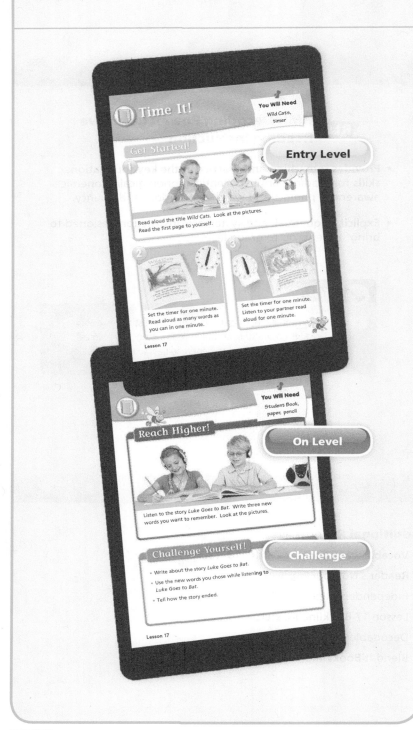

Word Study

Materials

- Context Cards: *practice, hurried, position, roared, extra, curb, cheered, final*
- Word Cards: *cry, fly, high, knight, pie, tie*
- Letter Cards: *ie, igh, y*
- Empty box labeled: "Put Cards Here"
- Books

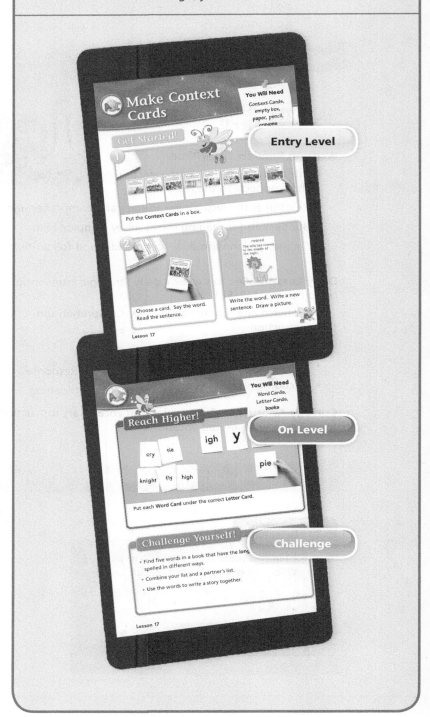

Assign Literacy Center activities during small group time. Each center contains three activities. Children who experience success with the entry-level activity move on to the on-level and challenge activities, as time permits.

Meaning Making

Effective Expression

Language Development

Content Knowledge

Foundational Skills

Think and Write

Materials

- Student Book
- Paper, pencil, crayons
- Child-made pages

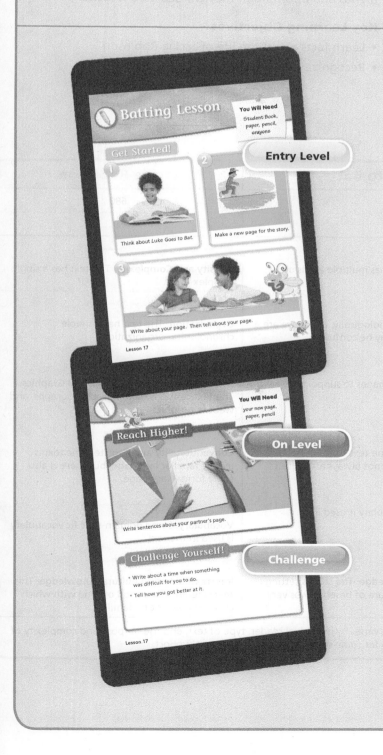

Independent Reading

Opportunities for Social Interaction Discussing books with classmates gives children the opportunity to share what they know and to learn about other books. Schedule time for sharing opportunities like these:

- **Book Talks and Reviews** Children work in small groups to talk about their books. They show the book, give the title, author, and a short summary. They tell what they liked or didn't like, and if they would recommend the book.

- **Book Sharing** Set up a basket or separate area in the library for sharing. Children place books they think others will like in this area.

- **Partner Reading** Partners read the same book. They alternate reading aloud sentences, paragraphs, or pages. Then they discuss what they have read.

- **Discussion Circles** Children who have read the same book or books on the same topic hold a discussion. You may want to appoint one group member to act as moderator to make sure that everyone has the opportunity to share.

See pp. T154–T155 for additional independent reading support. **ELA** RL.2.10, RI.2.10

Prepare for Complex Texts

Luke Goes to Bat
by Rachel Isadora

GENRE: Realistic Fiction

Why This Text?
Children need practice identifying fantasy and reality in stories. This realistic fiction story combines both realistic events and imagined ones through the main character, who likes to daydream.

Key Learning Objectives
- Understand the sequence of events in the story.
- Observe the difference between formal and informal language.

Jackie Robinson

GENRE: Informational Text

Why This Text?
Children will regularly encounter informational text on the Internet. This text is a biography that gives children exposure to the types of menus and information they will see on a website.

Key Learning Objectives
- Learn facts about the life of Jackie Robinson.
- Recognize the features of a website.

▲ TEXT COMPLEXITY RUBRIC

		Luke Goes to Bat	Jackie Robinson
Quantitative Measures	Lexile	430	680
	Guided Reading Level	K	L
Qualitative Measures	Purpose/Levels of Meaning	**Density and Complexity:** The text has multiple levels of meaning.	**Density and Complexity:** The text has a single complex topic.
	Text Structure	**Organization:** The text is told chronologically, but there are a few imaginative sequences that may be confusing.	**Organization:** The text has a simple chronological organization.
		Use of Images: The text relies on images to support comprehension in some areas.	**Use of Images, Text Features, and Graphics:** The text contains headings, photographs, and website graphics.
	Language Features	**Standard English and Variations:** The text contains both formal and informal English that is not always attributed.	**Conventionality and Register:** The text is mostly familiar language, but there is also some formal language.
		Vocabulary: Domain-specific vocabulary is used in explanations and dialogue.	**Vocabulary:** Some domain-specific vocabulary is used in the text.
	Knowledge Demands	**Intertextuality and Cultural Knowledge:** The story's setting represents a time in which the culture of baseball was very different than it is today.	**Intertextuality and Cultural Knowledge:** This text references a period of time with which children may not be familiar.
Reader/Task Considerations		Determine using the professional judgment of the teacher. This varies by individual reader, type of text, and the purpose and complexity of particular tasks. See **Reader and Task Considerations** on p. T125 for some suggestions for Anchor Text support.	

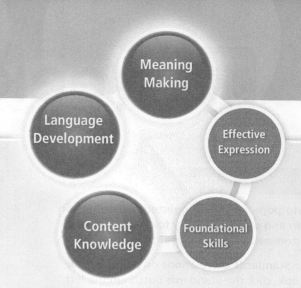

ENGLISH LANGUAGE SUPPORT Use the Text X-Ray below to prepare for teaching the Anchor Text *Luke Goes to Bat*. Use it to plan, support, and scaffold instruction in order to help children understand the text's **key ideas** and **academic language features**.

Zoom In on Key Ideas

Children should understand these **key ideas** after reading *Luke Goes to Bat*.

Key Idea | pp. 54–57

Luke really loves to play baseball, but he is not very good at it. The other kids won't let him play with them, so he just sits and watches them. In the evening, Luke goes up to the top of his apartment building to listen to the Dodgers game from nearby Ebbets Field.

Have children use the picture on pp. 56–57 to tell what Luke is imagining.

Key Idea | pp. 58–61

One day, Luke gets the chance to play ball with the other kids, but he strikes out. He goes home, where his grandma surprises him with tickets to a Dodgers game.

Have children tell how they know Luke is upset after he strikes out.

Key Idea | pp. 62–65

At the Dodgers game, Luke watches as his favorite player, Jackie Robinson, nearly strikes out but then hits a home run out of the park. Grandma tells Luke that even a player as good as Jackie Robinson has to keep trying.

Have children tell why Grandma feels Luke shouldn't give up trying.

Key Idea | pp. 66–73

Luke goes home and runs up to the top of his building. He sees the lights at Ebbets Field. He finds a ball and thinks it is the home run ball hit by Jackie Robinson! Then something special happens to Luke, and he promises he will never give up.

Have children tell how they know he took the advice Grandma and Jackie Robinson gave him.

Zoom In on Academic Language

Guide children at different proficiencies and skill levels to understand the structure and language of this text.

Focus: Text Level | pp. 58–60

Point out words that the boys use on these pages, such as *gonna, aw, mess up, stink*. Explain that these are examples of **informal language** in the text that the children use at home or when they are playing. Have the class echo-read this text with you, checking for understanding as you read.

Focus: Word Level | pp. 62–64

Point out **domain-specific vocabulary** related to baseball, such as *innings, bottom of the fourteenth, outs, curveball, strike*, and *umpire*. Explain these terms to children, acting out the actions when possible. Then have children look for other baseball words in the story.

Focus: Sentence Level | p. 65

Reread the second sentence with emphasis. Guide children to recognize the **sequence of events** in the sentence. Write the sentence on the board, and have children identify what Luke saw happen first, second, and third.

Focus: Text Level | pp. 68–71

Explain that the text makes it appear that Luke is really speaking to Jackie Robinson and seeing the teammates on the roof of his apartment. Explain that Luke is imagining these things. Have children refer to the pictures to explain how they know Luke is imagining these events.

Content and Language Instruction

Make note of additional **content knowledge** and **language features** children may find challenging in this text.

Weekly Planner

DAY 1

Materials
- Blend-It Books: Books 113–116
- Common Core Writing Handbook, Lesson 17
- Decodable Reader: *Bright Lights*
- GrammarSnap Video: Subject-Verb Agreement
- High-Frequency Word Cards 161–170
- Instructional Routines 3, 6, 11, 13
- Language Support Card, Lesson 17
- Letter Cards; Sound/Spelling Card: ice cream
- Literacy and Language Guide, pp. 88–89
- Projectables S1, 17.1, 17.2, 17.3
- Reader's Notebook Vol 2 pp. 16–17
- Retelling Cards 65–68
- Student Book pp. 48–73
- Vocabulary in Context Cards 129–136

DAY 2

Materials
- Decodable Reader: *Bright Lights*
- GrammarSnap Video: Subject-Verb Agreement
- Graphic Organizer 4
- High-Frequency Word Cards 161–170
- Instructional Routines 3, 12
- Letter Cards
- Literacy and Language Guide, pp. 88–89
- Projectables S1, 17.4, 17.5
- Reader's Notebook Vol 2 pp. 18–21
- Sound/Spelling Card: ice cream
- Student Book pp. 52–77
- Vocabulary in Context Cards 129–136

Whole Group

Daily Language
- Oral Vocabulary
- Phonemic Awareness
- Speaking and Listening

Day 1:
Opening Routines, T112–T113
Read Aloud "The Crowd Roared!" T114–T115
Phonemic Awareness, T116

Day 2:
Opening Routines, T140–T141
Phonemic Awareness, T142

Vocabulary
Text-Based Comprehension
- Skills and Strategies
- Craft and Structure

Day 1:
☑ **Introduce Target Vocabulary** T120–T121
☑ **Read and Comprehend** T122–T123
FIRST READ **Think Through the Text**
Read the Anchor Text: *Luke Goes to Bat,* T124–T137
Research/Media Literacy, T173

Day 2:
☑ **Dig Deeper,** T144–T145
- Sequence of Events
- Formal and Informal Language
SECOND READ **Analyze the Text**
Reread the Anchor Text: *Luke Goes to Bat,* T124–T135
Your Turn, T146–T147
Research/Media Literacy, T173

Foundational Skills
- Phonics and Word Recognition
- Fluency

Day 1:
☑ **Fluency**
Stress, T114
☑ **Phonics**
- Long *i* (*i, igh, ie, y*), T116–T118
Read *Bright Lights,* T119

Day 2:
☑ **Fluency**
Stress, T143
☑ **Phonics**
- Long *i* (*i, igh, ie, y*), T142–T143

Whole Group Language Arts

Spelling
Grammar
Writing

Day 1:
☑ **Spelling**
Long *i* (*i, igh, y*); Pretest T138
☑ **Grammar**
Subject-Verb Agreement, T138
Daily Proofreading Practice, T139
☑ **Narrative Writing:**
Story Paragraph
Introduce the Model, T139

Day 2:
☑ **Spelling**
Long *i* (*i, igh, y*), T148
☑ **Grammar**
Subject-Verb Agreement, T148
Daily Proofreading Practice, T149
☑ **Narrative Writing:**
Story Paragraph
Focus Trait: Development, T149

Small Group

Suggestions for Small Groups (See pp. T181–T199.)

Language Workshop

Designated English Language Support

Day 1:
Connect to Text: *Luke Goes to Bat*
Introduce Vocabulary Network: Words About Overcoming Problems

Day 2:
Expand Vocabulary Network
Collaborate: Ask and Answer Questions; Listen Attentively

---

iRead Use *iRead*, an adaptive digital foundational reading skills program, to personalize learning for students.

Integrated English Language Support
See page T103 for instructional support activities for Diverse Linguistic Learners.

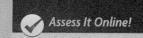 *Assess It Online!*
▶ Lesson 17 Assessment

DAY 3

Materials
- Cold Reads
- Decodable Reader: *Wild Cats*
- GrammarSnap Video: Subject-Verb Agreement
- Graphic Organizer 4
- High-Frequency Word Cards 161–170
- Instructional Routine 15
- Letter Cards; Picture Cards; Word Cards
- Literacy and Language Guide, pp. 88–89, 148–149
- Projectables 17.6, 17.7
- Reader's Notebook Vol 2 pp. 22–26
- Student Book pp. 52–73
- Vocabulary in Context Cards 129–136

Opening Routines, T150–T151
Phonemic Awareness, T152

Independent Reading, T154–T155
- Reader's Guide: *Luke Goes to Bat*
- Self-Selected Reading
- Self-Correction Strategies

Apply Vocabulary Knowledge, T156–T157

Research/Media Literacy, T173

☑ **Fluency**
Stress, T153
☑ **Phonics**
- Review, T152

☑ **Spelling**
Long *i (i, igh, y),* T158
☑ **Grammar**
Subject-Verb Agreement, T158
Daily Proofreading Practice, T159
☑ **Narrative Writing:**
Story Paragraph
Prewrite, T159

DAY 4

Materials
- Decodable Reader: *Wild Cats*
- High-Frequency Word Cards 161–170
- Instructional Routine 14
- Interactive Whiteboard Lesson: Antonyms
- Literacy and Language Guide, pp. 88–89
- Projectables 17.7, 17.8, 17.9
- Reader's Notebook Vol 2 pp. 27–29
- Sound/Spelling Cards: eagle, ocean
- Student Book pp. 78–81
- Vocabulary in Context Cards 129–136

Opening Routines, T160–T161
Phonemic Awareness, T162

Connect to the Topic
- Read Informational Text: *Jackie Robinson,* T164–T165
- Introduce Genre and Text Focus, T164
☑ **Compare Texts,** T165
☑ **Vocabulary Strategies,** Antonyms, T166–T167

Research/Media Literacy, T173

☑ **Fluency**
Stress, T163
☑ **Phonics**
- Phonics Review, T162–T163

☑ **Spelling**
Long *i (i, igh, y),* T168
☑ **Grammar**
Spiral Review, T168
Daily Proofreading Practice, T169
☑ **Narrative Writing:**
Story Paragraph
Draft, T169

DAY 5

Materials
- Blackline Masters: Writing Rubric, Proofreading Checklist
- Graphic Organizer 6
- High-Frequency Word Cards 161–170
- Interactive Whiteboard Lesson: Phonics: Words with Long *i (i, igh, ie, y)*
- Projectable 17.10
- Reader's Notebook Vol 2 p. 30
- Student Book pp. 82–85
- Vocabulary in Context Cards 129–136
- Close Reader, Lesson 17

Opening Routines, T170–T171
Speaking and Listening, T173

Close Reader
- Lesson 17
Extend the Topic
- Domain-Specific Vocabulary, T172
- Research/Media Skills: Compare and Contrast Media Messages, T173
- Optional Second Read: *Jackie Robinson,* T164–T165

☑ **Fluency**
Stress, T179
☑ **Phonics**
- Phonics Review, T171

☑ **Spelling**
Assess, T174
☑ **Grammar**
Subject-Verb Agreement, T174–T175
Daily Proofreading Practice, T176
☑ **Narrative Writing:**
Story Paragraph
Revise and Edit, T176–T177

 Tier II Intervention provides 30 minutes of additional daily practice with key parts of the core instruction. (See pp. S12–S21.)

Interpret: Analyze Language Choices
Unpack a Sentence

Produce: Write an Informational Report
Focus on How English Works: Use Conjunctions to Connect Ideas

Share and Reflect

DAY 1

Today's Goals

Vocabulary & Oral Language

- **Teacher Read Aloud:**
  "The Crowd Roared!"
- **Oral Vocabulary**
- **Listening Comprehension**
- **Introduce Vocabulary**

☑ TARGET VOCABULARY

practice	extra
hurried	curb
position	cheered
roared	final

Phonemic Awareness

- **Segment Phonemes**

Phonics & Fluency

- **Long** *i (i, igh, ie, y)*
- **Read Decodable Reader:**
  Bright Lights
- **Fluency:** Stress
- **High-Frequency Words**

Text-Based Comprehension

- **Read and Comprehend**
- **Read the Anchor Text:**
  Luke Goes to Bat

Grammar & Writing

- **Subject-Verb Agreement**
- **Narrative Writing:**
  Story Paragraph

Spelling

- **Long** *i (i, igh, y)*

Opening Routines

Warm Up with Wordplay

Share a Riddle

Display and read aloud the following riddle:

> ## How do baseball players stay cool?

Have children turn and talk to a partner to discuss their responses before you tell them the correct answer: *They sit next to the fans!* Remind them to use discussion rules.

Then discuss the multiple-meaning word *fan*. Tell children that a fan is someone who watches a baseball game, but it is also the name of a machine with spinning blades that keeps you cool in hot weather. Explain that this week, children will read a story about a boy who wants more than anything to play baseball. **ELA** SL.2.1a **ELD** ELD.PI.2.1

Daily Phonemic Awareness

Segment Phonemes

- *We're going to listen for sounds in words. Say this word:* kid. *What is the first sound you hear?* /k/ *What is the next sound you hear?* /ĭ/ Remind children that /ĭ/ is the short *i* sound. *What is the last sound you hear in the word kid?* /d/

- Continue with the word *kind*. Have children sound out the word and identify the phonemes. Say: *The vowel sound in* kind *is the long* i *sound,* /ī/.

- Continue with these words: *fin/find; kit/kite; stick/strike; bin/bind; rink/rind; bit/bite.*

Corrective Feedback

- If a child is unable to segment the phonemes, say the word, give correction, and model the task. Example: *The word is* sit. *The first sound is* /s/. *The next sound I hear is the short* i *sound,* /ĭ/. *The last sound that I hear is* /t/: /s/ /ĭ/ /t/, sit.

- Have children segment the words with you before doing the task on their own.

Daily High-Frequency Words

- Point to the High-Frequency Words on the Focus Wall. Say: *Our new High-Frequency Words for this week are* doing, else, *and* room. *Our review words are* any, blue, carry, studied, sure, teacher, *and* turned. *You will see these words in your reading.*

- Use <u>Instructional Routine 11</u> and **High-Frequency Word Card 161** to introduce the word *doing*.

- Repeat with **High-Frequency Word Cards 162–170** for the words *else, turned, blue, room, teacher, any, studied, carry,* and *sure*.
  ELA RF.2.3f

Corrective Feedback

- If a child does not recognize the word *doing*, say the correct word and have children repeat it. *Doing. What is the word?* doing

- Have children spell the word. *d-o-i-n-g How do we say this word?* doing

- Have children reread all of the cards in random order.

Daily Vocabulary Boost

- Have children think about a sport or competition in which they have taken part. Preview the Target Vocabulary by displaying the **Vocabulary in Context Cards** and discussing the words. For example, use sentences such as these to discuss the words *practice* and *roared*.

  When people practice *something, they learn to do it better.*

  The crowd roared *loudly when the baseball player hit a homerun.*

- Tell children that they will find these and other Vocabulary Words when they read *Luke Goes to Bat*.

practice
If you practice hitting the baseball every day, your hitting will get better.

Vocabulary in Context Cards
129–136

✓ **Target Vocabulary**

practice
hurried
position
roared
extra
curb
cheered
final

Teacher Read Aloud

▶ SHARE OBJECTIVES

- Listen to fluent reading.
- Retell key details from the story.
- Speak using complete sentences. LANGUAGE
- Identify and use prepositional phrases that tell "how" in sentences. LANGUAGE

PREVIEW
☑ TARGET VOCABULARY

hurried did something quickly

cheered shouted to show happiness

extra more of something

final last

practice to do an activity often to become better at it

curb the edge of a road

position the place where something or someone is supposed to be

roared shouted in a powerful voice

ENGLISH LANGUAGE SUPPORT

Comprehensible Input

All Proficiencies To assist children with accessing the content and topic of the Teacher Read Aloud, complete the Build Background activities on Lesson 17 **Language Support Card.**

Model Fluency

Stress Explain that when good readers read aloud, they say some words with more force, or stress. Stressing words gives some words more importance, creating meaning and understanding for the listener.

- Display Projectable 17.1 ⬈. As you read the second sentence, stress *finished*. Then reread the sentence, this time stressing *could*. Explain that the meaning of the text changes with which words are stressed. When the word *finished* is stressed, the idea that Minna must finish her homework is the most important idea. When the word *could* is stressed, watching soccer becomes just one option after finishing her homework. Then continue with the rest of the sentences.

- Read aloud the selection. Stress words correctly to emphasize the author's intended meaning. When finished, reread **Projectable 17.1** with children, reviewing with them which words to stress.

Listening Comprehension

Read aloud the story. Pause at the numbered stopping points to ask children the questions below. Discuss the meanings of the highlighted words, as needed, to support the discussion. Tell children they will learn more about the words later in the lesson. **ELA** SL.2.2 **ELD** ELD.PI.2.5

1 *Who is the main character?* Minna IDENTIFY STORY STRUCTURE

2 *What problem does Minna have?* Sample answer: She loves soccer, but she is afraid to join a team because she does not think she will play well. ANALYZE STORY STRUCTURE

3 *How does Javier respond when Minna tells him how she feels?* Sample answer: He gives her a private lesson. UNDERSTANDING CHARACTERS

4 *How is Minna different at the end of the story from how she was at the beginning of the story?* She has some experience playing soccer and feels confident enough to join a team. UNDERSTANDING CHARACTERS

💬 Classroom Collaboration

Support children as they work together to retell "The Crowd Roared!" in their own words. Remind them to use complete sentences in their retelling. **ELA** SL.2.2, SL.2.6 **ELD** ELD.PI.2.1, ELD.PI.2.5

🔍 Language Detective

How English Works: Prepositional Phrases Tell children that authors sometimes use phrases to add detail to their writing. Display and read an example, such as the last sentence in the first paragraph. Tell children that *above their heads* is a prepositional phrase that tells how. *How did they wave their arms? Above their heads.* Reread the paragraph, and have children give a thumbs-up when they hear the prepositional phrase. Guide children to write new sentences using phrases that tell how. **ELD** ELD.PII.2.5

The Crowd Roared!

1 After dinner, Minna **hurried** to do her homework. When she finished she could watch the end of the soccer game on TV. She loved watching soccer. She loved how the crowds shouted and **cheered** and waved their arms above their heads every time a player scored a goal.

Minna's mom came in to watch a bit too. She smiled when she saw how much Minna was enjoying the match.

"Why don't you join a team?" asked Minna's mom. "You might like playing soccer, you know."

But Minna didn't want to try. "I'll be no good at it," she complained. "I've never done it before. I don't like doing things I'm not good at."

Minna's mom shook her head. "Well, you'll never learn how if you don't try," she said.

The next day, Minna was walking home from school with her friend Javier. She was telling him about last night's match. It was **extra** special because her two favorite teams had played against each other. Minna was very happy with the **final** score—1 to 1—a tie. Neither of her teams had lost!

2 "Yeah, that sounds great," said Javier, sounding kind of bored. "I prefer to play soccer myself, not watch it on TV. You know," he said, perking up a bit, "the fall soccer season is about to start. You could join a team!"

Minna opened her mouth to reply. She was about to say the same thing to Javier that she had said to her mom.

"Well, I might like to," said Minna, "but the truth is I'm afraid I won't be any good. I don't know how to kick the ball correctly or pass. Everyone will laugh at me."

"Maybe," said Javier, "but who cares? It's true, it takes time to learn, but you'll get better every time you **practice**, and then you'll start to enjoy it more. I know that was true for me. Besides, even if you aren't the best at something, it can still be fun."

Minna and Javier had reached his house. This was where they usually said goodbye. Javier pointed to the **curb** and shouted, "Sit there. I'll be back in a minute."

When Javier came out, he was carrying a soccer ball. "Let's go to the park," he said. "I can show you some basics."

3 For the next hour, Javier gave Minna her own private soccer lesson. He showed her the correct **position** of her leg when kicking and the best ways to control the ball.

Javier set their backpacks a few yards apart on the grass to act as goal posts. He played goalie, and Minna tried to kick the ball past him.

At first Javier stopped every kick that Minna made. When it was almost time to go home, Minna kicked one past him!

In her head, Minna could see the crowd waving their arms above their heads. She could hear them as they **roared** with one mighty voice, "GOAL!"

Minna and Javier picked up their things and headed home.

4 "Thanks," said Minna. "You were right. Even if I'm not the best, playing soccer would be a lot of fun. I think I'll give it a try."

Phonics

SHARE OBJECTIVES

- Identify sounds in words with long *i* spelled *i*, *igh*, *ie*, *y*.
- Learn the spelling-sound correspondences for vowel teams *(igh, ie)* (vowel team syllables) and other spellings for long *i* (*i, igh, ie, y*).
- Blend and decode regularly spelled words with long *i* spelled *i, igh, ie, y*.

SKILLS TRACE

Words with Long *i* (*i, igh, ie, y*)	
▶ Introduce	pp. T116–T117, T142–T143
Differentiate	pp. T184–T185
Reteach	p. T198
Review	pp. T162, T263, T352, T363
Assess	Weekly Tests, Lesson 17

ENGLISH LANGUAGE SUPPORT

Comprehensible Input

Emerging Reinforce the meanings of words in the Phonics lesson using **Picture Cards** *(tie, knight, pie, fly)* and gestures *(sigh, thigh, cry)*. Provide additional practice saying each word as you emphasize the long *i* sound. Have children repeat each word after you and then match the word to the image or gesture.

Expanding Display several words from the lesson, such as *tie, knight, pie, fly, sigh, thigh,* and *cry*. Read the words aloud with children and then have children read the words chorally. Have partners practice reading the words. Monitor their pronunciation of the various spellings for long *i* and provide corrective feedback as needed.

Bridging Display words with the long *i* sound spelled *i, igh, ie,* or *y*. Discuss meanings. Have children use the words in sentences.

Words with Long *i* (*i, igh, ie, y*)

ENGLISH LANGUAGE SUPPORT Explain that unlike most languages, in English, long vowel sounds can be spelled many different ways. For example, in Spanish the sound /ē/, as in *rico*, is always spelled with an *i*, but the /ē/ sound in English can be spelled *e*-consonant-*e*, *ee*, *ea*, and other ways. The long *i* sound in English can also be spelled many different ways including *i*-consonant-*e*, *i*, *ie*, *igh*, and *y*. Write the words *mine, mind, might, tie, try*. Underline the letters in each word that make the long *i* sound and read the words with children. **ELD** ELD.PIII.2

Phonemic Awareness Warm-Up *I'll say a word. You tell the sounds you hear and name the vowel sound. I'll do it first. Listen:* kind. *Now I'll say each sound:* /k/ /ī/ /n/ /d/. *Let's do it together. Say the word* kind. *What sounds do you hear?* /k/ /ī/ /n/ /d/ *Which sound is the vowel sound?* /ī/ *What do we call that sound?* long i

Let's do some more. You say the sounds in these words and name the vowel sound: right, /r/ /ī/ /t/, *long* i; fin, /f/ /ī/ /n/, *short* i; dry, /d/ /r/ /ī/, *long* i; wild, /w/ /ī/ /l/ /d/, *long* i; trick, /t/ /r/ /ĭ/ /k/, *short* i; tie /t/ /ī/, *long* i.

1 Teach/Model

Sound/Spelling Card Display the card for *ice cream*. Name the picture and say the beginning sound. Have children repeat after you. *Listen:* ice cream, /ī/. *Now you say it.*

- Say the sound and give the spelling. *Ice cream begins with the long i sound* /ī/. Point out on the card the spelling patterns *i, ie, igh,* and *y*. *The letters* i, ie, igh, *or* y *can stand for the long* i *sound* /ī/ *at the beginning, middle, or end of a word.*

- Write and read *kind*. Point out the /ī/ spelling, *i*. *This is the word* kind. *The letter* i *stands for the long* i *sound* /ī/ *in* kind. *The letter* i *can stand for* /ī/ *at the beginning of a word but usually stands for* /ī/ *in the middle of a word, especially in the patterns* ild *and* ind. Read the word together: kind.

- Write and read *tie*. Point out the /ī/ spelling, *ie*. *This is the word* tie. *The letters* ie *together stand for the long* i *sound* /ī/ *at the end of* tie. *The letters* ie *often stand for the long* i *sound* /ī/ *at the end of a word.* Read the word together: tie.

- Repeat with the *igh* and *y* spellings for /ī/, using the words *night* and *spy*. Explain that *y* can stand for the long *i* sound /ī/ at the end of a one-syllable word.

i
i_e
ie
igh
—y

2 Guided Practice

Continuous Blending Routine Use Instructional Routine 3 to model blending *light*.

- Display **Letter Cards** *l, igh, t*. Name the letters. Remind children that *i, igh, ie,* or *y* can stand for the /ī/ sound.

- Blend the sounds, stretching out the word while pointing to each letter in a sweeping motion. *Listen: /l/ /ī/ /t/.* Have children blend with you. *Blend with me: /l/ /ī/ /t/, light.* Then have children blend on their own.

Blending Lines

Blend Words Have children read the following words chorally; provide Corrective Feedback as needed. Help children compare the sounds and spellings in each line.

1. sit	sight	flit	flight	fit	fight
2. my	might	tie	tight	fry	fright
3. die	thigh	why	sigh	wild	knight

Transition to Longer Words Have children read the following words chorally. Ask children to identify known word parts in each longer word that helped them decode it.

4. high	highway	try	trying	light	delight
5. cry	cried	ply	reply	kind	kindly
6. spy	spying	bind	blind	pie	pies

Challenge Call on above-level children to read the words in Line 7 and discuss the elements. Then have the class read the sentences chorally.

7. midnight mighty supply multiply item wildflower
8. Ty is <u>doing</u> something <u>else</u> tonight.
9. I'm <u>sure</u> Kim will be selling her pies. **ELA** RF.2.3a, RF.2.3b, RF.2.3c

3 Apply

Have partners take turns rereading Blending Lines 1–3 and 4–6. On a sheet of paper, have children make four columns and label them *i, igh, ie,* and *y*. Tell children to sort the words into lists according to their long *i* spelling. Have partners read the lists of sorted words. **ELA** RF.2.3a, RF.2.3b

Distribute <u>Reader's Notebook Volume 2 page 16</u> or <u>leveled practice</u> in Grab-and-Go™ Resources to children to complete independently.

Corrective Feedback When a child mispronounces a letter-sound, highlight that letter, restate its sound, have children repeat the sound, and then guide them to blend the word. See the example below.

Decoding Error:
A child reads *light* in Line 4 as *lit*.

Correct the error. Say the word and remind children that /ī/ can be spelled *i, igh, ie,* or *y*. *The word is* light. *The letters* igh *together stand for the sound* /ī/.

Model as you touch the letters. *I'll blend: /l/ /ī/ /t/. What is the word?* light

Guide *Let's blend together: /l/ /ī/ /t/. What is the word?* light

Check *You blend. /l/ /ī/ /t/ What is the word?* light

Reinforce Go back three or four words and have children continue reading. Make note of errors and review those words during the next lesson.

 Go to pp. T184–T185 for additional phonics support.

DAY 1

Phonics

▶ **SHARE OBJECTIVES**

- Write words with the long *i* sound spelled *i, igh, ie, y*.
- Read on-level text with long *i* words spelled *i, igh, ie, y* and High-Frequency Words.
- Practice reading fluently, placing stress on important words.

▶ **DICTATION SENTENCES**

- **mind** Do you *mind* if I wait here?
- **fly** We will *fly* home on a jet.
- **might** Jill *might* go with us.
- **tie** I will *tie* string around the package.
- **dry** The towels aren't *dry* yet.
- **sight** You use your sense of *sight* to see.

ENGLISH LANGUAGE SUPPORT

Use Visuals and Gestures

All Proficiencies Use **Picture Cards**, objects, photographs, simple sketches, gestures, and pantomime to help convey the meanings of words in the dictation. Have children say each word with you as you present its meaning. For example, use **Picture Cards** *fly* and *tie* to help show the meanings of those words. Discuss the fact that these words have other meanings as well. Gesture to a child's laced shoes, and say *We tie our shoes every morning.* Display a photograph of a plane and say *I will fly away on a plane.* Display a photo of a clothes dryer or a clothesline and say *We use this to dry our clothes.* Then say the words at random and ask children to match the word to an image or gesture.

Blend-It Books

To provide reading practice with new sound/spellings in decodable texts, see **Blend-It Books** 113–116.

Write Words with Long *i* (*i, igh, ie, y*)

1 Teach/Model

Connect Sounds to Spelling Review **Sound/Spelling Card** *ice cream.* Tell children that they will write words with different spellings for the long *i* sound /ī/.

Use Instructional Routine 6 ⬀ to dictate the first sentence at left. *Listen as I say a word and use it in a sentence.*

- Model how to spell the word *mind.* *The first sound I hear in mind is /m/. I know that m stands for the sound /m/, so I'll start by writing m. I remember that i by itself is one way to spell the long i sound /ī/, so I'll write i next. The final two sounds in mind are /n/ /d/; I'll write the letters n and d. Then I'll reread to check:* mind.

2 Guided Practice

Connect Sounds to Writing Continue the dictation, using the sentences at left.

- Have children say each dictation word aloud after you. Then have them identify the sounds they hear at the beginning, middle, and end and write the letters that spell each sound. **ELA** RF.2.3b, L.2.2d

- Remind children to write only the dictation word.

3 Apply

Read aloud the following decodable sentence for children to write. Remind children to look at the Focus Wall if they need help spelling *doing* or *else.* Then have children read the sentence aloud. **ELA** RF.2.3f, L.2.2d

> Why might you be <u>doing</u> something <u>else</u> this week?

Print the dictation words and decodable sentence for children to check their work.

Decodable Reader

Read *Bright Lights*

Review /ī/ and High-Frequency Words Review **Sound/Spelling Card** *ice cream* and the High-Frequency Words *any*, *blue*, *carry*, *doing*, *else*, *room*, *studied*, *sure*, *teacher*, and *turned*. Tell children that the story includes many words with the long *i* sound /ī/ as well as some High-Frequency Words.

Preview Have children read the title, browse the beginning pages, and discuss what they think the story is about.

Use Projectable S1 to review the **Phonics/Decoding Strategy.** Model the strategy using the title.

Have children read the first page silently. Then ask a child to read the page aloud as others follow. Repeat for each page.

ENGLISH LANGUAGE SUPPORT Guide children whose first language uses different conventions to identify statements and questions in the story. Remind them that statements are sentences that tell something and end with a period. Questions are sentences that ask something. They end with a question mark.
ELD ELD.PIII.2

If children make more than six total errors, use the **Corrective Feedback** steps to help them reread aloud with accuracy. If they make fewer than six errors, have them reread and retell the story.

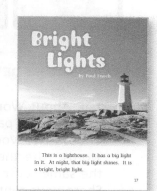

This is a lighthouse. It has a big light in it. At night, that big light shines. It is a bright, bright light.

17

Decodable Reader

Corrective Feedback When a child mispronounces a word, point to the word and say it. Call attention to the element that was mispronounced, say the sound, and then guide children to read the word. See the example below.

Decoding Error:
A child reads *bright* on page 1 as *bit*.

Correct the error. Say the word. *That word is* bright. *The letters* igh *stand for the long i sound /ī/.*

Guide Have children repeat the word. *What is the word?* bright

Check *Go back to the beginning of the sentence and read it again.*

Reinforce Record the error and review the word again before children reread the story.

Go to pp. T184–T185 for additional phonics support.

Fluency: Stress

Remind children that when good readers read aloud, their reading sounds as if they are telling a story to a friend. Good readers say important words with more force, or stress. Write and read aloud the following sentences:

> This is a lighthouse.
> It has a big light in it.

Model Fluency and Stress Read each sentence in a monotone and ask children whether your reading sounds interesting and is easy to understand. Then model using appropriate stress. *Listen to which words I say a little louder.* Reread the sentences fluently and have children repeat each one. *Let's read the sentences together. Say important words with a little more force, or stress.*

ENGLISH LANGUAGE SUPPORT As children read, monitor their pronunciation of words with the long *i* sound /ī/. Provide modeling and support as needed. **ELD** ELD.PIII.2

Responding Have children scan the text. Ask volunteers to identify and read details that tell why lighthouses are important. **ELA** RI.2.1

Reread for Fluency Use Instructional Routine 13 to reread *Bright Lights* with children. Remind children to make their voices louder to stress important words.
ELA RF.2.4b

DAY 1

Introduce Vocabulary

▶ SHARE OBJECTIVES

- Acquire and use vocabulary. LANGUAGE
- Use a variety of vocabulary in shared language activities. LANGUAGE
- Create complete sentences using multiple Vocabulary words. LANGUAGE

Teach

Display and discuss the **Vocabulary in Context Cards,** using the routine below.

1 Read and pronounce the word. Read the word once alone and then together.

2 Explain the word. Read aloud the explanation under *What Does It Mean?*

ENGLISH LANGUAGE SUPPORT Review these cognates with Spanish-speaking students.

- posición (position)
- prácticas (practice)

3 Discuss vocabulary in context. Together, read aloud the sentence on the front of the card. Help children explain and use the word in new sentences.

4 Engage with the word. Ask and discuss the *Think About It* question with children.

Practice/Apply

Give partners or small groups one or two **Vocabulary in Context Cards.** Help children complete the *Talk It Over* activities for each card. **ELA** RF.2.3f **ELD** ELD.PII.2.3a

Read aloud and have children complete the activity at the top of **Student Book** p. 48.

Then guide children to complete the Language Detective activity. Work with them to create sentences using the two Vocabulary words they chose. Have children share the sentences with the class. **ELA** RF.2.3f, SL.2.6, L.2.6 **ELD** ELD.PI.2.1, ELD.PI.2.12b

---

Lesson 17

Vocabulary in Context

🔍 **LANGUAGE DETECTIVE**

Talk About Words
Work with a partner. Choose two Vocabulary words. Use them in the same sentence. Share your sentences with the class.

48   **ELA** L.2.1f, L.2.6 **ELD** ELD.PI.2.12b

▶ Read each Context Card.

▶ Make up a new sentence that uses a Vocabulary word.

1   practice
If you practice hitting the baseball every day, your hitting will get better.

2   hurried
The soccer player hurried to stop the ball. He moved fast.

ENGLISH LANGUAGE SUPPORT

Comprehensible Input

Emerging Have children complete sentence frames about each Vocabulary word. Example: *It wasn't a bad accident, but the car did hit the _____.* **ELD** ELD.PI.2.12b

Expanding Ask children questions to confirm their understanding. Example: *What position are you in now?* **ELD** ELD.PI.2.12b

Bridging Have partners write questions and answers using Vocabulary words. Example: *When is the final class of the year?* **ELD** ELD.PI.2.12b

③ position

The batter is in position to hit the baseball.

④ roared

The crowd roared loudly as the player caught the ball.

⑤ extra

The extra players for the football team sat on the bench.

⑥ curb

After skating, the girl rested on the curb outside her house.

⑦ cheered

The audience clapped and cheered as the player scored a goal.

⑧ final

When the game ended, the final score was four to two.

49

FORMATIVE ASSESSMENT ▲ **RtI**

3
2
1

Are children able to understand and use Target Vocabulary words?

IF...	THEN...
children struggle,	▶ use **Vocabulary in Context Cards** and differentiate **Vocabulary Reader**, *The Brooklyn Dodgers*, for Struggling Readers, p. T186. *See also Intervention Lesson 17, pp. S12–S21.*
children are on track,	▶ use **Vocabulary in Context Cards** and differentiate **Vocabulary Reader**, *The Brooklyn Dodgers*, for On-Level Readers, p. T186.
children excel,	▶ differentiate **Vocabulary Reader**, *The Brooklyn Dodgers*, for Advanced Readers, p. T187.

SMALL GROUP Options

Vocabulary Reader, pp. T186–T187
Scaffold instruction to the English learner's proficiency level.

ENGLISH LANGUAGE SUPPORT

More Vocabulary Practice

Emerging/Expanding Distribute Chant, EL17.5 ⬚. Read the title aloud and have children repeat. Have children look at the title, images, and other information on the page. Then have them predict what they think the chant will be about.

- As you read the chant aloud, display the Context Cards for *cheered, hurried, roared,* and *final*. After you read the chant, have children choral read it with you.

- Have small groups act out playing baseball. Tell them to use short phrases or sentences to describe their actions.

- Allow children to include language from the chant. Encourage them to use high-utility words. **ELD** ELD.PI.2.1, ELD.PI.2.6, ELD.PI.2.12b

---

Read and Comprehend

▶ SHARE OBJECTIVES

- Identify the order of events in a story.
- Recount what happened in a story in order.
- Visualize story details as you read.
- Access prior knowledge to exchange information about a topic. LANGUAGE

☑ TARGET STRATEGY

Sequence of Events

- Read the top section of **Student Book** p. 50 with children.

- Remind children that events are things that happen in a story. Those things happen in order, or *sequence of events*.

- Point out that signal words such as *first, next, last, then,* and *finally* can help readers figure out the sequence of events.

- Draw children's attention to the graphic organizer on **Student Book** p. 50. Tell them that, as they read, they will use this flow chart to record the sequence of events by writing important events in each box as they read the story.

- Explain that at the end of the story, they will use the chart to retell the events in the order in which they happened. **ELA** RL.2.2 **ELD** ELD.PI.2.6

ENGLISH LANGUAGE SUPPORT Draw a flow chart on the board, and write *First, Next,* and *Last* in the appropriate boxes. Have children think of something they do each day, such as feed their pet. Ask them to think about the steps they follow to do this task. Then have them either write or draw the steps in the boxes on their graphic organizer in order.

Read and Comprehend

☑ TARGET SKILL

Sequence of Events In *Luke Goes to Bat*, the author tells about Luke and the things that happen to him one summer. The order in which events happen is called the **sequence of events**. Putting these events in order in a chart like the one below can help you understand the story.

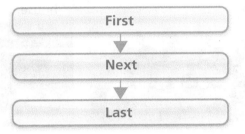

☑ TARGET STRATEGY

Visualize As you read, use text evidence to picture what is happening. This will help you understand and remember important ideas and details.

50   **ELA** RL.2.2, SL.2.1a, SL.2.3 **ELD** ELD.PI.2.1, ELD.PI.2.3, ELD.PI.2.6

Comprehensible Input

Emerging Perform a series of events such as closing a door, sitting down, and reading a book. Retell the events using signal words such as *first, next,* and *last.* Then have children complete sentence frames such as

_____ I closed the door. _____ I sat down. _____ I read a book. *first, next, last*
ELD ELD.PII.2.2

Expanding Perform a series of events. Ask children questions such as *What did I do first? next? last?* Have children answer in phrases or complete sentences. Sample answer: *First you closed the door.* **ELD** ELD.PII.2.2

Bridging Ask children to retell the sequence of events describing what they did when they woke up this morning. Remind them to use signal words. **ELD** ELD.PII.2.2

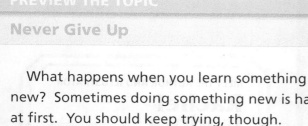

What happens when you learn something new? Sometimes doing something new is hard at first. You should keep trying, though. Think about the things that you can do now that were difficult at first. You learned many of the things you can do today by doing them over and over.

In *Luke Goes to Bat*, you will read about a boy who does not give up.

💬 Talk About It

How does practicing a new skill help you? Share your ideas with the class.

▸ Take turns speaking.

▸ Listen carefully to others.

▸ Ask questions if you don't understand.

51

COMPREHENSION STRATEGIES

Use the following strategies flexibly as you read with children by modeling how they can be used to improve comprehension and understanding of a text. See scaffolded support for the strategy shown in boldface during this week's reading.

- **Monitor/Clarify**
- **Summarize**
- **Infer/Predict**
- **Visualize**
- **Analyze/Evaluate**
- **Question**

Use Strategy Projectables 🔗 S1–S8, for additional support.

🔸 DOMAIN: Values
LESSON TOPIC: Never Give Up

✅ TARGET STRATEGY

Visualize

- Read the bottom section of **Student Book** p. 50 with students. Tell students that when you visualize something, you see a picture in your mind.

- Explain that when readers visualize what the author is describing, it can help them enjoy and remember the sequence of events in a story.

- Then explain that you will guide them to use this strategy when you read *Luke Goes to Bat* together.

PREVIEW THE TOPIC

Never Give Up

- Tell children that today they will begin to read *Luke Goes to Bat*.

- Read the information at the top of **Student Book** p. 51 with children.

- Have children share their experiences of when things have been difficult at first and they wanted to give up. Have them tell whether they chose to keep trying or to give up and why.

Talk About It

- Read the collaborative discussion prompt with children. Remind them to ask and answer questions if something isn't understood.

- Before children share their sentences with the class, tell them that it is important to stay on topic during a conversation. This means that everything partners say builds an answer to the prompt. Have a volunteer be the Helper. This child's role is to help the group to stay on topic. Guide children to make a list of the ways the Helper can get a conversation back on track.

- Remind children to follow other discussion rules, such as asking and answering questions, as they share their ideas. **ELA** SL.2.1a, SL.2.3 **ELD** ELD.PI.2.1, ELD.PI.2.3

ENGLISH LANGUAGE SUPPORT Use the image on Lesson 17 **Language Support Card** to review the lesson topic with children. Guide children to share and summarize what they have learned. **ELD** ELD.PI.2.1, ELD.PI.2.12a

DAY 1

Read the Anchor Text

 GENRE

Realistic Fiction

- Read the genre information on **Student Book** p. 52 with children.

- Preview the selection with children, and model identifying the characteristics of realistic fiction.

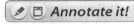 *Realistic fiction is made up, but it tells about people and events that could happen in real life.* Luke Goes to Bat *is a story about a boy who dreams of playing baseball. This could have happened, even if it is made-up. I think this story is realistic fiction.*

- As you preview, ask children to identify other features of realistic fiction. Point out Jackie Robinson and explain that he was a real baseball player. Tell children that Ebbets Field was a real baseball stadium many years ago and that Brooklyn is a real place in New York City.

ELA RL.2.10 **ELD** ELD.PI.2.6

ENGLISH LANGUAGE SUPPORT Guide children at the emerging and expanding levels to complete the Academic English activities on Lesson 17 **Language Support Card.** **ELD** ELD.PII.2.6

Lesson 17
ANCHOR TEXT

Luke Goes to Bat
RACHEL ISADORA

 GENRE

Realistic fiction is a story that could happen in real life. As you read, look for:

- ▶ characters who act like real people
- ▶ a setting that could be a real place

52 **ELA** RL.2.2, RL.2.10, L.2.3a **ELD** ELD.PI.2.4, ELD.PI.2.6, ELD.PI.2.7, ELD.PI.2.8

MEET THE AUTHOR AND ILLUSTRATOR
Rachel Isadora

Rachel Isadora grew up wanting to be a ballerina. She was so shy that she wouldn't dance in front of her class until she had practiced the steps in an empty room. Later, she injured her foot and couldn't dance anymore.

She decided to become an artist instead. Today, Ms. Isadora writes and illustrates children's books about ballet, music, and baseball.

Scaffold Close Reading

Strategies for Annotation	Think Through the Text	Analyze the Text	Independent Reading
	FIRST READ	SECOND READ	
Annotate it! As you read the selection with children, look for this icon **Annotate it!** for opportunities to annotate the text collaboratively as a class.	Develop comprehension through • Guided Questioning • Target Strategy: Visualize • Vocabulary in Context	Support analyzing short sections of text: • Sequence of Events • Formal and Informal Language Use directed note-taking by working with children to complete a graphic organizer during reading. Distribute copies of Graphic Organizer 4 Flow Chart.	• Children analyze the text independently, using the Reader's Guide on Reader's Notebook Volume 2 pp. 23–24 . (See pp. T154–T155 for instructional support.) • Children read independently in a self-selected trade book.

LUKE GOES TO BAT

by Rachel Isadora

ESSENTIAL QUESTION

Why is it important to keep trying even if something is difficult to do?

53

READER AND TASK CONSIDERATIONS

ELA RL.2.1, SL.2.4, SL.2.6
ELD ELD.PI.2.1, ELD.PI.2.6, ELD.PI.2.12a

Determine the level of additional support your children will need to read and comprehend *Luke Goes to Bat* successfully.

READERS

- **Motivate** Ask children to share their experiences with playing baseball.

- **Access Knowledge and Experiences** Review with children the word web you completed as part of the Talk It Over activity on the back of Lesson 17 **Language Support Card.** Ask children to share with a partner experiences they've had learning from people who are special to them. Encourage them to use complete sentences as they share.

TASKS

- **Increase Scaffolding** Stop periodically as you read to have children ask and answer questions about what they've read.

- **Foster Independence** Prompt children to ask questions about the text every few pages, and have the rest of the class share ideas about how to answer the questions. Have children raise their hand if they think the answer makes sense based on information in the text.

ESSENTIAL QUESTION

- Read aloud the Essential Question on **Student Book** p. 53. *Why is it important to keep trying even if something is difficult to do?* Then tell children to think about this question as they read *Luke Goes to Bat.*

Predictive Writing

- Tell children to write the Essential Question.

- Explain that they will write what they expect *Luke Goes to Bat* to be about. Ask them to think about how the Essential Question relates to what they noticed while previewing the selection or what they already know about the Essential Question from their own experiences or past readings.

- Guide children to think about the genre of the selection as they write.

Set Purpose

- Read aloud the title and the author's name. Ask children to describe the illustration they see on **Student Book** p. 53. Explain that good readers set a purpose for reading, based on their preview of the selection and what they know about realistic fiction.

- Model setting a reading purpose.

Think Aloud *I like baseball, and I learned from my preview that the baseball player Jackie Robinson is in this story. I think this selection might be about a boy and Jackie Robinson. I'll read to find out.*

- Have children set their own purpose for reading. Ask several children to share their purpose for reading. **ELA** RF.2.4a, RL.2.10

ENGLISH LANGUAGE SUPPORT To help make the text accessible to all children, consider modifications such as these:

- Use gestures and objects as you describe each photo to help children understand the nouns and verbs and what is happening in each scene.

- Allow children to listen to audio of the selection as they read along.

It was Brooklyn. It was summer. It was baseball. All day long the kids on Bedford Avenue played stickball in the streets. Except for Luke.

"When you're older," his big brother, Nicky, told him. "He's just a squirt," one of the other kids said, laughing. So Luke watched the games from the curb, and then he'd practice. **1**

He threw a ball against the wall next to the deli. He practiced his swing over and over again. He ran as fast as he could up and down the block.

He wanted to be ready when it was time. **2**

54

55

ENGLISH LANGUAGE SUPPORT

Use Visuals

Emerging Show the **Online Picture Card** for *ball*. Have children point to the pictures and say the words.

Expanding Show children the **Online Picture Card** for *ball*. Ask children to complete using descriptive words: *A baseball is _____. A basketball is _____.*

Bridging Have children use the illustrations on **Student Book** pp. 54–55 to predict what might happen next in the story and why.

FIRST READ

Cite Text Evidence

Think Through the Text

1 *How does Luke feel when the other kids won't let him play? He feels sad and disappointed.* **ELA** RL.2.3 **ELD** ELD.PI.2.6

2 *What clues in the text help you understand the meaning of the word practice? Luke watches the other kids play together. Then he throws the ball and swings the stick over and over again and runs as fast as he can. Practice must mean doing something over and over again to get better at it.* **ELA** L.2.4a **ELD** ELD.PI.2.6

ENGLISH LANGUAGE SUPPORT Tell children that the word *practice* has a cognate in Spanish: *prácticas*. Remind children to look for cognates as they read to help them figure out the meanings of key words.

FOR STUDENTS WITH DISABILITIES Allow children who have difficulty answering questions verbally additional time to formulate their answers. Cue the child that he or she will answer the next question.

And at night, whenever the Dodgers were playing, Luke hurried up to the roof, where he could see the lights of Ebbets Field. When he heard the crowd go wild, he imagined his favorite player, Jackie Robinson, had hit a home run.

Someday, Luke thought, I will hit a home run, too.

56   57   3

---

3 *In the picture, what is happening on Luke's roof?* a Dodger's baseball game *What details from the story tell you that Luke is imagining a game on his roof? The picture shows the Dodgers playing on a roof, but we know they really play in a ballpark. The baseball players are in black and white, and Luke is in color.*

ELA RL.2.1, RL.2.3

ENGLISH LANGUAGE SUPPORT *Use these frames to support participation. Luke is watching a _____ on his roof.* baseball game *The players are in black and white, but Luke is in _____.* color   **ELD** ELD.PI.2.6

✓ **TARGET STRATEGY | Visualize**

Use the Visualize strategy to help children picture the setting of the story. Model the strategy:

Think Aloud   *The story starts in summer. I can picture in my mind the hot, busy city street where the kids play ball. The picture shows buildings, Ebbets Field, and a roof, so I imagine I can hear the sounds of cars and people at a baseball stadium.*

◗ **DOMAIN: Life Science**

LESSON TOPIC: Growing Up

Cross-Curricular Connection Talk with children about Luke and how he might feel knowing that the other kids can do things that he cannot do. Point out that everyone grows up at his or her own pace, and it's important to treat others with kindness no matter what they can or cannot do. Remind children that everyone has feelings that can be hurt, and it is important to treat others in a way that will not hurt their feelings.

Finally, one morning, the team was short a player.

"Franky had to go to his aunt's!"

"Who we gonna get?"

"Hey," said Luke, "what about me?"

Everyone was quiet.

"Aw, come on," said his brother.

"Give him a chance."

"We got nobody else."

"He better not mess up."

They put him in left field. No balls came his way, so he just stood there.

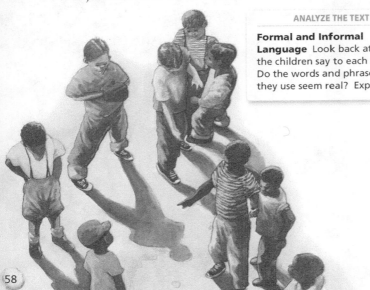

ANALYZE THE TEXT

Formal and Informal Language Look back at what the children say to each other. Do the words and phrases that they use seem real? Explain.

When it was his turn up at bat, Luke took a few practice swings, then stepped up to the plate.

"I'll show them," Luke muttered.

The ball whizzed past.

"Strike one!"

Luke held the bat higher.

"Strike two!"

Luke was barely in position when the next ball flew past and the catcher yelled, "Out!"

④ ⑤

58

59

ENGLISH LANGUAGE SUPPORT

Comprehensible Input

Emerging Reread **Student Book** p. 58. Reread "He better not mess up." Ask children for another meaning for the word *mess*.

Expanding Ask children to tell how they know that Luke does not hit the ball when at bat. *He makes two strikes, then the catcher yells "out."* **ELD** ELD.PI.2.6

Bridging Ask children to give examples of informal dialogue on **Student Book** p. 58. **ELD** ELD.PI.2.6, ELD.PI.2.7

FIRST READ

Cite Text Evidence

Think Through the Text

④ *What happens when a ball player is "in position"?* The ball player steps up to the plate and is ready to swing the bat.

ENGLISH LANGUAGE SUPPORT Tell children that the word *position* has a cognate in Spanish: *posición*. Remind children to look for cognates as they read to help them figure out the meanings of key words.

⑤ *What happened when Luke first asked he if could play ball?* The kids laughed at him, so he sat at the curb. *What happened next that makes the older kids decide that Luke can play?* Franky can't play, and there is no one else to take his place. *What happens when Luke finally does play ball?* He strikes out. **ELA** RL.2.1, RL.2.3

ENGLISH LANGUAGE SUPPORT Provide sentence frames to encourage participation. *When Luke first asked to play, the kids _____. laugh Then they let Luke play because _____ is not there. Franky Luke tries to hit the ball, but he _____. strikes out* **ELD** ELD.PI.2.6

"You stink," Luke heard.

He got up to bat one more time but struck out again.

"Sometimes it just goes that way," his brother told him.

6

Franky came back in the afternoon, so Luke spent the rest of the day on the curb. He was sure they'd never let him play again.

60

Grandma was in the kitchen when he got home.

"I finally got a chance to play with the team," Luke told her.

Grandma could tell that the game hadn't gone well. "Not everyone plays like Jackie Robinson all the time," she said. "Not even Jackie Robinson."

Luke didn't smile.

"By the way," Grandma said, "are you doing anything tomorrow night?"

Luke shrugged.

"Well, if you're so busy, someone else will have to go with me to the game at Ebbets Field."

"What? You mean a real game?"

Grandma held up two tickets.

7

61

6 *How does Luke's brother show that he cares about Luke? He tries to make Luke feel better after Luke strikes out.* **ELA** RL.2.3

ENGLISH LANGUAGE SUPPORT Tell children that the expression *sometimes it just goes that way* is another way of saying that things won't always go the way you want them to. Explain that Luke's brother says it because he knows Luke feels disappointed about striking out in the game. He wants to help Luke remember that everyone has disappointments sometimes. **ELD** ELD.PI.2.6, ELD.PI.2.7

7 *What happens to Luke after he strikes out the second time? Franky comes back, so Luke spends the rest of the day sitting on the curb. He goes home and tells his grandmother what happened. She says it's okay and tells him she is taking him to a Dodger's game.* **ELA** RL.2.7 **ELD** ELD.PI.2.6

SECOND READ   DAY 2

Analyze the Text

Formal and Informal Language

Read the Analyze the Text box on **Student Book** p. 58 with children. Remind children that sometimes an author uses informal, or casual, familiar language to make characters seem more real. Have children point out examples of children using informal language. *"Who we gonna get?"* and *"He better not mess up,"* for example. Discuss what each example of informal language on p. 58 means. Then ask children to look for more examples of informal language as they read. **ELA** L.2.3a **ELD** ELD.PI.2.6

🖉 📋 *Annotate it!* Work with children to highlight examples of informal language in the text.

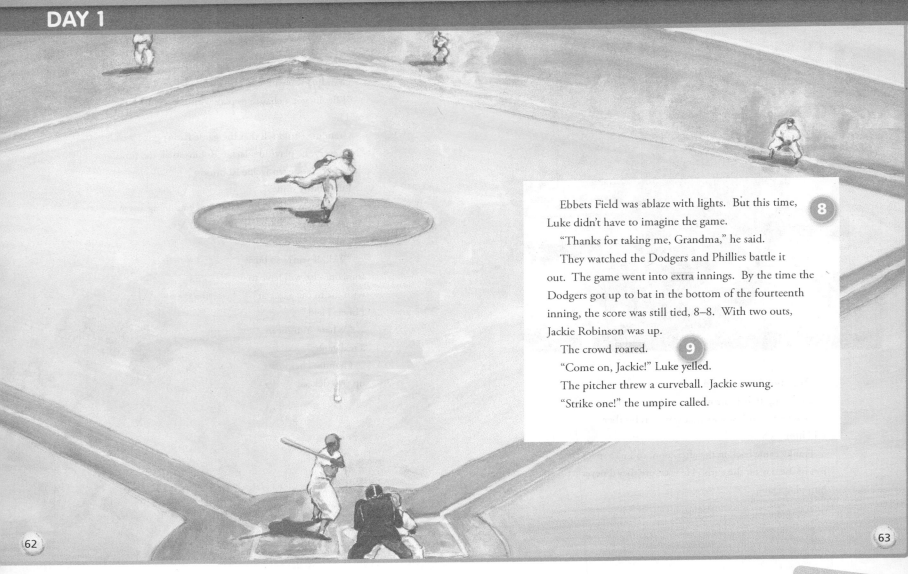

Ebbets Field was ablaze with lights. But this time, Luke didn't have to imagine the game. **8**

"Thanks for taking me, Grandma," he said.

They watched the Dodgers and Phillies battle it out. The game went into extra innings. By the time the Dodgers got up to bat in the bottom of the fourteenth inning, the score was still tied, 8–8. With two outs, Jackie Robinson was up.

The crowd roared. **9**

"Come on, Jackie!" Luke yelled.

The pitcher threw a curveball. Jackie swung.

"Strike one!" the umpire called.

62   63

ENGLISH LANGUAGE SUPPORT

Idiomatic Language

Emerging Explain to children the term *dug his feet into the dirt.* Then pantomime digging your feet into the ground. **ELD** ELD.PI.2.6

Expanding Ask children to describe how they know what Grandma means when she says, *"See, you can't give up."* **ELD** ELD.PI.2.6

Bridging Ask children how they know what the author means: *"They watched the Dodgers and the Phillies battle it out."* **ELD** ELD.PI.2.6

FIRST READ

Cite Text Evidence

Think Through the Text

8 *What words does the author use to help you visualize the baseball park?* Ebbets Field was ablaze with lights. **ELA** RL.2.4 **ELD** ELD.PI.2.6

9 *Why do people say that crowds roar?* **Sample answer:** *When everyone cheers at once, it sounds like a giant animal roaring.* **ELA** L.2.5a

ENGLISH LANGUAGE SUPPORT Remind children that authors use different kinds of verbs to describe what someone or something does. Point out that the author used the verb *roared* to help readers understand how loud the crowd was. Have children discuss why an audience would roar at a baseball game. **ELD** ELD.PI.2.7

✅ PHONICS/DECODING STRATEGY

Use Projectable S1 to help children apply the Phonics/Decoding strategy while reading **Student Book** pp. 62–63. Write *lights* and model blending the sounds: /l/ /ī/ /t/ /z/. Reread the sentence to make sure *lights* makes sense. Have children identify other words on **Student Book** pp. 62–63 that have the long *i* sound. *time, tied, strike*

The pitcher wound up. He threw a fastball and Jackie missed.

"Strike two!"

Three balls followed.

All eyes at Ebbets Field rested on Jackie. The Dodgers could still win.

Luke shouted with the crowd. "Give it to 'em, Jackie! You show 'em!"

Jackie looked around from under his cap, then dug his feet into the dirt.

The pitcher began his windup. "You can do it, Jackie," Luke whispered. "You can do it."

64

Suddenly, Luke heard the loud crack of a bat. When he looked up, the ball was flying over his head, flying over the scoreboard, flying over the walls of Ebbets Field! The crowd went wild!

10

Luke stood up on his seat and cheered, "You showed 'em, Jackie!"

"What a game!" Grandma said. "See, you can't give up. Even Jackie Robinson's got to keep trying."

Luke didn't answer.

11

65

---

10 *What words help you understand the sound Luke hears when Jackie hits the ball?* **loud crack of a bat**

ENGLISH LANGUAGE SUPPORT Point out the phrase *crack of a bat* and explain that the author uses these words to help readers understand what it sounds like when Jackie hits the ball. Then pretend to swing a bat and make the sound of the bat as it hits the ball. **ELD** ELD.PI.2.7

11 *What happens after Jackie Robinson has two strikes and three balls?* **He hits a home run and scores.** *What does Grandma say to Luke after that?* **Even Jackie Robinson has to keep trying.**
ELA RL.2.1, RL.2.7 **ELD** ELD.PI.2.6

ENGLISH LANGUAGE SUPPORT

How English Works: Interpretive

Prepositional Phrases Remind children that authors sometimes use small groups of words called phrases to add detail to their writing. Read the first paragraph on page 65 aloud, emphasizing the phrases *over his head, over the scoreboard,* and *over the walls of Ebbets Field.* Discuss with children how these phrases add details that help them to picture what is happening in the text. **ELD** ELD.PII.2.5

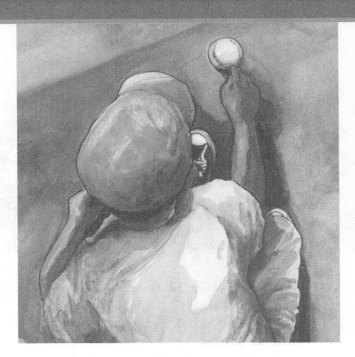

When Luke got home, he ran up to the roof. The lights were going out at Ebbets Field.

"Come on down! It's bedtime!" Nicky called.

Just then, Luke saw a ball lying on the ground.

"Look!" he said, picking it up. "This is the home run ball that Jackie Robinson hit tonight!"

"Naw. That's just some old ball a kid hit up on the roof," Nick said, laughing, as he went downstairs. **13**

12

66

67

FORMATIVE ASSESSMENT RtI

3
2
1

Visualize IF children have difficulty applying the Visualize strategy, **THEN** use this model:

 Think Aloud

To visualize, I can look back at the text and pictures. I can use details about the baseball field to create a picture of the game in my mind. I can use the author's words to help me hear the sounds of the baseball game.

FIRST READ

Cite Text Evidence

Think Through the Text

12 *What does Luke do right after the game is over?* He runs up to the roof. *Based on what you know about Luke, why do you think he runs to the roof?* Sample answer: *He wants to see the lights of Ebbets Field one more time and remember what happened at the game.* **ELA** RL.2.3, RL.2.7

ENGLISH LANGUAGE SUPPORT Provide sentence frames to encourage participation. *After he gets home, Luke goes _____. to the roof I think he goes there because _____. he wants to see the lights of Ebbets Field* **ELD** ELD.PI.2.6

13 *Why does Luke believe the ball he finds is the one Jackie Robinson hit?* Sample answer: *Luke saw the ball fly high in the air and out of the ballpark. Luke has a strong imagination.* **ELA** RL.2.1, RL.2.7 **ELD** ELD.PI.2.6

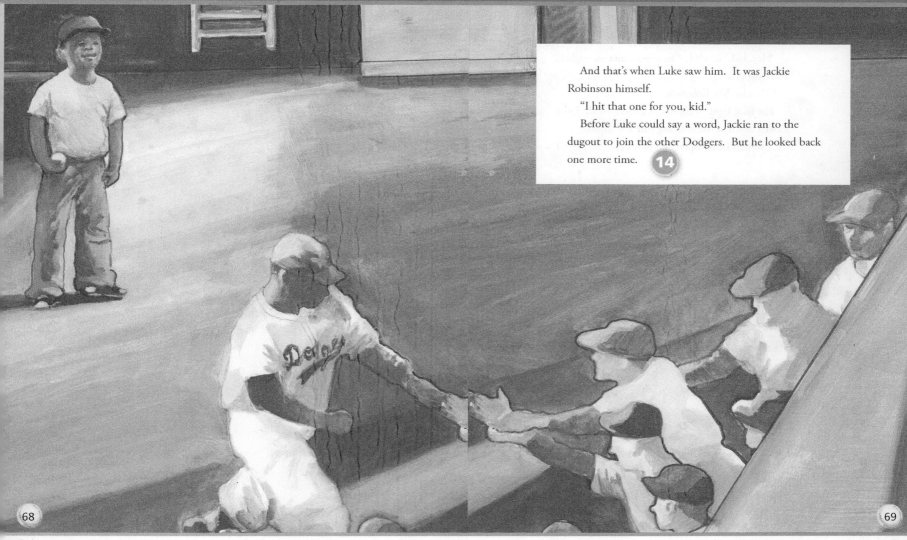

And that's when Luke saw him. It was Jackie Robinson himself.

"I hit that one for you, kid."

Before Luke could say a word, Jackie ran to the dugout to join the other Dodgers. But he looked back one more time. **14**

68

69

14 *Do you think Luke really sees and talks to Jackie Robinson or does he just imagine it? What clues from the story make you think so?* He imagines it. No one else is on the roof when Luke sees Jackie. Jackie goes back to the dugout, but there cannot be a dugout on the roof. Luke imagined the Dodgers on the roof at the beginning of the story. **ELA** RL.2.7

ENGLISH LANGUAGE SUPPORT Point to the dugout and name it for children. Have children repeat the noun and discuss why the dugout cannot really be on Luke's roof. **ELD** ELD.PI.2.6

✅ **TARGET STRATEGY | Visualize**

Tell children to practice the Visualize strategy as they read **Student Book** pp. 68–69. Have children discuss the pictures they have in their minds of what Luke sees on the roof after the game. Have children use details from the text and pictures to support what they visualize. **ELD** ELD.PI.2.6

"Hey, kid," he said. "Your grandma was right. You can't give up."

"Thanks, Mr. Robinson."

15 The final lights went out at Ebbets Field. Luke looked down at the winning ball and smiled.

"I won't," he whispered to himself.

70

71

DOMAIN: Values

LESSON TOPIC: Never Give Up

Cross-Curricular Connection Tell children that Jackie Robinson was the first African American man to play in major league baseball. Ask children what qualities Jackie Robinson might have had that made him never give up. Sample answers: *He kept practicing; he had to be better than a lot of people to be the first African American to play in major league baseball; he had to believe in his abilities as a ballplayer.*

FIRST READ

Cite Text Evidence

Think Through the Text

15 *What happens after Jackie looks back one more time at Luke on the roof? He tells Luke not to give up. Why do you think Luke needs this advice? He struck out when he played the day before. He may be thinking of giving up.* **ELA** RL.2.1

ENGLISH LANGUAGE SUPPORT Provide sentence frames to encourage participation. *Jackie tells Luke not to _____. give up I think Luke needs this advice because _____. he struck out last time he played* **ELD** ELD.PI.2.6

And he didn't. **16**

ANALYZE THE TEXT

Sequence of Events Think about the story's events. What lesson does Luke learn?

16 *What do you think will happen the next time Luke gets to play baseball? Why?* **Sample answer:** *He'll keep trying his best. He'll be able to hit the ball. I think this because the picture shows him hitting the ball.* **ELA** RL.2.7 **ELD** ELD.PI.2.3, ELD.PI.2.6

Collaborative Conversation

Remind children that they have been reading about a boy who loves baseball. Working in groups, have children describe how Luke changed by the end of the story. Tell them to refer to the text and illustrations to describe how the story events affected Luke. To encourage multiple exchanges, remind them of the following frequently used phrases and explain the meaning of each: Can you say more? Can you give an example? **ELA** RL.2.3, SL.2.1a, SL.2.1c, L.2.6 **ELD** ELD.PI.2.1, ELD.PI.2.6

SECOND READ   **DAY 2**   *Analyze the Text*

Sequence of Events

Read the Analyze the Text box on **Student Book** p. 73 with children. Then distribute Graphic Organizer 4 .

Display Projectable 17.4, and tell children that you will work together to start filling in the flow chart by listing events from the story in order. Guide children to write a few events. Then have them complete the flow chart with a partner and use it to retell the story. Explain that they should use the completed graphic organizer to explain how the sequence of events contributes to the lesson that Luke learns. **ELA** RL.2.2 **ELD** ELD.PI.2.6

🖊 📄 *Annotate it!* Work with children to highlight sentences that help them understand the lesson Luke learned.

Guided Retelling

Oral Language

Use the retelling prompts on the **Retelling Cards** to guide children to retell the story.

ELA RL.2.2 **ELD** ELD.PI.2.6, ELD.PI.2.12a

front

Grade 2, Lesson 17
Luke Goes to Bat
RETELLING CARD 1

Talk About It

What game do the kids in Luke's neighborhood enjoy playing in the summer?

Why won't the other children let Luke play?

What does Luke do when the other boys tell him he can't play with them?

back

front

Grade 2, Lesson 17
Luke Goes to Bat
RETELLING CARD 2

Talk About It

What happens when the team does not have enough players?

How do the other children feel about letting Luke play?

back

front

back

front

back

RETELLING RUBRIC

4	**Highly Effective**	The retelling names the characters, describes the setting and the problem, and tells important events in order. It includes several details and tells how the problem was solved.
3	**Generally Effective**	The retelling names the characters and tells most of the important events in order, including how the problem was solved. It includes some details.
2	**Somewhat Effective**	The retelling includes a few elements of the story, but omits important characters or events and provides few details.
1	**Ineffective**	The reader is unable to provide an accurate retelling of *Luke Goes to Bat*.

ENGLISH LANGUAGE SUPPORT

Review Key Ideas

All Proficiencies Pronounce and explain *retell*, reminding children that when they retell a story they are describing the main events in the order they happened. Page through *Luke Goes to Bat* with children and share the following sentence frames to help them retell the selection.

When Luke's brother lets him play baseball with him, Luke _____. strikes out Luke's grandmother takes him to see _____. Jackie Robinson and the Dodgers After the game, he imagines he sees _____ on his roof. Jackie Robinson Jackie tells him not to _____. give up **ELD** ELD.PI.2.6, ELD.PI.2.12a

DAY 1

Grammar Subject-Verb Agreement

▶ **SHARE OBJECTIVES**

- **Grammar** Use subject-verb agreement. LANGUAGE
- **Spelling** Spell words with long *i* (*i, igh,* and *y*).
- **Writing** Identify the characteristics of a good narrative. LANGUAGE

ENGLISH LANGUAGE SUPPORT

Language Transfer

All Proficiencies Before teaching subject-verb agreement, provide students with more practice identifying subjects and verbs. Write simple sentences on the board, such as: *Rick rides his bike. The cats jump high.* Have children come to the board and circle the verbs. Then have them underline the subject.

Linguistic Transfer In many languages, *i, igh,* and *y* represent sounds other than /ī/. Before beginning the lesson, use familiar, high-frequency English words such as *mind, blind, might, fight, my,* and *by* to provide explicit instruction. **ELD** ELD.PIII.2

1 Teach/Model

Subjects and Verbs Display <u>Projectable 17.2</u> ⬀. Remind children that a verb names the action in a sentence. The subject tells who or what does the action.

- In a sentence that tells about now, singular subjects use a verb that ends in *-s.* Plural subjects use verbs without the *-s.* Model using the correct verb ending with singular and plural subjects. Write these example sentences: *The boy (throw/ throws) the ball. The boys (throw/throws) the ball.*

- Repeat with the examples in the box on the projectable.

Think Aloud To find the correct form of a verb, I ask this Thinking Question: When should I add -s to the end of a verb that tells about now? I know that if the subject of a sentence that tells about now is singular, I add -s to the verb. In The boy stops the ball, boy is singular, so the verb stops ends in -s.

ENGLISH LANGUAGE SUPPORT Tell children that the Spanish cognates for *subject* and *verb* are *sujeto* and *verbo,* respectively.

2 Guided Practice/Apply

- Have children use the Thinking Question to complete the sentences on **Projectable 17.2.**

- Distribute <u>Reader's Notebook Volume 2 page 17</u> ⬀ to children to complete independently.

- For additional support, have children view the <u>GrammarSnap Video</u> ⬀ that supports Lesson 17. **ELD** ELD.PII.2.3a

Spelling Long *i (i, igh, y)*

SPELLING WORDS AND SENTENCES

BASIC

1. **night*** I go to sleep at *night.*
2. **kind** We like that *kind* of cereal.
3. **spy** The hero in the story was a *spy.*
4. **child** A young person is a *child.*
5. **light** I turned out the *light.*
6. **find** I cannot *find* my watch.
7. **right*** I throw with my *right* hand.
8. **high** The building is ten stories *high.*
9. **wild*** A wolf is a *wild* animal.
10. **July** We take a vacation in *July.*

11. **fry** We are going to *fry* fish.
12. **sigh** I heard my father *sigh* as he wiped up the milk.

REVIEW

13. **by** I put my jacket *by* my books.
14. **why** *Why* is the dog barking?

CHALLENGE

15. **behind** I always sit *behind* the driver.
16. **lightning** During the storm, *lightning* lit the sky.

*A form or forms of these words appear in the literature.

Administer the Pretest

Say each Spelling Word. Then say it in the sentence and repeat the word. Have children write the word. **ELA** L.2.2d

Teach the Principle

- Review the **Sound/Spelling Card** *ice cream.* Point to each long *i* spelling, and say a spelling word to match. Write *kind, night,* and *spy.* Then read each word aloud.

- Explain that the long *i* vowel sound can be spelled *i, igh,* and *y.*

Model a Word Sort

Model sorting words based on the spelling of the long *i* sound. Present the Model the Sort lesson on page 88 of the **Literacy and Language Guide.**

Narrative Writing Introduce the Model

1 Teach/Model

Story Paragraph Tell children that this week they will be writing a story paragraph. Then display and read aloud Projectable 17.3 ⌐.

- Use the labels for paragraph 1 on the projectable to identify dialogue, events, and exact words.

- Read and discuss the Writer's Checklist about stories.

Writer's Checklist

What Makes a Great Story?

- There is action. Something interesting happens.

- **Dialogue** tells what the characters are like.

- **Events** are told in an order that makes sense.

- **Exact words** tell how the characters feel.

- The sentences read smoothly.

2 Guided Practice/Apply

- Read paragraph 2 on the projectable with children. Label the dialogue, events, and exact words.

- Ask children what events happened before Kit, Mom, and Baby Brother waited at the airport. *Daddy went away and was gone a long time.* Ask children why the writer chose to tell that event out of time order. Have them provide reasons for their answers.

Model Study Ask children to work with a partner to write another sentence to add to the end of the second paragraph. The sentence should make sense coming at the end of the paragraph and should include something that shows how a character feels. *Possible response: "I'm so glad you're home, Daddy," said Kit.*

ELA W.2.3, W.2.4, W.2.10 **ELD** ELD.PI.2.10, ELD.PII.2.1

Daily Proofreading Practice

The s̶e̶e̶t̶ on my bike is too h̶i̶.̶ dad
         seat   high
will make it r̶i̶t̶s̶.
              right

Performance Task

Children may prewrite, draft, revise, and publish their narrative writing task through *my*WriteSmart beginning on Day 3.

Additional support for Narrative Writing appears in the **Common Core Writing Handbook,** Lesson 17.

DAY 2

Today's Goals

Vocabulary & Oral Language

 TARGET VOCABULARY

practice	extra
hurried	curb
position	cheered
roared	final

Phonemic Awareness
- **Segment Phonemes**

Phonics & Fluency
- **Long *i*** (*i, igh, ie, y*)
- **Fluency:** Stress
- **Read Decodable Reader:**
  Bright Lights
- **High-Frequency Words**

Text-Based Comprehension
- **Dig Deeper:** Use Clues to Analyze the Text
- **Sequence of Events**
- **Formal and Informal Language**
- **Reread the Anchor Text:**
  Luke Goes to Bat

Grammar & Writing
- **Subject-Verb Agreement**
- **Narrative Writing:** Story Paragraph
- **Trait:** Development

Spelling
- **Long *i*** (*i, igh, y*)

Opening Routines

Warm Up with Wordplay

Make a Rhyme

Display and read aloud the following word: *ball*.

Have children work with partners to come up with as many words that rhyme with *ball* as they can. When children are ready, compile their words on the board. Depending on the words that children suggest, you may want to add others.

ball	**tall**	**fall**
stall	**hall**	**call**
wall	**mall**	**crawl**

Have children suggest opening lines for a poem, ending with one of the rhyming words. Let children choose their favorite opening line, and then, as a class, write a short poem using the rhyming words in the list. **ELA** W.2.7 **ELD** ELD.PI.2.2

Daily Phonemic Awareness

Segment Phonemes

- *Listen to these words:* mint, thin, did. *What vowel sound do you hear?* short i *Now listen to these words:* sight, fly, kind. *What vowel sound do you hear?* long i

- *Let's sound out some of these words together. Say this word:* mint. *What is the first sound you hear?* /m/ *What is the next sound you hear?* /ĭ/ *What is that sound called?* short i *What sound do you hear after /ĭ/?* /n/ *What is the last sound you hear?* /t/

- Continue with the words *wild, might, thin, dry, tiger, pilot, slip,* and *fry.*
  ELA RF.2.3a

Corrective Feedback

- If a child is unable to segment the phonemes, say the word, give correction, and model the task. Example: *The word is* wild. *The first sound I hear in* wild *is* /w/. *The next sound I hear is* /ī/, *the long i sound. The next sound I hear in* wild *is* /l/. *The last sound I hear is* /d/, wild.

- Have children segment the words with you before doing the task on their own.

Daily High-Frequency Words

- Point to **High-Frequency Word Card 163,** *else.*

- *Say the word.* else *Spell the word.* e-l-s-e. *Write the word. Check the word.*

- Repeat the procedure with the new words *doing* and *room* and with review words *any, blue, carry, studied, sure, teacher,* and *turned.* **ELA** RF.2.3f

Blast Off!

- Display **High-Frequency Word Card 163** *else.*

- Tell children to crouch and then jump as they say each letter of the word *else.*

- Repeat the activity for each of this week's High-Frequency Words.

Corrective Feedback

- If a child does not recognize the word *else,* say the correct word and have children repeat it. *Else. What is the word?* else

- Have children spell the word. *e-l-s-e How do we say this word?* else

- Have children reread all of the cards in random order.

Daily Vocabulary Boost

- Review Target Vocabulary and definitions with children. (See p. T114.) Remind children that they heard these words in the Read Aloud "The Crowd Roared!"

- Recall the article with children as you guide them to interact with each word's meaning.

  The match was extra special *to Minna. What have you done lately that was* extra *special to you?*

  Javier said, "You'll get better every time you practice.*" What are some things that you* practice?

  Minna learned the correct position *for her leg when kicking the ball. Put your body in a relaxed* position.

- Continue with children in the same manner, using *hurried, roared, cheered, final,* and *curb.* **ELA** L.2.6

Vocabulary in Context Cards 129–136

☑ **Target Vocabulary**

practice
hurried
position
roared
extra
curb
cheered
final

Phonics

- Identify sounds in words with long *i* spelled *i, igh, ie, y.*
- Blend, read, and build words with vowel teams *(igh, ie)* (vowel team syllables) and other spellings for long *i (i, y).*
- Reread on-level text with long *i* words spelled *i, igh, ie, y* and High-Frequency Words for fluency practice.

▶ **SKILLS TRACE**

Words with Long *i (i, igh, ie, y)*	
Introduce	**pp. T116–T117, T142–T143**
Differentiate	pp. T184–T185
Reteach	p. T198
Review	pp. T162, T263, T352, T363
Assess	Weekly Tests, Lesson 17

ENGLISH LANGUAGE SUPPORT

Comprehensible Input

Emerging Reinforce and clarify the meanings of words in Blending Lines 1–3 by saying a sentence missing the last word; have children point to and say the word that completes the sentence. Examples: *I use my eyes for my sense of _____.* sight *The angry dogs had a _____.* fight *My little sister gave me her jacket. It is too _____.* tight

Expanding Ask children to use each word in Blending Lines 1–3 in a sentence to show meaning. Clarify any unfamiliar words using simple definitions. Monitor pronunciation of the target words and provide modeling and additional practice as needed.

Bridging Have partners give each other clues to guess the meanings of selected words in Blending Lines. Monitor and provide corrective feedback as needed.

Words with Long *i (i, igh, ie, y)*

Phonemic Awareness Warm-Up *I'll say a word. You say the sounds you hear and name the vowel sound. I'll do it first. Listen:* might. *Now I'll say each sound:* /m/ /ī/ /t/. *Let's do it together. Say the word* might. *What sounds do you hear?* /m/ /ī/ /t/ *Which sound is the vowel?* /ī/ *What do we call that sound?* long i

Now you do it. Say the sounds you hear in these words and name the vowel sound: sight, /s/ /ī/ /t/, *long* i; sit, /s/ /ĭ/ /t/, *short* i; dried, /d/ /r/ /ī/ /d/, *long* i; rind, /r/ /ī/ /n/ /d/, *long* i; pick, /p/ /ĭ/ /k/, *short* i; cry, /k/ /r/ /ī/, *long* i.

1 Teach/Model

Continuous Blending Routine

Use Instructional Routine 3 to model blending *right.*

- Display **Letter Cards** *r, igh, t.* Point out the letters *igh* that make the long *i* sound.
- Blend the sounds, stretching out the word while pointing to each letter in a sweeping motion: /r/ /ī/ /t/.
- Have children blend the sounds and say the word with you, and then have children blend and say the word on their own. *Blend with me:* /r/ /ī/ /t/. *Now you blend the sounds.* /r/ /ī/ /t/, right

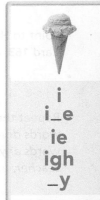

2 Guided Practice

Blending Lines

Blend Words Repeat the blending routine with the first two words in Line 1 below; help children compare the words. Point to each word as children read the entire line chorally. Continue with the remaining lines. Then call on volunteers to reread selected words until children can identify the words quickly.

1. sit	sight	flit	flight	fit	fight
2. my	might	tie	tight	fry	fright
3. die	thigh	why	sigh	wild	knight

Transition to Longer Words Use a similar process for Lines 4–6.

4. high	highway	try	trying	light	delight
5. cry	cried	ply	reply	kind	kindly
6. spy	spying	bind	blind	pie	pies

Challenge Call on above-level children to read the words in Line 7. Then have the class read the sentences chorally.

7. midnight   mighty   supply   multiply   item   wildflower
8. Ty is <u>doing</u> something <u>else</u> tonight.
9. I'm <u>sure</u> Kim will be selling her pies.

Build Words Use **Letter Cards** to model how to spell *flight*. *The first sounds in* flight *are the blended sounds /f/ /l/. The two letters f and l stand for those sounds. The next sound I hear is /ī/. In this word, the letters igh stand for /ī/. The letter t stands for the final sound, /t/. Now read the word with me:* flight.

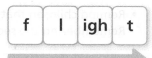

- Guide children to identify sounds and spell *lie, sigh, mailbox, fry, street,* and *pilot.* Individuals can spell the words with **Letter Cards** while other children check their work. **ELA** RF.2.3b, L.2.2d

Have children select three words from Blending Lines and write them on a separate sheet of paper. Tell children to underline the letter or letters in each word that make the /ī/ sound. Have children use each word in a sentence. Write some of the words on the board and call on volunteers to blend and read these words. **ELA** RF.2.3a, RF.2.3b

Distribute <u>Reader's Notebook Volume 2 page 18</u> or <u>leveled practice</u> in Grab-and-Go™ Resources for children to complete independently.

Practice Fluency

Use <u>Instructional Routine 12</u> to have partners read the **Decodable Reader** *Bright Lights*.

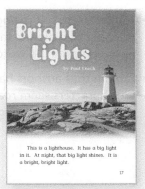

This is a lighthouse. It has a big light in it. At night, that big light shines. It is a bright, bright light.

17

Decodable Reader

Corrective Feedback
When a child mispronounces a letter-sound, highlight that letter, restate its sound, have children repeat the sound, and then guide them to blend the word. See the example below.

Decoding Error:
A child reads *fight* in Line 1 as *fit*.

Correct the error. Say the word and remind children that /ī/ can be spelled *i, igh, ie,* or *y. The word is* fight. *The letters* igh *together stand for the long i sound /ī/.*

Model as you touch the letters. *I'll blend: /f/ /ī/ /t/. What is the word?* fight

Guide *Let's blend together: /f/ /ī/ /t/. What is the word?* fight

Check *You blend. /f/ /ī/ /t/ What is the word?* fight

Reinforce Go back three or four words and have children continue reading. Make note of errors and review those words during the next lesson.

Go to pp. T184–T185 for additional phonics support.

Dig Deeper: Use Clues to Analyze the Text

▶ **SHARE OBJECTIVES**
- Identify the order of events in a story.
- Recount what happened in a story. LANGUAGE
- Visualize story details as you read.

ENGLISH LANGUAGE SUPPORT

Expand Language Production

Emerging Reread **Student Book** p. 57. Ask questions with one- and two-word answers: *Who plays at Ebbets Field? the Dodgers* Expand the response by saying, *The Dodgers play at Ebbets Field.*

Expanding Have children read the text on **Student Book** pp. 58–59. Ask questions about the sequence of events. Have children respond in complete sentences.

Bridging Have partners look at **Student Book** pp. 68–69 and discuss how they know that Luke is imagining that he meets Jackie Robinson on the rooftop. **ELD** ELD.PI.2.6

Text-Based Comprehension

1   Teach/Model

Terms About Literature

sequence of events the order in which things happen

dialogue a conversation between two or more characters

Remind children that they have just read *Luke Goes to Bat,* a realistic fiction story about the things that happen to a boy one summer. Read **Student Book** p. 74 with children.

- Remind children that events of a story are written in a certain order. Remembering the sequence of events can help readers retell a story.

ENGLISH LANGUAGE SUPPORT Tell children that the words *sequence of events* have a cognate in Spanish: *secuencia de eventos.* Remind children that certain words such as *first, then, next,* and *finally* are often used to show sequence, or the order that things happened.

- When readers retell story events, they can think about how a character learns a lesson in a story. This helps readers to find out the important message, or lesson to be learned, in a story.

- Remind children that a flow chart can help readers organize the sequence of events in a story.

- Then discuss the flow chart using this model.

> **Think Aloud**   *I can use this flow chart to organize the sequence of events in a story. As I read through the story, I can ask myself,* What happens first? What happens next? *and* What happens last? *and write these events on the flow chart. When I look back at it, I can use it to retell the story events. This helps me figure out how characters learn from the events in a story.*

Next, read the top of **Student Book** p. 75 with children.

- Tell children that *dialogue* refers to the words that the characters say. Point to an example of dialogue in *Luke Goes to Bat.* Explain that children can find dialogue by looking for the words inside of quotation marks.

- Explain that authors have the characters use formal or informal language to make the characters seem real. Tell children that they will be looking for examples of formal or informal language in the dialogue as they read the story again.

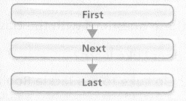

Q BE A READING DETECTIVE

Dig Deeper

Use Clues to Analyze the Text

Use these pages to learn about Sequence of Events and Formal and Informal Language. Then read *Luke Goes to Bat* again. Use what you learn to understand it better.

Sequence of Events

Luke Goes to Bat is about events that happen to a boy named Luke. The events in the story happen in order. Knowing the **sequence of events** can help you understand the story.

As you read, think about what happens and what the characters learn from the events. Then think about the lesson that you can learn. You can use a chart like the one below to show the order of events.

> First
>
> ↓
>
> Next
>
> ↓
>
> Last

Formal and Informal Language

Authors write **dialogue** to show what characters say. Sometimes the way a character speaks is **formal,** or follows correct grammar rules. Sometimes it is **informal,** or more relaxed. In *Luke Goes to Bat*, the boys sometimes use informal language as they talk to each other. An author uses formal and informal language to make what the characters say seem real.

ELA RL.2.2, L.2.3a ELD ELD.PI.2.4, ELD.PI.2.6, ELD.PI.2.7, ELD.PI.2.8

---

2 Guided Practice/Apply

Analyze the Text

Begin a second read of *Luke Goes to Bat* with children. Use the stopping points and instructional support to guide them to think more deeply about the text.

- Formal and Informal Language, p. T129
  ELA L.2.3a ELD ELD.PI.2.4, ELD.PI.2.6, ELD.PI.2.7, ELD.PI.2.8

- Sequence of Events, p. T135 ELA RL.2.2 ELD ELD.PI.2.6, ELD.PII.2.2

Directed Note Taking The graphic organizer will be completed with children during a second read on p. T135. ELA RL.2.2 ELD ELD.PI.2.6, ELD.PII.2.2

FORMATIVE ASSESSMENT ▲ RtI

Are children able to identify the sequence of events in a story?

IF...	THEN...
children struggle,	use **Differentiate Comprehension** for Struggling Readers, p. T188. See also Intervention Lesson 17, pp. S14–S15.
children are on track,	use **Differentiate Comprehension** for On-Level Readers, p. T188.
children excel,	use **Differentiate Comprehension** for Advanced Readers, p. T189.

 Differentiate Comprehension, pp. T188–T189 *Scaffold instruction to the English learner's proficiency level.*

DAY 2

Your Turn

Cite Text Evidence

▶ SHARE OBJECTIVES

- Recount a story to determine its moral, lesson, or message.
- Write an opinion piece about a topic or book.
- Add details to sentences by adding prepositional phrases. LANGUAGE

RETURN TO THE ESSENTIAL QUESTION

As partners discuss the Essential Question, have them discuss the benefits and rewards of continuing to try when something is difficult. Ask partners to share why they feel it's important to keep trying. Have them tell a story about a time they had to keep trying. Ask children to think about what might have happened if they hadn't kept trying. Remind children to follow the rules of discussion, ask questions when they don't understand, and to respect the opinions of their partners.

ELA SL.2.1a, SL.2.1c, SL.2.4 **ELD** ELD.PI.2.1, ELD.PI.2.6, ELD.PI.2.12a

 Classroom Conversation Have children continue their discussion of *Luke Goes to Bat* by reminding them that the characters in a story can learn lessons from the events in the story. As children discuss the questions on **Student Book** p. 76, remind them to follow the rules of discussion and build on things others say to keep the discussion going. Have them decide what the story's message really is. *Don't give up; keep trying.*

ELA RL2.2, SL.2.1a **ELD** ELD.PI.2.1, ELD.PI.2.6

ENGLISH LANGUAGE SUPPORT Use sentence frames such as the following to support discussion.

Luke learns that ____.

When Jackie Robinson almost struck out, Luke learned that ____.

The next time Luke plays baseball, he might ____. I know this might happen because ____.

As children share their ideas, have them use gestures and refer to the story for help completing the sentence frames. **ELD** ELD.PI.2.6, ELD.PI.2.12a

---

Your Turn

RETURN TO THE ESSENTIAL QUESTION

Turn and Talk **Why is it important to keep trying even if something is difficult to do?** Take turns sharing your ideas. Use text evidence from *Luke Goes to Bat* to support what you say. Ask questions if you need more information about what your partner says.

Classroom Conversation

Now talk about these questions with the class.

1. What lesson does Luke learn?
2. How does it help Luke to see Jackie Robinson almost strike out?
3. What might happen the next time Luke plays baseball with his friends? Use text evidence to explain your answer.

ELA RL.2.2, RL.2.7, W.2.1, W.2.4, W.2.10, SL.2.1a, SL.2.1c **ELD** ELD.PI.2.1, ELD.PI.2.6, ELD.PI.2.10, ELD.PI.2.11, ELD.PI.2.12a

ENGLISH LANGUAGE SUPPORT

How English Works: Collaborative

Prepositional Phrases Before children begin discussing why it is important to keep trying, have them think about how they will add detail while sharing. Using the following sentence, review adding details with prepositional phrases: *Luke wanted to hit the ball hard with the bat.* Remind children that prepositional phrases tell *how, when,* or *where.* Help children at different proficiency levels think about their topics and make lists of prepositional phrases to use during their discussions. **ELD** ELD.PII.2.5

WRITE ABOUT READING

Response Look back at pages 66–71. How do the pictures show you what is real and what Luke is imagining? Does this help you understand the story? Write a paragraph to explain what you think.

Writing Tip

Remember that a pronoun can take the place of a noun. Use a pronoun instead of using the same noun over and over.

77

WRITE ABOUT READING — Performance Task

Tell children they will write a response to the story that gives an opinion about *Luke Goes to Bat*.

- Remind children that an opinion is the way a person feels about something, and there are no right or wrong answers.

- Have children look back in the story to pages 66–71. Remind them that some parts of the story happen in Luke's imagination. Ask: *What does this tell you about Luke? Why do you think the author wrote the story this way? Does it help you understand the reason why Luke didn't give up?* Have all children participate in the discussion.

- Tell children to end their paragraph by restating their opinion.

Writing Tip Make sure children read the Writing Tip before they begin writing. Remind children of the pronouns *he, she, they, you,* and *we.* **ELA** RL.2.7, W.2.1, W.2.4, W.2.10, L.2.1f **ELD** ELD.PI.2.11

See **Analytic Writing Rubric** on p. R17.

WriteSmart Have children complete the Write About Reading activity through *my*WriteSmart. Children will read the prompt within *my*WriteSmart and have access to multiple writing resources, including the Student eBook, Writing Rubrics, and Graphic Organizers.

ENGLISH LANGUAGE SUPPORT

Comprehensible Input

All Proficiencies Before children begin writing, review what Luke imagined. Ask children if they've ever been in a situation where they imagined what their parents or teacher might say to them about something. Ask them to tell how they know that Luke is imagining this scene. For children who need support, provide the sentence frames: *I can tell what is real in the story because _____. The parts of the story Luke imagines are _____. The pictures (do/do not) help me understand the story because _____.* **ELD** ELD.PI.2.10, ELD.PI.2.11, ELD.PI.2.12a

Grammar Subject-Verb Agreement

► SHARE OBJECTIVES

- **Grammar** Use subject-verb agreement. LANGUAGE
- **Spelling** Spell words with long *i* (*i, igh,* and *y*).
- **Handwriting** Write Spelling Words.
- **Writing** Use dialogue in a narrative to tell readers what characters are like. LANGUAGE

ENGLISH LANGUAGE SUPPORT
Comprehensible Input

All Proficiencies Provide English learners more support with subject-verb agreement. Remind children that the subject tells who does the action, and the verb names the action. Have children complete sentence frames with the correct forms of *play: Luke plays baseball with Franky. They play on the same team.* Repeat with sentences with *run, catch, miss, wash.* Encourage them to point out the different spellings of the verb. **ELD** ELD.PII.2.3a

Primary-Language Support Sometimes first-language partners can work on projectables together. They can use their first language to talk about the items and to explain how they answered each one.

1 Teach/Model

Subjects and More Verbs Display Projectable 17.5 ⬒. Remind children that they should use the correct form of the verb to match the subject of a sentence that tells about something happening now. Explain that they will add -*es* to verbs that end with *s, sh, ch, tch, z,* or *x* to match a singular subject. Write the example sentences: *The boy splashes in the water. The boys splash in the water.*

Think Aloud *To identify the correct verb ending to use, I ask this Thinking Question: When should I add -es to the end of a verb that tells about now? If the subject is singular, such as boy, I add -s or -es at the end of the verb. I add -es if the verb ends with s, sh, ch, tch, z, or x. Splash ends in sh so splashes is correct. If the subject is plural, such as boys, I do not add -s or -es, so splash is correct.*

FOR STANDARD ENGLISH LEARNERS Some children may omit the final *s* from third-person present-tense regular verbs. They may say *he walk* instead of *he walks.* Guide children to complete sentence frames with the Standard English subject-verb agreement, such as *I _____ (walk/walks) home from school.*

2 Guided Practice/Apply

- Use the Thinking Question to complete the activity on **Projectable 17.5** with children.

- To reinforce concepts as needed play the GrammarSnap Video ⬒ that supports this lesson.

- Distribute Reader's Notebook Volume 2 page 20 ⬒ to children to complete independently. **ELD** ELD.PII.2.3a

Spelling Long *i* (*i, igh, y*)

SPELLING WORDS

BASIC

night*	July
kind	fry
spy	sigh
child	**REVIEW**
light	by
find	why
right*	**CHALLENGE**
high	behind
wild*	lightning

*A form or forms of these words appear in the literature.

Teach/Word Sort

- Review **Sound/Spelling Card** *ice cream. What sound do you hear at the beginning of ice cream? /ī/ This sound can be spelled* i, igh, *and* y.

- Draw a three-column chart. Have children write long *i* spelling words under each heading.

i	*igh*	*y*
wild	light	spy
child	night	fry

- Distribute Reader's Notebook Volume 2 p. 19 ⬒ to children to complete independently. **ELA** L.2.2d

Guess My Category

For additional practice with the Spelling Words, guide children to complete the Guess My Category activity on page 88 of the **Literacy and Language Guide.**

Handwriting

Model how to form the Basic Words *night, kind, spy, child, light,* and *find.* Handwriting models are available on pp. R24–R29 and on the Handwriting Models Blackline Masters ⬒. Remind children to write legibly and stay within the margins. **ELA** L.2.1g

Narrative Writing Focus Trait: Development

1 Teach/Model

Dialogue Explain that writers use dialogue to show more about a character. The words used in dialogue show what characters are like and how they feel.

- Remind children that the words they choose for character dialogue can show a character's personality and feelings.

- Remind them to use quotation marks to show the exact words a character says.

- Read and discuss this model.

Connect to *Luke Goes to Bat*	
Instead of this...	**...the author wrote this.**
Luke told Jackie to hit the ball.	Luke shouted with the crowd. "Give it to 'em, Jackie! You show 'em!" (p. 64)

- *How do the author's sentences show how Luke feels?* The dialogue shows that Luke believes Jackie can hit the ball. It also shows that he is excited.

2 Guided Practice/Apply

- Write: *Luke shrugged.*

- Direct children to **Student Book** p. 61 of *Luke Goes to Bat*. Point out that he shrugs to answer his grandmother's question. Ask children to replace the words *Luke shrugged* with a sentence of dialogue. Possible response: *"I think I'll practice hitting the ball."*

- Write: *"Thanks for taking me, Grandma," he said.* Ask children to reread **Student Book** p. 63, and then add a sentence of dialogue to give Grandma's answer. Possible response: *"I wouldn't have missed it for the world," said Grandma.*

- Ask children to work in pairs to write more dialogue between Luke and his grandmother. Remind them to use quotation marks. Ask partners to share their dialogue.

- Distribute Reader's Notebook Volume 2 page 21 to children to complete independently. **ELA** W.2.3, W.2.4, W.2.10 **ELD** ELD.PI.2.10

Daily Proofreading Practice

The crowd ~~roored~~ roared ⊙≡ the score was a ~~ty~~ tie.

ENGLISH LANGUAGE SUPPORT

Comprehensible Input

All Proficiencies Have children practice writing dialogue with partners. Provide a list of several very simple sentences, such as *I like puppies*, and have one partner choose one to read to their partner. The partner then puts it into writing using quotation marks and attributes the quote to their partner. For example, *"I like puppies," said Maria.* Provide assistance for those who need it.

myWriteSmart Children may prewrite, draft, revise, and publish their narrative writing task through *my*WriteSmart beginning on Day 3.

DAY 3

Today's Goals

Vocabulary & Oral Language
• Apply Vocabulary Knowledge

☑ **TARGET VOCABULARY**

practice	extra
hurried	curb
position	cheered
roared	final

Phonemic Awareness
• Segment Phonemes

Phonics & Fluency
• Compound Words
• Read Decodable Reader: *Wild Cats*
• Fluency: Stress
• High-Frequency Words

Text-Based Comprehension
• Independent Reading
• Reader's Guide
• Self-Selected Reading

Grammar & Writing
• Subject-Verb Agreement
• Narrative Writing:
  Story Paragraph

Spelling
• Long *i* (*i, igh, y*)

Opening Routines

Warm Up with Wordplay

Two Words

Tell children that they will each think of two words that describe Luke in the story *Luke Goes To Bat*. Ask them to write their ideas on a sheet of paper. Then collect the responses and write them on the board.

lonely	sad	patient
determined	lucky	excited

Ask children to choose a word from the list and use it in a sentence about Luke. Give them the following sentence starter:

Luke is _____ because _____. **ELA** L.2.6

Daily Phonemic Awareness

Segment Phonemes

- *Listen to this word:* light. *What is the first sound you hear?* /l/ *What sound do you hear next?* /ī/ *What sound do you hear last?* /t/

- Repeat the activity with the word *lit*. Remind children that the vowel sound they hear in *lit* is the short *i* sound /ĭ/.

- Continue the activity with these words: *night/knit, sit/sight, spy/spin, fly/fleet/flight, might/mitt, bin/bind.* **ELA** RF.2.3a

Corrective Feedback

- If a child is unable to segment the phonemes, say the word, give correction, and model the task. Example: *The word is spy. The first sound is /s/. The next sound I hear is /p/. The final sound that I hear is /ī/.*

- Have children segment the words with you before doing the task on their own.

Daily High-Frequency Words

- Point to **High-Frequency Word Card 162,** *sure.*

- *Say the word.* sure *Spell the word.* s-u-r-e *Write the word. Check the word.*

- Repeat the procedure with the new words *doing* and *room,* and with review words *any, blue, carry, else, studied, teacher,* and *turned.* **ELA** RF.2.3f

Hopscotch

- Create a hopscotch grid on the floor using masking tape. Write each letter of the word *sure* in a box. Write the whole word *sure* at the top.

- Have children hop from letter to letter, in the right order, to say and spell *sure.* Have them say the word. Repeat with more words, as time allows.

Corrective Feedback

- If a child does not recognize the word *sure,* say the correct word and have children repeat it. Sure. *What is the word?* sure

- Have children spell the word. s-u-r-e *How do we say this word?* sure

- Have children reread all of the cards in random order.

Daily Vocabulary Boost

- Guide children to interact with the Target Vocabulary using the following discussion starters.

  Tell what will happen if you practice playing the guitar.

  Show how you would walk if you hurried.

  Describe the position of your body before you jump.

- Have children work together to explain *practice, hurried,* and *position* in their own words. Make sure children follow appropriate rules for discussion, such as listening to speakers, taking turns, and staying on topic. **ELA** SL.2.1a, L.2.6 **ELD** ELD.PI.2.1

hurried
The soccer player hurried to stop the ball. He moved fast.

Vocabulary in
Context Cards 129–136

☑ **Target Vocabulary**

practice
hurried
position
roared
extra
curb
cheered
final

Phonics

▶ **SHARE OBJECTIVES**

- Substitute final syllables in compound words.
- Blend and decode regularly spelled compound words.
- Read on-level text with long *i* words spelled *i*, *igh*, *ie*, *y* and High-Frequency Words fluently.

FORMATIVE ASSESSMENT **RtI**

Corrective Feedback When a child mispronounces a word, point to the word and say it. Call attention to the element that was mispronounced, and then guide them to read the word. See the example below.

Decoding Error:
A child has trouble identifying the two words in a compound word.

Correct the error. Write the word *rain* on one card and *drop* on another. Say the words. *The words are* rain *and* drop. Hold the word cards together. *If we put the words together, we make the word* raindrop.

Model as you touch the word parts. *I'll read:* rain, drop, raindrop.

Guide *Let's read together:* rain, drop, raindrop. *What is the word?* raindrop

Check *You read the word:* raindrop *What is the word?* raindrop

Reinforce Say other compound words. Have children identify and read slowly the two words that make up the compound word, and then read the whole word faster. Make note of errors and review those words during the next lesson.

 Go to p. 190 for additional phonics and fluency support.

Cumulative Review

Phonemic Awareness Warm-Up *Let's substitute final syllables in compound words. I'll do it first. Listen:* sunshine. *Now listen as I change* shine *in* sunshine *to* light: sunlight.

Now you do it. Say the word seashell. *Change* shell *in* seashell *to* shore. seashore *Change* bow *in* rainbow *to* drop. raindrop *Change* flake *in* snowflake *to* man. snowman

Review Compound Words Remind children that sometimes two words are put together to make a new, longer word called a compound word.

- Display **Picture Cards** and **Word Cards** *snow* and *man*. Have children name each picture.

- Move the **Word Cards** together as you say each word. *When I put the words* snow *and* man *together, what compound word do I make?* snowman

Write and Read Compound Words Write the compound word *raindrop* on the board. Explain to children that recognizing the smaller words that make up the compound word will help them read the compound word. Cover *drop* and have children read *rain*. Then cover *rain* and have children read *drop*.

- Write these words on the board: *rainbow, sunlight, sunshine, backpack, baseball, daydream, paintbrush, railroad.* Work with children to read the two smaller words and then the compound word.

- Have partners work together to list compound words using the following words as one part of the compound: *tooth* toothpaste, toothbrush, toothpick; *book* bookcase, bookshelf, bookworm, bookstore; *black* blackboard, blackberries, blackbird. Then have partners read their lists to each other.

Practice Fluency

Use <u>Instructional Routine 15</u> to have partners read the **Decodable Reader** *Wild Cats*.

Decodable Reader

Fluency

Stress

1 Teach/Model

Explain that when good readers read aloud, the sound of their voice is sometimes softer and sometimes louder. Good readers stress important words in the text by saying them a little louder or stronger than other words.

Display Projectable 17.6 and read aloud the first paragraph. As you read each sentence, model how to use stress to add interest and emphasis to the reading. Record the words you stressed.

2 Guided Practice

Have children return to p. 55 of *Luke Goes to Bat* in the **Student Book**. Reread the first two sentences together. Point out the words you stress and discuss why those words get more emphasis. Have children select another sentence and choose the words they will stress. Have them read their sentences aloud.

3 Apply

Have partners take turns reading **Student Book** p. 55 to each other two or three times. Remind them to stress words to emphasize the author's meaning. **ELA** RF.2.4a, RF.2.4b

Distribute Reader's Notebook Volume 2 page 22 or leveled practice in Grab-and-Go™ Resources to children to complete independently.

▶ SHARE OBJECTIVE
- Read fluently, placing appropriate stress on important words.

ENGLISH LANGUAGE SUPPORT

Evaluating Fluency

All Proficiencies It is important to note that English learners can demonstrate fluency while still struggling with English pronunciation. Children's accents should never be a factor in evaluating fluency. Rather than interrupting an English learner's fluency practice to focus on pronunciation, sometimes children can be asked to focus on one sound that they produce as they record themselves reading. This way, children are not overwhelmed. Have children record, listen, and then record again to demonstrate improvement.

HOUGHTON MIFFLIN HARCOURT

JOURNEYS

Cold Reads

GRADE 2

Cold Reads: Support for fluent reading and comprehension

Independent Reading

▶ SHARE OBJECTIVES

- Read and comprehend literature.
- Ask and answer questions about what you read.
- Use evidence from the text to answer questions and support opinions. LANGUAGE
- Read independently from a "just right" book.
- Self-correct word recognition.

ENGLISH LANGUAGE SUPPORT

Review Key Ideas

Emerging Ask children *yes/no* questions about the selection. **ELD** ELD.PI.2.6

Expanding Ask children some details about the story, such as, *Where does Luke live?* and *What does Luke find on the roof?* **ELD** ELD.PI.2.6

Bridging Have children write a paragraph about a time when they did not give up, just like Luke. **ELD** ELD.PI.2.10

Reader's Guide

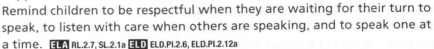

Revisit the Anchor Text Lead children in a brief discussion about *Luke Goes to Bat*. Have them retell important events in the order they happened and summarize what the story is about. Remind children to be respectful when they are waiting for their turn to speak, to listen with care when others are speaking, and to speak one at a time. **ELA** RL.2.7, SL.2.1a **ELD** ELD.PI.2.6, ELD.PI.2.12a

Have children read *Luke Goes to Bat* on their own. Then distribute Reader's Notebook Volume 2 pages 23–24 ⬀ and have children complete them independently. **ELA** RL.2.1, RL.2.7 **ELD** ELD.PI.2.6

FOR STUDENTS WITH DISABILITIES Some children may need assistance to participate in small-group or whole-class discussions. Provide sentence prompts and sentence starters as needed. Allow children to use drawings and gestures as part of their responses.

Model Questioning Demonstrate generating a question about *Luke Goes to Bat*. For example, write this question on the board: *Is Luke like anyone I know?* Reread **Student Book** p. 55 together to respond to the question. **ELA** RL.2.1 **ELD** ELD.PI.2.6

Generate Questions Have children generate questions about *Luke Goes to Bat*. Ask children to share their questions. Begin a class discussion of questions that children have in common or that are most significant to their understanding of the story. Remind children to be sure to keep to the topic and listen carefully to their classmates. **ELA** RL.2.1, SL.2.1a **ELD** ELD.PI.2.1, ELD.PI.2.6

Self-Selected Reading

Five Finger Rule Tell children that when they select books for reading, they should make sure the book is not too easy or too difficult. Teach them the Five Finger Rule for choosing a "just right" book.

- Choose a book that interests you, and read the first page or two.

- Put one finger up for every word you don't know.

- If five of your fingers go up while reading, choose another book.

- If only two or three fingers go up, you've found a "just right" book.

- If no fingers or only one finger go up, this book is too easy for you.

Review with children why it is important to choose a book that is neither too easy nor too difficult. **ELA** RL.2.10, RI.2.10

Self-Correction Strategies

Self-Correct Word Recognition Tell children that sometimes when reading, they might notice that something does not make sense. Explain that often when this happens, it is because they have misread a word. It will help to go back to where the reading stopped making sense to look for a word that might have been read incorrectly.

Model stopping to learn a new word with the word *ablaze* on **Student Book** p. 63. Read and reread the word, the sentence, and the paragraph. As a class, talk about clues in the context that help you figure out the meaning of this word.

Have partners take turns reading aloud to each other from their self-selected books. Ask them to pay attention to whether what they are reading makes sense and to use context to self-correct word recognition. Reaffirm that rereading new words in context makes them easier to understand. **ELA** RF.2.4c

---

ENGLISH LANGUAGE SUPPORT

"Just Right" Books for ELs

All Proficiencies Start a conversation about how to choose a "just right" book. Model the Five Finger Rule for children. Then guide them to use it on books they have chosen. Invite children to come up with their own methods for choosing a "just right" book and discuss them with the group.

Apply Vocabulary Knowledge

- Use words and phrases acquired through conversations, reading and being read to, and responding to texts. LANGUAGE
- Identify real-life connections between words and their use. LANGUAGE
- Talk about words that have more than one meaning. LANGUAGE

ENGLISH LANGUAGE SUPPORT

Access Prior Knowledge

Emerging Have children tell about a time when someone excluded them. Were others right to exclude them? What did the children do to feel better?

Expanding Ask children to tell if they were ever persistent and what or who encouraged them to keep trying.

Bridging Have partners talk about something they like to practice a lot, such as a sport, a dance, a language, or a musical instrument. **ELD** ELD.PI.2.1

☑ Review Target Vocabulary

Review with children the Vocabulary in Context Cards in **Student Book** pp. 48–49. Call on children to read the context sentences and explain how the photograph demonstrates the meaning of the word.

Enrich Vocabulary Write the following Related Words on the board. Read each word aloud, and have children repeat after you. Then read the child-friendly explanation for each word. Connect each word's meaning to the story *Luke Goes to Bat* by writing the context sentences on the board and reading them aloud. **ELA** L.2.5a

persistent: If you kept trying even when something was hard, you were persistent. *Luke was persistent at playing baseball.*

encouraged: If you helped someone feel courage and hope, you encouraged him or her. *Luke encouraged Jackie Robinson by yelling from the stands.*

treat: When you pay for a friend's lunch, you treat him or her to lunch, especially when you do it for fun! *Luke's grandmother decided to treat him to a baseball game.*

Make Connections Discuss all of the words using the items below to help children make connections between vocabulary words and their use.
ELA L.2.5a **ELD** ELD.PI.2.1, ELD.PI.2.12a, ELD.PI.2.12b

- Tell about a time you got an **extra** serving of something you like to eat.
- What happens if you don't **practice** something that is new to you?
- Stand on one foot. Can you stay in that **position** long?
- Tell about a time you **hurried**.
- How do you feel when you **treat** someone to something?
- What is something you have to be **persistent** about practicing to learn?
- How can a **curb** be helpful?
- Tell about a time you **cheered**.
- Tell about a time you **encouraged** someone.
- What are some feelings children have on the **final** day of the school year?
- How would you feel if a lion **roared** right next to you?

Dictionary Skills

Discuss Multiple Entries Use the word *treat* to begin a discussion about words that have more than one dictionary entry.

Look up *treat* in an online dictionary or a classroom dictionary. Point out how related meanings of *treat* are all listed together. Point out the part of speech. Write on the board the sentence *I will treat you to lunch.* Ask children whether *treat* is a person, place, or thing (a noun), or an action word (a verb) in this sentence.

Ask children to read the definitions of *treat* as a noun and a verb. As a class, think of sentences that use *treat* as a noun and as a verb. Have them decide which entry gives the best definition of *treat* as it is used in the example sentence. Remind children to take turns speaking and to listen when others are speaking. **ELA** SL.2.1a, L.2.4e **ELD** ELD.PI.2.1

FOR STUDENTS WITH DISABILITIES To help children focus during group discussions, agree on a simple gesture, such as nodding three times or giving a thumbs-up, for children to use when they agree with another child's point during a discussion. Before the discussion, remind children about the gesture. Model the gesture when you agree with something someone adds to a discussion.

QUICKWRITE Read aloud each question below. Pause a few minutes between each item to allow children to write a response. **ELA** L.2.6

1. What would you like someone to **treat** you to?

2. Who has **encouraged** you the most?

3. When might it be bad to be **persistent**?

ENGLISH LANGUAGE SUPPORT Write the following sentence frames on the board to support children in writing: *I would like someone to treat me to _____. It would make me feel _____. My _____ has encouraged me by _____. You should not be persistent when _____.* Read the sentence frames aloud with children. Ask them to write to complete the sentences. **ELD** ELD.PI.2.10

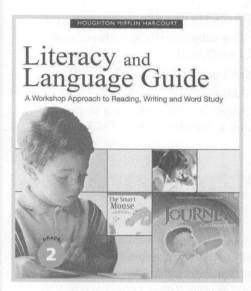

For additional practice with the lesson's Target Vocabulary words, use the activities on pages 148–149 of the **Literacy and Language Guide.**

- Introduce Target Vocabulary; Prefix *re-*
- Word Pairs
- Twenty Questions
- "Because" Sentences
- Vocabulary Web

Grammar Subject-Verb Agreement

▶ SHARE OBJECTIVES

- **Grammar** Use subject-verb agreement with pronouns. LANGUAGE
- **Spelling** Spell words with long *i* (*i*, *igh*, and *y*).
- **Writing** Choose a topic, and use a sequence chart to plan a narrative. LANGUAGE

ENGLISH LANGUAGE SUPPORT

Linguistic Transfer

All Proficiencies English learners often have difficulty with subject-verb agreement. Chant simple pronoun-verb sentences, using different verbs for each set: *He plays; She plays; It plays. I play; You play; We play; They play. He eats; She eats; It eats. I eat; You eat; We eat; They eat.* Have children provide their own examples. Write them, circling the pronoun and underlining the verb ending.

Linguistic Transfer There is no verb agreement in Cantonese, Vietnamese, Hmong, Tagalog, or Haitian Creole. English learners may omit the *-s* or *-es* endings on singular verbs. Provide practice with singular subject pronouns and verbs, for example, *She plays baseball.* **ELD** ELD.PIII.2

1 Teach/Model

Pronouns and Verbs Remind children that they must use the correct form of a verb to match the subject in a sentence that tells about now. Review with *The girl practices. The girls practice.*

- Review that pronouns can take the place of nouns and that pronouns can sometimes be the subject of a sentence.
- Explain that *he*, *she*, and *it* are pronouns that take the place of singular nouns. When *he*, *she*, or *it* is the subject of a sentence that tells about now, use a verb that ends in *-s* or *-es*. Write examples on the board: *He runs fast. She catches the bus.*
- When the pronoun *I*, *you*, *they*, or *we* is the subject of a sentence that tells about now, do not add *-s* or *-es* to the verb. Write examples on the board: *I run fast. You play well. We ride bikes.*

2 Guided Practice/Apply

- Write sentences on the board: *You (hit, hits) the ball with the bat. She (chase/chases) the ball. I (catch, catches) the ball. They (cheer/cheers) for the team.*
- Work with children to write each sentence correctly.
- To reinforce concepts as needed, play the GrammarSnap Video that supports this lesson.
- Distribute Reader's Notebook Volume 2 page 26 to children to complete independently. **ELD** ELD.PII.2.3a

Spelling Long *i (i, igh, y)*

SPELLING WORDS

BASIC

night*	July
kind	fry
spy	sigh
child	**REVIEW**
light	by
find	why
right*	**CHALLENGE**
high	behind
wild*	lightning

*A form of this word appears in the literature.

Segment Sounds

- Model segmenting sounds. *Listen as I say the word night: nniiight. Listen for the /ī/ sound in the word night. Now you say it with me: nniiight.*
- Repeat with *child* and *July*. Tell children that saying sounds slowly will help them spell words.

Build Words with *igh*

- Use **Letter Cards** to model building *night*. Have children read the word with you and begin to list the Spelling Words.

- Have partners use **Letter Cards** to build words with *i*, *igh*, and *y* and add them to their lists.
- Have partners read and spell words they built using **Letter Cards**.
- Distribute Reader's Notebook Volume 2 page 25 to children to complete independently. **ELA** L.2.2d

Word Hunt

For additional practice with the Spelling Words, have children complete the Word Hunt activity on page 89 of the **Literacy and Language Guide.**

Narrative Writing Prewrite

1 Teach/Model

Sequence of Events Teach children to write events in the order in which they happen. Remind children that when events are out of order, a story will not make sense to readers.

Connect to *Luke Goes to Bat*

Out of Order	Correct Order
Jackie struck out. "Strike three!" the umpire called. Jackie swung.	Jackie swung. "Strike three!" the umpire called. Jackie struck out.

- *What makes the second passage easier to understand? The second passage tells the events in the order they happened.*

2 Guided Practice/Apply

Story Paragraph Display Projectable 17.7. Read the prompt aloud.

- Work with children to complete the Flow Chart.
- Save the completed Flow Chart for Day 4.

Think Aloud *My story will be about how a girl meets her hero, an astronaut. What is the first thing that happens? Kira wins a trip to Florida to meet her hero. I'll write that in the first box. Then I will tell about what happens when she gets there.*

Prewriting Read together the prompt on **Projectable 17.7**. Distribute Graphic Organizer 4: Flow Chart. Have children brainstorm ideas for heroes they know or would like to meet. Point out that the heroes can be in their family, in the community, or in the wider world. Then have children complete their own Flow Chart using their own idea or one from the discussion. Remind them to add details about when and where their story takes place.
ELA W.2.3, W.2.4, W.2.10 **ELD** ELD.PI.2.10, ELD.PII.2.1

Daily Proofreading Practice

Now the basebal player hit the ball.
It goes hi through the air.

ENGLISH LANGUAGE SUPPORT

How English Works: Productive

Prepositional Phrases Before children begin drafting their stories, have them think about how they will add detail as they write. Using the following sentence, review adding details with prepositional phrases: *Kira wins a trip to Florida.* Remind children that prepositional phrases tell *how, when,* or *where.* Help children at different proficiency levels think about their topics and make lists of prepositional phrases to use while drafting. **ELD** ELD.PII.2.5

WriteSmart Have children prewrite their narrative writing task through *my*WriteSmart.

Today's Goals

Vocabulary & Oral Language
- **Vocabulary Strategies:**
  Antonyms

☑ **TARGET VOCABULARY**

practice	extra
hurried	curb
position	cheered
roared	final

Phonemic Awareness
- **Segment Phonemes**

Phonics & Fluency
- **Long *i* (*i, igh, ie, y*)**
- **Fluency:** Stress
- **Read Decodable Reader:** *Wild Cats*
- **High-Frequency Words**

Text-Based Comprehension
- **Connect to the Topic**
- **Read Informational Text:**
  Jackie Robinson
- **Compare Texts**

Grammar & Writing
- **Spiral Review:** Kinds of Sentences
- **Narrative Writing:** Story Paragraph

Spelling
- **Long *i* (*i, igh, y*)**

Opening Routines

Warm Up with Wordplay

Using Vocabulary

Remind children that they learned three new vocabulary words: *treat, persistent, encouraged*. Have children read the words with you and explain their meaning. Review the explanations on p. T156, if necessary.

Display the words, along with the sentences below. Tell children that they will use these words to help a girl named Mia list the top three reasons why her soccer coach is great.

Top Three Reasons Why My Coach Is Great

1. She _____ me to try out for goalie.
2. She knew I would improve if I practiced and was _____.
3. She would _____ the team to pizza on Fridays!

Have partners write each sentence, filling in the correct Related Word. Then have children read and discuss their sentences.

ELA L.2.5a

Daily Phonemic Awareness

Segment Phonemes

- *Listen to this word:* mild. *What is the first sound you hear?* /m/ *What sound do you hear next?* /ī/ *What's the next sound?* /l/ *What's the final sound?* /d/

- Repeat the activity with the word *pry*. Remind children that the vowel sound they hear is /ī/, the long *i* sound.

- Continue the activity with the words *flight, tied, pit, sigh, by, lid, lied,* and *fly*. **ELA** RF.2.3a

Corrective Feedback

- If a child is unable to identify each sound, say the word, give correction, and model the task. Example: *The word is pry. The first sound I hear is /p/. The next sound I hear is /r/. The last sound I hear is /ī/.*

- Have children segment the word with you and then continue on their own.

Daily High-Frequency Words

- Point to **High-Frequency Word Card 166,** *room*.

- *Say the word.* room *Spell the word.* r-o-o-m *Write the word. Check it.*

- Repeat the routine with new words *doing* and *else*, and with review words *any, blue, carry, studied, sure, teacher,* and *turned*. **ELA** RF.2.3f

Crossword Puzzle

- Have children use any High-Frequency Words they want to make a crossword puzzle.

r			
e	l	s	e
a		u	
d		r	
y		e	

Corrective Feedback

- If a child does not recognize the word *room*, say the correct word and have children repeat it. room. *What is the word?* room

- Have children spell the word. r-o-o-m *How do we say this word?* room

- Have children reread all of the cards in random order.

Daily Vocabulary Boost

- Guide children to interact with Target Vocabulary by asking the following questions. Remind them to speak clearly when participating in the discussion.

  Why would you spend extra time on your homework?

  Where do you find a curb? What is important about a curb?

  Describe a time when you cheered.

  How might you feel on the final day of vacation?

- Have children work together to explain *extra, curb, cheered,* and *final* in their own words. Make sure children follow appropriate rules for discussion, such as listening to speakers, taking turns, and staying on topic. **ELA** SL.2.1a, L.2.6 **ELD** ELD.PI.2.1

cheered
The audience clapped and cheered as the player scored a goal.

GO TEAM

Vocabulary in Context Cards 129–136

☑ **Target Vocabulary**

practice
hurried
position
roared
extra
curb
cheered
final

Phonics

▶ **SHARE OBJECTIVES**

- Review words with long *i* spelled *i, igh, ie, y.*
- Review and sort words with vowel teams *ee, ea* (vowel team syllables) and words with long *o* spelled *o, oa, ow.*

▶ **SKILLS TRACE**

Words with Long *i* (*i, igh, ie, y*)	
Introduce	pp. T116–T117, T142–T143
Differentiate	pp. T184–T185
Reteach	p. T198
▶ Review	**pp. T162, T263, T352, T363**
Assess	Weekly Tests, Lesson 17

ENGLISH LANGUAGE SUPPORT

Comprehensible Input

All Proficiencies Preview the word pairs in the Write and Read Words activity to check on children's understanding of the words' meanings. Display each pair of words. Ask a question to help get at the meaning of each word, for example: *What is something a shy person might do? Is a sly person clever or silly?* Use children's responses to determine if they need a simple definition, example, or image to prepare them to participate in the activity.

Review Words with Long *i* (*i, igh, ie, y*)

Phonemic Awareness Warm-Up *I'll say a word. You say the sounds you hear and name the vowel sound. I'll do it first. Listen: spy. Now listen as I say each sound: /s/ /p/ /ī/. Let's do it together. Say: spy. What sounds do you hear? /s/ /p/ /ī/ Which sound is the vowel sound? /ī/ What do we call that sound? long i*

Now you do it. Say the sounds you hear in these words and name the vowel sound: sly, /s/ /l/ /ī/, long i; kick, /k/ /ĭ/ /k/, short i; ship, /sh/ /ĭ/ /p/, short i; right, /r/ /ī/ /t/, long i; flip, /f/ /l/ /ĭ/ /p/, short i; fright, /f/ /r/ /ī/ /t/, long i; child, /ch/ /ī/ /l/ /d/, long i; my, /m/ /ī/, long i; sift, /s/ /ĭ/ /f/ /t/, short i; bind, /b/ /ī/ /n/ /d/, long i; lie, /l/ /ī/, long i.

Write and Read Words Remind children that /ī/, the long *i* sound, can be spelled *i, igh, ie,* or *y.* Write *find, might, lie,* and *fly* in four columns on the board as shown below. Have children read the words and copy them on a sheet of paper. Then read each of the following questions aloud. Ask children to say the word that answers the question and listen for the long *i* sound. Then have them write the word in the column below the word with the same long *i* spelling.

1. If someone is tricky, is that person *sly* or *shy*? *sly*

2. If it is a dessert with fruit, is it *pie* or *rye*? *pie*

3. If you do a nice thing, are you *wild* or *kind*? *kind*

4. If a light hurts your eyes, is it *bright* or *mild*? *bright*

5. If you cook meat, do you *spy* or *fry*? *fry*

6. If you think, do you use your *mind* or your *might*? *mind*

7. If you fly in a plane, is it a *sight* or a *flight*? *flight*

8. If you fix your laces, do you *try* them or *tie* them? *tie*

Ask children to read their word groups aloud. Use the **Corrective Feedback** steps if children need additional help. **ELA** RF.2.3b

find	might	lie	fly
kind	*bright*	*pie*	*sly*
mind	*flight*	*tie*	*fry*

Cumulative Review

Phonemic Awareness Warm-Up *Listen to the words and tell which two words have the same middle vowel sound. I'll do it first. Listen: team, seep, soap. I hear the middle vowel sound /ē/ in team and seep.*

Now you do it. Tell which two words have the same middle vowel sound: leaf, lame, green, **leaf, green**; toast, beast, float, **toast, float**; freeze, grown, most, **grown, most**; feel, stream, bowl, **feel, stream**; rope, meet, foam, **rope, foam**; coach, tree, cream, **tree, cream**.

Sort Words by Sound Review **Sound/Spelling Cards** *eagle* and *ocean*. Remind children that the /ē/ sound can be spelled *ee* or *ea*, and the /ō/ sound can be spelled *o, oa,* or *ow.*

- Write these words on the board and have children read them: *reason, agree, floating, eager, owner, slow, treat, deal, boast, clean, crow, thrown, fifteen, croak, cargo, creek.*

- Have partners work together to copy each word onto an index card. Tell them to shuffle the cards and place them face-down in rows.

- Have partners alternate turning over two cards and reading the words. If the long vowel sounds in the words match and the words are read correctly, the child keeps the cards.

- If the vowel sounds do not match or the words are read incorrectly, the cards are returned face-down. Play continues until all cards are gone. The child with the most cards wins.

ELA RF.2.3a, RF.2.3b, RF.2.3c

e
e_e
ee
ea
_y
_ie_
_ey
(c)ei

o
o_e
oa
ow
_oe

Corrective Feedback When a child mispronounces a word, point to the word and say it. Call attention to the element that was mispronounced, say the sound, and then guide children to read the word. See the example below.

Decoding Error:
In the Write and Read Words activity, a child reads *fry* as *free*.

Correct the error. Review the **Sound/Spelling Card** *ice cream.* Then say the word and the sound. *The word is* fry. *The letter* y *often stands for the long* i *sound at the end of a one-syllable word.*

Model as you touch the letters. *I'll blend: /f/ /r/ /ī/,* fry.

Guide *Let's blend together: /f/ /r/ /ī/,* fry. *What's the word?* fry

Check *You blend: /f/ /r/ /ī/ What's the word?* fry

Reinforce Have children go back and reread the word group for that spelling on their list.

Practice Fluency

Use Instructional Routine 14 ⎘ to reread the **Decodable Reader** *Wild Cats* with children.

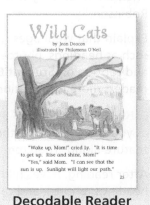

Decodable Reader

☑ **GENRE**

Informational text gives facts about a topic. This is a website.

☑ **TEXT FOCUS**

A **website** is an online collection of pages about a topic. As you read, pay attention to how the website looks. Which parts would help you move to another part of the website?

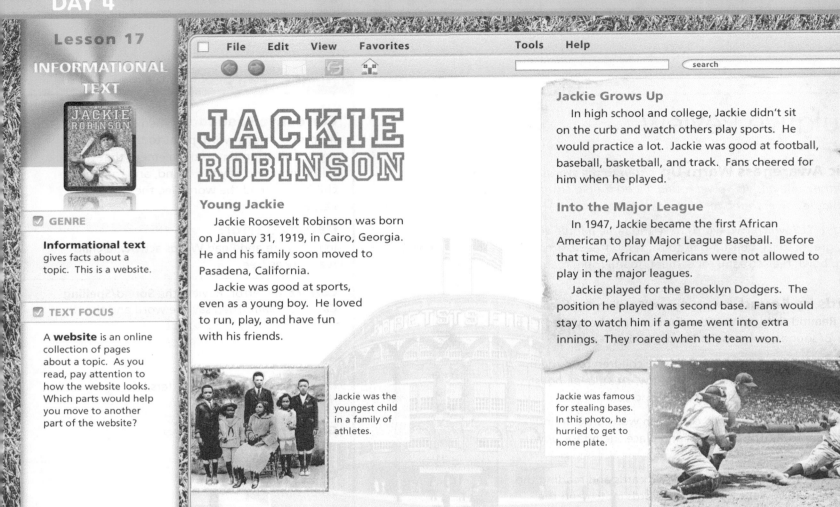

File   Edit   View   Favorites   Tools   Help

search

JACKIE ROBINSON

Young Jackie

Jackie Roosevelt Robinson was born on January 31, 1919, in Cairo, Georgia. He and his family soon moved to Pasadena, California.

Jackie was good at sports, even as a young boy. He loved to run, play, and have fun with his friends.

Jackie was the youngest child in a family of athletes.

Jackie Grows Up

In high school and college, Jackie didn't sit on the curb and watch others play sports. He would practice a lot. Jackie was good at football, baseball, basketball, and track. Fans cheered for him when he played.

Into the Major League

In 1947, Jackie became the first African American to play Major League Baseball. Before that time, African Americans were not allowed to play in the major leagues.

Jackie played for the Brooklyn Dodgers. The position he played was second base. Fans would stay to watch him if a game went into extra innings. They roared when the team won.

Jackie was famous for stealing bases. In this photo, he hurried to get to home plate.

78   ELA RI.2.5, RI.2.10 ELD ELD.PI.2.6, ELD.PII.2.1   79

DOMAIN: Values

LESSON TOPIC: Never Give Up

Cross-Curricular Connection Lead a discussion about what it means to be a hero. Then discuss Jackie Robinson's contribution to the sport of baseball. Ask children if they think that Jackie Robinson was a hero, and have them give reasons that support their opinions. Then ask children to name some people they think are heroes or actions that people might take that make them heroes.

Connect to the Topic: Informational Text
Introduce Genre and Text Focus

- Read with children the genre and text focus information on **Student Book** p. 78. Then tell them they will read a webpage of an encyclopedia entry called "Jackie Robinson."

- Explain that webpages can have the same types of features as a print encyclopedia, such as headings, photos, and captions. Point to and name the title, heading, photo, and caption on **Student Book** p. 78. Ask children to tell how these features give readers more information about a topic.

  ENGLISH LANGUAGE SUPPORT Have children point to the features on the page as you name them. As they point to each one, have them say the name of the feature aloud. Then remind them of the purpose of the feature.

- After reading, have children locate specific information in the text using the headings, photos, and captions. **ELA** RL.2.5

File　Edit　View　Favorites　Tools　Help

Jackie Retires

Jackie played his final game on September 30, 1956. After that, he worked hard to change laws that were unfair to African Americans.

In honor of Jackie, no other major league baseball player will ever wear the number 42 again.

80

 ## Compare Texts

Luke Goes to Bat ・ Jackie Robinson

TEXT TO TEXT

Share Differences Think about why the authors wrote *Luke Goes to Bat* and *Jackie Robinson*. How is the author's purpose for writing the story different from the author's purpose for making the website? Share your ideas with a partner.

TEXT TO SELF

Write a Story Have you ever worked hard to get good at something the way Luke did? Write sentences about your experience.

TEXT TO WORLD

Connect to Technology Luke watched baseball at Ebbets Field. How might seeing a game in person be different from seeing it on television? Share your opinion with a partner.

ELA RI.2.6, W.2.3, W.2.4, W.2.8, W.2.10 **ELD** ELD.PI.2.6, ELD.PI.2.10, ELD.PI.2.12a

81

Compare Texts

TEXT TO TEXT

Share Differences Remind children of the different reasons an author may write a selection. Be sure that children first identify the author's purpose for each text and then discuss how the purposes are different. **ELA** RL.2.6

ENGLISH LANGUAGE SUPPORT Tell children the author's purpose for writing *Luke Goes to Bat* was to tell a story. The author's purpose for writing "Jackie Robinson" was to tell the reader about an important person. Ask children to tell if they agree with those statements and to tell why.

ELD ELD.PI.2.1, ELD.PI.2.3, ELD.PI.2.6, ELD.PI.2.11

TEXT TO SELF

Write a Story Tell children to pay attention to the sequence of events as they write their sentences. *First, write about which activity you wanted to do better. Then tell how you practiced your activity. Finish by explaining how you have improved.* **Answers will vary.**

ELA W.2.3, W.2.4, W.2.5 **ELD** ELD.PI.2.10

TEXT TO WORLD

Connect to Technology Review with children that to visualize is to create a picture in your mind. Have children visualize watching a game on television and compare the mental picture to a real event. *Sample answer: You probably get to see the game better on television. You hear an announcer. The roar of the crowd is probably louder when you are at the game. At the game, you might catch a foul ball and you might smell different foods, like popcorn.*

ELD ELD.PI.2.1, ELD.PI.2.3, ELD.PI.2.11

Vocabulary Strategies

▶ **SHARE OBJECTIVES**
- Identify and understand antonyms using sentence context. LANGUAGE
- Use word-learning strategies independently. LANGUAGE

▶ **SKILLS TRACE**

Antonyms	
Introduce	**T166–T167**
Differentiate	T196–T197
Reteach	T199
Assess	Weekly Tests, Lesson 17

ENGLISH LANGUAGE SUPPORT

Build Background

Emerging Tell children opposites cannot both be true. Say, *If I'm happy, I can't be sad. Happy and sad are opposites.* Repeat with other words.

Expanding Have children write simple statements such as *It is nighttime.* Then tell the opposite. One by one, have children read their statements and then say the opposite of what they wrote.

Bridging Tell children that *happy* has several opposites, including *unhappy* and *sad.* Have children list other words with multiple opposites. **ELD** ELD.PI.2.8

Antonyms

1   Teach/Model

Terms About Language

antonyms words that have opposite, or very different, meanings

Spanish cognate: antónimo

ENGLISH LANGUAGE SUPPORT Preteach antonyms. Point out that *hot* is the antonym of *cold*. Write *hurried*. Hurried *means "moved quickly." What word means the opposite of* hurried? Slowed *means "moved less quickly."* Hurried *and* slowed *are antonyms.* Write *big, soft,* and *sweet.* Have children work in pairs to identify an antonym for each word. Then, discuss answers as a class. **ELD** ELD.PI.2.1

- Explain that antonyms are words that have opposite, or very different, meanings.

- Tell children that they can use clues in a sentence or in nearby sentences to identify an unknown word's antonym and figure out its meaning.

- Point out that sometimes a word has more than one antonym.

- Write the following sentence on the board:

> The white dog was <u>frisky</u>, but the brown dog seemed tired and stayed still on his bed.

Think Aloud *I'm not sure what* frisky *means. I'll look at nearby words and sentences for clues. I know that the word* but *often signals that things are being compared. I see the words* tired *and* stayed still *in the second part of the sentence. I know they mean that the brown dog didn't move. I think those are antonyms for* frisky. *The opposite of* tired *and* stayed still *must mean the white dog moved a lot and wasn't tired. I think* frisky *must mean moving about a lot in a lively way.*

- Ask children what they could do to make sure that they have the correct meaning for *frisky*. *look up the word in a dictionary*

2 Guided Practice

- Display the top half of <u>Projectable 17.8</u> and read the sentences aloud.

- Help children use context to figure out the meanings of the underlined words. Then have them find the words' antonyms in the word bank and use them to fill in the sentence frames.

- If children incorrectly identify a word as an antonym, remind them that antonyms have opposite meanings.

- Display the chart on the bottom half of **Projectable 17.8.** Have children use the antonym pairs they identified to complete the chart.

3 Apply

- Remind children that looking around a word for context clues can help them understand word meaning. Have them apply Step 1 of the **Vocabulary Strategy** to deepen their understanding of the words used to complete the sentence frame. Have children discuss which words in the sentences helped them understand the meaning of the antonyms. **ELA** L.2.4a

ENGLISH LANGUAGE SUPPORT Write these frames on the board, and help children use them to respond: *Antonyms do not mean the same thing. They have different meanings. I think the antonyms in those sentences are _____ and _____ because _____.* **ELD** ELD.PI.2.7, ELD.PI.2.12b

- Have partners work together to write brief definitions for one pair of antonyms.

- Distribute <u>Reader's Notebook Volume 2 page 27</u> or <u>leveled practice</u> in Grab-and-Go™ Resources to children to complete independently.

Interactive Whiteboard Lesson Use **Vocabulary Strategies: Antonyms** to learn about these words with opposite meanings. **ELA** L.2.4a

FORMATIVE ASSESSMENT RtI

Are children able to identify and understand antonyms?

IF...	THEN...
children struggle,	▶ use Struggling Readers lesson, p. T194.
children are on track,	▶ use On-Level Readers lesson, p. T194.
children excel,	▶ use Advanced Readers lesson, p. T195.

 Differentiate Vocabulary Strategies: pp. T194–T195. *Scaffold instruction to the English learner's proficiency level.*

Grammar Spiral Review: Kinds of Sentences

▶ SHARE OBJECTIVES

- **Grammar** Review kinds of sentences. LANGUAGE
- **Spelling** Spell words with long *i* (*i, igh,* and *y*).
- **Handwriting** Write Spelling Words.
- **Writing** Draft a narrative. LANGUAGE

ENGLISH LANGUAGE SUPPORT

Access Prior Knowledge

All Proficiencies Demonstrate that the way a sentence is said tells what kind of sentence it is. Say, *Where is the desk?* Look around. *The desk is here.* Point to it. Have children repeat each sentence, using your intonation and gestures. Repeat with other sentences based on objects and people in the room. Write a few of the sentences on the board, underlining the capital letter at the beginning and circling the end mark. Have children identify each kind of sentence.

1 Teach/Model

Kinds of Sentences Review the kinds of sentences.

- An *exclamation* shows a strong feeling such as excitement, surprise, or fear. An exclamation ends with an exclamation point.
- A *statement* tells something. A statement ends with a period.
- A *command* tells someone to do something. A command usually begins with a verb and ends with a period.
- A *question* asks something. It ends with a question mark and starts with a question word such as *Did, Can, What, Where, Why, How,* or *When.*

ENGLISH LANGUAGE SUPPORT Review capital and lowercase letters. Remind children that all sentences in English begin with a capital letter. Page through the selection and have children find the capital letters at the beginning of each sentence.

2 Guided Practice/Apply

- Write: *Did you see the game? Angel hit a home run! Tell Angel to come here. I want to talk to him.* Work with children to identify each kind of sentence.
- Have children underline the capital letter at the beginning of each sentence and circle the end punctuation mark.
- Have partners write an example of each kind of sentence. Then have them read their sentences aloud and identify each kind of sentence.
- Distribute Reader's Notebook Volume 2 page 29 ⬚ and have children complete it independently.

Spelling Long *i (i, igh, y)*

SPELLING WORDS

BASIC

night*	July
kind	fry
spy	sigh
child	REVIEW
light	by
find	why
right*	REVIEW
high	behind
wild*	lightning

*A form or forms of these words appear in the literature.

Connect to Writing

- Ask children to use the Spelling Words to write sentences about someone who is special to them.
- Have them proofread their sentences. Then have children read their sentences aloud.
- As a class, have children say each word and spell it aloud.
- Distribute Reader's Notebook Volume 2 p. 28 ⬚ to children to complete independently. **ELA** L.2.2d

Handwriting

Model how to form the Basic Words *right, high, wild, July, fry,* and *sigh.* Handwriting models are available on pp. R24–R29 and on the Handwriting Models Blackline Masters ⬚. Remind children to write legibly and stay within the margins. **ELA** L.2.1g

Blind Writing Sort

For additional practice with the Spelling Words, have children complete the Blind Writing Sort activity on page 89 of the **Literacy and Language Guide.** **ELA** L.2.2d

Narrative Writing Draft

1 Teach/Model

Avoiding Stringy Sentences Tell children that sentences that are too long can be difficult or confusing to read. Explain that writers can break long, stringy sentences into shorter sentences to make writing clearer. Write the following sentences.

Connect to *Luke Goes to Bat*	
Weak	**Strong**
Luke went to the game, and he went with his grandma, and he saw Jackie Robinson play.	Luke went to the game. He went with his grandma, and he saw Jackie Robinson play.

• *Why is the second example clearer? The two shorter sentences are easier to read than the long, stringy one.*

2 Guided Practice/Apply

Story Paragraph Review the Flow Chart on Projectable 17.7 ◰ from Day 3. Display Projectable 17.9 ◰, and work with the class to draft a story paragraph.

• As you draft, use the Think Aloud to model avoiding stringy sentences.

Think Aloud *I want to write about what happens when Kira is in Florida. I won't put all the details into one sentence because that would be hard to read.*

Drafting Have children begin drafting their own stories using their Flow Charts from Day 3. Remind children to include details and dialogue as they write about the events in order.

ELA W.2.3, W.2.4, W.2.10 **ELD** ELD.PI.2.10, ELD.PII.2.1

ENGLISH LANGUAGE SUPPORT

Comprehensible Input

All Proficiencies Tell children that sometimes it's better to break longer sentences up if they tell about too many ideas and are confusing. Provide children several examples of sentences that are too long. Work with them to divide the sentences up in appropriate ways.

myWriteSmart Have children draft their narrative writing task through *my*WriteSmart.

DAY 5

Today's Goals

Vocabulary & Oral Language
- Domain-Specific Vocabulary
- Speaking & Listening

☑ TARGET VOCABULARY

practice	extra
hurried	curb
position	cheered
roared	final

Phonemic Awareness
- Segment Phonemes

Phonics & Fluency
- Interactive Whiteboard Lesson
- High-Frequency Words

Text-Based Comprehension
- Extend the Topic
- Research/Media Skills: Compare and Contrast Media Messages

Assess & Reteach
- Assess Skills
- Respond to Assessment

Grammar & Writing
- Subject-Verb Agreement
- Narrative Writing: Story Paragraph

Spelling
- Long *i* (*i, igh, y*)

Opening Routines

Warm Up with Wordplay

Alike and Not Alike

Tell children that today, they will work with partners to think of two games that are alike but also different.

Display and read aloud the following example:

> ### stickball and baseball
> **They are both played by hitting a ball.
> One is played with a stick, and one is played with a bat.**

Have partners come up with two other games, and write ways in which they are alike and different. Provide suggestions, if needed: soccer/hockey, dodgeball/tag, kickball/baseball, checkers/chess. **ELA** SL.2.1b **ELD** ELD.PI.2.1

Interactive Whiteboard Lesson

For cumulative review, use **Phonics: Words with Long *i* (*i, igh, ie, y*)** to reinforce blending, reading, and building decodable words with long *i* spelled *i*, *igh*, *ie*, or *y*. **ELA** RF.2.3a, RF.2.3b, RF.2.3c, RF.2.3e

Daily Phonemic Awareness

Segment Phonemes

- *You are going to listen to some words with the long* i, /ī/, *and short* i, /ĭ/, *vowel sounds. The first word is* bright. *What sounds do you hear?* /b/ /r/ /ī/ /t/ *What vowel sound do you hear?* /ī/, *long* i

- Continue with children, using these words: *pin, pie, list, lie, right, wrist, sky, skip, trip, try.* **ELA** RF.2.3a

Corrective Feedback

- If a child is unable to identify and segment the phonemes, say the first word, give correction, and model the task. Example: *The word is* pin. *The first sound I hear is* /p/. *The next sound I hear in* pin *is* /ĭ/. *The last sound I hear is* /n/. *The vowel sound in* pin *is short* i, /ĭ/.

- Have children segment the words with you before doing the task on their own.

Daily High-Frequency Words

- Point to **High-Frequency Word Card 167**, *teacher*.

- *Say the word.* teacher *Spell the word.* t-e-a-c-h-e-r *Write the word. Check the word.*

- Repeat the procedure with words from this week (*any, carry, studied, turned*) and words from last week (*something, said, gone*). **ELA** RF.2.3f

Word Box

- Write this week's and last week's High-Frequency Words on multiple slips of paper. Place the slips in a box.

- Have children take turns selecting a slip of paper and reading the word aloud.

Corrective Feedback

- If a child does not recognize the word *any*, say the correct word and have children repeat it. *Any. What is the word?* any

- Have children spell the word. *a-n-y How do we say it?* any

- Have children reread all of the cards in random order.

Daily Vocabulary Boost

- Reread "The Crowd Roared!" aloud to children. (See p. T115.)

- As you read each Target Vocabulary word in the selection, pause to have a child explain or describe its meaning.

- After reading, review the Target Vocabulary and the definitions. (See p. T114.) Challenge children to use the words in their everyday speech. **ELA** L.2.6 **ELD** ELD.PI.2.5

final
When the game ended, the final score was four to two.

0402

Vocabulary in Context Cards 129–136

☑ **Target Vocabulary**

practice
hurried
position
roared
extra
curb
cheered
final

DAY 5

DOMAIN: **Values**

LESSON TOPIC: Never Give Up

Extend the Topic

► SHARE OBJECTIVES

- Acquire and use domain-specific vocabulary. LANGUAGE
- Participate in conversations about a topic. LANGUAGE
- Build on what others say in conversations by linking comments. LANGUAGE
- Ask for clarification or explanation about topics or texts under discussion. LANGUAGE

Words About the Topic: Never Give Up

- **determined** strong minded, firm
- **morals** doing what is right
- **respect** admire, believe in

Domain-Specific Vocabulary

Introduce Words About the Topic Remind children that this week's topic is Never Give Up. Display the words shown at left. Tell children that these are words that can help them learn more about the topic. Read aloud the meaning of each word, and have children respond to the following prompts. **ELA** L.2.5a, L.2.6

- *You have made up your mind and won't let anything get in your way. What word describes your attitude?* determined
- *Someone who is always helpful to others has good_____.* morals
- *Name one person you respect. Discuss students' responses.*

ENGLISH LANGUAGE SUPPORT Guide children to interact with the words by discussing as a class questions such as these: *What are you determined to do? In addition to being helpful, what are some other morals that people have? When you respect someone, how might you show it?* **ELD** ELD.PI.2.1, ELD.PI.2.12a

Interact with the Words Have children work in small groups to create a Four-Square Map for each of the domain-specific words. For each of the domain-specific words, children should fold a blank sheet of paper into four equal sections. Work with them to follow the steps below for each word. As needed, display the meanings of the words on the board. Ask individual children to use the words in a sentence orally. Then write the sentence on the board for other children to copy.

1 In the first corner, draw a picture for the word.

2 In the second corner, write the meaning of the word.

3 In the third corner, write a sentence using the word.

4 In the fourth corner, write the word.

When groups have finished, have them share their Four-Square Maps with the class. **ELA** L.2.5a, L.2.6 **ELD** ELD.PI.2.1

Research and Media Literacy: Performance Task
Compare and Contrast Media Messages

Media Messages Talk to the class about media messages. Ask: *Should you automatically believe everything you see or read? No* Point out that people have to think about and evaluate the information they get from television, the radio, and the Internet.

Evaluate Website Remind children that they must always have adult permission and supervision when they are using the Internet. Direct the children's attention to *Jackie Robinson* on **Student Book** p. 78. This website should be evaluated like all others. Do they think the information presented is trustworthy? Why or why not? **ELD** ELD.PI.2.3, ELD.PI.2.11

Compare Advertisements Display two advertisements (from print media or the Internet) that advertise the same type of product, such as different brands of cars or shoes. Have the children compare and contrast the two. What are the advertisements trying to sell? How are they trying to sell it? What claims do the advertisements make?

Evaluate Advertisements Tell children to use the following tips to decide whether the information presented in the advertisements is useful and true.

• Is it possible to research the information in the advertisement to determine if it's true?

• Compare the information with what you already know.

• Remember that people may only give information that supports their point of view.

Have a class discussion as the children evaluate the advertisements. They should be prepared to ask and answer questions as needed. Remind them to build the conversation by linking to what others have said. **ELA** SL.2.1b, SL.2.1c **ELD** ELD.PI.2.1

Evaluate Media Messages In groups, have children evaluate and discuss more advertisements. Remind them to use the evaluation tips listed above. **ELD** ELD.PI.2.1

Skill Focus: Use Evidence Explain to children that when they research information and write reports, they should use evidence to support their opinions. This will help to show their readers that they have thought about their opinion and based it on facts. Then provide the following scenario:

• *You are writing a report about Jackie Robinson. You wrote the following opinion:* I think Jackie Robinson was a good athlete. *Then you found some sources to support your opinion. Which sentence has information that supports your opinion?*

Jackie Roosevelt Robinson was born in Cairo, Georgia.

Jackie was the youngest child in a family of athletes.

In high school and college, Jackie practiced a lot. **ELA** RI.2.1, W.2.1, W.2.8

Day 1 Discuss Media Messages

Day 2 Evaluate Website

Day 3 Compare Advertisements

Day 4 Evaluate and Discuss as a Class

Day 5 Evaluate and Discuss in Groups

ENGLISH LANGUAGE SUPPORT
Use Language Models

All Proficiencies As children discuss and evaluate advertisements and trustworthy media sites, remind them that it is important to stay on topic. Then model the rule for children and discuss what might happen when this rule is not followed. Have children think about this and practice it during their conversations. Afterwards, have volunteers share examples of how they stayed on topic. **ELD** ELD.PI.2.1

Grammar Weekly Review: Subject-Verb Agreement

▶ **SHARE OBJECTIVES**

- **Grammar** Proofread for subject-verb agreement. LANGUAGE
- **Spelling** Assess words with long *i* (*i, igh,* and *y*).

ENGLISH LANGUAGE SUPPORT

How English Works: Productive

Subject-Verb Agreement Prepare sets of strips with subject pronouns and regular verbs, some with *-s* and some without. Use capital letters on the pronouns and periods after the verbs. Have children work in small groups to combine the strips in as many ways as possible. Have them write each complete sentence. **ELD** ELD.PII.2.3a

1 Review/Practice

Subjects and Verbs Review subject-verb agreement, including that a pronoun can be the subject of a sentence. Read together the text on **Student Book** p. 82.

- *When the pronoun* he, she, *or* it *comes before a verb that tells about now, add -s or -es to the verb.*
- *When the pronoun* I, we, you *or* they *comes before a verb that tells about now, do not add -s or -es.*
- Read and discuss the examples in the chart.
- Direct children to the Try This! activity at the bottom of the page. Support children as they write the sentences correctly.

2 Connect to Writing

- Read together **Student Book** p. 83. Tell children that they should proofread their writing to make sure the verbs have the correct endings. Then read and discuss the examples.
- Together, read the directions for Connect Grammar to Writing ⎘ at the bottom of the page. Support children as they make sure they have written the correct verb with each pronoun.
- Distribute Reader's Notebook Volume 2 page 30 ⎘ to children to complete independently. **ELD** ELD.PII.2.3b

Spelling Long *i* (*i, igh, y*)

SPELLING WORDS AND SENTENCES

BASIC

1. **night*** I sleep at *night*.
2. **kind** We like that *kind* of cereal.
3. **spy** The hero in the story was a *spy*.
4. **child** A young person is a *child*.
5. **light** I turned out the *light*.
6. **find** I cannot *find* my watch.
7. **right*** I throw with my *right* hand.
8. **high** The building is ten stories *high*.
9. **wild*** A wolf is a *wild* animal.

10. **July** We take a vacation in *July*.
11. **fry** We are going to *fry* fish.
12. **sigh** I heard my father *sigh* as he wiped up the milk.

REVIEW

13. **by** I put my jacket *by* my books.
14. **why** *Why* is the dog barking?

CHALLENGE

15. **behind** I always sit *behind* the driver.
16. **lightning** During the storm, *lightning* lit the sky.

*A form or forms of these words appear in the literature.

Assess
Say each Spelling Word, read aloud its sentence, and then repeat the word. Have children write the word. **ELA** L.2.2d

Corrective Feedback
Review any words that children misspell. If children misspell two or more words, then revisit the Day 2 Guess My Category activity on page 88 of the **Literacy and Language Guide**.

Grammar

Pronouns and Verbs A **verb** can name an action that is happening now. A **pronoun** can tell who or what is doing the action. If the pronoun *he*, *she*, or *it* comes before a verb that tells about now, add *-s* or *-es* to the verb. If the pronoun *we*, *I*, or *they* comes before a verb that tells about now, do not add *-s* or *-es*.

Add *-s* or *-es* to Verb	No Change to Verb
He hits the ball.	We hit the ball.
She catches the ball.	I catch the ball.
It breaks the window.	They break the window.

Try This! Choose the correct verb to complete each sentence. Then write the sentence correctly.

❶ We (watch, watches) the game.

❷ She (play, plays) well.

❸ They (buy, buys) new bats.

❹ It (roll, rolls) toward second base.

82   ELD ELD.PII.2.3b

Edit your writing carefully. Make sure the verbs that go with the pronouns have the correct endings.

Singular Pronoun and Verb	Plural Pronoun and Verb
He looks at the ticket.	We walk to the seats.
She pitches to the batter.	They watch the game together.

Connect Grammar to Writing

When you edit your story paragraph, be sure you have written the correct verb to go with each pronoun.

83

1. We watch the game.

2. She plays well.

3. They buy new bats.

4. It rolls toward second base.

Narrative Writing Revise and Edit

▶ **SHARE OBJECTIVE**

- **Writing** Revise, edit, and publish a narrative.
LANGUAGE

Daily Proofreading Practice

child
The ~~childe~~ speaks to Jackie
       ^
                    wishes   night
robinson. He ~~wishs~~ the ~~nigt~~
═══   ^   ^
would never end.

√myWriteSmart Have children revise, proofread, and publish their narrative writing task through *my*WriteSmart.

1 Teach/Model

Story Paragraph: Development Remind children that writers use dialogue to show what characters are like and how they feel.

- Read the top of **Student Book** p. 84 with the class. Discuss the revisions made by the student writer, Nick.

- *How does the dialogue Nick added to his story make the characters seem more real?*

- To see and discuss revisions made by Nick, display Projectable 17.10 ⌐.

- Point out how Nick applied these skills: adding dialogue and using words that tell how characters feel.

2 Guided Practice/Apply

Story Paragraph Read and discuss Nick's Final Copy on **Student Book** p. 85.

- Discuss the Reading as a Writer questions.

Revising Support children as they revise their stories. Have them use the Writing Rubric Blackline Master ⌐ to evaluate their stories. Remind them to include dialogue in their revisions.

Proofreading For proofreading support, have children use the Proofreading Checklist Blackline Master ⌐.

Handwriting If you have children write their final pieces rather than use digital tools, tell them to focus on using their best handwriting. *See also pp. R24–R29 for handwriting support.*

Publishing Have children make a neat final copy and share their writing.

ELA W.2.3, W.2.4, W.2.5, W.2.10, L.2.1g **ELD** ELD.PI.2.10, ELD.PII.2.1

Narrative Writing ✓my WriteSmart

✓ **Development** Dialogue is what the characters say in a **story**. Dialogue can show what your characters are like.

Nick drafted a story about a girl who meets her favorite writer. Later, he added dialogue to show how his characters act and how they feel.

Writing Checklist

☑ **Organization**
Do things happen in a way that makes sense?

☑ **Development**
Did I use dialogue to tell what the characters are like?

☑ **Elaboration**
Do the words I chose show how the characters feel?

☑ **Conventions**
Did I use different types of sentences?

Revised Draft

"There he is! " Tonya shouted.
^ Today, Tonya was going to
meet her hero. Shane Jonas
was signing his books at the
bookstore. Shane wrote stories
about Tik and Tak. Tonya had
read them all.
"Hi," Shane said as
^ Tonya and her dad walked
"What's your name? " Then he
up to the table. ~~Shane Jonas~~
^
reached out to shake her hand.

Final Copy

Tonya and Her Hero
by Nick Haswell

"There he is!" Tonya shouted. Today, Tonya was going to meet her hero. Shane Jonas was signing his books at the bookstore. Shane wrote stories about Tik and Tak. Tonya had read them all.

"Hi," Shane said as Tonya and her dad walked up to the table. "What's your name?" Then he reached out to shake her hand.

"I'm Tonya, and this is my dad," Tonya said. "I love your books!"

"I love to hear that," Shane replied. After that he smiled and wrote a long note in her book.

Reading as a Writer

How does dialogue show more about the characters? Where can you add dialogue in your story?

I added dialogue to tell more about what my characters are like.

84   ELA W.2.3, W.2.4, W.2.5, W.2.10 ELD ELD.PI.2.10, ELD.PI.2.12b, ELD.PII.2.1

85

NARRATIVE WRITING RUBRIC   See also the Multipurpose Writing Rubric on p. R18.

Score	4	3	2	1	NS
Purpose/Organization	The narrative is clear and well organized. It is appropriately sequenced and has closure. • Plot contains a well-elaborated event or a short sequence of events • Setting and characters are included and well-maintained • Plot events follow a logical sequence • Includes an effective conclusion	The narrative is generally clear and organized. The sequence is adequately maintained, and the plot has closure. • Plot contains a well-elaborated event or a short sequence of events • Characters and setting are included and adequately maintained • Plot events follow an understandable sequence • Includes an adequate conclusion	The narrative is somewhat organized but may be unclear in parts. The sequence is weak. The plot lacks closure. • Minimal development of plot • Characters and setting are included but are minimally maintained • Sequence of events is poorly organized • Conclusion is inadequate or missing	The narrative's focus is unclear, and it is poorly organized. The narrative lacks sequence and has no closure. • Little or no plot • No attempt to maintain characters or setting • Sequence of events is not organized • Conclusion is missing	• not intelligible • not written in English • not on topic • contains text copied from another source • does not address the purpose for writing
Development/ Elaboration	The narrative includes effective elaboration, and details describing actions, thoughts, and feelings. • Clear effort to develop experiences, characters, setting, and events • Contains strong use of details • Writer uses temporal words to signal the order of events	The narrative includes adequate elaboration, and details describing actions, thoughts, and feelings. • Some attempt to develop experiences, characters, setting, and events • Contains adequate use of details • Contains adequate use of temporal words to signal the order of events	The narrative includes only partial or ineffective elaboration. The narrative includes some details. • Little attempt to develop experiences, characters, setting, and events • Contains weak use of details • Contains little use of temporal words. • Order of events is not clear	The narrative provides little or no elaboration and few details. • No attempt to develop experiences, characters, setting, and events • Few or no details • No use of temporal words • Order of events is confusing	• not intelligible • not written in English • not on topic • contains text copied from another source • does not develop the writing

Score	2	1	0	NS
Conventions	The narrative demonstrates adequate command of conventions. • Consistent use of complete sentences, correct sentence structures, punctuation, capitalization, grammar, spelling	The narrative demonstrates partial command of conventions. • Limited use of complete sentences, correct sentence structures, punctuation, capitalization, grammar, spelling	The narrative demonstrates little or no command of conventions. • Does not use complete sentences, correct sentence structures, punctuation, capitalization, grammar, spelling	• not intelligible • not written in English • not on topic • contains text copied from another source

 # Formative Assessment

Weekly Tests

At the end of the lesson, administer the Weekly Test. This will give you a **snapshot of how children are progressing** with the Reading and Language Arts skills in this lesson and can give you **guidance on grouping, reteaching, and intervention**: Suggestions for adjusting instruction based on these results can be found on the next page.

Access Through Accommodations

When you administer the Weekly Test, some children may have problems accessing all or parts of the assessment. The purpose of the Weekly Test is to determine children's ability to complete the Reading and Language Arts tasks they learned in this lesson. Any barriers to them accessing the tasks demanded of them should be lowered so they can focus on skill demonstration.

When choosing accommodations, you will want to avoid invalidating the test results if you are measuring a child's reading skill. For example, you will not want to read aloud the passage. The following accommodations, if needed, will not interfere with the Weekly Test's validity:

- Read aloud the assessment directions and item prompts. If children are English learners, read aloud the assessment directions and item prompts in the child's native language, if possible.

- Define any unknown words in the directions or item prompts that do not give away the answers to the items.

- Allow for a break during the assessment.

- Simplify the language of assessment directions and item prompts.

- Administer the assessment in a smaller group setting.

- Administer the assessment on a computer or other electronic device.

- Provide audio amplification equipment, colored overlays, or visual magnifying equipment to maintain visual/audio attention and access.

- Allow children to complete the assessment items orally or by having another person transcribe their responses.

Using Data to Adjust Instruction

Use children's scores on the Weekly Test to determine Small Group placement, reteaching, and potential for intervention.

☑ VOCABULARY AND COMPREHENSION

Sequence of Events; Formal and Informal Language; Anchor Text

Target Vocabulary; Antonyms

IF STUDENT SCORES...	
...at acceptable,	**...below acceptable,**
THEN continue core instruction.	**THEN** use Reteach Comprehension Skill and Vocabulary Strategies lessons. For struggling students, administer the *Intervention Assessments* to determine if students would benefit from intervention.

☑ PHONICS

Long i (i, igh, ie, y)

IF STUDENT SCORES...	
...at acceptable,	**...below acceptable,**
THEN continue core instruction.	**THEN** use Reteach Phonics lesson. Administer the *Intervention Assessments* to determine if students would benefit from intervention.

☑ LANGUAGE ARTS

Subject-Verb Agreement

IF STUDENT SCORES...	
...at acceptable,	**...below acceptable,**
THEN continue core instruction.	**THEN** use Reteach Language Arts lesson. Administer the *Intervention Assessments* to determine if students would benefit from intervention.

☑ FLUENCY

Fluency Plan

Assess one group per week using the <u>Fluency Tests</u> in the *Grab-and-Go*™ Resources. Use the suggested plan at the right.

● Struggling Readers	Weeks 1, 2, 3
▲ On Level	Week 2
■ Advanced	Week 5

IF...	
...students are reading on-level text fluently,	**...students are reading below level,**
THEN continue core instruction.	**THEN** provide additional fluency practice using the **Student Book,** the **Cold Reads,** and the Leveled Readers. For struggling students, administer the *Intervention Assessments* to determine if students would benefit from intervention.

HOUGHTON MIFFLIN HARCOURT

JOURNEYS

Cold Reads

2

The **Cold Reads** passages increase gradually in Lexile® measures throughout the year, from below grade level to above grade level.

- Each passage is accompanied by several selected-response questions and one constructed-response prompt, requiring children to read closely, answer questions at substantial DOK levels, and cite text evidence.

- The **Cold Reads** may be used to provide practice in reading increasingly complex texts and to informally monitor children's progress.

- The **Cold Reads** may be used to estimate children's Lexile® levels in order to recommend appropriately challenging books for small-group instruction or independent reading.

Turn the page for more information about using FORMATIVE ASSESSMENT for **ELD AND INTERVENTION.**

Assess It Online!
► Language Workshop Assessment Handbook
► Intervention Assessments

Formative Assessment for ELD and Intervention

Formative Assessment for English Learners

English learners should engage in the same rigorous curriculum and formative assessment as other students. However, it is important to remember that English learners face a dual challenge: they are strengthening their abilities *to use* English at the same time that they are learning challenging content *through* English. Use the following strategies and resources for ongoing assessment of English language development, in addition to the assessments you use with all children:

- A combination of **observational measures,** such as listening in as children read aloud or participate in collaborative conversations. Be prepared to provide **"just-in-time" scaffolding** to support students. For example, if children are retelling a story, you could help them use sentence structures with past-tense verbs and time-order transition words.

- **Constructive feedback** that focuses on communication and meaning-making. Avoid overcorrecting in a way that makes English learners reluctant to speak up. You might try recasting a child's statement more correctly, making a note to address the target form more directly during Designated ELD time.

- **Student self-assessment,** through children's own notes in their vocabulary notebooks or other learning journals. If possible, meet with each child to review his or her self-assessments and provide encouragement and feedback.

- **Formative assessment** notes that are integrated into the Language Workshop Teacher's Guide for use during Designated ELD.

- **Language Workshop Assessment Handbook** for longer-cycle assessment to make sure students are progressing in their English development.

Response to Intervention  **RtI**

Use the Weekly Tests and Benchmark and Unit Tests, along with your own observations, to determine if individual students are not responding to primary instruction and need additional testing to identify specific needs for targeted intervention.

Intervention Assessments

Assessment for Intervention

Administer these assessments to

- children who are receiving supplemental intervention to gauge progress toward exit from the intervention program.

- children who demonstrate lack of success with Weekly Tests, Benchmark and Unit Tests, and core instruction to determine if they might benefit from additional practice or intervention.

SMALL GROUP

Differentiate Phonics
- Long *i* (*i, igh, ie, y*)

Vocabulary Reader
- *The Brooklyn Dodgers*

Differentiate Comprehension
- Sequence of Events
- Visualize

Differentiate
Phonics & Fluency
- Cumulative Review
- Stress

Leveled Readers
- ⬤ *The Winning Hit*
- ▲ *Take Me Out to the Ballpark*
- ◼ *The New Field*
- ◆ *The Summer of Baseball Parks*

Differentiate
Vocabulary Strategies
- Antonyms

Options for Reteaching
- Phonics
- Language Arts
- Vocabulary Strategies
- Comprehension

Literacy Centers

Independent Practice
- Word Study, T106
- Think and Write, T107
- Comprehension and Fluency, T106

Small Group Plan
Differentiated Instruction

		DAY 1	DAY 2	DAY 3
Teacher-Led	**Struggling Readers**	**Vocabulary Reader,** *The Brooklyn Dodgers,* Differentiated Instruction, p. T186 **Differentiate Phonics:** Long *i* (*i, igh, ie, y*), p. T184 **English Language Support,** pp. T185, T187	**Differentiate Comprehension:** Sequence of Events; Visualize, p. T188 **Reread** *Bright Lights* **English Language Support,** p. T189	**Leveled Reader** *The Winning Hit,* p. T192 **Differentiate Phonics:** Cumulative Review, p. T190 **English Language Support,** Leveled Reader Teacher's Guide, p. 5
	On Level	**Vocabulary Reader,** *The Brooklyn Dodgers,* Differentiated Instruction, p. T186 **English Language Support,** pp. T185, T187	**Differentiate Comprehension:** Sequence of Events; Visualize, p. T188 **Reread** *Bright Lights* **English Language Support,** p. T189	**Leveled Reader** *Take Me Out to the Ballpark,* p. T193 *The Summer of Baseball Parks,* p. T195 **Differentiate Fluency:** Stress, p. T191 **English Language Support,** Leveled Reader Teacher's Guide, p. 5
	Advanced	**Vocabulary Reader,** *The Brooklyn Dodgers,* Differentiated Instruction, p. T187 **English Language Support,** pp. T185, T187	**Differentiate Comprehension:** Sequence of Events; Visualize, p. T189 **English Language Support,** p. T189	**Leveled Reader** *The New Field,* p. T194 **Differentiate Fluency:** Stress, p. T191 **English Language Support,** Leveled Reader Teacher's Guide, p. 5
What are my other children doing?	**Struggling Readers**	**Word Building:** Build and read Spelling Words • Leveled Practice, SR17.1	**Partners:** Vocabulary in Context Cards 129–136 **Partners:** Reread *Bright Lights* • Leveled Practice, SR17.2	**Partners:** Reread Leveled Reader *The Winning Hit* • Leveled Practice, SR17.3
	On Level	**Word Building:** Build and read Long *i* (*i, igh, ie, y*) words using Letter Cards **Complete** Reader's Notebook, pp. 16–17 or Leveled Practice, EL17.1	**Target Vocabulary:** Practice reading using Vocabulary in Context Cards 129–136 **Reread** *Bright Lights* **Complete** Reader's Notebook, pp. 18–21 or Leveled Practice, EL17.2	**Partners:** Reread Leveled Reader *Take Me Out to the Ballpark* or *The Summer of Baseball Parks* **Complete** Reader's Notebook, pp. 22–26 or Leveled Practice, EL17.3
	Advanced	**Vocabulary in Context Cards** 129–136 *Talk It Over* activities • Leveled Practice, A17.1	**Reread** *Luke Goes to Bat* **Student Book,** pp. 52–73 • Leveled Practice, A17.2	**Partners:** Reread Leveled Reader *The New Field* • Leveled Practice, A17.3

For strategic intervention for this lesson, see pp. S12–S21.

DAY 4	DAY 5	English Language Support
Differentiate Vocabulary Strategies: Antonyms, p. T196 **Reread** *Wild Cats* **English Language Support,** p. T197	**Options for Reteaching,** pp. T198–T199 **Reread** *Bright Lights* or *Wild Cats* or one of this week's Blend-It Books.	*Use the Leveled Reader Teacher's Guide to support ELs during differentiated instruction.*
Differentiate Vocabulary Strategies: Antonyms, p. T196 **Reread** *Wild Cats* **English Language Support,** p. T197	**Options for Reteaching,** pp. T198–T199 **Reread** *Bright Lights* or *Wild Cats*	
Differentiate Vocabulary Strategies: Antonyms, p. T197 **English Language Support,** p. T197	**Options for Reteaching,** pp. T198–T199 **Reread** *Bright Lights* or *Wild Cats*	

- **Characteristics of the Text** (p. 1)

  Identify challenging language features, such as text structure, literary features, complex sentences, and vocabulary.

- **Cultural Support/Cognates/Vocabulary** (p. 5)

  Explain unfamiliar features of English and help ELs transfer first-language knowledge.

- **Oral Language Development** (p. 5)

  Check comprehension using dialogues that match children's proficiency levels.

Book Share

Use this routine at the end of the week to show children that they have become experts on their Leveled Readers.

Step 1:

Help each group write a presentation of their Leveled Reader **Responding** page. Use the following routine:

- Briefly tell what your book is about.

- Show your graphic organizer and explain what you added to complete it.

- Tell about your favorite part of the book.

Every child should have his or her own presentation to share with a new group.

Step 2:

Have children number off. Assign places in the classroom for 1s to gather, 2s, and so on. Help children find their new groups.

Step 3:

Have children take turns sharing their book presentations in the new groups. Continue until all children have finished sharing. Encourage children to ask questions. Give the following frames for support.

Can you tell me more about _____?

I wonder why _____?

What do you think about _____?

DAY 4	DAY 5
Partners: Reread *Wild Cats* • Leveled Practice, SR17.4	**Partners:** Choose among the stories for this week to reread • Complete and share Literacy Center activities
Reread *Wild Cats* **Complete** Reader's Notebook, pp. 27–29 or Leveled Practice, EL17.4	**Partners:** Reread Leveled Reader *Take Me Out to the Ballpark* or *The Summer of Baseball Parks* • Complete and share Literacy Center activities • Self-Selected Reading **Complete** Reader's Notebook, p. 30
Partners: Reread *Jackie Robinson,* Student Book, pp. 78–81 • Leveled Practice, A17.4	**Partners:** Reread Leveled Reader *The New Field* • Complete and share Literacy Center activities • Self-Selected Reading

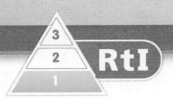

Differentiate Phonics
Words with Long *i* (*i, igh, ie, y*)

Struggling Readers

 ELA RF.2.3b
ELD ELD.PI.2.1

I DO IT

- Display **Letter Cards** *s, igh, t*. Review the long *i* vowel sound and the *igh* spelling.

- Use Instructional Routine 3 to model how to blend and read the word.

- Blend the sounds. *Listen: /s/ /ī/ /t/, sight. Have children blend with you. Now you blend the sounds: /s/ /ī/ /t/, sight.*

- Repeat with *try, pie,* and *kind*, pointing out the *y, ie,* and *i* spellings for the long *i* sound.

- Review long *i* words in the **Decodable Reader** *Bright Lights*.

WE DO IT

- Dispay the **Sound/Spelling Card** *ice cream*. Review the *i, igh, ie,* and *y* spellings for long *i*.

- Ask children to name the /ī/ word in each of the following word pairs: *rip, right; tin, tie; kin, kind; pup, pry.*

- Help children blend the sounds to read the words below. Use the **Corrective Feedback** steps if children need additional help.

reply	fright	lie	china
sunlight	pie	kind	July

YOU DO IT

- Have partners take turns using **Letter Cards** to build words with long *i* spelled *i, igh, ie,* and *y*.

- Have children record their words and read the list to the group.

FORMATIVE ASSESSMENT RtI

Corrective Feedback
When a child mispronounces a word, point to the word and say it. Call attention to the element that was mispronounced, say the sound, and then guide children to read the word. See the example below.

Phonics Error:
A child reads *kind* with the short *i* sound.

Correct the error. Say the word and the vowel sound. *The word is kind; the letter i stands for the sound /ī/.*

Model as you touch the letters. *I'll blend: /k/ /ī/ /n/ /d/. What is the word? kind*

Guide *Let's blend together: /k//ī/ /n/ /d/. What is the word? kind.*

Check *You blend. /k/ /ī/ /n/ /d/ What is the word? kind*

Reinforce Go back three or four words and have children continue reading. Make note of errors and review those words during the next lesson.

English Language Support

ELD ELD.PI.2.1

Provide Struggling Readers, On Level, and Advanced ELs proficiency-level support during differentiated instruction. Give children extra practice blending words.

- Write the word *find* on the board. Say the word, sound by sound, and then say the whole word: */f/ /ī/ /n/ /d/, find.* Underscore the *i* and say: *The letter* i *stands for the long* i *sound in* find. Repeat, using these words to show the different long *i* spelling patterns: *might, pie, spy.*

Emerging

- Point to each letter in the word *find* as you say its sound. Have children repeat each sound after you. Then say the whole word and have children repeat.

Expanding

- After you have modeled blending the sounds and saying the word *find,* have children join you as you repeat the process.

Bridging

- After you have modeled blending the sounds and saying the word *find,* write *might.* Have children use the same process to blend the sounds and say that word.

On Level

See Literacy Centers—Unit 4 Lesson 17 Word Study

If children have time after completing the purple activity, have them try moving on to the blue activity.

Advanced

See Literacy Centers—Unit 4 Lesson 17 Word Study

If children have time after completing the blue activity, have them reread **Decodable Reader** *Bright Lights* or another book independently.

Vocabulary Reader
The Brooklyn Dodgers

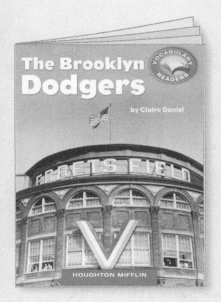

Summary

The Dodgers have always been a great baseball team. Now they are in Los Angeles, but people in New York still cheer for them.

☑ **TARGET VOCABULARY**

practice	extra
hurried	curb
position	cheered
roared	final

Struggling Readers

ELA L.2.4a, L.2.6
ELD ELD.PI.2.1, ELD.PI.2.5

- Explain to children that the Brooklyn Dodgers began as a baseball team in New York City. They were the first major league team to have an African American player, Jackie Robinson.

- Guide children to preview the selection. Ask children to describe the images, using Target Vocabulary when possible.

- Have children read the selection aloud. When you come to an unfamiliar word (or phrase), guide children to use context clues to determine the meanings. As necessary, use the **Vocabulary in Context Cards** to review the meanings of the Target Vocabulary.

- Have partners work together to complete the Responding page. Then review the directions on Blackline Master 17.4 and guide children to complete it.

On Level

ELA L.2.4a, L.2.6
ELD ELD.PI.2.1, ELD.PI.2.5

- Explain to children that the Brooklyn Dodgers were one of the first professional baseball teams. In 1947, Jackie Robinson joined the Dodgers, becoming the first African American major league player.

- As children preview the selection, tell them that they may find some unfamiliar words (or phrases) in the text, including the Target Vocabulary. Encourage them to use context, the words, phrases, and sentences around the unfamiliar word (or phrase), to find clues as to the meaning of the unfamiliar word (or phrase).

- Have partners take turns reading the selection aloud. Have them pause when they come to an unfamiliar word (or phrase) to use context clues to determine its meaning.

- Assign the Responding page and Blackline Master 17.4. Review the directions. Have children discuss their responses with a partner.

Advanced

ELA L.2.4a, L.2.6
ELD ELD.PI.2.1, ELD.PI.2.5

- Have children preview the selection and visualize what it was like to go to a Brooklyn Dodgers game many years ago. Have them use information from the preview and their prior knowledge.

- Remind children to use context clues to help them determine the meanings of unfamiliar words (or phrases).

- Have children work with partners to alternate reading pages aloud. Have them think about which words to stress as they read.

- Assign the Responding page and Blackline Master 17.4 ⧉. For the Write About It activity, remind children to include facts and details to support their ideas.

English Language Support

ELD ELD.PI.2.1

Provide Struggling Readers, On Level, and Advanced ELs proficiency-level support during differentiated instruction.

Emerging

- Preview pictures from *The Brooklyn Dodgers* and use them to preteach the meanings of common sports terms such as *cheered*, *roared*, and *position*. Ask simple yes/no questions to check children's understanding of the terms.

Expanding

- Give children sentence frames they can use to respond to the Write About It activity. Display the frames and have children complete them with words from the selection or with other words they know to describe what spectators do. For example: *People _____ when their team wins a game.*

Bridging

- Remind children that in addition to using context clues, they can also use a dictionary or thesaurus to look up the meaning of an unfamiliar word. Encourage children to write down each unknown word and a simple synonym or definition next to it.

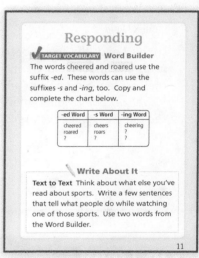

Responding

✔ **TARGET VOCABULARY** **Word Builder**

The words cheered and roared use the suffix -*ed*. These words can use the suffixes -*s* and -*ing*, too. Copy and complete the chart below.

-ed Word	-s Word	-ing Word
cheered	cheers	cheering
roared	roars	?
?	?	?

Write About It

Text to Text Think about what else you've read about sports. Write a few sentences that tell what people do while watching one of those sports. Use two words from the Word Builder.

11

The Brooklyn Dodgers, p. 11

Differentiate Comprehension
Sequence of Events; Visualize

Struggling Readers

ELA RL.2.2
ELD ELD.PI.2.1, ELD.PII.2.1

I DO IT

- Explain that visualizing what you read can help you understand the sequence of events.

- Read aloud **Student Book** p. 65 of *Luke Goes to Bat* and model visualizing to identify a sequence of events.

> **Think Aloud** *The ball goes flying over Luke's head, the scoreboard, and the walls of Ebbets Field. In my mind, I see the ball reaching higher and higher. Visualizing helps me remember what the ball flew over first, second, and third.*

WE DO IT

- Have children read **Student Book** p. 63. Ask them to visualize the events, from the beginning of the game until Jackie Robinson's turn at bat.

- Work with children to make a list of the events: First, Next, and Last.

- Write the sequence of events on the board.

YOU DO IT

- Have children review the entire selection.

- Have children visualize the story as they complete a Flow Chart with major story events. Remind them to keep the events in sequence.

- Point out that the sentences on their Flow Chart form a summary of the story. Have children share their summaries.

On Level

ELA RL.2.2
ELD ELD.PI.2.1, ELD.PII.2.1

I DO IT

- Read aloud **Student Book** p. 58. Explain that illustrations can help readers visualize a story to establish the sequence of events.

- Model using the pictures on **Student Book** pp. 58–59 to visualize the sequence of events.

> **Think Aloud** *I see the kids arguing, and then Luke missing the ball. This helps me to visualize the order in which Luke was allowed to play, but then struck out.*

WE DO IT

- Have children visualize the events as you read aloud the last three paragraphs of **Student Book** p. 61.

- Ask volunteers to pantomime Luke's activities.

- Work together to list events. Point out that the author does not tell every little detail; the reader has to infer some events.

YOU DO IT

- Have children complete a Flow Chart for this selection. The chart should be labeled "First, Next, and Last."

- Pass out index cards. Have partners work together to write the events that go with each section of the flow chart. One event should go on each card.

- Have partners take turns putting the cards in order and retelling the story. Point out that they have just summarized *Luke Goes to Bat*.

Advanced

ELA RL.2.2
ELD ELD.PI.2.1, ELD.PII.2.1

I DO IT

- Read aloud **Student Book** p. 61. Tell children that they can visualize characters' body language to understand, or infer, unstated events in a story.
- Model visualizing characters' body language on **Student Book** p. 61.

> **Think Aloud** *The story says that Grandma can tell the game went badly. I can infer that Luke looks sad. He might be slumping his shoulders or looking at the floor.*

WE DO IT

- Have children read **Student Book** pp. 59–60. Guide them to visualize Luke's body language.

- *What does the illustration on p. 59 show? How does Luke look different on p. 60? Which story details support this idea? On p. 59, Luke looks like he's concentrating. On p. 60, he looks unhappy. The story says he believes he'll never be asked to play again.*

YOU DO IT

- Have children use their Flow Charts to write a summary of the main events of the story.

- Have them explain the parts of the story that were real and the parts that Luke imagined.

- Have children share their summaries with the group. Encourage them to adjust their sequence of events based on the discussion.

English Language Support

ELD ELD.PI.2.1, ELD.PII.2.2

Provide Struggling Readers, On Level, and Advanced ELs proficiency-level support during differentiated instruction.

Emerging

- Lead children on a picture walk through *Luke Goes to Bat*. Guide them to retell the events by asking simple questions. For example, point to the illustration on pp. 54–55 and ask: *Where is Luke? What is Luke doing?* Point to the picture on pp. 56–57 and ask: *What is Luke doing here? How do you think Luke feels? Who is he watching?*

Expanding

- As children read the selection with others in their group, guide them to list key story events. Give them index cards and have them write each event on a separate card. Prompt children to arrange the events in sequence. Then help them write the events in order on their Flow Charts.

Bridging

- Prompt children to retell the selection in their own words. Ask: *What is this story mostly about? Who are the characters in the story? What happens at the beginning of the story? What happens in the middle? What happens at the end?* Guide children to complete their Flow Charts by writing the events in sequence.

Differentiate Phonics and Fluency

ELD ELD.PIII.2

Struggling Readers

Phonics

Cumulative Review

I DO IT

- Write *mailbox* on the board. Read the word aloud.
- Point out the two words that form the compound word. *I hear and see two small words in the word* mailbox: mail *and* box.
- Explain that *mailbox* is a compound word—a word made up of two smaller words.

WE DO IT

- Write *seashell* on the board.
- Have children use **Letter Cards** to build *seashell*.
- Tell them to find the two small words in *seashell* and separate them by moving their **Letter Cards**.

- Have children read *sea* and *shell*. Then have them put the two words back together and read *seashell*.
- Repeat with *rainbow*.

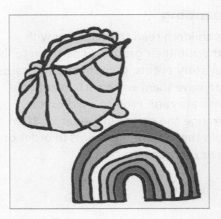

YOU DO IT

- Have partners build *anthill, baseball,* and *pancake* using **Letter Cards**.
- Have them identify and read the smaller words in each compound word. Provide **Corrective Feedback as needed.**

FORMATIVE ASSESSMENT RtI

Corrective Feedback
When a child mispronounces a word, point to the word and say it. Call attention to the element that was mispronounced, say the sound, and then guide children to read the word. See the example below.

Phonics Error:
A child identifies the two smaller words in *anthill* as *an* and *thill*.

Correct the error. Say the word slowly, emphasizing the two smaller words. *The word is* anthill: ant, hill.

Model using **Letter Cards** to show the two smaller words that make up *anthill*.

Guide *Let's read the two smaller words:* ant, hill. *Let's read the compound word:* anthill.

Check Have children use their **Letter Cards** to show the two words that make up *anthill*.

Reinforce Have children continue to build and identify words. Note any errors and review those words during later lessons.

All Levels

ELA RF.2.4b

Fluency

Stress

I DO IT

- Write: *When Luke got home, he ran up to the roof.*

- Model reading the sentence with appropriate stress.

- Use a Think Aloud as you underline the words in the sentence that you emphasize.

  Think Aloud *As I look at this sentence, I think about which words I should say a little louder or stronger than the others. By reading some words a little louder or stronger, listeners will know what words are important. I will reread the sentence, giving stress to the words home, ran, and roof.*

WE DO IT

- Choose two sentences from *The New Field, The Winning Hit, Take Me Out to the Ballpark,* and *The Summer of Baseball Parks,* and write them on the board.

- Have children take a few minutes to review the sentences and read them silently.

- Then work with children to underline words that should be stressed, or said a little louder or stronger, during reading.

- Have children take turns reading the sentences. Remind them to make their voice sound louder as they read words they want to emphasize. Provide **Corrective Feedback.**

YOU DO IT

- Have partners choose a page from a **Leveled Reader** and take turns reading aloud. Remind them to emphasize important words.

- Monitor and provide **Corrective Feedback** as needed.

FORMATIVE ASSESSMENT

Corrective Feedback Work with children to correct errors, following the model below.

Fluency Error:
A child has difficulty with emphasizing important words.

Correct the error. Remind children that when we read aloud, our voice should sound louder as we read words we want to stand out.

Model by reading a few sentences from a **Leveled Reader.** Show children how you change your voice to emphasize important words and give meaning to the text.

Guide by reading a sentence together with children, stressing important words.

Check by asking children to read aloud a sentence on their own.

Reinforce Have children go back a sentence or two and begin reading on their own again.

Leveled Readers

TARGET SKILL
Sequence of Events

TARGET STRATEGY
Visualize

TARGET VOCABULARY

cheered	curb
extra	final
hurried	position
practice	roared

ELA RL.2.1, RL.2.5, RF.2.4b
ELD ELD.PI.2.1, ELD.PI.2.6, ELD.PII.2.1

Struggling Readers

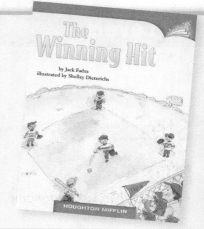

The Winning Hit

Summary Liz and Andy are twins who always practice baseball together. Liz proves to be just as good a player when Andy, the star on the team, gets hurt.

Genre: Realistic Fiction

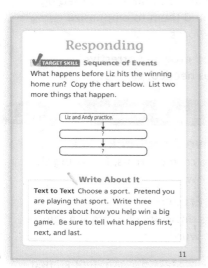

Responding

TARGET SKILL Sequence of Events
What happens before Liz hits the winning home run? Copy the chart below. List two more things that happen.

> Liz and Andy practice.
> ↓
> ?
> ↓
> ?

Write About It

Text to Text Choose a sport. Pretend you are playing that sport. Write three sentences about how you help win a big game. Be sure to tell what happens first, next, and last.

11

The Winning Hit, p. 11

Introducing the Text

- Explain that Andy and Liz always practice baseball together, but only Andy plays on the team. When Andy gets hurt, Liz gets to show her skills.

- Remind children that using a Flow Chart can help them organize the sequence of events and infer unstated events.

Supporting the Reading

- **p. 6** *What happens after Andy's team is winning?* The other team is winning, but then the score is tied.

- **p. 7** *When you read the words on p. 7, "It went up and up and up. Andy ran to catch it," what do you picture in your mind?* I can see a picture of a baseball going high into the air and Andy running very fast to catch it.

Discussing and Revisiting the Text

Critical Thinking After they discuss the book, have children read the instructions on the top half of Responding p. 11 in *The Winning Hit.*

- Have partners identify story events that happen before Liz hits the winning home run.

- Have them add events to <u>Blackline Master 17.5</u>.

FLUENCY: STRESS Model reading with correct stress. Then have partners echo-read p. 2, paying attention to proper stress.

On Level

ELA RL.2.1, RL.2.5, RF.2.4b
ELD ELD.PI.2.1, ELD.PI.2.6, ELD.PII.2.1

Take Me Out to the Ballpark

Summary Grandpa finds out that Shea Stadium is going to be torn down. So he and his grandson Evan decide to go to baseball games in old baseball parks before they are torn down, too.

Genre: Realistic Fiction

Introducing the Text

- Explain that sometimes old baseball parks are torn down so new ones can be built. Many people go to games at old parks because they like the history of the parks.

- Remind children that authors do not always describe every event in a sequence. Good readers use their own knowledge and clues from the text to visualize events.

Supporting the Reading

- **p. 12** *What picture can you see in your head when Grandpa and Evan watch a night game at Wrigley Field? I can picture a dark sky and lots of bright lights on the field. The lights almost make the field look like it is daytime.*

- **p. 13** *What happens after Grandpa and Evan return home from Chicago? They talk about their favorite parts of their trip.*

Discussing and Revisiting the Text

Critical Thinking After they discuss the book, have children read the instructions on the top half of Responding p. 15 in *Take Me Out to the Ballpark*.

- Have children discuss the order Grandpa and Evan visit the ballparks.

- Have children fill in Blackline Master 17.6 📄.

FLUENCY: STRESS Have children practice reading their favorite parts of *Take Me Out to the Ballpark*. Model using the correct stress. Children's reading should sound like natural speech.

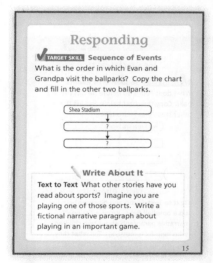

Take Me Out to the Ballpark, p. 15

Leveled Readers

TARGET SKILL
Sequence of Events

TARGET STRATEGY
Visualize

TARGET VOCABULARY

cheered	curb
extra	final
hurried	position
practice	roared

ELA RL.2.1, RL.2.5, RF.2.4b
ELD ELD.PI.2.1, ELD.PI.2.6, ELD.PII.2.1

Advanced

The New Field

Summary Miguel and his friends love two things: playing baseball and rooting for Pedro Sanchez, the best player in the major leagues, who grew up in their town. Pedro comes home to build the kids a new field.

Genre: Realistic Fiction

Introducing the Text

- Explain that Miguel and his friends will have their dream come true when Pedro Sanchez, their hero, returns to his hometown to fix up the ball field.

- Remind children that keeping track of the sequence of events will help them better understand the story. Readers can also visualize what happens before, after, or between the events the author describes to get a better picture of what is going on in the story.

Supporting the Reading

- **p. 2** *What happened after Pedro left the Dominican Republic to become a baseball player? He became the best player in the league.*

- **p. 13** *Picture in your mind what the new baseball field looks like. What do you see? I see a new field, with dark green grass, new bases, a new dugout, new stands for the people to sit on, and a newly painted scoreboard.*

Discussing and Revisiting the Text

Critical Thinking After they discuss the book, have children read the instructions on the top half of Responding p. 15 in *The New Field*.

- Have children visualize Pedro Sanchez as he gets up to bat.

- Have them list events in sequence on Blackline Master 17.7 ↗.

FLUENCY: STRESS Have children practice reading with correct stress, so their reading sounds like natural speech. Tell them to practice with their favorite parts of *The New Field*.

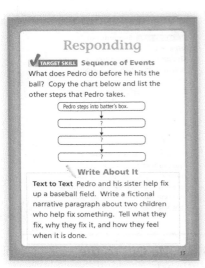

The New Field, p. 15

English Language Support

ELD ELD.PI.2.1, ELD.PI.2.6, ELD.PII.2.1

The Summer of Baseball Parks

Summary Grandpa and Evan love baseball. One summer, Grandpa hears that Shea Stadium is closing for good. Evan and Grandpa drive to watch baseball games at old baseball parks around the country.

Genre: Realistic Fiction

Introducing the Text

- Explain that Grandpa and Evan love baseball. One summer they drive to the most famous old baseball parks to watch games before the old parks are gone.

- Remind children that good readers use text details and their own knowledge to help them put story events in the right order.

Supporting the Reading

- **p. 10** *Wrigley Field is in the middle of a city. Picture in your mind what might be around Wrigley Field. What do you see?* I see cars, other buildings, and many people walking around.

- **pp. 10–12** *Where did Grandpa and Evan go after they saw a game at Fenway Park?* They went to Wrigley Field in Chicago.

Discussing and Revisiting the Text

Critical Thinking After they discuss the book, have children read the instructions at the top half of Responding p. 15 in *The Summer of Baseball Parks*.

- Have children work in pairs to identify the parks Grandpa and Evan visit.

- Have children complete Blackline Master 17.8 .

FLUENCY: STRESS Remind children that stress is saying some words with more force. Have children practice reading a favorite part of *The Summer of Baseball Parks* with correct stress.

Responding

✔ TARGET SKILL **Sequence of Events**
After Shea Stadium, which ballpark do Evan and Grandpa visit next? Which do they visit last? Copy the chart and write in the other ballparks.

| Shea Stadium |
| ? |
| ? |

Write About It

Text to Text Think of another story you read about a sport. Pretend that you are playing that sport. Then write a paragraph about playing an exciting game. Tell what happens first, next, and last.

The Summer of Baseball Parks, p. 15

Differentiate Vocabulary Strategies
Antonyms

Struggling Readers

ELA L.2.4a
ELD ELD.PI.2.1

I DO IT

- Explain that antonyms are words that have opposite, or very different, meanings.

- Tell children that they can use context clues in a sentence, or in a nearby sentence, to figure out a word's antonym. Identifying antonyms can help children figure out the meaning of an unfamiliar word (or phrase).

WE DO IT

- Write *Melissa was disappointed when she lost her purse, but she was happy when she found it.*

- Discuss with children the meaning of *happy.* Then help children use context clues to identify the antonym of *happy.* *disappointed*

- Guide children to use their understanding of *happy* and context clues to figure out the meaning of *disappointed. not happy, sad*

YOU DO IT

- Write *My lips turned blue because it was cold outside. The soup was too hot for me to eat.*

- Have children use context clues to identify the antonyms in the sentences. *cold, hot* Have children use *hot* in a new context sentence.

On Level

ELA RF.2.4c, L.2.4a
ELD ELD.PI.2.1

I DO IT

- Tell children that antonyms are words that have opposite, or very different, meanings.

- Remind them that they can use context clues in a sentence to figure out a word's antonym. Identifying antonyms can help children figure out the meaning of an unfamiliar word.

WE DO IT

- Write *Steve has <u>less</u> hair than Bob but more hair than Fred. My dinner was so <u>hot</u> that it burned my tongue, but the ice cream was so cold that my tongue froze.*

- Help children use context clues to determine the meanings of the two underlined words.

- Have children identify the antonyms for *less* and *hot* in the sentences.

YOU DO IT

- Have children work with partners. Tell children that the two sentences on the board are the first sentences of two different stories.

- Have partners choose a sentence and then write the second sentence of that story. The sentence they write should include a pair of antonyms.

Advanced

ELA RF.2.4c, L.2.4a
ELD ELD.PI.2.1

I DO IT

- Write *dirty, clean, neat,* and *spotless.*
- Explain that words with opposite, or very different, meanings are called *antonyms.*
- Point out that words can have more than one antonym. For example, *clean, neat,* and *spotless* are all antonyms for *dirty.*
- Point out that *clean* and *spotless* are synonyms.

WE DO IT

- Ask children to suggest other words that could have multiple antonyms. List the suggested words and their antonyms on the board.
- If there is a question about whether or not two words are antonyms, use a dictionary to confirm that the words have opposite, or very different, meanings.

YOU DO IT

- Have partners choose a word and its antonyms from the list.
- Have them work together to write a short paragraph that includes sentences using the word and one or more of its antonyms.

English Language Support

ELD ELD.PI.2.1

Provide Struggling Readers, On Level, and Advanced ELs proficiency-level support during differentiated instruction.

Emerging

- Point out to children that because antonyms are opposites, they can find the meaning of a word's antonym by adding *not* before the word.
- Ask: *What is the opposite of happy?* not happy What is a word that means not happy? sad
- Guide children to understand that just as a word can have multiple synonyms, it can also have multiple antonyms.

Expanding

- Before children take part in the You Do It or We Do It activities for their group, remind them that context clues can help them figure out a word's antonym. Model with this example:
- Write *Tom has more money than Lily* and *The dresses look different.*
- Write *Lily has _____ money than Tom* and *The dresses do not look the _____.*
- Write *less, same.* Have children use the words to fill in the frames and identify the antonym pairs. more/less; different/same

Bridging

- As children complete the You Do It activity for their group, have them use the word *not* to help them find the correct antonyms.
- Pair children with more proficient speakers. Have children read their sentences aloud to their partners and have them suggest different antonyms to use in their sentences.

Options for Reteaching

ELA RF.2.3b **ELD** ELD.PI.2.1

Reteach Phonics

Words with Long *i (i, igh, ie, y)*

I DO IT

- Display **Sound/Spelling Card** *ice cream.* Name the picture and say the sound. Have children repeat after you. *Listen: ice cream, /ī/. Now you say it.*

- One at a time, write the words *kind, night, tie,* and *spy* on the board. Blend and read the word. Point out the spelling for long *i.*

WE DO IT

- Write *silent* on the board. Use Instructional Routine 3 🔗 to blend the sounds, stretching out the word while pointing to each letter in a sweeping motion.

- Have children blend and read *silent* with you. Then have them blend and read it on their own.

- Repeat the routine with *thigh, lie,* and *myself.*

YOU DO IT

- Have partners work together to read **Decodable Reader** *Wild Cats.*

Decodable Reader

ELD ELD.PI.2.1

Reteach Language Arts

Subject-Verb Agreement

I DO IT

- Remind children that subjects and verbs need to match. If a singular pronoun or a singular noun comes before the verb, the verb should end in *-s* or *-es.*

- Write the following sentences: *She swing the bat. She swings the bat.*

Think Aloud *Which sentence is correct? I know that if he, she, or it comes before the verb, the verb should end in -s or -es. She comes before the verb, so She swings the bat is correct.*

WE DO IT

- Write the following sentences: *The boy toss the ball. The boy tosses the ball.*

- Ask, *Which sentence is correct? The boy tosses the ball. Why? The boy is just one boy, so the verb should end in -s or -es.*

- Repeat with these sentences: *It falls on the grass. It fall on the grass. It falls on the grass.*

YOU DO IT

- Ask children to write three or four sentences that begin with *he, she,* or *it.* Remind them to make sure the verb ends the correct way.

- Have children exchange papers with a partner and check each other's work.

Reteach Vocabulary Strategies

ELA L.2.4a ELD ELD.PI.2.1

Antonyms

I DO IT

- Remind children that antonyms are words that have opposite, or very different, meanings.

- Tell children that they can use antonyms as context clues.

- Explain that identifying antonyms can help children figure out the meaning of an unfamiliar word.

WE DO IT

- Write *Mia was calm before the party but became excited as soon as the guests arrived.* Have children read aloud the sentences.

- Model how to apply the **Vocabulary Strategy** to figure out the meaning of *calm*.

> **Think Aloud** *I'm not sure what* calm *means. I'll look at the words and phrases nearby for clues. I see the word* but *and I know that word often signals an opposite. I see the word* excited. *I think that* calm *and* excited *are antonyms. I think* calm *means "not excited."*

YOU DO IT

- Provide the following words. Have children copy them and write their antonyms: *hot, thin, true, first, stop, lost, forget, small, right, high.* Provide **Corrective Feedback** if children need additional support.

- Have partners choose an antonym pair and write a sentence or two using both words. Have them read their sentences aloud to each other.

Reteach Comprehension Skill

ELA RL.2.2 ELD ELD.PI.2.1, ELD.PI.2.6, ELD.PII.2.1

Sequence of Events

I DO IT

- Remind children that events in a selection often happen in a certain order. This time order is known as a *sequence of events.* Readers should note the sequence of events so that the selection will make sense.

WE DO IT

- Model how to identify the time sequence of the events of the ball game on **Student Book** pp. 63–65.

> **Think Aloud** *The events in this story seem to be mentioned in the order that they actually happen. In the third paragraph on p. 63, I see a description of things that happen in the game. The Dodgers and Phillies are playing a game. The game goes into extra innings. Jackie Robinson comes up to bat.*

- Help volunteers identify the sequence of events of Jackie Robinson's turn at bat.

YOU DO IT

- Distribute Graphic Organizer 4 [↗]: **Flow Chart.**

- Have children list the events that happen on **Student Book** pp. 59–60. Sample answer: *Luke takes a few practice swings; Luke gets three strikes; Luke strikes out again; Franky comes back; Luke has to sit out.*

- Have partners work together to complete the Flow Chart.

- Review the completed Flow Charts.

Teacher Notes

Anchor
Text

Poems About
Reading
and
Writing

Paired
Selection

LESSON
18

JOURNEYS

DIGITAL RESOURCES

Teacher Dashboard

Log onto the Teacher Dashboard and *my***SmartPlanner**. Use these searchable tools to customize lessons that achieve your instructional goals.

Interactive Whiteboard Lessons

- Vocabulary Strategies: Suffixes *-y, -ful*
- Phonics: Words with the Long *e* Sound for *y* and Changing *y* to *i*

- Write About Reading
- Narrative Writing: Descriptive Paragraph

 **Assess It Online!**

- Weekly Tests
- Assessment-driven instruction with prescriptive feedback

Student eBook

✎ 🗅 Annotate it! **Strategies for Annotation**

Guide children to use digital tools for close reading.

Children may also use the interactive features in their Student eBooks to respond to prompts in a variety of ways, including:

- short-answer response
- drag-and-drop
- spoken response
- multiple choice
- fill-in-the-blank
- drawing

 High-Interest Informational Texts and Multimedia

hmhfyi.com

Have children explore the FYI website for additional information about topics of study.

ENGLISH LANGUAGE SUPPORT

Culturally Responsive Teaching

Read About It, Write About It Tell children that this week, they will be reading and thinking about why reading and writing are important.

- Create a text-rich environment by providing a broad range of books, articles, and stories that cover a variety of topics. Include books and resources in English learners' first languages in the collection.

- Encourage children to make their own reading and writing choices. Invite children to share stories they have read or written.

- Interview children, or have partners interview each other, about types of books and stories they especially enjoy reading. Begin a "Check Out These Titles" classroom display to which children can add favorite topics and titles.

Promote Access and Cultural Awareness Include books at different reading levels. For emerging English learners, provide books in which pictures support the meaning of the text. Promote cultural awareness by including texts that highlight different countries, cultures, and traditions.

Language Support Card

Use the Lesson 18 Language Support Card to activate prior knowledge, frontload vocabulary, and teach academic English.

 Use the Text X-Ray on page T209 to review the language demands of *My Name Is Gabriela* with the needs of English learners in mind.

Language Workshop for Designated ELD

- Connection to Essential Question
- Vocabulary Network
- Focus on Interacting in Meaningful Ways
- Discussion Frames
- How English Works
- Word Learning Strategies

You may wish to use the following suggestions to modify instruction for some children, according to their needs.

Learner's Journal

Keeping a Learner's Journal can help children see themselves as successful, growing learners. Developing a sense of ownership in children can motivate them to reach their highest potential. Have children add to their Learner's Journal for this lesson. Depending on children's needs and skills, have them record information about what they are learning. Some examples:

- Day 1: Vocabulary: *accepted, pretend, express, prize, taught, wonder, grand, fluttering*
- Day 2: The title of the Anchor Text, *My Name Is Gabriela,* and words or pictures about the text
- Day 3: Write and draw about something new they learned about why reading and writing are important. To help, you might want to discuss with children the Essential Question and their ideas about it.
- Day 4: Write one or more words they have learned to spell this week.
- Day 5: Write about how they are becoming better writers. For example, "I am learning to write a descriptive paragraph."

Student eBook

- **Audio** can be activated to support fluency, decoding, and comprehension.
- **Alternative Text** provides spoken information that can be used in place of the information provided in the book's images.
- **Vocabulary Pop-Ups** contain point-of-use definitions for selection vocabulary.

History-Social Science

Create a Personal Time Line Have children create a personal time line of important events in their lives.

- Prepare a simple time line frame that children will complete with important events from their lives.
- Review *My Name Is Gabriela* and guide children to point out important events Gabriela shares, such as teaching herself to read, becoming a teacher and writer, and her travels to other countries.
- Using your own or Gabriela's life as an example, model creating a time line on the board and add important events. Point out that the time line shows events in the order in which they occurred.
- Distribute time line frames to children and guide them to complete their own personal time lines. Encourage them to include important events, such as learning to read and write, the birth of siblings, special events or trips, family moves, and accomplishments they recall fondly or take pride in. Explain that they do not have to include specific dates and years, but the events should appear in the order in which they occurred.
- Have children share and discuss their timelines in small groups.

LESSON 18

Our Focus Wall

ANCHOR TEXT

My Name Is Gabriela
Biography

Paired Selection

Poems About Reading and Writing
Poetry

ESSENTIAL QUESTION

Why are reading and writing important?

FOUNDATIONAL SKILLS

☑ High-Frequency Words

always	mother
anything	soon
been	under
draw	watch
friends	words

Phonics

The Long e Sound for *y*
Changing *y* to *i*

Fluency

Expression

READING LITERATURE & INFORMATIONAL TEXT

Comprehension Skills and Strategies

☑ TARGET SKILL
• Understanding Characters
• Author's Word Choice

☑ TARGET STRATEGY
• Analyze/Evaluate

LANGUAGE

☑ Target Vocabulary

accepted	pretend
express	prize
taught	wonder
grand	fluttering

Vocabulary Strategies

Suffixes -*y* and -*ful*

Grammar

The Verb *Be*

Spelling

The Long e Sound for *y*

happy	carry
pretty	lucky
baby	only
very	sunny
puppy	penny
funny	city

WRITING

Writing

Narrative Writing:
Descriptive Paragraph
Focus Trait: Elaboration

ANCHOR TEXT

My Name Is Gabriela
GENRE: Biography

21st Century Theme: Global Awareness

 Prepare for Complex Texts For a comprehensive overview and analysis of key ideas and academic language features of this lesson's Anchor Text, see pages T208–T209.

Poems About Reading and Writing
GENRE: Poetry

Digital Resources

▶ eBook: Annotate it!

▶ Interactive Whiteboard Lessons
  • Vocabulary Strategies: Suffixes -y, -ful
  • Phonics: Words with the Long e Sound for y and Changing y to i

▶ Multimedia Grammar Glossary

▶ mySmartPlanner

▶ Parent Resource

● Additional Resources

• Vocabulary in Context Cards 137–144
• Reader's Notebook, pp. 31–45
• Independent Reading

• Lesson 18 Blackline Masters
• Decodable Readers
• Blend-It Books 117–120

Vocabulary Reader

All About Chile
by Monica Brown

HOUGHTON MIFFLIN

- **Vocabulary Reader**
  for all levels

  Provide strategic scaffolding to support all students in reading on-level text and in acquiring general academic and domain-specific vocabulary. Use the instructional supports on pp. T286–T287 or the Leveled Reader Teacher's Guide.

  Guided Reading Level: K
  Lexile: 550
  DRA: 20
  Leveled Reader Teacher's Guide

Weekly Leveled Readers

Guide children to read and comprehend additional texts about the lesson topic.
Use the instructional supports on pp. T292–T295 or the Leveled Reader Teacher's Guides.

Struggling Readers
Guided Reading Level: K
Lexile: 390
DRA: 20
Leveled Reader Teacher's Guide

On Level
Guided Reading Level: M
Lexile: 540
DRA: 28
Leveled Reader Teacher's Guide

Advanced
Guided Reading Level: P
Lexile: 660
DRA: 38
Leveled Reader Teacher's Guide

English Language Learners
Guided Reading Level: M
Lexile: 500
DRA: 28
Leveled Reader Teacher's Guide

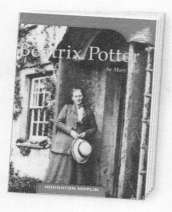   

Meaning Making

Language Development

Effective Expression

Content Knowledge

Foundational Skills

Language Workshop for Designated ELD

- Provides an additional hour of daily instruction for targeted language support.

- **Supports English learners** at three different proficiency levels as they dig deeper into the language of the lesson texts.

- Guides students in collaboration, interpretation, and production of English.

Lesson 18 Focus

Collaborate: Offer Opinions with Learned Phrases

Interpret: Analyze Language Choices

Produce: Give Presentations; Recount Experiences

How English Works: Condense Clauses

Vocabulary Network

Intervention

 Strategic Intervention Tier II

Write-In Reader: *Pat Mora*

- Interactive worktext with selection that connects to the lesson topic
- Reinforces the lesson's vocabulary and comprehension
- Builds skills for reading increasingly complex texts
- Online version with dual-speed audio and follow-text

Daily Lessons See this week's daily Strategic Intervention Lesson on pp. S22–S31.

- Preteach and reteach daily instruction
- Oral Grammar
- Words to Know
- Decoding
- Comprehension
- Fluency
- Grammar
- Written Response
- Unpack Meaning

Curious About Words Provides oral vocabulary instruction for children with limited vocabularies.

HMH Decoding Power: Intensive Reading Instruction

- **Provides reteaching and practice in the key foundational skills** for reading: print concepts, phonological/phonemic awareness, phonics and word recognition, and fluency.

- **Explicit, sequential, and systematic instruction** designed to bring students up to grade level.

✓ Assess It Online!

▶ **Intervention Assessments** place individual students within the system, ensure students are making satisfactory progress, and provide a measure of student readiness to exit the system.

What My Other Students Are Doing

Digital Resources

▶ Literacy Centers: Word Study, Think and Write, Comprehension and Fluency

● **Additional Resources**

- Vocabulary in Context Cards 137–144
- Reader's Notebook, pp. 31–45
- Independent Reading
- Lesson 18 Blackline Masters
- Decodable Readers
- Blend-It Books 117–120

Comprehension and Fluency

Materials
- Student Book
- Decodable Reader: *Bunny and the Penny*
- Audio
- Paper and pencil

Word Study

Materials
- Letter Cards: *f, l, u, t, t, e, r, i, n, g*
- Paper, pencil, crayons
- Children's lists of words

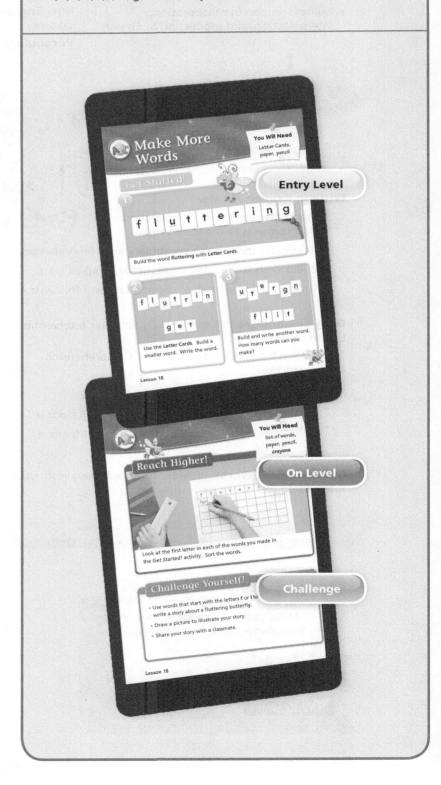

Assign Literacy Center activities during small group time. Each center contains three activities. Children who experience success with the entry-level activity move on to the on-level and challenge activities, as time permits.

Meaning Making

Effective Expression

Language Development

Content Knowledge

Foundational Skills

Think and Write

Materials
- Student Book
- Paper, pencil, crayons
- Construction paper
- Blank cards

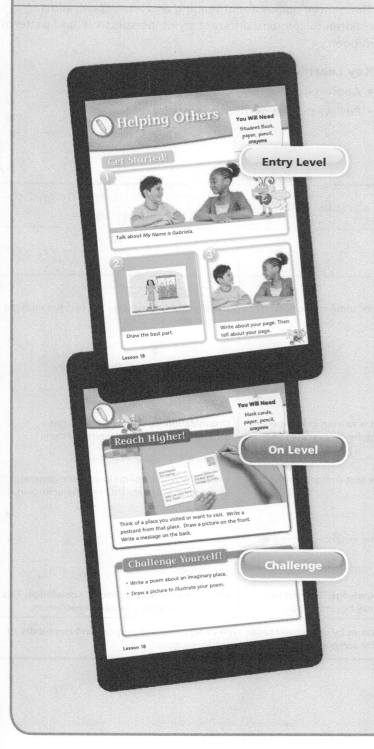

Helping Others

You Will Need
Student Book, paper, pencil, crayons

Get Started!

Entry Level

1 Talk about *My Name Is Gabriela.*

2 Draw the best part.

3 Write about your page. Then tell about your page.

Lesson 18

Reach Higher!

You Will Need
blank cards, paper, pencil, crayons

On Level

Think of a place you visited or want to visit. Write a postcard from that place. Draw a picture on the front. Write a message on the back.

Challenge Yourself!

Challenge

- Write a poem about an imaginary place.
- Draw a picture to illustrate your poem.

Lesson 18

Independent Reading

Writing in Response to Books Writing in response to texts prompts children to think more deeply about the text. Vary the kinds of writing you ask children to do to keep them engaged and motivated to write about their independent reading.

- **Planning for Book Talks** Children make brief notes or drawings to bring to Book Talk discussions. They can focus on a particular scene or a part that they really like.

- **Book Reviews** Children draw posters or make bookmarks to tell others about their books.

- **Reactions to Texts** Children write on index cards. They write the title, author, and something they like or do not like about the book. They post it on a bulletin board near the classroom library.

- **Alternate Ending** Children draw or write a different ending to the book and tell a classmate how their ending is different from the book's real ending.

See pp. T254–T255 for additional independent reading support. **ELA** RL.2.10, RI.2.10

Prepare for Complex Texts

My Name Is Gabriela
by Monica Brown

GENRE: Biography

Why This Text?

Children will regularly encounter biographies about important people in independent reading and on the Internet. This text is about someone who worked hard to make her dreams come true.

Key Learning Objectives

- Learn about the person presented in the biography.
- Notice words the author has chosen to convey meaning.

Poems About Reading and Writing
by Patricia and Fredrick McKissack, Richard Armour, and Beatrice Schenk de Regniers

GENRE: Poetry

Why This Text?

These three poems about reading and writing will allow children to compare different styles, perspectives, and patterns in poetry.

Key Learning Objectives

- Appreciate different forms of poetry.
- Review the use of rhythm in poetry.

▲ TEXT COMPLEXITY RUBRIC

		My Name Is Gabriela	Poems About Reading and Writing
Quantitative Measures	Lexile	830	NP
	Guided Reading Level	N	K
Qualitative Measures	Purpose/Levels of Meaning	**Figurative Language:** The text contains some metaphors.	**Density and Complexity:** The text has multiple related themes. **Figurative Language:** The poems use personification and imagery.
	Text Structure	**Genre:** The text is a biography, but it is written in first-person point of view, as if it is an autobiography.	**Organization:** Each of the poems has a different rhythm and rhyming pattern.
	Language Features	**Standard English and Variations:** The text contains both familiar and poetic language. **Sentence Structure:** The text has many instances of complex sentence structure.	**Vocabulary:** The poems have some general academic vocabulary that may be unknown.
	Knowledge Demands	**Subject Matter Knowledge/Prior Knowledge:** The text has some geographical references that may be unfamiliar.	**Life Experiences/Background Knowledge:** This text includes mostly familiar experiences.
Reader/Task Considerations		Determine using the professional judgment of the teacher. This varies by individual reader, type of text, and the purpose and complexity of particular tasks. See **Reader and Task Considerations** on p. T225 for some suggestions for Anchor Text support.	

Meaning Making

Language Development

Effective Expression

Content Knowledge

Foundational Skills

TEXT X-RAY

ENGLISH LANGUAGE SUPPORT Use the Text X-Ray below to prepare for teaching the Anchor Text *My Name Is Gabriela*. Use it to plan, support, and scaffold instruction in order to help children understand the text's **key ideas** and **academic language features**.

Zoom In on Key Ideas
Children should understand these **key ideas** after reading *My Name Is Gabriela*.

Key Idea | pp. 92–97

Gabriela Mistral grew up in the country of Chile. As a child, she had a lot of imagination and loved the sound of words.

Have children tell how they know Gabriela liked to imagine things.

Key Idea | pp. 98–101

Young Gabriela liked to write poems and tell stories. She used to play school with the other children and taught them their ABCs.

Have children name some things Gabriela liked to do as a child that they also like to do.

Key Idea | pp. 102–103

When Gabriela became an adult, she became a real teacher. She also continued to write poems and stories.

Have children tell how what Gabriela did as a little girl helped her when she was an adult.

Key Idea | pp. 104–109

Gabriela traveled to many different countries, sharing her poems and stories. She received a very important award for her writing.

Have children tell why they think winning the Nobel Prize for Literature was a special event for Gabriela Mistral.

Zoom In on Academic Language
Guide children at different proficiencies and skill levels to understand the structure and language of this text.

Focus: Text Level | pp. 92–95

This text is a **biography,** which is the story of a real person's life, written by someone else. This biography is unusual, though, because it is written in **first-person point of view.** Point out to children that the story is written as if Gabriela is telling it. Have them point to words in the text, such as *me* and *I,* that show this.

Focus: Word Level | p. 96

Point out the **imagery** *rolling off my tongue,* and write the phrase on the board. Tell children that in the context of the sentence, the narrator is saying that she loves the way words sound as she says them. Explain that this kind of description makes the author's words more interesting to read.

Focus: Sentence Level | p. 103

Reread the second paragraph with children. Point out that the two sentences in this paragraph use examples to explain something. The first sentence gives a topic, *poems,* and then gives details about the types of poems: *happy poems, sad poems, stories of mothers and children.* Guide children to point out the topic and details of the second sentence.

Content and Language Instruction

Make note of additional **content knowledge** and **language features** children may find challenging in this text.

Weekly Planner

my SmartPlanner

Auto-populates the suggested five-day lesson plan and offers flexibility to create and save customized plans from year to year.

See **Standards Correlations** on p. C1. In your eBook, click the Standards button in the left panel to view descriptions of the standards on the page.

DAY 1

Materials

- Blend-It Books: Books 117–118
- Common Core Writing Handbook, Lesson 18
- Decodable Reader: *Bunny and the Penny*
- High-Frequency Word Cards 171–180
- Instructional Routines 7, 11, 12
- Language Support Card, Lesson 18
- Letter Cards
- Literacy and Language Guide, pp. 90–91
- Projectables S1, 18.1, 18.2, 18.3
- Reader's Notebook Vol 2 pp. 31–32
- Retelling Cards 69–72
- Sound/Spelling Card: eagle
- Student Book pp. 86–109
- Vocabulary in Context Cards 137–144

DAY 2

Materials

- Decodable Reader: *Bunny and the Penny*
- Graphic Organizer 2
- High-Frequency Word Cards 171–180
- Instructional Routines 3, 15
- Letter Cards
- Literacy and Language Guide, pp. 90–91
- Projectables 18.4, 18.5
- Reader's Notebook Vol 2 pp. 33–36
- Student Book pp. 90–113
- Vocabulary in Context Cards 137–144

Whole Group

Daily Language
- Oral Vocabulary
- Phonemic Awareness
- Speaking and Listening

Vocabulary

Text-Based Comprehension
- Skills and Strategies
- Craft and Structure

Foundational Skills
- Phonics and Word Recognition
- Fluency

DAY 1

Opening Routines, T212–T213
Read Aloud "Doctor Salk's Treasure," T214–T215
Phonemic Awareness, T216

☑ **Introduce Target Vocabulary,** T220–T221
☑ **Read and Comprehend** T222–T223
FIRST READ **Think Through the Text**
Read the Anchor Text: *My Name Is Gabriela*, T224–T235

☑ **Fluency**
Expression, T214
☑ **Phonics**
- The Long *e* Sound for *y*, T216–T218
Read *Bunny and the Penny*, T219

DAY 2

Opening Routines, T238–T239
Phonemic Awareness, T240

☑ **Dig Deeper,** T242–T243
- Understanding Characters
- Author's Word Choice
SECOND READ **Analyze the Text**
Reread the Anchor Text: *My Name Is Gabriela*, T224–T234
Your Turn, T244–T245

☑ **Fluency**
Expression, T241
☑ **Phonics**
- The Long *e* Sound for *y*, T240–T241

Whole Group Language Arts

Spelling

Grammar

Writing

DAY 1

☑ **Spelling**
Long *e* Spelled *y*; Pretest, T236
☑ **Grammar**
The Verb *Be*, T236
Daily Proofreading Practice, T237
☑ **Narrative Writing:**
Descriptive Paragraph
Introduce the Model, T237

DAY 2

☑ **Spelling**
Long *e* Spelled *y*, T246
☑ **Grammar**
The Verb *Be*, T246
Daily Proofreading Practice, T247
☑ **Narrative Writing:**
Descriptive Paragraph
Focus Trait: Elaboration, T247

Small Group

 Suggestions for Small Groups (See pp. T281–T299.)

Language Workshop

Designated English Language Support

DAY 1

Connect to Text: *My Name Is Gabriela*
Introduce Vocabulary Network: Words About Reading and Writing

DAY 2

Expand Vocabulary Network
Collaborate: Offer Opinions

iRead™ Use *iRead*, an adaptive digital foundational reading skills program, to personalize learning for students.

Integrated English Language Support
See page T203 for instructional support activities for Diverse Linguistic Learners.

Assess It Online!
▶ Lesson 18 Assessment

DAY 3	DAY 4	DAY 5
Materials	**Materials**	**Materials**
• Blend-It Books: Books 119–120	• Decodable Reader: *Puppies*	• Blackline Masters: Writing Rubric, Proofreading Checklist
• Cold Reads	• High-Frequency Word Cards 171–180	• High-Frequency Word Cards 171–180
• Decodable Reader: *Puppies*	• Instructional Routine 15	• Interactive Whiteboard Lesson: Phonics: Words with the Long *e* Sound for *y*; Changing *y* to *i*
• High-Frequency Word Cards 171–180	• Interactive Whiteboard Lesson: Suffixes -*y* and -*ful*	• Listening Log
• Letter Cards	• Letter Cards	• Projectable 18.10
• Literacy and Language Guide, pp. 90–91, 150–151	• Literacy and Language Guide, pp. 90–91	• Reader's Notebook Vol 2 p. 45
• Projectables 18.6, 18.7	• Projectables S8, 18.7, 18.8, 18.9	• Student Book pp. 118–121
• Reader's Notebook Vol 2 pp. 37–41	• Reader's Notebook Vol 2 pp. 42–44	• Vocabulary in Context Cards 137–144
• Sound/Spelling Card: eagle	• Sound/Spelling Cards: ice cream, eagle	• Close Reader, Lesson 18
• Student Book pp. 90–109	• Student Book pp. 114–117	
• Vocabulary in Context Cards 137–144	• Vocabulary in Context Cards 137–144	
Opening Routines, T248–T249 **Phonemic Awareness,** T250	**Opening Routines,** T260–T261 **Phonemic Awareness,** T262	**Opening Routines,** T270–T271 **Speaking and Listening,** T273
Independent Reading, T254–T255 • Reader's Guide: *My Name Is Gabriela* • Self-Selected Reading • Self-Correction Strategies **Apply Vocabulary Knowledge,** T256–T257	**Connect to the Topic** • Read Poetry: *Poems About Reading and Writing*, T264 • Introduce Genre and Text Focus, T264 ☑ **Compare Texts,** T265 ☑ **Vocabulary Strategies,** Suffixes -*y*, -*ful*, T266–T267	**Close Reader** • Lesson 18 **Extend the Topic** • Domain-Specific Vocabulary, T272 • Speaking and Listening: Recount an Experience, T273 • Optional Second Read: *Poems About Reading and Writing*, T264
☑ **Fluency** Expression, T253 ☑ **Phonics** • Changing *y* to *i*, T250–T251 **Read** *Puppies*, T252	☑ **Fluency** Expression, T262 ☑ **Phonics** • Phonics Review, T262–T263	☑ **Fluency** Expression, T279 ☑ **Phonics** • Phonics Review, T278
☑ **Spelling** Long *e* Spelled *y*, T258 ☑ **Grammar** The Verb *Be*, T258 Daily Proofreading Practice, T259 ☑ **Narrative Writing:** Descriptive Paragraph Prewrite, T259	☑ **Spelling** Long *e* Spelled *y*, T268 ☑ **Grammar** Spiral Review, T268 Daily Proofreading Practice, T269 ☑ **Narrative Writing:** Descriptive Paragraph Draft, T269	☑ **Spelling** Assess, T274 ☑ **Grammar** The Verb *Be*, T274–T275 Daily Proofreading Practice, T276 ☑ **Narrative Writing:** Descriptive Paragraph Revise and Edit, T276–T277

 Tier II Intervention provides 30 minutes of additional daily practice with key parts of the core instruction. (See pp. S22–S31.)

Interpret: Distinguish Effects of Language Choice
Unpack a Sentence

Produce: Plan a Presentation
Focus on How English Works: Use Conjunctions to Condense Ideas

Share and Reflect

DAY 1

Today's Goals

Vocabulary & Oral Language
- **Teacher Read Aloud:**
  "Doctor Salk's Treasure"
- **Oral Vocabulary**
- **Listening Comprehension**
- **Introduce Vocabulary**

☑ TARGET VOCABULARY

accepted	pretend
express	prize
taught	wonder
grand	fluttering

Phonemic Awareness
- **Identify Sound Placement**

Phonics & Fluency
- **Long e Sound for y**
- **Read Decodable Reader:**
  Bunny and the Penny
- **Fluency:** Expression
- **High-Frequency Words**

Text-Based Comprehension
- **Listening Comprehension**
- **Read and Comprehend**
- **Read the Anchor Text:**
  My Name Is Gabriela

Grammar & Writing
- **The Verb be**
- **Narrative Writing:**
  Descriptive Paragraph

Spelling
- **Long e Spelled y**

Warm Up with Wordplay

Share a Brain Teaser

Display and read aloud the following brain-teaser:

> ## How many books can you put into an empty backpack?

Have children turn and talk to a partner to discuss possible responses. If no one figures it out, tell the answer: *One. After that it's not an empty backpack!*

Discuss the importance of listening carefully to a problem, question, or set of directions. Tell children that sometimes all it takes is a word or two to change the whole meaning of a sentence. For example, the word *empty* makes a big difference in the meaning of the question above and how it is answered. **ELA** SL.2.1a **ELD** ELD PI.2.1

Daily Phonemic Awareness

Identify Sound Placement

- Say the word *mean*. *What vowel sound do you hear?* /ē/

- Say the word *puppy*. *What is this word?* *puppy* Ask: *Where do you hear the /ē/ sound in* puppy? *at the end; the final sound* Sound out the word. Have children repeat after you.

- Help children identify the position of the /ē/ sound as you say the following words: *steam, baby, penny, silly, clean, easy, lucky, heavy, eat, behind.*

Corrective Feedback

- If a child is unable to identify sound placement, say the word, give correction, and model the task. Example: *The word is* puppy. *The /ē/ sound is at the end of the word, in the second syllable. Say it with me,* /p/ /ŭ/ /p/ /ē/, puppy. *Now you say it.*

- Have children repeat on their own, and then continue with other words.

Daily High-Frequency Words

- Point to the High-Frequency Words on the Focus Wall. Say: *This week, our new High-Frequency Word is* words. *Our review words are* always, anything, been, draw, friends, mother, soon, under, *and* watch.

- Use <u>Instructional Routine 11</u> and **High-Frequency Word Card 171** to introduce the new word *words*.

- Repeat with **High-Frequency Word Cards 172–180** for review words *always, anything, been, draw, friends, mother, soon, under,* and *watch.*
  ELA RF.2.3f

Corrective Feedback

- If a child does not recognize the word *words*, say the correct word and have children repeat it. *Words. What is the word?* words

- Have children spell the word. *w-o-r-d-s How do we say it?* words

- Have children reread all of the cards in random order.

Daily Vocabulary Boost

- Preview the Target Vocabulary by displaying the **Vocabulary in Context Cards** and discussing the words. For example, use sentences such as these to discuss the words *pretend, prize,* and *wonder.*

  It is easy to pretend to be in a make-believe place from a book or a movie.

  She won a prize because she was such a good writer.

  It is normal for children to wonder what will happen in the future.

- Tell children that they will find these and other Vocabulary Words when they read *My Name Is Gabriela.*

Vocabulary in Context Cards 137–144

☑ **Target Vocabulary**

accepted

express

taught

grand

pretend

prize

wonder

fluttering

Teacher Read Aloud

▶ SHARE OBJECTIVES

- Listen to fluent reading.
- Retell key ideas and details from text read aloud. LANGUAGE
- Identify and use action verbs. LANGUAGE

PREVIEW
☑ TARGET VOCABULARY

wonder to think about something you are not sure about

taught to have helped someone learn something

accepted to have agreed with something

fluttering waving or moving rapidly

express to show or describe something

prize an award

pretend not real

grand big or impressive

ENGLISH LANGUAGE SUPPORT

Comprehensible Input

All Proficiencies To assist children with accessing the content and topic of the Teacher Read Aloud, complete the Build Background activities on Lesson 18 **Language Support Card.**

Model Fluency

Expression Explain that when good readers read aloud, they make their voice show feelings. This is called *expression.*

- Display Projectable 18.1 ⌐. As you read the first paragraph, do so with no expression. Then reread it using appropriate expression for each sentence.

- Point out that the text sounds different when correct expression is used.

- Reread the paragraph together with children. Use correct expression to emphasize the text's meaning. Then read the remainder of the article aloud.

Listening Comprehension

Read aloud the selection. Pause at the numbered stopping points to ask children the questions below. Discuss the meanings of the highlighted words, as needed, to support the discussion. Tell children they will learn more about the words later in the lesson. **ELA** SL.2.2 **ELD** ELD.PI.2.5

(1) *What is the first paragraph about? Sample answer: It describes the symptoms of a frightening disease.* MAIN IDEA AND DETAILS

(2) *The writer used the word* horrible *to describe polio. Is this a fact or an opinion?* opinion *What type of writing is this likely to be?* persuasive *What might the author be trying to convince you to believe? Sample answer: Curing polio was important. Dr Salk was an important man; we should respect people who make the world better.* FACT AND OPINION

(3) *What is the selection mostly about? Sample answer: a man named Jonas Salk who made a medicine that cured polio* MAIN IDEA AND DETAILS

💬 Classroom Collaboration

Ask children to retell the most important parts of "Doctor Salk's Treasure." *There was a time when polio was a feared disease. Dr. Jonas Salk invented a cure. People around the world were thankful.*
ELA SL.2.2 **ELD** ELD.PI.2.1, ELD.PI.2.5, ELD.PI.2.12a

🔍 Language Detective

How English Works: Verb Types Explain to children that authors use different kinds of verbs to describe what someone or something does. Tell children that *doing* verbs show action. Reread the fourth paragraph, emphasizing the following doing verbs as you read them: *working, made, tested, accepted, fluttering, waited, showed, worked, called.* Explain what each verb describes as you write it on the board. Then reread the fifth paragraph, and have children give a thumbs up when they hear a doing verb. *trying, spent, working, won, earn* Guide children to practice writing sentences that contain doing verbs.
ELD ELD.PII.2.3a

Doctor Salk's Treasure

1 Imagine being afraid that a fever or a sore throat could mean something far worse than a cold or flu. Not long ago, children would go to sleep feeling a little sick and wake up unable to move their legs. Sometimes they could not even breathe. Some of these children could not walk for the rest of their lives.

2 These horrible things happened because of a disease called polio. Luckily, we don't have to worry about polio today. Why, you **wonder**? You are safe because of Dr. Jonas Salk.

Jonas Salk **taught** at a school for doctors. He was interested in keeping people well by helping them fight diseases like polio. In the 1950s, he worked at finding a way to make the terrible disease go away forever.

After working long and hard, Dr. Salk and his team made a medicine to protect children from polio. At first they were not sure if it would work. The medicine had to be tested before it was **accepted** for human use. Imagine Dr. Salk's heart **fluttering** with nervousness as he waited for the test results. Imagine the look on his face when the results showed that the medicine worked. Dr. Salk's treatment kept children safe from polio! People all over the world called to **express** an interest in this new vaccine.

Dr. Salk never stopped trying to help people. He spent the rest of his life working to find cures for other diseases. In 1956, he won an important **prize** for his work, the Albert Lasker Award. Dr. Salk would go on to earn many other awards.

3 During your free time, do you ever act like a **pretend** doctor? Do you ever help others in different ways? It is a **grand** feeling to know that you can do something to make the world a better place.

Phonics

- Identify the position of the long *e* sound in words.
- Identify the spelling *y* for the long *e* sound.
- Blend and decode regularly spelled words with the long *e* sound for *y*.

▶ **SKILLS TRACE**

Words with the Long *e* Sound for *y*	
Introduce	pp. T216–T217, T240–T241
Differentiate	pp. T284–T285
Reteach	p. T298
Review	pp. T263, T352, T363
Assess	Weekly Tests, Lesson 18

ENGLISH LANGUAGE SUPPORT

Comprehensible Input

Emerging Say each of the following words from the Phonics lesson and demonstrate meaning (suggested actions are in parentheses); have children repeat each word: *baby* (rock a baby); *penny* (show a penny); *copy* (copy from the board); *lazy* (yawn and stretch). Show each action again, and encourage children to name the word that matches.

Expanding Focus children's attention on the second syllable of *baby, penny, copy,* and *lazy* by saying each word and then repeating just the first syllable; have children provide the second syllable before saying the whole word again. Monitor their pronunciation and provide corrective feedback. As needed, use the word in a context phrase or give a simple definition.

Bridging Check children's understanding of the words used in the Phonics lesson by asking for the word in a phrase or short sentence that shows meaning.

Words with the Long *e* Sound for *y*

ENGLISH LANGUAGE SUPPORT Multiple spellings for the same vowel sound are common in English, unlike many other languages. Tell children that the letter *i* spells the long *e* sound in Spanish (for example, *niña* (girl) or *comida* (meal), but in English, there are many more ways to spell the same sound. Review previously learned spellings by writing these words for children to read with you; underline the spelling for long *e* in each: *he, tree, bean, compete*. You may want to add that another English spelling for /ē/ is just like the one in Spanish; write the word *pizza* for children to read with you; have them name the letter that spells /ē/. **ELD** ELD.PIII.2

Phonemic Awareness Warm-Up *I'm going to say a word with the long e sound /ē/ and tell whether the sound is in the beginning, middle, or end of the word. Listen: lady. I hear /ē/ at the end of lady. Say lady with me: lady. Where in the word do you hear /ē/? at the end*

Let's do some more. Listen as I say a word; you tell whether you hear /ē/ at the beginning, middle, or end of the word: baby, **end**; *tiny,* **end**; *wheel,* *middle*; *even,* *beginning*; *funny,* **end**; *please,* *middle*; *eastern,* *beginning*; *tricky,* **end**; *January,* **end**

1 Teach/Model

Sound/Spelling Card Display the **Sound/Spelling Card** for *eagle.* Name the picture and say the sound /ē/ for children to repeat.

e
e_e
ee
ea
_y
_ie_
_ey
(c)ei

- **Say the sound and introduce the spelling *y*.** *Eagle begins with the long e vowel sound /ē/. The letter y can spell the sound /ē/ at the end of a word that has two or more syllables.*

- **Write and read *baby*.** *This is the word* baby. *It has two syllables. Clap the syllables with me: ba-by.* Point to each syllable as you tell about its sounds and letters. *The letters* b, a *spell the first syllable of* baby. *It is an open syllable, and the vowel sound for a is long: /bā/. The second syllable has the letters* b, y. *The letter y stands for the long e vowel sound /ē/ at the end of the second syllable, /bē/.* Point to each syllable of *baby* as children read it with you and then blend the syllables to read the word aloud.

- **Write and read *penny*.** *This is the word* penny. *Clap the syllables with me: pen-ny. The letters* p, e, n *spell the first syllable of* penny. *It is a closed syllable, and the vowel sound is short e: /pĕn/. The second syllable has the letters* n, y. *The letter y stands for the long /ē/ sound at the end of the syllable: /nē/. Let's read each syllable and then blend them to read the whole word:* pen-ny, penny.

- Repeat the process, using the words *happy, lady,* and *easy.*

2 Guided Practice

Continuous Blending Routine Use the routine to model blending *lady* one syllable at a time. Display **Letter Cards** *l, a, d, y*.

- Blend the sounds in each syllable and then blend the syllables. *Listen: /l/ /ā/, /d/ /ē/; la-dy; lady.* Have children blend with you in the same way.

Blending Lines

Blend Words Have children read the following words chorally; provide Corrective Feedback as needed. Help children compare the sounds and spellings they notice in each line.

1. bay	by	baby	may	my	mommy
2. say	messy	shy	pushy	tiny	try
3. funny	fly	play	happy	skinny	sky

Transition to Longer Words Have children read the following words chorally. Ask children to identify known word parts in each longer word that helped them decode it.

4. snowy	shady	sleepy	puppy	silly	bunny
5. berry	body	daddy	pony	foggy	jelly
6. creamy	cherry	nosy	city	shiny	easy

Challenge Call on above-level children to read the words in Line 7 and discuss the elements. Then have the class read the sentences chorally.

> 7. empty angry copying unlucky blueberry carrying
> 8. Did my <u>words</u> make that tiny baby cry?
> 9. I <u>always</u> carry my lucky penny. **ELA** RF.2.3c, RF.2.3e

3 Apply

Have partners take turns rereading Blending Lines 1–3 and 4–6. Then tell partners to choose pairs of words that can be used together in a sentence, such as *messy jelly, sleepy bunny, foggy city.* Have them choose one sentence to use as a caption for a drawing.

Distribute <u>Reader's Notebook Volume 2 page 31</u> or <u>leveled practice</u> in Grab-and-Go™ Resources to children to complete independently.

FORMATIVE ASSESSMENT ▲ RtI

Corrective Feedback When a child mispronounces a letter-sound, highlight that letter, restate its sound, have children repeat the sound, and then guide them to blend the word. See the example below.

Decoding Error:
A child reads *silly* in Line 4 as *sly*.

Correct the error. Say the correct word. Identify the syllables. *The word is silly. The first syllable is sil. The second syllable is ly: sil-ly, silly.*

Model as you cover the word one syllable at a time. *The letters s, i, l spell the syllable sil. The letters l, y spell the second syllable. The sound for y in the second syllable is /ē/. The second syllable is ly. I'll blend the syllables to say the word: sil-ly, silly.*

Guide *Let's blend the syllables together: sil-ly. What is the word?* silly

Check *You read the two syllables.* sil-ly *What is the word?* silly

Reinforce Go back three or four words and have children continue reading. Make note of errors and review those words during the next lesson.

 Go to pp. T284–T285 for additional phonics support.

DAY 1

Phonics

▶ SHARE OBJECTIVES

- Write words with the long *e* sound for *y*.
- Read decodable text with words containing the long *e* sound for *y* and High-Frequency Words.
- Practice reading fluently with expression (prosody).

▶ DICTATION SENTENCES

- **tiny** A baby has *tiny* feet.
- **bunny** That *bunny* is so soft.
- **silly** The clown acted so *silly*.
- **berry** This *berry* tastes sweet.
- **lady** The *lady* wore a red hat.
- **story** Tell me a funny *story*.

ENGLISH LANGUAGE SUPPORT

Use Visuals and Gestures

All Proficiencies Support children's understanding of the words in the dictation sentences by offering simple definitions or examples accompanied by images or gestures; for example: *Tiny things are very little. An ant is tiny.* Ask children a *yes/no* question about the word; for example: *Is this dot tiny?* Prompt them to use the word in a phrase or sentence; for example; *Yes, the dot is tiny;* or *Yes, it is tiny.*

Blend-It Books

To provide reading practice with new sound/spellings in decodable texts, see **Blend-It Books** 117–118.

Write Words with the Long *e* Sound for *y*

1 Teach/Model

Connect Sounds to Spelling Use **Sound/Spelling Card** *eagle* to review the long *e* sound /ē/. Tell children that they will write words in which the letter *y* spells the long *e* sound.

Use Instructional Routine 7 ⤢ to dictate the first word at the left. *Listen as I say a word and use it in a sentence.*

- Model how to spell the word *tiny*. *I hear two syllables in the word tiny, ti-ny. The first syllable is /tī/. It begins with /t/, so I write t. The syllable ends with long i /ī/, so I write i. The second syllable in tiny begins with the sound /n/, so I write n. The final sound is /ē/. I remember that in a two-syllable word, long e can be spelled y. I write y. I'll reread to check: tiny.*

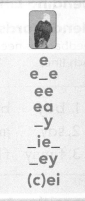

e
e_e
ee
ea
_y
_ie_
_ey
(c)ei

2 Guided Practice

Connect Sounds to Writing Continue the dictation, using the sentences at left.

- Have children say each dictation word aloud after you. Remind them to think about the two syllables they hear in the word, identify the sounds they hear at the beginning, middle, and end of each one, and write the letters that spell each sound. **ELA** L.2.2d

- Remind children to write only the dictation word.

3 Apply

Read aloud the following decodable sentence for children to write. Remind children to look at the Focus Wall if they need help spelling *friends*. **ELA** RF.2.3f, L.2.2d

> This tiny puppy and I are <u>friends</u>.

Print the dictation words and decodable sentence for children to check their work.

Decodable Reader

Read *Bunny and the Penny*

Review the Long e Sound for *y* and High-Frequency Words Review **Sound/Spelling Card** *eagle*. Then review High-Frequency Words *always, anything, been, draw, friends, mother, soon, under, watch,* and *words.*

Preview Have children read the title, browse beginning pages, and discuss what they think the story is about.

Use Projectable S1 to review the **Phonics/Decoding Strategy.** Model the strategy using the title. Have children read the first page silently. Then ask a child to read the page aloud as others follow. Repeat for each page.

ENGLISH LANGUAGE SUPPORT Offer support as needed in drawing meaning from complex sentences such as *"Maybe I can get a treat mom might like more than a cherry and a berry,"* Bunny thought. Prompt children to break the sentence into its component ideas by identifying words to complete spoken sentences like these: *Maybe I can get a (treat). It will be a treat for (mom). Mom might like the treat more than a (cherry). She might like it more than a (berry).*

If children make more than six total errors, use the **Corrective Feedback** steps to help them reread aloud with accuracy. If they make fewer than six errors, have them reread and retell the story.

> Bunny and the Penny
>
> On a chilly, breezy spring day, Bunny went hopping along. It was sunny and bright as she went up a long, winding path. She saw a penny on the path.
>
> 33

Decodable Reader

Fluency: Expression

Tell children that when good readers read aloud, they add interest and enjoyment to their reading by reading with expression. Write the following sentences on the board and read them aloud:

> "You can get a cherry and a berry," said Nanny Goat. "Yummy treats!"

Model Fluency and Expression Read each sentence in a monotone and ask children whether it sounds interesting. *Listen to how I show the character's feelings as I reread.* Reread the sentences fluently and expressively. *Let's read the sentences together. We'll say the words to show how Nanny Goat feels about these treats.*

ENGLISH LANGUAGE SUPPORT As children read, monitor their decoding of words with final *y*. Provide modeling and support as needed. **ELD** ELD.PIII.2

Responding Have children review the story. Ask them why Bunny asks the mothers a question. Tell children to write a sentence about what Bunny wants to know and a sentence about how Bunny finds the answer. **ELA** RL.2.1

Reread for Fluency Use Instructional Routine 12 to have children read *Bunny and the Penny* chorally. Remind children to reread to correct any mistakes and to use their voice to show how the characters feel. **ELA** RF.2.4a, RF.2.4b

Corrective Feedback When a child mispronounces a word, point to the word and say it. Call attention to the element that was mispronounced, say the sound, and then guide children to read the word. See the example below.

Decoding Error:
A child reads *shiny* on page 2 as *shy.*

Correct the error. *That word is* shiny. *It has two syllables:* shi-ny, shiny.

Guide Have children repeat the word. *What is the word?* shiny

Check *Go back to the beginning of the sentence and read it again.*

Reinforce Record the error and review the word again before children reread the story.

SMALL GROUP Options

Go to pp. T284–T285 for additional phonics support.

DAY 1

Introduce Vocabulary

▶ SHARE OBJECTIVES

- Acquire and use vocabulary. LANGUAGE
- Use a variety of vocabulary in shared language activities. LANGUAGE
- Identify and change the tense of a verb in a sentence. LANGUAGE

Teach

Display and discuss the **Vocabulary in Context Cards,** using the routine below.

1 Read and pronounce the word. Read the word once alone and then together.

2 Explain the word. Read aloud the explanation under *What Does It Mean?*

ENGLISH LANGUAGE SUPPORT Review these cognates with Spanish-speaking students.

- aceptó (accepted)
- expresar (express)
- premio (prize)

3 Discuss vocabulary in context. Together, read aloud the sentence on the front of the card. Help children explain and use the word in new sentences.

4 Engage with the word. Ask and discuss the *Think About It* question with children.

Practice/Apply

Give partners or small groups one or two **Vocabulary in Context Cards.** Help children complete the *Talk It Over* activities for each card. **ELA** RF.2.3f **ELD** ELD.PII.2.3a

Read aloud and have children complete the activity at the top of **Student Book** p. 86.

Then guide children to complete the Language Detective activity. Work with them to identify the verb and its tense in each sentence. Have children share their new sentences. **ELA** RF.2.3f, SL.2.6, L.2.6 **ELD** ELD.PI.2.1, ELD.PI.2.12b, ELD.PII.2.3b

Lesson 18

🔍 LANGUAGE DETECTIVE

Talk About Words A verb's tense tells if something happened in the past, is happening now, or will happen in the future. Work with a partner. Find the Vocabulary words that are verbs. Then say the sentence again with the verb in a different tense.

86

ELA L.2.1f, L.2.6
ELD ELD.PI.2.12b, ELD.PII.2.3a, ELD.PII.2.3b

Vocabulary in Context

▶ **Read each** Context Card.

▶ **Talk about a picture. Use a different Vocabulary word from the one in the card.**

1 **accepted**
The student gave the teacher an apple. She accepted it.

2 **express**
You can express your ideas by writing a story.

ENGLISH LANGUAGE SUPPORT

Comprehensible Input

Emerging Use gestures to demonstrate the meanings of *accepted* and *fluttering.* Have children repeat the gestures and say the words with you. **ELD** ELD.PI.2.12b

Expanding Ask children questions to confirm their understanding. Example: *What prize do you want to win?* **ELD** ELD.PI.2.12b

Bridging Have partners write questions and answers using Vocabulary words. Example: *Why might my heart be fluttering?* **ELD** ELD.PI.2.12b

3 taught

This teacher taught his class a new word.

4 grand

A grand award is a top prize in a contest.

5 pretend

This girl is not a real doctor. She is a pretend doctor.

6 prize

The best speller received first prize in the spelling bee.

7 wonder

The children wonder when the caterpillar will become a butterfly.

8 fluttering

The butterfly is fluttering its wings as it flies. The wings move quickly.

87

DAY 1

FORMATIVE ASSESSMENT RtI

Are children able to understand and use Target Vocabulary words?

IF...	THEN...
children struggle,	▶ use **Vocabulary in Context Cards** and differentiate **Vocabulary Reader**, *All About Chile*, for Struggling Readers, p. T286. *See also Intervention Lesson 18, pp. S22–S31.*
children are on track,	▶ use **Vocabulary in Context Cards** and differentiate **Vocabulary Reader**, *All About Chile*, for On-Level Readers, p. T286.
children excel,	▶ differentiate **Vocabulary Reader**, *All About Chile*, for Advanced Readers, p. T287.

SMALL GROUP Options

Vocabulary Reader, pp. T286–T287
Scaffold instruction to the English learner's proficiency level.

ENGLISH LANGUAGE SUPPORT

More Vocabulary Practice

Emerging/Expanding Distribute Dialogue, EL18.5 📄. Read the title aloud and have children repeat. Have children look at the title, images, and other information on the page. Then have them predict what they think the dialogue will be about.

- As you read the dialogue aloud, display the Context Cards for *express*, *taught*, *fluttering*, and *accepted*. After you read the dialogue, have partners read the dialogue together.

- Have children draw a picture of something they would love to write about.

- Have partners use their imaginations to tell each other stories about their pictures.

- Allow children to include language from the dialogue. Encourage them to use high-utility words. **ELD** ELD.PI.2.1, ELD.PI.2.12b

Read and Comprehend

Read and Comprehend

▶ SHARE OBJECTIVES

- Figure out a character's feelings and traits based on their actions, speech, and relationships.
- Use knowledge of characters to analyze and evaluate texts.
- Access prior knowledge to exchange information about a topic. LANGUAGE

☑ TARGET SKILL

Understanding Characters

- Read the top section of **Student Book** p. 88 with children.

- Remind children that authors write about what characters do and say and how characters solve problems. Paying attention to what the characters say, feel, and do helps readers understand characters' *traits*, or qualities.

- Explain that in a biography, the author wants the readers to learn about an important person. The author includes details to help the reader understand what that person is like and why he or she is important.

- Draw children's attention to the graphic organizer on **Student Book** p. 88. Tell them that, as they read, they can use this three-column chart to record characters' traits, thoughts, words, and actions. Guide them to complete the chart using Dr. Salk as the character.

- Explain that taking note of a character's traits will help them gain a deeper understanding of what they're reading and help them identify the main purpose of the selection. **ELA** RI.2.6 **ELD** ELD.PI.2.6

ENGLISH LANGUAGE SUPPORT Draw a three-column chart on the board with the headings *character; words, thoughts, actions;* and *traits.* Using a movie or television show that all of the children are familiar with, fill in the chart using one of the characters. **ELD** ELD.PI.2.1, ELD.PI.2.3, ELD.PI.2.11

☑ TARGET SKILL

Understanding Characters *My Name Is Gabriela* is a true story that tells about the poet Gabriela Mistral. Pay attention to what Gabriela says and does. Use these clues and other text evidence to understand Gabriela and why the author wrote about her. You can write details in a chart like this.

Character	Words, Thoughts, Actions	Trait

☑ TARGET STRATEGY

Analyze/Evaluate To **analyze** as you read, think about the author's words and story events. Then **evaluate**, or decide, how the words and events help you understand what is important in the text.

88 **ELA** RI.2.6, SL.2.1a **ELD** ELD.PI.2.1, ELD.PI.2.3

ENGLISH LANGUAGE SUPPORT

Sentence Frames

Emerging Guide children to complete these sentence frames: *My name is _____. I am _____. (friendly/nice) I am _____. (smart/funny)* Have them repeat the responses in complete sentences. **ELD** ELD.PI.2.1

Expanding Have children complete these sentence frames with words that describe their traits: *I am _____ and _____.* Sample answers: *smart, funny* **ELD** ELD.PI.2.1

Bridging Have children recall a character they have read about. The character can be a person or an animal. Ask them to discuss the character's traits using the sentence frame *The character was _____ and _____.* **ELD** ELD.PI.2.1

People have been reading and writing for thousands of years. Writing is a way to record information. We can still read things that were written long ago. Some of your favorite books might be very old. Some day in the future, people may read what you write today!

In *My Name Is Gabriela*, you will read about Gabriela Mistral. She was a poet who knew that reading and writing are important.

Think | Write | Pair | Share

How do you feel about reading and writing poetry? Make a list of words that describe your feelings. Share your list with a partner. Take turns speaking. Do you have any words that are the same? Share your list with the class.

89

COMPREHENSION STRATEGIES

Use the following strategies flexibly as you read with children by modeling how they can be used to improve comprehension and understanding of a text. See scaffolded support for the strategy shown in boldface during this week's reading.

- **Monitor/Clarify**
- **Visualize**
- **Summarize**
- **Analyze/Evaluate**
- **Infer/Predict**
- **Question**

Use Strategy Projectables ⬚, S1–S8, for additional support.

DOMAIN:
Communication

LESSON TOPIC: Reading and Writing

✔ TARGET STRATEGY

Analyze/Evaluate

- Read the bottom of **Student Book** p. 88 with children. Tell them that they can think about, or evaluate, the story's events to decide how they feel about what they are reading.

- Tell children to use their three-column chart to help them analyze, or study details of the story.

- Then explain that you will help them use this strategy as you read *My Name Is Gabriela*.

PREVIEW THE TOPIC

Reading and Writing

- Tell children that today they will begin to read *My Name Is Gabriela*. Read the information at the top of **Student Book** p. 89 with children.

- Explain that people have used reading and writing to communicate for thousands of years. Before written language, people communicated by drawing and painting. Evidence of this has been found in caves, structures, and ruins.

- Discuss with children the many ways that people communicate today using reading and writing.

Think-Write-Pair-Share

- Read the collaborative discussion prompt with children.

- Before children share their lists, explain that they can help each other in a discussion by asking open questions. Point out that open questions cannot be answered with *yes* or *no*. Give children several examples of open vs. closed questions. **Open:** What do you think about this story? **Closed:** Did you like this story? Then have children practice writing their own open questions.

- Remind children to follow other discussion rules, such as taking turns speaking, as they share their ideas. **ELA** SL.2.1a, SL.2.3 **ELD** ELD.PI.2.1, ELD.PI.2.3

ENGLISH LANGUAGE SUPPORT Use the image on Lesson 18 **Language Support Card** to review the lesson topic with children. Guide them to share and summarize what they have learned.
ELD ELD.PI.2.1, ELD.PI.2.12a

DAY 1

Read the Anchor Text

☑ **GENRE**

Biography

- Read the genre information on **Student Book** p. 90 with children.

- Preview the selection with children, and model identifying the characteristics of a biography.

Think Aloud *Biographies tell true stories about the lives of real people. My Name Is Gabriela is about a girl who lived in Chile and grew up to win the Nobel Prize. These things could really happen, so I think this selection may be a biography.*

- As you preview, ask children to identify other features of a biography. **ELA** RI.2.10 **ELD** ELD.PI.2.6

ENGLISH LANGUAGE SUPPORT Guide children at the emerging and expanding levels to complete the Academic English activities on Lesson 18 **Language Support Card.** **ELD** ELD.PII.2.3b

Lesson 18

ANCHOR TEXT

☑ **GENRE**

A **biography** tells about events in a person's life. As you read, look for:

▶ information about why a person is important

▶ events in time order

MEET THE AUTHOR

Monica Brown

Monica Brown's daughters think it's pretty cool to have a mom who's an author. At book signings, "They'll walk up and announce that it was their Mommy who wrote this book," Ms. Brown says. The family lives in Arizona, not far from the Grand Canyon.

MEET THE ILLUSTRATOR

John Parra

John Parra grew up in California in a home filled with Mexican art, food, and traditions. Today, Mr. Parra's colorful artwork can be seen in galleries, on posters and CD covers, and in the pages of children's books.

90   **ELA** RI.2.6, RI.2.10 **ELD** ELD.PI.2.6

Scaffold Close Reading

Strategies for Annotation

🖉 📋 **Annotate it!**

As you read the selection with children, look for this icon 🖉 📋 *Annotate it!* for opportunities to annotate the text collaboratively as a class.

Think Through the Text

FIRST READ

Develop comprehension through
- Guided Questioning
- Target Strategy: Analyze-Evaluate
- Vocabulary in Context

Analyze the Text

SECOND READ

Support analyzing short sections of text:
- Understanding Characters
- Author's Word Choice

Use directed note-taking by working with children to complete a graphic organizer during reading. Distribute copies of Graphic Organizer 2 📄: Column Chart.

Independent Reading

- Children analyze the text independently, using the Reader's Guide on Reader's Notebook Volume 2 pp. 38–39 📄. (See pp. T254–T255 for instructional support.)
- Children read independently in a self-selected trade book.

My Name is Gabriela

by Monica Brown   illustrated by John Parra

ESSENTIAL QUESTION

Why are reading and
writing important?

91

ESSENTIAL QUESTION

- Read aloud the Essential Question on **Student Book** p. 91: *Why are reading and writing important?* Then tell children to think about this question as they read *My Name Is Gabriela*.

Predictive Writing

- Tell children to write the Essential Question.

- Explain that they will write about what they expect *My Name Is Gabriela* to be about. Ask them to think about how the Essential Question relates to what they noticed while previewing the selection or what they already know about the Essential Question from their own experiences or past readings.

- Guide children to think about the genre of the selection as they write.

Set Purpose

- Explain that good readers set a purpose for reading, based on their preview of the selection and what they know about the genre.

- Model setting a reading purpose.

> **Think Aloud** *I know Gabriela Mistral was a great writer, but I want to know why she started writing. I will read the selection to find out.*

- Have children set their own purpose for reading. Ask several children to share their purpose for reading. **ELA** RF.2.4a, RI.2.10

READER AND TASK CONSIDERATIONS

ELA RI.2.1, SL.2.4, SL.2.6
ELD ELD.PI.2.1, ELD.PI.2.6, ELD.PI.2.12a

Determine the level of additional support your children will need to read to comprehend *My Name Is Gabriela* successfully.

READERS

- **Motivate** Ask children to tell what they feel makes a good teacher.

- **Access Knowledge and Experience** Review with children the word web you completed as part of the Talk It Over activity on the back of Lesson 18 **Language Support Card**. Ask children to share with a partner experiences they've had with one or more of the items on the web. Encourage them to use complete sentences as they share.

TASKS

- **Increase Scaffolding** Stop periodically to discuss unfamiliar places and determine correct pronunciation.

- **Foster Independence** Have children ask questions about the text every few pages, and flag the pages with self-stick notes. Then have children share their questions with classmates and discuss possible answers.

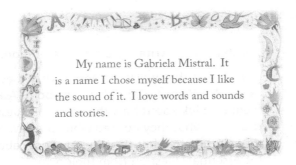

My name is Gabriela Mistral. It is a name I chose myself because I like the sound of it. I love words and sounds and stories.

92

93

Use Visuals

Emerging Show children the **Online Picture Card** for *book*. Have children complete: *I carry books in a _____. I put books in a _____.* **ELD** ELD.PI.2.6

Expanding Use the illustrations on p. 93 to practice directional words. Ask, *Where is the apple? Where is the rooster? Where is the butterfly?* **ELD** ELD.PI.2.6

Bridging Have children use the illustrations on pp. 94–95 to predict what might happen next. **ELD** ELD.PI.2.6

Cite Text Evidence

Think Through the Text

1 *Look at the picture of Gabriela Mistral on page 93. What do you think the things around Gabriela stand for? How might they help you learn about Gabriela?* Sample answer: *I think the books and the pen stand for reading and writing, because the text says Gabriela loves words. The palm trees might stand for where she is from, and the globe might stand for travel.*
ELA RI.2.7
ENGLISH LANGUAGE SUPPORT Point to the butterfly, the rooster, the monkey, and the palm trees and name them for children. Have children repeat the nouns and use them to answer the question. **ELD** ELD.PI.2.6

✅ **PHONICS/DECODING STRATEGY**

Use Projectable S1 ⬚ to help children apply the Phonics/Decoding strategy while reading **Student Book** pp. 92–93. Write *stories*. Explain that the word *stories* is the plural form of the word *story*. When we add the ending *-es*, the *y* in *story* changes to an *i*. As they read, have children identify words in which *y* was changed to *i*.

When I was a little girl, I lived with my mother and Emelina, my sister, in a small house in the beautiful Elqui Valley in Chile. From my bedroom window I could see the Andes Mountains.

When I couldn't sleep I would look up at the mountains and wonder what could be beyond them. Zebras with polka dots? Rainbow-colored flowers? Angels reading books?

2

94

95

2 *What do you know about Gabriela by the end of page 95? How would you describe her?* **Sample answers:** *She is creative, independent, female, a sister, a daughter, from Chile, curious. She likes words, sounds, stories.* **ELA** RI.2.1 **ELD** ELD.PI.2.6

ENGLISH LANGUAGE SUPPORT Tell children that the word *flower* has a cognate in Spanish: *flor*. Remind children to look for cognates as they read to help them figure out the meanings of key words.

☑ **TARGET STRATEGY | Analyze/Evaluate**

Use the Analyze/Evaluate strategy to help children examine what they are reading and figure out the author's purpose for writing these paragraphs. Model the strategy:

Think Aloud *The author says that Gabriela thinks of zebras with polka dots, rainbow-colored flowers, and angels reading books. With these words, I think the author does a good job of telling us that Gabriela has a good imagination.* **ELD** ELD.PI.2.6

I loved words—I liked the sounds they made rolling

off my tongue and I liked the

way they could express how I felt.

When I saw a butterfly fluttering, I noticed the way

the words fluttering butterfly sounded together—like a poem.

96

I taught myself to read so that I could read other people's words and stories. I read stories about princes and princesses, about monsters, and about birds and flowers.

ANALYZE THE TEXT

Author's Word Choice
What words does the author use to tell how Gabriela feels about words?

97

ENGLISH LANGUAGE SUPPORT

Comprehensible Input

Emerging Use the **Online Picture Card** for *bird* to ask yes/no questions about birds such as, *Do birds have wings, feathers, and feet?*

Expanding Pantomime a butterfly fluttering. Ask, *What kinds of things flutter?*

Bridging Ask students to give examples of poetry on p. 96. *butterfly fluttering* Ask them why the words sound like a poem.

FIRST READ

Cite Text Evidence

Think Through the Text

3 *What words does the author use to tell about Gabriela's feelings?* loved, liked *Why do you think Gabriela felt this way?* She loved words and liked the way they made sounds, expressed feelings, and could sound like a poem. *What words does the author use to describe how it feels to speak words?* rolling *What words does the author use to describe how a butterfly moves?* fluttering

ENGLISH LANGUAGE SUPPORT Explain to children that the author uses the phrase *rolling off my tongue* to help readers understand why Gabriela loves words. It means that Gabriela loves the way the words feel when she says them. **ELD** ELD.PI.2.6, ELD.PI.2.7

> I also liked to write poems, sing songs, and tell stories using the words that I knew. I told stories about happy times and sad times, about mothers and babies and little children. **4** **5**

98

99

4 *What kinds of stories does Gabriela tell? She tells stories about happy times, sad times, mothers, babies, and little children.*
ELA RI.2.2 **ELD** ELD.PI.2.6

5 *What details on page 98 support the main idea that Gabriela loves words? Writing poems, singing songs, and telling stories all use words.* **ELA** RI.2.1

ENGLISH LANGUAGE SUPPORT Provide this sentence frame to encourage participation. *Gabriela liked to use the words she knew to write poems, _____, and _____. songs; stories*
ELD ELD.PI.2.6

SECOND READ **DAY 2** *Analyze the Text*

Author's Word Choice

Remind children that authors use sensory words to describe what things are like. These sensory words describe how something looks, smells, tastes, sounds, or feels. The author chooses these words carefully so the reader understands more about what the author is trying to explain. Read the Analyze the Text box with children and have them answer the question. *loved, liked.* Then have children tell what they think the author's purpose is for using those words to describe Gabriela's feelings.
ELA RI.2.6 **ELD** ELD.PI.2.6

🖊🗂 *Annotate it!* Work with children to highlight sensory words in the selection.

I liked to play school with the children of my village. I pretended to be the teacher, and my friends, Sofía, Ana, and Pedro, were my pupils.

Pedro would always say that I was mean because I made him write his ABCs until he knew all the letters of the alphabet. But I told him that the alphabet is important. How else would he create words and tell his stories without it?

100

In our pretend class we sang songs like:
     The baby chicks are saying,
     Peep, peep, peep.
     It means they're cold and hungry.
     It means they need some sleep.
That was Sofía's favorite song. During recess we had fun, running and chasing and laughing and playing. **6** **7**

101

FORMATIVE ASSESSMENT 3 2 1 RtI

Analyze/Evaluate IF children have difficulty applying the Analyze/Evaluate strategy, **THEN** use this model:

> **Think Aloud** *The picture on page 100 shows Gabriela teaching children, but when I read the text, I know that she is pretending to be a teacher. I look for phrases like "When I was a little girl" or "When I grew up" to help me figure out the story of Gabriela's life.*

Cite Text Evidence

FIRST READ

Think Through the Text

6 *How do the illustrations on pages 100–101 seem like what happens in real school?* **The children have books and pencils and are listening to the teacher. They also play games, sing songs, and have recess.** **ELA** RI.2.7 **ELD** ELD.PI.2.6

7 *Why does Pedro think Gabriela is mean?* **She makes him learn to write his ABCs.** *Why does Gabriela think the alphabet is important?* **because you need to know the alphabet to create words and tell stories.** **ELA** RI.2.1

ENGLISH LANGUAGE SUPPORT Provide sentence frames to support participation. *Pedro said Gabriela was mean because she made him _____.* learn the alphabet *Gabriela says the alphabet is _____.* important *You need to know the alphabet to create _____ and tell _____.* words; stories **ELD** ELD.PI.2.6

When I grew up I became a real teacher and writer. I taught the children of Chile, and many of my students became teachers themselves.

I still wrote poems—happy poems, sad poems, stories of mothers and children. But I also wrote poems about animals—about parrots and peacocks and even rats!

8

ANALYZE THE TEXT

Understanding Characters What does the author want you to know about how Gabriela feels about teaching and learning? How do you know?

102   103

---

8 *Does it surprise you that Gabriela grows up to become a teacher? Use evidence from the text to explain your answer.* Sample answer: *No, she liked to pretend to be a teacher when she was a child, so it is not surprising that she became a teacher as a grown-up.* **ELA** RI.2.7

ENGLISH LANGUAGE SUPPORT Provide sentence frames to encourage participation. *I am/am not surprised Gabriela became a teacher because* _____. **ELD** ELD.PI.2.3, ELD.PI.2.6, ELD.PI.2.11

☑ **TARGET STRATEGY|** Analyze/Evaluate

Tell children to practice the Analyze/Evaluate strategy as they read **Student Book** pp. 102–103. Have children recall how Gabriela learned to read and what she liked to do as a child. *She taught herself to read. She liked to pretend to be a teacher.* Ask children how well the selection helped them understand what happened to Gabriela as she grew up. Then have them tell how they used the strategy to follow the story of Gabriela's life. **ELD** ELD.PI.2.6

SECOND READ   **DAY 2**   *Analyze the Text*

Understanding Characters

Read the Analyze the Text box on **Student Book** p. 103 with children. Then display Projectable 18.4 🔗 and distribute Graphic Organizer 2 🔗. Tell children that you will work together to complete the graphic organizer.

Remind children that in a biography, the author wants to describe an important person and to give details about how that person thinks, feels, and acts. Prompt them to add events from the selection, how Gabriela feels or reacts to those events, and what that tells them about on the graphic organizer. Then have them use the graphic organizer to answer the question on p. 103. **ELA** RI.2.6 **ELD** ELD.PI.2.6

✏ 🖺 *Annotate it!* Work with children to highlight words in the text that tell the reader what is important to Gabriela.

I also traveled to far away places. I never saw
zebras with polka dots or rainbow-colored flowers,
but I met wonderful children and their teachers.
I traveled to Europe—to France and Italy. **9**

104

I traveled to Mexico.

105

ENGLISH LANGUAGE SUPPORT

Review Key Ideas

Emerging *Where does Gabriela travel? Who does
Gabriela meet?* **ELD** ELD.PI.2.6

Expanding Have children use words and phrases to
describe the skyscrapers and buildings in the illustrations on pp. 104–106. **ELD** ELD.PI.2.6

Bridging Have partners use the illustrations on
pp. 104–106 to compare and contrast the places that
Gabriela visited. **ELD** ELD.PI.2.6

FIRST READ

Think Through the Text

9 *Besides teaching and writing, what did Gabriela do when she grew up?
She traveled to faraway places and met many people. Why do you think
Gabriela met children and their teachers when she traveled? She was a
teacher and she wanted to learn about teachers and children in other
countries.* **ELA** RI.2.1 **ELD** ELD.PI.2.6

STANDARD ENGLISH LEARNERS Children may double the inflected -*ed*
ending of past tense regular verbs or add -*ed* to irregular forms that are
already in the past tense. Explain to children that they add -*ed* to most
verbs to show that the action took place in the past. Model with sentences
such as: *I traveled to Europe. We kicked the ball*. Then explain that some
verbs have special past tense forms and do not need -*ed* at the end. Give
examples such as *meet/met; write/wrote; teach/taught*. Ask children to say
a sentence that tells about something they did in the past. Correct their
verb usage if necessary.

I traveled to the United States.

Everywhere I went, I wrote and taught and met teachers. I saw how all over the world, people wanted their children to learn.

106

My stories traveled the world with me. People liked to read my happy stories, my sad stories, my stories of women and children, my stories of parrots and peacocks, of old lions and of the fisherfolk, who slept in the sand and dreamt of the sea. **10** **11**

107

10 *How does the illustration on page 107 relate to what is going on in Gabriela's biography?* The illustration shows many of the things she wrote about in her stories. **ELA** RI.2.7 **ELD** ELD.PI.2.6

11 *Why do you think the author wrote this biography?* Sample answer: *To teach about an important poet and teacher, and to get children interested in reading and in writing stories and poems* **ELA** RI.2.6

ENGLISH LANGUAGE SUPPORT Provide sentence frames to encourage participation. *I think the author wrote this biography to _____.* **ELD** ELD.PI.2.3, ELD.PI.2.6

ENGLISH LANGUAGE SUPPORT

How English Works: Interpretive

Verb Types Remind children that authors use different kinds of verbs to describe what someone or something does. Tell children that *doing* verbs show action. Read page 106 aloud, emphasizing the words *traveled, wrote, taught,* and *met*. Explain what each verb describes as you write it on the board. Guide children to practice writing sentences that contain *doing* verbs. **ELD** ELD.PII.2.3a

And because people from all over the world loved my stories so, I was given a very special prize—the Nobel Prize for Literature.

When I accepted the grand award, I thought of the beautiful mountains outside of my window in Chile, of my mother and sister, of the children of my village, and of all the stories that still need to be told.

12

108

109

2-9_RFLESE869911_U4AT18.indd 108   5/25/12

◇ **DOMAIN: Communication**

LESSON TOPIC: Reading and Writing

Cross-Curricular Connection Tell children that the Nobel Prize is an award given every year to people who do something very special. Explain that Gabriela Mistral was the first Hispanic woman to win a Nobel Prize for Literature, or writing. Ask children why they think Gabriela's contributions to literature are important. Sample answers: *She wrote poetry and stories about many things. She taught children from all cultures that it is important to learn how to read and write.*

FIRST READ

Cite Text Evidence

Think Through the Text

12 *What do you think the author means by "all of the stories that still need to be told?"* Sample answer: *There are many more stories that need to be written about different things from all over the world.* **ELA** RI.2.1 **ELD** ELD.PI.2.6

💬 Collaborative Conversation

Remind children they have been reading a biography of Gabriela Mistral. Working in groups, have children discuss how Gabriela shared the things she loved most with others. Tell them to refer to the text and the illustrations to support their discussion. Remind children to listen carefully, take turns while speaking, and build on the comments of others. Call on groups to share their responses with the class.

ELA RI.2.1, SL.2.1a, SL.2.1b **ELD** ELD.PI.2.1, ELD.PI.2.6, ELD.PI.2.12a

Guided Summary

Oral Language

Use the retelling prompts on the **Retelling Cards** to guide children to summarize the selection.

ELA RI.2.2 **ELD** ELD.PI.2.6, ELD.PI.2.12a

front

front

Talk About It

Who is the woman in the picture?

What are some things she likes?

What are some objects that you see around the woman? What do you think they mean?

back

Talk About It

What does Gabriela become when she grows up?

Where does Gabriela go?

How does Gabriela share her love for words with others?

back

front

Talk About It

What does Gabriela teach the other children in the village?

Do you think Gabriela was a good teacher? Why?

back

Talk About It

What award does Gabriela receive?

What do the objects in the picture tell about Gabriela's life?

back

front

SUMMARIZING RUBRIC

4	**Highly Effective**	The summary gives the events of Gabriela's life in the correct sequence. Many details are included, including Gabriela's love of words and writing, sharing stories, and acceptance of the Nobel Prize.
3	**Generally Effective**	The summary states some details about Gabriela as a girl and then as an adult. Gabriela's love of words and sharing stories are included.
2	**Somewhat Effective**	The summary gives a few general statements in no clear sequence.
1	**Ineffective**	The reader is unable to provide an accurate summary of *My Name Is Gabriela*.

ENGLISH LANGUAGE SUPPORT

Review Key Ideas

All Proficiencies Pronounce and explain *summarize*, reminding children that when they summarize they are telling the main idea and one or two details. Page through *My Name is Gabriela* with children and share the following sentence frames to help them summarize the selection.

When Gabriela was a little girl, she lived in _____. Chile She loved the sound of _____. words Gabriela liked to write poems and tell _____. stories She grew up to become a _____ and a _____. teacher; writer

ELD ELD.PI.2.6, ELD.PI.2.12a

Grammar The Verb *Be*

▶ **SHARE OBJECTIVES**

- **Grammar** Use forms of the verb *be*. LANGUAGE
- **Spelling** Spell words with the long *e* sound spelled *y*.
- **Writing** Identify the characteristics of a good descriptive paragraph. LANGUAGE

ENGLISH LANGUAGE SUPPORT

Linguistic Transfer

Emerging Write sentence frames using *be* in the present. For example: *Sam and Jose are boys. I am here.* Ask children to complete them.

Expanding Have children create simple sentence frames with the verb *be* for their partners to complete.

Bridging Have children write a short paragraph using all forms of *be* in the present (*am, is, are*).

All Proficiencies Have children write a short paragraph using all forms of *be* in the present (*am, is, are*).

Linguistic Transfer Some children may have language transfer difficulty with the long *e* sound spelled *y*; that *y* can also make the long *i* sound may add to confusion. Provide ample opportunities for children to read aloud words in which *y* stands for long *i* and in which *y* stands for long *e* to contrast the sounds. **ELD** ELD.PIII.2

1 Teach/Model

Using *am, is,* and *are* Display Projectable 18.2 ⬚. Explain that *am, is,* and *are* are all forms of the verb *be*. Add that *am, is,* and *are* tell about something that is happening in the present. Model identifying the correct form of *be* in this example sentence: *The snow is falling.*

Think Aloud *To identify the correct form of be to use, I ask this Thinking Question: Does the subject tell about one or more than one, or is the subject I? The subject tells about one thing, the snow. The verb is should be used.*

- Review the other examples in the box on **Projectable 18.2**.

FOR STANDARD ENGLISH LEARNERS Some children may need help mastering grammar rules of Standard English when speaking or writing. Children, especially those who use Mexican American Language and Chicano English, may drop the linking verb from present-tense sentences. Remind children to say each verb clearly. Say the following sentences and have children repeat the verbs: *The boys are here; She is happy; We are in school.* Use additional sentences as necessary.

2 Guided Practice/Apply

- Read the three sentences in item 1 with children. Guide them to use the Thinking Question to identify and underline the sentence that has the form of the verb *be* that agrees with the sentence's subject. Work with children to choose the correct subject/verb agreement in the remaining sentences on the projectable.

- Distribute Reader's Notebook Volume 2 page 32 ⬚ to children to complete independently. **ELD** ELD.PII.2.3b

Spelling Long *e* Spelled *y*

SPELLING WORDS AND SENTENCES

BASIC

1. *happy** I smile when I am *happy*.
2. *pretty* That blue dress is *pretty*.
3. *baby** Our *baby* brother is cute.
4. *very* It is *very* cold outside.
5. *puppy* Our *puppy* is a poodle.
6. *funny* My aunt told a *funny* joke.
7. *carry* The bag was too heavy to *carry*.
8. *lucky* We were *lucky* the storm missed our town.
9. *only* This is my *only* pair of shoes.

10. *sunny* It will be *sunny* all day.
11. *penny* A *penny* is only one cent.
12. *city* We moved to a big *city*.

REVIEW

13. *tiny* My sock has a *tiny* hole.
14. *many* There are *many* children.

CHALLENGE

15. *sorry* I am *sorry* we missed the bus.
16. *noisy* The crowd at the game was *noisy*.

**A form of this word appears in the literature.*

Administer the Pretest

Say each Spelling Word. Then say it in a sentence and repeat the word. Have children write the word. **ELA** L.2.2d

Teach the Principle

- Review **Sound/Spelling Card** *eagle*. Point to the *e* as you say *eagle*. Write *pretty*, underlining the *y*. Then read the word aloud. Explain that the /ē/ sound can also be spelled with *y*.

Model a Word Sort

Model sorting words based on the single or double consonants before the long *e* sound spelled *y*. Present the Model the Sort lesson on page 90 of the **Literacy and Language Guide**.

Narrative Writing Introduce the Model

1 Teach/Model

Descriptive Paragraph Tell children that this week they will be writing a descriptive paragraph. Ask children to describe an object that you hold up for the class to see. Then display and read aloud Projectable 18.3 .

- Use the labels for paragraph 1 on the projectable to identify the lead sentence and sense words.

- Read and discuss these features.

Writer's Checklist

What Makes a Great Descriptive Paragraph?

- A **lead sentence** clearly tells what you are describing.

- Details show your readers what it was like to be there.

- **Sense words** tell what you saw, heard, felt, tasted, or smelled.

- Some words compare what you are describing to something else.

2 Guided Practice/Apply

- With children, label the lead sentence and sense words in paragraph 2 on the projectable.

Model Study Read aloud the second paragraph. Have children work with a partner to find another sense word that could replace *cozy*. Possible response: *"The kitchen felt warm . . . "* **ELA** W.2.3, W.2.4, W.2.10 **ELD** ELD.PI.2.10, ELD.PII.2.1, ELD.PII.2.4

Daily Proofreading Practice

night
At nigh she looks at the mountains⊙
She wonder what lies beyond theem.

Performance Task

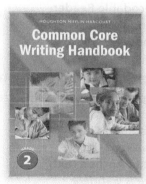

Children may prewrite, draft, revise, and publish their narrative writing task through *my*WriteSmart beginning on Day 3.

Common Core Writing Handbook

Additional support for Narrative Writing appears in the **Common Core Writing Handbook,** Lesson18.

DAY 2

Today's Goals

Vocabulary & Oral Language
☑ **TARGET VOCABULARY**

accepted	pretend
express	prize
taught	wonder
grand	fluttering

Phonemic Awareness
- Identify Sound Placement

Phonics & Fluency
- Long *e* Sound for *y*
- **Fluency:** Expression
- **Read Decodable Reader:**
  Bunny and the Penny
- High-Frequency Words

Text-Based Comprehension
- **Dig Deeper:** Use Clues to Analyze the Text
- **Understanding Characters**
- **Author's Word Choice**
- **Reread the Anchor Text:**
  My Name Is Gabriela

Grammar & Writing
- **The Verb** *be*
- **Narrative Writing:**
  Descriptive Paragraph
- **Trait:** Elaboration

Spelling
- Long *e* Spelled *y*

Opening Routines

Warm Up with Wordplay

Names with Long e

Tell children that you are forming a club for people whose names end with the long e sound. Have children respond with a thumbs up for *Yes*, thumbs down for *No* for members of the club. Say the following names: *Marlee, Jadin, José, Mariana, Akimi, Rick, Rory, Ty, Julia.*

Have children work with partners to come up with other members of the club. Display the names on the board.

Terry	Mary	Ellie
Freddy	Willie	Amy

Daily Phonemic Awareness

Identify Sound Placement

- *Listen for the sounds in this word: seed. Say it with me, /s/ /ē/ /d/, seed. What is the vowel sound? /ē/ Is the vowel sound at the beginning, middle, or end of the word? middle*

- Continue the activity with the word *snappy.* Have children identify the vowel sound /ē/ and its position.

- Ask children to identify the position of the /ē/ sound in the following words: *green, funny, carry, heat, city.*

Corrective Feedback

- If a child is unable to identify sound placement, say the word, give correction, and model the task by first segmenting the word into its sounds, then identifying the position of the target sounds.

- Have children repeat with you and then continue on their own.

Daily High-Frequency Words

- Point to **High-Frequency Word Card 172,** *mother.*

- *Say the word. mother Spell the word. m-o-t-h-e-r Write the word. Check the word.*

- Repeat with this week's new word *words,* and with review words *always, anything, been, draw, friends, soon, under,* and *watch.*
  ELA RF.2.3f

Lead a Cheer

- Choose a child to be the cheerleader. Have him or her call out each letter of a High-Frequency Word while the class responds.

- Give me an *M! M!* Give me an *O! O!* Give me a *T! T!* Give me an *H! H!* Give me an *E! E!* Give me an *R! R!* What does that spell? *MOTHER!*

- Repeat for the remaining words.

Corrective Feedback

- If a child does not recognize the word *mother,* say the correct word and have children repeat it. *Mother. What is the word? mother*

- Have children spell the word. *m-o-t-h-e-r How do we say this word? mother*

- Have children reread all of the cards in random order.

Daily Vocabulary Boost

- Use page T214 to review Target Vocabulary with children. Remind them that they heard these words in "Doctor Salk's Treasure." Recall the article as you guide children to interact with each word.

- *Luckily, we don't have to worry about polio today. "Why not?" you wonder. What kinds of things do you wonder about?*

- *Jonas Salk taught other doctors. Have you ever taught someone?*

- *Dr. Salk's heart was fluttering with nervousness as he waited for the test results. Name something you might feel or see fluttering.*

- Continue with children in the same manner, using *accepted, express, grand, pretend,* and *prize.* **ELA** L.2.6

**Vocabulary in Context
Cards 137–144**

☑ **Target Vocabulary**

accepted

express

taught

grand

pretend

prize

wonder

fluttering

Phonics

▶ **SHARE OBJECTIVES**

- Identify the position of the long e sound in words.
- Blend, build, and decode regularly spelled words with the long e sound for y.
- Reread text with words with the long e sound for y and High-Frequency Words for fluency practice.

▶ **SKILLS TRACE**

Words with the Long e Sound for y	
Introduce	**pp. T216–T217, T240–T241**
Differentiate	pp. T284–T285
Reteach	p. T298
Review	pp. T263, T352, T363
Assess	Weekly Tests, Lesson 18

ENGLISH LANGUAGE SUPPORT

Comprehensible Input

Emerging Help children match words to meanings in Blending Lines. Use objects, gestures, and facial expressions to accompany simple context sentences; for example: *This desk is messy; I'm too shy to talk; It's not nice to be pushy; This doll has a skinny waist.* Have children repeat the word.

Expanding Use the words in Blending Lines to point out that a final y in a two-syllable word may be a suffix added to a base word. Prompt children to identify the base word in each of the following words: *messy, pushy, funny, skinny, snowy, shady, sleepy, foggy, creamy, nosy, shiny.* Use both the base word and the adjective with the suffix -y in a brief sentence to show the connection in meaning.

Bridging Check children's understanding of words used in Blending Lines that may be unfamiliar by asking for the word in a phrase or short sentence that shows meaning.

Words with the Long e Sound for y

Phonemic Awareness Warm-Up *I'll say a word with the long e sound /ē/ and tell whether the sound /ē/ is at the beginning, middle, or end of the word. Listen: lucky. I hear /ē/ at the end of lucky. Now you try one. Listen: stream. Do you hear /ē/ at the beginning, middle, or end of stream? middle Let's try some more:* happy, *end;* leash, *middle;* eel, *beginning;* easel, *beginning;* queen, *middle*

Review **Sound/Spelling Cards** *eagle,* pointing out the y spelling for the long e sound /ē/.

Continuous Blending Routine Use Instructional Routine 3 ⬆ to model blending *happy,* one syllable at a time.

- Blend the sounds in each syllable and then blend the syllables. *Listen: /h/ /ă/ /p/, /ē/; hap-py; happy.* Have children blend with you in the same way.

h	a	p	p	y

e
e_e
ee
ea
_y
_ie_
_ey
(c)ei

2 Guided Practice

Blending Lines

Blend Words Repeat the blending routine with the first two words in Line 1 below; help children compare the words and sounds. Point to each word as children read the entire line chorally. Continue with the remaining lines. Then call on volunteers to reread selected words until children can identify the words quickly.

1. bay	by	baby	may	my	mommy
2. say	messy	shy	pushy	tiny	try
3. funny	fly	play	happy	skinny	sky

Transition to Longer Words Use a similar process for Lines 4–6.

4. snowy	shady	sleepy	puppy	silly	bunny
5. berry	body	daddy	pony	foggy	jelly
6. creamy	cherry	nosy	city	shiny	easy

Challenge Call on above-level children to read the words in Line 7. Then have the class read the sentences chorally.

7. empty angry copying unlucky blueberry carrying
8. Did my <u>words</u> make that tiny baby cry?
9. I <u>always</u> carry my lucky penny. **ELA** RF.2.3c, RF.2.3e

Build Words Model how to spell the word *fifty*.
I hear two syllables in fifty: fif-ty. I'll spell one syllable at a time. The sounds in the first syllable are fif. I hear /f/, so I write f; /i/ so I write i; /f/, so I write f. The sounds in the second syllable are /tē/. The first sound is /t/, so I write t. I know that a final long e sound /ē/ in a two-syllable word can be spelled with y, so I write y. I'll reread to check: fifty.

f i f t y

• Guide children to spell the words *lucky, why, pony,* and *windy*. Individuals can spell the words with **Letter Cards** while others check their work. **ELA** L.2.2d

3 **Apply**

Have partners take turns rereading Blending Lines 1–3 and 4–6. Ask each partner to choose ten words from Blending Lines and sort them into two lists. Then tell partners to exchange lists, read each list of words they receive, and identify the sorting criteria used. **ELA** RF.2.3c, L.2.2d

Distribute <u>Reader's Notebook Volume 2 page 33</u> or <u>leveled practice</u> in Grab-and-Go™ Resources for children to complete independently.

Practice Fluency

Use <u>Instructional Routine 15</u> to have partners read the **Decodable Reader** *Bunny and the Penny*. Remind children to read with expression.

Bunny and the Penny

On a chilly, breezy spring day, Bunny went hopping along. It was sunny and bright as she went up a long, winding path. She saw a penny on the path.

33

Decodable Reader

Corrective Feedback
When a child mispronounces a letter-sound, highlight that letter, restate its sound, have children repeat the sound, and then guide them to blend the word. See the example below.

Decoding Error:
A child reads *skinny* in Line 3 as *skin*.

Correct the error. Say the correct word. Identify the syllables. *The word is* skinny. *The first syllable is* skin. *The second syllable is* ny: skin-ny, skinny.

Model as you cover the word one syllable at a time. *The letters* s, k, i, n *spell the syllable* skin. *The letters* n, y *spell the second syllable. The sound for y in the second syllable is* /ē/. *The second syllable is* ny. *I'll blend the syllables to say the word:* skin-ny, skinny.

Guide *Let's blend the syllables together:* skin-ny. *What is the word?* skinny

Check *You read the two syllables.* skin-ny *What is the word?* skinny

Reinforce Go back three or four words and have children continue reading. Make note of errors and review those words during the next lesson.

SMALL GROUP Options

Go to pp. T284–T285 for additional phonics support.

SECOND READ

Dig Deeper: Use Clues to Analyze the Text

- Figure out a character's feelings and traits based on his or her actions, speech, and relationships.
- Identify words and phrases that supply story details. LANGUAGE

ENGLISH LANGUAGE SUPPORT

Linguistic Transfer

Emerging Have children identify the cognate for *biography* (*biografía*). Tell children that a biography is a written story of a person's life. Have children complete the sentence frame: *This biography is about _____.*

Expanding If appropriate, have children skim through the story and identify and name related words in Spanish and their English cognates.

Bridging Have partners look back through the text and review the highlighted vocabulary words. Have them write a sentence using each word. If appropriate, have them tell if any of these words have Spanish cognates. **ELD** ELD.PI.2.1, ELD.PI.2.2

Text-Based Comprehension

1   Teach/Model

Terms About Informational Text

characters the people and animals in a story

traits ways of speaking and acting that show what someone is like

Remind children that they have just read *My Name Is Gabriela,* a biography about a girl who becomes a poet. Read **Student Book** p. 110 with children.

- Tell children that in order to understand characters and character traits, they should study what characters say, think, and do.
- Point out that in a biography, the author wants to tell about an important person.
- Then discuss the three-column chart using this model.

Think Aloud
I can use this three-column chart to record details about Gabriela. As I read the biography, I pay attention to what Gabriela says, thinks, and does. I write the important details in the chart, such as what Gabriela said or thought, and what this tells me about her. At the end of the story, I can use the information in the chart to form opinions about Gabriela.

Next, read the top of **Student Book** p. 111 with children.

- Remind children that authors choose their words carefully. Authors often use words that describe something, or that tell how something looks, smells, sounds, tastes, or feels. Explain that sensory words help us to imagine things with our five senses, telling us exactly what something is like.

ENGLISH LANGUAGE SUPPORT Tell children that the word *describe* has a cognate in Spanish: *describir*.

- Have children look at **Student Book** p. 96. Ask, *What phrase helps you imagine how it feels to speak words?* **rolling off my tongue** *What word does the author use to help you imagine how a butterfly moves?* **fluttering**
- Ask children to imagine a dog. Then ask them to imagine the following dogs: a spotted dog, a soft dog, a howling dog, a wet and stinky dog. Have children tell how these sensory words changed their idea of a dog. Then have children suggest sensory words that could describe a butterfly.

Q BE A READING DETECTIVE

Dig Deeper

Use Clues to Analyze the Text

Use these pages to learn about Understanding Characters and Author's Word Choice. Then read *My Name Is Gabriela* again. Use what you learn to understand it better.

Understanding Characters

My Name Is Gabriela is a biography that tells about a poet named Gabriela. In a biography, the author gives details to help the reader understand what the person is like. You can use a chart like the one below to show details about Gabriela. The text evidence you write can help you figure out why she is important.

Character	Words, Thoughts, Actions	Trait

Author's Word Choice

An author chooses strong words to help tell about places, characters, and things. Words and phrases can help the reader picture what the author is telling about. For example, an author might use the words *tiny* and *colorful* to tell about a butterfly. As you read, look for words that tell how things look, feel, and sound.

110 ELA RI.2.6 ELD ELD.PI.2.6, ELD.PI.2.7

111

---

2 Guided Practice/Apply

Analyze the Text

Begin a second read of *My Name Is Gabriela* with children. Use the stopping points and instructional support to guide them to think more deeply about the text.

• Understanding Characters, p. T231 ELA RI.2.6 ELD ELD.PI.2.6

• Author's Word Choice, p. T229 ELA RI.2.6 ELD ELD.PI.2.6, ELD.PI.2.7

Directed Note Taking The graphic organizer will be completed with children during a second read on p. T231. ELA RI.2.6 ELD ELD.PI.2.6

FORMATIVE ASSESSMENT △ RtI

Are children able to identify the main purpose of a story?

IF...	THEN...
children struggle,	use **Differentiate Comprehension** for Struggling Readers, p. T288. See also Intervention Lesson 18, pp. S24–S25
children are on track,	use **Differentiate Comprehension** for On-Level Readers, p. T288.
children excel,	use **Differentiate Comprehension** for Advanced Readers, p. T289.

 Differentiate Comprehension, pp. T288–T289
Scaffold instruction to the English learner's proficiency level.

Your Turn

Cite Text Evidence

▶ **SHARE OBJECTIVES**

- Describe why reading and writing are important.
- Write a response to literature that gives information or explains.
- Use verbs for a set purpose when speaking. LANGUAGE

RETURN TO THE ESSENTIAL QUESTION

As partners discuss the Essential Question—*Why are reading and writing important?*—have them use text evidence to support their thinking. Ask children to draw from their own experiences and what they have read as they discuss key details from the text. Remind children that when having a discussion, they can gain more understanding about a topic if they ask and answer questions about something their discussion partner says.

ELA SL.2.1a, SL.2.1c, SL.2.3, SL.2.4 **ELD** ELD.PI.2.1, ELD.PI.2.6, ELD.PI.2.12a

Classroom Conversation Have children continue their discussion of *My Name Is Gabriela* by answering the questions. Remind them that a character's thoughts, words, and actions can tell a lot about what the character is like. Have children decide if the author's purpose for writing the selection fits with the genre of the selection, Biography. Have all children participate in the discussion and follow rules for discussion.

ELA RI.2.1, RI.2.6, SL.2.1a **ELD** ELD.PI.2.1, ELD.PI.2.6

ENGLISH LANGUAGE SUPPORT Use sentence frames such as the following to support discussion.

Gabriela was important because ____.

Gabriela got ideas for her stories from ____.

I think the author wrote about Gabriela to ____. I think this because ____.

As children share their ideas, have them use gestures and refer to the story for help completing the sentence frames. **ELD** ELD.PI.2.6, ELD.PI.2.12a

---

Your Turn

RETURN TO THE ESSENTIAL QUESTION

 Why are reading and writing important? Talk to a partner about your ideas. Look back at *My Name Is Gabriela* for text evidence to support what you say. Be sure to ask questions if you need more information about what your partner says.

Classroom Conversation

Now talk about these questions with the class.

1. What events in this biography explain how Gabriela became important?

2. How did Gabriela get ideas for her stories?

3. Why do you think the author wrote about Gabriela? Use text evidence to help you answer.

ELA RI.2.1, RI.2.6, W.2.2, W.2.4, W.2.10, SL.2.3 **ELD** ELD.PI.2.1, ELD.PI.2.6, ELD.PI.2.10

ENGLISH LANGUAGE SUPPORT

How English Works: Collaborative

Verb Types Before children begin discussing item 1, have them think about the verb types that they will use when sharing. Review some verb types and purposes with children, such as how doing verbs show action. Help children at different proficiency levels think about their topics and make short lists of verbs to use while sharing. **ELD** ELD.PII.2.3a

Performance Task

WRITE ABOUT READING

Response How would you describe Gabriela? Write a paragraph telling what she is like. Use text evidence from the words and pictures to help you.

Writing Tip

Make sure that each sentence has a verb with the correct ending to match its subject.

113

WRITE ABOUT READING — Performance Task

Tell children they will write a response to the story that describes what Gabriela is like.

- Help children begin by listing words that describe Gabriela, using the text and illustrations. Tell them to think about Gabriela as a child and then as an adult.

- Remind children that they can tell a lot about a character's traits by their words, actions, and feelings. Have children use the completed graphic organizer to guide their writing.

Writing Tip Make sure children read the Writing Tip before they begin writing. Remind children that every sentence must have a subject and a verb. A subject can be a proper noun like a name, or a pronoun like *she*, *he*, *they*, or *we*. Point out that verbs can be action verbs like *sing*, *play*, *dance*, *write*, *travel*, and *read*. **ELA** W.2.2, W.2.4, W.2.10, L.2.1f

See **Analytic Writing Rubric** on p. R17.

 Have children complete the Write About Reading activity through *my*WriteSmart. Children will read the prompt within *my*WriteSmart and have access to multiple writing resources, including the Student eBook, Writing Rubrics, and Graphic Organizers.

ENGLISH LANGUAGE SUPPORT

Comprehensible Input

All Proficiencies Before children begin writing, review the list of words that the class made to describe Gabriela. Have children act out these words, if possible, or provide an example of these describing words. Ask them to write down two or three of these describing words that they want to include in their paragraph. For children who need support, provide the sentence frame: *Gabriela was _____ because the selection says _____.* **ELD** ELD.PI.2.10, ELD.PI.2.12a

Grammar The Verb *Be*

▶ **SHARE OBJECTIVES**

- **Grammar** Use forms of the verb *be*. LANGUAGE
- **Spelling** Spell words with the long e sound spelled *y*.
- **Handwriting** Write Spelling Words.
- **Writing** Use sense words to describe. LANGUAGE

ENGLISH LANGUAGE SUPPORT

Comprehensible Input

All Proficiencies Identify an event that happened in the past. For example, say and write: *It was sunny yesterday.* Compare to an event in the present: *It is cloudy today.* Have children say other sentences in the past or present tense. Have the class identify whether they are in the past or present. **ELD** ELD.PII.2.3b

Preview Lesson Preview the lesson in children's first language if another teacher who speaks a language other than English is available. After the preview, ask volunteers to translate the main points of the lesson back into English.

1 Teach/Model

Using was and were Display Projectable 18.5. Explain that *was* and *were* are also forms of the verb *be*. Point out that *was* and *were* tell about something that happened in the past. Model identifying the correct form of *be* in this example sentence: *The party was fun.*

Think Aloud *To identify the correct form of be to use, I ask this Thinking Question: Does the subject tell about one or more than one, or is the subject I? The subject tells about one thing, the party. The verb was should be used.*

- Repeat with the next example.

FOR STANDARD ENGLISH LEARNERS Standard English learners may use *be* in place of past-tense forms of *to be*. Explain to children that the verb *be* is used as part of a verb phrase, and is not used on its own. Write the forms of *be* and review them with children. Model with sentences such as: *I was here. We were working. They were sleepy. She was singing.* Have children generate additional sentences with the correct form of *be*.

2 Guided Practice/Apply

- Guide children to write the sentences on **Projectable 18.5**. Have children use the Thinking Question to identify the correct form of the verb *be* to agree with each sentence's subject.

- Distribute Reader's Notebook Volume 2 page 35 to children to complete independently. **ELA** L.2.1d **ELD** ELD.PII.2.3b

Spelling Long e Spelled *y*

SPELLING WORDS

BASIC

happy*	sunny
pretty	penny
baby*	city
very	**REVIEW**
puppy	tiny
funny	many
carry	**CHALLENGE**
lucky	sorry
only	noisy

A form or forms of these words appear in the literature.

Teach/Word Sort

- Review **Sound/Spelling Card** *eagle*. *What sound do you hear at the beginning of eagle?* /ē/ *This is the long e sound. The letter y can also stand for the /ē/ sound.*

- Draw a two-column chart. Have children write Spelling Words in each column. Tell them to write words that have a single consonant in one column and words that have double consonants in the other column.

- Distribute Reader's Notebook Volume 2 p. 34 to children to complete independently. **ELA** L.2.2d

Pattern Sort

For additional practice with the Spelling Words, guide children to complete the Pattern Sort activity on page 90 of the **Literacy and Language Guide.**

Handwriting

Model how to form the Basic Words *happy, pretty, baby, very, puppy,* and *funny.* Handwriting models are available on pp. R24–R29 and on the Handwriting Models Blackline Masters . Remind children to write legibly and stay within the margins. **ELA** L.2.1g

Narrative Writing Focus Trait: Elaboration

1 Teach/Model

Sense Words Explain that good writers use words that tell what they see, hear, feel, taste, or smell. These are called sense words.

- Tell children that sense words appeal to the five senses: sight, sound, touch, taste, and smell.

- Explain that choosing words that tell about senses can help readers feel as if they are at the scene.

Connect to *My Name Is Gabriela*	
Instead of this...	**...the author wrote this.**
I loved words.	"I loved words—I liked the sounds they made rolling off my tongue and I liked the way they could express how I felt." (p. 96)

- *Why is the author's sentence a better description? Sense words help the reader understand how words sounded to the author.*

2 Guided Practice/Apply

- Write: *Zebras sing.*

- Ask children to look at the illustration of imaginary zebras on **Student Book** pp. 94–95. Have them brainstorm sense words that tell more about the zebras. List their suggestions. Possible responses: *black and white stripes, pink and blue polka dots, soft and furry, two, singing sweet-sounding songs*

- Write a couple of sentences that children suggest using the list of sense words. Possible responses: *Two zebras sing sweet-sounding songs. The black and white zebras are soft and furry.*

- Write: *I see a bridge.*

- Ask children to look at the picture on **Student Book** p. 106. Ask them to describe something in the scene by writing a sentence that uses sense words and, if possible, also some details that answer the question *Where?* Possible responses: *I see a long, busy bridge. I see a tiny, yellow tugboat going under the bridge.*

- Distribute <u>Reader's Notebook Volume 2 page 36</u> to children to complete independently. **ELA** W.2.3, W.2.4, W.2.10 **ELD** ELD.PI.2.10, ELD.PII.2.4, ELD.PII.2.5

Daily Proofreading Practice

it's a <u>sunny</u> day at the market. <u>a</u> mother

plays with her <del>babee</del>. (baby)

ENGLISH LANGUAGE SUPPORT

Comprehensible Input

All Proficiencies Provide children with word webs to complete the activity. Have them brainstorm different sense words on the webs to use to complete the activity and the Reader's Notebook page.

myWriteSmart Children may prewrite, draft, revise, and publish their narrative writing task through *my*WriteSmart beginning on Day 3.

DAY 3

Today's Goals

Vocabulary & Oral Language
• Apply Vocabulary Knowledge

☑ **TARGET VOCABULARY**

accepted	pretend
express	prize
taught	wonder
grand	fluttering

Phonemic Awareness
• Blending Phonemes

Phonics & Fluency
• **Changing y to i**
• **Read Decodable Reader:** *Puppies*
• **Fluency:** Expression
• **High-Frequency Words**

Text-Based Comprehension
• **Independent Reading**
• **Reader's Guide**
• **Self-Selected Reading**

Grammar & Writing
• **The Verb** *be*
• **Narrative Writing:** Descriptive Paragraph

Spelling
• **Long e Spelled** *y*

Opening Routines

Warm Up with Wordplay

Two Words

Children have been reading about a woman named Gabriela. Have each child think of two words that describe Gabriela. Ask them to write their ideas on paper. Then collect the responses and write them on the board.

Chile	**writer**
traveler	**poet**
teacher	**prizewinner**

Ask children to read the words and discuss whether each word describes Gabriela well, using examples from the story. **ELA** L.2.5a, L.2.6

Daily Phonemic Awareness

Blending Phonemes

- *Listen to these sounds: /p/ /ĕ/ /n/ /ē/. Blend the sounds. What's the word?* penny *Say the word with me.* penny *Now listen to these sounds: /p/ /ĕ/ /n/ /ē/ /z/. Blend the sounds. What's the word?* pennies *What sound did we add?* /z/

- *Now let's try this word:* bunny. *How would you change the word to mean more than one bunny?* bunnies *What sound did you add?* /z/

- Continue the activity with the words *baby* and *puppy*.

Corrective Feedback

- If a child is unable to blend the sounds, provide correction, and model the task. Example. *Listen to these sounds: /b/ /ā/ /b/ /ē/. I blend the sounds quickly:* baby. *The word is* baby.

- Have children blend the sounds with you before doing the task on their own.

Daily High-Frequency Words

- Point to **High-Frequency Word Card 173**, *friends.*

- *Say the word.* friends *Spell the word.* f-r-i-e-n-d-s *Write the word. Check the word.*

- Repeat the procedure with the words *always, anything, been, draw, mother, soon, under, watch,* and *words.* **ELA** RF.2.3f

Word Search

- Create a word search puzzle that includes the words *always, anything, been, draw, friends, mother, soon, under, watch,* and *words.*

- Have children draw a ring around each word and then read them aloud.

Corrective Feedback

- If a child does not recognize the word *friends,* say the correct word and have children repeat it. *Friends. What is the word?* friends

- Have children spell the word. *f-r-i-e-n-d-s How do we say this word?* friends

- Have children reread all of the cards in random order.

Daily Vocabulary Boost

- Guide children to interact with the Target Vocabulary, using these questions. Remind them to speak clearly during the discussion.

  What do you think makes something a good prize?

  Would you rather have a pretend dog or a real dog?

  Have you ever accepted a gift? How did you feel?

- Have children work together to explain *prize, pretend,* and *accepted* in their own words. Make sure children follow appropriate rules for discussion, such as listening to speakers, taking turns, and staying on topic. **ELA** SL.2.1a, L.2.6 **ELD** ELD PI.2.1

pretend
The girl is not a real doctor.
She is a pretend doctor.

Vocabulary in Context Cards 137–144

☑ **Target Vocabulary**

accepted
express
taught
grand
pretend
prize
wonder
fluttering

Phonics

▶ **SHARE OBJECTIVES**
- Add and take away sounds to form new words.
- Blend and decode regularly spelled words ending with *-es*.

▶ **SKILLS TRACE**

Changing *y* to *i*	
▶ Introduce	pp. T250–T251
Differentiate	p. T290
Review	p. T262
Assess	Weekly Tests, Lesson 18

ENGLISH LANGUAGE SUPPORT
Comprehensible Input

Emerging Speakers of Spanish are familiar with forming plurals by adding a final /s/, but speakers of Chinese, Korean, and other Asian languages may need additional support with the concept. Hold up one penny while saying "one penny" and have children repeat after you. Show two or more pennies as you emphasize the added sound /z/ in *pennies,* and have children repeat. **ELD** ELD.PIII.2

Expanding Check children's understanding of the words used in the Phonics lesson by naming each (*penny, baby, fly, copy*), using it as a singular noun in a short context sentence, and asking children to say the plural form in a phrase or sentence. Then use *fly/flies* and *copy/copies* as verbs, and prompt children to use each in a sentence similar to yours; for example: *Planes fly. One plane flies. I copy from the board. He copies from the board.*

Bridging For words in Blending Lines that may be unfamiliar to children, offer context sentences, pictures, or objects to support their understanding.

Changing *y* to *i*

ENGLISH LANGUAGE SUPPORT The sound /z/ may be difficult for many English learners, including speakers of Spanish and Asian languages. Have children study your mouth position as you elongate the sound; as they imitate the sound, encourage them to feel the vibration in their throat. Point out that in words that end with a vowel sound, such as *tree, day, go,* and *fly,* adding the ending *-s* or *-es* adds the sound /z/. Have children listen as you say these words ending with /z/; prompt them to identify the final sound and practice saying the word: *trees, days, goes, flies, pennies, puppies, berries.* Use each word in a brief sentence to reinforce meaning. **ELD** ELD.PIII.2

Phonemic Awareness Warm-Up *I'll say a word and then add or take away a sound to make a new word. Listen:* penny. *Now I'll add the sound /z/ at the end. Listen:* pennies. *Do it with me. Say* penny *and then add /z/ at the end:* penny, pennies. *Now you do it. Say* ponies. ponies *Take away the sound /z/ at the end. What is the new word?* pony *Say* copy. copy *Add /z/ at the end.* copies *Say* tries. tries *Take away /z/ at the end:* try *Say* kitties. kitties *Take away /z/ at the end.* kitty

1   Teach/Model

Introduce Changing *y* to *i* Use **Sound/Spelling Card** *eagle* to review the long e sound spelled *y,* as in *pony* and *tiny.*

Continue in the same way with words ending with long *i* spelled *y,* using the **Sound/Spelling Card** *ice cream* and the words *try, tries.* Explain that *y* is also changed to *i* before the new verb ending: *I try. He tries.*

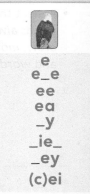

- Write and read *penny.* *The word* penny *ends with the vowel* y *and the long e sound /ē/.*

- Write and read *pennies.* Circle the *i* and underline the ending *-es. The letter* y *in* penny *changes to* i *before the ending* -es. Point out that the ending *-es* turns the word into its plural form, meaning "more than one." Show the *ie* spelling for long e on **Sound/Spelling Card** *eagle.* Point to *ie* in *pennies,* and have children say the sound.

- Follow a similar process with *dry* and *dries.*

Write and Read Words On the board, write the words *puppy, lady, study; fly, cry, carry.* For each word, model changing *y* to *i* before adding the ending *-es* to make the plural form of the word or the new verb form. Read each word with children and ask them to use the word in a sentence.

2 Guided Practice

Continuous Blending Routine Use the routine to model blending *jellies* one syllable at a time. Display **Letter Cards** *j, e, l, l, i, e, s.*

- Blend the sounds in each syllable and then blend the syllables. *Listen: /j/ /ĕ/ /l/, /ē/ /z/;* jel-lies; jellies. Have children blend with you in the same way.

Blending Lines

Blend Words Have children read the following words chorally; provide Corrective Feedback as needed. Help children compare the sounds and spellings they notice in each line.

1. try	tries	cry	cries	fly	flies
2. penny	pennies	berry	berries	puppy	puppies
3. pony	ponies	lady	ladies	duty	duties

Transition to Longer Words Have children read the following words chorally. Ask children to identify known word parts in each longer word that helped them decode it.

4. candies	marries	fries	cherries	rubies	cities
5. bellies	stories	babies	kitties	buddies	daisies
6. studies	bunnies	lilies	bodies	carries	pansies

Challenge Call on above-level children to read the words in Line 7 and tell what elements helped them decode the words. Then have the class read the sentences chorally.

7. entries houseflies strawberries families worries replies
8. My <u>friends</u> <u>always</u> try to play with puppies.
9. At night, I <u>watch</u> my bunnies act very silly.

3 Apply

Have partners take turns rereading Blending Lines 1–3 and 4–6. Together, have them choose four words with endings to record. Tell them to write the base word beside each word with the ending and to use each word as a caption for side-by-side pictures. **ELA** RF.2.3d

Distribute Reader's Notebook Volume 2 page 37 or leveled practice in Grab-and-Go™ Resources for children to complete independently.

FORMATIVE ASSESSMENT 3 2 1 **RtI**

Corrective Feedback When a child mispronounces a letter-sound, highlight that letter, restate its sound, have children repeat the sound, and then guide them to blend the word. See the example below.

Decoding Error:
A child reads *daisies* in Line 5 as *dazes*.

Correct the error. Say the correct word. *The word is* daisies. *The letters* i, e, s *spell the sounds /ēz/.*

Model as you identify the base word and ending. *The base word is* daisy. *The y in* daisy *changes to* i *before the added ending -es. The word* daisy *becomes* daisies.

Guide *Let's say the sounds for i-e-s together: /ēz/. Let's read the word together:* daisies. *What is the word?* daisies

Check *You read the word.* daisies

Reinforce Go back three or four words and have children continue reading the word lists. Make note of errors and review those words during the next lesson.

 Go to p. T290 for additional phonics support.

Blend-It Books

To provide reading practice with new sound/spellings in decodable texts, see **Blend-It Books** 119–120.

Decodable Reader

▶ SHARE OBJECTIVE

• Accurately read text with words with the long *e* sound for *y*, words ending with *-ies*, and High-Frequency Words.

FORMATIVE ASSESSMENT	3 2 1	RtI

Corrective Feedback When a child mispronounces a word, point to the word and say it. Call attention to the element that was mispronounced, say it correctly, and then guide children to read the word. See the example below.

Decoding Error:
A child reads *carries* on page 2 as *cars*.

Correct the error. Say the word. *That word is* carries. *The letters* i, e, s *at the end spell /ēz/.*

Guide Have children repeat the word. *What is the word?* carries

Check *Go back to the beginning of the sentence and read it again.*

Reinforce Record the error and review the word again before children reread the story.

Go to p. T290 for additional phonics support.

Read *Puppies*

Review Changing *y* to *i* and High-Frequency Words Display the words shown below and read them with children to review words in which *y* changes to *i* before the ending *-es*.

Decodable Reader

cry	cries
bunny	bunnies
city	cities

Review the High-Frequency Words *always*, *anything*, *been*, *draw*, *friends*, *mother*, *soon*, *under*, *watch*, and *words*. Tell children that the story they will read has many of this week's High-Frequency Words as well as words in which *y* has changed to *i* before the ending *-es*.

Preview Have children read the title, browse beginning pages, and discuss what they think the text is about. Ask children for some questions that might be answered in the text. Tell children to think about the answers to questions about puppies that they find in this informational text.

ENGLISH LANGUAGE SUPPORT Point out the word *grassy* and the grass in the photograph. Help children recognize that "a grassy place" is covered in grass.

Fluency: Expression Tell children to read with expression by using their voice to show feeling. Remind them to look for question marks and exclamation points to guide their reading and to decide which words to say most strongly.

Read Have children read the first page of *Puppies* silently. Remind them to read familiar words quickly and correctly. Then ask a child to read the page aloud using appropriate expression. Call on individuals to identify words with the ending *-es* and any High-Frequency Words. Repeat for each page.

Responding Ask children what questions are answered in this informational text. Have partners take turns rereading a part of the text that answers the question, "What do puppies need?" **ELA** RI.2.1, RI.2.2, RF.2.4a

Fluency

Expression

1 Teach/Model

Tell children that good readers add interest and enjoyment to their reading by reading with expression. Explain that when readers read with expression, they use their voice to express, or show, the characters' or the author's thoughts and feelings.

Display Projectible 18.6 . As you read the sentences fluently, model appropriate expression. Go back to circle punctuation that was a clue to expressive reading and underline words you emphasized.

2 Guided Practice

Have children return to p. 103 of *My Name is Gabriela* in the **Student Book**. Tell children to think about how Gabriela Mistral might sound if she were telling her story to a friend. Model reading the page with expression. Have children read with you.

3 Apply

Suggest that partners try reading the same passage with varied feelings (such as happy, sad, excited, or bored) to see how expression can impact the meaning of the text.

Then have partners take turns reading the page to each other several times using appropriate expression. **ELA** RF.2.4b

▶ **SHARE OBJECTIVE**

• Read fluently with expression (prosody).

> SMALL GROUP Options
>
> **Go to p. T291 for additional fluency support.**

ENGLISH LANGUAGE SUPPORT

Partner Reading

All Proficiencies English language learners may be paired with readers who are more fluent and can provide a model, help with word recognition, and provide feedback. One method of partner reading is to have the stronger reader read a paragraph first. The less fluent reader then reads the same text aloud while the stronger reader provides feedback and encouragement. The less fluent reader rereads the passage until he or she can read it independently.

Cold Reads: Support for fluent reading and comprehension

DAY 3

Independent Reading

▶ **SHARE OBJECTIVES**
- Read and comprehend informational text.
- Ask and answer questions about what you read.
- Use evidence from the text to answer questions and support opinions. LANGUAGE
- Read independently from a "just right" book.
- Read aloud with expression.

ENGLISH LANGUAGE SUPPORT

Review Key Ideas

Emerging Ask children *yes/no* questions about the selection. **ELD** ELD.PI.2.6

Expanding Ask children some details about the story, such as *Where does Gabriela live as a little girl?* and *What special prize did Gabriela win?* **ELD** ELD.PI.2.6

Bridging Have children summarize the passage, discussing each different thing that Gabriela did/accomplished in her life. **ELD** ELD.PI.2.6

Reader's Guide

Revisit the Anchor Text Lead children in a brief discussion about *My Name Is Gabriela*. Have them recount the important events and summarize what the selection is about. Remind children to be respectful when they are waiting for their turn to speak, to listen with care when others are speaking, and to speak one at a time. **ELA** RI.2.2, SL.2.1a **ELD** ELD.PI.2.1, ELD.PI.2.6, ELD.PI.2.12a

Have children read *My Name Is Gabriela* on their own. Then distribute Reader's Notebook Volume 2 pages 38–39 🔗 and have children complete them independently. **ELA** RI.2.1 **ELD** ELD.PI.2.6

Model Questioning Demonstrate generating a question about *My Name is Gabriela*. For example: *What did Gabriela like to read about?* Reread **Student Book** p. 97 with children to respond to the question. **ELA** RI.2.1 **ELD** ELD.PI.2.6

Generate Questions Have children work independently or collaboratively to generate questions about *My Name Is Gabriela*. Ask children to share their questions. Begin a class discussion of questions that children have in common or that are most significant to their understanding of the selection. Remind them to follow the rules for discussions. **ELA** RI.2.1, SL.2.1a **ELD** ELD.PI.2.1, ELD.PI.2.6

Self-Selected Reading

Take a Picture Walk Tell children that one way to decide which book to read is to take a picture walk through the book. Good readers learn about a book before they commit themselves to reading it. Discuss the following points with children:

- Often, informational text has photos and literature has illustrations.
- Pictures can tell us about the topic of an informational text. We can learn about some key details by reading captions.
- Illustrations can tell us about the genre of a story, the kinds of events that take place, and the characters in the story.

After taking a picture walk, think about whether this book looks interesting and enjoyable. Is it "just right" for you? Tell children that if the book does not seem interesting and enjoyable, they should find another book, and preview it with a picture walk. **ELA** RL.2.10, RI.2.10

Self-Correction Strategies

Read for Fluency and Expression Remind children that we communicate not just through words, but through how we express words. Punctuation guides us in reading with expression. Model reading with expression from *My Name Is Gabriela*. Have children join you in echo reading a section from the selection, then have them choral read the same section with you.

Have partners practice reading aloud to each other from their self-selected books. Ask them to focus on reading aloud with expression. Remind children to use context to confirm or self-correct word recognition and understanding, and to reread as necessary to improve accuracy, rate, and expression. **ELA** RF.2.4b

---

ENGLISH LANGUAGE SUPPORT

"Just Right" Books for ELs

All Proficiencies All children, but especially English learners, benefit from seeing themselves in the books they read. Give English learners opportunities to self-select a "just right" book from an author, illustrator, or photographer that shares their cultural background or that has characters from their culture.

Apply Vocabulary Knowledge

▶ SHARE OBJECTIVES

- Use words and phrases acquired through conversations, reading and being read to, and responding to texts. LANGUAGE
- Identify real-life connections between words and their use. LANGUAGE
- Use print and digital dictionaries. LANGUAGE

ENGLISH LANGUAGE SUPPORT
Build Background

Emerging Have children discuss places they would like to take a journey. Take note of their ideas on the board.

Expanding Have children talk about the kind of professional activities they would like to perform when they are adults. They may want to use the sentence frame *Since I am very good at _____, as an adult, I would like to be a professional _____.*

Bridging Ask partners to tell each other a kind of prize they would like to win and what they are doing toward that end. **ELD** ELD.PI.2.1

☑ Review Target Vocabulary

Review with children the Vocabulary in Context Cards on **Student Book** pp. 86–87. Call on children to read the context sentences and explain how the photograph demonstrates the meaning of the word.

Enrich Vocabulary Write the following Related Words on the board. Read each word aloud, and have children repeat after you. Then read the child-friendly explanation for each word. Connect each word's meaning to the selection *My Name Is Gabriela* by writing the context sentences on the board and reading them aloud. **ELA** L.2.5a

educator: An educator is someone who teaches. *Gabriela Mistral loved her job as an educator.*

inspiration: When someone is an inspiration to others, he or she is admired because they fill others with encouragement or excitement. *Gabriela is an inspiration to many people because of what she did with her life.*

journey: A journey is a trip from one place to another. *She would often take a journey to far-away countries.*

professional: If people do something as an important part of their work, you can call them professional. *Gabriela Mistral grew up to be a professional poet.*

Make Connections Discuss all of the words using the items below to help children make connections between vocabulary words and their use. **ELA** L.2.5a **ELD** ELD.PI.2.1, ELD.PI.2.12a, ELD.PI.2.12b

- What might you like to win a *prize* for one day?
- What type of building or place might be called *grand*?
- Tell about a time you saw something *fluttering*.
- Have you ever acted like a *pretend* teacher or fireman? Tell about it.
- Who *taught* you how to tie your shoes?
- Is a coach an *educator*? Why or why not?
- What would you take with you on a *journey* to the beach?
- Who is an *inspiration* to you? Why?
- How do you *express* your thoughts and feelings?
- What is something you *wonder* about the future?
- What *professional* activities will you do when you are grown?
- What might a person do after he or she has *accepted* an award?

Dictionary Skills

Discuss Using a Dictionary Discuss with children how to look up a word in a print or digital dictionary.

Ask children to tell what they can do if they do not know the meaning of a word. Have them point out the guide words at the top of the page and describe how the words are ordered.

Have partners work together and take turns looking up the new words *educator, inspiration, journey,* and *professional*. If necessary, point out the base word of each to help children locate the word. Have children read aloud each definition. Have peer tutors help children who were not able to find the words.

ELA SL.2.1a, L.2.4e **ELD** ELD.PI.2.1

QUICKWRITE Read aloud each question below. Pause a few minutes between each item to allow children to write a response. **ELA** L.2.6

1. Name an **educator** who taught you something important.

2. How can you be an **inspiration** to others?

3. Tell about a short **journey** you have taken.

4. When should you ask for a **professional** opinion about something?

ENGLISH LANGUAGE SUPPORT Write the following sentence frames on the board to support children in writing: *An educator who taught me something important is _____. He/she taught me _____. I can be an inspiration to others by _____. I took a short journey when I went to _____. On my journey, I saw _____. It's a good idea to ask for a professional opinion when _____.* Read the sentence frames aloud with children. Ask them to write to complete the sentences.

ELD ELD.PI.2.10

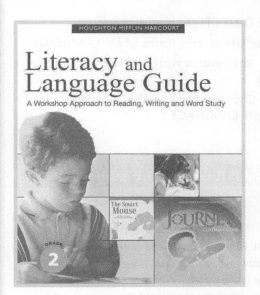

For additional practice with the lesson's Target Vocabulary words, use the activities on pages 150–151 of the **Literacy and Language Guide**.

- Introduce Target Vocabulary; Base Words and Endings -er, -est
- Word Sort
- Glossary Snapshots
- Act Out the Words
- Word Associations

Grammar The Verb *Be*

▶ **SHARE OBJECTIVES**
- **Grammar** Use correct forms of *be*. LANGUAGE
- **Spelling** Spell words with the long e sound spelled *y*.
- **Writing** Choose a topic, and plan a descriptive paragraph. LANGUAGE

ENGLISH LANGUAGE SUPPORT

Comprehensible Input

All Proficiencies Identify an event that happened in the past. For example, say and write: *We were adding numbers yesterday.* Ask, *Is were talking about something in the present or in the past?* past Have children say other sentences that happen in the past or in the present. Have the class identify whether they are in the past or present. **ELD** ELD.PII.2.3b

Linguistic Transfer The verb be can be left out of a sentence in Cantonese, Hmong, Vietnamese, and Haitian Creole. If students say *I happy* instead of *I am happy,* provide extra practice with sentences containing forms of the verb *be,* for example, *She is happy. We are happy.* **ELD** ELD.PIII.2

---

1 | Teach/Model

Using Being Verbs Review with children how to choose the correct form of the verb *be.*

- Remind children that the form of the verb must agree with the subject of the sentence.

- Review the examples and the Thinking Questions from Day 1 and Day 2.

ENGLISH LANGUAGE SUPPORT Provide children with additional practice using *being* verbs. Have partners complete sentence frames with forms of the verb *be.* For example: *Today _____ Monday. Yesterday _____ cold.*

2 | Guided Practice/Apply

- Write: *The children are skipping. The playground were busy.* Work with children to decide whether the subject-verb agreement in each sentence is correct. *Is the first sentence about one child or more than one?* more than one *Is are the correct form of the verb be to use with a subject that is more than one?* yes

- Repeat the procedure with the second sentence. *Does playground name one or more than one?* one *Is were the correct form of the verb be to use with a subject that is one?* no, should be was

- Have children write sentences using each form of the verb *be (am, is, are, was,* and *were).* Have them check that they used the correct verb for the subject in each sentence.

- Distribute Reader's Notebook Volume 2 page 41 to children to complete independently. **ELA** L.2.1d **ELD** ELD.PII.2.3a

---

Spelling Long e Spelled *y*

SPELLING WORDS

BASIC

happy*	sunny
pretty	penny
baby*	city
very	**REVIEW**
puppy	tiny
funny	many
carry	**CHALLENGE**
lucky	sorry
only	noisy

A form of this word appears in the literature.

Segment Sounds
- Model segmenting sounds. *Listen to me as I say the word* pretty: prettyyy. *Try to hear the long* e *sound in the word* pretty. *Now you say it with me:* prettyyy.

- Repeat with *only* and *puppy.* Tell children that saying sounds slowly will help them spell the words.

Build Words with Long *e* for *y*
- Use **Letter Cards** to model building *sunny.* Have children read the word with you and begin a list of Spelling Words.

- Have partners use **Letter Cards** to build Spelling Words with long e spelled *y* and add them to their lists.

- Have partners read and spell words they built using **Letter Cards.**

- Distribute Reader's Notebook Volume 2 page 40 to children to complete independently. **ELA** L.2.2d

Blind Writing Sort

For additional practice with the Spelling Words, have children complete the Blind Writing Sort activity on page 91 of the **Literacy and Language Guide.**

Narrative Writing Prewrite

1 Teach/Model

Showing Rather Than Telling Explain to children that they should use words that show, rather than just tell, when they write a descriptive paragraph.

- *A good descriptive paragraph makes your readers feel as if they were there.*

Weak Telling Sentence	Strong Showing Sentence
The cat was pretty.	The cat had shiny and soft white fur and sky-blue eyes.

- *Telling says that something is true, while showing gives details that help readers paint pictures in their minds.*

- *What makes the second sentence stronger? The sentence shows that the cat is pretty by using words to describe what it looked like.*

2 Guided Practice/Apply

Descriptive Paragraph Display Projectable 18.7 ⬀. Read the prompt aloud.

- Have children work with you to complete the Column Chart.

Think Aloud *I am going to write about my kitchen. I'll use a Column Chart to help me think of sense words. Where shall I start? I'll start with things I see. I see a bowl of red apples, so I will write that in the chart under What I See. I also see a yellow mixer and an old wooden spoon. I'll write those also.*

- Work with children to complete their own Column Charts. Save the completed Column Charts for Day 4.

Prewriting Reread together the prompt on **Projectable 18.7**. Work with children to list some ideas of places, animals, or things to describe. Have children draw their own Column Charts with the heads: *What I See, What I Hear, What I Feel, What I Taste, What I Smell*. Then tell them to complete their Column Charts using their five senses to describe their topic. Remind them that details can also answer the questions *When? Where?* or *How?* **ELA** W.2.3, W.2.4, W.2.10 **ELD** ELD.PI.2.10, ELD.PII.2.1, ELD.PII.2.4, ELD.PII.2.5

Daily Proofreading Practice

This toy cost only a penny. I am buying it for my friend.

ENGLISH LANGUAGE SUPPORT

How English Works: Productive

Verb Types Before children begin drafting their descriptive paragraphs, have them think about the verb types that they will use as they write. Tell children that *doing* verbs will work best with this type of paragraph because they will be describing senses. Give examples such as *I smell _____, I hear _____, I see _____*, and explain that these are all doing verbs. Help children at different proficiency levels think about their topics and make short lists of verbs to use while drafting.

ELD ELD.PII.2.3a

---

my WriteSmart Have children prewrite their narrative writing task through *my*WriteSmart.

DAY 4

Today's Goals

Vocabulary & Oral Language
- **Vocabulary Strategies:**
  Suffixes -*y* and -*ful*

☑ **TARGET VOCABULARY**

accepted	pretend
express	prize
taught	wonder
grand	fluttering

Phonemic Awareness
- **Blend Phonemes**

Phonics & Fluency
- **Changing *y* to *i***
- **Fluency:** Expression
- **Read Decodable Reader:** *Puppies*
- **High-Frequency Words**

Text-Based Comprehension
- **Connect to the Topic**
- **Read Poetry:**
  Poems About Reading and Writing
- **Compare Texts**

Grammar & Writing
- **Spiral Review:** Writing Quotations
- **Narrative Writing:**
  Descriptive Paragraph

Spelling
- **Long e Spelled *y***

Opening Routines

Warm Up with Wordplay

Using New Vocabulary

Write this week's Related Words on the board: *educator, inspiration, journey, professional*. Have children read the words with you and discuss their definitions.

Display these sentence pairs and read them with children. Explain that the first sentence in each pair has a clue that will help them complete the second sentence.

> **I want to be a teacher when I grow up.**
> **I will be an _____.**
> **We took a trip all the way to Canada.**
> **It was a long _____.**
> **Today's rainbow gave Rose an idea for a story.**
> **The rainbow was an _____.**
> **Andy's profession is plumbing.**
> **He is a _____ plumber.**

Have partners work together to complete each sentence frame. Have them write the new sentences and then read the sentence pairs to the class. Ask children to point out the clues that helped them.

ELA L.2.6

Daily Phonemic Awareness

Blend Phonemes

- *Listen: /l/ /ā/ /d/ /ē/ . What's the word?* lady *Now listen again: /l/ /ā/ /d/ /ē/ /z/. What's the word?* ladies *What sound did I add that made the word mean "more than one lady"?* /z/

- *Now it's your turn. Say this word: /s/ /ĭ/ /t/ /ē/.* city *What word means "more than one city"?* cities *What sound did you add?* /z/

- Continue the activity with the words *party, cherry, baby, kitty, pony, puppy, fairy,* and *berry.*

Corrective Feedback

- If a child is unable to blend the sounds, say the word, give correction, and model the task. Example: *The word is pony. I can add the /z/ sound at the end of pony to make it plural. Listen:* ponies.

- Have children blend the words with you before doing the task on their own.

Daily High-Frequency Words

- Point to **High-Frequency Word Card 171**, *words.*

- *Say the word.* words *Spell the word.* w-o-r-d-s *Write the word. Check it.*

- Repeat the routine with the words *always, anything, been, draw, friends, mother, soon, under,* and *watch.* **ELA** RF.2.3f

Spell It

- Provide children with **Letter Cards**.

- Have them take turns using the cards to spell the word *words* correctly.

- Repeat for all of this week's High-Frequency Words.

Corrective Feedback

- If a child does not recognize the word *anything*, say the correct word and have children repeat it. *Anything. What is the word?* anything

- Have children spell the word. *a-n-y-t-h-i-n-g How do we say this word?* anything

- Have children reread all of the cards in random order.

Daily Vocabulary Boost

- Guide children to interact with Target Vocabulary by asking the following questions. Remind them to speak clearly when participating in the discussion.

  What is one way you express your feelings?

  What is a time when you accepted someone's apology? What did you say?

  Have you ever seen anything grand? What made it grand?

- Have children work together to explain *express, accepted,* and *grand* in their own words. Make sure children follow appropriate rules for discussion such as listening to speakers, taking turns, and staying on topic. **ELA** SL.2.1a, L.2.6 **ELD** ELD.PI.2.1

fluttering
The butterfly is fluttering its wings as it flies. The wings move quickly.

Vocabulary in Context Cards 137–144

☑ **Target Vocabulary**

accepted
express
taught
grand
pretend
prize
wonder
fluttering

Phonics

▶ **SHARE OBJECTIVES**

- Blend, build, and decode words in which a final *y* has changed to *i* before *-es*.
- Review and sort words with long *i* spelled *i, igh, ie, y* and words with long *e* spelled *y*.

▶ **SKILLS TRACE**

Changing *y* to *i*	
Introduce	pp. T250–T251
▶ Review	**p. T262**
Assess	Weekly Tests, Lesson 18

▶ **SKILLS TRACE**

Long *e* spelled *y*	
Introduce	pp. T142–T143, T216–T217
▶ Review	**p. T263, T352, T363**
Assess	Weekly Tests, Lesson 18

ENGLISH LANGUAGE SUPPORT

Comprehensible Input

All Proficiencies Review the singular and plural forms of the words in Make and Read Words to prepare children for the activity. Write each base word on a card or paper slip: *city, fry, bunny, puppy, candy, copy.* Review meanings by asking children to give an example or describe each one. Use the plural form of each word in a phrase or short sentence; for example: *Here are three candies; I made many copies of this page; I ate French fries.* Have children repeat the plural form and identify the displayed base word that matches.

Review Changing *y* to *i*

Phonemic Awareness Warm-Up *I'll say a word and then add or take away a sound to make a new word. Listen:* lady. *Now I'll add the sound /z/ at the end. Listen:* ladies. *Do it with me. Say* lady *and then add /z/ at the end:* lady, ladies.

Now you do it. Say cubbies. cubbies *Take away the sound /z/ at the end. What is the new word?* cubby *Say* daisy. daisy *Add /z/ at the end.* daisies *Say* flies. flies *Take away /z/ at the end.* fly

Make and Read Words Remind children that a final *y* after a consonant changes to *i* before the ending *-es*. Illustrate by writing the word *penny* and having children tell you how to change it into *pennies.*

Display base words such as the following: *city, fry, bunny, puppy, candy, copy.* Read the words aloud with children.

Then tell partners to build each word using **Letter Cards**. Tell them to take turns changing the *y* to *i* and adding the ending *-es.* Have partners read each word together. Then ask individuals to come to the board to write the words with endings. **ELA** RF.2.3d

city/cities   fry/fries
bunny/bunnies   . copy/copies

Practice Fluency

Use Instructional Routine 15 to have partners reread **Decodable Reader** *Puppies.* Remind children to practice reading with expression.

Decodable Reader

Review Words with Long *i* (*i, igh, ie, y*) and the Long *e* Sound for *y*

Phonemic Awareness Warm-Up *I will say a word and then change the vowel sound to make a new word. Listen to the word:* leaf. *Now listen as I change the long* e *vowel sound /ē/ in* leaf *to a long i vowel sound /ī/:* life. *Let's do one together. Repeat this word after me:* free. *What is the vowel sound in* free? long e /ē/ *Let's change it to long* i, /ī/. *What is the new word?* fry

Continue by having children change the long *e* vowel sound in each of the following words to a long *i* vowel sound to make a new word: *wheel,* while; *see,* sigh; *tea,* tie; *me,* my; *feet,* fight

Word Sort Display **Sound/Spelling Cards** *ice cream* and *eagle* to review the spellings *i, igh, ie, y* for long *i* and the spelling *y* for long *e*. List the following words on the board; ask children to read each one, to tell whether it has a long *i* or a long *e* sound in it, and to identify the spelling for you to underline: *find, high, pie, try, funny.*

Work with children to brainstorm more words with long *i* spelled *i, igh, ie, y* and more two-syllable words with long *e* spelled *y*. Display the words randomly on the board. Have partners read the words and list them in two columns by vowel sound: *Long i, Long e.* Ask children to read their lists aloud. Have them tell how they knew which word to list in each column.

ELA RF.2.3a, RF.2.3b, RF.2.3c, RF.2.3e

i
i_e
ie
igh
_y

e
e_e
ee
ea
_y
_ie_
_ey
(c)ei

Corrective Feedback When a child mispronounces a word, point to the word and say it. Call attention to the element that was mispronounced, say the sound, and then guide children to read the word. See the example below.

Decoding Error:
In Make and Read Words, a child reads *candies* with a long *i*.

Correct the error. Say the correct word. *The word is* candies. *The letters* i, e, s *spell the sounds /ēz/.*

Model as you identify the base word and ending. *The base word is* candy. *The final* y *in* candy *changed to* i *before the added ending* -es. *The word* candy *becomes* candies.

Guide *Let's say the sounds for* i, e, s *together:* /ēz/. *Let's read the word together:* candies. *What is the correct word?* candies

Check *You read the word.* candies

Reinforce Record the error and review the word again at the end of the activity.

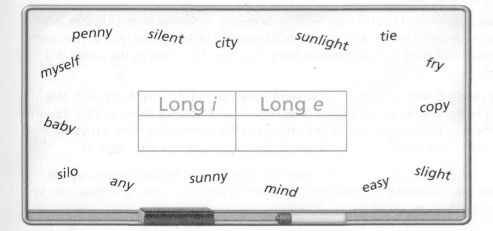

penny   silent   city   sunlight   tie

myself   fry

Long *i*	Long *e*

baby   copy

silo   any   sunny   mind   easy   slight

Lesson 18

POETRY

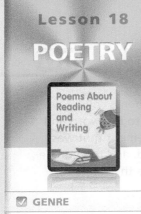

Poems About
Reading
and Writing

☑ **GENRE**

Poetry uses the sound of words to show pictures and feelings.

☑ **TEXT FOCUS**

Rhythm is a pattern of beats, like music. The words and phrases in poetry can give it rhythm and meaning.

Poems About
Reading
and Writing

When you read a poem, do you pretend to be in the poem? When you write a poem, do you express wonder about things? These poems are about reading and writing.

Share the Adventure

Pages and pages
A seesaw of ideas—
Share the adventure

Fiction, nonfiction:
Door to our past and future
Swinging back and forth

WHAM! The book slams shut,
But we read it together
With our minds open

*by Patricia and
Fredrick McKissack*

The Period

Fat little period, round as a ball,
You'd think it would roll,
But it doesn't
At all.
Where it stops,
There it plops,
There it stubbornly stays,
At the end of a sentence
For days and days.

"Get out of my way!"
Cries the sentence. "Beware!"
But the period seems not to hear
     or to care.
Like a stone in the road,
It won't budge, it won't bend.
If it spoke, it would say to a sentence,
"The end."

by Richard Armour

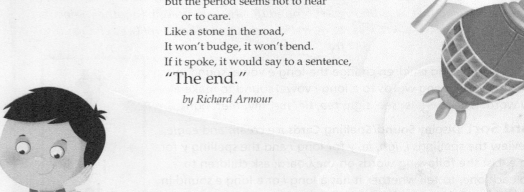

LESSON TOPIC: Reading and Writing

Cross-Curricular Connection Tell children that many people have made contributions through their writings. Authors, presidents, singers, and poets are just some of them. Read aloud poetry written by African American, Hispanic, American Indian, or female poets. Have children discuss which poems they like and tell why.

FOR STUDENTS WITH DISABILITIES
Some children may need help to distinguish between the literal and figurative meaning of a word or phrase. Model using context clues to figure out the meaning and how to use a dictionary or thesaurus. Create a class notebook with examples of multiple-meaning words, their definitions, example sentences, and illustrations.

Connect to the Topic: Poetry
Introduce Genre and Text Focus

- Read with children the genre and text focus information on **Student Book** p. 114. Then tell them they will read three poems about reading and writing. Remind children that poets choose words that help readers imagine how things look, sound, smell, taste, or feel.

- Explain that lines of poetry have rhythm, or strong and weak beats. Rhythm in a poem is similar to the beat of a drum in a song. Tell children that, just as they can tap their toes along to their favorite song, they can clap along to the words in a poem.

- Have children read the poems on **Student Book** pp. 114–115. With children, clap along to the rhythm of the poems "The Period" and "Keep a Poem in Your Pocket." Ask them to tell how the words and phrases in the poems give them a rhythm. *Some of the words rhyme and the words have a beat like a song.* **ELA** RL.2.4

ENGLISH LANGUAGE SUPPORT Point out examples of figurative language in "Share the Adventure" for children. Ask them to tell what is being represented in the poem. *Seesaw, doors, book*

Keep a Poem in Your Pocket

Keep a poem in your pocket
and a picture in your head
and you'll never feel lonely
at night when you're in bed.

The little poem will sing to you
the little picture bring to you
a dozen dreams to dance to you
at night when you're in bed.

So—
Keep a picture in your pocket
and a poem in your head
and you'll never feel lonely
at night when you're in bed.

by Beatrice Schenk de Regniers

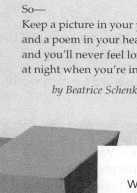

Write a Poem

Write a poem about your favorite book. Think about how you can use rhythm, rhyme, and repetition to make your poem fun to read. Share your poem with a partner. Talk about how the words add rhythm and meaning.

116

Compare Texts

TEXT TO TEXT

Connect to Poetry Gabriela Mistral loved to read and write. Look back at the poems you just read. Which poem do you think Gabriela would have liked the best? Write a few sentences to give your opinion. Give reasons using text evidence from *My Name Is Gabriela*.

TEXT TO SELF

Tell a Story How does Gabriela help people learn? How has a teacher made a difference in your life? Tell a partner. Use facts and details to tell what happened.

TEXT TO WORLD

Find Facts Gabriela grew up in Chile. Use the index of a reference book to look up information about Chile. Make two fact cards with information you learned.

> Chile is over 4,000 kilometers long from north to south.

ELA RI.2.5, W.2.1, W.2.4, W.2.10, SL.2.4 ELD ELD.PI.2.6, ELD.PI.2.10, ELD.PI.2.11, ELD.PI.2.12a

117

Compare Texts

TEXT TO TEXT

Connect to Poetry Ask children to skim back through the story to help them explain which poem Gabriela would like the best. Guide children to ask themselves questions about how Gabriela feels about reading and writing. Their own answers should help them write their responses. ELA RI.2.1, W.2.1, W.2.4, W.2.10 ELD ELD.PI.2.1, ELD.PI.2.3, ELD.PI.11

ENGLISH LANGUAGE SUPPORT
Provide sentence frames for children to share their opinion. For example, *I think Gabriela Mistral would like ____ because ____.*
ELD ELD.PI.2.1, ELD.PI.2.3, ELD.PI.6, ELD.PI.2.11

TEXT TO SELF

Tell a Story Tell children to practice good discussion skills such as speaking clearly and in complete sentences. Remind children that they should speak loudly enough for their partner to hear what they say. Explain that when telling about something that happened to them, they should use facts and details and tell events in order.
ELA SL.2.4 ELD ELD.PI.2.12a

TEXT TO WORLD

Find Facts Point to Chile on a map. Then direct children to reference books in the classroom. Point out the index, and model using it to find an entry about Chile. *Sample answer: Chile is a country in South America. The climate is different in different parts of Chile because it is so long. The Pacific Ocean forms one of its borders, and the Andes Mountains form the other.* ELA RI.2.5

DAY 4

Vocabulary Strategies

▶ **SHARE OBJECTIVES**

- Use knowledge of suffixes *-y* and *-ful* to determine word meanings. LANGUAGE
- Use word-learning strategies independently. LANGUAGE

▶ **SKILLS TRACE**

Suffixes *-y* and *-ful*	
▶ **Introduce**	**Unit 1 pp. T258–T259**
Differentiate	T296–T297
Reteach	T299
Assess	Weekly Tests, Lesson 18

ENGLISH LANGUAGE SUPPORT

Use Visuals

Emerging Write *play, sleep, -y,* and *-ful* on index cards. Hold the cards together and show children how words are formed. Say each word that is formed and then discuss word meaning.

Expanding Write *-y* and *-ful* on the board. Explain that adding these suffixes to the end of a word sometimes requires you to drop the final *e*. Point out the base words in *sparkly* and *wrinkly.* Discuss word meaning.

Bridging Explain that suffixes *-ful* and *-y* can be added to some words but not others. Have partners choose a word on their own, add a suffix, and check a dictionary to see if it is a word. **ELD** ELD.PI.2.1

Suffixes *-y* and *-ful*

> ## 1   Teach/Model

Terms About Language

base word a word to which prefixes and/or suffixes are added; for example, the base word of *unwholesome* is *whole.* A base word is also called a root word.

suffix an ending that, when attached to the end of a base word (or root word), changes the meaning of the word

---

ENGLISH LANGUAGE SUPPORT Preteach suffixes *-y* and *-ful.* Write *beautiful, sleepy,* and *wordy.* Underline the suffix in each word. Have partners try to identify the root word in each word and discuss what each word might mean. **ELD** ELD.PI.2.1

- Explain that *-y* and *-ful* are suffixes that attach to the end of a base word (or root word), changing the meaning of the word by forming a new word.

- Explain that *-y* and *-ful* both mean "full of."

- Remind children that looking for word parts such as suffixes and base words (or root words) can help them figure out a word's meaning.

- Write the following words on the board: *joyful, sparkly, forgetful, messy.*

- Display the Projectable S8 and model using the **Vocabulary Strategy** to figure out the meaning of the word *joyful.*

> **Think Aloud**   *I see the suffix* -ful *and the base word* joy. *I learned that the suffix* -ful *means "full of," and I know that* joy *means "happiness." The word* joyful *means "full of happiness."*

- Help children apply the **Vocabulary Strategy** to figure out the meanings of other words on the board.

- Explain that sometimes words ending in *-y* do not always have the meaning of "full of." For example, *story, quarry,* and *hurry.* Children can look for word parts they know to decide if the ending *-y* means "full of" or not.

2 Guided Practice

- Display the top half of <u>Projectable 18.8</u> and read the sentences aloud.

- Have children identify the words with *-y* or *-ful* suffixes. Circle each word.

- Display the chart at the bottom half of <u>Projectable 18.8</u>. Break the circled words into base words (or root words) and suffixes and complete the chart.

3 Apply

- Have children apply the **Vocabulary Strategy** to each word. Discuss the meanings of each word ending in *-y* or *-ful*.

ENGLISH LANGUAGE SUPPORT Write these frames on the board, and help children use them to participate: *The suffix ___ means ___. I think the word ___ means ___ because ___.*

- Have children use what they know about the meaning of suffixes to tell the meaning of each word with the added suffix *-y* or *-ful*. Then have children use the context of the sentence to verify that the word makes sense in the sentence. **ELA** L.2.4a

- Distribute <u>Reader's Notebook Volume 2 page 42</u> or <u>leveled practice</u> in Grab-and-Go™ Resources to children to complete independently.

Interactive Whiteboard Lesson Use **Vocabulary Strategies: Suffixes *-y, -ful*** to learn the meanings of these suffixes.

Are children able to use knowledge of suffixes *-y* and *-ful* to determine word meanings?

IF...	THEN...
children struggle,	▶ use **Differentiate Vocabulary Strategies** for Struggling Readers, p. T296.
children are on track,	▶ use **Differentiate Vocabulary Strategies** for On-Level Readers, p. T296.
children excel,	▶ use **Differentiate Vocabulary Strategies** for Advanced Readers, p. T297.

Differentiate Vocabulary Strategies: pp. T296–T297.
Scaffold instruction to the English learner's proficiency level.

Grammar Spiral Review: Writing Quotations

▶ **SHARE OBJECTIVES**

- **Grammar** Review writing quotations. LANGUAGE
- **Spelling** Spell words with the long e sound spelled *y*.
- **Handwriting** Write Spelling Words.
- **Writing** Draft a descriptive paragraph. LANGUAGE

ENGLISH LANGUAGE SUPPORT

Access Prior Knowledge

All Proficiencies Recall that a quotation is a person's exact words. Say, *A quotation needs four things: quotation marks, a comma, capitalization, and an end mark.* Organize children into mixed-proficiency small groups and say a simple sentence, such as: *I like to cook.* Have groups work together to write your quotation. *Possible response: My teacher said, "I like to cook."*

1 Teach/Model

Writing Quotations Review with children that quotations show a speaker's exact words. Recall the rules for placing quotation marks around a speaker's exact words.

- *Use a comma after words such as* said *and* asked.
- *Begin the first word inside the quotation marks with a capital letter.*
- *Put the end mark inside the quotation marks.*

ENGLISH LANGUAGE SUPPORT Have partners each share a sentence that tells about something fun they have recently done. Partners can write down what each person says in quotation marks. **ELD** ELD.PI.2.1

2 Guided Practice/Apply

- Write the following sentences on the board:

  1. **He said come with me.** *He said, "Come with me."*

  2. **I asked, Where are we going.** *I asked, "Where are we going?"*

  3. **He said I thought you might want to go to the zoo.** *He said, "I thought you might want to go to the zoo."*

  4. **I shouted What a great surprise!** *I shouted, "What a great surprise!"*

- Have children rewrite each sentence correctly.

- Distribute Reader's Notebook Volume 2 page 44 and have children complete it independently.

Spelling Long *e* Spelled *y*

SPELLING WORDS

BASIC

happy*	sunny
pretty	penny
baby*	city
very	**REVIEW**
puppy	tiny
funny	many
carry	**CHALLENGE**
lucky	sorry
only	noisy

*A form of this word appears in the literature.

Connect to Writing

- Have children use the Spelling Words to write a sentence or two about why it is important to help others.

- Have them proofread their sentences and read them aloud.

- As a class, have children say each word and spell it aloud.

- Distribute Reader's Notebook Volume 2 p. 43 to children to complete independently. **ELA** L.2.2d

Handwriting

Model how to form the Basic Words *carry, lucky, only, sunny, penny,* and *city.* Handwriting models are available on pp. R24–R29 and on the Handwriting Models Blackline Masters. Remind children to write legibly and stay within the margins. **ELA** L.2.1g

Word Hunt

For additional practice with the Spelling Words, have children complete the Word Hunt activity on page 91 of the **Literacy and Language Guide.** **ELA** L.2.2d

Narrative Writing Draft

1 Teach/Model

Similes and Metaphors Explain that writers can compare what they are describing to something else. Two kinds of comparisons are similes and metaphors.

- A **simile** compares two different things using the words *like* or *as*.

- A **metaphor** compares two different things without using *like* or *as*.

Simile	Metaphor
His footsteps sounded like thunder in the hallway.	His footsteps were thunder in the hallway.

- *What makes the first example a simile? It uses the word* like *to compare his footsteps to thunder. What makes the second example a metaphor? It compares footsteps and thunder but it does not use* like *or* as.

2 Guided Practice/Apply

Descriptive Pararagraph Review the Column Chart on Projectable 18.7 ⬚ from Day 3. Then display for children Projectable 18.9 ⬚.

- Use the Think Aloud to model how to create similes and metaphors.

> **Think Aloud** *What can I compare the hissing steam to? I know that cats hiss too, so I will compare the sound of the hissing steam to a hissing cat.*

Drafting Then have children begin drafting their own descriptive paragraphs using their prewriting Column Charts from Day 3. Remind them to include details that use their senses and tell about when, where, or how something happens.

ELA W.2.3, W.2.4, W.2.10 **ELD** ELD.PI.2.10, ELD.PII.2.1, ELD.PII.2.4, ELD.PII.2.5

Daily Proofreading Practice

Becky said, "the city looks nice."

Mom said, "The lights are pretty."

ENGLISH LANGUAGE SUPPORT

Comprehensible Input

All Proficiencies Explain that similes and metaphors are ways to add more details to their paragraphs. Have children use their column chart from Day 3 to expand on ideas using similes and metaphors. Ask children to think of what some of the items on their charts remind them of. For example, maybe the heat of the oven reminds them of a hot summer day. Guide children to find appropriate examples on their charts to write similes or metaphors for.

 Have children draft their narrative writing task through *my*WriteSmart.

Today's Goals

Vocabulary & Oral Language
- Domain-Specific Vocabulary
- Speaking & Listening

☑ **TARGET VOCABULARY**

accepted	pretend
express	prize
taught	wonder
grand	fluttering

Phonemic Awareness
- Identify Sound Placement

Phonics & Fluency
- Interactive Whiteboard Lesson
- High-Frequency Words

Text-Based Comprehension
- Extend the Topic
- Speaking and Listening:
  Recount an Experience

Assess & Reteach
- Assess Skills
- Respond to Assessment

Grammar & Writing
- The Verb *be*
- Narrative Writing:
  Descriptive Paragraph

Spelling
- Long *e* Spelled *y*

Opening Routines

Warm Up with Wordplay

Write a Poem

Display and read aloud the following words: *read* and *write*. Have children work with partners to come up with as many words that rhyme with these as they can. When children are ready, compile their words on the board.

read	need	deed
lead	seed	speed
write	light	night
fright	bite	sight

Have children suggest an opening line for a poem, ending with one of the rhyming words. Let them choose their favorite opening line, and then, as a class, write a short poem that uses both *read* and *write*, along with at least one rhyming word for each.

ELA W.2.7 **ELD** ELD.PI.2.2

Interactive Whiteboard Lesson

For cumulative review, use **Phonics: Words with Long e Sound for y and Changing y to i** to reinforce blending, reading, and building decodable words with long e spelled *y* and their plural forms. **ELA** RF.2.3e

Daily Phonemic Awareness

Identify Sound Placement

- *Listen to this word: only. What is the vowel sound at the end of the word only?* /ē/ *Where in the word is the /ē/ sound? at the end* Explain that the long e sound /ē/ in *only* is in the second syllable.

- As you say the following words, have children identify where they hear the /ē/ sound (beginning, middle, or end) in each one: *slippery, tiny, meet, many, easy, shiny, queen, sunny, eagle, clean, nightly.*

Corrective Feedback

- If a child cannot identify sound placement, say the word. Give correction. Model the task. *The word is only. Listen and clap the syllables: on-ly. The long e sound is at the end of the word, in the second syllable.*

- Have the child clap syllables of the word and identify where long e is. Have them proceed on their own.

Daily High-Frequency Words

- Point to **High-Frequency Word Card 176**, *watch*.
- *Say the word. watch Spell the word. w-a-t-c-h Write it. Check the word.*
- Repeat with new words *always, anything, mother, under,* and *words* and review words *carry, doing, else, sure,* and *turned.* **ELA** RF.2.3f

Light the Word

- Display this week's **High-Frequency Word Cards**.
- Give children clues to each word, such as *This word starts with m and ends with r.*
- Give one child a flashlight and turn out the lights. Have the child shine the light on the word and read it.

Corrective Feedback

- If a child does not recognize the word *watch*, say the correct word and have children repeat it. *Watch. What is the word? watch*
- Have children spell the word. w-a-t-c-h *How do we say this word? watch*
- Have children reread all of the cards.

Daily Vocabulary Boost

- Reread "Doctor Salk's Treasure" aloud to children. (See pp. T214–T215.)

- As you read each Target Vocabulary word in the article, have children explain or describe its meaning.

- After reading, review Target Vocabulary and the definitions. (See p. T214.) Challenge children to use the words in their everyday speech. **ELA** L.2.6 **ELD** ELD PI.2.5

accepted
The student gave the teacher an apple. She accepted it.

Vocabulary in Context Cards 137–144

☑ **Target Vocabulary**

accepted
express
taught
grand
pretend
prize
wonder
fluttering

DAY 5

⟶ DOMAIN: **Communication**
LESSON TOPIC: Reading and Writing

Extend the Topic

▶ **SHARE OBJECTIVES**

- Acquire and use domain-specific vocabulary. LANGUAGE
- Participate in conversations about a topic. LANGUAGE
- Tell a story or recount an experience with facts and details. LANGUAGE

Words About the Topic:
Reading and Writing

- **print** writing (such as writing that appears in newspapers, magazines, and books)
- **journalist** a person who reports the news (in writing, on the radio, on television)
- **exchange** to give something in return for something else
- **publish** to produce and distribute a piece of work

Domain-Specific Vocabulary

Introduce Words About the Topic Remind children that this week's topic is Reading and Writing. Display the words shown at left. Tell children that these are words that can help them learn more about the topic. Read aloud the meaning of each word, and have children respond to the following prompts. **ELA** L.2.5a, L.2.6

- *What is the job of a journalist? investigating, interviewing people, writing a report, giving readers and listeners information*
- *Would you prefer to be a journalist who works for a newspaper, a magazine, or on television? Tell the reasons. Discuss students' responses.*
- *On some holidays, people _____ gifts. exchange*
- *What are some ways you can publish your work? Discuss students' responses.*

FOR STUDENTS WITH DISABILITIES To help children maintain their focus, intersperse periods of sitting still with prompted physical movements. If children begin to lose focus or fidget, have them remember where they are in a task and then stretch or walk around the room, and then go back to what they were doing at their seats.

Interact with the Words Have children work in small groups to create a Four-Square Map for each of the domain-specific words. For each of the domain-specific words, children should fold a blank sheet of paper into four equal sections. Work with them to follow the steps below for each word. As needed, display the meanings of the words on the board. Ask individual children to use the words in a sentence orally. Then write the sentence on the board for other children to copy.

1 In the first corner, draw a picture for the word.

2 In the second corner, write the meaning of the word.

3 In the third corner, write a sentence using the word.

4 In the fourth corner, write the word.

When groups have finished, have them share their Four-Square Maps with the class. **ELA** L.2.5a, L.2.6 **ELD** ELD.PI.2.1

ENGLISH LANGUAGE SUPPORT Guide children to interact with the words by discussing as a class questions such as these: *What print source do you rely on most to find out news? What words might describe a journalist? What would you like to exchange with a friend? What is the name of your favorite book that has been published?* **ELD** ELD.PI.2.1, ELD.PI.2.12a

Speaking and Listening:
Recount an Experience

Telling About an Experience Remind children about the main character in the book *My Name Is Gabriela*. Gabriela Mistral played school when she was a child, and when she grew up she became a teacher. In the book Gabriela tells about her experiences.

Display and read aloud the Tips for Telling About an Experience. Explain that:

• Telling the events in order will make it easy for listeners to follow what happened. The more facts and details you give, the more the listeners will understand what happened and how it made you feel.

• Using complete sentences makes what you say sound more important and polished. If you don't speak loudly and clearly enough to be heard, there's no point in speaking at all!

Teacher's Example Inform the class that you are going to give an example of how to tell about an experience. Tell the class about a time when someone taught you something. When you have finished, reread each tip above, and have children explain how you demonstrated that tip.

Practice in Pairs Tell children that they will be telling the class about an experience they've had. In pairs, have children think about a time when someone taught them to do something. Have them write down notes about their experience to refer to as they tell the story. Remind them to follow the tips from the chart and to think about the sequence of events, add important details, and provide a conclusion. Then have partners take turns explaining and sharing their experiences. They should also share how the experiences made them feel.

ENGLISH LANGUAGE SUPPORT Guide children to condense their ideas as they plan their presentation. Instead of using repetitive sentences such as *I went to the store. I went to my neighbor's house. Then I went home,* guide them to see how sentences sound better when combined, such as *I went to the store, to my neighbor's house, and then home.* **ELD** ELD.PII.2.7

Presentations After children have practiced with a partner, have them share their experiences with the class. Remind them to speak loudly and clearly and to use complete sentences. Allow time for questions at the end of each presentation. Remind children to ask questions to clarify, or help them understand, things the speaker said. Explain that they can also ask questions to get more information from the speaker or to understand the topic better. Reinforce children's examples of good questions by stating whether the question helps them clarify comprehension, get more information, or understand the topic better.
ELA SL.2.3, SL.2.4, SL.2.4a **ELD** ELD.PI.2.1, ELD.PI.2.9, ELD.PI.2.12a

Skill Focus: Identify Ideas and Supporting Evidence Explain to children that authors often give evidence, or reasons, to support their ideas. When they hear texts read aloud, they should listen for evidence to support ideas, too. Read aloud a portion of *My Name Is Gabriela*. Then ask children these questions:

• *Which details that you heard support the idea that Gabriela was determined to succeed?*

• *Which ideas that you heard support the fact that Gabriela loved words?*
ELA SL.2.2, SL.2.3 **ELD** ELD.PI.2.6

TIPS FOR TELLING ABOUT AN EXPERIENCE

1. **Tell events in order.**

2. **Tell facts and details to explain what happened and how it made you feel.**

3. **Use complete sentences.**

4. **Speak loud enough to be heard clearly.**

ENGLISH LANGUAGE SUPPORT

Use Sentence Frames

All Proficiencies Before children begin their discussions, explain what it means to describe people, places, things, and events. Point out that to describe something is to tell what it looks like. Explain that to describe an event is to tell what it feels like to be there. Model the describing skill for children using the following frames.

_____ *is an example of* _____.

_____ *is called* _____.

_____ *looks like* _____.

_____ *feels like* _____.

Point out that the verbs *is, are, can,* and *has* are often used when describing. Have children practice describing things and events in their conversations leading up to recounting a personal experience.
ELD ELD.PI.2.1, ELD.PI.2.12a

Grammar Weekly Review: The Verb *Be*

▶ **SHARE OBJECTIVES**

- **Grammar** Use correct forms of *be*. LANGUAGE
- **Spelling** Assess words with the long *e* sound spelled *y*.

ENGLISH LANGUAGE SUPPORT

How English Works: Productive

The Verb *Be* Remind children they should use *am, is,* or *was* if a sentence tells about one noun and *are* or *were* if a sentence is about more than one. Have partners make up sentences using the verbs *am, is, was, are,* or *were.* Call on partners to read them aloud. Have the class raise one hand if the sentence tells about one, and raise both hands if the sentence tells about more than one. **ELD** ELD.PII.2.3b

1 Review/Practice

The Verb *be* Read together the text on **Student Book** p. 118. Remind children that the following are all forms of the verb *be: am, is, are, was, were.*

- *The verbs am, is, and are tell about something happening now.*
- *The verbs was and were tell about something in the past.*
- Remind children to use *am, is,* or *was* if the sentence tells about one. Use *are* or *were* if the sentence tells about more than one.
- Have children complete the Try This! activity on the bottom of the page. Support them as they choose the correct form of the verb *be*. **ELD** ELD.PII.2.3b

2 Connect to Writing

- Read together **Student Book** p. 119. Review with children that they can combine two sentences that have the same subject. Read and discuss the examples in the chart.
- Ask, *Which sentences are choppy? Which sentence is smoother?*
- Together, read the directions for Connect Grammar to Writing [↗ at the bottom of the page. Provide support as children revise their paragraphs to combine sentences.
- Distribute Reader's Notebook Volume 2 page 45 [↗ to children to complete independently. **ELA** W.2.5 **ELD** ELD.PII.2.3b, ELD.PII.2.6

Spelling Long *e* Spelled *y*

SPELLING WORDS AND SENTENCES

BASIC

1. *happy** I smile when I am *happy.*
2. *pretty* That blue dress is *pretty.*
3. *baby** Our *baby* brother is cute.
4. *very* It is *very* cold outside.
5. *puppy* Our *puppy* is a poodle.
6. *funny* My aunt told a *funny* joke.
7. *carry* The bag was too heavy to *carry.*
8. *lucky* We were *lucky* the storm missed our town.
9. *only* This is my *only* pair of shoes.

10. *sunny* It will be *sunny* all day.
11. *penny* A *penny* is only one cent.
12. *city* We moved to a big *city.*

REVIEW

13. *tiny* My sock has a *tiny* hole.
14. *many* There are *many* children.

CHALLENGE

15. *sorry* I am *sorry* we missed the bus.
16. *noisy* The crowd at the game was *noisy.*

**A form of this word appears in the literature.*

Assess

Say each Spelling Word, read aloud its sentence, and then repeat the word. Have children write the word. **ELA** L.2.2d

Corrective Feedback

Review any words that children misspell. If children misspell two or more words, then revisit the Day 2 Pattern Sort activity on page 90 of the **Literacy and Language Guide.**

Grammar

The Verb be The **verbs** *am*, *is*, and *are* tell about something that is happening now. The verbs *was* and *were* tell about something that happened in the **past.** Use *am*, *is*, or *was* if the sentence tells about one noun. Use *are* or *were* if the sentence tells about more than one.

Now	In the Past
I am tired.	I was awake last night.
Ann is a teacher.	Ann was a teacher last year, too.
The boys are in Chile.	The boys were in Mexico last week.

Try This! Choose the correct verb to complete each sentence. Then write the sentence correctly.

1. Gabriela (is, are) famous.
2. Her students (was, were) grateful.
3. Her books (is, are) easy to find.
4. My grandfather (was, were) a big fan.

118 | ELA L.2.1d, L.2.1f ELD ELD.PII.2.3b, ELD.PII.2.6

You can combine sentences that have the same subject and verb. This will make your writing smoother.

Short, Choppy Sentences
The boy is a good reader.
The boy is a good writer.

Smoother Sentence
The boy is a good reader and writer.

Connect Grammar to Writing

When you revise your paragraph that describes, try combining sentences with the same subject and verb.

119

Try This!

1. Gabriela is famous.

2. Her students were grateful.

3. Her books are easy to find.

4. My grandfather was a big fan.

ENGLISH LANGUAGE SUPPORT

Comprehensible Input

Emerging Read the Try This! sentences aloud with each of the verb choices. Ask, *Which sentence is correct?* Reveal the answer and explain why it is correct. Have children say the sentence with the correct verb in place. ELD ELD.PII.2.3a

Expanding Have children identify the subject in each Try This! sentence and tell if it is singular or plural. Provide these sentence frames: *The subject in this sentence is _____. The correct verb is _____.* ELD ELD.PII.2.3a

Bridging Have children work with a partner to complete the Try This! activity. Have them write additional sentences using different subjects with the verbs in each sentence. ELD ELD.PII.2.3a

Narrative Writing Revise and Edit

▶ **SHARE OBJECTIVE**

- **Writing** Revise, edit, and publish a descriptive paragraph.

ENGLISH LANGUAGE SUPPORT

Peer-Supported Learning

All Proficiencies Provide ELL students with additional practice with sense words. Draw a five-column chart on the board. Use simple sketches for column titles: eye (look), hand (feel), nose (smell), ear (sound), and lips (taste). Work with children to brainstorm sense words for each category. Prompt them by asking questions, such as: *What words tell how something looks?* Have children work with a partner to add some of these words to their paragraphs where appropriate.

See the Peer Conference Forms in the *ELL Teacher's Handbook.*

Daily Proofreading Practice

gabriela wrote ~~meny~~ **many** stories. She won a Nobel ~~Prise~~ **Prize**.

WriteSmart Have children revise, proofread, and publish their narrative writing task through *my*WriteSmart.

---

1 Teach/Model

Descriptive Paragraph: Elaboration Remind children that choosing words that appeal to the five senses can make a description more real.

- Read the top of **Student Book** p. 120 with the class. Discuss the revisions made by the student writer, Alice.

- *How do Alice's revisions show the reader what the beach is like? She added words about how things looked, smelled, sounded, tasted, and felt.*

- To see and discuss revisions made by Alice, display Projectable 18.10 ⬀.

- Point out how Alice applied these skills: adding sense words and introducing the topic at the beginning.

2 Guided Practice/Apply

Descriptive Paragraph Read and discuss Alice's Final Copy on **Student Book** p. 121.

- Discuss the **Reading as a Writer** questions.

Revising Have children use the Writing Rubric Blackline Master ⬀ to evaluate their paragraphs. Have children suggest places where more details, including details that answer the questions *When? Where?* or *How?* can be added to the paragraph.

Proofreading Provide support as children proofread their paragraphs. Then have them use the Proofreading Checklist Blackline Master ⬀.

Handwriting If you have children write their final pieces rather than use digital tools, tell them to focus on using their best handwriting. *See also pp. R24–R29 for handwriting support.*

Publishing Have children make a final digital or paper copy and share their writing. **ELA** W.2.3, W.2.4, W.2.5, W.2.10, L.2.1g **ELD** ELD.PI.2.10, ELD.PII.2.1, ELD.PII.2.4, ELD.PII.2.5

Narrative Writing WriteSmart

☑ **Elaboration** You can use sense words to tell how things look, feel, smell, sound, and taste.

Alice wrote a draft of a **description.** She wanted to tell about her favorite place. Later, she added sense words to make her description come alive.

Writing Checklist

☑ **Purpose**
Did I make the readers feel like they are there?

☑ **Organization**
Did I start by telling what I am describing?

☑ **Elaboration**
Did I use sense words to tell more?

☑ **Conventions**
Have I combined ideas and sentences when I can?

Revised Draft

My family goes to Long

Beach almost every summer.

I love it at the beach. I

like walking on the ⌃soft, hot sand. I

love to listen to the ⌃pounding waves hit

the shore. The many smells

of ⌃spicy food make me hungry. My

brother usually buys me an ⌃a big, cool ice

cream cone. ⌃ It always tastes delicious!

Final Copy

Our Summers at Long Beach
by Alice O'Brien

My family goes to Long Beach almost every summer. I love it at the beach. I like walking on the soft, hot sand. I love to listen to the pounding waves hit the shore. The many smells of spicy food make me hungry. My brother usually buys me a big, cool ice cream cone. It always tastes delicious!

Reading as a Writer

Which sense words did Alice add? What sense words can you add to your story?

I used sense words to tell the reader more about how things look, feel, smell, taste, and sound.

120 | ELA W.2.3, W.2.4, W.2.5, W.2.10 ELD ELD.PI.2.10, ELD.PI.2.12b, ELD.PII.2.4

121

NARRATIVE WRITING RUBRIC   See also the Multipurpose Writing Rubric on p. R18.

Score	4	3	2	1	NS
Purpose/Organization	The narrative is clear and well organized. It is appropriately sequenced and has closure. • Plot contains a well-elaborated event or a short sequence of events • Setting and characters are included and well-maintained • Plot events follow a logical sequence • Includes an effective conclusion	The narrative is generally clear and organized. The sequence is adequately maintained, and the plot has closure. • Plot contains a well-elaborated event or a short sequence of events • Characters and setting are included and adequately maintained • Plot events follow an understandable sequence • Includes an adequate conclusion	The narrative is somewhat organized but may be unclear in parts. The sequence is weak. The plot lacks closure. • Minimal development of plot • Characters and setting are included but are minimally maintained • Sequence of events is poorly organized • Conclusion is inadequate or missing	The narrative's focus is unclear, and it is poorly organized. The narrative lacks sequence and has no closure. • Little or no plot • No attempt to maintain characters or setting • Sequence of events is not organized • Conclusion is missing	• not intelligible • not written in English • not on topic • contains text copied from another source • does not address the purpose for writing
Development/Elaboration	The narrative includes effective elaboration, and details describing actions, thoughts, and feelings. • Clear effort to develop experiences, characters, setting, and events • Contains strong use of details • Writer uses temporal words to signal the order of events	The narrative includes adequate elaboration, and details describing actions, thoughts, and feelings. • Some attempt to develop experiences, characters, setting, and events • Contains adequate use of details • Contains adequate use of temporal words to signal the order of events	The narrative includes only partial or ineffective elaboration. The narrative includes some details. • Little attempt to develop experiences, characters, setting, and events • Contains weak use of details • Contains little use of temporal words. • Order of events is not clear	The narrative provides little or no elaboration and few details. • No attempt to develop experiences, characters, setting, and events • Few or no details • No use of temporal words • Order of events is confusing	• not intelligible • not written in English • not on topic • contains text copied from another source • does not develop the writing

Score	2	1	0	NS
Conventions	The narrative demonstrates adequate command of conventions. • Consistent use of complete sentences, correct sentence structures, punctuation, capitalization, grammar, spelling	The narrative demonstrates partial command of conventions. • Limited use of complete sentences, correct sentence structures, punctuation, capitalization, grammar, spelling	The narrative demonstrates little or no command of conventions. • Does not use complete sentences, correct sentence structures, punctuation, capitalization, grammar, spelling	• not intelligible • not written in English • not on topic • contains text copied from another source

Formative Assessment

Weekly Tests

At the end of the lesson, administer the Weekly Test. This will give you a **snapshot of how children are progressing** with the Reading and Language Arts skills in this lesson and can give you **guidance on grouping, reteaching, and intervention.** Suggestions for adjusting instruction based on these results can be found on the next page.

Access Through Accommodations

When you administer the Weekly Test, some children may have problems accessing all or parts of the assessment. The purpose of the Weekly Test is to determine children's ability to complete the Reading and Language Arts tasks they learned in this lesson. Any barriers to them accessing the tasks demanded of them should be lowered so they can focus on skill demonstration.

When choosing accommodations, you will want to avoid invalidating the test results if you are measuring a child's reading skill. For example, you will not want to read aloud the passage. The following accommodations, if needed, will not interfere with the Weekly Test's validity:

- Read aloud the assessment directions and item prompts. If children are English learners, read aloud the assessment directions and item prompts in the child's native language, if possible.

- Define any unknown words in the directions or item prompts that do not give away the answers to the items.

- Allow for a break during the assessment.

- Simplify the language of assessment directions and item prompts.

- Administer the assessment in a smaller group setting.

- Administer the assessment on a computer or other electronic device.

- Provide audio amplification equipment, colored overlays, or visual magnifying equipment to maintain visual/audio attention and access.

- Allow children to complete the assessment items orally or by having another person transcribe their responses.

Using Data to Adjust Instruction

Use children's scores on the Weekly Test to determine Small Group placement, reteaching, and potential for intervention.

☑ VOCABULARY AND COMPREHENSION

Understanding Characters; Author's Word Choice; Anchor Text

Target Vocabulary; Suffixes -y and -ful

IF STUDENT SCORES...

...at acceptable,	...below acceptable,
THEN continue core instruction.	**THEN** use Reteach Comprehension Skill and Vocabulary Strategies lessons. For struggling students, administer the *Intervention Assessments* to determine if students would benefit from intervention.

☑ PHONICS

The Long e Sound for y; Changing y to i

IF STUDENT SCORES...

...at acceptable,	...below acceptable,
THEN continue core instruction.	**THEN** use Reteach Phonics lesson. Administer the *Intervention Assessments* to determine if students would benefit from intervention.

☑ LANGUAGE ARTS

The Verb *Be*

IF STUDENT SCORES...

...at acceptable,	...below acceptable,
THEN continue core instruction.	**THEN** use Reteach Language Arts lesson. Administer the *Intervention Assessments* to determine if students would benefit from intervention.

☑ FLUENCY

Fluency Plan

Assess one group per week using the <u>Fluency Tests</u> [↗ in the *Grab-and-Go™* Resources. Use the suggested plan at the right.

🔵 **Struggling Readers**	Weeks 1, 2, 3
🔺 **On Level**	Week 2
🟥 **Advanced**	Week 5

IF...

...students are reading on-level text fluently,	...students are reading below level,
THEN continue core instruction.	**THEN** provide additional fluency practice using the **Student Book,** the **Cold Reads,** and the Leveled Readers. For struggling students, administer the *Intervention Assessments* to determine if students would benefit from intervention.

JOURNEYS

Cold Reads

2

The ***Cold Reads*** passages increase gradually in Lexile® measures throughout the year, from below grade level to above grade level.

- Each passage is accompanied by several selected-response questions and one constructed-response prompt, requiring children to read closely, answer questions at substantial DOK levels, and cite text evidence.

- The ***Cold Reads*** may be used to provide practice in reading increasingly complex texts and to informally monitor children's progress.

- The ***Cold Reads*** may be used to estimate children's Lexile® levels in order to recommend appropriately challenging books for small-group instruction or independent reading.

→

Turn the page for more information about using **FORMATIVE ASSESSMENT** for **ELD AND INTERVENTION.**

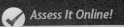
Formative Assessment for ELD and Intervention

Formative Assessment for English Learners

English learners should engage in the same rigorous curriculum and formative assessment as other students. However, it is important to remember that English learners face a dual challenge: they are strengthening their abilities *to use* English at the same time that they are learning challenging content *through* English. Use the following strategies and resources for ongoing assessment of English language development, in addition to the assessments you use with all children:

- A combination of **observational measures,** such as listening in as children read aloud or participate in collaborative conversations. Be prepared to provide **"just-in-time" scaffolding** to support students. For example, if children are retelling a story, you could help them use sentence structures with past-tense verbs and time-order transition words.

- **Constructive feedback** that focuses on communication and meaning-making. Avoid overcorrecting in a way that makes English learners reluctant to speak up. You might try recasting a child's statement more correctly, making a note to address the target form more directly during Designated ELD time.

- **Student self-assessment,** through children's own notes in their vocabulary notebooks or other learning journals. If possible, meet with each child to review his or her self-assessments and provide encouragement and feedback.

- **Formative assessment** notes that are integrated into the Language Workshop Teacher's Guide for use during Designated ELD.

- **Language Workshop Assessment Handbook** for longer-cycle assessment to make sure students are progressing in their English development.

Response to Intervention  **RtI**

Use the Weekly Tests and Benchmark and Unit Tests, along with your own observations, to determine if individual students are not responding to primary instruction and need additional testing to identify specific needs for targeted intervention.

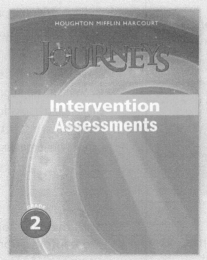

Intervention Assessments

Assessment for Intervention

Administer these assessments to

- children who are receiving supplemental intervention to gauge progress toward exit from the intervention program.

- children who demonstrate lack of success with Weekly Tests, Benchmark and Unit Tests, and core instruction to determine if they might benefit from additional practice or intervention.

SMALL GROUP

Differentiate Phonics
- The Long *e* Sound for *y*

Vocabulary Reader
- *All About Chile*

Differentiate Comprehension
- Understanding Characters
- Analyze/Evaluate

Differentiate
Phonics & Fluency
- Changing *y* to *i*
- Expression

Leveled Readers
- ⬤ *Beatrix Potter*
- ▲ *The Life of Jack Prelutsky*
- ⬛ *The Life of Langston Hughes*
- ◆ *Jack Prelutsky*

Differentiate
Vocabulary Strategies
- Suffixes *-y* and *-ful*

Options for Reteaching
- Phonics
- Language Arts
- Vocabulary Strategies
- Comprehension

Literacy Centers

Independent Practice
- Word Study, T206
- Think and Write, T207
- Comprehension and Fluency, T206

		DAY 1	DAY 2	DAY 3
Teacher-Led	**Struggling Readers**	**Vocabulary Reader,** *All About Chile,* Differentiated Instruction, p. T286 **Differentiate Phonics:** Long *e* Sound for *y*, p. T284 **English Language Support,** pp. T285, T287	**Differentiate Comprehension:** Understanding Characters; Analyze/Evaluate, p. T288 **Reread** *Bunny and the Penny* **English Language Support,** p. T289	**Leveled Reader** *Beatrix Potter,* p. T292 **Differentiate Phonics:** Changing *y* to *i*, p. T290 **English Language Support,** Leveled Reader Teacher's Guide, p. 5
	On Level	**Vocabulary Reader,** *All About Chile,* Differentiated Instruction, p. T286 **English Language Support,** pp. T285, T287	**Differentiate Comprehension:** Understanding Characters; Analyze/Evaluate, p. T288 **Reread** *Bunny and the Penny* **English Language Support,** p. T289	**Leveled Reader** *The Life of Jack Prelutsky,* p. T293 *Jack Prelutsky,* p. T295 **Differentiate Fluency:** Expression, p. T291 **English Language Support,** Leveled Reader Teacher's Guide, p. 5
	Advanced	**Vocabulary Reader,** *All About Chile,* Differentiated Instruction, p. T287 **English Language Support,** pp. T285, T287	**Differentiate Comprehension:** Understanding Characters; Analyze/Evaluate, p. T289 **English Language Support,** p. T289	**Leveled Reader** *The Life of Langston Hughes,* p. T294 **Differentiate Fluency:** Expression, p. T291 **English Language Support,** Leveled Reader Teacher's Guide, p. 5
What are my other children doing?	**Struggling Readers**	**Word Building:** • Leveled Practice, SR18.1	**Partners:** Vocabulary in Context Cards 137–144 **Partners:** Reread *Bunny and the Penny* • Leveled Practice, SR18.2	**Partners:** Reread Leveled Reader *Beatrix Potter* • Leveled Practice, SR18.3
	On Level	**Word Building:** Build and read words with long *e* sound for *y* using Letter Cards **Complete** Reader's Notebook, pp. 31–32 or Leveled Practice, EL18.1	**Target Vocabulary:** Practice reading using Vocabulary in Context Cards 137–144 **Reread** *Bunny and the Penny* **Complete** Reader's Notebook, pp. 33–36 or Leveled Practice, EL18.2	**Partners:** Reread Leveled Reader *The Life of Jack Prelutsky* or *Jack Prelutsky* **Complete** Reader's Notebook, pp. 37–41 or Leveled Practice, EL18.3
	Advanced	**Vocabulary in Context Cards** 137–144 *Talk It Over* activities • Leveled Practice, A18.1	**Reread** *My Name Is Gabriela,* **Student Book,** pp. 90–109 • Leveled Practice, A18.2	**Partners:** Reread Leveled Reader *The Life of Langston Hughes* • Leveled Practice, A18.3

For strategic intervention for this lesson, see pp. S22–S31.

DAY 4	DAY 5	English Language Support

DAY 4

Differentiate Vocabulary Strategies: Suffixes -*y*, -*ful*, p. T296
Reread *Puppies*
English Language Support, p. T297

Differentiate Vocabulary Strategies: Suffixes -*y*, -*ful*, p. T296
Reread *Puppies*
English Language Support, p. T297

Differentiate Vocabulary Strategies: Suffixes -*y*, -*ful*, p. T297
English Language Support, p. T297

Partners: Reread *Puppies*
• Leveled Practice, SR18.4

Reread *Puppies*
Complete Reader's Notebook, pp. 42–44 or Leveled Practice, EL18.4

Partners: Reread *Poems About Reading and Writing,* **Student Book,** pp. 114–117
• Leveled Practice, A18.4

DAY 5

Options for Reteaching, pp. T298–T299
Reread *Bunny and the Penny* or *Puppies* or one of this week's Blend-It Books.

Options for Reteaching, pp. T298–T299
Reread *Bunny and the Penny* or *Puppies* or one of this week's Blend-It Books.

Options for Reteaching, pp. T298–T299
Reread *Bunny and the Penny* or *Puppies* or one of this week's Blend-It Books.

Partners: Choose among stories for this week to reread
• Complete and share Literacy Center activities

Partners: Reread Leveled Reader *The Life of Jack Prelutsky* or *Jack Prelutsky*
• Complete and share Literacy Center activities
• Self-Selected Reading
Complete Reader's Notebook, p. 45

Partners: Reread Leveled Reader *The Life of Langston Hughes*
• Complete and share Literacy Center activities
• Self-Selected Reading

English Language Support

Use the Leveled Reader Teacher's Guide to support ELs during differentiated instruction.

- **Characteristics of the Text** (p. 1)

  Identify challenging language features, such as text structure, literary features, complex sentences, and vocabulary.

- **Cultural Support/Cognates/Vocabulary** (p. 5)

  Explain unfamiliar features of English and help ELs transfer first-language knowledge.

- **Oral Language Development** (p. 5)

  Check comprehension using dialogues that match children's proficiency levels.

Book Share

Use this routine at the end of the week to show children that they have become experts on their Leveled Readers.

Step 1:

Help each group write a presentation of their Leveled Reader **Responding** page. Use the following routine:

- Briefly tell what your book is about.

- Show your graphic organizer and explain what you added to complete it.

- Tell about your favorite part of the book.

Every child should have his or her own presentation to share with a new group.

Step 2:

Have children number off. Assign places in the classroom for 1s to gather, 2s, and so on. Help children find their new groups.

Step 3:

Have children take turns sharing their book presentations in the new groups. Continue until all children have finished sharing. Encourage children to ask questions. Give the following frames for support.

Can you tell me more about _____?

I wonder why _____?

What do you think about _____?

Differentiate Phonics
Words with the Long *e* Sound for *y*

Struggling Readers

ELA RF.2.3b
ELD ELD.PI.2.1

I DO IT

- Display **Picture Card** *penny*. Name the picture, emphasizing the final sound, /ē/.

- Write *penny* and underline *y*. *The letter y stands for the final sound /ē/ in penny.*

Use Instructional Routine 3 🔗 to model how to blend *penny*.

- Blend the sounds. *Listen: /p/ /ĕ/ /n/ /ē/, penny.* Have children blend with you. *Now you blend the sounds: /p/ /ĕ/ /n/ /ē/, penny.*

- Repeat with *bunny*, pointing out the *y* spelling for /ē/.

WE DO IT

- Say the following word pairs and have children identify the word with the final sound /ē/ in each of the pairs: *peace, pretty; city, sight; even, funny; keep, tricky.*

- On the board, write the following words: *pretty, city, funny, tricky, furry, lucky, messy, slippery, easy.*

- Help children blend the sounds to read the words. Use the **Corrective Feedback** steps if children need additional help.

YOU DO IT

- Have partners take turns using **Letter Cards** to create words with long *e* spelled *y*.

- Have children record the words they make and read the list to the group.

- Have children reread the **Decodable Reader** *Bunny and the Penny*.

FORMATIVE ASSESSMENT

Corrective Feedback

When a child mispronounces a word, point to the word and say it. Call attention to the element that was mispronounced, say the sound, and then guide children to read the word. See the example below.

Phonics Error:

A child reads *lucky* with long *i*.

Correct the error. Say the word and the sound. *The word is* lucky; *the letter* y *stands for the final sound /ē/ in* lucky.

Model as you touch the letters. *I'll blend: /l/ /ŭ/ /k/ /ē/. What's the word?* lucky

---

Guide *Let's blend together: /l/ /ŭ/ /k/ /ē/. What's the word?* lucky

---

Check *You blend. /l/ /ŭ/ /k/ /ē/ What's the word?* lucky

Reinforce Go back two words and have children continue reading. Make note of errors and review those words during the next lesson.

English Language Support

ELD ELD.PI.2.1

Provide Struggling Readers, On Level, and Advanced ELs proficiency-level support during differentiated instruction. Give children in all groups extra practice identifying words that contain long e spelled y.

- Explain that the spelling *y* stands for the sound /ē/ at the end of a word with two or more syllables.

- Write and say the words *muddy* and *sunny*. Underline the long e spelling in each word. Blend the words and have children repeat after you.

- Have children identify more words containing the long e sound for *y*. Children may refer to the **Decodable Reader** *Bunny and the Penny* or think of words on their own.

Emerging	**Expanding**	**Bridging**
• Write the words *candy, copy, pony,* and *story*. Read each word aloud. Help children point out the long e spelling in each word.	• Write *candy, copy, pony,* and *story*. Have children read the words and copy them on a sheet of paper. Have children underline the long e spelling in each word.	• Have children write three or four words that contain long e spelled *y*. Have children use two of their words in a complete sentence. Have children share their sentences.

On Level

See Literacy Centers—Unit 4 Lesson 18 Word Study

If children have time after completing the purple activity, have them try moving on to the blue activity.

Advanced

See Literacy Centers—Unit 4 Lesson 18 Word Study

If children have time after completing the blue activity, have them reread the **Decodable Reader** *Bunny and the Penny* or another book independently.

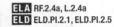
Vocabulary Reader
All About Chile

Summary

Chile is a country in South America with many places to visit and sites to see. People in Chile are very friendly.

☑ **TARGET VOCABULARY**

accepted	pretend
express	prize
taught	wonder
grand	fluttering

Struggling Readers

ELA RF.2.4a, L.2.4a
ELD ELD.PI.2.1, ELD.PI.2.5

- Explain to children that Chile is a country in South America with many beautiful landscapes and friendly people.

- Guide children to preview the selection. Ask children to describe the images, using Target Vocabulary when possible.

- Have children alternate reading pages of the selection aloud. Guide them to use context to determine the meanings of unfamiliar words (or phrases). As necessary, use the **Vocabulary in Context Cards** to review how the Target Vocabulary words are used.

- Have partners work together to complete the Responding page. Then review the directions on Blackline Master 18.4 and guide children to complete it.

On Level

ELA RF.2.4a, L.2.4a
ELD ELD.PI.2.1, ELD.PI.2.5

- Explain to children that Chile is a unique country with many beautiful landscapes. Guide children to preview the selection.

- Remind children that context clues can help them determine the meaning of an unfamiliar word (or phrase).

- Have children alternate reading pages of the selection aloud. Tell them to use context clues to confirm their understanding of how Target Vocabulary words are used and to learn the meanings of unfamiliar words (or phrases).

- Assign the Responding page and Blackline Master 18.4. Review the directions with children. Have children discuss their responses with a partner.

Advanced

ELA RF.2.4a, L.2.4a
ELD ELD.PI.2.1, ELD.PI.2.5

- Explain to children that Chile is a unique country with many beautiful landscapes. Guide children to preview the selection.

- Remind children that context clues can help them determine the meaning of an unfamiliar word (or phrase).

- Have children alternate reading pages of the selection aloud. Tell them to use context clues to confirm their understanding of how Target Vocabulary words are used and to learn the meanings of unfamiliar words (or phrases).

- Assign the Responding page and Blackline Master 18.4 [ ]. Review the directions with children. Have children discuss their responses with a partner.

English Language Support

ELD ELD.PI.2.1

Provide Struggling Readers, On Level, and Advanced ELs proficiency-level support during differentiated instruction.

Emerging

- Help children prepare for the Word Builder activity on the Responding page. Use the **Vocabulary in Context Card** for *prize* to teach the meaning of the word.

- Then help children brainstorm other examples of prizes and help them fill out the word web with their responses.

Expanding

- Help children prepare for the Write About It activity on the Responding page. Give them sentence frames they can copy and complete to tell about what makes their prize of choice special. For example: _____ *is a special type of prize. It is special because* _____.

Bridging

- Have partners preview the Vocabulary Reader by studying the images and summarizing what they see. Then have partners read sections to each other, stopping to use context to define unknown words. Use the following frames to support participation: *I think the word* _____ *means* _____ *because* _____.

Responding

✓ **TARGET VOCABULARY** **Word Builder**
Make a word web around the word *prize*. What things can be a prize? Copy this word web and add more words.

trophy — prize — ?
money — ?

✓ **Write About It**
Text to World Choose a prize from the Word Builder. Write a few sentences about the prize and what makes it special.

11

All About Chile, p. 11

Differentiate Comprehension
Understanding Characters; Analyze/Evaluate

Struggling Readers

ELA RI.2.6
ELD ELD.PI.2.1, ELD.PI.2.6

I DO IT

- Point out that readers make decisions about characters by analyzing what they do and say.

- Read aloud **Student Book** p. 95. Model analyzing details to evaluate characters.

  Think Aloud *This page tells what Gabriela imagined. I think Gabriela would be a great friend because she would use her imagination to play fun games.*

WE DO IT

- Have children read **Student Book** pp. 100–101.

- Have each child identify the details that describe Gabriela as a pretend teacher. As children share each detail, have them tell how it affected their opinion of Gabriela.

- Use these details from the selection to create a Column Chart on the board, labeling the charts three columns: Words, Thoughts, Actions.

YOU DO IT

- Have children complete a Column Chart about Gabriela.

- Provide time for children to share their charts with a partner.

- Encourage partners to notice whether their opinions about Gabriela are the same or different.

On Level

ELA RI.2.6
ELD ELD.PI.2.1, ELD.PI.2.6

I DO IT

- Read aloud **Student Book** p. 97. Explain that the author tells two things Gabriela did. We can figure out several things about Gabriela just from these two details.

- Use Projectable S7 to model analyzing details to evaluate characters.

  Think Aloud *The selection says that Gabriela taught herself to read, and that she read about many things. Some kids read about many things, but not many teach themselves to read. Gabriela must have been a very smart child!*

WE DO IT

- Help children to continue working with p. 97. Ask, *What else can you learn about Gabriela from this page?*

- Have children suggest Gabriela's character traits. Ask them to support their responses with ideas from the text.

- Help children create a Column Chart for p. 97.

YOU DO IT

- Ask children to create Column Charts to show traits they believe Gabriela has. Remind them to support the traits with text details.

- Provide time for small groups to share their Column Charts with each other.

- Then ask the groups to discuss this question: *Would you like to have a friend like Gabriela? Why or why not?*

Advanced

ELA RI.2.6
ELD ELD.PI.2.1, ELD.PI.2.6

I DO IT

- Point out that readers put together ideas from different parts of a text to form opinions.

- Read aloud **Student Book** p. 103. Model using ideas from different parts of the text to evaluate the character.

  Think Aloud *This page says that many of Gabriela's students became teachers. This detail makes me think that her students must have admired her and wanted to be like her.*

WE DO IT

- Have children read **Student Book** p. 108 independently.

- Ask, *What do you learn about the kind of person Gabriela was from the details on this page?*

- Discuss with children what in Gabriela's childhood led her to become this kind of person. Ask, *Why might people admire Gabriela?*

YOU DO IT

- Ask children to create a Column Chart to show Gabriela's character traits. Encourage them to add as many columns as necessary.

- Then ask children to think of a short description of Gabriela's personality. Tell them to support their ideas with details from their Column Chart.

- Allow children to create a drawing of Gabriela to accompany their description.

English Language Support

ELD ELD.PI.2.1

Provide Struggling Readers, On Level, and Advanced ELs proficiency-level support during differentiated instruction.

Emerging

- Before children fill in their Column Charts, have them look at and use the illustrations in *My Name Is Gabriela*. Ask them to use their own words to describe Gabriela.

- Ask children why they think the illustrator chose to include details such as butterflies in the drawings.

Expanding

- As children fill in their Column Charts, work with them to come up with words that describe Gabriela, such as *teacher*. Ask children to match each word with one of the illustrations and describe what the picture tells them about the character. Have children pick out other words or phrases that describe Gabriela.

Bridging

- As children fill in their Column Charts, have them think about why Gabriela chose to travel the world. Have them scan the selection for details and use them to write one or two sentences about this.

- Have children think about which places Gabriela visited. They can look for the information in the text and in the selection's illustrations. Ask them to say what Gabriela's travels tell them about her personality.

Differentiate Phonics and Fluency

Struggling Readers

ELA RF.2.3b, RF.2.3e
ELD ELD.PIII.2

Phonics

Changing *y* to *i*

I DO IT

- Display **Letter Cards** *l, a, d, y*. Use <u>Instructional Routine 3</u> to blend and read *lady*.

- Use *lady* in a sentence. *The kind lady at the store helped me choose a gift for my mom.*

- Use **Letter Cards** *i, e, s* to model changing the *y* in *lady* to *i* and adding the ending *-es*. *To make the word ladies, I change the* y *in* lady *to* i *and add the ending* -es.

- Use the **Continuous Blending Routine** to blend and read *ladies*. Then use *ladies* in a sentence.

| l | a | d | i | e | s |

The ladies in the book group all agreed that the story was well written.

Repeat the procedure with the words *penny* and *pennies*.

WE DO IT

- Display **Letter Cards** *d, a, i, s, y*. Blend and read *daisy*. Then have children blend and read the word with you.

| d | a | i | s | y |

- Ask a volunteer to use *daisy* in a sentence. Then ask: *How can you change the word* daisy *to* daisies? *We can change the* y *to* i *and add* -es.

- Work with children to use **Letter Cards** *i, e, s* to change the *y* in *daisy* to *i* and add the ending *-es*.

| d | a | i | s | i | e | s |

- Blend and read *daisies* together. Then ask a volunteer to use the word in a sentence.

- Have children use **Letter Cards** to build *puppy*. Repeat the procedure above to have children build *puppies*. Provide **Corrective Feedback** as needed.

YOU DO IT

- Have children use **Letter Cards** to build and read the words *penny/pennies, lady/ladies, baby/babies,* and *pony/ponies*.

- Have partners take turns using the words in sentences.

FORMATIVE ASSESSMENT  RtI

Corrective Feedback

When a child mispronounces a word, point to the word and say it. Call attention to the element that was mispronounced, say the sound, and then guide children to read the word. See the example below.

Phonics Error:

A child builds *puppies* as *puppes*.

Correct the error. Say the word. *The word is* puppies; *the* y *in* puppy *is changed to* i *before adding* -es.

Model using **Letter Cards** to build *puppies*. *I'll change the* y *in* puppy *to* i *before I add* -es.

Guide *What do you need to do to the final* y *in* puppy *before you can add* -es? *Change the* y *to* i.

Check *You spell* puppy. *p-u-p-p-y Now spell* puppies. *p-u-p-p-i-e-s*

Reinforce Have children practice building more words. Note any errors and review those words during later lessons.

All Levels

ELA RF.2.4b

Fluency

Expression

I DO IT

- Write this sentence from *My Name is Gabriela*: *But I also wrote poems about animals—about parrots and peacocks and even rats!*

- Use a Think Aloud as you look at the sentence and decide how to read with expression.

> **Think Aloud** *As I look at this sentence, I think about how I can use my voice to show the author's feelings about the subject. I'll look at the punctuation in the sentence for clues about how to read it. The dash shows that I should pause in the middle of the sentence. The exclamation mark tells me to show excitement in my voice. I'll also underline important words to remind myself to be more expressive when I read them.*

- Model reading the sentence with appropriate expression.

WE DO IT

- Write two sentences from *Beatrix Potter*, *The Life of Jack Prelutsky*, *The Life of Langston Hughes*, and *Jack Prelutsky*.

- Have individuals circle punctuation they can use as clues for how to read the sentences with expression.

- Then ask volunteers to underline important words and phrases they will read with expression. Remind them to think about the author's or the characters' feelings about the subjects.

- Have children take turns reading the sentences with expression.

YOU DO IT

- Have partners choose a page from a **Leveled Reader** and take turns reading aloud.

- Monitor and provide **Corrective Feedback** as needed.

FORMATIVE ASSESSMENT **RtI**

Corrective Feedback Work with children to correct errors, following the model below.

Fluency Error:
A child reads a sentence in a monotone voice.

Correct the error. Remind children to read as if they are telling a story to a friend.

Model reading a sentence with expression. *Listen to how my voice shows emotion as I read this sentence.*

Guide children to make their voices higher or lower and louder or softer as they read.

Check that children can read the sentence with appropriate expression.

Reinforce Have children go back a sentence or two and begin reading on their own again.

Leveled Readers

☑ **TARGET SKILL**
Understanding Characters

☑ **TARGET STRATEGY**
Analyze/Evaluate

☑ **TARGET VOCABULARY**

accepted	express
fluttering	grand
pretend	prize
taught	wonder

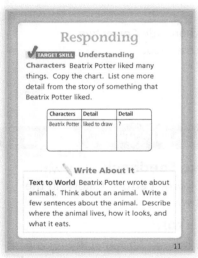

Beatrix Potter, p. 11

Struggling Readers

ELA RI.2.1, RF.2.4a, RF.2.4b
ELD ELD.PI.2.1, ELD.PI.2.6

Beatrix Potter

Summary Beatrix Potter began drawing pictures of animals and nature when she was young. Then she began writing stories about her pictures and became a children's author.

Genre: Biography

Introducing the Text

- Explain that Beatrix Potter was a children's author who loved to write stories about animals and draw her own pictures.

- Remind children that using a Column Map can help them keep track of information about characters.

Supporting the Reading

- **pp. 4–5** *Think about the facts you read on these pages. Do you think the author did a good job of telling about Beatrix Potter's life? Why?* **Sample answer:** *Yes, I think the author did a good job of telling about Beatrix Potter's life because I learned what she liked as a young girl, how she became an artist, and what she did with her art.*

- **p. 8** *Why do you think Beatrix Potter moved to the country and lived on a farm?* *She still loved animals and nature and wanted to be near them.*

Discussing and Revisiting the Text

Critical Thinking After they discuss the book, have children read the instructions on the top half of Responding p. 11 in *Beatrix Potter*.

- Have partners complete Blackline Master 18.5 .

FLUENCY: EXPRESSION Model reading p. 6 with expression. Then have partners echo-read p. 6 and focus on reading with expression.

On Level

ELA RI.2.1, RF.2.4a, RF.2.4b
ELD ELD.PI.2.1, ELD.PI.2.6

 ## *The Life of Jack Prelutsky*

Summary Jack Prelutsky didn't like poetry when he was young. It didn't make him laugh. When Jack was older, he began to write funny and scary poems that people loved.

Genre: Biography

Introducing the Text

• Explain that Jack Prelutsky is a poet who loves to write funny poems for children and adults.

• Remind children that they should look for and keep track of information that will help them better understand the person in the biography better.

Supporting the Reading

• **p. 3** *Why didn't Jack like poetry when he was growing up? What does this tell you about him?* When Jack was growing up, he didn't like poetry because it didn't make him laugh; it tells me that Jack likes to laugh.

• **pp. 3–7** *What do these pages tell us about Jack Prelutsky? Did the author do a good job of introducing you to this poet? Explain.* **Sample answer:** *The pages tell facts about Jack Prelutsky's life. Yes, the author did a good job because I feel like I know a lot about Jack Prelutsky now.*

Discussing and Revisiting the Text

Critical Thinking After they discuss the book, have children read the instructions on the top half of Responding p. 15 in *The Life of Jack Prelutsky.*

• Have children write details in the appropriate columns to complete Blackline Master 18.6 .

FLUENCY: EXPRESSION Have children practice reading their favorite parts of *The Life of Jack Prelutsky* using punctuation marks as a guide to help them read with expression.

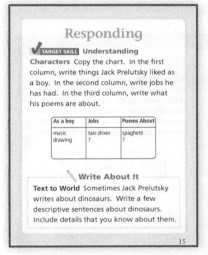

The Life of Jack Prelutsky, p. 15

Leveled Readers

☑ **TARGET SKILL**
Understanding Characters

☑ **TARGET STRATEGY**
Analyze/Evaluate

☑ **TARGET VOCABULARY**

accepted	express
fluttering	grand
pretend	prize
taught	wonder

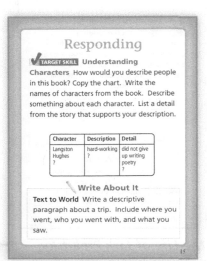

The Life of Langston Hughes, p. 15

Advanced

ELA RI.2.1, RF.2.4a, RF.2.4b
ELD ELD.PI.2.1, ELD.PI.2.6

 The Life of Langston Hughes

Summary Langston Hughes wrote poetry all the time when he was young, and he won poetry awards. His father didn't want him to be a poet. This made it hard for Langston.

Genre: Biography

Introducing the Text

- Explain that Langston Hughes was a poet who wrote about the people in the neighborhoods, cities, and other places where he lived and visited.

- Point out that biographies give important facts. As they are reading, children should look for and record information about the subject to help them better understand the person's life and personality.

Supporting the Reading

- **pp. 12–13** *How does the author help you get to know Langston Hughes better by writing about his trip to Africa? He wrote poetry about the people and sent it back to the United States to be published. I think that he was proud to be an African American.*

- **p. 14** *When do these events happen in Langston's life? Do you think the author did a good job by including these events? Why?* **Sample answer:** *They take place toward the end of Langston's life. I think the author did a good job by including these events because a biography can tell about a person's entire life.*

Discussing and Revisiting the Text

Critical Thinking After they discuss the book, have children read the instructions on the top half of Responding p. 15 in *The Life of Langston Hughes.*

- Have children work individually or in pairs to read the character details.

- Have them complete Blackline Master 18.7 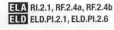.

FLUENCY: EXPRESSION Have children practice reading their favorite parts of *The Life of Langston Hughes,* focusing on reading with expression.

English Language Support

ELD ELD.PI.2.1, ELD.PI.2.6

◆ *Jack Prelutsky*

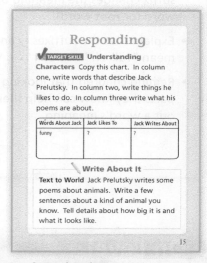

Summary Jack Prelutsky is a poet who had many different jobs. First he was a singer, but later Jack decided to write poems.

Genre: Biography

Introducing the Text

• Explain that Jack Prelutsky, the poet, had many jobs before he started to write poetry.

• Remind children that they can use a Column Map to help keep track of details they learn about each character as they read.

Supporting the Reading

• **p. 3** *Why didn't Jack like the poems he read when he was a boy?* He didn't like them because he thought they were boring.

• **p. 5** *This page tells about things Jack did before he started to write poetry. Did the author do a good job by telling these things? Why?* **Sample answer:** *The author did a good job because these are things that tell about Jack and his life. They tell that Jack likes many other things besides poetry.*

Discussing and Revisiting the Text

Critical Thinking After they discuss the book, have children read the instructions on the top half of Responding p. 15 in *Jack Prelutsky*.

• Have them write details in the appropriate columns on <u>Blackline Master 18.8</u>.

FLUENCY: EXPRESSION Have children listen as you read p. 10 with appropriate expression. Have them echo-read, using appropriate expression.

Responding

✓ **TARGET SKILL** **Understanding Characters** Copy this chart. In column one, write words that describe Jack Prelutsky. In column two, write things he likes to do. In column three write what his poems are about.

Words About Jack	Jack Likes To	Jack Writes About
funny	?	?

✎ **Write About It**

Text to World Jack Prelutsky writes some poems about animals. Write a few sentences about a kind of animal you know. Tell details about how big it is and what it looks like.

15

Jack Prelutsky, p. 15

Differentiate Vocabulary Strategies
Suffixes -y, -ful

Struggling Readers

ELA RF.2.3d, L.2.4c
ELD ELD.PI.2.1

I DO IT

- Display the word: *fluttering*. Then write the base word (or root word) *flutter* on the board.

- Explain that suffixes are word parts added to the ends of words. Adding a suffix changes the meaning of the base word (or root word).

- Explain that the suffixes -y and -ful mean "full of."

- Remind children that looking for word parts they know can help them to figure out a word's meaning.

WE DO IT

- Write *flutter* + *y* = *fluttery* on the board.

- Tell children that the base word (or root word) *flutter* means "to move quickly or lightly."

- Ask children to use their knowledge of the suffix -y to figure out what the new word *fluttery* means.

- Have children check a print or digital dictionary to verify that their definitions are correct.

YOU DO IT

- Write *sleep* + *y* = *sleepy* and *joy* + *ful* = *joyful* on the board.

- Have children look up *sleep* and *joy* in a print or digital dictionary. Then work with partners to use their knowledge of word parts to figure out the meanings of *sleepy* and *joyful*.

On Level

ELA RF.2.3d, L.2.4c
ELD ELD.PI.2.1

I DO IT

- Remind children that a suffix is a word part added to the end of a word.

- Explain that the suffixes -y and -ful mean "full of."

- Explain that words ending in -y do not always have the meaning "full of." Some examples are *ready, jury,* and *pretty*.

- Tell children that they can look for word parts they know to decide whether the ending -y is actually a suffix meaning "full of."

WE DO IT

- On the board, list the words *silly, doubtful, useful, awful, healthy, playful,* and *salty*.

- Go through the list together and identify word parts to decide which of the words have a suffix with the meaning "full of."

- Circle the words for which the ending -y is not a suffix meaning "full of."

YOU DO IT

- Have children choose two words from the list and use their knowledge of word parts to figure out the words' meanings. Children can use a print or digital dictionary to confirm their understanding.

- Have children write a sentence for each word.

Advanced

ELA RF.2.3d, L.2.4c
ELD ELD.PI.2.1

I DO IT

- Write the following words on the board: *hope, dirt, luck, use.*

- Explain that adding a suffix to these words can change their meaning.

- Remind children that the suffixes *-ful* and *-y* mean "full of."

WE DO IT

- Have children add the correct suffix, either *-y* or *-ful*, to each base word (or root word).

- Offering feedback as needed, have children use their knowledge of suffixes to explain the meaning of each new word.

- Have children use print or digital dictionaries to verify their explanations.

YOU DO IT

- Have children list other words they know that contain the suffixes *-y* and *-ful*. Remind them that not all words that end in *-y* and *-ful* have the meaning "full of," and clarify misunderstandings as needed.

- Have children choose two words from the list and write a sentence that includes both words.

English Language Support

ELD ELD.PI.2.1

Provide Struggling Readers, On Level, and Advanced ELs proficiency-level support during differentiated instruction.

Emerging

- As children complete the We Do It activity for their group, allow them to look up the base words or root words in a print or digital dictionary.

- Confirm that children understand the meaning of the base or root word. Ask: *What is another word that is similar to this word?* Then have children add both suffixes to each word and ask them which new words are familiar or sound right.

Expanding

- As children complete the We Do It activity for their group, have them tell the definition of the base or root word to a partner. Have the partner add the appropriate suffix and state the definition of the new word. Then have partners trade roles.

Bridging

- If children are having trouble completing the You Do It activity for their group, allow them to look up the words with their suffixes in a dictionary or thesaurus. Then ask: *How can you use this word to describe someone or something?* Guide them to complete their sentences with support as needed.

Options for Reteaching

ELA RF.2.3e **ELD** ELD.PI.2.1

Reteach Phonics

Words with the Long *e* Sound for *y*

I DO IT

- Display the **Picture Card** and **Word Card** for *baby*. Read the word aloud, emphasizing the final sound, /ē/.

- Review the long *e* sound for *y*. *The letter y can stand for the sound /ē/ at the end of a word with two or more syllables.* Repeat *baby*, clapping the syllables.

- Write and read *funny*. Point out the long *e* sound for *y*, and clap the syllables as you repeat *funny*.

WE DO IT

- Write *lucky* on the board. Blend and read the word. Then have children blend and read the word with you.

- Ask a volunteer to circle the letter that stands for the final sound, /ē/.

- Together with children, repeat the word and clap the syllables.

- Repeat the process with the words *city*, *happy*, and *penny*.

YOU DO IT

- Have partners work together to read the **Decodable Reader** *Puppies*.

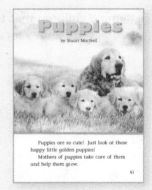

Decodable Reader

ELA L.2.1d **ELD** ELD.PI.2.1, ELD.PII.2.3a

Reteach Language Arts

The Verb *be*

I DO IT

- Write: *is, am, are*. *These verbs tell about now.*

- Write: *was, were*. *These verbs tell about the past.*

- Circle *is, am,* and *was*. *These verbs tell about one.*

- Put a box around *are* and *were*. *These verbs tell about more than one.*

- Write: *The boys is loud. She are late.* Model fixing each sentence with the correct form of *be*.

WE DO IT

- Work together to write two or three sentences describing your classroom. Use the verb *be*.

- Have partners work together to write two or three more sentences describing your classroom. Have them use the verb *be*.

- Check their work for subject-verb agreement and correct any errors.

YOU DO IT

- Have children write two or three more sentences describing their home. Have them use the verb *be*.

- Check their work for subject-verb agreement and correct any errors.

Reteach Vocabulary Strategies

ELD ELD.PI.2.1

Suffixes -y, -ful

I DO IT

- Explain that identifying word parts, such as prefixes, suffixes, and base words (or root words), can help children figure out the meaning of an unfamiliar word.

- Remind children that both suffixes -y and -ful mean "full of."

WE DO IT

- Display Projectable 18.8 .

- Help children identify words containing the word parts -y and -ful.

- Model how to apply the **Vocabulary Strategy** to figure out the meaning of the word *flowery*.

  Think Aloud *I know the word part -y means "full of." I also recognize the word* flower. *I think the meaning of this word is "full of flowers."*

- Have a child look up *flowery* in a print or digital dictionary and read the definition.

YOU DO IT

- Provide children with several words with -y and -ful endings.

- Have them use their knowledge of word parts to determine each word's meaning.

- Have them confirm their understanding by looking up the words in a print or digital dictionary.

- Provide corrective feedback if children need additional support.

Reteach Comprehension Skill

ELA RI.2.6 ELD ELD.PI.2.1, ELD.PI.2.6

Understanding Characters

I DO IT

- Remind children that authors tell what characters do and say, how they act with other people, and how they solve problems.

- Explain that characters' words, thoughts, feelings, and actions are clues to understanding their traits.

WE DO IT

- Have children read **Student Book** p. 100. Then have them identify what the actions described on the page tell them about Gabriela.

- Model how to use text clues and knowledge of people to figure out what she is like.

  Think Aloud *On this page, we learn about how Gabriela played "pretend school" with the children in her village. She helped her friends learn their ABCs so that they could read and write. These details tell me that she liked to imagine and pretend things. The other thing it tells me is that she cared a lot about passing on her learning to others.*

YOU DO IT

- Distribute Graphic Organizer 1 : **Column Chart**.

- Have children list details about the character, Gabriela, using pp. 95–96. *Gabriela liked to read, play, teach, and pretend.* Then have children list their own experiences that are similar to Gabriela's. Ask children to make inferences about what Gabriela was like, based on text details and their own experiences.

- Review and discuss the completed Column Charts.

Teacher Dashboard

Log onto the Teacher Dashboard and *my*SmartPlanner. Use these searchable tools to customize lessons that achieve your instructional goals.

Interactive Whiteboard Lessons

- Vocabulary Strategies: Shades of Meaning
- Phonics: Words with *ar*

- Write About Reading
- Narrative Writing: Fictional Story

 **Assess It Online!**

- Weekly Tests
- Assessment-driven instruction with prescriptive feedback

Student eBook

 Annotate it! Strategies for Annotation

Guide children to use digital tools for close reading.

Children may also use the interactive features in their Student eBooks to respond to prompts in a variety of ways, including:

- short-answer response
- drag-and-drop
- spoken response
- multiple choice
- fill-in-the-blank
- drawing

fyi hmhfyi.com

High-Interest Informational Texts and Multimedia

Have children explore the FYI website for additional information about topics of study.

Culturally Responsive Teaching

Signs Are Everywhere! Tell children that this week, they will be reading and thinking about how signs are helpful.

- Lead a class discussion about how signs help people. Ask children to name, describe, or draw signs they have seen, such as street and traffic signs, railroad signs, construction signs, and store signs. Discuss the role of sign colors, and how they have meaning or draw attention.

- Invite English learners to share examples of signs from their home regions, and to explain what they know about the signs' meanings.

- Have partners take a walk around school and record notes about or photograph signs they find.

- Encourage children to create funny signs, as Norman does in *The Signmaker's Assistant,* and post them in a "Silly Signs" classroom display.

Act It Out Develop understanding for English learners by reading aloud and acting out the meaning of common signs, such as *Push, Pull, Enter, Exit, Keep Off the Grass, Open,* and *Closed.* Model reading aloud each sign, acting it out, and then have children do the same.

Language Support Card

Use the Lesson 19 Language Support Card to activate prior knowledge, frontload vocabulary, and teach academic English.

 Use the Text X-Ray on page T309 to review the language demands of *The Signmaker's Assistant* with the needs of English learners in mind.

Language Workshop for Designated ELD

- Connection to Essential Question
- Vocabulary Network
- Focus on Interacting in Meaningful Ways
- Discussion Frames
- How English Works
- Word Learning Strategies

You may wish to use the following suggestions to modify instruction for some children, according to their needs.

Learner's Journal

Keeping a Learner's Journal can help children see themselves as successful, growing learners. Developing a sense of ownership in children can motivate them to reach their highest potential. Have children add to their Learner's Journal for this lesson. Depending on children's needs and skills, have them record information about what they are learning. Some examples:

- Day 1: Vocabulary: *assistant, tearing, agreed, wisdom, polite, cleared, failed, trouble*
- Day 2: The title of the Anchor Text, *The Signmaker's Assistant,* and words or pictures about the text
- Day 3: Write and draw about something new they learned about how signs are helpful. To help, you might want to discuss with children the Essential Question and their ideas about it.
- Day 4: Write one or more words they have learned to spell this week.
- Day 5: Write about how they are becoming better writers. For example, "I am learning to write a fictional story."

Student eBook

- **Audio** can be activated to support fluency, decoding, and comprehension.
- **Alternative Text** provides spoken information that can be used in place of the information provided in the book's images.
- **Vocabulary Pop-Ups** contain point-of-use definitions for selection vocabulary.

Math

Recognize and Draw Sign Shapes Use common traffic and street signs to have children recognize and draw geometric shapes with specific attributes.

- Collect images of a variety of traffic and street signs of different shapes, such as street and speed limit signs (rectangles), *Yield* and *No Passing* signs (triangles), a school warning sign (pentagon), and a stop sign (octagon).
- Present signs one at a time and guide children to tell what information each sign provides. Invite them to name the shape of each sign, and describe each shape's attributes, such as the number of sides, and that its sides are straight. Record children's observations on the board.
- Have children use crayons and markers to draw one or more of the signs. Tell them to write a sentence that describes the sign's shape.

LESSON 19

Our Focus Wall

ANCHOR TEXT

Paired Selection

The Signmaker's Assistant
Humorous Fiction

The Trouble with Signs
Play

ESSENTIAL QUESTION

How are signs helpful?

FOUNDATIONAL SKILLS

☑ High-Frequency Words

are	is
baby	please
didn't	sound
good	talk
I'll	too

Phonics

Words with *ar*

Fluency

Phrasing: Punctuation

READING LITERATURE & INFORMATIONAL TEXT

Comprehension Skills and Strategies

☑ TARGET SKILL
• Text and Graphic Features
• Point of View

☑ TARGET STRATEGY
• Question

LANGUAGE

☑ Target Vocabulary

assistant	tearing
agreed	wisdom
polite	cleared
failed	trouble

Vocabulary Strategies

Shades of Meaning

Grammar

Commas in Dates and Places

Spelling

Words with *ar*

car	party
dark	hard
arm	farm
star	start
park	part
yard	spark

WRITING

Writing

Narrative Writing:
Fictional Story

Focus Trait: Organization

Whole Group Resources

The Signmaker's Assistant
GENRE: Humorous Fiction
21st Century Theme: Global Awareness

Prepare for Complex Texts For a comprehensive overview and analysis of key ideas and academic language features of this lesson's Anchor Text, see pages T308–T309.

The Trouble with Signs
GENRE: Play

Digital Resources

▶ eBook: Annotate it!

▶ Interactive Whiteboard Lessons
   • Vocabulary Strategies: Shades of Meaning
   • Phonics: Words with *ar*

▶ Multimedia Grammar Glossary

▶ *my*SmartPlanner

▶ Parent Resource

Additional Resources

• Vocabulary in Context Cards 145–152
• Reader's Notebook, pp. 46–60
• Independent Reading

• Lesson 19 Blackline Masters
• Decodable Readers
• Blend-It Books 121–122

Language
Development

Meaning
Making

Effective
Expression

Content
Knowledge

Foundational
Skills

LINGUISTICALLY DIVERSE LEARNERS

∨ Integrated English Language Support

Interacting in Meaningful Ways

Classroom Conversations
- Talk About It, p. T323
- Collaborative Conversation, pp. T314, T336, T346, T372
- Turn and Talk, p. T346

Interactive and Collaborative Writing
- Fictional Story, p. T349
- Write About Reading, p. T347

Learning About How English Works

Scaffold the Texts
- Text X-Ray: Focus on Academic Language, p. T309
- Condensing Ideas, p. T333

Communicative Modes
- Interpretive, p. T314
- Collaborative, pp. T320, T346
- Productive, p. T359

Using Foundational Literacy Skills

Support Linguistic Transfer
- Words with *ar*, p. T316
- *r*-Controlled Vowel Sound, p. T338
- Comma Usage in Dates, p. T358

Fluency: Phrasing: Punctuation, pp. T353, T391

Phonics, pp. T316–T317, T318, T342–T343, T352, T362–T363, T384–T385, T390

Apply Language Skills
- Commas in Dates and Places, pp. T374–T375

ASSESSMENT

Formative Assessment
- Phonics: Words with *ar*, pp. T317, T343
- Target Vocabulary, p. T321
- Decodable Reader, p. T319
- Target Skill: Text and Graphic Features, p. T345
- Vocabulary Strategies: Shades of Meaning, p. T367
- Using Data to Adjust Instruction, p. T379

✓ Assess It Online!
- Weekly Test

Performance Tasks
- Write About Reading, p. T347
- Fictional Story, p. T339

⌄ Vocabulary Reader

Signs Are Everywhere
by Myka-Lynne Sokoloff

HOUGHTON MIFFLIN

 Vocabulary Reader
for all levels

Provide strategic scaffolding to support all students in reading on-level text and in acquiring general academic and domain-specific vocabulary. Use the instructional supports on pp. T386–T387 or the Leveled Reader Teacher's Guide.

Guided Reading Level: J

Lexile: 380
DRA: 18

Leveled Reader Teacher's Guide 🔗

⌄ Weekly Leveled Readers

Guide children to read and comprehend additional texts about the lesson topic.
Use the instructional supports on pp. T392–T395 or the Leveled Reader Teacher's Guides.

Struggling Readers

Guided Reading Level: I
Lexile: 240
DRA: 16
Leveled Reader Teacher's Guide 🔗

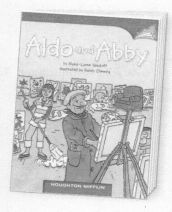

On Level

Guided Reading Level: K
Lexile: 300
DRA: 20
Leveled Reader Teacher's Guide 🔗

Advanced

Guided Reading Level: L
Lexile: 450
DRA: 24
Leveled Reader Teacher's Guide 🔗

English Language Learners

Guided Reading Level: K
Lexile: 270
DRA: 20
Leveled Reader Teacher's Guide 🔗

Language Workshop for Designated ELD

- Provides an additional hour of daily instruction for targeted language support.

- **Supports English learners** at three different proficiency levels as they dig deeper into the language of the lesson texts.

- Guides students in collaboration, interpretation, and production of English.

Lesson 19 Focus

Collaborate: Gain and Hold the Floor

Interpret: Describe Ideas

Produce: Write Collaboratively; Retell Texts

How English Works: Comprehend/ Compose Texts

Vocabulary Network

Meaning Making

Language Development

Effective Expression

Content Knowledge

Foundational Skills

Intervention

Strategic Intervention Tier II

Write-In Reader: *The Big City*

- Interactive worktext with selection that connects to the lesson topic
- Reinforces the lesson's vocabulary and comprehension
- Builds skills for reading increasingly complex texts
- Online version with dual-speed audio and follow-text

Daily Lessons See this week's daily Strategic Intervention Lesson on pp. S32–S41.

- Preteach and reteach daily instruction
- Oral Grammar
- Words to Know
- Decoding
- Comprehension
- Fluency
- Grammar
- Written Response
- Unpack Meaning

Curious About Words Provides oral vocabulary instruction for children with limited vocabularies.

HMH Decoding Power: Intensive Reading Instruction

- **Provides reteaching and practice in the key foundational skills** for reading: print concepts, phonological/phonemic awareness, phonics and word recognition, and fluency.

- **Explicit, sequential, and systematic instruction** designed to bring students up to grade level.

✓ *Assess It Online!*

▶ **Intervention Assessments** place individual students within the system, ensure students are making satisfactory progress, and provide a measure of student readiness to exit the system.

What My Other Students Are Doing

Digital Resources

▶ Literacy Centers: Word Study, Think and Write, Comprehension and Fluency

◉ **Additional Resources**

- Vocabulary in Context Cards 145–152
- Reader's Notebook, pp. 46–60
- Independent Reading
- Lesson 19 Blackline Masters
- Decodable Readers
- Blend-It Books 121–122

Comprehension and Fluency

Materials

- Student Book
- Decodable Reader: *Darling Starling*
- Audio
- Paper and pencil

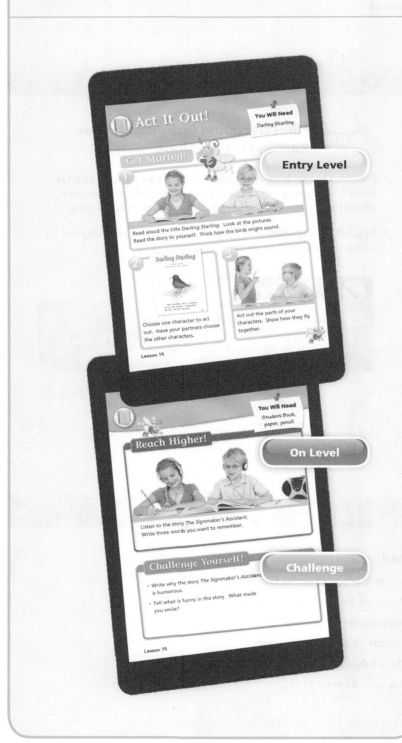

Word Study

Materials

- Picture Cards and Word Cards: *car, farm, jar, scarf, yard, yarn*
- Letter Cards: *d, ar, k; s, t, ar; p, ar, t, y; h, ar, d; s, p, ar, k; s, m, ar, t*
- Paper and pencil

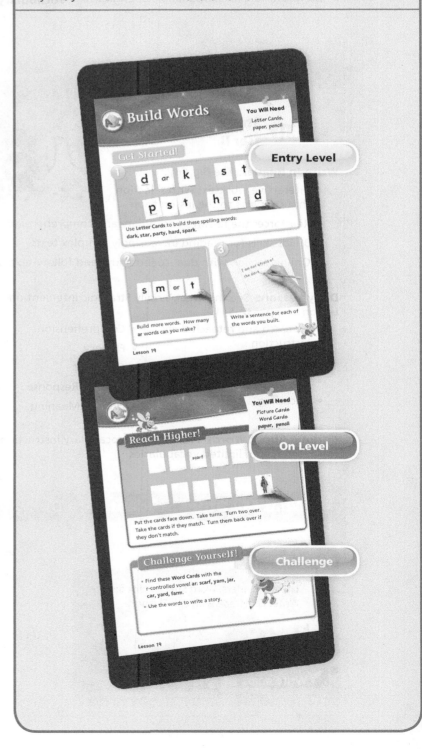

Assign Literacy Center activities during small group time. Each center contains three activities. Children who experience success with the entry-level activity move on to the on-level and challenge activities, as time permits.

Meaning Making

Effective Expression

Language Development

Content Knowledge

Foundational Skills

Think and Write

Materials

- Poster board
- Scissors and tape
- Child-made signs
- Paper, pencil, crayons, markers

Make a Sign

You Will Need
poster board, markers, crayons, scissors, tape

Get Started!

Entry Level

1. Think about a sign that would tell people to do funny things. Make the sign.

2. WALK BACKWARDS
Cut your sign into an appropriate shape.

3. WALK BACKWARDS
Hang your sign in the classroom.

Lesson 19

You Will Need
your sign, paper, pencil, crayons

Reach Higher!

On Level

WALK BACKWARDS
LOOK UP!

Tell about your sign. Then write a sentence about it.

Challenge Yourself!

Challenge

- Draw a picture of people obeying your sign.
- Write a sentence or two to go with your picture.

Lesson 19

Independent Reading

Teacher Modeling Modeling how to select appropriate books and books of interest is helpful to children who have difficulty choosing books. Select a book and do two brief Think Alouds—one in favor of reading the book and the other to demonstrate deciding not to read the book. Below are some example Think Alouds for a nonfiction book.

- **PRO:** *I'm interested in (topic). The title of this book has (topic) in it, so the whole book is probably about (topic). Each page has a picture with a caption that gives me more information. When I read the first two pages, I see a few words that are hard for me. I've read other books by this author, and I have enjoyed them. I think I'll give this book a try.*

- **CON:** *I'm interested in (topic). The title of this book includes (topic), but it also has other topics. Maybe the whole book isn't about what I want. When I read the first two pages, there are a lot of words that I don't know. I think this book might be too hard right now. I'll try another book.*

If a child consistently selects books that are too challenging for him or her, have the child explain why he or she has chosen a particular book before beginning to read. Guide the child to a more appropriate book, as necessary.

See pp. T354–T355 for additional independent reading support. ELA RL.2.10, RI.2.10

Prepare for Complex Texts

Anchor Text

The Signmaker's Assistant
by Tedd Arnold

GENRE: Humorous Fiction

Why This Text?

Children will encounter humorous fiction in textbooks and through independent reading. This text exposes children to subtle humor by combining details in the text and the art.

Key Learning Objectives

• Learn how words and art interact to convey meaning.

• Examine narrator's point of view.

Paired Selection

The Trouble with Signs *by Bebe Jaffe*

GENRE: Play

Why This Text?

Children should be exposed to a variety of fiction genres, including plays. This play includes basic drama elements, such as stage directions.

Key Learning Objectives

• Compare two texts about signs.

• Examine how a play uses dialogue.

TEXT COMPLEXITY RUBRIC

		The Signmaker's Assistant	The Trouble with Signs
Quantitative Measures	Lexile	810	NP
	Guided Reading Level	N	L
Qualitative Measures	Purpose/Levels of Meaning	**Density and Complexity:** The text has multiple levels of meaning.	**Figurative Language:** The text has many instances of figurative language.
	Text Structure	**Organization:** The text has shifting perspectives and multiple points of view.	**Genre:** The genre is familiar to children but contains new elements.
		Use of Images: The text has images that are critical to comprehension of the story.	
	Language Features	**Sentence Structure:** The text includes sentences with adjective and adverb phrases that increase sentence length.	**Dialogue:** The text includes dialogue that is directly attributed to a character, but the reader must attend to stage directions.
		Vocabulary: The text includes unfamiliar vocabulary that may need support.	**Conventionality and Register:** The text includes many examples of figurative language that may be unfamiliar.
	Knowledge Demands	**Life Experiences/Background Knowledge:** The events in the story require some experience with signs and the importance they have in a community.	**Life Experiences/Background Knowledge:** This play requires some previous experience with signs and with figurative language.
Reader/Task Considerations		Determine using the professional judgment of the teacher. This varies by individual reader, type of text, and the purpose and complexity of particular tasks. See **Reader and Task Considerations** on p. T325 for some suggestions for Anchor Text support.	

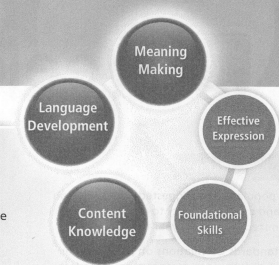

ENGLISH LANGUAGE SUPPORT Use the Text X-Ray below to prepare for teaching the Anchor Text *The Signmaker's Assistant*. Use it to plan, support, and scaffold instruction in order to help children understand the text's **key ideas** and **academic language features**.

Zoom In on Key Ideas

Children should understand these **key ideas** after reading *The Signmaker's Assistant*.

Key Idea | pp. 128–131

Young Norman works for the old signmaker in town. He sees that the people obey the signs, such as *STOP* and *ENTER*. He decides to make his own signs.

Have children tell why the signmaker might want Norman to only help out around the shop and not to make all of the signs.

Key Idea | pp. 132–139

Norman puts up silly signs such as *BUY NORMAN A PRESENT* and *EAT YOUR HAT* while the signmaker is out of town. Norman laughs at the people who follow his signs.

Have children tell why these signs cause problems for the town.

Key Idea | pp. 140–143

The townspeople become angry. They think the old signmaker is playing tricks on them. They tear down all the signs, even the good ones. Having no signs in town causes a lot of trouble.

Have children tell why they think the townspeople took down the good signs along with the silly signs.

Key Idea | pp. 144–149

Norman finally realizes how much trouble he has caused. He knows he has to find a way to make everything all right in town again.

Have children explain whether or not Norman apologizing was a brave thing to do.

Zoom In on Academic Language

Guide children at different proficiencies and skill levels to understand the structure and language of this text.

Focus: Word Level | pp. 129–130

Write the word *assistant* on the board. Remind children that an assistant is a helper. Explain that there are many types of helpers. Read the sentences before and after the word *assistant,* and have children tell what Norman did for the signmaker, or what kind of assistant he was.

Focus: Text Level | pp. 136–139

Tell children that the illustrations on these pages help to tell the story. Explain that it is important to study what is happening in them to understand the story's events. Guide children to determine how the words on the signs in each picture cause a problem for the townspeople. Ask children to tell if they find any of these events funny.

Focus: Sentence Level | p. 142

Reread the first sentence with children. Write the **prepositional phrase** *In the evening* on the board. Guide them to understand that this phrase adds a detail; it tells *when* something happened. Have them look for other phrases that tell when something happened.

Content and Language Instruction

Make note of additional **content knowledge** and **language features** children may find challenging in this text.

Weekly Planner

my SmartPlanner

Auto-populates the suggested five-day lesson plan and offers flexibility to create and save customized plans from year to year.

See **Standards Correlations** on p. C1. In your eBook, click the Standards button in the left panel to view descriptions of the standards on the page.

	DAY 1	**DAY 2**
	Materials	**Materials**
	• Blend-It Books: Books 121–122	• Decodable Reader: *Darling Starling*
	• Common Core Writing Handbook, Lesson 19	• Graphic Organizer 1
	• Decodable Reader: *Darling Starling*	• High-Frequency Word Cards 181–190
	• High-Frequency Word Cards 181–190	• Instructional Routine 15
	• Instructional Routines 3, 6, 11, 12	• Letter Cards
	• Language Support Card, Lesson 19	• Literacy and Language Guide, pp. 92–93
	• Letter Cards	• Projectables S1, 19.4, 19.5
	• Literacy and Language Guide, pp. 92–93	• Reader's Notebook Vol 2 pp. 48–51
	• Projectables S1, 19.1, 19.2, 19.3	• Sound/Spelling Card: artist
	• Reader's Notebook Vol 2 pp. 46–47	• Student Book pp. 126–153
	• Retelling Cards 73–76	• Vocabulary in Context Cards 145–152
	• Sound/Spelling Card: artist	
	• Student Book pp. 122–149	
	• Vocabulary in Context Cards 145-152	

Whole Group

	DAY 1	**DAY 2**
Daily Language • Oral Vocabulary • Phonemic Awareness • Speaking and Listening	**Opening Routines,** T312–T313 **Read Aloud** "Wild Friends, Wow!" T314–T315 **Phonemic Awareness,** T316	**Opening Routines,** T340–T341 **Phonemic Awareness,** T342
Vocabulary **Text-Based Comprehension** • Skills and Strategies • Craft and Structure	☑ **Introduce Target Vocabulary,** T320–T321 ☑ **Read and Comprehend** T322–T323 **FIRST READ Think Through the Text** Read the Anchor Text: *The Signmaker's Assistant,* T324–T337	☑ **Dig Deeper,** T344–T345 • Text and Graphic Features • Point of View **SECOND READ Analyze the Text** Reread the Anchor Text: *The Signmaker's Assistant,* T324–T336 **Your Turn,** T346–T347
Foundational Skills • Phonics and Word Recognition • Fluency	☑ **Fluency** Phrasing: Punctuation, T314 ☑ **Phonics** • Words with *ar,* T316–T318 **Read** *Darling Starling,* T319	☑ **Fluency** Phrasing: Punctuation, T343 ☑ **Phonics** • Words with *ar,* T342–T343

Whole Group Language Arts

	DAY 1	**DAY 2**
Spelling **Grammar** **Writing**	☑ **Spelling** Words with *ar;* Pretest, T338 ☑ **Grammar** Commas in Dates and Places, T338 Daily Proofreading Practice, T339 ☑ **Narrative Writing:** Fictional Story Reading/Writing Workshop Introduce the Model, T339	☑ **Spelling** Words with *ar,* T348 ☑ **Grammar** Commas in Dates and Places, T348 Daily Proofreading Practice, T349 ☑ **Narrative Writing:** Fictional Story Reading/Writing Workshop Focus Trait: Organization, T349

Small Group

Suggestions for Small Groups (See pp. T381–T399.)

Language Workshop

	DAY 1	**DAY 2**
Designated English Language Support	**Connect to Text:** *The Signmaker's Assistant* **Introduce Vocabulary Network:** Words About Signs	**Expand Vocabulary Network** **Collaborate:** Offer Opinions

iRead Use *iRead*, an adaptive digital foundational reading skills program, to personalize learning for students.

Integrated English Language Support

See page T303 for instructional support activities for Diverse Linguistic Learners.

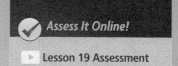 **Assess It Online!**

▶ Lesson 19 Assessment

DAY 3

Materials
- Cold Reads
- Decodable Reader: *Going to the Farm*
- High-Frequency Word Cards 181–190
- Instructional Routine 12
- Letter Cards
- Literacy and Language Guide, pp. 92–93, 152–153
- Projectable 19.6
- Reader's Notebook Vol 2 pp. 52–56
- Student Book pp. 126–149
- Vocabulary in Context Cards 145–152

Opening Routines, T350–T351
Phonemic Awareness, T352

Independent Reading, T354–T355
- Reader's Guide: *The Signmaker's Assistant*
- Self-Selected Reading
- Self-Correction Strategies

Apply Vocabulary Knowledge, T356–T357

☑ **Fluency**
Phrasing: Punctuation, T353
☑ **Phonics**
- Phonics Review, T352

☑ **Spelling**
Words with *ar*, T358
☑ **Grammar**
Commas in Dates, Places, and Letters, T358
Daily Proofreading Practice, T359
☑ **Narrative Writing:**
Fictional Story
Reading/Writing Workshop
Prewrite, T359

DAY 4

Materials
- Decodable Reader: *Going to the Farm*
- Graphic Organizer 10
- High-Frequency Word Cards 181–190
- Instructional Routine 14
- Interactive Whiteboard Lesson: Shades of Meaning
- Letter Cards
- Literacy and Language Guide, pp. 92–93
- Projectables 19.7, 19.8
- Reader's Notebook Vol 2 pp. 57–59
- Sound/Spelling Cards: ice cream, eagle
- Student Book pp. 154–157
- Vocabulary in Context Cards 145–152

Opening Routines, T360–T361
Phonemic Awareness, T362

Connect to the Topic
- Read Play: *The Trouble with Signs*, T364–T365
- Introduce Genre and Text Focus, T364
☑ **Compare Texts,** T365
☑ **Vocabulary Strategies,** Shades of Meaning, T366–T367

☑ **Fluency**
Phrasing: Punctuation, T363
☑ **Phonics**
- Phonics Review, T362–T363

☑ **Spelling**
Words with *ar*, T368
☑ **Grammar**
Spiral Review, T368
Daily Proofreading Practice, T369
☑ **Narrative Writing:**
Fictional Story
Reading/Writing Workshop
Prewrite, T369

DAY 5

Materials
- Graphic Organizer 6
- High-Frequency Word Cards 181–190
- Interactive Whiteboard Lesson: Phonics: Words with *ar*
- Listening Log
- Reader's Notebook Vol 2 p. 60
- Student Book pp. 158–161
- Vocabulary in Context Cards 145–152
- Close Reader, Lesson 19

Opening Routines, T370–T371
Speaking and Listening, T373

Close Reader
- Lesson 19
Extend the Topic
- Domain-Specific Vocabulary, T372
- Speaking and Listening: Matching Game: Synonyms, T373
- Optional Second Read: *The Trouble with Signs*, T364–T365

☑ **Fluency**
Phrasing: Punctuation, T379
☑ **Phonics**
- Phonics Review, T371

☑ **Spelling**
Assess, T374
☑ **Grammar**
Commas in Dates and Places, T374–T375
Daily Proofreading Practice, T376
☑ **Narrative Writing:**
Fictional Story
Reading/Writing Workshop
Prewrite, T376–T377

 Tier II Intervention provides 30 minutes of additional daily practice with key parts of the core instruction. (See pp. S32–S41.)

Interpret: Understand Text Elements
Unpack a Sentence

Produce: Write a Description
Focus on How English Works:
Understand Text Structure

Share and Reflect

DAY 1

Today's Goals

Vocabulary & Oral Language
- **Teacher Read Aloud:**
  "Wild Friends, Wow!"
- **Oral Vocabulary**
- **Listening Comprehension**
- **Introduce Vocabulary**

☑ TARGET VOCABULARY

assistant	tearing
agreed	wisdom
polite	cleared
failed	trouble

Phonemic Awareness
- **Substitute Phonemes**

Phonics & Fluency
- **Words with** *ar*
- **Read Decodable Reader:**
  Darling Starling
- **Fluency:** Phrasing: Punctuation
- **High-Frequency Words**

Text-Based Comprehension
- **Listening Comprehension**
- **Read and Comprehend**
- **Read the Anchor Text:**
  The Signmaker's Assistant

Grammar & Writing
- **Commas in Dates and Places**
- **Narrative Writing:** Fictional Story

Spelling
- **Words with** *ar*

Opening Routines

Warm Up with Wordplay

Share a Riddle

Display and read aloud the following riddle:

> ## What are three fast ways to share information?

Have children discuss possible answers before telling them: *Telephone, television, and tell-a-friend!* Remind them to use discussion rules. Display the answers.

Ask children to explain why the riddle is funny. If necessary, point out that after hearing *telephone* and *television*, we expect to hear another way to communicate that starts with *tele-*. *Tell-a-friend* is funny because we don't expect it.

ELA SL.2.1a **ELD** ELD.PI.2.1

Daily Phonemic Awareness

Substitute Phonemes

- *Today we are going to listen to sounds in words. Listen to this word: cat. What sounds do you hear? /k/ /ă/ /t/ Now we're going to change one sound in the word to make a new word. Let's change the /ă/ sound to the /är/ sound. What are the sounds? /k/ /är/ /t/ What is the new word?* cart

- Have children continue with the words *stay/star, back/bark, hat/heart,* and *fame/farm.*

Corrective Feedback

- If a child is unable to make a substitution, say the word, give correction, and model the task. Example: *The word is cat. I can change the /ă/ sound in cat to /är/ and make a new word, cart. Cat—cart.*

- Have children try once with you before doing it on their own. Continue with the other words.

Daily High-Frequency Words

- Point to the High-Frequency Words on the Focus Wall. Say: *This week, our new High-Frequency Words are* didn't, I'll, *and* sound. *Our review words are these words:* are, baby, good, is, please, talk, *and* too.

- Use <u>Instructional Routine 11</u> and **High-Frequency Word Card 182** to introduce the word *I'll.*

- Repeat the procedure with **High-Frequency Word Cards 181** and **190** for new words *didn't* and *sound* and with **High-Frequency Word Cards 183–189** for review words *are, baby, good, is, please, talk,* and *too.*
  ELA RF.2.3f

Corrective Feedback

- If a child does not recognize the word *I'll,* say the correct word and have children repeat it. I'll. *What is the word? I'll*

- Have children spell the word. *I-'-l-l How do we say this word? I'll*

- Have children reread all of the cards in random order.

Daily Vocabulary Boost

- Have children think about signs they have seen around town or in school. Preview the Target Vocabulary by displaying the **Vocabulary in Context Cards** and discussing the words. For example, use sentences such as these to discuss the words *trouble, failed,* and *agreed.*

  People had trouble understanding the new signs at the park.

  A man got a ticket because he failed to follow the rules on the signs.

  Everyone agreed to make new signs that everyone could understand.

- Tell children that they will find these and other Vocabulary Words when they read *The Signmaker's Assistant.*

1 assistant
The assistant is helping to put up this sign.

Vocabulary in
Context Cards 145–152

☑ **Target Vocabulary**

assistant
agreed
polite
failed
tearing
wisdom
cleared
trouble

Teacher Read Aloud

▶ SHARE OBJECTIVES

- Listen to fluent reading.
- Ask and answer questions about what you hear.
- Retell important ideas and details. LANGUAGE
- Identify and use connecting words in sentences. LANGUAGE

PREVIEW
☑ TARGET VOCABULARY

agreed to have said yes to something

trouble problems

cleared to have taken things away from someplace

failed did not succeed

polite respectful

assistant someone who helps another person

tearing damaging something by pulling it apart

wisdom good sense of judgment

ENGLISH LANGUAGE SUPPORT

Comprehensible Input

All Proficiencies To assist children with accessing the content and topic of the Teacher Read Aloud, complete the Build Background activities on Lesson 19 **Language Support Card**.

Model Fluency

Phrasing: Punctuation Explain that when good readers read aloud, they use punctuation to help them group words that go together.

- Display Projectable 19.1 ⌐. As you read each sentence, model how to pause briefly for punctuation within and at the end of sentences. Model changing your voice at the end of a sentence for exclamation points and question marks.

- Reread the text together with children, having them pause briefly at the punctuation throughout and change their tone of voice appropriately for end punctuation. Then read the remainder of the story aloud. **ELA** RF.2.4b

Listening Comprehension

Read aloud the selection. Pause at the numbered stopping points to ask children the questions below. Discuss the meanings of the highlighted words, as needed, to support the discussion. Tell children they will learn more about the words later in the lesson. **ELA** SL.2.2 **ELD** ELD.PI.2.5

1 *What is Wild Friends?* Sample answer: a group whose members take a pledge to protect and support wild animals MAIN IDEA AND DETAILS

2 *What do you expect to read about in the section* Whooping Crane Day in New Mexico? *Sample answer: a holiday related to Whooping Cranes* TEXT FEATURES

3 *Which heading helps you find the promise kids make when they join Wild Friends?* Wild Friend Pledge TEXT FEATURES

4 *What was the author's purpose in writing "Wild Friends, Wow!"?* Sample answer: to persuade people to join an organization AUTHOR'S PURPOSE

5 *How did the author show that it would be a good idea to join Wild Friends? Sample answer: The author said,* Everyone needs friends. *The author gave an example of Wild Friends being helpful to Whooping Cranes.* PERSUASION

💬 Classroom Collaboration

Have children ask questions about any part of the text they want to understand better. Guide them to answer the questions before answering the questions yourself. **ELA** SL.2.1c, SL.2.2, SL.2.3 **ELD** ELD.PI.2.1, ELD.PI.2.5

🔍 Language Detective

How English Works: Condensing Ideas Explain to children that sometimes authors need to join more than one sentence to give an exact idea. Reread the last sentence of the third paragraph. Write the sentence on the board, and explain that it is made up of the two ideas. Tell children that the author combined the two sentences into one sentence and used the word *and* to connect the ideas. Then display the following sentences: *Some people work hard to protect animals. Some people work hard to teach others about animals.* Have partners talk about how they can combine these sentences. **ELD** ELD.PII.2.7

Wild Friends, Wow!

1 Do you need friends? I bet your answer is "Yes! Of course!" Everybody needs friends. Animals do, too. Animals in New Mexico are very lucky. They have Wild Friends. Wild Friends is a group of students and teachers who have **agreed** to help wildlife.

A Beautiful Friend

Whooping Cranes, huge snow-white birds, were in **trouble**. Marshes where they made their nests were being drained and **cleared** for houses and other buildings. Whooping Cranes needed a friend.

The Wild Friends worked hard to help the Whooping Cranes. If they had **failed**, New Mexico could have lost this beautiful bird forever. Many students wrote **polite** letters to lawmakers. They told others about what was happening to the Whooping Cranes. In other words, each student became the Whooping Crane's personal **assistant**. Because of the students' hard work, Whooping Cranes have returned to New Mexico, and October 21 is now Whooping Crane Day!

Whooping Crane Day in New Mexico

2 On October 21, 1998, people in New Mexico celebrated the first Whooping Crane Day. They gathered in front of the state capitol in Santa Fe with a five-foot crane they had made out of paper. It was windy, so students stood around it in a circle to protect it from **tearing**. Then three students danced in Whooping Crane costumes.

Since then, hundreds of students in New Mexico (and other states, too!) have become Wild Friends. Every Wild Friends member makes a pledge similar to the one below.

Wild Friend Pledge:

3 I am a friend of wild creatures.
I support the Earth's wildlife.
I promise to study wildlife and to learn others' opinions
    and points of view.
I will work to write laws that help wildlife and will talk to
    lawmakers about wildlife's needs.

4 5 Acting with **wisdom** will help us to protect life on Earth. The Wild Friends organization urges "all citizens to study ways to be friends with each other and to protect the wild creatures among us." As any Wild Friends member could tell you, helping someone in need gives you a great feeling—kind of like flying in a clear blue sky surrounded by graceful snow-white birds.

Phonics

▶ **SHARE OBJECTIVES**

- Substitute sounds in words.
- Learn the sound/spelling for *ar*.
- Blend and decode regularly spelled words with *ar* (*r*-controlled vowel syllable).

▶ **SKILLS TRACE**

Words with *ar*	
Introduce	pp. T316–T317, T342–T343
Differentiate	pp. T384–T385
Reteach	p. T398
Review	pp. T362, T452, T463
Assess	Weekly Tests, Lesson 19

ENGLISH LANGUAGE SUPPORT

Comprehensible Input

Emerging Reinforce the meanings of words in the Phonics lesson using **Picture Cards** (*yarn, farm, scarf, yard*) and gestures, objects, or simple sketches (for example, *park, arm, marches, carpet, postcard*). Provide additional practice saying each word as you emphasize the /är/ sound. Have children repeat. **ELD** ELD.PIII.2

Expanding Have children use **Letter Cards** to make the word *am*. Ask them to read the word. Then guide children to change *am* to *arm* by adding an *r* after the *a*. Help them read the new word and use it in a sentence. Repeat with *had, cat, ban, ham, mash,* and *at*. Monitor their pronunciation and provide corrective feedback as needed. **ELD** ELD.PIII.2

Bridging Display the words *artist, garden, barn,* and *start*. Ask children to read the words and choose two to use in sentences.

Words with *ar*

ENGLISH LANGUAGE SUPPORT Speakers of Spanish and most Asian languages may have difficulty with the way vowels in English change when they are followed by an *r*. Explain that in English, vowels can sound a little different before the /r/ sound. Read aloud words such as *car, star, jar, part, dark,* and *yard,* and have students chorally repeat each word, say just the vowel sound, and then say the whole word again. Use each word in a sentence to reinforce meaning. **ELD** ELD.PIII.2

Phonemic Awareness Warm-Up *I'll say a word and then make a new word by changing one of the sounds. Listen:* back. *I'll change the /ă/ in* back *to /är/:* bark. *Now you try it with me. Change the /ă/ in* back *to /är/. Say the new word with me:* bark. *Now you do it. Change the /ă/ in* make *to /är/.* mark *Change the /ŏ/ in* shock *to /är/.* shark *Change the /ē/ in* bean *to /är/.* barn *Change the /ō/ in* foam *to /är/.* farm *Change the /ă/ in* had *to /är/.* hard

1　Teach/Model

Sound/Spelling Card Display the card for *artist*. Name the picture and say the beginning sound. Have children repeat after you. *Listen:* artist, /är/. *Now you say it.*

- Say the sound and give the spelling. *Artist begins with the sound /är/. The letters* ar *together stand for the sound /är/. The letters* ar *can stand for /är/ at the beginning, middle, or end of a word.*

- Write and read *sharp*. Point out the /är/ spelling, *ar. This is the word* sharp. *The vowel* a *is followed by* r. *The letters* ar *together stand for the sound /är/ in* sharp. **Read the word together:** *sharp.*

- Write and read *party*. Point out the /är/ spelling, *ar. This is the word* party. *The letters* ar *together stand for the sound /är/ in* party. **Read the word together:** *party.*

- Repeat the procedure with the word *park.*

2 Guided Practice

Continuous Blending Routine Use Instructional Routine 3 to model blending *dark*.

- Point to the **Sound/Spelling Card** *artist* and remind children that knowing the sound/spelling *ar* can help them read words.

d | ar | k

- Display **Letter Cards** *d, ar,* and *k*.

- Blend the sounds. Listen: /d/ /är/ /k/. Have children blend with you and then say the word. *Now you blend the sounds: /d/ /är/ /k/, dark.*

Blending Lines

Blend Words Have children read the following words chorally; provide Corrective Feedback as needed. Help children compare the sounds and spellings in each line.

1. pack	park	chain	chart	far	farm
2. cat	cart	shark	shack	bark	bake
3. aim	arm	scale	scarf	marches	matches

Transition to Longer Words Have children read the following words chorally. Ask children to identify known word parts that help them decode each longer word.

4. spark	sparkle	car	carpet	yard	barnyard
5. smart	outsmart	mark	market	part	partner
6. tar	target	card	postcard	harm	harmful

Challenge Call on above-level children to read the words in Line 7 and discuss the elements. Then have the class read the sentences chorally.

7. carnival   lumberyard   discard   gardener   faraway   alarming
8. The tiny <u>baby</u> started to cry in the dark.
9. We <u>didn't</u> travel <u>too</u> far in the large car.

3 Apply

Have partners take turns rereading Blending Lines 1–3 and 4–6. Then give children two index cards. Ask them to think of and write a riddle for an *ar* word on one side of each card and the answer on the other, for example: *This is the sound a dog makes.* (bark) Ask pairs to exchange cards and see if they can answer their partner's riddles.

Distribute Reader's Notebook Volume 2 page 46 or leveled practice in Grab-and-Go™ Resources to children to complete independently.

Corrective Feedback When a child mispronounces a letter-sound, highlight that letter, restate its sound, have children repeat the sound, and then guide them to blend the word. See the example below.

Decoding Error:
A child reads *chart* in Line 1 as *chat*.

Correct the error. Review the **Sound/Spelling Card** *artist*. Then say the word and the sound. *The word is* chart. *The letters* ar *stand for the sound /är/.*

Model as you touch the letters. *I'll blend: /ch/ /är/ /t/. What is the word?* chart

Guide *Let's blend together: /ch/ /är/ /t/. What is the word?* chart

Check *You blend. /ch/ /är/ /t/ What is the word?* chart

Reinforce Go back three or four words and have children continue reading. Make note of errors and review those words during the next lesson.

SMALL GROUP Options   **Go to pp. T384–T385 for additional phonics support.**

DAY 1

Phonics

▶ **SHARE OBJECTIVES**

- Write words with *ar*.
- Read on-level text with *ar* words (*r*-controlled vowel syllable) and High-Frequency Words.
- Practice reading fluently using appropriate phrasing (prosody).

▶ **DICTATION SENTENCES**

- **smart** A *smart* dog can do tricks.
- **bark** I can hear the dog *bark*.
- **chart** I'll read the words on the *chart*.
- **far** We drove *far* to get to the beach.
- **yarn** My grandma knitted blue *yarn* to make a sweater.
- **card** I got a *card* in the mail.

ENGLISH LANGUAGE SUPPORT

Use Visuals and Gestures

All Proficiencies Use pictures, objects, and gestures to help reinforce the meanings of the dictation words and sentences. For example, show the **Picture Card** for *yarn*. Point to a classroom chart, saying *This chart shows our classroom helpers.* Draw or display a greeting card and say *I always send my friend a card on her birthday.* Have children repeat your sentences.

Blend-It Books

To provide reading practice with new sound/spellings in decodable texts, see **Blend-It Books** 121–122.

Write Words with *ar*

1   Teach/Model

Connect Sounds to Spelling Review **Sound/Spelling Card** *artist*. Tell children that now they will write words with the sound /är/.

Use Instructional Routine 6 ⤴ to dictate the first word at left. *Listen as I say a word and use it in a sentence.*

- Model how to spell *smart*. *The word* smart *begins with the blend /s/ /m/. The blend /s/ /m/ is spelled* sm, *so I write* sm. *The middle sound in* smart *is /är/. I remember that the /är/ sound is spelled with the letters* ar *together, so I write the letters* ar *next. The final sound in* smart *is /t/. It is spelled* t, *so I write* t *last. Then I reread to check:* smart.

2   Guided Practice

Connect Sounds to Writing Continue the dictation, using the sentences at left.

- Have children say each dictation word aloud after you. Then have them identify the sounds they hear at the beginning, middle, and end and write the letters that spell each sound. **ELA** L.2.2d
- Remind children to write only the dictation word.

3   Apply

Read aloud the following decodable sentence for children to write. Remind children to look at the Focus Wall if they need help spelling *didn't* or *I'll*. **ELA** L.2.2d

> Dad <u>didn't</u> park the car, so <u>I'll</u> do it.

Print the dictation words and decodable sentence for children to check their work.

Decodable Reader

Read *Darling Starling*

Review /är/ and High-Frequency Words Review **Sound/Spelling Card** *artist* and the High-Frequency Words *are, baby, didn't, good, I'll, is, please, sound, talk,* and *too.*

Preview Have children read the title, browse the beginning pages, and discuss what they think the story is about.
Use Projectable S1 🔗 to review the **Phonics/Decoding Strategy.** Model the strategy using the title. Have children read the first page silently. Then ask a child to read the page aloud as others follow. Repeat for each page.

ENGLISH LANGUAGE SUPPORT Explain that the words *Cheep, cheep, cheep* (page 4) stand for the sounds the birds make. Ask children to tell the equivalent words in a language they know. Point out that these words are inside quotation marks, which show readers that a character is speaking. Have children identify the quotation marks on page 4 and read the words the characters are saying. **ELD** ELD.PIII.2

If children make more than six total errors, use the **Corrective Feedback** steps to help them reread aloud with accuracy. If they make fewer than six errors, have them reread and retell the story.

Darling Starling

This is Darling. She is a starling. She is a city starling. Darling likes city life. She likes city rain.

Decodable Reader

Fluency: Phrasing and Punctuation

Tell children that good readers read groups of words that make sense together. They look at punctuation for clues about how to group words. Write the following sentence on the board:

> Starlings play and eat with each other, as well.

Model Phrasing Read the sentence without phrasing or pausing at the comma. Then model using appropriate phrasing, prompted by the punctuation. Pause briefly after the comma and read the words *as well* as a group. *Listen to how I read groups of words together and pause briefly after the comma.* Reread the sentence fluently and have children repeat. *Let's read the sentence together. Pause briefly after the comma. Say the words after the comma as a group.*

ENGLISH LANGUAGE SUPPORT As children read, monitor their pronunciation of words with *ar.* Provide modeling and support as needed. **ELD** ELD.PIII.2

Responding Have children use details from the story to make a sequence chart that tells what Darling and her two best friends do, beginning with their meeting at the city park and ending with Bart Lark's party. **ELA** RL.2.1

Reread for Fluency Use Instructional Routine 12 🔗 to reread *Darling Starling* with children. Remind them to look at the punctuation for clues about how to read words together as a group. **ELA** RF.2.4b

---

Corrective Feedback When a child mispronounces a word, point to the word and say it. Call attention to the element that was mispronounced, say the sound, and then guide children to read the word. See the example below.

Decoding Error:
A child reads *starling* on page 1 as *sterling.*

Correct the error. Say the word. *That word is* starling. *The letters* ar *stand for the /är/ sound.*

Model Have children repeat the word. *What is the word?* starling

Check *Go back to the beginning of the sentence and read it again.*

Reinforce Record the error and review the word again before children reread the story.

 Go to pp. T384–T385 for additional phonics support.

Introduce Vocabulary

▶ **SHARE OBJECTIVES**
- Acquire and use vocabulary. LANGUAGE
- Use a variety of vocabulary in shared language activities. LANGUAGE
- Discuss practical uses of Vocabulary words in speaking or writing. LANGUAGE

Teach

Display and discuss the **Vocabulary in Context Cards,** using the routine below.

1 Read and pronounce the word. Read the word once alone and then together.

2 Explain the word. Read aloud the explanation under *What Does It Mean?*

ENGLISH LANGUAGE SUPPORT Review this cognate with Spanish-speaking children.

- asistente (assistant)

3 Discuss vocabulary in context. Together, read aloud the sentence on the front of the card. Help children explain and use the word in new sentences.

4 Engage with the word. Ask and discuss the *Think About It* question with children.

Practice/Apply

Give partners or small groups one or two **Vocabulary in Context Cards.** Help children complete the *Talk It Over* activities for each card. **ELA** RF.2.3f **ELD** ELD.PII.2.3a

Read aloud and have children complete the activity at the top of **Student Book** p. 122.

Then guide children to complete the Language Detective activity. Remind children of discussion rules and about taking turns when speaking with a partner. Encourage them to share their ideas with the class. **ELA** RF.2.3f, L.2.6 **ELD** ELD.PI.2.1, ELD.PI.2.12b

Lesson 19

SIGNMAKER'S ASSISTANT

The Trouble with Signs

🔍 **LANGUAGE DETECTIVE**

Talk About Words
Work with a partner. Think about times when you might use each Vocabulary word in speaking or writing. Do you and your partner have similar ideas or different ideas?

122 **ELA** L.2.5a, L.2.6 **ELD** ELD.PI.2.4, ELD.PI.2.12b

Vocabulary in Context

▶ Read each Context Card.

▶ Ask a question that uses one of the Vocabulary words.

1 **assistant**
The assistant is helping to put up this sign.

2 **agreed**
The people agreed that this road needed a stop sign.

ENGLISH LANGUAGE SUPPORT

Comprehensible Input

Emerging Use gestures to demonstrate the meanings of *tearing, agreed,* and *cleared.* Have children repeat the gestures and say the words with you. **ELD** ELD.PI.2.12b

Expanding Ask children questions to confirm their understanding. Example: *How do people gain wisdom?* **ELD** ELD.PI.2.12b

Bridging Have partners write questions and answers using Vocabulary words. Example: *Why should you be polite?* **ELD** ELD.PI.2.12b

3 polite

This sign reminds children to be polite, or nice, to others.

4 failed

The sign failed to keep the dog off the grass.

5 tearing

The worker is tearing apart this old sign.

6 wisdom

The words of wisdom on this billboard teach us to act the right way.

7 cleared

The crossing guard cleared the way so these children could cross.

8 trouble

Without signs, drivers would have trouble knowing when to stop.

123

FORMATIVE ASSESSMENT **RtI**

Are children able to understand and use Target Vocabulary words?

IF...	THEN...
children struggle,	▲ use **Vocabulary in Context Cards** and differentiate **Vocabulary Reader,** *Signs Are Everywhere,* for Struggling Readers, p. T386. *See also Intervention Lesson 19, p. S33.*
children are on track,	▲ use **Vocabulary in Context Cards** and differentiate **Vocabulary Reader,** *Signs Are Everywhere,* for On-Level Readers, p. T386.
children excel,	▲ differentiate **Vocabulary Reader,** *Signs Are Everywhere,* for Advanced Readers, p. T387.

SMALL GROUP Options

Vocabulary Reader, pp. T386–T387
Scaffold instruction to the English learner's proficiency level.

ENGLISH LANGUAGE SUPPORT

More Vocabulary Practice

Emerging/Expanding Distribute Dialogue, EL19.5 ⬚. Read the title aloud and have children repeat. Have children look at the title, images, and other information on the page. Then have them predict what they think the dialogue will be about.

• As you read the dialogue aloud, display the Context Cards for *trouble, cleared, tearing,* and *agreed.* After you read the dialogue, have children read the dialogue aloud with a partner.

• Have children draw signs they see every day, such as stop signs. Have them use phrases or short sentences to describe the purpose of each sign they drew.

• Allow children to include language from the dialogue. Encourage them to use high-utility words. **ELD** ELD.PI.2.1, ELD.PI.2.12b

DAY 1

Read and Comprehend

▶ **SHARE OBJECTIVES**

- Use text and graphic features to support understanding.
- Ask and answer questions while reading to guide comprehension.
- Access prior knowledge to exchange information about a topic. LANGUAGE

 TARGET SKILL

Text and Graphic Features

- Read the top section of **Student Book** p. 124 with children.
- Ask children to recall how using the pictures or photos in a selection can help the reader understand what is happening.
- Explain that the pictures will be very important in the story they will be reading. As children read the story, they should look at the pictures and read the signs in the pictures. They should then think about how the pictures go together with the words to tell the story.
- Draw attention to the graphic organizer. Explain to children that they will keep track of the pictures in a column chart as they read. Explain that when they come to a picture, they can describe the picture in the first column, the page number of the picture, and the purpose of the picture. Using this graphic organizer will help them better understand the story. **ELA** RL.2.7 **ELD** ELD.PI.2.6

ENGLISH LANGUAGE SUPPORT Draw a three-column chart on the board with the headings *Sign, Location,* and *Purpose.* Have children think of signs that are around their school to fill in the chart. **ELD** ELD.PI.2.1

 # Read and Comprehend

✓ **TARGET SKILL**

Text and Graphic Features Pictures in a story are kinds of **graphic features.** These features can help readers to better understand what they read.

As you read *The Signmaker's Assistant*, look carefully at the signs in the pictures. They can help you figure out what is happening in the story. A chart like the one below can help you keep track of what the pictures tell you.

Picture	Page Number	Purpose

✓ **TARGET STRATEGY**

Question Ask questions about what you are reading. Look for text evidence to answer your questions.

124 **ELA** RL.2.1, SL.2.1a, SL.2.1b **ELD** ELD.PI.2.1, ELD.PI.2.3

ENGLISH LANGUAGE SUPPORT

Comprehensible Input

Emerging Explain that an assistant helps someone do a job. Have children look at the cover picture. Ask, *Who is the signmaker's assistant? What do you think he does?* **ELD** ELD.PI.2.1, ELD.PI.2.3

Expanding Read aloud the first three paragraphs of p. 130. Help children use context clues and picture clues to figure out the meaning of *assistant.* **ELD** ELD.PI.2.1

Bridging Ask, *Why would a signmaker need an assistant?* Have children tell a partner about a time when they were someone's assistant. **ELD** ELD.PI.2.1, ELD.PI.2.3

Signs

Signs are everywhere. Signs help you find things you need, and they help you stay safe. For example, there are signs at the grocery store that help you find the food you want. Signs on the road help drivers know how to drive safely.

In *The Signmaker's Assistant*, you will read about what happens when someone changes the signs in a town.

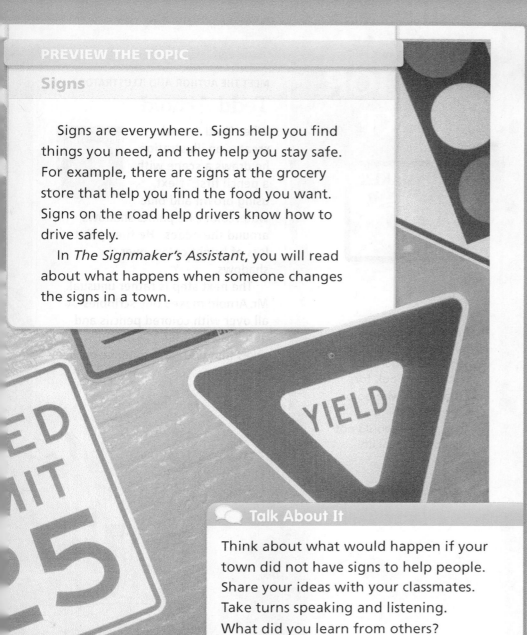

Talk About It

Think about what would happen if your town did not have signs to help people. Share your ideas with your classmates. Take turns speaking and listening. What did you learn from others?

125

COMPREHENSION STRATEGIES

Use the following strategies flexibly as you read with children by modeling how they can be used to improve comprehension and understanding of a text. See scaffolded support for the strategy shown in boldface during this week's reading.

- **Monitor/Clarify**
- **Summarize**
- **Infer/Predict**
- **Visualize**
- **Analyze/Evaluate**
- **Question**

Use Strategy Projectables ⬀, S1–S8, for additional support.

⬭ DOMAIN: Communication
LESSON TOPIC: Signs

✅ **TARGET STRATEGY**

Question

- Read the bottom of **Student Book** p. 124 with children. Tell them that as they read, they should stop occasionally to check their understanding. They can do this by asking themselves questions.

- Provide examples of questions that children could ask themselves, such as *What just happened? Why did the character act the way he did? What do the pictures show and how do they help me understand what I am reading?* Children should answer the questions before continuing to read.

- Explain that you will guide them to practice using the strategy when you read *The Signmaker's Assistant* together. **ELA** RL.2.1 **ELD** ELD.PI.2.6

PREVIEW THE TOPIC

Signs

- Tell children that today they will begin reading *The Signmaker's Assistant*. Read the information at the top of **Student Book** p. 125 with children.

- Ask children to name signs they see around them. If needed, use prompts such as, *What traffic signs have you seen? What signs do you see in store windows?* List the signs children name.

- Explain that signs are a way of giving information in a shortened way, and that the information on many signs helps keep people safe.

Talk About It

- Read the collaborative discussion prompt with children.

- Before the discussion, explain that when responding to a comment, a person can agree, disagree, share a similar idea, or ask a question. Model the skill using the following example.
  Student A: I feel good when I help people.
  Student B: I agree. It makes me feel good, too.

- After the discussion, have children share examples of how they responded to other's comments and what they learned. **ELA** SL.2.1a, SL.2.1b **ELD** ELD.PI.2.1, ELD.PI.2.3

ENGLISH LANGUAGE SUPPORT Use the image on Lesson 19 **Language Support Card** to review the lesson topic with children. Guide children to share and summarize what they have learned.
ELD ELD.PI.2.1, ELD.PI.2.12a

DAY 1

Read the Anchor Text

 GENRE

Humorous Fiction

- Read the genre information on **Student Book** p.126 with children.

- Preview the selection with children, and model identifying the characteristics of humorous fiction.

 Authors write humorous fiction to make the reader laugh. In humorous fiction, characters often do foolish things that have funny results. As I look through some of the pictures in this story, I see some silly signs. I also see people doing peculiar things. I think this story is humorous fiction.

- As you preview, ask children to point out additional examples that would lead them to think the selection is humorous fiction.
ELA RL.2.10 **ELD** ELD.PI.2.6

ENGLISH LANGUAGE SUPPORT Guide children at the emerging and expanding levels to complete the Academic English activities on Lesson 19 **Language Support Card.** **ELD** ELD.PII.2.3b, ELD.PII.2.5

Lesson 19

ANCHOR TEXT

MEET THE AUTHOR AND ILLUSTRATOR

Tedd Arnold

When Tedd Arnold creates an illustration, he draws a scene with a pencil first. Next, using brown and blue watercolors, he paints shadows around the edges. He then paints lots of bright colors over the shadows.

The next step is rather unusual. Mr. Arnold makes tiny scribbles all over with colored pencils and outlines everything in black. It takes him two days to make each illustration.

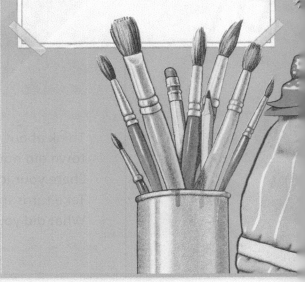

 GENRE

Humorous fiction is a story that is written to make the reader laugh. As you read, look for:

- ▶ characters who do or say funny things
- ▶ events that would not happen in real life

126 **ELA** RL.2.6, RL.2.7, RL.2.10
ELD ELD.PI.2.6, ELD.PI.2.7

Scaffold Close Reading

Strategies for Annotation

✎ 🖻 *Annotate it!*

As you read the selection with children, look for this icon ✎ 🖻 *Annotate it!* for opportunities to annotate the text collaboratively as a class.

Think Through the Text
FIRST READ

Develop comprehension through
- Guided Questioning
- Target Strategy: Question
- Vocabulary in Context

Analyze the Text
SECOND READ

Support analyzing short sections of text:
- Text and Graphic Features
- Point of View

Use directed note-taking with children to complete a graphic organizer during reading. Distribute copies of Graphic Organizer 1 🖻: Column Chart.

Independent Reading

- Children analyze the text independently, using the Reader's Guide on Reader's Notebook Volume 2 pp. 53–54 🖻. (See pp. T354–T355 for instructional support.)
- Children read independently in a self-selected trade book.

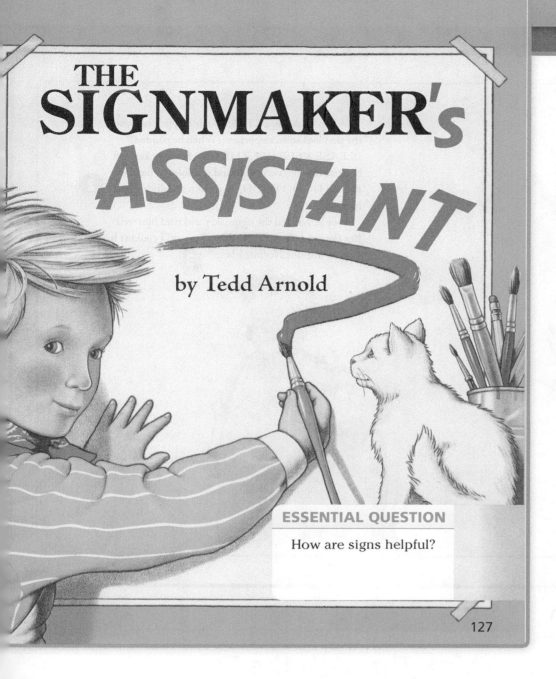

THE SIGNMAKER'S ASSISTANT

by Tedd Arnold

ESSENTIAL QUESTION

How are signs helpful?

127

READER AND TASK CONSIDERATIONS

ELA RL.2.2, SL.2.4, SL.2.6
ELD ELD.PI.2.1, ELD.PI.2.6, ELD.PI.2.12a

Determine the level of additional support your children will need to read and comprehend *The Signmaker's Assistant* successfully.

READERS

- **Motivate** Ask children to share times that they have been an assistant. What did they get to do? Was following rules important?

- **Access Knowledge and Experiences** Review with children the chart you completed as part of the Talk It Over activity on the back of Lesson 19 **Language Support Card**. Ask children to share with a partner experiences they've had with the sign types on the chart. Encourage them to use complete sentences.

TASKS

- **Increase Scaffolding** Stop periodically as you read to have children retell story events in order.

- **Foster Independence** Have children read the story in small groups. Have them assign parts and read the story as Readers' Theater.

ESSENTIAL QUESTION

- Read aloud the Essential Question on **Student Book** p. 127: *How are signs helpful?* Then tell children to think about this question as they read *The Signmaker's Assistant*.

Predictive Writing

- Tell children to write the Essential Question.

- Explain that they will write what they expect *The Signmaker's Assistant* to be about. Ask them to think about how the Essential Question relates to what they noticed while previewing the selection or what they already know about the Essential Question from their own experiences or past readings.

- Guide children to think about the genre of the selection as they write.

Set Purpose

- Explain that good readers think ahead and set a purpose for reading. They think about the title of the selection and what they have seen as they previewed. Then they ask themselves what they want to find out as they read the selection.

- Model setting a reading purpose.

Think Aloud *I think the illustrations will make this story fun to read. There is a lot of detail in the illustrations, so I am going to read the words carefully to understand exactly what is going on in the pictures.*

- Have children set their own purposes for reading. Ask several children to share their purposes with the class. **ELA** RF.2.4a, RL.2.10

Everyone in town agreed. The old signmaker did the finest work for miles around. Under his brush ordinary letters became beautiful words—words of wisdom, words of warning, or words that simply said which door to use. 1

When he painted STOP, people stopped because the sign looked so important. When he painted PLEASE KEEP OFF THE GRASS, they kept off because the sign was polite and sensible. When he painted GOOD FOOD, they just naturally became hungry. 2

People thanked the signmaker and paid him well. But the kind old man never failed to say, "I couldn't have done it without Norman's help." 3

128   129

DOMAIN: Communication

LESSON TOPIC: Signs

Cross-Curricular Connection Discuss with children the kind of information given by such traffic signs as stop signs, one-way street signs, and curvy road signs. Point out that these signs are a quick way of telling people the rules of a road. Ask children why it is important to pay close attention to road signs like these. Lead children to recognize that traffic signs keep people safe.

FIRST READ

Cite
Text Evidence

Think Through the Text

1. *What three kinds of words did the signmaker put on his signs?* **words of wisdom, words of warning, words that say which door to use** *What might be an example of "words of wisdom"?* **be kind to others** *What might be an example of "words of warning"?* **beware of the dog**
   ELA RL.2.1 **ELD** ELD.PI.2.6

2. *Why do the townspeople follow the signmaker's signs so carefully?* **They trust him because he makes good signs.** **ELA** RL.2.1 **ELD** ELD.PI.2.6

3. *What does the signmaker do when people thank him?* **He says he couldn't have done it without Norman's help.** *What does this tell you about the signmaker?* **He is nice. He appreciates Norman's help.** **ELA** RL.2.7

   ENGLISH LANGUAGE SUPPORT Provide sentence frames to encourage participation. *The signmaker says he couldn't have done it without _____. Norman's help I think the signmaker is _____ to have Norman's help. grateful, happy* **ELD** ELD.PI.2.6

Norman was the signmaker's assistant. Each day after school he cut wood, mixed colors, and painted simple signs.

"Soon I will have a shop of my own," said Norman. "Perhaps," answered the signmaker, "but not before you clean these brushes."

One day after his work was done, Norman stood at a window over the sign shop and watched people. They stopped at the STOP sign. They entered at the ENTER sign. They ate under the GOOD FOOD sign.

"They do whatever the signs say!" said Norman to himself. "I wonder . . ." He crept into the shop while the signmaker napped. With brush and board he painted a sign of his own. **4**

130

131

☑ **TARGET STRATEGY | Question**

Reread aloud the text in **Student Book** pp. 130–131. Remind children that it is useful to ask questions as they read stories to check that they understand what is happening. Then model the strategy:

Think Aloud *I wonder what Norman actually does for the signmaker. I can find out by rereading the page. I see that Norman cuts wood, mixes colors, paints simple signs, and cleans the signmaker's brushes.*

4 *What kind of sign do you think Norman will make?* **Possible response:** *funny signs* **ELA** RL.2.3 **ELD** ELD.PI.2.6

ENGLISH LANGUAGE SUPPORT Tell children that the word *assistant* has a cognate in Spanish: *asistente*. Remind children to look for cognates as they read to help them figure out the meanings of key words.

Early the next morning he put up the sign, then ran back to his window to watch.

"No school?" muttered the principal. "How could I forget such a thing?"

132

"No one informed me," said the teacher.

"Hooray!" cheered the children, and everyone went home.

5

"This is great!" cried Norman. He looked around town for another idea. "Oh," he said at last, "there is something I have always wanted to do."

6

> **ANALYZE THE TEXT**
>
> **Point of View** How does the principal feel about school being closed? How do the children feel?

133

FIRST READ

Cite Text Evidence

Think Through the Text

5 *Why does everyone believe the "No School Today" sign?* **People do whatever the signs say. People trust the signmaker's signs.**
ELA RL.2.1

ENGLISH LANGUAGE SUPPORT Provide sentence frames to help children describe why the people followed the *No School Today* sign. *When people see the signmaker's signs they always _____. follow them People think _____ made the* No School Today *sign. the signmaker They do not know that _____ is playing a trick.* Norman **ELD** ELD.PI.2.6

6 *What happens after Norman sees the children go home from school?* **He looks around for another idea for a sign.** **ELA** RL.2.3 **ELD** ELD.PI.2.6

☑ **PHONICS/DECODING STRATEGY**

Use Projectable S1 to help children apply the Phonics/Decoding strategy while reading **Student Book p. 135.** Write and read aloud *park, large,* and *started.* Circle the letters *ar,* pronounce the sounds they make together, and then have children read the words—/p/ /är/ /k/, /l/ /är/ /j/, /s/ /t/ /är/ /t/ /əd/.

The following day Norman jumped from the top of the fountain in the park. As he swam, he thought to himself, I can do lots of things with signs. Ideas filled his head.

That afternoon when Norman went to work, the signmaker said, "I must drive to the next town and paint a large sign on a storefront. I'll return tomorrow evening, so please lock up the shop tonight."

7

As soon as the signmaker was gone, Norman started making signs. He painted for hours and hours and hours.

8

134

135

---

7 *What does the signmaker ask Norman to do when he must go out of town?* **Lock up the shop.** *What does the signmaker think of Norman?* **The signmaker thinks he can trust Norman to take care of the shop.** **ELA** RL.2.1 **ELD** ELD.PI.2.6

8 *Think about the two signs that Norman has made. What have they told people to do?* **not to go to school, to swim in the park fountain** *Why did Norman make these signs?* **They looked like fun things to do.** *What kinds of signs do you think Norman will make while the signmaker is away?* **Sample answer:** *signs that tell people to do things that Norman would enjoy.* **ELA** RL.2.1

ENGLISH LANGUAGE SUPPORT Provide sentence frames and help children use them to make predictions. *Norman made those signs because _____.* **they were fun** *I think Norman will make signs that _____ because _____.* **tell people to do more things Norman will like; that will be fun for him** **ELD** ELD.PI.2.3, ELD.PI.2.6, ELD.PI.2.11

SECOND READ **DAY 2** *Analyze the Text*

Point of View

Remind children that different story characters often see the same event in different ways. Readers can see the different *points of view* of different characters through the words they say. Read the Analyze the Text box on **Student Book** p. 133 with children. Have children reread what the principal said and then what the children said. Then have children answer the questions. *The principal was confused because she did not remember canceling school. The children were happy.* **ELA** RL.2.6 **ELD** ELD.PI.2.6

🖉 📋 *Annotate it!* Work with children to highlight the text that shows the different feelings that the principal, the children, and Norman have about the *No School Today* sign.

9

In the morning people discovered new signs all around town.

ANALYZE THE TEXT

Text and Graphic Features What makes Norman's signs so funny?

136

137

Think Through the Text

9 *Why do you think the author wrote* The Signmaker's Assistant? *Support your answer with details from pages 136–137.* Sample answer: *I think the author wrote this selection to make readers laugh. I think this because pages 136–137 show people doing silly things that no one would do in real life.*

ENGLISH LANGUAGE SUPPORT Provide sentence frames and help children use them to give and support their opinions. *I think the author wrote* The Signmaker's Assistant *to make readers _____. laugh I think this because _____. the story is funny* **ELD** ELD.PI.2.3, ELD.PI.2.6, ELD.PI.2.11

138

139

Look closely at the pictures on pages 138–139. What do the signs say? *STOP/ANTS CROSSING. GARBAGE DUMP.* How do people respond to the signs? *They stop their vehicles to let ants cross. They dump garbage in front of the grocery store.* Why doesn't the author write about what the townspeople are doing? Sample answer: *The illustrations show people doing silly things, and the signs in the pictures explain why they are doing them.* **ELA** RL.2.7

ENGLISH LANGUAGE SUPPORT Provide sentence frames and help children to use them to describe the illustrations on pages 138–139. *The sign says _____. The picture shows _____.* **ELD** ELD.PI.2.6

Text and Graphic Features

Read the Analyze the Text box on **Student Book** p. 136 with children. Then display Projectable 19.4 and distribute Graphic Organizer 1. Tell children that you will work together to complete the graphic organizer.

Remind children of the importance of looking at both the text and the pictures in a story. Have children read the signs on p. 136 and describe what people do after reading them. Point out that this information is presented in the pictures, not the words. Guide them to complete the graphic organizer using the pictures on pp. 136–139. Then have them use the graphic organizer to answer the question on p. 136. **ELA** RL.2.7 **ELD** ELD.PI.2.6

✏ 🗎 Annotate it! Work with children to highlight the sentences that tell what the townspeople do when they realize they've been tricked.

Norman watched it all and laughed until tears came to his eyes. But soon he saw people becoming angry.

"The signmaker is playing tricks," they shouted. "He has made fools of us!"

The teacher tore down the NO SCHOOL TODAY sign. Suddenly people were tearing down all the signs—not just the new ones but every sign the signmaker had ever painted. **11**

140

Then the real trouble started. Without store signs, shoppers became confused. Without stop signs, drivers didn't know when to stop. Without street signs, firemen became lost.

141

FORMATIVE ASSESSMENT 3 2 1 **RtI**

Question IF children have difficulty applying the Question strategy, **THEN** use this model:

> *Think Aloud*
>
> *After I read page 140, I asked myself: What is in the picture? Which signs were torn down? I read the signs and discover that both silly and important signs were torn down. I think that this may be a problem.*

Think Through the Text

11 *What happens after the townspeople realize that they have been tricked? They become angry and tear down all the signs in town.* **ELA** RL.2.1, RL.2.3

ENGLISH LANGUAGE SUPPORT Remind children that authors often use connecting words to help readers understand the order in which things happen in the story. Read pages 140–141 with children, emphasizing the words *soon, suddenly,* and *then.* Discuss with children how these words help them understand the order of events after the townspeople realize they've been tricked. **ELD** ELD.PI.2.6, ELD.PII.2.2

☑ **TARGET STRATEGY | Question**

Tell children to practice the Question strategy as they reread **Student Book** p. 140 silently to themselves and look closely at the pictures. Ask children to point out where they used the strategy to help them clarify what is happening. **ELA** RL.2.1 **ELD** ELD.PI.2.6

In the evening when the signmaker returned from his work in the next town, he knew nothing of Norman's tricks. An angry crowd of people met him at the back door of his shop and chased him into the woods.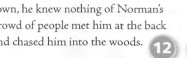

As Norman watched, he suddenly realized that without signs and without the signmaker, the town was in danger.

"It's all my fault!" cried Norman, but no one was listening.

142

143

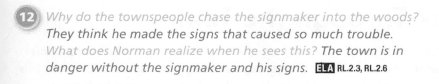

12 *Why do the townspeople chase the signmaker into the woods?* *They think he made the signs that caused so much trouble.* *What does Norman realize when he sees this?* *The town is in danger without the signmaker and his signs.* **ELA** RL.2.3, RL.2.6

ENGLISH LANGUAGE SUPPORT Provide sentence frames to encourage participation. *The townspeople chase the signmaker because _____. they think he played a trick on them Norman knows that the town is in danger without _____. the signmaker and his signs* **ELD** ELD.PI.2.6

13 *Why do the townspeople become angry at the signmaker instead of at Norman?* *They assume the signmaker is the person who has tricked them. They do not know that it was Norman.* **ELA** RL.2.3, RL.2.6 **ELD** ELD.PI.2.6

ENGLISH LANGUAGE SUPPORT

How English Works: Interpretive

Condensing Ideas Remind children that authors may join two short sentences into one to make an idea more exact. Read the last sentence on page 142 aloud and write it on the board. Explain that it is made up of two ideas: *An angry crowd of people met him at the back door of his shop* and *An angry crowd of people chased him into the woods.* Tell children that the author condensed, or combined, the two sentences using the word *and.* Then display the following sentences: *Norman painted new signs. Norman caused a lot of trouble.* Have partners talk about how they can combine these sentences. **ELD** ELD.PII.2.7

Late that night the signmaker returned and saw a light on in his shop. Norman was feverishly painting.

144

While the town slept and the signmaker watched, Norman put up stop signs, shop signs, street signs, danger signs, and welcome signs; in and out signs, large and small signs, new and beautiful signs. He returned all **14** his presents and cleared away the garbage at the grocery store. It was morning when he finished putting up his last sign for the entire town to see. **15**

145

ENGLISH LANGUAGE SUPPORT

Use Visuals

Emerging Have children look at the pictures and describe two of the signs. **ELD** ELD.PI.2.6

Expanding Ask children, *Are the signs funny? Which is the funniest?* **ELD** ELD.PI.2.6

Bridging Ask children, *What signs do you see in your neighborhood? What do they look like? What do they tell people to do?*

FIRST READ

Cite
Text Evidence

Think Through the Text

14 *What does Norman do after he puts up the new signs?* He returns all his presents and clears away the garbage at the grocery store. *What does this tell you about how he is feeling now?* He is very sorry and he feels ashamed. **ELA** RL.2.3

ENGLISH LANGUAGE SUPPORT Provide sentence frames to encourage participation. *After Norman puts up the new signs he returns his _____ and clears away _____.* presents; the garbage *I think Norman is feeling _____.* sorry for what he did **ELD** ELD.PI.2.6

15 *What does Norman's last sign say?* Don't blame the signmaker. I tricked you and I'm sorry. *How is this sign different from the other signs he made? It doesn't tell people to do silly things and is an apology note.* **ELA** RL.2.1 **ELD** ELD.PI.2.6

16 Then Norman packed his things and locked up the shop. But as he turned to go, he discovered the signmaker and all the townspeople gathered at the door.

"I know you're angry with me for what I did," said Norman with downcast eyes, "so I'm leaving."

"Oh, we were angry all right!" answered the school principal. "But we were also fools for obeying such signs without thinking." **17**

146

147

16 *Why does Norman pack his things?* **He is leaving the signmaker's shop because he is ashamed of what he has done. He thinks everyone will be mad at him.** ELA RL.2.3 ELD ELD.PI.2.6

17 *What do the townspeople learn about following signs?* **They learn that it is foolish to follow signs without thinking.** ELA RL.2.1

ENGLISH LANGUAGE SUPPORT Provide this sentence frame to encourage participation. *The townspeople learn they should not follow signs without _____.* thinking ELD ELD.PI.2.6

"You told us you are sorry," said the signmaker, "and you fixed your mistakes. So stay, and work hard. One day this shop may be yours." **18**

"Perhaps," answered Norman, hugging the old man, "but not before I finish cleaning those brushes." **19**

148

149

FIRST READ

Cite
Text Evidence

Think Through the Text

18 *What does the signmaker say to Norman?* Because Norman apologized and made up for his mistakes, he can stay and he may someday own the shop. *What does this tell you about the signmaker?* He is kind and forgiving. **ELA** RL.2.3, RL.2.6 **ELD** ELD.PI.2.6

19 *What does cleaning the brushes stand for at the end of the story?* Norman is trying to make a fresh start, and he will obey the signmaker. **ELA** RL.2.1 **ELD** ELD.PI.2.6

 Collaborative Conversation

Working in groups, have children discuss whether they think the townspeople can trust Norman. Before children begin their discussions, remind them that one of the reasons to have conversations is to listen to many opinions. Model the following sentence starters for giving a different opinion: *I don't agree with you because _____. I understand, but _____.*

ELA SL.2.1a, SL.2.6, L.2.6 **ELD** ELD.PI.2.1, ELD.PI.2.3

Guided Retelling

Oral Language

Use the retelling prompts on the **Retelling Cards** to guide children to tell the story.

ELA RL.2.2 **ELD** ELD.PI.2.6, ELD.PI.2.12a

front

Talk About It

What do the people in the town think of the signmaker's work?

Who is the boy in the picture? What is his job?

What does he notice about the people below?

back

front

Talk About It

Who made the signs in the picture?

What effect do the signs have on people? How can you tell?

back

front

Talk About It

What trouble happens after the people take down the signs?

Who is the signmaker running from? Why?

What are some words that you could use to describe how the signmaker might feel?

back

front

Talk About It

How does Norman fix what he did?

Do the townspeople also blame themselves? Why or why not?

What lesson does Norman learn? What lesson to the townspeople learn?

back

RETELLING RUBRIC

4	Highly Effective	The retelling names the characters, describes the problem, and tells important events in order. It includes several details and tells how the problem was solved.
3	Generally Effective	The retelling names the characters and tells most of the important events in order, including how the problem was solved. It includes some details.
2	Somewhat Effective	The retelling includes a few elements of the story, but omits important characters or events and provides few details.
1	Ineffective	The reader is unable to provide any accurate elements of *The Signmaker's Assistant*.

ENGLISH LANGUAGE SUPPORT

Review Key Ideas

All Proficiencies Pronounce and explain *retell*, reminding children that when they retell a story they are describing the main events in the order they happened. Page through *The Signmaker's Assistant* with children and share the following sentence frames to help them retell the selection.

Norman is the signmaker's _____. assistant He decides to trick the townspeople by _____ . making funny signs The townspeople get angry at _____ . the signmaker Norman tells the signmaker and the townspeople _____ . he is sorry **ELD** ELD.PI.2.6, ELD.PI.2.12a

Grammar Commas in Dates and Places

▶ **SHARE OBJECTIVES**
- **Grammar** Use commas in dates. LANGUAGE
- **Spelling** Spell words with *ar*.
- **Writing** Identify the characteristics of a good narrative. LANGUAGE

ENGLISH LANGUAGE SUPPORT

Comprehensible Input

Emerging Write today's date. Write the comma in a different color. Explain that dates are written: month, day, year. Write a date without the comma. Say, *Is this date written correctly? no What does it need to be correct? a comma Where do I write the comma? between the number of the day and the year*

Expanding Write several dates without commas. Guide children to add commas in a different color to the dates you have written.

Bridging Ask partners to ask each other when they were born and write the date.

All Proficiencies: Linguistic Transfer As the /r/ sound may not exist or may be pronounced differently in many languages other than English, the *r*-controlled vowel sound /är/ may be difficult for children. Demonstrate mouth and tongue positions and provide time for children to practice the sound. **ELD** ELD.PIII.2

1 Teach/Model

Commas in Dates Display Projectable 19.2 ⬚. Explain to children how to use commas in sentences with dates.

ENGLISH LANGUAGE SUPPORT Tell children that the Spanish cognate for *comma* is *coma*.

- Tell children that a comma is used between the number of the day and the year to separate them, but not between the month and the day. Tell them the year is always listed last.

- Model identifying the correct place to put a comma in this example sentence: *Papa built the fruit stand on May 15, 2010.*

Think Aloud To identify the correct place to put the comma, I ask this Thinking Question: *Which number shows the day, and which number shows the year? The number 15 is the day of the month, and 2010 is the year. The comma belongs between these two numbers.*

2 Guided Practice/Apply

- Complete the examples on **Projectable 19.2** with children.

- Have children use the Thinking Question to identify the correct place in each sentence to put the comma.

- Distribute Reader's Notebook Volume 2 page 47 ⬚ to children to complete independently.

Spelling Words with *ar*

SPELLING WORDS AND SENTENCES

BASIC

1. **car** Our *car* has four doors.
2. **dark** It gets *dark* at night.
3. **arm** I fell and broke my *arm*.
4. **star** The sun is a *star*.
5. **park*** We play soccer in the *park*.
6. **yard** Grass grows in the *yard*.
7. **party** Come to the *party*!
8. **hard*** He skates on the *hard* ice.
9. **farm** We grow corn on our *farm*.

10. **start** The game will *start* late.
11. **part** A dial is *part* of a clock.
12. **spark** A *spark* starts the fire.

REVIEW

13. **art** We painted in *art* class.
14. **jar** The jelly is in the glass *jar*.

CHALLENGE

15. **carpet** *Carpet* covers the floor.
16. **apartment** My brother lives in an *apartment*.

A form of this word appears in the literature.

Administer the Pretest
Say each Spelling Word. Then read aloud its sentence and repeat the word. Have children write the word. **ELA** L.2.2d

Teach the Principle
- Review the sound and spelling on **Sound/Spelling Card** *artist*. Point to *ar* as you say *artist*. Write *dark* and *yard*, underlining the *ar* in each word. Then read each word aloud. Explain that the /är/ sound can be spelled with the letters *ar*.

Model a Word Sort
Model sorting words based on the location of the /är/ sound spelled *ar*. Present the Model the Sort lesson on page 92 of the **Literacy and Language Guide**.

Narrative Writing Introduce the Model

1 Teach/Model

Fictional Story Display and read aloud <u>Projectable 19.3</u>.

• Use the labels on **Projectable 19.3** to identify the characteristics of a good story and examples of interesting details.

• Read and discuss the Writer's Checklist about stories.

Writer's Checklist

What Makes a Great Story?

• It has a **beginning**, **middle**, and **end**.

• It has interesting **details** about the **setting**, **characters**, and their **problem**.

• The **events** are in an order that makes sense.

2 Guided Practice/Apply

• Reread and discuss **Projectable 19.3**.

Model Study Ask: *What is the problem? A white crane was tangled in string. What did Alika do to try to solve the problem? She tried to free the crane, and then ran to get her father. How was the problem finally solved? Alika talked softly to the crane. Her father gently cut the string, and the crane was able to fly away.*

ELA W.2.3, W.2.4, W.2.10 **ELD** ELD.PI.2.10, ELD.PII.2.1

ENGLISH LANGUAGE SUPPORT Discuss the meaning of the words *problem* and *solution* with children. Give them simple problems and ask them what the solution might be. Give sample problems such as *I dropped my pencil, I forgot my lunch,* or *My shoe is untied.* Have children tell how they would solve those problems by using the sentence frame *I would solve that problem by ____.*

Daily Proofreading Practice

the asistant painter made a funny
sign. It ~~were~~ for the ~~arte~~ sale.

Performance Task

Children may prewrite, draft, revise, and publish their narrative writing task through *my*WriteSmart beginning on Day 3.

Additional support for Narrative Writing appears in the **Common Core Writing Handbook,** Lesson 19.

DAY 2

Today's Goals

Vocabulary & Oral Language

 TARGET VOCABULARY

assistant	tearing
agreed	wisdom
polite	cleared
failed	trouble

Phonemic Awareness
- Substitute Phonemes

Phonics & Fluency
- Words with *ar*
- **Fluency:** Phrasing: Punctuation
- **Decodable Reader:** *Darling Starling*
- High-Frequency Words

Text-Based Comprehension
- **Dig Deeper:** Use Clues to Analyze the Text
- Text and Graphic Features
- Point of View
- **Reread the Anchor Text:** *The Signmaker's Assistant*

Grammar & Writing
- **Commas in Dates and Places**
- **Narrative Writing:** Fictional Story
- **Trait:** Organization

Spelling
- Words with *ar*

Opening Routines

Warm Up with Wordplay

How Do They Go Together?

Display and read aloud the following:

> **Turn Off Cell Phones**
>
> **Keep Off the Grass**
>
> **Don't Walk**

Have children turn and talk with partners about what these commands have in common. (They are all words that might appear on a sign.) Remind them to use discussion rules.

Ask partners to think of and share with the class other phrases they see on signs.

ELA SL.2.1a **ELD** ELD.PI.2.1

Daily Phonemic Awareness

Substitute Phonemes

- *I am going to say a word and then change the vowel sound to make a new word. Say the word after me:* had. Model how to make a new word by changing the vowel sound to /är/: /h/ /ă/ /d/; /h/ /är/ /d/.

- Have children continue with the words *ham/harm, pack/park, bay/bar,* and *am/arm.*

Corrective Feedback

- If a child is unable to make a substitution, provide correction and model the task. Example: *Listen to this word:* had, /h/ /ă/ /d/. *Change* /ă/ *to* /är/. *What is the new word?* hard

- Have children repeat once with you before doing it on their own. Have them continue with the other words.

Daily High-Frequency Words

- Point to **High-Frequency Word Card 181**, *didn't.*
- *Say the word.* didn't *Spell the word.* d-i-d-n-'-t *Write the word. Check the word.*
- Repeat the routine with new words *I'll* and *sound* and with review words *are, baby, good, is, please, talk,* and *too.* **ELA** RF.2.3f

Letter Play

- Provide dried beans, rice, or macaroni. Write each High-Frequency Word on a slip of paper.
- Have partners take turns taking a slip of paper, reading the word aloud, and then using one of the materials to spell the word.

Corrective Feedback

- If a child does not recognize the word *didn't,* say the correct word and have children repeat it. Didn't. *What is the word?* didn't
- Have children spell the word. d-i-d-n-'-t *How do we say this word?* didn't
- Have children reread all of the cards in random order.

Daily Vocabulary Boost

- Review the Target Vocabulary (p. T314). Remind children that they heard these words in the Read Aloud, "Wild Friends, Wow!" Recall the article with children as you guide them to interact with each word's meaning.

Wild Friends is a group of students and teachers who have agreed to help wildlife. Name something your friends agreed on.

Whooping Cranes, huge snow-white birds, were in trouble. Have you ever helped a person or animal in trouble? How?

Many students wrote polite letters to lawmakers. Describe a time when you were very polite to someone.

- Continue with children in the same manner with *assistant, failed, tearing, wisdom,* and *cleared.* **ELA** L.2.6

Vocabulary in Context Cards 145–152

☑ **Target Vocabulary**

assistant
agreed
polite
failed
tearing
wisdom
cleared
trouble

Phonics

▶ SHARE OBJECTIVES

- Substitute sounds in words.
- Blend, build, and read regularly spelled words with *ar* (*r*-controlled vowel syllable).
- Reread text with *ar* words and High-Frequency Words for fluency practice.

▶ SKILLS TRACE

Words with *ar*	
Introduce	**pp. T316–T317, T342–T343**
Differentiate	pp. T384–T385
Reteach	p. T398
Review	pp. T362, T452, T463
Assess	Weekly Tests, Lesson 19

ENGLISH LANGUAGE SUPPORT

Use Visuals and Gestures

All Proficiencies Continue to reinforce the meanings of words children decode in Blending Lines. Use visuals, such as **Picture Cards** *farm, scarf,* and *yard*, as well as gestures and pantomime, to help clarify word meaning. Reinforce the meanings of the words *cart* and *market* as you show a photograph or illustration of a market and use the words in sentences such as *We put food in a cart at the market.* Demonstrate marching and playing an instrument while saying *The band marches down the street.* Have children repeat your sentences as they point to the related image or imitate your gestures.

Words with *ar*

Phonemic Awareness Warm-Up *Today we are going to substitute vowel sounds in words to create new words. I'll do it first. Listen:* pat. *Now listen as I change the /ă/ in* pat *to /är/:* part. *Now let's do it together. Say:* pat. *Change the /ă/ in* pat *to /är/. What's the new word?* part

Let's do some more. Change the /ā/ in lake *to /är/.* lark *Change the /ă/ in* pack *to /är/.* park *Change the /ā/ in* make *to /är/.* mark *Change the /ă/ in* ham *to /är/.* harm *Change the /ā/ in* fame *to /är/.* farm

1 Teach/Model

Review **Sound/Spelling Cards** *artist.* Remind children that the letters *ar* together stand for the /är/ sound.

Continuous Blending Routine Use the routine to model blending *harm*, displaying **Letter Cards** *h, ar,* and *m.* Name the letters.

- Blend the sounds, stretching out the word while pointing to each letter in a sweeping motion. *Listen: /h/ /är/ /m/.*
- Have children blend the sounds and say the word with you.

2 Guided Practice

Blending Lines

Blend Words Repeat the blending routine with the first two pairs of words in Line 1 below; help children compare the sounds and spellings. Point to each word as children read the entire line chorally. Continue with the remaining lines. Then call on volunteers to reread selected words until children can identify the words quickly.

1. pack	park	chain	chart	far	farm
2. cat	cart	shark	shack	bark	bake
3. aim	arm	scale	scarf	marches	matches

Transition to Longer Words Use a similar process for Lines 4–6.

4. spark	sparkle	car	carpet	yard	barnyard
5. smart	outsmart	mark	market	part	partner
6. tar	target	card	postcard	harm	harmful

Challenge Call on above-level children to read the words in Line 7. Then have the class read the sentences chorally.

7. carnival lumberyard discard gardener faraway alarming
8. The tiny <u>baby</u> started to cry in the dark.
9. We <u>didn't</u> travel <u>too</u> far in the large car.

Build Words Model how to spell the word *charm*, using **Letter Cards**. *The letters* ch *together stand for the first sound, /ch/. The next sound in* charm *is /är/. The letters* ar *together stand for the vowel sound /är/. The last sound in* charm *is /m/. The letter* m *stands for /m/. Now read the word with me:* charm.

- Guide children to identify sounds and spell the words *scarf, hilly, start, target, harvest,* and *muddy*. Call on children to spell words with **Letter Cards** while others check their work. **ELA** L.2.2d

3 Apply

Have partners take turns rereading Blending Lines 1–3 and 4–6. Then ask them to think about the sounds as they write these words: *yard, chart, arm, carpet,* and *market*. Have partners check their spelling using Blending Lines, and then work together to use each word in a sentence. **ELA** L.2.2d

Distribute Reader's Notebook Volume 2 page 48 or leveled practice in Grab-and-Go™ Resources for children to complete independently.

Practice Fluency

Use Instructional Routine 15 to have partners read the **Decodable Reader** *Darling Starling*. Remind them to look for groups of words that go together to make their reading sound natural.

Darling Starling
by Mary James
illustrated by Judy Lanfredi

This is Darling. She is a starling.
She is a city starling. Darling likes
city life. She likes city rain.

Decodable Reader

DAY 2

SECOND READ

Dig Deeper: Use Clues to Analyze the Text

▶ **SHARE OBJECTIVES**

- Use information in illustrations and words to demonstrate understanding of characters, setting, or plot. LANGUAGE
- Recognize differences in points of view of characters.

ENGLISH LANGUAGE SUPPORT

Use Visuals

Emerging Explain that readers can learn things just by looking at pictures. Ask children to point to Norman in the illustrations. What can readers learn from noticing how often he appears? *He is the main character.* **ELD** ELD.PI.2.6

Expanding Have children ask a question about the story and use information from one of the illustrations to answer it. **ELD** ELD.PI.2.6

Bridging Ask children to look for details in the pictures that do not appear in the story's words. Ask how this adds to the story. **ELD** ELD.PI.2.6

Text-Based Comprehension

1 Teach/Model

Terms About Literature

graphic features photos or drawings, such as maps or charts, that stand for ideas or add details to the text

point of view the way a character or person thinks about an event

---

- Explain that authors use graphic features, such as pictures, to make their ideas clearer. Often pictures tell parts of a story.

ENGLISH LANGUAGE SUPPORT Tell children that the words *graphic feature* have a cognate in Spanish: *elemento gráfico*. Show children some maps, charts, or newspapers to help them better understand graphic features. Point out that the word *map* also has a Spanish cognate: *mapa*.

- Tell children that good readers look at all the words and graphics on a page and then think about how they go together. *Sometimes we can figure out what is happening in a story just from the words. Other times, we may have to use pictures to understand the characters' actions.*

- Discuss the column chart, using this model.

  Think Aloud *This column chart can help me figure out the information the author gives through the pictures. For example, if I look at page 132, I see a sign that says NO SCHOOL TODAY. The picture shows the principal, who is confused, and many students. In my chart under, Text or Graphic Feature, I write, "a school with a NO SCHOOL TODAY sign." In the second column, I write the page number. In the third column, I write the picture's purpose: to show that Norman has made a sign telling people not to go to school today. Now I will think about what the words said and figure out how the words and picture go together. The sign made everyone confused.*

- Next, read **Student Book** p. 151 with children. Point out that people looking at the same events may see things in a completely different way.

- Give students examples. For instance, say, *Suppose a friend drops a brand-new toy into the mud. You may think that is funny. Now think about how your friend might feel. He or she may feel very sad, angry, or afraid he/she will get in trouble. The two of you will have different points of view.*

Q BE A READING DETECTIVE

Dig Deeper

Use Clues to Analyze the Text

Use these pages to learn about Text and Graphic Features and Point of View. Then read *The Signmaker's Assistant* again. Use what you learn to understand it better.

Text and Graphic Features

In *The Signmaker's Assistant,* you read about a boy who changed all of the signs in his town. The pictures, or **graphic features,** in this story help you understand what is happening. You have to read the signs in the pictures to understand the problem.

When you read, use a chart like the one below to list the graphic features in the story and what they tell you about the characters, setting, or plot.

Text or Graphic Feature	Page Number	Purpose

150

Point of View

Characters in a story sometimes think about the same event in different ways. Each character has a different **point of view.** Look at page 140 again. Think about how the characters feel when Norman changes the signs. Norman thinks it is funny, but the townspeople are angry. As you read a character's words, think about how he or she might feel about what is happening.

151

---

2 Guided Practice/Apply

Analyze the Text

Begin a second read of *The Signmaker's Assistant* with children. Use the stopping points and instructional support to guide children to analyze the text:

- Text and Graphic Features, p. T331 ELA RL.2.7 ELD ELD.PI.2.6

- Point of View, p. T329 ELA RL.2.6 ELD ELD.PI.2.6, ELD.PI.2.7

Directed Note Taking The graphic organizer will be completed with children during the second read on p. T331. ELA RL.2.7 ELD ELD.PI.2.6

FORMATIVE ASSESSMENT   RtI

Are children able to use text and graphic features to answer questions?

IF...	THEN...
children struggle,	use **Differentiate Comprehension** for Struggling Readers, p. T388. See also Intervention Lesson 19, pp. S34–S35.
children are on track,	use **Differentiate Comprehension** for On-Level Readers, p. T388.
children excel,	use **Differentiate Comprehension** for Advanced Readers, p. T389.

Differentiate Comprehension, pp. T388–T389
Scaffold instruction to the English learner's proficiency level.

Your Turn

Cite
Text Evidence

▶ SHARE OBJECTIVES

- Use text and graphic features to support understanding.
- Write dialogue for a short play.
- Condense ideas to create precise and detailed sentences in shared language activities. LANGUAGE

RETURN TO THE ESSENTIAL QUESTION

As children respond to the Essential Question, ask them to look back at the story to identify different signs. List them on the board. Then have children name signs from their own community. Remind them to think about traffic signs, signs on stores, and billboard signs. List these signs. Have children discuss which signs help keep them safe and which give them information. Remind children to listen carefully to what others say and to build on the ideas that other children express. **ELA** SL.2.1a, SL.2.1b **ELD** ELD.PI.2.1, ELD.PI.2.3, ELD.PI.2.6, ELD.PI.2.12a

Classroom Conversation Have children take a picture walk through *The Signmaker's Assistant* as they briefly recount the events of the story. Have them consider where in the story the author used pictures to get his ideas across. Have children discuss the kind of person Norman is and how the events of the story changed Norman. Finally, point out that characters in stories often learn important lessons. Have them discuss the lesson Norman learned. **ELA** RL.2.2, RL.2.7, SL.2.1a **ELD** ELD.PI.2.1, ELD.PI.2.3, ELD.PI.2.6, ELD.PI.2.11

ENGLISH LANGUAGE SUPPORT Use sentence frames such as the following to support discussion.

It was important to look at the pictures as I read the story because ____.

I think Norman is sorry for tricking the town because ____.

Norman learned that ____.

As children share their ideas, have them use gestures and refer to the story for help completing the sentence frames. **ELD** ELD.PI.2.6, ELD.PI.2.12a

---

Your Turn

RETURN TO THE ESSENTIAL QUESTION

Turn and Talk

How are signs helpful?
Think about the signs in *The Signmaker's Assistant.* Then think about signs that you have seen in your town. Discuss your ideas with a partner. Add your own ideas to what he or she says.

Classroom Conversation

Now talk about these questions with the class.

1. How do the words and illustrations work together to help you understand this story?

2. Why do you think Norman is sorry for tricking the town? Explain your answer using text evidence.

3. What lesson does Norman learn?

152 **ELA** RL.2.2, RL.2.6, RL.2.7, W.2.3, W.2.4, W.2.10, SL.2.1b **ELD** ELD.PI.2.1, ELD.PI.2.6, ELD.PI.2.10

ENGLISH LANGUAGE SUPPORT

How English Works: Collaborative

Condensing Ideas Before children begin discussing the Essential Question, help them focus on using sentences that are detailed and that give exact messages. Tell children that sometimes a more exact sentence can be made from two shorter sentences. Show children the following example: *Signs are important. Signs are helpful.* Then provide a revised sentence, and explain how it was condensed. Help children at different proficiency levels condense sentences to use during their discussions. **ELD** ELD.PII.2.3a

Performance Task

WRITE ABOUT READING

Response Think about how the signmaker and Norman treat each other. Work with a partner. Write a short play about Norman and the signmaker. Show how they act toward each other during one part of the story. Take turns acting out each character's lines. Use a different voice for each character to show how each is feeling.

Writing Tip

When you write a play, write each character's name followed by what he or she says.

153

WRITE ABOUT READING

Performance Task

Remind children that individual characters in plays say things that convey actions and feelings. Write on the board a formatted example of dialogue from the story, such as:

Principal: (muttering) *No school? How could I forget such a thing?* Teacher: (confused) *No one informed me!*

Have partners select brief sections of the story. Tell partners they may use the exact words that characters say, or invent dialogue. They can include in parentheses the way the character is feeling or how the character is moving.

Have partners act out their dialogue, using characters' voices. Ask partners to express their feelings and point of view through their voices and to move as they think the characters would.

Writing Tip Make sure children read the Writing Tip before they begin writing. Encourage children to look back at a Readers' Theater script if they need help in formatting their scripts correctly. **ELA** RL.2.6, W.2.3, W.2.4, W.2.10, L.2.1f

See **Analytic Writing Rubric** on p. R17.

 Have children complete the Write About Reading activity through *my*WriteSmart. Children will read the prompt within *my*WriteSmart and have access to multiple writing resources, including the Student eBook, Writing Rubrics, and Graphic Organizers.

ENGLISH LANGUAGE SUPPORT

Comprehensible Input

All Proficiencies Before children begin writing, guide them to act out a part of the story. For example, use the illustration on **Student Book** p. 129 as a guide. Point out that the signmaker was always very kind to Norman. Have children act out how the signmaker might have asked Norman to do something in the shop and what Norman would have said in response. Then guide children to put the sentences into play form. **ELD** ELD.PI.2.10, ELD.PI.2.12a

Grammar Commas in Dates and Places

▶ SHARE OBJECTIVES

- **Grammar** Use commas with place names.
- **Spelling** Spell words with *ar*. LANGUAGE
- **Handwriting** Write Spelling Words.
- **Writing** Write a strong beginning, middle, and ending for a narrative. LANGUAGE

ENGLISH LANGUAGE SUPPORT

Comprehensible Input

All Proficiencies Have children name your city or town and state. Write the combination without the comma. Invite children to insert the comma in the place name. Continue the activity by having children name other town and state combinations.

Primary-Language Support Emerging English learners may benefit from responding in their first language to begin with, followed by responding in English. This is a scaffold that can be removed gradually as students gain proficiency in English.

1 Teach/Model

Commas with Place Names Display Projectable 19.5 ⬆. Explain to children how to use a comma with names of places.

- Explain that a comma belongs between the name of the city or town and the name of the state. Tell them the state is always listed last in a place name.

- Model identifying the correct place to put a comma in this example sentence: *Jake owns a store in Chicago, Illinois.*

Think Aloud *To identify the correct place to put a comma in a place name, I ask this Thinking Question: Which word is the name of the city or town, and which word is the name of the state? Chicago is the city, and Illinois is the state. So the comma goes between Chicago and Illinois.*

FOR STANDARD ENGLISH LEARNERS Display a map of the United States and have children point to a location they would like to visit. Write the cities and states on the board. Model adding the comma to one example. Then have children come up and add the comma to their answers.

2 Guided Practice/Apply

- Complete other examples on **Projectable 19.5** with children.

- Have children use the Thinking Question to correctly identify the name of the city and the state and the correct place to put the comma to separate them.

- Distribute Reader's Notebook Volume 2 page 50 ⬆ to children to complete independently.

Spelling Words with *ar*

SPELLING WORDS

BASIC

car	start
dark	part
arm	spark
star	**REVIEW**
park*	art
yard	jar
party	**CHALLENGE**
hard*	carpet
farm	apartment

*A form or forms of these words appear in the literature.

Teach/Word Sort

- Review **Sound/Spelling Card** *artist*. *What sound do you hear at the beginning of* artist? /är/ *How is the /är/ sound spelled?* ar

- Draw a two-column chart with the headings *One Consonant* and *Two Consonants*.

- Guide children in writing Spelling Words in each column. Words that begin with a single consonant should go in one column, and words that begin with two consonants should go in the other column. Then have children write in other *ar* words they know.

- Distribute Reader's Notebook Volume 2 p. 49 ⬆ to children to complete independently. **ELA** L.2.2d

Guess My Category

For additional practice with the Spelling Words, guide children to complete the Guess My Category activity on page 92 of the **Literacy and Language Guide.**

Handwriting

Model how to form the Basic Words *car, dark, arm, star, park,* and *yard.* Handwriting models are available on pp. R24–R29 and on the Handwriting Models Blackline Masters ⬆. Remind children to write legibly and stay within the margins. **ELA** L.2.1g

Narrative Writing Focus Trait: Organization

1 Teach/Model

Beginning, Middle, and End Remind children that a good story has a beginning, a middle, and an end. Tell children that good persuasive essays have a clear purpose. Part of the purpose of a persuasive essay is to state the goal of the essay and provide supporting facts.

- The beginning introduces the characters, the setting, and the problem.

- The middle shows the characters working to solve the problem.

- The end shows how the problem was solved.

- Discuss the beginning, middle, and end of *The Signmaker's Assistant*. Identify the beginning, middle, and end. Then identify the elements of each.

Beginning	Introduces characters (signmaker and Norman)
	Introduces the setting (town)
	Introduces the problem (The townspeople obey all the signs they see, so Noman decides to put up some silly signs.)
Middle	The townspeople do what the silly signs say.
	The townspeople get angry.
End	Norman says he's sorry.
	The townspeople realize that they should think before they obey signs. They forgive Norman.

2 Guided Practice/Apply

- Write: "*Everyone in town agreed. The old signmaker did the finest work for miles around.*"

- Ask children to explain why this is a good beginning. Possible response: *It introduces the character (the signmaker) and the setting (the town). It is interesting and makes the reader want to read more about the signmaker.*

- Distribute Reader's Notebook Volume 2 page 51 to children to complete independently. **ELA** W.2.4, W.2.10 **ELD** ELD.PI.2.10, ELD.PII.2.1

Daily Proofreading Practice

art
The arts store opened on
                                    park
May 1, 2008. it is next to the parke.

ENGLISH LANGUAGE SUPPORT

Visual Aids

All Proficiencies Provide a visual aid for children to symbolize beginning, middle, and end. For example, this may be a train engine, car, and caboose, or the head, body, and tail of a caterpillar. Have children draw pictures for *The Signmaker's Assistant* for each part of the story in the appropriate section of the visual.

my WriteSmart Children may prewrite, draft, revise, and publish their narrative writing task through *my*WriteSmart beginning on Day 3.

DAY 3

Today's Goals

Vocabulary & Oral Language
• Apply Vocabulary Knowledge

☑ **TARGET VOCABULARY**

assistant	tearing
agreed	wisdom
polite	cleared
failed	trouble

Phonemic Awareness
• Substitute Phonemes

Phonics & Fluency
• Long *i* (*i, igh, ie, y*)
• Long *e* sound for *y*
• Read Decodable Reader: *Going to the Farm*
• Fluency: Phrasing: Punctuation
• High-Frequency Words

Text-Based Comprehension
• Independent Reading
• Reader's Guide
• Self-Selected Reading

Grammar & Writing
• Commas in Dates, Places, and Letters
• Narrative Writing: Fictional Story

Spelling
• Words with *ar*

Opening Routines

Warm Up with Wordplay

Change a Word

Tell children that you will read some sentences where the short *a* sound in a word should be changed to the sound /är/ to make sense (as in *ban* should be *barn*).

Display the following sentences and have children read along with you:

> **I found the missing pat for the puzzle.**
> **Put the books on the cat.**
> **It is not had to clean up.**
> **I will write your names on the chat.**

Reread each sentence, and have children identify the incorrect word. Then have them provide the correct word. Replace the word on the board as it is provided.

Daily Phonemic Awareness

Substitute Phonemes

- *We can change a sound in a word to make a new word. Listen:* dot. *What sounds do you hear?* /d/ /ŏ/ /t/ *Let's change the /ŏ/ sound to the /är/ sound. What are the sounds now?* /d/ /är/ /t/ *What word does it make?* dart

- Have children continue with the words *foam/farm, mat/mart, code/card,* and *much/march.*

Corrective Feedback

- If a child is unable to make a substitution, say the word, give correction, and model the task. Example: *The word is* dot. *I can change the /ŏ/ sound in* dot *to /är/ and make a new word,* dart. *Dot–dart.*

- Have children repeat the words with you. Then have them say the words on their own and continue with other words.

Daily High-Frequency Words

- Point to **High-Frequency Word Card 183,** *please.*

- *Say the word.* please *Spell the word.* p-l-e-a-s-e *Write the word. Check the word.*

- Repeat the procedure with the words *are, baby, didn't, good, I'll, is, sound, talk,* and *too.* **ELA** RF.2.3f

Hopscotch

- Create a hopscotch pattern on the floor with masking tape. Write one letter from the word *please* in each box and then write the whole word at the top.

- Invite children to hop from one letter to the next, saying each letter to spell the word. Have them say the word.

- Repeat the activity for the words *I'll* and *didn't.*

Corrective Feedback

- If a child does not recognize the word *please,* say the correct word and have children repeat it. Please. *What is the word?* please

- Have children spell the word. p-l-e-a-s-e *How do we say this word?* please

- Have children reread all of the cards in random order.

Daily Vocabulary Boost

- Guide children to interact with the Target Vocabulary by asking the following questions. Remind them to speak clearly when participating in discussion.

  If you had an assistant, what would your assistant do?

  Tell about someone you know who has a lot of wisdom.

  What are some ways to be polite?

- Have children work together to explain *assistant, wisdom,* and *polite* in their own words. Make sure children follow appropriate rules for discussion, such as listening to speakers, taking turns, and staying on topic. **ELA** SL.2.1a, L.2.6 **ELD** ELD.PI.2.1

Vocabulary in Context Cards 145–152

☑ **Target Vocabulary**

assistant

agreed

polite

failed

tearing

wisdom

cleared

trouble

DAY 3

Phonics

▶ **SHARE OBJECTIVES**

- Identify sounds in words.
- Read and sort words with long e spelled *y* and long *i* spelled *i, igh, ie, y,* including vowel teams (vowel team syllables) and two-syllable words with long vowels.
- Read text with *ar* words (*r*-controlled vowel syllables) and High-Frequency Words.

FORMATIVE ASSESSMENT · **RtI**

Corrective Feedback When a child mispronounces a letter-sound, highlight that letter, restate its sound, have children repeat the sound, and then guide them to blend the word. See the example below.

Decoding Error: A child sorts *baby* under the long *i* spelling.

Correct the error. Say the correct word. *The word is* baby. *It ends with the long* e *sound /ē/, spelled with the letter* y.

Model *Listen: /b/ /ā/, /b/ /ē/. What's the vowel sound at the end of* baby? */ē/ The letter* y *often stands for the sound /ē/ at the end of a word with two or more syllables. The letter* y *stands for the sound /ē/ in* baby.

Guide *Let's read together:* baby. *What is the final sound? /ē/*

Check *What letter stands for the long* e *sound /ē/ in* baby? y

Reinforce Record the error and review the word again before the next lesson.

Go to p. T390 for additional phonics support.

Cumulative Review

Phonemic Awareness Warm-Up *I'll say a word. You say the sounds you hear and name the vowel sound. I'll do it first. Listen:* sky. *Now I'll say each sound: /s/ /k/ /ī/. Let's do it together. Say:* sky. *What sounds do you hear? /s/ /k/ /ī/ Which sound is the vowel sound? /ī/ What do we call that sound?* long i

Now you say the sounds in these words and name the vowel sound(s): tight, */t/ /ī/ /t/, long* i; baby, */b/ /ā/, /b/ /ē/, long a and long e;* child, */ch/ /ī/ /l/ /d/, long* i; pie, */p/ /ī/, long* i; ivy, */ī/, /v/ /ē/, long i and long e;* mighty, */m/ /ī/, /t/ /ē/, long i and long e.*

Word Sort Write the following words on the board in random order: *baby, silent, city, cry, pilot, fried, flight, mind, flying, funny, high, lady, lie, night, penny, pie, copy, sunlight, July, sigh, child, thigh, tie, myself, spider.*

- Have partners take turns reading the words and identifying the long vowel sounds. Have them sort the words according to the vowel sound they hear, long e or long *i*. Use the **Corrective Feedback** steps if children need additional help.

- Call on children to read aloud the words in each group. Challenge them to further sort the long *i* words according to their spelling pattern—*i, igh, ie,* or *y.*

Write and Sort Words Have partners write more words with the vowel spelling patterns for long *i (i, igh, ie, y)* and the long e sound for *y.* Then have partners exchange words with another pair of children, read the words aloud, and sort the words according to sound and spelling patterns. **ELA** RF.2.3b, RF.2.3c, RF.2.3e

Practice Fluency

Use Instructional Routine 12 ⤤ to have children read the **Decodable Reader** *Going to the Farm* chorally, using appropriate phrasing.

Going to the Farm

Marge and Carl had never been on a farm. Their home is in Star City. Marge and Carl lived high up, far above Star City streets.

37

Decodable Reader

Fluency

Phrasing: Punctuation

1 Teach/Model

Explain that when good readers read aloud, they group words together in ways that make sense. Good readers use the punctuation for clues about which words go together and where to pause.

Display Projectable 19.6 . As you read each sentence aloud, model how to pause after phrases. Write a slash mark after each phrase to illustrate. Draw attention to the commas that indicate the reader should pause briefly, and to the end marks that indicate the reader should take a longer pause. Also point out phrases where there is no punctuation. Then read the sentences together, pausing briefly at the end of each phrase and for a longer time at the end of each sentence.

2 Guided Practice

Have children return to page 135 of *The Signmaker's Assistant* in the **Student Book**. Reread the first paragraph chorally. Ask a volunteer to explain how she or he used the punctuation to group words to read together.

3 Apply

Have pairs take turns reading the page to each other two or three times, using appropriate phrasing. **ELA** RF.2.4a, RF.2.4b

Tell partners to help each other go back to any phrases that caused difficulty and reread them correctly. Point out that rereading phrases correctly will increase their understanding of the text.

Distribute Reader's Notebook Volume 2 page 52 or leveled practice in Grab-and-Go™ Resources for children to complete independently.

▶ **SHARE OBJECTIVE**
- Read fluently, using appropriate phrasing (prosody).

SMALL GROUP Options

Go to p. T391 for additional fluency support.

ENGLISH LANGUAGE SUPPORT

Audio Support

All Proficiencies English learners may benefit from recording themselves as they read during fluency practice. Have children choose a portion of a text that they are familiar with and have read several times. Give English learners a focus for the reading such as phrasing. Have children record themselves and play back the recording. As children listen, tell them to follow along in the text and mark places in the text where they need more practice. Have children practice and record again to improve their oral reading fluency.

Cold Reads: Support for fluent reading and comprehension

Independent Reading

▶ **SHARE OBJECTIVES**
- Read and comprehend literature.
- Ask and answer questions about what you read.
- Use evidence from the text to answer questions and support opinions. LANGUAGE
- Read independently from a "just right" book.
- Read for fluency and understanding.

ENGLISH LANGUAGE SUPPORT

Review Key Ideas

Emerging Ask children *yes/no* questions about the selection. **ELD** ELD.PI.2.6

Expanding Ask children some details about the story, such as, *What was the first sign that Norman painted?* and *Why did Norman apologize?* **ELD** ELD.PI.2.6

Bridging Have children summarize the selection, discussing what they learn at the end of the story. **ELD** ELD.PI.2.6

Reader's Guide

Revisit the Anchor Text Lead children in a brief discussion about *The Signmaker's Assistant*. Have them recount the main events in order, summarize what the story is about, and tell the lesson Norman learned. Tell them to build on others' talk in conversations by linking comments. Remind children to follow classroom rules for discussions. **ELA** RL.2.2, SL.2.1a, SL.2.1b **ELD** ELD.PI.2.1, ELD.PI.2.6, ELD.PI.2.12a

Have children read *The Signmaker's Assistant* on their own. Then distribute Reader's Notebook Volume 2 pages 53–54 ☐ and have children complete them independently. **ELA** RL.2.1, RL.2.7 **ELD** ELD.PI.2.6

Model Questioning Demonstrate generating a question about *The Signmaker's Assistant*. For example: *Why do the townspeople tear down all the signs?* Reread **Student Book** p. 140 with children, and look at the illustrations together to respond to the question. **ELA** RL.2.1 **ELD** ELD.PI.2.6

Generate Questions Have children work independently or collaboratively to generate questions about *The Signmaker's Assistant*. Ask children to share their questions. Begin a class discussion of questions that children have in common or that are most significant to their understanding of the story. Remind children to take turns speaking, listen carefully, and build on the comments of others. **ELA** RL.2.1, SL.2.1a, SL.2.1b **ELD** ELD.PI.2.1, ELD.PI.2.6

Self-Selected Reading

Read the Summary Tell children that before they select a book to read, they should learn something about the book. Guide children in selecting a book based on reading a summary using the following tips:

- Think of a topic or a kind of story that interests you, and find a book that looks like something you would like to read.
- Look at the picture on the cover of the book, and read the title and the author's name.
- Look for a summary of the book on the back cover or on the inside of the book jacket, and read about the book. Does this book have an interesting topic? Is it a story that sounds interesting?

Tell children that once they have selected a book, they should open the book and read one or two pages to be sure it is "just right." Tell children that although they liked the subject of the book, they might not like the way the book is written or the style of the writing. Then, it is okay to select another book following the same process from the beginning. **ELA** RL.2.10, RI.2.10

Self-Correction Strategies

Read for Fluency and Understanding Tell children that it is important to read accurately and make sure they understand what they are reading. If they come to a word they cannot read or understand, they should pause and reread to look for clues to help them understand the text.

Have partners practice reading aloud to each other from their self-selected books. Have them practice rereading parts of the text they do not understand to self-correct word recognition and understanding.

When one child has finished reading, his or her partner should provide feedback about accuracy. Then, have the partner read aloud from his or her book and receive feedback. Have each partner read one more time, trying to improve his or her accuracy. **ELA** RF.2.4c

Apply Vocabulary Knowledge

▶ **SHARE OBJECTIVES**

- Use words and phrases acquired through conversations, reading and being read to, and responding to texts. LANGUAGE
- Identify real-life connections between words and their use. LANGUAGE
- Use a glossary to locate words and to clarify meanings of words. LANGUAGE

ENGLISH LANGUAGE SUPPORT

Comprehensible Input

Emerging Ask children what would be a polite way to ask someone to help them with their homework.

Expanding Have children tell about a time they failed at something. Then ask what they learned and if they might like to try again. **ELD** ELD.PI.2.12a

Bridging Have children tell what kind of trade they think they would like to be an assistant for. Have them explain why. **ELD** ELD.PI.2.3, ELD.PI.2.11

☑ Review Target Vocabulary

Review with children the Vocabulary in Context Cards on **Student Book** pp. 122–123. Call on children to read the context sentences and explain how the photograph demonstrates the meaning of the word.

Enrich Vocabulary Write the following Related Words on the board. Read each word aloud, and have children repeat after you. Then read the child-friendly explanation for each word. Connect each word's meaning to the story *The Signmaker's Assistant* by writing the context sentences on the board and reading them aloud. **ELA** L.2.5a

FOR STUDENTS WITH DISABILITIES To help children recognize new vocabulary words, print each word on a self-stick note. Distribute the self-stick notes, and have children find each word in the text.

trade: A trade is a job where someone needs special skills. *The signmaker's trade was making signs.*

mischief: Mischief is bad behavior that causes others to be annoyed. *Norman's mischief made the townspeople angry.*

chaos: Chaos is total confusion. *Norman's prank created chaos.*

Make Connections Discuss all of the words using the items below to help children make connections between vocabulary words and their use.
ELA L.2.5a **ELD** ELD.PI.2.1, ELD.PI.2.12a, ELD.PI.2.12b

- What is a **trade** you would like to learn?

- What kind of **mischief** might a puppy get in trouble for?

- Tell about a time you experienced **chaos**.

- How do you stay out of **trouble**?

- When someone has **failed** at something, what would you tell that person to do next?

- Tell about a story you know that has words of **wisdom**.

- Ask for something in a **polite** way.

- What tools would you use if you were **tearing** down a house?

- When might a windshield on a car need to be **cleared**?

- If you had an **assistant**, what would you ask for help with?

- Tell about a time you **agreed** to do something for a friend.

Glossary Skills

Discuss Using a Glossary Use the glossary in the **Student Book** to discuss how to use a glossary. As needed, point out the location of the glossary in the back of the book, as well as how to use the guide words and the headings to help children find a word. Remind children that glossaries place words in alphabetical order.

Have partners work together and take turns looking up the Target Vocabulary words *wisdom, polite,* and *assistant.* Ask children to read the entries aloud and describe the features of each entry, such as the word, definition, and example sentence. Allow time for children who have difficulty finding the entries to ask questions and receive help. Have children verify that the glossary definition matches their understanding of the word's meaning. If it doesn't, discuss how the glossary definition or sample sentence helped them understand the word's meaning.

ELA SL.2.1a, L.2.4e **ELD** ELD.PI.2.1

QUICKWRITE Read aloud each question below. Pause a few minutes between each item to allow children to write a response. **ELA** L.2.6

1. What could happen if you get into **mischief**?

2. What could be the start of total **chaos**?

3. What **trade** would you enjoy?

ENGLISH LANGUAGE SUPPORT Write the following sentence frames on the board to support children in writing: *If I got into mischief, I might _____. _____ could lead to total chaos. A trade I would enjoy is _____.* Read the sentence frames aloud with children. Ask them to write to complete the sentences. **ELD** ELD.PI.2.10

For additional practice with the lesson's Target Vocabulary words, use the activities on pages 152–153 of the **Literacy and Language Guide.**

- Introduce Target Vocabulary; Prefix *im-*
- Idea Completion
- Homographs
- Riddles
- Synonyms

Grammar Commas in Dates, Places, and Letters

▶ SHARE OBJECTIVES

- **Grammar** Use commas in the date, greeting, and closing of a letter. LANGUAGE
- **Spelling** Spell words with *ar*.
- **Writing** Brainstorm possible problems and solutions for a narrative. LANGUAGE

ENGLISH LANGUAGE SUPPORT

Peer-Supported Learning

All Proficiencies Organize children into mixed-proficiency small groups. Write this letter on the board without commas: *Dear Sam, We are coming to see you on May 22, 2018. We will drive to Atlanta, Georgia. Your friend, Zoe.* Have groups work together to decide where to insert the commas using a different color. Ask them to write a similar letter.

Linguistic Transfer Children with literacy skills in Spanish may need additional practice writing dates. Point out that the name of the month should be capitalized. Have them practice the correct usage of the comma. **ELD** ELD.PIII.2

1 Teach/Model

Commas in Parts of a Letter Review where to place a comma in dates and place names. Explain that in a letter you also put a comma after the greeting and after the closing.

- Write *Dear Mary, Hello Max,* and *Dear Dad,* on the board. Circle each comma. *Each of these is called a greeting. Begin a letter with a greeting and put a comma after it.*

- Write *Your friend, Sincerely,* and *Best wishes,* on the board. Circle each comma. *Each of these is called a closing. End a letter with a closing and put a comma after it. Then write your name.*

2 Guided Practice/Apply

- Write the following letter on the board without commas.

> Dear Sophie,
>
> The toy store opened June 11, 2012. It is in Orlando, Florida.
>
> > Your friend,
> >
> > Elena

- Guide children to place the commas correctly. Then have them write a short letter that includes a greeting, a date and place, and a closing using commas correctly.

ENGLISH LANGUAGE SUPPORT Have volunteers read their letters aloud. Have children give a thumbs up when they hear a date or place that needs a comma.

- Distribute <u>Reader's Notebook Volume 2 page 56</u> ⟦⟧ to children to complete independently. **ELA** L.2.2b **ELD** ELD.PII.2.1

Spelling Words with *ar*

SPELLING WORDS

BASIC

car	start
dark	part
arm	spark
star	**REVIEW**
park*	art
yard	jar
party	**CHALLENGE**
hard*	carpet
farm	apartment

*A form of this word appears in the literature.

Segment Sounds

- Model segmenting sounds. Lift your hand each time you say a new sound. *I'll say words slowly. I will signal each time I say a new sound: /p/ /är/ /t/ /ē/. Now you say it with me: party.*

- Repeat with *park* and *start*. Tell children that saying a word sound by sound will help them spell it.

Build Words with *ar*

- Use **Letter Cards** to model building the word *farm*. Have children read the word with you and begin to list the Spelling Words.

- Have partners use **Letter Cards** to build words with *ar* and add each word to their lists.

- Have partners read and spell words they built using **Letter Cards**.

- Distribute <u>Reader's Notebook Volume 2 page 55</u> ⟦⟧ to children to complete independently. **ELA** L.2.2d

Open Sort

For additional practice with the Spelling Words, have children complete the Open Sort activity on page 93 of the **Literacy and Language Guide.**

Narrative Writing Prewrite

1 Teach/Model

Fictional Story: Brainstorming Problems and Solutions Remind children that a good story has a problem the characters try to solve. What happens to the characters in the story and how they solve the problem is called the *plot*.

- Write this prompt on the board and read it to children: *Write a story about a character who does something important or brave*.

- Model for children how to brainstorm possible problems and solutions for a story.

Think Aloud *I will brainstorm possible problems and solutions for my story. My characters are two birds who are best friends. I will think about possible problems they might have and different ways they can solve those problems.*

Possible Problem	Possible Solution
Robbie gets hurt and can't fly south.	Ramona stays with Robbie all winter.
Ramona is afraid to fly.	Robbie teaches Ramona to fly short distances.

2 Guided Practice/Apply

- Have children suggest and list other possible problems and solutions to add to the chart.

- Save your chart for use on Day 4.

Prewriting Reread with children the prompt on the board: *Write a story about a character who does something important or brave*. Have children begin exploring their topics by brainstorming possible problems and solutions in a chart similar to the one you made with the class. **ELA** W.2.3, W.2.4, W.2.10 **ELD** ELD.PI.2.10, ELD.PII.2.1

ENGLISH LANGUAGE SUPPORT Have children decide on characters for their stories. Remind them that the main character must have done something important or brave. Then have them discuss with partners what their character does and develop possible problems and solutions the character may encounter. **ELD** ELD.PII.2.1

Daily Proofreading Practice

Daily Proofreading Practice

We shopped at the ~~partey~~ party store on December 31, 2014. The store ~~were~~ was full of prety things.

Have children prewrite their narrative writing task through *my*WriteSmart.

Today's Goals

Vocabulary & Oral Language
- **Vocabulary Strategies:** Shades of Meaning

 TARGET VOCABULARY

assistant	**tearing**
agreed	**wisdom**
polite	**cleared**
failed	**trouble**

Phonemic Awareness
- **Substitute Phonemes**

Phonics & Fluency
- **Words with** *ar*
- **Fluency:** Phrasing: Punctuation
- **Decodable Reader:** *Going to the Farm*
- **High-Frequency Words**

Text-Based Comprehension
- **Connect to the Topic**
- **Read a Play:** *The Trouble with Signs*
- **Compare Texts**

Grammar & Writing
- **Spiral Review:** Proper Nouns
- **Narrative Writing:** Fictional Story

Spelling
- **Words with** *ar*

Opening Routines

Warm Up with Wordplay

Using New Vocabulary

Remind children that they learned these Related Vocabulary words in this lesson: *chaos, mischief, trade (n.)*. Display the words, have children read them with you, and have them provide definitions.

> **mischief**
>
> **trade**
>
> **chaos**

Tell children that they will use these words in a paragraph about a mouse that causes big trouble when he tries to build a house. Explain that building is a type of trade. Then have partners work together to write their paragraphs, including a title. When they are ready, have them read the paragraphs to the class and discuss how they used the vocabulary words.

ELA W.2.7, L.2.5a, L.2.6 **ELD** ELD.PI.2.2, ELD.PI.2.9

Daily Phonemic Awareness

Substitute Phonemes

- *Today, we are going to change one sound in a word to make a new word. Say pat. We can change the /ă/ in pat to /är/ to make a new word,* part.

- Have children continue with the words *coat/cart, pick/park, back/bark, shack/shark, dock/dark, spike/spark, pot/part.*

Corrective Feedback

- If a child is unable to make the substitution, say the word, give correction, and model the task. Example: *The word is* back. *I can change the /ă/ sound in* back *to /är/ and make a new word,* bark. Back— bark.

- Have children repeat once with you before doing it on their own.

Daily High-Frequency Words

- Point to **High-Frequency Word Card 185,** *good.*

- *Say the word.* good *Spell the word* g-o-o-d *Write the word. Check the word.*

- Repeat the procedure with the words *are, baby, didn't, I'll, is, please, sound, talk,* and *too.*

ELA RF.2.3f

Word Box

- Write this week's and last week's High-Frequency Words on multiple slips of paper. Place the papers in a box.

- Invite children to take turns selecting a paper and reading the word aloud.

- Have other children repeat the word each time.

- Continue until all the words have been read.

Corrective Feedback

- If a child does not recognize the word *good,* say the correct word and have children repeat it. Good. *What is the word?* good

- Have children spell the word. g-o-o-d *How do we say this word?* good

- Have children reread all of the cards in random order.

Daily Vocabulary Boost

- Guide children to interact with the Target Vocabulary by asking the following questions. Remind them to speak clearly during discussion.

Have you ever failed *to do something important? What happened?*

If I say the sky has cleared, *what does it look like?*

If you are tearing *a piece of paper, what does it look like?*

Have you ever helped someone who was in trouble? *What happened?*

- Have children work together to explain *failed, cleared, tearing,* and *trouble* in their own words. Make sure children follow appropriate rules for discussion, such as listening to speakers, taking turns, and staying on topic.

ELA SL.2.1a, L.2.6 **ELD** ELD.PI.2.1

tearing
The worker is tearing apart this old sign.

Vocabulary in Context Cards 145–152

☑ **Target Vocabulary**

assistant
agreed
polite
failed
tearing
wisdom
cleared
trouble

DAY 4

Phonics

▶ SHARE OBJECTIVES

- Blend, build, and decode regularly spelled words with *ar* (*r*-controlled vowel syllable).
- Sort and read words with long *e* spelled *y* and long *i* spelled *i, igh, ie, y,* including vowel teams (vowel team syllables).
- Generalize learned spelling patterns when writing.

▶ SKILLS TRACE

Words with *ar*	
Introduce	pp. T316–T317, T342–T343
Differentiate	pp. T384–T385
Reteach	p. T398
Review	**pp. T362, T452, T463**
Assess	Weekly Tests, Lesson 19

ENGLISH LANGUAGE SUPPORT

Comprehensible Input

All Proficiencies To reinforce and develop the meanings of words in the Make and Read Words activity, ask questions that include the words, for example: *What is something children do at a park? When does school start? What might you see inside a barn? How does someone become a star?* Ask children to respond with gestures, phrases, or sentences as they are able. Restate their responses in complete sentences and have children repeat.

Review Words with *ar*

Phonemic Awareness Warm-Up Have children listen for the word with the sound /är/ as you say each pair of words. Tell them to hold up one finger if they hear /är/ in the first word of the pair or two fingers if they hear /är/ in the second word. *I'll do it first. Listen:* chat/chart. *I hear /är/ in the second word,* chart, *so I'll hold up two fingers. You try it. Listen:* chat/chart. *Which word has the sound /är/?* chart *(two fingers)*

Now you do it. Listen for /är/ in the following words: bark/bake, *one finger;* artist/ate, *one finger;* spark/spade, *one finger;* chap/charm, *two fingers;* may/mark, *two fingers.*

Make and Read Words Remind children that the letters *ar* together can spell the sound /är/ at the beginning, middle, or end of a word.

- Write the word *mark* on the board. Have children build the word with **Letter Cards.** Then have them build more words with the sound /är/ by substituting different letters at the beginning and end of the word. Have children record the words they build.

mark	card	bar
park	yard	star
part	yarn	start
cart	barn	smart

- Have children read their list with a partner. Use the **Corrective Feedback** steps if children need help.

- Then have partners work together to build and read additional words with *ar.* If children have difficulty thinking of more words, suggest words like *market, garden, party, alarm, barnyard,* and *starlight.* Children may also refer to **Decodable Reader** stories *Darling Starling* and *Going to the Farm* for words with *ar.* ELA L.2.2d

Cumulative Review

Phonemic Awareness Warm-Up *Let's blend sounds to make words. I'll do it first. Listen: /n/ /ī/ /t/. What word do you hear?* night *Now you do it with me: /n/ /ī/ /t/,* night.

Now you listen and blend: /p/ /ĕ/ / /n/, /ē/, penny; */r/ /ī/ /t/,* right; */w/ /ī/ /l/ /d/,* wild; */l/ /ī/,* lie; */m/ /ī/ /t/, /ē/,* mighty; */s/ /p/ /ī/,* spy.

Word Ladders Review **Sound/Spelling Cards** *ice cream* and *eagle* with children. Remind them that the letters *i, ie, igh,* and *y* can all spell the long *i* sound /ī/. The letter *y* can spell the long *e* sound /ē/, at the end of a word with two or more syllables.

Have children work in pairs to create a word ladder for each spelling pattern: long *i* spelled *i, ie, igh,* and *y,* and long *e* spelled *y.* Tell them to write a different word with the given pattern on each rung of the ladder.

Tell children to think about and generalize what they know about the spelling patterns as they write new words for each pattern. **ELA** L.2.2d

Then have partners take turns reading aloud the words on each ladder. Have children use their word ladders to summarize what they have learned about the spellings for the long *i* sound and the long *e* sound for *y.* **ELA** RF.2.3b, RF.2.3e

FORMATIVE ASSESSMENT · RtI

Corrective Feedback When a child mispronounces a word, point to the word and say it. Call attention to the element that was mispronounced, say the sound, and then guide children to read the word. See the example below.

Decoding Error: A child reads *mark* in the Make and Read Words activity as *make*.

Correct the error. Review the **Sound/Spelling Card** *artist.* Write *mark* on the board. *The word is* mark. *The letters* ar *stand for the vowel sound /är/.*

Model as you touch the letters. *I'll blend: /m/ /är/ /k/. What is the word?* mark

Guide *Let's blend together: /m/ /är/ /k/. What is the word?* mark

Check *You blend. /m/ /är/ /k/ What is the word?* mark

Reinforce Have children continue reading words with *ar.* Make note of errors and review those words at the end of the lesson.

Practice Fluency

Use <u>Instructional Routine 14</u> to have children reread **Decodable Reader** *Going to the Farm.* Remind them to read fluently and smoothly, grouping words in ways that make sense as they read.

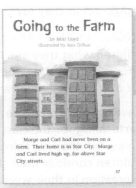

Going to the **Farm**
by Matt Lloyd
illustrated by Ana Ochoa

Marge and Carl had never been on a farm. Their home is in Star City. Marge and Carl lived high up, far above Star City streets.

57

Decodable Reader

☑ GENRE

A **play** is a story people act out.

☑ TEXT FOCUS

Dialogue is the talk between two or more people in a play. Dialogue helps the reader get to know each character's point of view through his or her own words.

The Trouble with Signs
by Bebe Jaffe

Cast of Characters
Ana
Ben

Ben: (steering a car) I'm glad we agreed to drive to the town meeting. We can look at the scenery.

Ana: (reading the pretend sign) Fresh berries. Turn left at the fork. Yum!

Ben: Where's the fork?

Ana: Do we need a fork to eat the berries?

Ben: I'm talking about a fork in the road!

Ana: I get it! You've got SO much wisdom, Ben.

Ben: I hope you are being polite and not teasing me.

Ana: (reading another sign) Do you have car trouble? Come to Polly's Place for some R and R. What's R and R?

Ben: R and R stands for Rest and Relaxation.

Fresh Berries
Turn left at the fork.

Polly's Place

154 ELA RL.2.6, RL.2.10 ELD ELD.PI.2.6

155

LESSON TOPIC: Signs

Cross-Curricular Connection Have children create safety signs for the classroom. Brainstorm the rules that students should follow. Then distribute materials for them to make signs. Have children present their signs to the class and explain the value and importance of their rules.

FOR STUDENTS WITH DISABILITIES
To help children with their oral reading fluency, have them listen to the audio of *The Trouble with Signs* as they read along. Have them play the audio a second time, this time reading aloud with the audio.

Connect to the Topic: Play
Introduce Genre and Text Focus

- Read with children the genre and text focus information on **Student Book** p. 154. Explain that a play is a story people act out for others to watch. The author of a play writes words for the actors to say aloud. This is called dialogue.

- Explain that the words in parentheses give information about how characters should act as they say their dialogue.

ENGLISH LANGUAGE SUPPORT Draw a pair of parentheses on the board and tell children what they are, having them repeat the word after you. Tell them that the information in the parentheses should be read silently, not aloud. Point to the first set of stage directions and have children act them out to check for understanding.

- Have partners read *The Trouble with Signs* silently and then choose parts. Before performing for the class, have partners practice reading their parts aloud several times. Tell them to think about the voices their characters would have. Then have children consider their character's point of view and how to convey this through the expression in their voice. **ELA** RL.2.6, RL.2.10

Ana: I'm glad that's cleared up, but do cars go to a special place for R and R?

Ben: (shaking his head) No, Ana. PEOPLE do.

Ana: Right! Listen to this sign! Have you failed in the kitchen? Are you tearing out your hair? Come to Carla's Cooking Class. Ouch! Do people tear their hair out because they overcooked a roast?

Ben: (losing patience) NO, Ana! That's just a saying. It means someone is getting frustrated.

Ana: Pull in! This is our meeting place.

Ben: Just in time! I'm tired of being your assistant.

156

Compare Texts

TEXT TO TEXT

Talk About Signs Think about the signs that Norman makes and the signs in *The Trouble with Signs*. How do the signs in each story make the characters confused? Talk about it with a partner.

TEXT TO SELF

Make a Sign Which sign from *The Signmaker's Assistant* do you think is the silliest? Make a silly sign for your classroom using words and pictures. Put it up for your class to see.

Make sure to laugh every 5 minutes!

TEXT TO WORLD

Connect to Social Studies Look through *The Signmaker's Assistant* for signs that are helpful to people. Make a list with a partner. Talk about why the signs are important.

ELA RL.2.1, RL.2.7 **ELD** ELD.PI.2.1, ELD.PI.2.6

157

Compare Texts

TEXT TO TEXT

Talk About Signs Tell children to look at the text and illustrations in both selections in order to answer the question. Have children pick particular signs from each story as a basis for their part of the discussion.
ELA RL.2.7 **ELD** ELD.PI.2.1, ELD.PI.2.3, ELD.PI.2.11

ENGLISH LANGUAGE SUPPORT Guide children to look back through both selections with you and look at the signs in the illustrations. Then have them tell what was happening and why the characters were confused.
ELD ELD.PI.2.1, ELD.PI.2.3, ELD.PI.2.6, ELD.PI.2.11

TEXT TO SELF

Make a Sign Ask children to review the pictures in *The Signmaker's Assistant*. Have them point out pictures of signs, as well as any sentences about signs. Have children tell which sign they thought was the silliest. Then guide children to make their own silly signs to display in the classroom. Signs should include pictures and words. Remind children to take care to use their best handwriting and to form letters properly. **ELA** L.2.1g

TEXT TO WORLD

Connect to Social Studies Draw a stop sign on the board. Say, *Stop signs help people by keeping them safe at intersections. Drivers see the sign and know to stop and check that their way is clear.* Ask partners to find signs in *The Signmaker's Assistant* that help people and discuss why these signs are important.

ENGLISH LANGUAGE SUPPORT Guide children to look back through both selections and find signs that are helpful, not silly. Have them tell why each one is helpful.
ELD ELD.PI.2.1, ELD.PI.2.3, ELD.PI.2.11

Vocabulary Strategies

SHARE OBJECTIVES

- Use verbs and adjectives that best fit your purpose in speaking or writing. LANGUAGE
- Identify shades of meaning among closely related verbs. LANGUAGE
- Identify shades of meaning among closely related adjectives. LANGUAGE

SKILLS TRACE

Shades of Meaning	
Introduce	**Unit 4 pp. T366–T367**
Differentiate	pp. T396–T397
Reteach	p. T399
Assess	Weekly Tests, Lesson 19

ENGLISH LANGUAGE SUPPORT

Access Prior Knowledge

Emerging Have children lightly toss a ball, eraser, or other small object to each other. Have them say *toss* after you. Then have them throw it a short distance and have them say *throw*. Explain the difference to them.

Expanding Discuss with children the difference between things (flowers, animals) that are cute, pretty, beautiful, or magnificent. **ELD** ELD.PI.2.8

Bridging Have children work in pairs to write or dictate things that are small and things that are tiny. **ELD** ELD.PI.2.1, ELD.PI.2.8

Shades of Meaning

1 Teach/Model

Terms About Language

synonyms Words that have the same meaning or almost the same meaning as another word are called *synonyms*.

ENGLISH LANGUAGE SUPPORT Preteach shades of meaning. Point out that *happy* and *overjoyed* are synonyms. *Overjoyed*, however, has a stronger feeling associated with it. Write *The signmaker's assistant cleans brushes. Then he scrubs his hands.* Cleans and scrubs are synonyms, but scrubs is a stronger word. To scrub is to clean by rubbing. Write *angry, wisdom,* and *tumbled*. Have partners use a thesaurus to find a synonym for each word. **ELD** ELD.PI.2.1, ELD.PI.2.8

- Remind children that *synonyms* are words that have the same or almost the same meaning.

- Explain that little differences in the meaning of words can make a big difference in meaning. *Good writers and speakers choose their words very carefully.*

- Write the following words on the board.

walk   creep   sneak

- Read each word. Then ask each of three children to demonstrate one of the actions *(walking, creeping,* and *sneaking)*. Have the three children start at the back of the classroom and move towards the front, demonstrating the meaning of their words. Provide quiet hints, as needed, to each child.

Think Aloud *If I say that* [name of student] *is* sneaking *to the front of the class, does that mean the same thing as saying that* [he/she] *is* walking *to the front of the class? No, because* sneaking *does mean moving, but it means moving in a secretive way.*

Also, if I say that someone is creeping *to the front of the class, does that mean the same thing as walking? No, because if the person is* creeping, *he or she is crouching down near the ground and moving very quietly. So these three words, while similar, have very different meanings.*

2 Guided Practice

- Display the top half of <u>Projectable 19.7</u> and read the sets of words aloud.

- Discuss the differences between *look, peek,* and *stare. Look means to use your eyes to search for something. Peek means to look quickly at something. Stare means to look at something for a long time.*

- Ask children which verb they would use in the sentences for item 1. Discuss their responses and reasons.

- Discuss the meanings of *thin, slender* and *scrawny*. Demonstrate the difference using a twig, a stick, and a branch. *Which is thin? Slender? Scrawny?*

3 Apply

- Read the remaining items on **Projectable 19.7** with children. Discuss any words that may be unknown to the children.

- Have children work with partners or independently to complete the items on the projectable. Ask them to look up any words in the dictionary that they are still confused about. Have them share their completed sentences with the class, acting out the meanings of the words if it is appropriate. **ELA** L.2.5b

ENGLISH LANGUAGE SUPPORT Say each word from the link, and read each sentence. Have children repeat each word, act it out, and define it. **ELD** ELD.PI.2.8

- Distribute <u>Reader's Notebook Volume 2 page 57</u> or <u>leveled practice</u> in Grab-and-Go™ Resources to children to complete independently.

 Interactive Whiteboard Lesson Use **Vocabulary Strategies: Shades of Meaning** to distinguish shades of meaning among verbs and adjectives that are synonyms. **ELA** L.2.5b

---

FORMATIVE ASSESSMENT · RtI

Are children able to choose appropriate words to communicate shades of meaning?

IF...	THEN...
children struggle,	▲ use **Differentiate Vocabulary Strategies** for Struggling Readers, p. T396.
children are on track,	▲ use **Differentiate Vocabulary Strategies** for On-Level Readers, p. T396.
children excel,	▲ use **Differentiate Vocabulary Strategies** for Advanced Readers, p. T397.

SMALL GROUP Options

Differentiate Vocabulary Strategies: pp. T396–T397
Scaffold instruction to the English learner's proficiency level.

ENGLISH LANGUAGE SUPPORT

Peer-Supported Learning

All Proficiencies Organize children into mixed-proficiency small groups to name additional words that show action (like *peek, look,* and *stare* or *toss, throw,* and *hurl*) and words that describe (like *thin, slender,* and *scrawny* or *shiny* and *bright*). Have group members take turns naming additional synonyms for these words. When children are finished with their lists, call on groups to share them with the class. Then have the class vote on which words are the most descriptive. Tell children they can use these words they learned when they speak and write. **ELD** ELD.PI.2.1, ELD.PI.2.8

Grammar Spiral Review: Proper Nouns

▶ SHARE OBJECTIVES
- **Grammar** Review how to write proper nouns correctly. LANGUAGE
- **Spelling** Spell words with *ar*.
- **Handwriting** Write Spelling Words.
- **Writing** Continue prewriting to plan a narrative. LANGUAGE

ENGLISH LANGUAGE SUPPORT

Access Prior Knowledge

All Proficiencies Write each day of the week using lowercase letters. Ask children to identify and correct the errors. Repeat with other types of proper nouns.

1 Teach/Model

Writing Proper Nouns Write examples on the board to review with children when to capitalize proper nouns.

ENGLISH LANGUAGE SUPPORT Remind Spanish speakers that both English and Spanish use capital letters for proper nouns; for example, people's names. However, English uses capitals in cases where Spanish does not, such as for days of the week.

- *The days of the week and the months of the year all begin with a capital letter.*
- *Each important word in the name of a holiday begins with a capital letter.*
- *Names of special things and places should be capitalized.*

2 Guided Practice/Apply

- Write these sentences on the board, and read them aloud.

  1. **The campers toast purepuff marshmallows at yellowstone national park.** *Purepuff Marshmallows, Yellowstone National Park*

  2. **Every year, thanksgiving falls on the fourth thursday in november.** *Thanksgiving, Thursday, November*

  3. **My birthday is the day after memorial day.** *Memorial Day*

- Help children rewrite each sentence by correctly capitalizing the proper nouns.

- Distribute Reader's Notebook Volume 2 page 59 and have children complete it independently. **ELA** L.2.2a

Spelling Words with *ar*

SPELLING WORDS

BASIC	
car	start
dark	part
arm	spark
star	**REVIEW**
park*	art
yard	jar
party	**CHALLENGE**
hard*	carpet
farm	apartment

*A form or forms of these words appear in the literature.

Connect to Writing
- Children use Spelling Words to write a sentence or two telling a story.
- Have them proofread their sentences. Then have children read their sentences aloud.
- As a class, practice the Spelling Words together. Say each word and spell it aloud with children.
- Distribute Reader's Notebook Volume 2 p. 58 to children to complete independently. **ELA** L.2.2d

Handwriting
Model how to form the Basic Words *party, hard, farm, start, part,* and *spark*. Handwriting models are available on pp. R24–R29 and on the Handwriting Models Blackline Masters . Remind children to write legibly and stay within the margins. **ELA** L.2.1g

Speed Sort
For additional practice with the Spelling Words, have children complete the Speed Sort activity on page 93 of the **Literacy and Language Guide**. **ELA** L.2.2d

Narrative Writing Prewrite

1 Teach/Model

Fictional Story: Details Tell children to include details in their stories that show the characters' feelings.

Connect to *The Signmaker's Assistant*	
Instead of this...	**The author wrote this...**
Norman watched it all.	"Norman watched it all and laughed until tears came to his eyes." (p. 140)

- *Why is the second sentence better? It shows how Norman feels about what he is watching. It helps you picture how hard he was laughing.*

2 Guided Practice/Apply

- Review the chart you made with the class on Day 3. Display Projectable 19.8 [.

- Create a Story Map. Model planning and writing details for the beginning, middle, and end of the story.

- As you work, use the Think Aloud to model adding details to the correct parts of the story.

- Save the completed chart for Day 1 of next week.

Think Aloud *I am writing about two birds named Robbie and Ramona. Robbie gets hurt when he is playing with Ramona. Now he can't fly south. This is the problem. I will write that in the Beginning box. I will add details to tell how Robbie got hurt.*

Prewriting Distribute Graphic Organizer 10 [. Have children use their problem and solution charts from Day 3 to complete their own Story Maps.
ELA W.2.3, W.2.4, W.2.10 **ELD** ELD.PI.2.10, ELD.PII.2.1

ENGLISH LANGUAGE SUPPORT

Comprehensible Input

All Proficiencies Have children work with partners to complete their own story maps. Using the visual aid from Day 2, allow children to draw what will happen in the story in the beginning, the middle, and the end of the story. Have them also list the characters and decide on a setting for their story. **ELD** ELD.PII.2.1

my WriteSmart Have children draft their narrative writing task through *my*WriteSmart.

Today's Goals

Vocabulary & Oral Language
- Domain-Specific Vocabulary
- Speaking & Listening

☑ TARGET VOCABULARY

assistant	tearing
agreed	wisdom
polite	cleared
failed	trouble

Phonemic Awareness
- Substitute Phonemes

Phonics & Fluency
- Interactive Whiteboard Lesson
- High-Frequency Words

Text-Based Comprehension
- Extend the Topic
- Speaking and Listening:
  Matching Game: Synonyms

Assess & Reteach
- Assess Skills
- Respond to Assessment

Grammar & Writing
- Commas in Dates and Places
- Narrative Writing: Fictional Story

Spelling
- Words with *ar*

Opening Routines

Warm Up with Wordplay

Write a Poem

Display and read aloud the following word: *sign*. Have children work with partners to come up with as many words that rhyme with *sign* as they can. When children are ready, compile their words on the board.

sign	**line**	**fine**
dine	**nine**	**pine**
shine	**mine**	**whine**

Have children suggest opening lines for a poem, ending with one of the rhyming words. Let children choose their favorite opening line, and then have them write short poems using rhyming words from the list. **ELA** W.2.7 **ELD** ELD.PI.2.2

Interactive Whiteboard Lesson

For cumulative review, use **Phonics: Words with _ar_** to reinforce blending, reading, and building decodable words with _ar_.

Daily Phonemic Awareness

Substitute Phonemes

- _We are going to change a sound in a word to make a new word. We can change the /ă/ in ban to /är/ to make the word barn._

- Have children substitute vowel sounds to make changes in other words such as _stay/star, cat/cart, foam/farm, dot/dart._

Corrective Feedback

- If a child is unable to make a substitution, provide correction and model the task. Example: _Listen:_ ban. _What is the vowel sound? /ă/ Change /ă/ to /är/. What is the new word?_ barn

- Have children repeat the first few words with you. Then have them continue on their own.

Daily High-Frequency Words

- Point to **High-Frequency Word Card 184**, _talk._

- _Say the word._ talk _Spell the word_ t-a-l-k _Write the word. Check it._

- Repeat the procedure with these words from this week _are, baby, I'll, please, sound_ and from last week _friends, mother, soon, under, words._ **ELA** RF.2.3f

Raise the Roof!

- Draw three houses on the board. Write _I'll_, _didn't_, and _please_ on the roofs.

- Explain to children that they will push their arms up to "raise the roof" each time they say a letter. Point to _didn't_ and read it aloud. Then demonstrate as children join in.

- Say: _d (push up), i (push up), d (push up), n (push up), apostrophe (push up), t (push up). What does it spell?_ _Didn't!_ Repeat for other words.

Corrective Feedback

- If a child does not recognize the word _sound_, say the correct word and have children repeat it: Sound. _What is the word?_ sound

- Have children spell the word. _s-o-u-n-d How do we say this word?_ sound

- Have children reread all of the cards in random order.

Daily Vocabulary Boost

- Reread "Wild Friends, Wow!" (p. T315) aloud to children.

- As you read each Target Vocabulary word in the article, pause to have a child explain or describe its meaning.

- After reading, review the Target Vocabulary and the definitions. (See p. T314.) Challenge children to use the words in their everyday speech. **ELA** L.2.6 **ELD** ELD.PI.2.5

trouble
Without signs, drivers would have trouble knowing when to stop.

Vocabulary in Context Cards 145–152

 **Target Vocabulary**

assistant
agreed
polite
failed
tearing
wisdom
cleared
trouble

DAY 5

Extend the Topic

▶ SHARE OBJECTIVES

- Acquire and use domain-specific vocabulary. LANGUAGE
- Participate in conversations about a topic. LANGUAGE
- Play a listening game.

Words About the Topic: Signs

- **advertise** to give information about something you wish to sell
- **announcement** something said publicly and officially
- **post** to place an announcement where people will see or hear it
- **beacon** a light or fire used to pass along a message

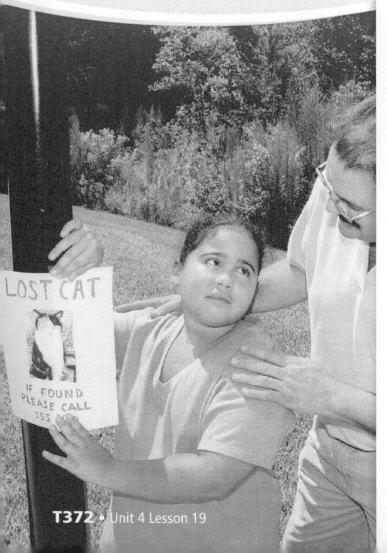

Domain-Specific Vocabulary

Introduce Words About the Topic. Remind children that this week's topic is Signs. Display the words shown at left. Tell children that these are words that can help them learn more about the topic. Read aloud the meaning of each word, and have children respond to the following prompts. **ELA** L.2.5a, L.2.6

- *Why would a company advertise?* to let people know about their products and to persuade people to buy them

- *You can be sure people will know about an event if you make an _____.* announcement

- *You can _____ a sign about a lost cat on a telephone pole.* post

- *What sorts of messages could you pass using a beacon?* only simple messages to people who know what the use of the beacon means

ENGLISH LANGUAGE SUPPORT Guide children to interact with the words by discussing as a class questions such as these: *How do toy companies advertise new toys? What important announcement did you hear recently? Where would be a good place to post a sign about a bike for sale? What would more likely have a beacon: a lighthouse or a birdhouse?* **ELD** ELD.PI.2.1, ELD.PI.2.12a

Interact with the Words Have children work in small groups to create a Four-Square Map for each of the domain-specific words. For each of the domain-specific words, children should fold a blank sheet of paper into four equal sections. Work with them to follow the steps below for each word. As needed, display the meanings of the words on the board. Ask individual children to use the words in a sentence orally. Then write the sentence on the board for other children to copy.

1 In the first corner, draw a picture for the word.

2 In the second corner, write the meaning of the word.

3 In the third corner, write a sentence using the word.

4 In the fourth corner, write the word.

When groups have finished, have them share their Four-Square Maps with the class.
ELA L.2.5a, L.2.6 **ELD** ELD.PI.2.1

Speaking and Listening:
Matching Game: Synonyms

Play a Matching Game Talk about shades of meaning in words. Remind children that some words mean almost the same thing. Tell them they are going to play a game where they match words that mean the same or almost the same thing.

Create a word card for each child in the class using an assortment of verbs and adjectives. Children will determine which of their classmates has a word card that is a synonym for their own card. Choose words that will provide children with 4–8 groups of synonyms, such as *look, peek, glare, stare; pleased, excited, happy, joyful; hop, jump, leap, spring; run, skip, trot, jog; big, huge, gigantic, enormous.*

Explain how to play the game. Players read their word silently to themselves. Then they begin moving around the room silently, looking at and reading each other's cards. When a player's card is a synonym of another player's card, the players sit down together. Play continues until all the children have joined a team. **ELD** ELD.PI.2.8

Discussion Have children on each team read their card aloud and act out its meaning. After all the words have been acted out, have children discuss how the meaning of each word in a group is a little different. Challenge each team to see how many other words with almost the same meaning they can think of. Remind children to raise their hands to speak and to listen to the ideas of others during the discussion. **ELA** SL.2.1a, L.2.5b **ELD** ELD.PI.2.1, ELD.PI.2.8

SHADES OF MEANING TIPS

1. **Look at the word and compare it to yours.**

2. **If you're unsure of a word, look it up in the dictionary.**

3. **When you find your group, sit down.**

4. **When sharing, raise your hand to speak, and listen to the ideas of everyone.**

ENGLISH LANGUAGE SUPPORT
Use Language Models

All Proficiencies Before children begin their discussions, reiterate what it means to respond to others' comments. Point out that when you respond to a comment, you can agree, disagree, share a similar idea, or ask a question. Model the skill for children using the following example. Help children identify the response.

Child A: *Look* is a synonym of *peek.*

Child B: I agree. Also, *stare* is another synonym of *look.*

After their discussions, have children share examples of how they responded to others' comments.
ELD ELD.PI.2.1, ELD.PI.2.8

Grammar Weekly Review: Commas in Dates and Places

▶ SHARE OBJECTIVES

- **Grammar** Proofread for commas in dates and place names. LANGUAGE
- **Spelling** Assess words with *ar*.
- **Writing** Revise and edit for commas, capital letters, and end marks. LANGUAGE

ENGLISH LANGUAGE SUPPORT

Peer-Supported Learning

All Proficiencies Organize students into mixed-proficiency small groups. Write these dates and places: *June 24 2010; January 1 2011; Doral Florida; Chicago Illinois.* Have children work together to write the dates and places correctly on paper. Help them figure out which of the words are the names of the cities or towns and which are the states.

1 Review/Practice

Commas in Dates and Places Read together the text at the top of **Student Book** p. 158. Discuss these rules.

- *Use a comma between the number of the day and the year.*
- *Use a comma between the name of a city or town and the name of a state.*
- Read and discuss the examples in the chart.
- Direct children's attention to the Try This! activity at the bottom of the page. Support children as they write each date or place correctly.

2 Connect to Writing

- Read together **Student Book** p. 159. Remind children that proofreading their work for the correct use of commas will make their writing easier to understand.
- Read and discuss the examples and the illustrations.

ENGLISH LANGUAGE SUPPORT Read the sign on page 159 aloud, modeling a pause where the commas occur in the place and date. Have children give a thumbs up when they hear the pause where a comma belongs.

- Together, read the directions for Connect Grammar to Writing ⌐ at the bottom of the page. Support children when they edit their writing for the correct use of commas, capital letters, and end marks.
- Distribute Reader's Notebook Volume 2 page 60 ⌐ to children to complete independently. **ELA** W.2.5

Spelling Words with *ar*

SPELLING WORDS AND SENTENCES

BASIC

1. **car** Our *car* has four doors.
2. **dark** It gets *dark* at night.
3. **arm** I fell and broke my *arm*.
4. **star** The sun is a *star*.
5. **park*** We play soccer in the *park*.
6. **yard** Grass grows in the *yard*.
7. **party** Come to the *party*!
8. **hard*** He skates on the *hard* ice.
9. **farm** We grow corn on our *farm*.

10. **start** The game will *start* late.
11. **part** A dial is *part* of a clock.
12. **spark** A *spark* started the fire.

REVIEW

13. **art** We painted in *art* class.
14. **jar** The jelly is in the glass *jar*.

CHALLENGE

15. **carpet** *Carpet* covers the floor.
16. **apartment** My brother lives in an *apartment*.

*A form of this word appears in the literature.

Assess

Say each Spelling Word, read aloud its sentence, and then repeat the word. Have children write the word. **ELA** L.2.2d

Corrective Feedback

Review any words that children misspell. If children misspell two or more words, then revisit the Day 2 Guess My Category activity on page 92 of the **Literacy and Language Guide.**

Grammar

Commas in Dates and Places Every day has a **date**. A date tells the month, the number of the day, and the year. Use a **comma** (,) between the number of the day and the year. Also use a comma between the name of a city or town and the name of a state.

Dates	Place Names
May 2, 2017	Austin, Texas
July 15, 2019	Westville, Idaho

 Write the underlined date or place correctly.

1. The signmaker opened his shop on June 4 1975.

2. The shop was in Columbus Ohio.

3. The boy started work on May 25 2018.

4. He came from Logan Utah.

Edit your writing carefully. Make sure you have used commas correctly when you write dates and names of places.

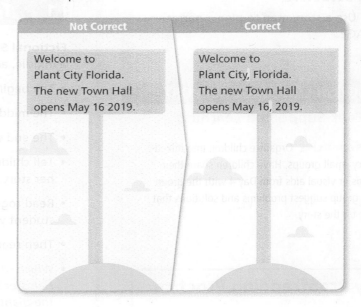

Not Correct	Correct
Welcome to Plant City Florida. The new Town Hall opens May 16 2019.	Welcome to Plant City, Florida. The new Town Hall opens May 16, 2019.

Connect Grammar to Writing

When you edit your story next week, be sure you have used commas, capital letters, and end marks correctly.

158   159

1. June 4, 1975

2. Columbus, Ohio

3. May 25, 2018

4. Logan, Utah

Narrative Writing Prewrite

▶ **SHARE OBJECTIVE**

- **Writing** Use a story map to plan a narrative.
LANGUAGE

ENGLISH LANGUAGE SUPPORT
Peer-Supported Learning

All Proficiencies Organize children into mixed-proficiency small groups. Have children share their story maps or visual aids from Day 4 with the group. Have the group suggest problems and solutions that will work for the story.

Daily Proofreading Practice

Mia got her pupy at the pet store
in Columbus Ohio. She hold it in
one arms.

WriteSmart Have children revise, proofread, and publish their narrative writing task through *my*WriteSmart.

1 Teach/Model

Fictional Story: Organization Remind children that a story has a beginning, a middle, and an end.

- The beginning introduces the characters, the setting, and the problem.
- The middle shows characters working to solve a problem.
- The end shows how the problem was solved.
- Tell children they will read how a student writer explored a topic and planned her story.
- Read together the top of **Student Book** p. 160 and the story ideas made by the student writer, Julie.
- Then read Julie's story map on p. 161.
- *Which of her ideas did Julie use in the beginning of the story? Girl has a pet; Hamster's name is Sparky. The middle? They meet a sad giant; Kids are afraid of the giant. The end? Pet has special powers; Sparky knows when things are wrong.*

2 Guided Practice/Apply

- Discuss the Reading as a Writer questions on **Student Book** p. 161.

Prewriting Ask children to check the ideas on their own Story Maps and rearrange them so they follow the pattern described above: The beginning of the story introduces the characters, the setting, and the problem. The middle has characters working to solve a problem. The story ends with the problem solved.

ELA W.2.3, W.2.4, W.2.10 **ELD** ELD.PI.2.10, ELD.PII.2.1

Reading-Writing Workshop: Prewrite

Narrative Writing

✔ Organization A **story** has a beginning, a middle, and an end. The events in a story should be told in an order that makes sense.

Julie made a list of ideas for her story. She crossed out the one that didn't belong. Then she used a story map to put her ideas in order.

Writing Process Checklist

▶ **Prewrite**
- ✔ Who are my characters?
- ✔ What happens at the beginning of the story?
- ✔ What happens in the middle?
- ✔ What happens at the end?
- Draft
- Revise
- Edit
- Publish and Share

Exploring a Topic

Girl has a pet.

~~She is a really good speller.~~

Pet has special powers.

They meet a sad giant.

Kids are afraid of the giant.

Hamster's name is Sparky.

Sparky knows when things are wrong.

Story Map

Beginning

Layla and Sparky go to the park.
They see a sign that the park is closed.

Middle

They find a crying giant.
The giant tells them why he is crying.
Kids are scared of him.

End

The kids see how gentle the giant is with Sparky.
The kids and the giant play together.

Reading as a Writer

What differences do you see between Julie's list and her story map? How will putting your ideas in a story map help you plan your story?

I put my ideas in an order that would make sense in my story.

160   **ELA** W.2.3, W.2.4, W.2.5, W.2.10 **ELD** ELD.PI.2.10, ELD.PI.2.12b, ELD.PII.2.1

161

NARRATIVE WRITING RUBRIC
See also the Multipurpose Writing Rubric on p. R18.

Score	4	3	2	1	NS
Purpose/ Organization	The narrative is clear and well organized. It is appropriately sequenced and has closure. • Plot contains a well-elaborated event or a short sequence of events • Setting and characters are included and well-maintained • Plot events follow a logical sequence • Includes an effective conclusion	The narrative is generally clear and organized. The sequence is adequately maintained, and the plot has closure. • Plot contains a well-elaborated event or a short sequence of events • Characters and setting are included and adequately maintained • Plot events follow an understandable sequence • Includes an adequate conclusion	The narrative is somewhat organized but may be unclear in parts. The sequence is weak. The plot lacks closure. • Minimal development of plot • Characters and setting are included but are minimally maintained • Sequence of events is poorly organized • Conclusion is inadequate or missing	The narrative's focus is unclear, and it is poorly organized. The narrative lacks sequence and has no closure. • Little or no plot • No attempt to maintain characters or setting • Sequence of events is not organized • Conclusion is missing	• not intelligible • not written in English • not on topic • contains text copied from another source • does not address the purpose for writing
Development/ Elaboration	The narrative includes effective elaboration, and details describing actions, thoughts, and feelings. • Clear effort to develop experiences, characters, setting, and events • Contains strong use of details • Writer uses temporal words to signal the order of events	The narrative includes adequate elaboration, and details describing actions, thoughts, and feelings. • Some attempt to develop experiences, characters, setting, and events • Contains adequate use of details • Contains adequate use of temporal words to signal the order of events	The narrative includes only partial or ineffective elaboration. The narrative includes some details. • Little attempt to develop experiences, characters, setting, and events • Contains weak use of details • Contains little use of temporal words. • Order of events is not clear	The narrative provides little or no elaboration and few details. • No attempt to develop experiences, characters, setting, and events • Few or no details • No use of temporal words • Order of events is confusing	• not intelligible • not written in English • not on topic • contains text copied from another source • does not develop the writing

Score	2	1	0	NS
Conventions	The narrative demonstrates adequate command of conventions. • Consistent use of complete sentences, correct sentence structures, punctuation, capitalization, grammar, spelling	The narrative demonstrates partial command of conventions. • Limited use of complete sentences, correct sentence structures, punctuation, capitalization, grammar, spelling	The narrative demonstrates little or no command of conventions. • Does not use complete sentences, correct sentence structures, punctuation, capitalization, grammar, spelling	• not intelligible • not written in English • not on topic • contains text copied from another source

 # Formative Assessment

Weekly Tests

At the end of the lesson, administer the Weekly Test. This will give you a **snapshot of how children are progressing** with the Reading and Language Arts skills in this lesson and can give you **guidance on grouping, reteaching, and intervention.**

Suggestions for adjusting instruction based on these results can be found on the next page.

Access Through Accommodations

When you administer the Weekly Test, some children may have problems accessing all or parts of the assessment. The purpose of the Weekly Test is to determine children's ability to complete the Reading and Language Arts tasks they learned in this lesson. Any barriers to them accessing the tasks demanded of them should be lowered so they can focus on skill demonstration.

When choosing accommodations, you will want to avoid invalidating the test results if you are measuring a child's reading skill. For example, you will not want to read aloud the passage. The following accommodations, if needed, will not interfere with the Weekly Test's validity:

- Read aloud the assessment directions and item prompts. If children are English learners, read aloud the assessment directions and item prompts in the child's native language, if possible.

- Define any unknown words in the directions or item prompts that do not give away the answers to the items.

- Allow for a break during the assessment.

- Simplify the language of assessment directions and item prompts.

- Administer the assessment in a smaller group setting.

- Administer the assessment on a computer or other electronic device.

- Provide audio amplification equipment, colored overlays, or visual magnifying equipment to maintain visual/audio attention and access.

- Allow children to complete the assessment items orally or by having another person transcribe their responses.

Using Data to Adjust Instruction

Use children's scores on the Weekly Test to determine Small Group placement, reteaching, and potential for intervention.

☑ VOCABULARY AND COMPREHENSION

Text and Graphic Features; Point of View; Anchor Text

Target Vocabulary; Shades of Meaning

IF STUDENT SCORES...

...at acceptable,	...below acceptable,
THEN continue core instruction.	**THEN** use Reteach Comprehension Skill and Vocabulary Strategies lessons. For struggling students, administer the *Intervention Assessments* to determine if students would benefit from intervention.

☑ PHONICS

Words with *ar*

IF STUDENT SCORES...

...at acceptable,	...below acceptable,
THEN continue core instruction.	**THEN** use Reteach Phonics lesson. Administer the *Intervention Assessments* to determine if students would benefit from intervention.

☑ LANGUAGE ARTS

Commas in Dates and Places

IF STUDENT SCORES...

...at acceptable,	...below acceptable,
THEN continue core instruction.	**THEN** use Reteach Language Arts lesson. For struggling students, administer the *Intervention Assessments* to determine if students would benefit from intervention.

☑ FLUENCY

Fluency Plan

Assess one group per week using the Fluency Tests ⬀ in the *Grab-and-Go*™ Resources. Use the suggested plan at the right.

● Struggling Readers	Weeks 1, 2, 3
▲ On Level	Week 2
■ Advanced	Week 5

IF...

...students are reading on-level text fluently,	...students are reading below level,
THEN continue core instruction.	**THEN** provide additional fluency practice using the **Student Book,** the **Cold Reads,** and the Leveled Readers. For struggling students, administer the *Intervention Assessments* to determine if students would benefit from intervention.

JOURNEYS

Cold Reads

HOUGHTON MIFFLIN HARCOURT

GRADE **2**

The ***Cold Reads*** passages increase gradually in Lexile® measures throughout the year, from below grade level to above grade level.

- Each passage is accompanied by several selected-response questions and one constructed-response prompt, requiring children to read closely, answer questions at substantial DOK levels, and cite text evidence.

- The ***Cold Reads*** may be used to provide practice in reading increasingly complex texts and to informally monitor children's progress.

- The ***Cold Reads*** may be used to estimate children's Lexile® levels in order to recommend appropriately challenging books for small-group instruction or independent reading.

Turn the page for more information about using **FORMATIVE ASSESSMENT** for **ELD AND INTERVENTION.**

Assess It Online!

▶ Language Workshop Assessment Handbook

▶ Intervention Assessments

Formative Assessment for ELD and Intervention

Formative Assessment for English Learners

English learners should engage in the same rigorous curriculum and formative assessment as other students. However, it is important to remember that English learners face a dual challenge: they are strengthening their abilities *to use* English at the same time that they are learning challenging content *through* English. Use the following strategies and resources for ongoing assessment of English language development, in addition to the assessments you use with all children:

- A combination of **observational measures,** such as listening in as children read aloud or participate in collaborative conversations. Be prepared to provide **"just-in-time" scaffolding** to support students. For example, if children are retelling a story, you could help them use sentence structures with past-tense verbs and time-order transition words.

- **Constructive feedback** that focuses on communication and meaning-making. Avoid overcorrecting in a way that makes English learners reluctant to speak up. You might try recasting a child's statement more correctly, making a note to address the target form more directly during Designated ELD time.

- **Student self-assessment,** through children's own notes in their vocabulary notebooks or other learning journals. If possible, meet with each child to review his or her self-assessments and provide encouragement and feedback.

- **Formative assessment** notes that are integrated into the Language Workshop Teacher's Guide for use during Designated ELD.

- **Language Workshop Assessment Handbook** for longer-cycle assessment to make sure students are progressing in their English development.

Response to Intervention

Use the Weekly Tests and Benchmark and Unit Tests, along with your own observations, to determine if individual students are not responding to primary instruction and need additional testing to identify specific needs for targeted intervention.

Intervention Assessments

Assessment for Intervention

Administer these assessments to

- children who are receiving supplemental intervention to gauge progress toward exit from the intervention program.

- children who demonstrate lack of success with Weekly Tests, Benchmark and Unit Tests, and core instruction to determine if they might benefit from additional practice or intervention.

Differentiate Phonics
- Words with *ar*

Vocabulary Reader
- *Signs Are Everywhere*

Differentiate Comprehension
- Text and Graphic Features
- Question

Differentiate
Phonics & Fluency
- Cumulative Review
- Phrasing: Punctuation

Leveled Readers
- ⬤ *Aldo and Abby*
- ▲ *Finding the Party*
- ⬛ *Too Many Signs!*
- ◆ *Sam Finds the Party*

Differentiate
Vocabulary Strategies
- Shades of Meaning

Options for Reteaching
- Phonics
- Language Arts
- Vocabulary Strategies
- Comprehension

Literacy Centers

Independent Practice
- Word Study, T306
- Think and Write, T307
- Comprehension and Fluency, T306

RtI Small Group Plan
Differentiated Instruction

		DAY 1	DAY 2	DAY 3
Teacher-Led	**Struggling Readers**	**Vocabulary Reader,** *Signs Are Everywhere,* Differentiated Instruction, p. T386 **Differentiate Phonics:** Words with *ar,* p. T384 **English Language Support,** pp. T385, T387	**Differentiate Comprehension:** Text and Graphic Features; Question, p. T388 **Reread** *Darling Starling* **English Language Support,** p. T389	**Leveled Reader** *Aldo and Abby,* p. T392 **Differentiate Phonics:** Cumulative Review, p. T390 **English Language Support,** Leveled Reader Teacher's Guide, p. 5
	On Level	**Vocabulary Reader,** *Signs Are Everywhere,* Differentiated Instruction, p. T386 **English Language Support,** pp. T385, T387	**Differentiate Comprehension:** Text and Graphic Features; Question, p. T388 **Reread** *Darling Starling* **English Language Support,** p. T389	**Leveled Reader** *Finding the Party,* p. T393 *Sam Finds the Party,* p. T395 **Differentiate Fluency:** Phrasing: Punctuation, p. T391 **English Language Support,** Leveled Reader Teacher's Guide, p. 5
	Advanced	**Vocabulary Reader,** *Signs Are Everywhere,* Differentiated Instruction, p. T387 **English Language Support,** pp. T385, T387	**Differentiate Comprehension:** Text and Graphic Features; Question, p. T389 **English Language Support,** p. T389	**Leveled Reader** *Too Many Signs!,* p. T394 **Differentiate Fluency:** Phrasing: Punctuation, p. T391 **English Language Support,** Leveled Reader Teacher's Guide, p. 5
What are my other children doing?	**Struggling Readers**	**Word Building:** Build and read Spelling Words • Leveled Practice, SR19.1	**Partners:** Vocabulary in Context Cards 145–152 **Partners:** Reread *Darling Starling* • Leveled Practice, SR19.2	**Partners:** Reread Leveled Reader *Aldo and Abby* • Leveled Practice, SR19.3
	On Level	**Word Building:** Build and read words with *ar* using Letter Cards **Complete** Reader's Notebook, pp. 46–47 or Leveled Practice, EL19.1	**Target Vocabulary:** Practice reading using Vocabulary in Context Cards 145–152 **Reread** *Darling Starling* **Complete** Reader's Notebook, pp. 48–51 or Leveled Practice, EL19.2	**Partners:** Reread Leveled Reader *Finding the Party* or *Sam Finds the Party* **Complete** Reader's Notebook, pp. 52–56 or Leveled Practice, EL19.3
	Advanced	**Vocabulary in Context Cards** 145–152 *Talk It Over* activities • Leveled Practice, A19.1	**Reread** *The Signmaker's Assistant,* **Student Book,** pp. 126–149 • Leveled Practice, A19.2	**Partners:** Reread Leveled Reader *Too Many Signs!* • Leveled Practice, A19.3

For strategic intervention for this lesson, see pp. S32–S41.

DAY 4	DAY 5	English Language Support

Differentiate Vocabulary Strategies: Shades of Meaning, p. T396
Reread *Going to the Farm*
English Language Support, p. T397

Options for Reteaching, pp. T398–T399
Reread *Darling Starling* or *Going to the Farm* or one of this week's Blend-It Books.

Differentiate Vocabulary Strategies: Shades of Meaning, p. T396
Reread *Going to the Farm*
English Language Support, p. T397

Options for Reteaching, pp. T398–T399
Reread *Darling Starling* or *Going to the Farm* or one of this week's Blend-It Books.

Differentiate Vocabulary Strategies: Shades of Meaning, p. T397
English Language Support, p. T397

Options for Reteaching, pp. T398–T399
Reread *Darling Starling* or *Going to the Farm* or one of this week's Blend-It Books.

Partners: Reread *Going to the Farm*
• Leveled Practice, SR19.4

Partners: Choose among the stories for this week to reread
• Complete and share Literacy Center activities

Reread *Going to the Farm*
Complete Reader's Notebook, pp. 57–59 or Leveled Practice, EL19.4

Partners: Reread Leveled Reader *Finding the Party* or *Sam Finds the Party*
• Complete and share Literacy Center activities
• Self-Selected Reading
Complete Reader's Notebook, p. 60

Partners: Reread *The Trouble with Signs,* **Student Book,** pp. 154–157
• Leveled Practice, A19.4

Partners: Reread Leveled Reader *Too Many Signs!*
• Complete and share Literacy Center activities
• Self-Selected Reading

English Language Support

Use the Leveled Reader Teacher's Guide to support ELs during differentiated instruction.

• **Characteristics of the Text** (p. 1)

  Identify challenging language features, such as text structure, literary features, complex sentences, and vocabulary.

• **Cultural Support/Cognates/Vocabulary** (p. 5)

  Explain unfamiliar features of English and help ELs transfer first-language knowledge.

• **Oral Language Development** (p. 5)

  Check comprehension using dialogues that match children's proficiency levels.

Book Share

Use this routine at the end of the week to show children that they have become experts on their Leveled Readers.

Step 1:

Help each group write a presentation of their Leveled Reader **Responding** page. Use the following routine:

• Briefly tell what your book is about.

• Show your graphic organizer and explain what you added to complete it.

• Tell about your favorite part of the book.

Every child should have his or her own presentation to share with a new group.

Step 2:

Have children number off. Assign places in the classroom for 1s to gather, 2s, and so on. Help children find their new groups.

Step 3:

Have children take turns sharing their book presentations in the new groups. Continue until all children have finished sharing. Encourage children to ask questions. Give the following frames for support.

Can you tell me more about _____?

I wonder why _____?

What do you think about _____?

Differentiate Phonics
Words with *ar*

Struggling Readers

ELA RF.2.3b
ELD ELD.PI.2.1

I DO IT

- Display the first page of the **Decodable Reader** *Darling Starling*. Read aloud the title. Emphasize the sound /är/ as you say each word.

- Write *darling* and underline *ar*. *The letters* ar *stand for the r-controlled vowel sound, /är/, in the word* darling.

Use <u>Instructional Routine 3</u> ↱ to model how to blend *darling*.

- Repeat with *starling*, pointing out the *ar* spelling.

- Review other *ar* words in *Darling Starling*.

WE DO IT

- Use **Sound/Spelling Card** *artist* to review /är/ spelled *ar*.

- Ask children to listen and name the /är/ word in each of the following pairs: *chart/chair, form/farm, head/hard*.

ar

- On the board, write the words shown below. Help children blend the sounds and read the words. Use the **Corrective Feedback** steps if children need additional help.

farm	dark	target	arctic
start	far	market	garden

YOU DO IT

- Have partners use **Letter Cards** to build words with *ar*. Provide **Corrective Feedback** as necessary.

- Have children record the words they build and read the list to the group.

FORMATIVE ASSESSMENT   3 2 1 **RtI**

Corrective Feedback
When a child mispronounces a word, point to the word and say it. Call attention to the element that was mispronounced, say the sound, and then guide children to read the word. See the example below.

Phonics Error:
A child reads *farm* as *form*.

Correct the error. Say the word and the vowel sound. *The word is* farm. *The letters* ar *stand for the sound /är/.*

Model as you touch the letters. *I'll blend: /f/ /är/ /m/. What is the word?* farm

Guide *Let's blend together: /f/ /är/ /m/. What is the word?* farm

Check *You blend. /f/ /är/ /m/ What is the word?* farm

Reinforce Have children continue reading the words on the board. Make note of errors and review those words during the next lesson.

English Language Support

ELD ELD.PIII.2

If appropriate, use Letter Cards to provide Struggling Readers, On Level, and Advanced ELs with proficiency-level support during differentiated instruction.

- Display **Letter Cards** *d*, *ar*, and *k*. Review the *ar* spelling of the sound /är/.

- Blend and read the word *dark*. *Listen: /d/ /är/ /k/, dark.* Have children blend and read the word with you. *Now you blend the sounds: /d/ /är/ /k/, dark.*

Emerging

- Write the word *pat*. Blend and read it with children. Then write *part* and blend and read it with children. Point out how the letter *r* changes the vowel sound from /ă/ to /är/. Repeat with *cat/cart* and *am/arm*.

Expanding

- Write a word ladder with these words: *jar, march, card, farm, yarn, bark, harm, far*. Have children take turns reading the words on the word ladder.

Bridging

- Display **Picture Card** *yard*. Have children use **Letter Cards** to build and read the picture name. Continue with **Picture Cards** *farm*, *jar*, *scarf*, *yarn*, and *car*.

On Level

See Literacy Centers—Unit 4 Lesson 19 Word Study

If children have time after completing the purple activity, have them try moving on to the blue activity.

Advanced

See Literacy Centers—Unit 4 Lesson 19 Word Study

If children have time after completing the blue activity, have them reread the **Decodable Reader** *Darling Starling* or another story independently.

Vocabulary Reader
Signs Are Everywhere

Summary

Signs can tell you what to do and what not to do. Signs can have words, numbers, and pictures.

☑ TARGET VOCABULARY

assistant	tearing
agreed	wisdom
polite	cleared
failed	trouble

Struggling Readers

ELA RF.2.4a, L.2.4a
ELD ELD.PI.2.1, ELD.PI.2.5

- Explain to children that signs are all over the place. They give people many kinds of important information.

- Guide children to preview the selection. Ask children to describe the images, using the Target Vocabulary words when possible.

- Have children alternate reading pages of the selection aloud. Guide them to use context to determine the meanings of unfamiliar words (or phrases). As necessary, use the **Vocabulary in Context Cards** to review how the Target Vocabulary words are used.

- Have partners work together to complete the Responding page. Then review the directions on Blackline Master 19.4 and guide children to complete it.

On Level

ELA RF.2.4a, L.2.4a
ELD ELD.PI.2.1, ELD.PI.2.5

- Explain to children that signs can use words, numbers, and pictures. Tell them that some signs tell us what to do and some tell us what not to do. Guide children to preview the selection.

- Remind children that context clues can help them determine the meaning of an unknown word (or phrase). Tell them to use context clues to confirm their understanding of how the Target Vocabulary words are used in the selection and to learn the meanings of unfamiliar words.

- Have children alternate reading pages of the selection aloud. Have them pause at unfamiliar words (or phrases) and use context clues to determine their meanings.

- Assign the Responding page and Blackline Master 19.4. Review the directions with children. Have children discuss their responses with a partner.

Advanced

ELA RF.2.4a, L.2.4a
ELD ELD.PI.2.1, ELD.PI.2.5

- Have children preview the selection and make predictions about what they will read, using information from the preview and their prior knowledge.

- Remind children to use context clues to help them determine the meanings of unfamiliar words (or phrases).

- Tell children to read the selection with a partner. Ask them to stop and discuss the meanings of unfamilar words (or phrases) as necessary.

- Assign the Responding page and Blackline Master 19.4 []. For the Write About It activity, remind children to include facts and details to support their ideas.

English Language Support

ELD ELD.PI.2.1

Provide Struggling Readers, On Level, and Advanced ELs proficiency-level support during differentiated instruction.

Emerging

- Help children express what they know about the selection to other children in their group. Show pictures of signs. Then display the following sentence frame: *I see _____ on this sign.* Have children choral-read the completed sentence frame with you. Guide them to use the frame to describe images on pages 3, 4, and 6 of the Vocabulary Reader.

Expanding

- Help children express what they see as they preview the Vocabulary Reader. Guide them to prepare for group discussions. Ask: *What do the signs on page 3 say? What does the sign on page 6 mean? What does the picture on page 6 show?*

Bridging

- Give children sentence frames they can use to respond to the Write About It activity. Have them copy and then complete the following frames: *The sign on _____ tells me to be polite. The sign says _____.*

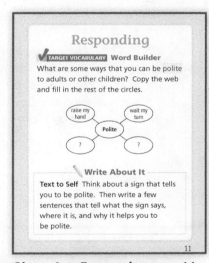

Responding

✓ **TARGET VOCABULARY** **Word Builder**

What are some ways that you can be polite to adults or other children? Copy the web and fill in the rest of the circles.

raise my hand — wait my turn — Polite — ? — ?

✏️ **Write About It**

Text to Self Think about a sign that tells you to be polite. Then write a few sentences that tell what the sign says, where it is, and why it helps you to be polite.

Signs Are Everywhere, p. 11

Differentiate Comprehension
Text and Graphic Features; Question

ELA RL.2.7
ELD ELD.PI.2.1, ELD.PI.2.6

Struggling Readers

I DO IT

- Explain that the authors use pictures to make ideas clearer.

- Read aloud **Student Book** p. 129. Model using the text to ask a question. Model using a picture to come up with an answer.

> **Think Aloud** *The signmaker says he had help from Norman. I wonder who Norman is. In the picture, the signmaker has his arm around the boy standing next to him. The boy is probably Norman.*

WE DO IT

- Have children read **Student Book** p. 131.

- *What do you want to know after reading this page? How might you find the answer to your question? What did Norman paint on the sign? I can read on and also look at the picture on the next page to find out.*

- Using the previous examples, start a Column Chart that identifies a text or graphic feature, the page it appears on, and its purpose.

YOU DO IT

- Have children continue filling out Column Charts for the story.

- Provide time for children to share their maps with a partner.

- Reinforce that readers get some information from the words and some from the pictures.

ELA RL.2.7
ELD ELD.PI.2.1, ELD.PI.2.6

On Level

I DO IT

- Read aloud **Student Book** p. 128. Explain that we can learn more about pictures by asking questions.

- Model forming and answering questions.

> **Think Aloud** *I look closely at the picture and see an old man holding a paint brush. I wonder who he is and what he is doing. The words say that the signmaker is old and that he uses a brush. I think the man is the signmaker, and he is painting a sign.*

WE DO IT

- Help children read **Student Book** p. 133.

- *What question do you have after you read this page? What has Norman always wanted to do?*

- Ask children to turn the next few pages and stop when they see a picture that answers their question. p. 134 Reread the first paragraph on **Student Book** p. 135 to confirm their answer.

- Help children begin a Column Chart showing their question and where they found the answer.

YOU DO IT

- Ask children to create Column Charts listing predictions and questions along with the page numbers of pictures and sentences that helped them answer their questions.

- Provide time for small groups to share their Column Charts with each other.

- Then ask the groups to discuss why the pictures are important in telling the story.

Advanced

ELA RL.2.7
ELD ELD.PI.2.1, ELD.PI.2.6

I DO IT

- Read aloud the first paragraph on **Student Book** p. 130. Model forming a question and identifying how a picture helps you answer it.

Think Aloud *Norman is an assistant. Assistants help people. I wonder if this picture can tell me something the author has not told me in words. I see that the paint brushes are dirty. Maybe Norman helps by cleaning them. I will read on to find out.*

WE DO IT

- Have children read **Student Book** p. 140.

- *After you read this page, what question do you have? What do you predict will happen? What will happen to the town without signs? People will be confused. They won't know what to do or where to go.*

- Have partners share predictions and questions they have about other parts of the story. Ask them to help each other find pictures and sentences that answer their questions.

YOU DO IT

- Ask children to create a Column Chart showing questions they had about the story and identifying page numbers of pictures and sentences that answered their questions.

- Then ask them to discuss whether this story would have been as good without the pictures. Have them support their answer with details from the story.

English Language Support

ELD ELD.PI.2.1

Provide Struggling Readers, On Level, and Advanced ELs proficiency-level support during differentiated instruction.

Emerging

- Use the following strategy to help children fill in the Column Charts.

- Have children point to their favorite picture from *The Signmaker's Assistant* and explain in their own words why they like it.

- Have children look for a sentence in the story that matches up with their favorite picture.

- Guide children to write the page number/s where the illustration and sentence appear in the column chart. Help them to add details next to the page number.

Expanding

- Page through *The Signmaker's Assistant* and talk about how the pictures and the words go together.

- Then display one page. Read the page to children and talk about how the picture adds to what the words say.

Bridging

- Discuss with children whether or not they prefer to read stories with pictures. Have children retell *The Signmaker's Assistant* using only the illustrations. Ask: *Did the story change when you used only the pictures to retell it? How did it change?*

Differentiate Phonics and Fluency

ELA RF.2.3c
ELD ELD.PIII.2

Struggling Readers

Phonics

Cumulative Review

I DO IT

- Show **Picture Card** *baby*. Name the picture and clap the syllables. *I hear the long e sound /ē/ at the end of the two-syllable word baby.*

- Write *baby* on the board and underline *y*. Explain that when a word with two or more syllables ends in *y*, the *y* usually has the sound /ē/.

- Write the words *find, knight, tie,* and *fly* on the board. Read the words aloud. *I hear the sound /ī/ in the middle of* find *and* knight *and at the end of* tie *and* fly.

- Underline the long *i* spelling in each word. Explain that *i, igh,* and *ie* can stand for the long *i* sound /ī/. Point out that the letter *y* also spells /ī/ at the end of one-syllable words.

WE DO IT

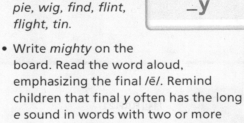

- Display **Sound/ Spelling Card** *ice cream*. Review the *i, igh, ie,* and *y* spellings for long *i*.

- Say these words and have children raise a hand each time they hear a word with /ī/: *mind, mint, pie, wig, find, flint, flight, tin.*

- Write *mighty* on the board. Read the word aloud, emphasizing the final /ē/. Remind children that final *y* often has the long *e* sound in words with two or more syllables.

- Write the words below on the board. Help children blend the sounds to read the words.

spider	tie	lucky	wild
reply	silly	bright	shy

Provide **Corrective Feedback** as necessary.

YOU DO IT

- Have partners use **Letter Cards** to build and read words with the long *i* spellings *i, igh, ie,* and *y* and the long *e* spelling *y*. Use the **Corrective Feedback** steps if children need additional help.

FORMATIVE ASSESSMENT **RtI**

Corrective Feedback
When a child mispronounces a word, point to the word and say it. Call attention to the element that was mispronounced, say the sound, and then guide children to read the word. See the example below.

Phonics Error:
Partners build *child* as *childe*.

Correct the error. Say the word and isolate the vowel sound. *The word is* child; *the letter* i *stands for the sound* /ī/.

Model using **Letter Cards** to build *child*. *I'll build* child: /ch/ ch, /ī/ i, /l/ l, /d/ d; child.

Guide *Let's build* child *together:* /ch/ ch, /ī/ i, /l/ l, /d/ d. *What is the word?* child

Check *You build* child. /ch/ ch, /ī/ i, /l/ l, /d/ d *What's the word?* child

Reinforce Have partners continue building words. Make note of errors and review those words during later lessons.

ELA RF.2.4b

All Levels

Fluency

Phrasing: Punctuation

I DO IT

- Write: *Without store signs, shoppers became confused.*

- Model reading the sentence with appropriate phrasing.

- Use a Think Aloud as you add slash marks to show how you grouped words to read together.

> **Think Aloud** *As I look at this sentence, I think about how I can make my reading sound natural and easy to understand. When we talk, we say groups of words that make sense together. We pause after groups of words so ideas don't run together. I'll group words when I read, too. I'll put a slash mark to show groups of words that go together. I'll look for commas, periods, and other punctuation marks to help me decide where to pause as I read.*

WE DO IT

- Choose two sentences from **Leveled Readers** *Too Many Signs!*, *Aldo and Abby*, *Sam Finds the Party*, and *Finding the Party* and write them on the board.

- Work with children to add slash marks to show phrasing. Provide **Corrective Feedback.**

- Have children take turns reading the sentences aloud. Tell them to use the slash marks to read groups of words that go together.

- Then have pairs of children take turns retelling what they have read.

YOU DO IT

- Have partners choose a page from a **Leveled Reader** and take turns reading aloud, using appropriate phrasing. Remind them to look at the punctuation for clues about grouping words.

- Monitor and provide **Corrective Feedback** as needed.

FORMATIVE ASSESSMENT

Corrective Feedback Work with children to correct errors, following the model below.

Fluency Error:
A child has difficulty with phrasing.

Correct the error. Remind children to look at the punctuation for clues about how to group words.

Model reading a sentence with appropriate phrasing: *When I read, I'll pause at commas, at end marks, and after groups of words that go together.*

Guide Have children echo your reading.

Check Have children read a sentence of their own with appropriate phrasing.

Reinforce Have children go back a sentence or two and begin reading on their own again.

Leveled Readers

☑ **TARGET SKILL**

Text and Graphic Features

☑ **TARGET STRATEGY**

Question

☑ **TARGET VOCABULARY**

agreed	assistant
cleared	failed
polite	tearing
trouble	wisdom

Responding

✔ **TARGET SKILL** Text and Graphic
Features Some pictures in *Aldo and Abby*
include labels. Copy the chart below. List
more labels. Then tell how the labels help
you understand the story better.

Page Number	Label	What It Tells You
2	artist	someone who paints
?	?	?
?	?	?

 Write About It

Text to Self Aldo and Abby agree to work
together. Write a few sentences about
two friends who work together.
Remember to tell the names of the
friends, why they work together, and
what they work on.

11

Aldo and Abby, p. 11

Struggling Readers

ELA RL.2.1, RL.2.7, RF.2.4b
ELD ELD.PI.2.1, ELD.PI.2.6

⬤ *Aldo and Abby*

Summary Aldo isn't a good artist until his assistant, Abby,
forgets to close the cans of paint. The dogs knock over the paint,
splashing it all over the paintings, and leaving paw prints on
them, too! Now everyone loves the paintings.

Genre: Humorous Fiction

Introducing the Text

- Abby is Aldo the painter's assistant. One day she makes a mistake that ends up helping Aldo.

- Remind children that using a graphic organizer to record clues and the page numbers of
important pictures will help them better understand what happens in the story.

Supporting the Reading

- **p. 7** *How does the picture on p. 7 help you understand what happened to Aldo's paintings? It
shows me that everything is a mess.*

- **p. 7** *What question would you ask yourself to figure out why the dogs got their paw prints
on the paintings?* **Sample answer:** *I might ask, "How did the dogs get paint on their feet?"*

Discussing and Revisiting the Text

Critical Thinking After they discuss the book, read with children the instructions on the
top half of Responding, p. 11 in *Aldo and Abby.*

- Have partners identify the picture labels and their corresponding page numbers that show
what happens to Aldo's paintings and why people like them now. Then have children
complete Blackline Master 19.5 ⬐.

FLUENCY: PHRASING/PUNCTUATION Model correct phrasing as you read aloud p. 9. Then
have children echo-read p. 9 and focus on using punctuation to help them read with proper
phrasing.

On Level

ELA RL.2.1, RL.2.7, RF.2.4b
ELD ELD.PI.2.1, ELD.PI.2.6

 ### *Finding the Party*

Summary Louisa and all her friends are trying to find Phil's party. They even have a map, but they can't find Phil's house. How does Sam help?

Genre: Humorous Fiction

Introducing the Text

- Explain that the children are using a map to find Phil's house. Why won't anyone listen to Sam?

- Remind children that authors often use pictures to give clues so readers know what is happening in the story. Sometimes readers know more than the characters in the story because readers see the clues in the pictures.

Supporting the Reading

- **pp. 5–6** *When you look at the picture on pp. 6–7, what do you and Sam see that the other characters do not see? We see balloons and a house that is decorated for a party. This is probably Phil's house.*

- **pp. 7–8** *What question would you ask yourself to figure out why no one is listening to Sam? I might ask, "Who is Sam trying to talk to? What does that person say?"*

Discussing and Revisiting the Text

Critical Thinking After they discuss the book, help children read the instructions on the top half of Responding, p. 15 in *Finding the Party*.

- Have children identify picture clues that show where Phil's house is.

- Have them write the page number and reason for each picture on Blackline Master 19.6.

FLUENCY: PHRASING/PUNCTUATION Have children practice reading their favorite parts of *Finding the Party*. Remind them that the punctuation marks are clues that will help their phrasing sound natural.

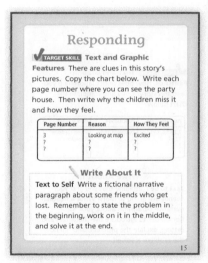

Responding

✓ **TARGET SKILL** **Text and Graphic Features** There are clues in this story's pictures. Copy the chart below. Write each page number where you can see the party house. Then write why the children miss it and how they feel.

Page Number	Reason	How They Feel
3	Looking at map	Excited
?	?	?
?	?	?

Write About It

Text to Self Write a fictional narrative paragraph about some friends who get lost. Remember to state the problem in the beginning, work on it in the middle, and solve it at the end.

15

Finding the Party, p. 15

☑ **TARGET SKILL**
Text and Graphic Features

☑ **TARGET STRATEGY**
Question

☑ **TARGET VOCABULARY**

agreed	assistant
cleared	failed
polite	tearing
trouble	wisdom

Leveled Readers

Advanced

ELA RL.2.1, RL.2.7, RF.2.4b
ELD ELD.PI.2.1, ELD.PI.2.6

 ### *Too Many Signs!*

Summary People in Happytown don't like it when they get tickets for not obeying the signs. When the mayor takes down the signs, everything goes wrong. Finally, they all agree that signs are good.

Genre: Humorous Fiction

Introducing the Text

- Explain that the people of Happytown find out what happens when they don't follow the signs and what happens when they don't have any signs at all.

- Remind children that authors use text and pictures to give information about what is happening in a story. When readers use the pictures to help them read, they understand the story better.

Supporting the Reading

- **p. 8** *Look at the picture on p. 8. What happens when there aren't any signs?* People crash into each other, fall, and are unhappy.

- **pp. 12–13** *What would you ask yourself to figure out why the townspeople want to meet with the mayor?* I might ask, "What is happening in town that might make the people upset?"

Discussing and Revisiting the Text

Critical Thinking After they discuss the book, have children read the instructions on the top half of Responding, p. 15 in *Too Many Signs!*

- Have children work individually or in pairs to find punctuation that helps them understand the story.

- Have children complete Blackline Master 19.7 [📄].

FLUENCY: PHRASING/PUNCTUATION Have children practice reading *Too Many Signs!* with phrasing and expression, remembering to use the punctuation as a guide.

Too Many Signs!, p. 15

ELD ELD.PI.2.1, ELD.PI.2.6

English Language Support

 ## *Sam Finds the Party*

Summary No one can find the party, even when they look at the map. Sam knows where the party is. Why won't anyone listen to her?

Genre: Humorous Fiction

Introducing the Text

- Explain that the children look at the map to try to find Phil's party, but they can't find the house. How does Sam help?

- Remind children that authors often put clues in the pictures, and that good readers look at the pictures to find the clues so they can better understand the story.

Supporting the Reading

- **p. 5** *Look at the words around the picture on p. 5. How do they help you know who the new boy in the picture is?* **The words tell me that the boy's name is Taylor. Now I know who he is.**

- **p. 9** *What would you ask yourself to figure out how Sam feels?* **I might ask, "How do I feel when people don't listen to me?"**

Discussing and Revisiting the Text

Critical Thinking After they discuss the book, read with children the instructions on the top half of Responding, p. 15 in *Sam Finds the Party*.

- Have them work individually or in pairs to find pictures and page numbers that show that Sam is the only person who knows where the party is.

- Have children complete Blackline Master 19.8 [↗].

FLUENCY: PHRASING/PUNCTUATION Have children practice reading their favorite parts of *Sam Finds the Party*. Point out the punctuation to help children with proper phrasing.

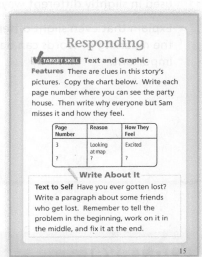

Responding

✓ **TARGET SKILL** **Text and Graphic Features** There are clues in this story's pictures. Copy the chart below. Write each page number where you can see the party house. Then write why everyone but Sam misses it and how they feel.

Page Number	Reason	How They Feel
3	Looking at map	Excited
?	?	?

Write About It

Text to Self Have you ever gotten lost? Write a paragraph about some friends who get lost. Remember to tell the problem in the beginning, work on it in the middle, and fix it at the end.

15

Sam Finds the Party, p. 15

Differentiate Vocabulary Strategies
Shades of Meaning

Struggling Readers

ELA L.2.5b
ELD ELD.PI.2.1, ELD.PI.2.8

I DO IT

- Remind children that synonyms are words that have the same or almost the same meaning.

- Explain that when synonyms have slightly different meanings, they are used in slightly different ways.

- Explain that even slight differences in the meaning of words can be important.

WE DO IT

- Display: *Tanya looked at the rain outside the window. Terence peeked at the cake in the oven.*

- Point out that *looked* and *peeked* are synonyms because they mean about the same thing: to use your eyes to examine something.

- Have children discuss the meanings of *look* and *peek*, finding clues in the sentence contexts. Ask, *If you're watching rain fall outside, are you in a hurry? If you're looking at a cake that's still in the oven, are you in a hurry?*

YOU DO IT

- Write the following sentences on the board: *I was late for dinner again. I ____ in the back door.*

- Have children work with their partners to decide whether *walked* or *sneaked* fits the sentence better. Encourage them to discuss the words' meanings and the sentence context.

- Have children write a sentence explaining why they chose the word they did.

On Level

ELA L.2.5b
ELD ELD.PI.2.1, ELD.PI.2.8

I DO IT

- Remind children that synonyms are words that have the same or almost the same meaning.

- Explain that when synonyms have slightly different meanings, they are used in slightly different ways. Explain that even slight differences in the meaning of words can be important.

- Tell children that they can often determine the different meanings of two synonyms by studying the words' contexts. Children can also look up words in a dictionary.

WE DO IT

- Display: *The right fielder hurled the ball toward home plate. My sister tossed me the magazine.*

- Point out that *hurled* and *tossed* are synonyms because they mean about the same thing: using your arm and hand to throw something.

- Have children discuss how the meanings of *hurled* and *tossed* are different. Encourage them to look for clues in the sentence contexts. Ask, *If you are throwing a ball from right field to home plate, how hard will you throw? If you are throwing someone a magazine, how hard will you throw?*

YOU DO IT

- Write the following sentences on the board: *The horse ____ over the fence. The frog ____ in the lake.*

- Have children work with their partners to decide which sentence is best completed with *hopped* and which is best completed with *leaped*. Encourage them to discuss the sentence contexts and to look the words up in a dictionary.

- Have children write their own sentences with *hopped* and *leaped*.

Advanced

ELA L.2.5b

I DO IT

- Remind children that synonyms are words that have the same or almost the same meaning.

- Explain that when synonyms have slightly different meanings, they are used in slightly different ways. Explain that even slight differences in the meaning can be important.

- Tell children that they can often determine the different meanings of two synonyms by studying the words' contexts or looking them up in a dictionary.

WE DO IT

- Display: *We couldn't stop laughing because the movie was* hilarious. *Our teacher told us a* funny *story.*

- Point out that *hilarious* and *funny* are synonyms because they mean about the same thing: causing smiles and laughter.

- Have children discuss how the meanings of *hilarious* and *funny* are different, finding clues in the sentence contexts. Ask, *How funny is something if you can't stop laughing? How funny are your teacher's stories?*

YOU DO IT

- Write the following words on the board: *quiet*, *silent*.

- Have children discuss with their partners how the words' meanings are slightly different. Encourage them to look up the words in a dictionary.

- Have children write two sentences, one using each word.

English Language Support

ELD ELD.PI.2.1, ELD.PI.2.8

Provide Struggling Readers, On Level, and Advanced ELs proficiency-level support during differentiated instruction.

Emerging

- As children complete the We Do It activity for their group, allow them to act out the words to emphasize the shades of meaning.

- Ask: *What was different when you acted out _____ from when you acted out _____?* Guide children to use their physical imitations of the words to find context clues in the sentences that indicate the shades of meaning.

Expanding

- As children complete the We Do It activity for their group, allow them to look up both words in a print or digital dictionary.

- Have children write down the definitions and compare them side by side. Tell them to circle any words that are similar in the definitions and underline the words that tell how they are different.

Bridging

- As children complete the You Do It activity for their group, have them include drawings with their sentences to help explain the shades of meaning.

- Provide sentence frames they can use to talk about their drawings: *I drew _____ to show _____.*

Differentiate Vocabulary Strategies • **T397**

Options for Reteaching

ELA RF.2.3b **ELD** ELD.PI.2.1

Reteach Phonics

Words with *ar*

I DO IT

- Display **Sound/Spelling Card** *artist*. Name the picture and say the sound, /är/. Have children repeat after you.

- Write *farm* and underline *ar*. Use Instructional Routine 3 🔲 to blend and read the word. *Listen: /f/ /är/ /m/*, farm. Have children repeat after you.

- Have children open to the first page of the **Decodable Reader** *Going to the Farm*.

WE DO IT

- Write *Marge* on the board and underline *ar*. Blend and read *Marge* with children.

- Have children find the name *Marge* on the page.

- Repeat the procedure with other words with *ar* in the **Decodable Reader** *Going to the Farm*.

YOU DO IT

- Have partners work together to read *Going to the Farm*.

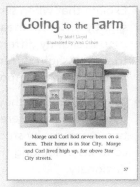

Decodable Reader

ELA L.2.2a **ELD** ELD.PI.2.1

Reteach Language Arts

Commas in Dates and Places

I DO IT

- *A comma is used between the day and year in a date. A comma is also used between a city and a state.*

- Write: *January 29 2010* and *El Paso Texas*. Model inserting commas.

- Think Aloud *I see a day and year in a date. The comma goes after the day and before the year:* January 29, 2010. *Which is the name of the state?* Texas. El Paso *must be the city. A comma goes between the city and the state.*

WE DO IT

- Work together to compose a story about a hero. Encourage children to use dates and places in the story.

- Guide children to identify where they need commas in dates and places in the story.

- Have children explain which words are dates and places.

YOU DO IT

- Ask children to write three or four sentences that tell when they went somewhere and where they went. Have them underline the dates and places. Then have them circle the commas in the dates and places.

- Invite children to explain whether each circled comma is in a date or a place.

ELA L.2.5b ELD ELD.PI.2.1, ELD.PI.2.8

Reteach Vocabulary Strategies

Shades of Meaning

I DO IT

- Remind children that *synonyms* are words that have the same or almost the same meaning.

- Once children know the meaning of a word, they can think of synonyms for it. Explain that replacing a word with a synonym won't change the meaning of the sentence very much, but the word and synonym will have slightly different shades of meaning.

WE DO IT

- Display Projectable 19.7 [✓]. Read the second sentence. Point to the boldface word (*cheered*) and reread it.

- Ask a volunteer to act out the word by pretending to cheer for a winning team.

  Think Aloud *I want to find a synonym of cheered. It should mean about the same thing—to shout encouragement. If I replace cheered with the synonym, the meaning of the sentence shouldn't change very much.*

- Have children find a synonym of *cheered* in the word bank. Write *yelled* above *cheered*. Reread the sentence with *yelled*.

- Have children compare the actions of cheering and yelling. How are they different? How are they similar?

YOU DO IT

- Have children work with their partners to choose the synonyms of the boldface words in Projectable 19.7 [✓].

- Have children write how each boldface word and its synonym are similar and how they are different.

ELA RL.2.7 ELD ELD.PI.2.1, ELD.PI.2.6

Reteach Comprehension Skill

Text and Graphic Features

I DO IT

- Remind children that authors choose charts, photos, maps, and other graphic features to go along with the ideas in their texts.

- Explain that sometimes authors use graphic features to make the ideas clearer. Other times, authors use graphic features to give more information or to explain it in a different way.

WE DO IT

- Have children read the story sentence on **Student Book** p. 136.

- Model how to figure out what information each graphic feature gives them and how that information connects with the text.

  Think Aloud *There really isn't much text on this page, but there is a lot to read. I read the words on all the funny signs Norman made and put up around town. Those signs tell me why the townspeople are doing strange things.*

- Help volunteers identify the text written into the illustrations on this page and tell why the signs are funny.

YOU DO IT

- Distribute Graphic Organizer 1: **Column Chart**.

- In the first and second column, have children list graphic features included on **Student Book** pp. 136–139 and the page number. Then have children list what they think should be the correct text for each funny sign shown in the artwork on these pages.

- Have partners work together to complete the Column Chart.

- Review the completed charts.

Teacher Notes

JOURNEYS

Anchor
Text

Paired
Selection

LESSON
20

DIGITAL RESOURCES

Teacher Dashboard

Log onto the Teacher Dashboard and *my*SmartPlanner.
Use these searchable tools to customize lessons that
achieve your instructional goals.

Interactive
Whiteboard Lessons

• Vocabulary Strategies: Prefix *over-*
• Phonics: Words with *or, ore*

 WriteSmart
• Write About Reading
• Narrative Writing:
  Fictional Story

✓ **Assess It Online!**

• Weekly Tests
• Assessment-driven instruction with prescriptive
  feedback

Student eBook

✏ ▯ **Annotate it!** Strategies for Annotation

Guide children to use digital tools for close reading.

Children may also use the interactive features in their
Student eBooks to respond to prompts in a variety of
ways, including:

• short-answer response	• drag-and-drop
• spoken response	• multiple choice
• fill-in-the-blank	• drawing

 fyi
hmhfyi.com
High-Interest Informational
Texts and Multimedia

Have children explore the FYI website for additional
information about topics of study.

ENGLISH LANGUAGE SUPPORT

Culturally Responsive Teaching

Hooray for Heroes! Tell children that this week, they
will be reading and thinking about what makes
someone a hero.

• Encourage small group discussions on topics related
  to heroes, such as favorite superheroes, heroes
  from the past and present, community heroes, and
  the qualities of a hero.

• Invite children to share books and comic books
  about heroes with special powers. Ask them to
  describe what makes each hero special, and guide
  them to identify elements of fantasy.

• Have children work independently to create an
  animal hero who has special powers. Encourage
  them to draw a picture, write a story, or sketch a
  comic book about their animal heroes' adventures.
  Invite children to share their work with the class or
  a small group.

Scaffold Instruction and Learning Use visuals with
English learners to present and discuss ideas about
heroes and elements of fantasy. Use simple sentence
structures to build ideas about heroes, and provide
word banks and sentence frames to help children
discuss ideas and form responses.

Language Support Card

Use the Lesson 20 Language Support Card to activate
prior knowledge, frontload vocabulary, and teach
academic English.

 **TEXT
X-RAY**
Use the Text X-Ray on page T409 to
review the language demands of
Dex: The Heart of a Hero with the
needs of English learners in mind.

Language Workshop for
Designated ELD

• Connection to Essential Question

• Vocabulary Network

• Focus on Interacting in Meaningful Ways

• Discussion Frames

• How English Works

• Word Learning Strategies

You may wish to use the following suggestions to modify instruction for some children, according to their needs.

Learner's Journal

Keeping a Learner's Journal can help children see themselves as successful, growing learners. Developing a sense of ownership in children can motivate them to reach their highest potential. Have children add to their Learner's Journal for this lesson. Depending on children's needs and skills, have them record information about what they are learning. Some examples:

- Day 1: Vocabulary: *depended, gazing, sore, hero, sprang, exercise, studied, overlooked*
- Day 2: The title of the Anchor Text, *Dex: The Heart of a Hero,* and words or pictures about the text
- Day 3: Write and draw about something new they learned about heroes. To help, you might want to discuss with children the Essential Question and their ideas about it.
- Day 4: Write one or more words they have learned to spell this week.
- Day 5: Write about how they are becoming better writers. For example, "I am learning to write a fictional story."

Student eBook

- **Audio** can be activated to support fluency, decoding, and comprehension.
- **Alternative Text** provides spoken information that can be used in place of the information provided in the book's images.
- **Vocabulary Pop-Ups** contain point-of-use definitions for selection vocabulary.

Health

Making Physical Activity a Habit Have children investigate and report on opportunities outside of school for regular participation in physical activity.

- Review how Dex realized that to be a hero, he needed strong muscles. Ask children to point out examples from *Dex: The Heart of a Hero* that tell how Dex trained and got regular exercise.
- Organize children into small groups to have a discussion about ways they can get exercise outside of school, such as running, swimming, riding a bike, or playing a sport. Have group members take turns recording ideas.
- Then have groups discuss ways they could make sure that physical exercise becomes a habit, such as using a calendar, keeping an exercise journal, or setting aside a period of time every day for any kind of physical activity. Have group members take turns recording ideas.
- Invite groups to share and discuss their ideas with another group. Have them choose the ones they like best and present them in a whole-class discussion.

Our Focus Wall

LESSON 20

ANCHOR TEXT

Paired Selection

Dex: The Heart of a Hero
Fantasy

Heroes Then and Now
Informational Text (Biography)

ESSENTIAL QUESTION

What makes someone a hero?

FOUNDATIONAL SKILLS

☑ High-Frequency Words

begins	laugh
being	ready
flower	stood
ground	tall
I've	very

Phonics

Words with *or, ore*

Fluency

Intonation

READING LITERATURE & INFORMATIONAL TEXT

Comprehension Skills and Strategies

☑ **TARGET SKILL**
• Compare and Contrast
• Figurative Language

☑ **TARGET STRATEGY**
• Monitor/Clarify

LANGUAGE

☑ Target Vocabulary

depended	gazing
sore	hero
sprang	exercise
studied	overlooked

Vocabulary Strategies

Prefix *over-*

Grammar

Commas in a Series

Spelling

Words with *or, ore*

horn	morning
story	shore
fork	short
score	born
store	tore
corn	forget

WRITING

Writing

Narrative Writing:
Fictional Story
Focus Trait: Organization

Whole Group Resources

ANCHOR TEXT

Dex: The Heart of a Hero
GENRE: Fantasy
21st Century Theme: Civic Literacy

Heroes Then and Now
GENRE: Informational Text

TEXT X-RAY

Prepare for Complex Texts For a comprehensive overview and analysis of key ideas and academic language features of this lesson's Anchor Text, see pages T408–T409.

Digital Resources

▶ **eBook: Annotate it!**

▶ **Interactive Whiteboard Lessons**
  • Vocabulary Strategies: Prefix *over-*
  • Phonics: Words with *or, ore*

▶ **GrammarSnap Videos**
  • Commas in a Series

▶ **Multimedia Grammar Glossary**

▶ ***my*SmartPlanner**

▶ **Parent Resource**

● Additional Resources

  • Vocabulary in Context Cards 153–160
  • Reader's Notebook, pp. 61–75
  • Independent Reading
  • Lesson 20 Blackline Masters
  • Decodable Readers
  • Blend-It Books 123–124

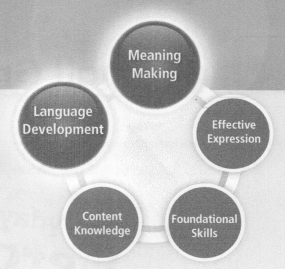

Meaning Making

Language Development

Effective Expression

Content Knowledge

Foundational Skills

LINGUISTICALLY DIVERSE LEARNERS

⌄ Integrated English Language Support

● Interacting in Meaningful Ways

Classroom Conversations
- Think-Write-Pair-Share, p. T423
- Collaborative Conversation, pp. T414, T436, T446, T472
- Turn and Talk, p. T446

Interactive and Collaborative Writing
- Fictional Story, p. T449
- Write About Reading, p. T447

● Learning About How English Works

Scaffold the Texts
- Text X-Ray: Focus on Academic Language, p. T409
- Connecting Ideas, p. T433

Communicative Modes
- Interpretive, pp. T414, T433
- Collaborative, pp. T420, T446
- Productive, pp. T459, T474

● Using Foundational Literacy Skills

Support Linguistic Transfer
- Words with *or, ore,* p. T416
- *r*-Controlled Vowel, p. T438
- Commas in a Series of Nouns, p. T458

Fluency: Intonation, p. T453

Phonics, pp. T416–T417, T418, T442–T443, T452, T462–T463, T488–T489, T494–T495

Apply Language Skills
- Commas in a Series, pp. T474–T475

⌄ Standard English Learners

- Voicing /s/ in Plurals, p. T464

ASSESSMENT

● Formative Assessment
- Phonics: Words with *or, ore,* pp. T417, T452
- Target Vocabulary, p. T421
- Decodable Reader, p. T419
- Target Skill: Compare and Contrast, p. T445
- Vocabulary Strategies: Prefix *over-,* p. T467
- Using Data to Adjust Instruction, p. T479

●  Assess It Online!
- Weekly Test

Performance Tasks	• Write About Reading, p. T447 • Fictional Story, p. T439

Small Group/Independent Resources

∨ Vocabulary Reader

Everyday Hero
by Jessica Quilty
illustrated by Julie Downing

HOUGHTON MIFFLIN

● **Vocabulary Reader**
for all levels

Provide strategic scaffolding to support all students in reading on-level text and in acquiring general academic and domain-specific vocabulary. Use the instructional supports on pp. T490–T491 or the Leveled Reader Teacher's Guide.

Guided Reading Level: I
Lexile: 600
DRA: 16

Leveled Reader Teacher's Guide

∨ Weekly Leveled Readers

Guide children to read and comprehend additional texts about the lesson topic.
Use the instructional supports on pp. T496–T499 or the Leveled Reader Teacher's Guides.

Struggling Readers
Guided Reading Level: I
Lexile: 310
DRA: 16
Leveled Reader Teacher's Guide

On Level
Guided Reading Level: J
Lexile: 410
DRA: 18
Leveled Reader Teacher's Guide

Advanced
Guided Reading Level: L
Lexile: 620
DRA: 24
Leveled Reader Teacher's Guide

English Language Support
Guided Reading Level: J
Lexile: 280
DRA: 18
Leveled Reader Teacher's Guide

Two Heroes

HOUGHTON MIFFLIN

Superheroes to the Rescue

HOUGHTON MIFFLIN

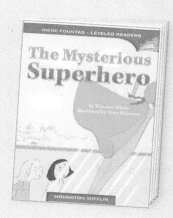

The Mysterious Superhero

HOUGHTON MIFFLIN

Superheroes Save the Day

HOUGHTON MIFFLIN

Language Workshop for Designated ELD

- Provides an additional hour of daily instruction for targeted language support.

- **Supports English learners** at three different proficiency levels as they dig deeper into the language of the lesson texts.

- Guides students in collaboration, interpretation, and production of English.

Lesson 20 Focus

Collaborate: Negotiate with Others

Interpret: Ask and Answer Questions

Produce: Use Technology; Give Presentations

How English Works: Possessive Pronouns

Vocabulary Network

Intervention

 Strategic Intervention Tier II

Write-In Reader: *Sue and the Tired Wolf*

- Interactive worktext with selection that connects to the lesson topic

- Reinforces the lesson's vocabulary and comprehension

- Builds skills for reading increasingly complex texts

Daily Lessons See this week's daily Strategic Intervention Lesson on pp. S42–S51.

- Preteach and reteach daily instruction
- Oral Grammar
- Words to Know
- Decoding
- Comprehension
- Fluency
- Grammar
- Written Response
- Unpack Meaning

Curious About Words Provides oral vocabulary instruction for children with limited vocabularies.

HMH Decoding Power: Intensive Reading Instruction

- **Provides reteaching and practice in the key foundational skills** for reading: print concepts, phonological/phonemic awareness, phonics and word recognition, and fluency.

- **Explicit, sequential, and systematic instruction** designed to bring students up to grade level.

✓ *Assess It Online!*

▶ **Intervention Assessments** place individual students within the system, ensure students are making satisfactory progress, and provide a measure of student readiness to exit the system.

What My Other Students Are Doing

Digital Resources

▶ Literacy Centers: Word Study, Think and Write, Comprehension and Fluency

 iRead

 myWriteSmart fyi hmhfyi.com Channel One News

● **Additional Resources**

- Vocabulary in Context Cards 153–160

- Reader's Notebook, pp. 61–75

- Independent Reading

- Lesson 20 Blackline Masters

- Decodable Readers

- Blend-It Books 123–124

Literacy Centers

Comprehension and Fluency

Materials

- Student Book
- Decodable Reader: *My Story*
- Audio
- Paper and pencil

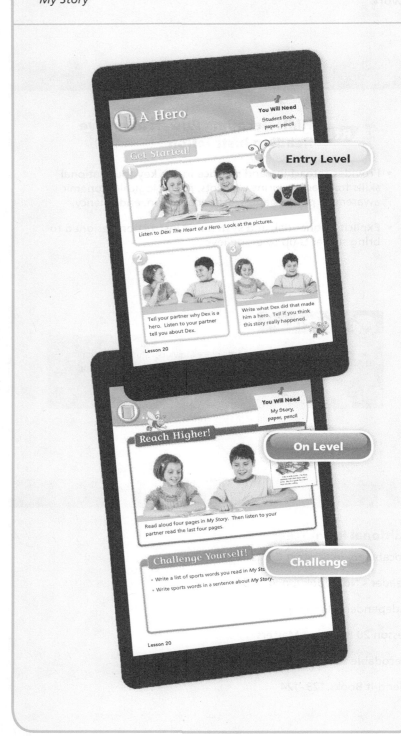

Word Study

Materials

- Sound/Spelling Cards: *artist, orange*
- Context Cards: *depended, sore, sprang, studied, gazing, hero, exercise, overlooked*
- Paper and pencil
- Blank cards
- Books
- Construction paper

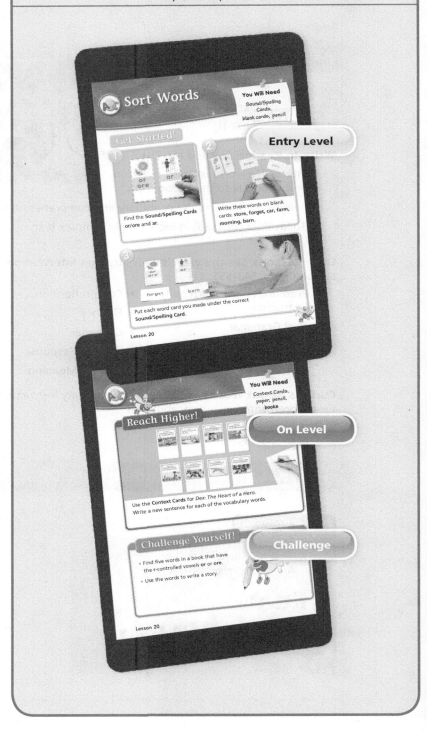

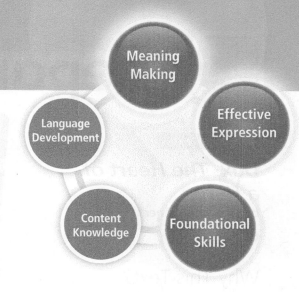

Assign Literacy Center activities during small group time. Each center contains three activities. Children who experience success with the entry-level activity move on to the on-level and challenge activities, as time permits.

Think and Write

Materials

- Picture Card: *prize*
- Paper, pencil, crayons
- Teacher-made word cards: *because, car, care, ready, school, walk, watch, work*

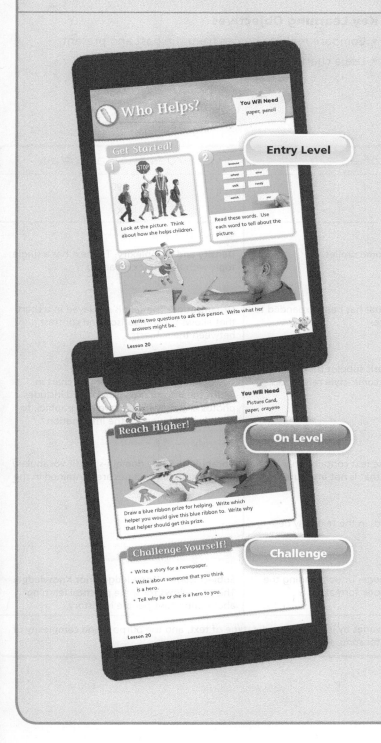

Who Helps?

You Will Need
paper, pencil

Get Started!

Entry Level

1. STOP

2. Read these words. Use each word to tell about the picture.

Look at the picture. Think about how she helps children.

3. Write two questions to ask this person. Write what her answers might be.

Lesson 20

You Will Need
Picture Card, paper, crayons

Reach Higher!

On Level

Draw a blue ribbon prize for helping. Write which helper you would give this blue ribbon to. Write why that helper should get this prize.

Challenge Yourself!

Challenge

- Write a story for a newspaper.
- Write about someone that you think is a hero.
- Tell why he or she is a hero to you.

Lesson 20

Independent Reading

Teacher and Librarian Recommendations

Teachers and media specialists can work together to select and feature books that might interest children in a particular classroom. Be sure to choose a variety of reading levels and topics, including books that will help children with projects or research related to what they are learning in Science or Social Studies.

Children's book award lists, which are updated each year, are a useful resource for selecting books that children will enjoy. Start with awards such as these:

- ALSC Notable Children's Books
- ALSC Newbery Medal and Honor Books, 1922-Present
- IRA Children's Choices

See pp. T454–T455 for additional independent reading support. **ELA** RL.2.10, RI.2.10

Dex: The Heart of a Hero
by Caralyn Buehner

GENRE: Fantasy

Why This Text?

Children should be exposed to a variety of fiction, including fantasies. This text is about a dog who has big dreams to be a hero.

Key Learning Objectives

- Compare and contrast how characters change in a story.
- Explain the meaning of figurative language, including similes.

Heroes Then and Now

GENRE: Informational Text

Why This Text?

Children will regularly encounter informational text in textbooks and on the Internet. This text is about people who have accomplished brave or remarkable things.

Key Learning Objectives

- Compare real-life heroes from the past and present.
- Use a chart to learn important information.

TEXT COMPLEXITY RUBRIC

		Dex: The Heart of a Hero	Heroes Then and Now
Quantitative Measures	Lexile	650	590
	Guided Reading Level	M	K
Qualitative Measures	Purpose/Levels of Meaning	**Figurative Language:** The text has some similes.	**Density and Complexity:** The text has a single topic with a complex meaning.
	Text Structure	**Genre:** The text is a familiar genre that has been expanded to include comic-style graphic references. **Organization:** The text has a very basic subplot that can be tracked using the story line and the comic-style references.	**Organization:** The text is displayed in a chart that allows for comparison and contrast between the subjects. **Use of Images and Graphics:** The chart in which the information is displayed includes photos and drawings, as well as graphics, to help the reader access the information.
	Language Features	**Standard English and Variations:** The text contains only familiar English and some dialogue that is not attributed. **Vocabulary:** Several vocabulary words in the text may be unfamiliar.	**Vocabulary:** Some domain-specific vocabulary and geographical names are contained in the text.
	Knowledge Demands	**Intertextuality and Cultural Knowledge:** Understanding the text relies on knowledge of comic book format.	**Subject Matter Knowledge/Prior Knowledge:** This text allows for some practical learning about important people in history.
Reader/Task Considerations		Determine using the professional judgment of the teacher. This varies by individual reader, type of text, and the purpose and complexity of particular tasks. See **Reader and Task Considerations** on p. T425 for some suggestions for Anchor Text support.	

Meaning Making

Language Development

Effective Expression

Content Knowledge

Foundational Skills

 TEXT X-RAY

ENGLISH LANGUAGE SUPPORT Use the Text X-Ray below to prepare for teaching the Anchor Text *Dex: The Heart of a Hero*. Use it to plan, support, and scaffold instruction in order to help children understand the text's **key ideas** and **academic language features**.

Zoom In on Key Ideas

Children should understand these **key ideas** after reading *Dex: The Heart of a Hero*.

Key Idea | pp. 168–170

Dex is a little dog. No one seems to notice him except Cleevis, a very large cat who makes fun of his size. Dex has big dreams of being a hero.

Have children use the pictures to tell what kind of hero Dex imagines himself being.

Key Idea | pp. 171–174

Dex starts training to be a hero. He runs and climbs and does push-ups to build his muscles. After a lot of hard work, Dex is ready.

Have children tell how they know that Dex is determined to make his dream come true.

Key Idea | pp. 175–179

Dex gets a red hero suit with a green cape. Cleevis still laughs at him, but soon Dex begins helping everyone who needs help. They call him Super Dog!

Have children tell why they think Dex doesn't let Cleevis's teasing bother him.

Key Idea | pp. 180–189

One night, Cleevis becomes stuck in a tree. Will Dex the Super Dog come to the rescue of the cat who makes fun of him?

Have children explain how Dex's dream comes true.

Zoom In on Academic Language

Guide children at different proficiencies and skill levels to understand the structure and language of this text.

Focus: Text Level | p. 170

Point out the **text box** at the bottom of the page. Tell children that the text is designed to look like a comic book because comic books are often about superheroes. Tell children that the author is showing how Dex is following his dream. Have children point out other boxes like this one.

Focus: Sentence Level | p. 175

Point out the words *fit like a glove*. Ask children to explain how a glove fits. Then ask children to tell if the details on the page support the idea that the suit fit well. Have children look for other examples of **figurative language** in the story.

Focus: Word Level | p. 181

Reread the second paragraph, emphasizing the **onomatopoeic** word *yeowling*. Remind children that Cleevis is a cat, and the word *yeowling* is describing the sound he is making. Ask children to tell why the author didn't use the word *meowing* or *purring* instead of *yeowling*.

Focus: Sentence Level | p. 182

Point out the **quotation marks** signifying **dialogue** in the second paragraph. Tell children that sometimes the author does not say who is speaking because it can be determined from following the conversation. Guide them to determine that it is Dex who is speaking in the second paragraph.

Content and Language Instruction

Make note of additional **content knowledge** and **language features** children may find challenging in this text.

Weekly Planner

DEX The Heart of a Hero

HEROES THEN AND NOW

my SmartPlanner

Auto-populates the suggested five-day lesson plan and offers flexibility to create and save customized plans from year to year.

See **Standards Correlations** on p. C1. In your eBook, click the Standards button in the left panel to view descriptions of the standards on the page.

	DAY 1	**DAY 2**
	Materials	**Materials**
	• Blend-It Books: Books 123–124	• Decodable Reader: *A Sporty Game*
	• Common Core Writing Handbook, Lesson 20	• GrammarSnap Video: Commas in a Series
	• Decodable Reader: *A Sporty Game*	• Graphic Organizer 14
	• GrammarSnap Video: Commas in a Series	• High-Frequency Word Cards 191–200
	• High-Frequency Word Cards 191–200	• Instructional Routines 3, 15
	• Instructional Routines 1, 3, 7, 11, 13	• Letter Cards
	• Language Support Card, Lesson 20	• Literacy and Language Guide, pp. 94–95
	• Letter Cards; Sound/Spelling Card	• Projectables 20.4, 20.5
	• Literacy and Language Guide, pp. 94–95	• Reader's Notebook Vol 2 pp. 63–66
	• Projectables S1, 19.8, 20.1, 20.2, 20.3	• Sound/Spelling Card: orange
	• Reader's Notebook Vol 2 pp. 61–62	• Student Book pp. 166–193
	• Retelling Cards 77–80	• Vocabulary in Context Cards 153–160
	• Student Book pp. 162–189	
	• Vocabulary in Context Cards 153–160	

Whole Group

Daily Language
• Oral Vocabulary
• Phonemic Awareness
• Speaking and Listening

DAY 1	**DAY 2**
Opening Routines, T412–T413	**Opening Routines,** T440–T441
Read Aloud "Ordinary Heroes," T414–T415	**Phonemic Awareness,** T442
Phonemic Awareness, T416	

Vocabulary
Text-Based Comprehension
• Skills and Strategies
• Craft and Structure

DAY 1	**DAY 2**
☑ **Introduce Target Vocabulary,** T420–T421	☑ **Dig Deeper,** T444–T445
☑ **Read and Comprehend,** T422–T423	• Compare and Contrast
FIRST READ **Think Through the Text**	• Figurative Language
Read the Anchor Text: *Dex: The Heart of a Hero*, T424–T437	**SECOND READ** **Analyze the Text**
	Reread the Anchor Text: *Dex: The Heart of a Hero*, T424–T436
	Your Turn, T446–T447

Foundational Skills
• Phonics and Word Recognition
• Fluency

DAY 1	**DAY 2**
☑ **Fluency**	☑ **Fluency**
Intonation, T414	Intonation, T443
☑ **Phonics**	☑ **Phonics**
• Words with *or, ore*, T416–T418	• Words with *or, ore*, T442–T443
Read *A Sporty Game*, T419	

Whole Group Language Arts

Spelling
Grammar
Writing

DAY 1	**DAY 2**
☑ **Spelling**	☑ **Spelling**
Words with *or, ore*; Pretest, T438	Words with *or, ore*, T448
☑ **Grammar**	☑ **Grammar**
Commas in a Series, T438	Commas in a Series, T448
Daily Proofreading Practice, T439	Daily Proofreading Practice, T449
☑ **Narrative Writing:**	☑ **Narrative Writing:**
Fictional Story	Fictional Story
Reading/Writing Workshop	Reading/Writing Workshop
Draft, T439	Focus Trait: Organization, T449

Small Group

Suggestions for Small Groups (See pp. T485–T503.)

Language Workshop

Designated English Language Support

DAY 1	**DAY 2**
Connect to Text: *Dex: The Heart of a Hero*	**Expand Vocabulary Network**
Introduce Vocabulary Network: Words About Heroes	**Collaborate:** Offer Opinions

iRead° Use iRead, an adaptive digital foundational reading skills program, to personalize learning for students.

Integrated English Language Support

See page T403 for instructional support activities for Diverse Linguistic Learners.

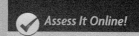 Assess It Online!

▶ Lesson 20 Assessment

DAY 3

Materials
- Cold Reads
- Decodable Reader: *My Story*
- GrammarSnap Video: Commas in a Series
- High-Frequency Word Cards 191–200
- Instructional Routine 13
- Letter Cards
- Literacy and Language Guide, pp. 94–95, 154–155
- Picture Card: jar
- Projectable 20.6
- Reader's Notebook Vol 2 pp. 67–71
- Student Book pp. 166–189
- Vocabulary in Context Cards 153–160
- Word Card: jar

Opening Routines, T450–T451
Phonemic Awareness, T452

Independent Reading, T454–T455
- Reader's Guide: *Dex: The Heart of a Hero*
- Self-Selected Reading
- Self-Correction Strategies
Apply Vocabulary Knowledge, T456–T457

☑ **Fluency**
Intonation, T453
☑ **Phonics**
- Phonics Review, T452

☑ **Spelling**
Words with *or, ore,* T458
☑ **Grammar**
Commas in a Series, T458
Daily Proofreading Practice, T459
☑ **Narrative Writing:**
Fictional Story
Reading/Writing Workshop
Draft, T459

DAY 4

Materials
- Decodable Reader: *My Story*
- High-Frequency Word Cards 191–200
- Instructional Routine 15
- Interactive Whiteboard Lesson: Prefix *-over*
- Literacy and Language Guide, pp. 94–95
- Projectables S8, 20.7
- Reader's Notebook Vol 2 pp. 72–74
- Sound/Spelling Cards: artist, orange
- Student Book pp. 194–197
- Vocabulary in Context Cards 153–160
- Writing Conference Form

Opening Routines, T460–T461
Phonemic Awareness, T462

Connect to the Topic
- Read Informational Text: *Heroes Then and Now,* T464–T465
- Introduce Genre and Text Focus, T464
☑ **Compare Texts,** T465
☑ **Vocabulary Strategies,** Prefix *-over,* T466–T467

☑ **Fluency**
Intonation, T463
☑ **Phonics**
- Phonics Review, T462–T463

☑ **Spelling**
Words with *or, ore,* T468
☑ **Grammar**
Spiral Review, T468
Daily Proofreading Practice, T469
☑ **Narrative Writing:**
Fictional Story
Reading/Writing Workshop
Draft and Revise, T469

DAY 5

Materials
- Blackline Masters: Writing Rubric, Proofreading Checklist
- Graphic Organizer 6
- High-Frequency Word Cards 191–200
- Interactive Whiteboard Lesson: Phonics: Words with *or, ore*
- Listening Log
- Projectable 20.8
- Reader's Notebook Vol 2 p. 75
- Student Book pp. 198–201
- Vocabulary in Context Cards 153–160
- Close Reader, Lesson 20

Opening Routines, T470–T471
Speaking and Listening, T473

Close Reader
- Lesson 20
Extend the Topic
- Domain-Specific Vocabulary, T472
- Speaking and Listening: Compare and Contrast, T473
- Optional Second Read: *Heroes Then and Now,* T464

☑ **Fluency**
Intonation, T479
☑ **Phonics**
- Phonics Review, T471

☑ **Spelling**
Assess, T474
☑ **Grammar**
Commas in a Series, T474–T475
Daily Proofreading Practice, T476
☑ **Narrative Writing:**
Fictional Story
Reading/Writing Workshop
Revise, Edit, Publish, T476–T477

 Tier II Intervention provides 30 minutes of additional daily practice with key parts of the core instruction. (See pp. S42–S51.)

Interpret: Ask and Answer Questions
Unpack a Sentence

Produce: Plan a Presentation
Focus on How English Works: Use Possessive Pronouns

Share and Reflect

DAY 1

Today's Goals

Vocabulary & Oral Language
- **Teacher Read Aloud:**
  "Ordinary Heroes"
- **Oral Vocabulary**
- **Listening Comprehension**
- **Introduce Vocabulary**

☑ TARGET VOCABULARY

depended	gazing
sore	hero
sprang	exercise
studied	overlooked

Phonemic Awareness
- **Substitute Phonemes**

Phonics & Fluency
- **Words with _or, ore_**
- **Read Decodable Reader:**
  A Sporty Game
- **Fluency:** Intonation
- **High-Frequency Words**

Text-Based Comprehension
- **Listening Comprehension**
- **Read and Comprehend**
- **Read the Anchor Text:**
  Dex: The Heart of a Hero

Grammar & Writing
- **Commas in a Series**
- **Narrative Writing:** Fictional Story

Spelling
- **Words with _or, ore_**

Opening Routines

Warm Up with Wordplay

Share a Riddle

Display and read aloud the following riddle:

> ## What gets larger the more you take away from it?

Have children turn and talk to a partner to discuss their responses before you tell them the correct answer: _a hole!_ Remind them to use discussion rules.

Discuss with children the fact that this riddle works because it misleads listeners. When most people hear that a thing is getting larger, they automatically think that something is being added to it. But what is being added to the hole is space!

ELA SL.2.1a **ELD** ELD.PI.2.1

Daily Phonemic Awareness

Substitute Phonemes

- *We're going to change a sound in a word to make a new word. Listen:* barn. *What are the sounds?* /b/ /är/ /n/ *Now change the /är/ to /ôr/. What is the new word?* born

- Have children continue with the following words: *part/port, coat/court, fake/fork, chair/chore, bear/bore, car/core.*

Corrective Feedback

- If a child is unable to make a substitution, say the word, give correction, and model the task. Example: *The word is barn. I can change the /är/ sound in barn to /ôr/ and make a new word,* born.

- Have children try once with you before doing it on their own. Continue with other words.

Daily High-Frequency Words

- Point to the High-Frequency Words on the Focus Wall. Say: *This week, our new High-Frequency Words are* being, I've, stood, *and* tall. *Our review words are* begins, flower, ground, laugh, ready, *and* very.

- Use <u>Instructional Routine 11</u> and **High-Frequency Word Card 191** to introduce the word *being.*

- Repeat the routine with **High-Frequency Word Cards 193–195** for new words *I've, tall, stood* and with **High-Frequency Word Cards 192** and **196–200** for review words *ready, very, ground, laugh, begins,* and *flower.*
ELA RF.2.3f

Corrective Feedback

- If a child does not recognize the word *being,* say the correct word and have children repeat it. Being. *What is the word?* being

- Have children spell the word. *b-e-i-n-g How do we say this word?* being

- Have children reread all of the cards in random order.

Daily Vocabulary Boost

- Preview the Target Vocabulary by displaying the **Vocabulary in Context Cards** and discussing the words. For example, use sentences such as these to discuss the words *gazing, hero,* and *sore.*

  I was gazing *at the beautiful sunset yesterday evening.*

  A hero *is brave, strong, and helpful.*

  Running very fast might make someone's legs sore.

- Tell children that they will find these and other Vocabulary Words when they read *Dex: The Heart of a Hero.*

Vocabulary in Context Cards 153–160

☑ **Target Vocabulary**

depended
sore
sprang
studied
gazing
hero
exercise
overlooked

Teacher Read Aloud

▶ SHARE OBJECTIVES

- Listen to intonation.
- Retell important ideas and details from a text read aloud. LANGUAGE
- Identify and use connecting words to connect ideas in sentences. LANGUAGE

PREVIEW
☑ TARGET VOCABULARY

gazing looking at something fondly

hero someone who is looked up to for doing something important or brave

sprang jumped up quickly

exercise activity that moves the body

sore a feeling of pain or discomfort

studied learned about a subject

depended counted on; relied on

overlooked didn't see; not noticed; looked past

ENGLISH LANGUAGE SUPPORT

Comprehensible Input

All Proficiencies To assist children with accessing the content and topic of the Teacher Read Aloud, complete the Build Background activities on Lesson 20 **Language Support Card.**

Model Fluency

Intonation Explain that when good readers read aloud, they use proper intonation to emphasize certain words and emotions. This means they change their voice so the listener can understand the mood of the story.

- Display Projectable 20.1 ⌐. As you read each sentence, model how to read with proper intonation for the purpose of the sentence. Point out that punctuation can give clues about where to put emphasis.

- Ask children to read the sentences aloud, practicing different intonations. Discuss how the meaning of the sentence can change depending on the intonation chosen. Then read the remainder of the story aloud. **ELA** RF.2.4b

Listening Comprehension

Read aloud the story. Pause at the numbered stopping points to ask children the questions below. Discuss the meanings of the highlighted words, as needed, to support the discussion. Tell children they will learn more about the words later in the lesson. **ELA** SL.2.2 **ELD** ELD.PI.2.5

1 *What is the setting of the first paragraph of "Ordinary Heroes"?* *an autumn Friday afternoon at school* IDENTIFY STORY STRUCTURE

2 *What does Meghan have to decide?* *Sample answer: She has to decide about whom to write her hero paragraph.* ANALYZE STORY STRUCTURE

3 *How does Meghan make her decision?* *She sees items that make her realize her family members are her heroes.* UNDERSTANDING CHARACTERS

4 *How are famous heroes and ordinary heroes both alike and different?* *Sample answer: All heroes are hardworking and do good things. Famous heroes are known to many, while ordinary heroes are known to a few, such as to family.* COMPARE AND CONTRAST

💬 Classroom Collaboration

Discuss "Ordinary Heroes" as a class. Ask children to recall words and phrases from the text that describe heroes. *famous, set a lot of records, exercise every day, played when their muscles were sore, studied very hard, always came through when Meghan depended on her for help, looked up to, wanted to be like them* **ELA** SL.2.2 **ELD** ELD.PI.2.1, ELD.PI.2.5, ELD.PI.2.12a

🔍 Language Detective

How English Works: Connecting Ideas Explain to children that authors use special words to connect, or put together, ideas in sentences. Tell children that *because, and, or,* and *but* are examples of connecting words. Reread the third sentence in the first paragraph, emphasizing the connecting word *but.* Explain the word's purpose, then write the sentence on the board. Reread the sentence, and have children give a thumbs up when they hear the connecting word. Guide children to write a new sentence using *but.* **ELD** ELD.PII.2.6

Ordinary Heroes

1 One chilly fall Friday afternoon, Meghan sat at her desk, **gazing** out the window. The trees were shedding their leaves like confetti, and the leaves rained down to the ground below, making a quilt of bright orange, red, yellow, and brown. Meghan wanted so badly to go out and play in the leaves, but the school bell would not ring for one more hour. Meghan sighed.

Her ears perked up as her teacher, Mrs. Blais, announced the homework assignment for the weekend.

2 "Class, this weekend I want you to write a paragraph about your **hero**. Tell me who this person is and what makes you look up to him or her."

Meghan's mind **sprang** to action. She started to think of all the posters she had hanging on her bedroom walls. On the wall behind her bed, she had a poster of Babe Ruth, the famous baseball player. She thought about all the records Ruth set during his career and how much the fans loved him. Was he a hero?, she wondered. She thought about the poster beside her bed. It was a picture of Olympic figure skater Kristi Yamaguchi landing after a big jump. The crowd in the background was clapping wildly. Is she a hero?, Meghan wondered. She considered that both athletes needed to **exercise** every day in order to do their jobs. They probably had to play or perform when their muscles were **sore** and tired. Meghan thought about how hard that must have been, but she still wasn't sure if they were heroes. She was stumped.

3 When Meghan got home from school, she tossed her backpack on the chair and went to find a snack. She saw her brother Kevin's social studies test taped to the refrigerator. At the top, it said, "100! Excellent work!" Meghan smiled. She knew that Kevin had **studied** very hard before that test, and she was happy for him.

On the counter, Meghan saw a note from her mother. It said, "Meg, I bought the materials for your science project. We will work on it together tomorrow. Love, Mom." Meghan smiled again. Her mom always came through when Meghan **depended** on her for help.

4 Just then a light bulb lit up over Meghan's head. She knew that she had **overlooked** the most obvious heroes: her family members! Meghan realized that even though they weren't famous, she looked up to everyone in her family, and, in some way, she wanted to be like each one of them. Now her biggest problem was deciding which one of them to write her paragraph about!

Phonics

- Substitute vowel sounds in words.
- Learn the sound/spellings for *or, ore*.
- Blend, build, and decode regularly spelled words with *or, ore* (*r*-controlled vowel syllable).

▶ **SKILLS TRACE**

<table>
<tr><td colspan="2">Words with or, ore</td></tr>
<tr><td>Introduce</td><td>pp. T416–T417, T442–T443</td></tr>
<tr><td>Differentiate</td><td>pp. T488–T489, T494</td></tr>
<tr><td>Reteach</td><td>p. T502</td></tr>
<tr><td>Review</td><td>pp. T452, T462–T463, Unit 5 T63</td></tr>
<tr><td>Assess</td><td>Weekly Tests, Lesson 20</td></tr>
</table>

ENGLISH LANGUAGE SUPPORT

Comprehensible Input

Emerging Use **Picture Card** *fork* and photographs or illustrations (*corn, fort, shore*) to reinforce the meanings of words used in the Phonics lesson. Use gestures and pantomime to demonstrate meanings for *more, score,* and *sore.* Say each word as you show the image or perform the action, having children repeat after you. Then say the words at random and have children match each word to an image or gesture.

Expanding Have partners work together to demonstrate understanding of lesson words by completing sentences such as these: *We eat food with a _____. At the beach we are near the _____. The soldiers live at the _____.* Reinforce meanings and pronunciations as needed.

Bridging Ask children to show understanding of lesson words such as *fork, corn, fort, shore,* and *more* by using them in meaningful phrases or complete sentences. Monitor their pronunciation of the /ôr/ sound, and provide modeling and feedback as needed.

Words with *or, ore*

ENGLISH LANGUAGE SUPPORT Speakers of Spanish and most Asian languages may have difficulty with the way vowels in English change when they are followed by an *r.* Explain that in English, vowels can sound a little different before the /r/ sound. Read aloud words such as *for, corn, score, and more,* and have students repeat each word chorally, say just the vowel sound, and then say the whole word again. Use each word in a sentence to reinforce meaning. **ELD** ELD.PIII.2

Phonemic Awareness Warm-Up *Let's change vowel sounds in words to make new words. I'll do it first. Listen:* park. *Listen as I change the /är/ in* park *to /ôr/:* pork. *Now you try it. Change the /är/ in* park *to /ôr/.* pork

Let's do some more. Change /ĕ/ in stem *to /ôr/.* storm *Change /ŏ/ in* shot *to /ôr/.* short *Change /ē/ in* feet *to /ôr/.* fort *Change /ŏ/ in* spot *to /ôr/.* sport *Change /är/ in* far *to /ôr/.* for *Change /ou/ in* house *to /ôr/.* horse

1   Teach/Model

Sound/Spelling Card Display the card for *orange.* Name the picture and say the sound. Have children repeat after you. *Listen:* orange, /ôr/. *Now you say it.*

- Say the sound and give the spelling. *Orange begins with the sound /ôr/. The letters* or *together stand for the sound /ôr/. The letters* or *usually stand for /ôr/ at the beginning or in the middle of a word.*

- Write and read *corn.* Point out the /ôr/ sound. *This is the word* corn. *The letters* or *together stand for the sound /ôr/ in* corn. Read the word together: *corn.*

- Repeat the procedure with the word *fork,* pointing out the /ôr/ sound and the letters that stand for it, *or.*

- Point out the spelling *ore* on the card. Say the word *more* as an example of a word with the *ore* spelling for /ôr/ and have children repeat it.

- Write and read *more.* Point out the /ôr/ spelling, *ore. This is the word* more. *The letters* ore *together stand for the sound /ôr/ in* more. *The letters* ore *usually stand for /ôr/ at the end of a word.* Read the word together: *more.*

- Repeat the procedure with the word *sore,* pointing out the /ôr/ sound and the letters that stand for it, *ore.*

2 Guided Practice

Continuous Blending Routine Use <u>Instructional Routine 3</u> to model blending *born*.

- Point to **Sound/Spelling Card** *orange* and remind children that knowing the sound/spellings *or* and *ore* can help them read words.

- Display **Letter Cards** *b, or,* and *n*.

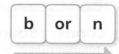

- Blend the sounds. *Listen: /b/ /ôr/ /n/.* Have children blend with you. *Now you blend the sounds and say the word: /b/ /ôr/ /n/,* born.

Blending Lines

Blend Words Have children blend and read the following words chorally; provide Corrective Feedback as needed. Help children compare the sounds and spellings they notice in each line.

1. or	for	fort	sort	short	snort
2. more	core	sore	store	score	shore
3. porch	story	north	snore	before	odor

Transition to Longer Words Have children read the following words chorally. Ask children to identify known word parts in each longer word that helped them decode it.

4. forever	forget	forest	forty	formal	normal
5. bored	adore	anymore	explore	stored	restore
6. color	honor	shoreline	ashore	offshore	shortly

Challenge Call on above-level children to read the words in Line 7 and discuss the elements. Then have the class read the sentences chorally.

7. boredom	orbiting	cordless	forecast	flavoring	ignore

8. A horse <u>stood</u> by the <u>tall</u> red barn.

9. The farm is <u>very</u> far north of the city. **ELA** RF.2.3e

3 Apply

Have partners take turns rereading Blending Lines 1–3 and 4–6. Then tell partners to identify rhyming words in Blending Lines and create lists of the words to use the next time they write a poem. **ELA** RF.2.3e

Distribute <u>Reader's Notebook Volume 2 page 61</u> or <u>leveled practice</u> in Grab-and-Go™ Resources to children to complete independently.

Phonics • **T417**

Phonics

▶ **SHARE OBJECTIVES**

- Write words with *or, ore.*
- Read on-level text with words with *or, ore* and High-Frequency Words.
- Practice reading fluently with intonation (prosody).

▶ **DICTATION SENTENCES**

- **form** An icicle will *form* as the dripping water freezes.
- **stormy** We are expecting *stormy* weather this weekend.
- **forget** Don't *forget* your homework.
- **wore** I *wore* my new sandals today.
- **core** Toss your apple *core* into the trash.
- **before** I ate breakfast *before* I came to school today.

ENGLISH LANGUAGE SUPPORT

Use Visuals and Gestures

All Proficiencies Use pantomime and visuals to reinforce the meanings of the dictation words and sentences. For example, show photographs or illustrations to discuss *stormy* and *core.* Pantomime the actions for *form, forget, wore,* and *before* as you use the word to describe what you are doing. Have children repeat the words after you. Finally, ask children to demonstrate understanding by completing sentences such as *You can use clay to form _____. We stay inside on a stormy day because _____. Today I wore _____.*

Blend-It Books

To provide reading practice with new sound/spellings in decodable texts, see **Blend-It Books** 123–124.

Write Words with *or, ore*

1 | Teach/Model

Connect Sounds to Spelling Review **Sound/Spelling Card** *orange.* Tell children that now they will write words with the sound /ôr/.

Use Instructional Routine 7 ⬚ to dictate the first sentence at left. *Listen as I say a word and use it in a sentence.*

- Use **Sound/Spelling Card** *orange* to review the /ôr/ sound. Then model how to spell the word *form. The word* form *begins with the /f/ sound. The /f/ sound is spelled f, so I'll write f. The middle sound in* form *is /ôr/. I remember /ôr/ is spelled* or, *so I write* or *next. The final sound in* form *is /m/. It is spelled m, so I write m last. Then I reread to check:* form

2 | Guided Practice

Connect Sounds to Writing Continue the dictation, using the sentences at left.

- Have children say each dictation word aloud after you. Then have them identify the sounds they hear at the beginning, middle, and end and write the letters that spell each sound. **ELA** L.2.2d

- Remind children to write only the dictation word.

3 | Apply

Read aloud the following decodable sentence for children to write. Remind children to look at the Focus Wall if they need help spelling *ready.* **ELA** RF.2.3f, L.2.2d

> Get <u>ready</u> for a storm from the north.

Print the dictation words and decodable sentence for children to check their work.

Decodable Reader

Read *A Sporty Game*

Review /ôr/ and High-Frequency Words Use Instructional Routine 1 to review **Sound/Spelling Card** *orange*. Also review the High-Frequency Words *begins, being, flower, ground, I've, laugh, ready, stood, tall,* and *very*.

Preview Have children read the title, browse beginning pages, and discuss what they think the story is about.

Use Projectable S1 to review the **Phonics/Decoding Strategy.** Model the strategy using the title.

Have children read the first page silently. Remind them to track the words from left to right as they read. Then ask a child to read the page aloud as others follow. Repeat for each page.

Decodable Reader

ENGLISH LANGUAGE SUPPORT Point out the quotation marks used to punctuate dialogue. Explain to children whose first language uses a different convention that in English quotation marks are used to set off a character's exact words. Guide English learners to identify and read examples of words, phrases, and sentences that story characters say. **ELD** ELD.PIII.2

If children make more than six total errors, use the **Corrective Feedback** steps to help them reread aloud with accuracy. If they make fewer than six errors, have them reread and retell the story.

Fluency: Intonation

Remind children that when good readers read aloud, their reading sounds as if they are telling a story or talking to a friend. The sound of their voice is sometimes higher and sometimes lower. Write and read aloud the following sentences:

> "I look so sporty," he said.
> "I've been waiting to be asked," said Luke.

Model Fluency and Intonation Read each sentence in a monotone and ask children whether it sounds natural and easy to understand. Then model using appropriate intonation. *Listen to the way my voice sounds higher and lower as I read the words.* Reread the sentences fluently and have children repeat.

ENGLISH LANGUAGE SUPPORT As children read, monitor their pronunciation of words with the /ôr/ sound. Provide modeling and support as needed. **ELD** ELD.PIII.2

Responding Ask children to read aloud sections of the text that tell some of the things Mort and Luke do together. Then have them write one sentence that tells what Mort and Luke do that makes them different from all the other players at Golf Park that day. **ELA** RL.2.1, RL.2.3

Reread for Fluency Use Instructional Routine 13 to reread *A Sporty Game* with children. Remind children to make the tone of their voices higher and lower to make their reading sound natural, as if they were talking to a friend. **ELA** RF.2.4b

FORMATIVE ASSESSMENT **RtI**

Corrective Feedback When a child mispronounces a word, point to the word and say it. Call attention to the element that was mispronounced, say the sound, and then guide children to read the word. See the example below.

Decoding Error:
A child reads *shorts* on page 1 as *shots*.

Correct the error. Say the word. *That word is* shorts. *The letters* or *spell the vowel sound /ôr/ in* shorts.

Guide Have children repeat the word. *What is the word?* shorts

Check *Go back to the beginning of the sentence and read it again.*

Reinforce Record the error and review the word again before children reread the story.

SMALL GROUP Options

Go to pp. T488–T489 for additional phonics support.

Introduce Vocabulary

▷ **SHARE OBJECTIVES**
- Acquire and use vocabulary. LANGUAGE
- Use a variety of vocabulary in shared language activities. LANGUAGE
- Find and use verbs in sentences in shared language activities. LANGUAGE

Teach

Display and discuss the **Vocabulary in Context Cards,** using the routine below.

1 Read and pronounce the word. Read the word once alone and then together.

2 Explain the word. Read aloud the explanation under *What Does It Mean?*

ENGLISH LANGUAGE SUPPORT Review these cognates with Spanish-speaking children.

- dependía (depended)
- ejercicio (exercise)
- héroe (hero)
- estudió (studied)

3 Discuss vocabulary in context. Together, read aloud the sentence on the front of the card. Help children explain and use the word in new sentences.

4 Engage with the word. Ask and discuss the *Think About It* question with children.

Practice/Apply

Give partners or small groups one or two **Vocabulary in Context Cards.** Help children complete the *Talk It Over* activities for each card. **ELA** RF.2.3f **ELD** ELD.PII.2.3a

Read aloud and have children complete the activity at the top of **Student Book** p. 162.

Then guide children to complete the Language Detective activity. Work with them to find the Vocabulary words that are verbs. Have children share their new sentences with the class. **ELA** RF.2.3f, L.2.6 **ELD** ELD.PI.2.1, ELD.PI.2.6, ELD.PI.2.12b

Lesson 20

🔍 **LANGUAGE DETECTIVE**

Talk About Words

Verbs are words that name actions. Work with a partner. Find the Vocabulary words that are verbs. What are your clues? Use the verbs in new sentences.

162   **ELA** L.2.1f, L.2.6 **ELD** ELD.PI.2.12b, ELD.PII.2.3a

Vocabulary in Context

▶ **Read each** Context Card.

▶ **Tell a story about two pictures. Use the Vocabulary words.**

① **depended**
The dog depended on its owner for food and water.

② **sore**
The dog hurt its paw. The paw is sore.

ENGLISH LANGUAGE SUPPORT

Comprehensible Input

Emerging Have children complete sentence frames about each Vocabulary word. For example: *Charlie depended on Maria for_____.* **ELD** ELD.PI.2.12b

Expanding Ask children questions to confirm their understanding. Example: *Why would you probably pass a test if you studied for it?* **ELD** ELD.PI.2.12b

Bridging Have partners write questions and answers using Vocabulary words. Example: *Who is your hero? Why?* **ELD** ELD.PI.2.12b

3 sprang

The cat saw the food. She sprang toward her dish.

4 studied

Before getting a puppy, the girl studied a book about dog care.

5 gazing

This dog is gazing, or looking closely, at a squirrel.

6 hero

This dog is a hero. It saved the boy from getting hurt.

7 exercise

A dog needs exercise every day. This dog wants to run fast.

8 overlooked

They overlooked, or didn't see, where the dog was hiding.

163

FORMATIVE ASSESSMENT **RtI**

Are children able to understand and use Target Vocabulary words?

IF...	THEN...
children struggle,	▲ use **Vocabulary in Context Cards** and differentiate **Vocabulary Reader,** *Everyday Hero,* for Struggling Readers, p. T490. *See also Intervention Lesson 20, p. S43.*
children are on track,	▲ use **Vocabulary in Context Cards** and differentiate **Vocabulary Reader,** *Everyday Hero,* for On-Level Readers, p. T490.
children excel,	▲ differentiate **Vocabulary Reader,** *Everyday Hero,* for Advanced Readers, p. T491.

SMALL GROUP Options

Vocabulary Reader, pp. T490–T491
Scaffold instruction to the English learner's proficiency level.

ENGLISH LANGUAGE SUPPORT

More Vocabulary Practice

Emerging/Expanding Distribute Chant, EL20.5 . Read the title aloud and have children repeat. Have children look at the title, images, and other information on the page. Then have them predict what they think the chant will be about.

- As you read the chant aloud, display the Context Cards for *hero, exercise, studied,* and *depended.* After you read the chant, reread and have children choral read after you.

- Have children draw a picture of what they imagine when they think of a hero.

- Have children explain why the person in their drawing is a hero.

- Allow children to include language from the chant. Encourage them to use high-utility words. **ELD** ELD.PI.2.1, ELD.PI.2.6, ELD.PI.2.12b

---

Read and Comprehend

▶ **SHARE OBJECTIVES**

- Compare and contrast characters in a story.
- Ask questions to monitor and clarify what is being read.
- Access prior knowledge to exchange information about a topic. LANGUAGE

☑ **TARGET SKILL**

Compare and Contrast

- Read the top section of **Student Book** p. 164 with children.

- Discuss the words *compare* and *contrast* with children.

- Point out that they can compare and contrast characters as they read. They can also look for ways characters change during a story, and compare and contrast how they were at the beginning and at the end. This can help them better understand the characters in a story and why they do the things they do.

- Draw attention to the graphic organizer. Identify it as a Venn diagram. Explain to children that they will use the words and pictures in the story and this diagram to compare and contrast two characters as they read. In the center, they can record how the characters are alike. In the outer ovals, they can write qualities that only Dex or Cleevis has.

- Explain that you will guide them to complete a graphic organizer like this one as they read.
  ELA RL.2.3, RL.2.4, RL.2.7 **ELD** ELD.PI.2.6

ENGLISH LANGUAGE SUPPORT Draw a Venn diagram on the board, and write *Cats* in the first oval, *Both* in the middle section, and *Dogs* in the second oval. Divide the children into small groups and have them think of at least one way that cats and dogs are alike and one way that they are different. Call on groups to share their thoughts as you write them on the board.
ELD ELD.PI.2.1, ELD.PI.2.3, ELD.PI.2.11

Read and Comprehend

☑ **TARGET SKILL**

Compare and Contrast In a story, the main characters will often go through some changes from the beginning to the end of a story. They grow and change because of the things that happen to them.

As you read *Dex: The Heart of a Hero*, you can compare and contrast to tell how Dex changes. You can use a diagram like the one below to **compare** things that are the same and **contrast** things that are different. Use the words and pictures in the story as text evidence for your ideas.

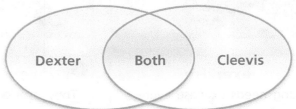

Dexter | Both | Cleevis

☑ **TARGET STRATEGY**

Monitor/Clarify If you don't understand why something is happening, stop and think. Find text evidence to figure out what doesn't make sense.

164   **ELA** RL.2.3, RL.2.4, RL.2.7, SL.2.1a **ELD** ELD.PI.2.1, ELD.PI.2.3, ELD.PI.2.6, ELD.PI.2.12a

---

ENGLISH LANGUAGE SUPPORT

Use Visuals

Emerging Use pictures or objects to teach the words *alike* and *different*. Have children complete this sentence frame: *These two things are _____.*
ELD ELD.PI.2.1, ELD.PI.2.3

Expanding Have partners find pictures of things that are alike and different. Have them quiz each other with the questions, *Are these alike? Are these different?*
ELD ELD.PI.2.1, ELD.PI.2.3

Bridging Have partners choose classroom objects that are alike and different. Have them compete with each other to create the longer list of how they are alike and how they are different.
ELD ELD.PI.2.1, ELD.PI.2.3

A hero is someone who has done something brave or good to help others. You may know of some famous heroes from history. For example, Martin Luther King, Jr. was a hero who helped change unfair laws. Not all heroes are famous. Most people feel that firefighters and police officers are heroes. The person who takes care of you or who teaches you might be a hero.

You will read about a dog that wants to be a hero in *Dex: The Heart of a Hero.*

Think | Write | Pair | Share

Think about who your hero is. It could be a family member, friend, or even someone famous. Write a few sentences about your hero to share with a partner. Then share your sentences with the class.

165

COMPREHENSION STRATEGIES

Use the following strategies flexibly as you read with children by modeling how they can be used to improve comprehension and understanding of a text. See scaffolded support for the strategy shown in boldface during this week's reading.

- **Monitor/Clarify**
- **Summarize**
- **Infer/Predict**
- Visualize
- Analyze/Evaluate
- Question

Use Strategy Projectables 🔗, S1–S8, for additional support.

DOMAIN: Civics

LESSON TOPIC: What Heroes Do

☑ TARGET STRATEGY

Monitor/Clarify

- Read the bottom of **Student Book** p. 164 with children. Tell them that they should make sure they understand what is happening as they read. They should stop and ask themselves, *What has happened so far? What have the characters done?* If they can't answer the questions, they should reread, read ahead, or look at illustrations.

- Tell children to pause when they come to words they do not know and ask, *What words around this word can help me figure out the meaning? What is in the picture that might help me?*

- Explain that you will help them use the strategy as you read *Dex: The Heart of a Hero* together.

PREVIEW THE TOPIC

What Heroes Do

- Tell children that today they will begin reading *Dex: The Heart of a Hero.* Read the information at the top of **Student Book** p. 165 with children.

- Ask children to name activities people do that are heroic. Then ask them for ways in which people like police officers and firefighters are heroic.

Think-Write-Pair-Share

- Read the collaborative discussion prompt with children.

- Before the discussions, explain that sometimes a conversation stops before it should. Tell them they can restart a conversation by asking an opinion question. Model some opinion questions. Have children practice using questions to restart conversations.

- After their discussions, have children share their sentences with the class. Remind them to follow discussion rules.

  ELA SL.2.1a **ELD** ELD.PI.2.1, ELD.PI.2.3, ELD.PI.2.12a

ENGLISH LANGUAGE SUPPORT Use the image on Lesson 20 **Language Support Card** to review the lesson topic with children. Guide children to share and summarize what they have learned.

ELD ELD.PI.2.1, ELD.PI.2.12a

DAY 1

Read the Anchor Text

☑ **GENRE**

Fantasy

- Read the genre information on **Student Book** p. 166 with children.

- Preview the selection with children, and model identifying the characteristics of fantasy.

  > **Think Aloud** *A fantasy is a story that has imaginary events and characters, such as animals that talk. Dex: The Heart of a Hero is about animals that act like people, so I think this selection is fantasy.*

- As you preview, ask children to point out additional examples that would lead them to think the selection is fantasy. **ELA** RL.2.10 **ELD** ELD.PI.2.6

ENGLISH LANGUAGE SUPPORT Guide children at the emerging and expanding levels to complete the Academic English activities on Lesson 20 **Language Support Card.** **ELD** ELD.PII.2.2

Lesson 20

ANCHOR TEXT

☑ **GENRE**

A **fantasy** is a story that could not happen in real life. As you read, look for:

► events that could not really happen
► characters that are not found in real life

MEET THE AUTHOR

Caralyn Buehner

As the mother of nine children, Caralyn Buehner squeezes in time for writing whenever she can. Once, while waiting for her sons' karate class to end, she started writing "Dexter was a little dog" on a pad. That's how the story of *Dex* began.

MEET THE ILLUSTRATOR

Mark Buehner

As you read *Dex*, look carefully at the pictures. Mark Buehner likes to hide bunnies, dinosaurs, cats, and mice in his drawings. In case you're wondering, Mr. Buehner is Caralyn Buehner's husband, and their last name is pronounced *Bee-ner*.

166　**ELA** RL.2.4, RL.2.7, RL.2.10
　　　ELD ELD.PI.2.6, ELD.PI.2.7

Scaffold Close Reading

Strategies for Annotation	**Think Through the Text** FIRST READ	**Analyze the Text** SECOND READ	**Independent Reading**
Annotate it! As you read the selection with children, look for this icon ✐ 🖥 *Annotate it!* for opportunities to annotate the text collaboratively as a class.	Develop comprehension through • Guided Questioning • Target Strategy: Monitor/Clarify • Vocabulary in Context	Support analyzing short sections of text: • Compare and Contrast • Figurative Language Use directed note-taking with children to complete a graphic organizer during reading. Distribute copies of Graphic Organizer 14 🖥: Venn Diagram.	• Children analyze the text independently, using the Reader's Guide on Reader's Notebook Volume 2 pp. 68–69 🖥. (See pp. T454–T455 for instructional support.) • Children read independently in a self-selected trade book.

DEX
The Heart of a Hero

by Caralyn Buehner
illustrated by Mark Buehner

ESSENTIAL QUESTION

What makes someone
a hero?

167

READER AND TASK CONSIDERATIONS

ELA RL.2.1, RL.2.2, SL.2.1c
ELD ELD.PI.2.1, ELD.PI.2.6, ELD.PI.2.12a

Determine the level of additional support your children will need to read and comprehend *Dex: The Heart of a Hero* successfully.

READERS

- **Motivate** Ask children to tell about superheroes they know of.

- **Access Knowledge and Experiences** Review with children the web you completed as part of the Talk It Over activity on the back of Lesson 20 **Language Support Card.** Ask children to share with a partner experiences they've had with one or more of the real-life heroes included on the web. Encourage them to use complete sentences as they share.

TASKS

- **Increase Scaffolding** Stop periodically as you read to have children retell story events in order.

- **Foster Independence** Prompt children to ask questions about the text every few pages, and have the rest of the class share ideas about how to answer the questions. Have children raise their hand if they think the answer makes sense based on information in the text.

ESSENTIAL QUESTION

- Read aloud the Essential Question on **Student Book** p. 167: *What makes someone a hero?* Then tell children to think about this question as they read *Dex: The Heart of a Hero*.

Predictive Writing

- Tell children to write the Essential Question.

- Explain that they will write what they expect *Dex: The Heart of a Hero* to be about. Ask them to think about how the Essential Question relates to what they noticed while previewing the selection or what they already know about the Essential Question from their own experiences or past readings.

- Guide children to think about the genre of the selection as they write.

Set Purpose

- Explain that good readers think ahead and set a purpose for reading. They think about the title and what they have seen as they previewed. Then they ask themselves what they want to find out as they read the selection.

- Model setting a reading purpose.

> **Think Aloud** *I know that make-believe stories are fun to read because I can use my imagination. I will read this story for fun, and I will read to learn why Dex has the heart of a hero.*

- Have children set their own purposes for reading. Ask several children to share their purposes with the class. **ELA** RF.2.4a, RL.2.10

ENGLISH LANGUAGE SUPPORT To help make the text accessible to all children, consider modifications such as these:

- Act out the verbs in the selection as you say each one.

- Allow children to listen to audio of the selection as they read along.

- Pair English learners with English-speaking peers and have them read the selection together.

DAY 1

Dexter was a little dog. His legs were little, his tail was little, his body was little. He looked like a plump sausage sitting on four little meatballs.

1   Being the size that he was, Dex was often overlooked. The other dogs grew tired of waiting for Dex to catch up when they played chase, and after a while they forgot to invite him at all. No one really seemed to notice him, except when Cleevis, the tomcat, demonstrated how he could stand right over Dex and not even ruffle his fur. 2

168

169

DOMAIN: Civics

LESSON TOPIC: What Heroes Do

Cross-Curricular Connection Help children list qualities that make someone a hero. Name heroic individuals with whom children are likely to be familiar, such as Abraham Lincoln, George Washington, Betsy Ross, and Francis Scott Key. Ask children to name qualities they associate with these people.

FIRST READ

Cite Text Evidence

Think Through the Text

1 *How do you think Dex feels about being overlooked? Why?* **Sample answer:** *He probably feels lonely and sad.* **ELA** RL.2.1 **ELD** ELD.PI.2.6

2 *How does Dex's size cause him problems? He has a hard time keeping up with the other dogs. The other animals make fun of him.* **ELA** RL.2.1 **ELD** ELD.PI.2.6

3 *How is the way Dex sees himself in his dreams different from the way he really is? In his dreams, Dex is a mighty hero. He can fly. In reality, he is just a small, ordinary dog.* **ELA** RL.2.7

ENGLISH LANGUAGE SUPPORT Tell children that the word *hero* has a cognate in Spanish: *héroe*. Remind children to look for cognates as they read to help them figure out the meanings of key words. **ELD** ELD.PI.2.6

FOR STUDENTS WITH DISABILITIES Some children may have difficulty keeping their place on a page of text. Provide an index card with a cutout window so children see only one line of text at a time. Have them move the card down the page as they read.

Yes, everything about Dex was little—except for his dreams. He wanted to be a HERO. He could just *see* it.

THE MIGHTY DEX FLEW UP INTO THE DARK AND STARRY NIGHT. . . .

③

170

But *wanting* and *being* are two different things. Dex lived on dreams until one day, after crawling out from under Cleevis yet again, he decided there had to be more to life than gazing at the underside of a cat. There had to be more to *him*. If he *could* be a hero, he *would*!

So Dex started training. He read every superhero comic book he could find. He watched every hero movie ever made. He went to the library.

④ FURIOUSLY HE STUDIED, KNOWING EVERYTHING DEPENDED ON HIM. . . .

171

④ *Look at the words in the boxes on pages 170–171. Where else have you seen this type of writing?* **a comic book** *Why do you think the author chose to use this style?* **to show that Dex dreams of being the kind of hero found in a comic book**

☑ **TARGET STRATEGY | Monitor/Clarify**

Reread aloud the first sentence on **Student Book** p. 171. Remind children that when they come across something they do not understand, they should stop and ask themselves, *How can I figure out what this means?* Then model the strategy:

Think Aloud *The phrase "wanting and being are two different things" does not make sense to me at first. I ask myself, how can I figure out the meaning of this phrase? I decide to read on, and I find out that Dex starts doing things that would help him become a hero instead of just dreaming about being a hero.*

Tell children to practice the Monitor/Clarify strategy as they continue reading. **ELD** ELD.PI.2.6

Dex figured that a hero must have strong muscles. He needed exercise, and lots of it!

Dex started trotting to the corner and back every morning. He hopped over every crack in the sidewalk.

He struggled to climb the garbage pile: up and over and down, then up and over and down again. All day long he worked, day after day. Even at bedtime, when he wanted to flop on the rug with his tongue hanging out, Dex forced himself to circle five extra times.

THE MIGHTY DEX PRESSED ON, THROUGH WIND AND RAIN AND STORM AND FATIGUE. . . .

172

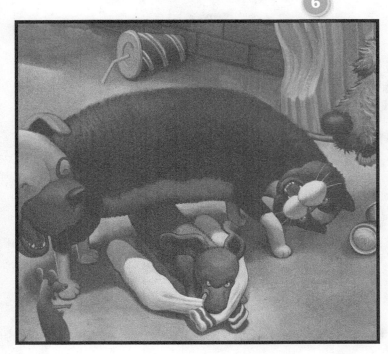

When it got easier to run to the corner and back, Dex did it again, and then again. Then he dragged a sock filled with sand as he ran, and then *two* socks. When Cleevis was bored and stood in the middle of the sidewalk to block his way, Dex dropped to the ground and slid right under him. He was too busy to be bothered by Cleevis.

173

ENGLISH LANGUAGE SUPPORT

Use Gestures

Emerging Pantomime exercising, and ask, *How do people get strong?*

Expanding Pantomime exercising, and ask children to write a sentence explaining the purpose of exercise.

Bridging Ask children to explain how exercise can make them stronger and more fit.

FIRST READ

Cite Text Evidence

Think Through the Text

☑ PHONICS/DECODING STRATEGY

Use Projectable S1 ↴ to help children apply the Phonics/Decoding strategy while reading **Student Book** pp. 172–173. Write and read aloud *corner, morning, forced,* and *bored.* Circle the letters *or* and *ore,* pronounce the sounds they make together, and then have children read the words—/c/ /or/ /n/ /er/, /m/ /or/ /n/ /ing/, /f/ /or/ /s/ /d/ , /b/ /or/ /d/. Have children read the words in the sentences on pp. 172–173 to ensure understanding.

5 *Why does a hero need to be strong?* Sample response: *He may need strength to rescue those who are in danger.* **ELA** RL.2.1 **ELD** ELD.PI.2.6

6 *How has Dex's attitude changed toward Cleevis?* Dex is too busy to let Cleevis bother him. **ELA** RL.2.1

ENGLISH LANGUAGE SUPPORT Have children look back at pages 168–169. Provide sentence frames to help them describe how Dex's attitude towards Cleevis has changed. *At the beginning of the story, Dex wishes Cleevis would not _____. stand over him After he starts exercising, Dex is too _____ to be bothered by Cleevis. busy* **ELD** ELD.PI.2.6

Dex was tired; he was sore. He was working so hard that he almost forgot what he was working for. But one night, as he dragged himself to bed after his last set of push-ups, Dex stopped in front of the mirror and flexed. He could feel them! He could see them! Muscles!

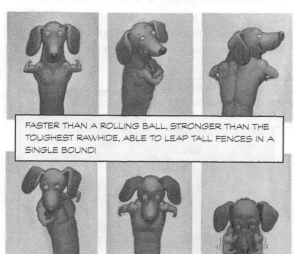

FASTER THAN A ROLLING BALL, STRONGER THAN THE TOUGHEST RAWHIDE, ABLE TO LEAP TALL FENCES IN A SINGLE BOUND!

Now Dex didn't "take" the stairs—he skimmed them! He leaped over hydrants; he vaulted up curbs. He could jump over the garbage mountain without touching the top! He could run like the wind; he felt as if his legs had springs! **7**

174

Only one thing was missing. Finally, a small brown package arrived. Dex ripped it open.

His HERO suit! It was red, with a shiny green cape, and it fit like a glove. Dex loved the way it felt, he loved the way it looked, and he loved the feeling he had when he put it on.

He was ready. **8**

ANALYZE THE TEXT

Figurative Language What does the author mean when she says that Dex's hero suit "fit like a glove"?

WITH THE COURAGE OF A LION, THE STRENGTH OF A BEAR, AND THE HEART OF A HERO . . .

175

---

7 *How has Dex changed since the beginning of the story?* **He is exercising more. He doesn't let Cleevis bother him. He is getting strong muscles.** ELA RL.2.5

ENGLISH LANGUAGE SUPPORT Remind children that authors use different kinds of verbs to describe what someone or something does. Tell children that *doing* verbs show action. Read the last paragraph on page 174 aloud, emphasizing the words *skimmed, leaped, vaulted, jump,* and *run.* Use gestures to explain what each verb means, and guide children to use them in sentences that describe how Dex has changed. ELD ELD.PI.2.6, ELD.PII.2.3a

8 *The last sentence on page 175 is, "He was ready." What causes Dex to feel ready?* **He has exercised, he has muscles, and he has a hero suit.** *Why is the hero suit important?* **It makes Dex feel strong and confident.** ELA RL.2.1 ELD ELD.PI.2.6

SECOND READ   DAY 2   *Analyze the Text*

Figurative Language

Read the Analyze the Text box on p. 175 with children. Remind them that authors make comparisons using the words *like* and *as* to show how things are alike and to create stronger pictures in the reader's mind. Ask, *How does a glove fit? It fits your hand perfectly. What does "fit like a glove mean"? fit perfectly* ELA RL.2.4 ELD ELD.PI.2.6

[✏️ 🖥 *Annotate it!*] Work with children to highlight comparisons the author makes on pages 174–175.

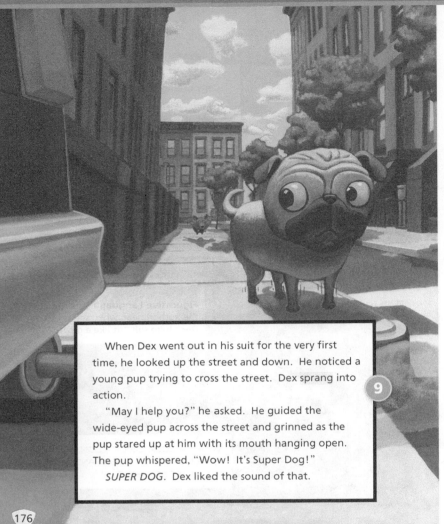

When Dex went out in his suit for the very first time, he looked up the street and down. He noticed a young pup trying to cross the street. Dex sprang into action.

"May I help you?" he asked. He guided the wide-eyed pup across the street and grinned as the pup stared up at him with its mouth hanging open. The pup whispered, "Wow! It's Super Dog!"

SUPER DOG. Dex liked the sound of that.

⑨

176

Of course, when Cleevis saw Dex, he just had to comment.

"Hey Dex, where's the party?"

Dex was so busy that he was able to ignore Cleevis—for the most part. The only time his face ever got red was when Cleevis yelled, "Where'd you get that dress-up?" Dex had to wonder if Cleevis saw anything but the suit. Didn't he understand that the suit was just a way to let people know he was there to help?

⑩

THE SUN GLINTED OFF OF HIS EMERALD CAPE AS SUPER DOG RACED TO THE RESCUE. . . .

177

DOMAIN: Social Relationships

DOMAIN: Friendship

Cross-Curricular Connection Remind children that it is important to be kind not only to friends, but to all people. Point out that part of being kind is thinking about other people's feelings. Discuss with children that Cleevis says things to make others laugh, but these are hurtful words because they are unkind to Dex. Explain that it is important to think about how your words make others feel, and asking yourself how you would feel if you were spoken to in the same way is one way of being kind to others. Then work with children to make a list of ways that they can respond if they hear someone use hurtful words.

FIRST READ

Cite Text Evidence

Think Through the Text

⑨ *How did Dex move when he sprang into action? He moved quickly. Why did the author use the word* sprang, *instead of using the word* moved? *Springing into action sounds like something a superhero would do.*
ELA RL.2.4

ENGLISH LANGUAGE SUPPORT Point out that the author uses the action word *sprang* to let the reader know that Dex moved quickly when he saw that someone needed help. Provide this sentence frame to guide children to compare Dex's actions with those of a superhero. *Superheroes spring into action to _____.* **ELD** ELD.PI.2.7

⑩ *What is Cleevis's attitude toward Dex? He thinks of Dex as the same old little dog and doesn't realize the changes that have taken place. What doesn't Cleevis understand about the suit? It makes Dex feel strong and confident, and it shows others that Dex is there to help.* **ELA** RL.2.3 **ELD** ELD.PI.2.6

There was a mouse he saved from a sewer,

a purse snatcher he tackled;

he fixed his neighbor's sprinkler;

178

he found a lost kitten, pulled a rat away from a live wire,

tracked down a lost wallet, put out a trash fire,

and organized a neighborhood cleanup day.

It seemed that now, whenever anyone needed help, they turned to Dex, and Dex had never been happier.

11 12 179

---

11 *What are pages 178–179 mostly about?* the different ways Dex helps others **ELA** RL.2.1 **ELD** ELD.PI.2.6

12 *How does helping others make Dex feel?* happy, proud, satisfied *How can you tell?* The story says he "had never been happier" and the pictures show him looking happy and confident. He keeps on helping others. **ELA** RL.2.7

ENGLISH LANGUAGE SUPPORT Provide sentence frames to encourage participation. *The pictures show that Dex is doing things to _____.* help others *The text says that Dex had never been _____.* happier **ELD** ELD.PI.2.6

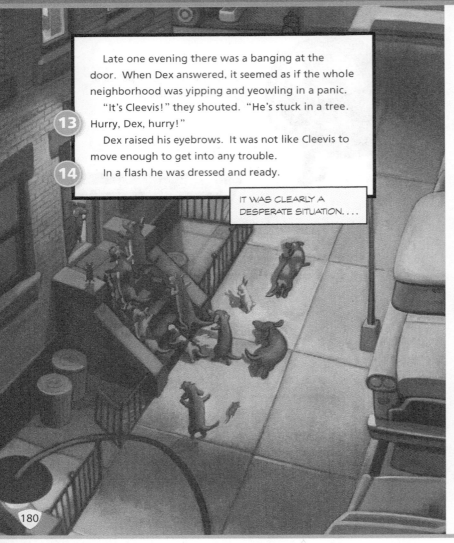

Late one evening there was a banging at the door. When Dex answered, it seemed as if the whole neighborhood was yipping and yeowling in a panic.

"It's Cleevis!" they shouted. "He's stuck in a tree. Hurry, Dex, hurry!"

Dex raised his eyebrows. It was not like Cleevis to move enough to get into any trouble.

In a flash he was dressed and ready.

IT WAS CLEARLY A DESPERATE SITUATION. . . .

(13)

(14)

180

As he got closer, Dex could see Cleevis. He had been chasing a squirrel to the top of the tree, but had slipped and was hanging by one claw from a slender branch.

He was yeowling for all he was worth.

"I'm slipping!" Cleevis screeched. "Help me!"

Dex looked desperately around for something to climb on. There were no boxes or ladders, not even any trash cans. Then Dex looked at the crowd.

OH, NO!

181

FORMATIVE ASSESSMENT 3 2 1 RtI

Monitor/Clarify IF children have difficulty applying the Monitor/Clarify strategy, THEN use this model:

Think Aloud *I am not sure what a teeter-totter is. I read that it "catapults" Dex into the air, but I don't know what catapulting means. Then I look at the pictures. I see a seesaw, and Dex has rocketed into the air.*

Cite
Text Evidence

Think Through the Text

(13) *How do the animals feel when they bang on Dex's door?* scared, upset *What details support this idea?* **They are yipping and yeowling in a panic, and they tell Dex to hurry.** ELA RL.2.1

ENGLISH LANGUAGE SUPPORT Point out the words *yipping* and *yeowling* on page 180. Explain that the author uses these sound words to help the reader understand what the neighborhood sounded like the night that Cleevis got stuck in a tree. ELD ELD.PI.2.7

(14) *The author says that Dex was dressed and ready "in a flash." What does a "flash" mean?* a sudden burst, like a flash of light *What does it mean "to be ready in a flash"?* to be ready very quickly ELA RL.2.4 ELD ELD.PI.2.7

"Quick, everybody!" Dex shouted. "I've got an idea!" Dex leaped onto the end of the teeter-totter facing the tree, pushing it to the ground.

"Everybody on the other end! One! Two! Three!!!!"

All the animals jumped together on the other end of the teeter-totter, catapulting Dex into the air. He soared over the crowd, his ears and cape streaming **(15)** out behind him. . . .

182

THE MIGHTY DEX FLEW UP INTO THE DARK AND STARRY NIGHT. . . .

183

---

(15) *Why does Dex ask all the animals to jump on the other end of the teeter-totter?* **This will send Dex flying into the air.** *Do you think this is a good plan? Why or why not?* **Sample answer: Yes, because Dex will land in the tree near Cleevis so he can help Cleevis get down.** **ELA** RL.2.1

ENGLISH LANGUAGE SUPPORT Provide sentence frames to encourage participation. *I think using the teeter-totter is a _____ idea because _____.* **good; it will help Dex save Cleevis** **ELD** ELD.PI.2.6

☑ **TARGET STRATEGY| Monitor/Clarify**

Tell children to practice the Monitor/Clarify strategy as they reread **Student Book** p. 180 silently to themselves and to look closely at the pictures. Ask them to clarify anything that does not make sense about Dex's plan to help Cleevis. Tell them to use techniques such as looking carefully at the illustrations, rereading, and reading ahead. **ELA** RL.2.7 **ELD** ELD.PI.2.6

ENGLISH LANGUAGE SUPPORT

How English Works: Interpretive

Connecting Ideas Remind children that authors use special words to connect, or put together, ideas in sentences. Tell children that *because, and, or,* and *but* are examples of connecting words. Read the first paragraph on page 181 aloud, emphasizing the word *but.* Explain its purpose, and have children write a new sentence containing the connecting word *but.* **ELD** ELD.PII.2.6

Dex scrambled onto the branch next to Cleevis. Quickly he pulled off his cape and tied its four corners onto the screeching cat.

"Jump!" Dex shouted. "Jump, Cleevis!"

184

185

ENGLISH LANGUAGE SUPPORT

Use Visuals

Emerging Drop a tissue from a good height and let it float to the ground. Ask, *How is this tissue like Dex's cape?* **ELD** ELD.PI.2.6

Expanding Drop a tissue to the ground. Ask children to write a sentence comparing the tissue to Dex's cape. **ELD** ELD.PI.2.6

Bridging Ask children to explain why Dex's cape can work like a parachute. **ELD** ELD.PI.2.6

FIRST READ

Cite Text Evidence

Think Through the Text

16 *Why do you think Dex ties his cape onto Cleevis before telling him to jump?* **The cape will act as a parachute and help Cleevis float to the ground safely.** **ELA** RL.2.1 **ELD** ELD.PI.2.6

17 *Will it be difficult for Cleevis to let go and jump? Why or why not?* **Sample answer: Yes, because it's a long way to the ground, and he might not believe that the parachute will work.** *How does Cleevis feel about jumping? How can you tell?* **He is afraid to jump. The text says he is screeching and he looks scared in the picture.** **ELA** RL.2.3

ENGLISH LANGUAGE SUPPORT Remind children that authors build noun phrases to add details about people, places, and things. Point out the noun phrase *screeching cat* and explain that the author used this phrase to add details about Cleevis. Encourage them to use the noun phrase as they answer the question. **ELD** ELD.PI.2.6, ELD.PII.2.4

18 With an ear-piercing shriek, Cleevis let go. The billowing cape caught the air and parachuted the big cat to the ground. Dex backed up and slid to the ground amidst the cheers of the crowd.

186

Dex was bruised and tired, but he forgot his discomfort as Cleevis sheepishly lumbered over, still tangled in the green cape.

"Thanks, Dex. You really are a hero!" 19

187

18 *How do you think Cleevis felt when he let go?* scared *What detail in the text lets you know this is how he feels?* He lets out an ear-piercing shriek. ELA RL.2.1 ELD ELD.PI.2.6

19 *How do the animals in the crowd feel about what Dex did?* They are happy and excited. *How can you tell?* They are cheering. *How does Cleevis feel toward Dex now?* He thinks he is a hero. ELA RL.2.3, RL.2.7

ENGLISH LANGUAGE SUPPORT Provide sentence frames to encourage participation. *The animals in the crowd _____ after Dex saves Cleevis.* cheer *Cleevis tells Dex he is a _____.* hero ELD ELD.PI.2.6

WITH TWICE THE BRAINS AND TRIPLE THE BRAWN, OUR HEROES FORGE ON, EVER READY TO LEND A HELPING PAW!

(20) Dex didn't think he could feel any better, but he did—just a little—the next day, when Cleevis sidled up next to him and whispered, "Say, Dex, could I be your partner?"

Dex looked the big tomcat up and down. It would take a *lot* of work to turn Cleevis into a hero. He could hardly wait. (21)

"Sure," said Dex with a grin. "Sure."

ANALYZE THE TEXT

Compare and Contrast How has Cleevis changed by the end of the story?

188

189

FIRST READ

Cite Text Evidence

Think Through the Text

(20) *Why does Cleevis want to be Dex's partner now?* Sample response: *He admires him; he wants to do the exciting things Dex is doing; he wants to help others, too.* **ELA** RL.2.1

(21) *Why can Dex "hardly wait" to turn Cleevis into a partner?* Sample responses: *He wants a hero sidekick; he will enjoy training Cleevis; it will be better to have Cleevis on his side for a change* **ELA** RL.2.1

Collaborative Conversation

Working in groups, have children discuss whether they think Dex and Cleevis will make a good team. Tell them to refer to the text and illustrations to support their responses. Remind children to listen carefully, take turns while speaking, stay on topic, and use complete sentences when they speak. Call on groups to share their responses with the class.
ELA SL.2.1a, SL.2.1b **ELD** ELD.PI.2.1, ELD.PI.2.3, ELD.PI.2.6, ELD.PI.2.11

SECOND READ **DAY 2**

Analyze the Text

Compare and Contrast

Read the Analyze the Text box on **Student Book** p. 188 with children. Then display Projectable 20.4 and distribute Graphic Organizer 14. Tell children that you will work together to complete the graphic organizer.

Remind children that to compare, they should look for ways in which things are the same; to contrast, they should look for ways in which things are different. Guide children to complete the graphic organizer with ways that Cleevis acted at the beginning and end of the story. Then have them use the graphic organizer to answer the question in the Analyze the Text box. **ELA** RL.2.1 **ELD** ELD.PI.2.6

Annotate it! Work with children to highlight sentences that show how Cleevis feels about Dex at the beginning of the story and at the end of the story.

Guided Retelling

Oral Language

Use the retelling prompts on the **Retelling Cards** to guide children to retell the story.

ELA RL.2.2 **ELD** ELD.PI.2.6, ELD.PI.2.12a

front

Talk About It

How is Dex different from the other animals? How is he the same?

How does the author use food to describe how Dex looks?

How does Dex feel about the way the other animals treat him?

back

front

Talk About It

What goal does Dex set for himself? How does he try to change?

How does the author make the story like a comic book? Why do you think the author does this?

back

front

Talk About It

How has Dex changed since the beginning of the story?

How do the other animals treat him differently now?

What does it mean to be a hero? Is Dex a hero?

back

WITH TWICE THE BRAINS AND TRIPLE THE BRAWN, OUR HEROES FORGE ON, EVER READY TO LEND A HELPING PAW!

front

Talk About It

What is Dex's idea to get Cleevis out of the tree? Does it work?

Why does Cleevis change his mind about Dex? Do you think Dex forgives Cleevis for teasing him before?

Do you think Dex and Cleevis will make a good team? Why or why not?

back

RETELLING RUBRIC	
4 Highly Effective	The retelling names the characters, describes the problem, and tells important events in order. It includes several details and tells how the problem was solved.
3 Generally Effective	The retelling names the characters and tells most of the important events in order, including how the problem was solved. It includes some details.
2 Somewhat Effective	The retelling includes a few elements of the story but omits important characters or events and provides few details.
1 Ineffective	The reader is unable to provide an accurate retelling of *Dex: The Heart of a Hero*.

ENGLISH LANGUAGE SUPPORT

Review Key Ideas

All Proficiencies Pronounce and explain *retell*, reminding children that when they retell a story they are describing the main events in the order they happened. Page through *Dex: The Heart of a Hero* with children and share the following sentence frames to help them retell the selection.

Dex was little, but he wanted to be a _____. hero
Cleevis the cat _____ him. teases Dex exercises and starts doing things to _____. help others When Cleevis gets caught in a tree, Dex _____. rescues him Cleevis asks Dex if they can be _____. partners

ELD ELD.PI.2.6, ELD.PI.2.12a

Grammar Commas in a Series

▶ **SHARE OBJECTIVES**

- **Grammar** Use commas in sentences with a series of nouns. LANGUAGE
- **Spelling** Spell words with *or, ore*.
- **Writing** Begin to draft a narrative. LANGUAGE

ENGLISH LANGUAGE SUPPORT
Comprehensible Input

Emerging Ask, *What do we need to do a math lesson?* Say, *We need books, pencils, and paper.* Then write the sentence without any commas. Have children insert the commas using a different color.

Expanding Say, *I like red.* Have children say which colors they like. Then write on the board, *We like red.* Have children complete the sentence adding one color each. Have them use a different color for commas.

Bridging Have children write a sentence with commas that lists three items they need to go to the beach.

Linguistic Transfer The /r/ sound may not exist or may be pronounced differently in many languages. The *r*-controlled vowel sound /ôr/ may be difficult for children. Provide additional practice time for these words. **ELD** ELD.PIII.2

1 Teach/Model

Commas in a Series of Nouns Display Projectable 20.2 ⬀. Say, *I like to eat corn, peas, and potatoes.* Point out that *corn, peas,* and *potatoes* are nouns. Explain that writers often list nouns in a series.

- Now explain that a comma is used after each noun except for the last noun. Point out that a comma comes before the word *and*.

- Model identifying the correct place to put commas in the example sentence: *My turtle eats melon, grapes, and lettuce.*

Think Aloud *To find out where to put commas, I ask this Thinking Question: Are there three or more nouns listed in a series? The nouns melon, grapes, and lettuce are listed in a series. I should use a comma after all but the last one.*

2 Guided Practice/Apply

- Complete other examples on **Projectable 20.2** with children. Have children use the Thinking Question to find the correct place to put commas in a series of nouns.

ENGLISH LANGUAGE SUPPORT Read the sentences on **Projectable 20.2** aloud, modeling a slight pause where the commas belong. Have children repeat after you and discuss where the commas should be in the sentence.

- Distribute Reader's Notebook Volume 2 page 62 ⬀ to children to complete independently.

- For additional support, have children view the GrammarSnap Video ⬀ that supports Lesson 20.

Spelling Words with *or, ore*

SPELLING WORDS AND SENTENCES

BASIC WORDS

1. **horn** The car *horn* is loud.
2. **story** We read a *story* every night.
3. **fork** You use a *fork* to eat.
4. **score** What is the game's *score*?
5. **store** Dad buys food at the *store*.
6. **corn** I like to eat *corn* on the cob.
7. **morning*** We eat breakfast every *morning*.
8. **shore** Waves roll onto the *shore*.
9. **short** *Short* is the opposite of tall.

10. **born** I was *born* on July 26.
11. **tore** I *tore* my pants when I fell down.
12. **forget** Don't *forget* to walk the dog.

REVIEW WORDS

13. **for** I bought gifts *for* my friends.
14. **more** We have *more* than we need.

CHALLENGE WORDS

15. **report** I wrote a book *report*.
16. **force** The *force* of the storm was strong.

*A form of this word appears in the literature.

Administer the Pretest
Say each Spelling Word. Then say it in a sentence and repeat the word. Have children write the word. **ELA** L.2.2d

Teach the Principle
- Review **Sound/Spelling Card** *orange*. Point to the *or* as you say *orange*. Write *tore*, underlining *ore*. Then read the word aloud.

- Explain that /ôr/ can be spelled with the letters *or* or the letters *ore*.

Model a Word Sort
Model sorting words based on the location of the /ôr/ sound. Present the Model the Sort lesson on page 94 of the **Literacy and Language Guide**.

Narrative Writing Draft

1 Teach/Model

Fictional Story Display the completed prewriting Projectable 19.8 ⬈ from the previous week. Reread and discuss the prompt.

- Use the Setting, Characters, and Beginning sections of the Story Map to model drafting the first paragraph of a story. Add transition words such as *One day* and *At long last* into the story to help readers be able to follow the sequence. Point out when you use details to describe when, where, or how something happens, such as *His wing was stuck in the branches.* The phrase *in the branches* describes where his wing was stuck. Display Projectable 20.3 ⬈. Use the Think Aloud and the first sample paragraphs to model drafting.

> **Think Aloud** *In the first paragraph of my story, I'll introduce its setting and characters. I will include details that describe what the characters are like. I especially want to make sure readers understand the characters are robins. I also want readers to know what the problem in the story is. Next I will write about how Robbie gets stuck in the branches.*

2 Guided Practice/Apply

- With children, use the Middle section of the Story Map on **Projectable 19.8** to draft the second paragraph of the story.

- *What should the second paragraph of the story mostly be about?* **how Robbie and Ramona work to solve the problem**

Drafting Review the prompt: *Write a story about a character who does something important or brave.* Remind children that they began prewriting their own stories to this prompt last week. Then have them begin drafting their stories using their Story Maps from the previous week. Remind children to include details that describe their characters' actions, thoughts, and feelings. Allow children to refer back to **Projectable 20.3** as they write to remember how to add transition words and details about when, where, and how things happen. Encourage children to use digital media, such as a word processing program, to draft their fictional narrative.

ELA W.2.3, W.2.4, W.2.6, W.2.10 **ELD** ELD.PI.2.10, ELD.PII.2.1, ELD.PII.2.2, ELD.PII.2.5

Performance Task

WriteSmart Children may prewrite, draft, revise, and publish their narrative writing task through *my*WriteSmart beginning on Day 3.

Additional support for Narrative Writing appears in the **Common Core Writing Handbook,** Lesson 20.

DAY 2

Today's Goals

Vocabulary & Oral Language

☑ **TARGET VOCABULARY**

depended	gazing
sore	hero
sprang	exercise
studied	overlooked

Phonemic Awareness

- Substitute Phonemes

Phonics & Fluency

- **Words with** *or, ore*
- **Fluency:** Intonation
- **Read Decodable Reader:** *A Sporty Game*
- **High-Frequency Words**

Text-Based Comprehension

- **Dig Deeper:** Use Clues to Analyze the Text
- **Compare and Contrast**
- **Figurative Language**
- **Reread the Anchor Text:** *Dex: The Heart of a Hero*

Grammar & Writing

- **Commas in a Series**
- **Narrative Writing:** Fictional Story
- **Trait:** Organization

Spelling

- **Words with** *or, ore*

Opening Routines

Warm Up with Wordplay

Two Words

Tell children that they will each think of two words that describe Dexter. Ask them to write their ideas on a sheet of paper. Then collect the responses and write them on the board.

small	strong-willed
helpful	smart
annoying	generous
brave	cute

After making sure children understand the meanings of all the words, ask them to pick one they did not know before and use it in a sentence. Have children share their sentences with the class. **ELA** L.2.6

Daily Phonemic Awareness

Substitute Phonemes

- *I am going to say a word and then change the vowel sound to make a new word.* Say the word *form*. Model how to make a new word by changing the vowel sound to /är/: /f/ /ôr/ /m/; /f/ /är/ /m/.

- Have children substitute long, short, or other *r*-controlled vowels to make new words, such as *star/stir, hose/horse, hen/horn, card/cord, far/for, speak/spark.*

Corrective Feedback

- If a child is unable to make a substitution, provide correction and model the task. Example: *Listen:* form. *What sounds do you hear?* /f/ /ôr/ /m/ *Change* /ôr/ *to* /är/. *What is the new word?* farm

- Have children repeat once with you. Then have them continue with the other words on their own.

Daily High-Frequency Words

- Point to **High-Frequency Word Card 193**, *I've.*

- *Say the word.* I've *Spell the word.* I-'-v-e *Write the word. Check the word.*

- Repeat the routine with the new words *being, stood, tall* and the review words *begins, flower, ground, laugh, ready, very.* **ELA** RF.2.3f

Hopscotch

- Create a hopscotch pattern on the floor with masking tape. Write one letter from the word *I've* in each box and then write the whole word at the top.

- Have children hop from one letter to the next, saying each letter to spell the word. Have them say the word.

- Repeat the activity for the words *being* and *ready.*

Corrective Feedback

- If a child does not recognize the word *I've*, say the correct word and have children repeat it. *I've. What is the word?* I've

- Have children spell the word. I-'-v-e *How do we say this word?* I've

- Have children reread all of the cards in random order.

Daily Vocabulary Boost

- Review Target Vocabulary and the definitions. (See p. T414.) Remind children that they heard these words in "Ordinary Heroes." Recall story events with children as you guide them to interact with each word's meaning.

  "Meghan's mind sprang to action." Could Meghan think of any ideas? Explain your answer.

  "She knew that Kevin had studied very hard before that test." Explain why Kevin was ready to take the test.

  "Her mom always came through when Meghan depended on her for help." Tell about a time when someone depended on you.

- Continue in the same manner, using the words *overlooked, gazing, hero, exercise,* and *sore.* **ELA** L.2.6

sprang
The cat saw the food. She sprang toward her dish.

Vocabulary in Context Cards 153–160

✔ Target Vocabulary

depended

sore

sprang

studied

gazing

hero

exercise

overlooked

DAY 2

Phonics

▶ **SHARE OBJECTIVES**

- Substitute vowel sounds in words to make new words.
- Blend, build, and decode regularly spelled words with *or, ore* (r-controlled vowel syllable).
- Reread on-level text with words with *or, ore* and High-Frequency Words for fluency practice.

▶ **SKILLS TRACE**

Words with *or, ore*	
Introduce	**pp. T416–T417, T442–T443**
Differentiate	pp. T488–T489, T494
Reteach	p. T502
Review	pp. T462–T463, Unit 5 T63
Assess	Weekly Tests, Lesson 20

ENGLISH LANGUAGE SUPPORT

Comprehensible Input

All Proficiencies Continue to reinforce the meanings and pronunciations of the words children decode in Blending Lines. Use a word in a simple sentence, such as "I can smell the odor of flowers." Have children repeat your sentence. Then have them say the sentence again, completing it with a word(s) that they choose: *I can smell the odor of [pizza].* Repeat with other words in Blending Lines, for example: *May I have more ___ ? At the shore we can ___. We can see ___ in the forest .*

Words with *or, ore*

Phonemic Awareness Warm-Up *Let's change vowel sounds in words to make new words. I'll do it first. Listen:* hen. *Now listen as I change the /ĕ/ in* hen *to /ôr/:* horn. *Now you try it. Say:* hen. *Change the /ĕ/ in* hen *to /ôr/. What is the word?* horn

Let's do some more. Change the /ă/ in pack *to /ôr/.* pork *Change the /är/ in* car *to /ôr/.* core *Change the /ĕ/ in* stem *to /ôr/.* storm *Change the /ôr/ in* born *to /är/.* barn

1   Teach/Model

Review **Sound/Spelling Card** *orange, /ôr/.* Remind children that the letters *or* and *ore* spell the sound /ôr/.

Continuous Blending Routine
Use Instructional Routine 3 to model blending *stork,* displaying **Letter Cards** *s, t, or, k.*

- Blend the sounds, stretching out the word while pointing to each letter in a sweeping motion. *Listen: /s/ /t/ /ôr/ /k/.*
- Have children blend the sounds and say the word with you. Then have children blend and read on their own. *You blend the sounds. /s/ /t/ /ôr/ /k/,* stork

2   Guided Practice

Blending Lines

Blend Words Repeat the blending routine with the first two words in Line 1 below; help children compare the words. Point to each word as children read the entire line chorally. Continue with the remaining lines. Then call on volunteers to reread selected words until children can identify the words quickly.

1. or	for	fort	sort	short	snort
2. more	core	sore	store	score	shore
3. porch	story	north	snore	before	odor

Transition to Longer Words Use a similar process for Lines 4–6.

4. forever	forget	forest	forty	formal	normal
5. bored	adore	anymore	explore	stored	restore
6. color	honor	shoreline	ashore	offshore	shortly

Challenge Call on above-level children to read the words in Line 7. Then have the class read the sentences chorally.

7. boredom   orbiting   cordless   forecast   flavoring   ignore
8. A horse <u>stood</u> by the <u>tall</u> red barn.
9. The farm is <u>very</u> far north of the city. **ELA** RF.2.3e

Build Words Use **Letter Cards** to model how to spell *snore*.
I know that the letters s and n stand for the blended /s/ /n/ sounds. The next sound is /ôr/. The letters o, r, and e usually stand for the /ôr/ sound when it comes at the end of a word. I write each letter in order: s-n-o-r-e. Now read the word with me: snore.

- Guide children to identify sounds and spell *north, forty, charm, score, ignore,* and *shore.* Individuals can spell with **Letter Cards** while others check their work. **ELA** L.2.2d

3 Apply

Have partners take turns rereading Blending Lines 1–3 and 4–6. Then tell each partner to choose any ten words and decide how to sort them. For example, they might sort according to the spelling of the /ôr/ sound or by number of syllables. Have partners read aloud each other's sorted words and identify the sorting criteria. **ELA** RF.2.3e, L.2.2d

Distribute <u>Reader's Notebook Volume 2 page 63</u> or <u>leveled practice</u> in Grab-and-Go™ Resources for children to complete independently.

Practice Fluency

Use <u>Instructional Routine 15</u> to have children read the **Decodable Reader** *A Sporty Game.*

Decodable Reader

FORMATIVE ASSESSMENT RtI

Corrective Feedback When a child mispronounces a letter-sound, highlight that letter, restate its sound, have children repeat the sound, and then guide them to blend the word. See the example below.

Decoding Error:
A child reads *shore* in Line 2 as *share.*

Correct the error. Review **Sound/Spelling Card** *orange.* Then say the word and the sound. *The word is* shore. *The letters o r together stand for the sound /ôr/.*

Model as you touch the letters. *I'll blend: /sh/ /ôr/. What is the word?* shore

Guide *Let's blend together: /sh/ /ôr/. What is the word?* shore

Check *You blend. /sh/ /ôr/ What is the word?* shore

Reinforce Go back two or three words and have children continue reading. Make note of errors and review those words during the next lesson.

SMALL GROUP Options Go to pp. T488–T489 for additional phonics support.

Dig Deeper: Use Clues to Analyze the Text

▶ **SHARE OBJECTIVES**
- Compare and contrast characters in a story.
- Understand comparisons created by similes. LANGUAGE

ENGLISH LANGUAGE SUPPORT

Expand Language Production

Emerging Present similes. Have children complete simple similes, such as *The man was as strong as _____. The hat was as green as _____.*

Expanding Ask children to create similes out of simple descriptions. For example, *The kitten was funny* could be turned into *The kitten was as funny as a clown.* **ELD** ELD.PII.2.4

Bridging Have children look for similes in other stories or poems and share them with the class. **ELD** ELD.PI.2.6

Text-Based Comprehension

1 Teach/Model

Terms About Literature

compare to find ways that things are the same

contrast to find ways that things are different

simile a comparison that uses *like* or *as*

Remind children that they have just read a fantasy story titled *Dex: The Heart of a Hero* about a dog that turns himself into a hero.

- Read **Student Book** p. 190 with children. Tell children that they can compare and contrast many parts of a text, such as the characters. Point out that both Dex and Cleevis changed their ideas and feelings from the beginning of the story to the end. Children can compare and contrast two different characters, or they can compare and contrast how much one character has changed.

- Discuss the Venn diagram, using this model.

  Think Aloud
  This Venn diagram can help me figure out ways in which Dex and Cleevis were alike and different. I'm going to think about the beginning of the story. Dex and Cleevis were alike because they didn't help others, so I'll write that for Both. At the beginning, Dex was weak, slow, and timid, so I'll write that for Dex. Cleevis was mean and annoying, so I'll write that for Cleevis. Then I can easily use this information to see how Dex and Cleevis were alike and different.

Next, read **Student Book** p. 191 with children. Tell children some common similes, such as "as busy as a bee" and "like two peas in a pod."

ENGLISH LANGUAGE SUPPORT Reiterate that the words *like* and *as* are often used to compare two similar things. When we contrast things, we look at how they are different. Point out that *diferente* is a Spanish cognate for *different*.

- Have children look at **Student Book** p. 168. Ask them to locate a simile that uses *like* and describes Dex. *like a plump sausage sitting on four little meatballs*

- Have children complete some similes, such as the following:

  as pretty as _____; the sky looked like _____

  as tall as _____; the grass looked like _____

🔍 BE A READING DETECTIVE

Dig Deeper

Use Clues to Analyze the Text

Use these pages to learn about Comparing and Contrasting and Figurative Language. Then read *Dex: The Heart of a Hero* again. Use what you learn to understand it better.

Compare and Contrast

In *Dex: The Heart of a Hero*, some of the characters change during the story. You can **compare** the characters' thoughts and feelings at the beginning and the end of the story by telling how they are the same. You can **contrast** by telling how they are different.

Words and pictures from the story are clues about how the characters change. Use a diagram like this for the beginning of the story and another for the end. Show how the characters changed.

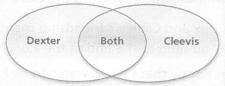

Dexter — Both — Cleevis

Figurative Language

Authors sometimes tell how two things are the same using the word *like* or *as*. This is called a **simile**. A simile helps readers picture story details in their mind. For example, *The dog ran as fast as lightning* is a simile. The dog can't really run as fast as lightning, but the simile helps the reader understand that the dog is running fast. Look for examples of similes as you reread *Dex: The Heart of a Hero*.

190 ELA RL.2.3, RL.2.4, RL.2.7 ELD ELD.PI.2.6, ELD.PI.2.7

191

---

2 Guided Practice/Apply

Analyze the Text

Begin a second read of *Dex: The Heart of a Hero* with children. Use the stopping points and instructional support to guide children to analyze the text:

- Compare and Contrast, p. T436 ELA RL.2.3, RL.2.7 ELD ELD.PI.2.6

- Figurative Language, p. T429 ELA RL.2.4 ELD ELD.PI.2.6, ELD.PI.2.7

Directed Note Taking Projectable 20.4 🔗 will be completed with children during the second read on p. T436. ELA RL.2.3, RL.2.7 ELD ELD.PI.2.6

FORMATIVE ASSESSMENT   RtI

Can children compare and contrast elements of the story?

IF...	THEN...
children struggle,	use **Differentiate Comprehension** for Struggling Readers, p. T492. See also Intervention Lesson 20, pp. S44–S45.
children are on track,	use **Differentiate Comprehension** for On-Level Readers, p. T492.
children excel,	use **Differentiate Comprehension** for Advanced Readers, p. T493.

 Differentiate Comprehension, pp. T492–T493
Scaffold instruction to the English learner's proficiency level.

DAY 2

Your Turn

Cite
Text Evidence

▶ SHARE OBJECTIVES

- Compare and contrast story characters.
- Write a reading response that expresses an opinion.
- Combine clauses to connect ideas in shared language activities. LANGUAGE

RETURN TO THE ESSENTIAL QUESTION

Have partners create web diagrams and write the word *hero* in the center circle. Have partners write as many attributes as they can think of for heroes in the other circles. Tell children to think back to what made Dexter a hero and to list his characteristics in their diagrams as well as to think of the attributes of other people they think of as heroes. Have children follow discussion rules and express their ideas as clearly as possible as they build on the ideas of their partners.

ELA SL.2.1a, SL.2.1b **ELD** ELD.PI.2.1, ELD.PI.2.3, ELD.PI.2.6, ELD.PI.2.12a

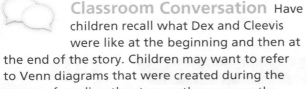

Classroom Conversation Have children recall what Dex and Cleevis were like at the beginning and then at the end of the story. Children may want to refer to Venn diagrams that were created during the course of reading the story as they answer the questions. For question 3, brainstorm the names of superheroes and have children tell what they know about the heroes before comparing them with Dex.

ELA RL.2.1, RL.2.3, SL.2.1a **ELD** ELD.PI.2.1, ELD.PI.2.3, ELD.PI.2.6, ELD.PI.2.11

ENGLISH LANGUAGE SUPPORT Use sentence frames such as the following to support discussion.

At the beginning of the story, Dex and Cleevis ____. At the end of the story, Dex and Cleevis ____.

Dex is happy that Cleevis wants to be his partner at the end because ____.

Dex is like the superhero ____ because ____.

As children share their ideas, have them use gestures and refer to the story for help completing the sentence frames. **ELD** ELD.PI.2.6, ELD.PI.2.12a

---

Your Turn

RETURN TO THE ESSENTIAL QUESTION

 Turn and Talk

What makes someone a hero? Discuss with a partner. Find text evidence from *Dex: The Heart of a Hero* to support your ideas. Speak one at a time. Add your own ideas to what your partner says.

Classroom Conversation

Now talk about these questions with the class.

1. How does Dex and Cleevis's friendship change from the beginning to the end of the story?

2. Why is Dex happy that Cleevis wants to be his partner at the end of the story?

3. Think of other superhero stories you know. How is Dex like the superheroes in those stories?

192 **ELA** RL.2.1, RL.2.3, W.2.1, W.2.4, W.2.10, SL.2.1a, SL.2.1b **ELD** ELD.PI.2.1, ELD.PI.2.6, ELD.PI.2.10, ELD.PI.2.11, ELD.PII.2.2

ENGLISH LANGUAGE SUPPORT

How English Works: Collaborative

Connecting Ideas Before children begin discussing item 1, have them plan to use connecting words when sharing. Tell children that speakers use special words to connect, or put together, ideas in sentences. Give the following examples: *because, and, or,* and *but.* Provide a model sentence such as this one: *Dex was weak in the beginning of the story, but he was strong at the end.* Help children at different proficiency levels build lists of connecting words to use during their discussions. **ELD** ELD.PII.2.6

Performance Task

WRITE ABOUT READING

Response Think about how Dex helped Cleevis. Would you have helped someone who had been mean to you in the past? Write a paragraph to share your opinion.

Writing Tip

Use linking words, such as *so* or *because,* to connect reasons with your ideas.

193

WRITE ABOUT READING

Have children discuss the way Cleevis acted toward Dex. Then have them describe the way Dex saved Cleevis. Ask, *If you were Dex, would you have helped Cleevis? Why or why not?*

Have children share ideas about helping those who have been mean to them. Then have children write paragraphs. Tell children to follow these guidelines.

- Write your opinion in your first sentence. Include a reason for your opinion in the same sentence, using a linking word.

- Write at least two more sentences that explain why you have your opinion.

Writing Tip Make sure children read the Writing Tip before they begin writing. Model sentences with the words *so* and *because* as linking words. For example, *I think I would help people in trouble even though they have been mean because you should help anyone who is in trouble,* or *I think you should help people who have been mean so that they will change the way they act.* **ELA** W.2.1, W.2.4, W.2.10, L.2.1f

See **Analytic Writing Rubric** on p. R17.

myWriteSmart Have children complete the Write About Reading activity through *my*WriteSmart. Children will read the prompt within *my*WriteSmart and have access to multiple writing resources, including the Student eBook, Writing Rubrics, and Graphic Organizers.

ENGLISH LANGUAGE SUPPORT

Comprehensible Input

All Proficiencies Before children begin writing, ask them to think about someone who has been mean to them in the past. Then have them think about that person needing help with something serious. For children who need support, provide the sentence frame *I (would/would not) help someone who has been mean to me before because _____.* Remind them not to use the name of the person who was mean to them in their sentences. **ELD** ELD.PI.2.10, ELD.PI.2.12a

Grammar Commas in a Series

▶ **SHARE OBJECTIVES**

- **Grammar** Use commas in a series of single verbs. LANGUAGE
- **Spelling** Spell words with *or, ore*.
- **Handwriting** Write Spelling Words.
- **Writing** Continue to draft a narrative using digital tools, if possible. LANGUAGE

ENGLISH LANGUAGE SUPPORT
Peer-Supported Learning

All Proficiencies Organize children into mixed-proficiency small groups. Have a child stand, jump, and clap. Say, *(Name) stands, jumps, and claps.* Then write the sentence without any commas. Have children insert the commas. Have groups work together to write sentences with a series of verbs. Suggest sentence starters *I like, I can,* or *I need.*

Preview Lesson Preview the lesson in children's first language if another teacher who speaks a language other than English is available. After the preview, ask volunteers to translate the main points of the lesson back into English.

---

1 Teach/Model

Commas in a Series of Verbs Display Projectable 20.5 ⬚. Say, *I like to eat, walk, run, and jump.* Point out that *eat, walk, run,* and *jump* are verbs. Explain that writers can list verbs in a series. Explain how to write a series of verbs using commas.

- Tell children that a comma is used after each verb except the last verb. Point out that a comma comes before the word *and.*

- Model identifying the correct place to put commas in this example sentence: *The puppy plays, sleeps, and barks.*

> **Think Aloud** To find out where to put commas in a series of verbs, I ask this Thinking Question: *Are there three or more verbs listed in a series?* The verbs *plays, sleeps,* and *barks* are listed in a series. I should use a comma after each verb except the last one, where there is a period.

2 Guided Practice/Apply

- Complete other examples on **Projectable 20.5** with children.

- Have children use the Thinking Question to correctly identify where to place the commas in the sentences.

- Distribute Reader's Notebook Volume 2 page 65 ⬚ to children to complete independently.

- To reinforce the concepts as needed, play the GrammarSnap Video ⬚ that supports this lesson.

Spelling Words with *or, ore*

SPELLING WORDS

BASIC

horn	born
story	tore
fork	forget
score	**REVIEW**
store	for
corn	more
morning*	**CHALLENGE**
shore	report
short	force

*A form of this word appears in the literature.

Teach/Word Sort

- Review **Sound/Spelling Card** *orange. What sound do you hear at the beginning of orange?* /ôr/ *How can the /ôr/ sound be spelled?* *or* and *ore*

- Draw a two-column chart. Label it *or* and *ore*. Have children write Spelling Words under each head.

or	ore
horn	store
fork	tore

- Distribute Reader's Notebook Volume 2 p. 64 ⬚ to children to complete independently. **ELA** L.2.2d

Open Sort

For additional practice with the Spelling Words, guide children to complete the Open Sort activity on page 94 of the **Literacy and Language Guide.**

Handwriting

Model how to form the Basic Words *horn, story, fork, score, store,* and *corn.* Handwriting models are available on pp. R24–R29 and on the Handwriting Models Blackline Masters ⬚. Remind children to write legibly and stay within the margins. **ELA** L.2.1g

Narrative Writing Focus Trait: Organization

1 Teach/Model

Fictional Story: Interesting Beginnings Explain that when people write stories, they want the beginning to grab the reader's attention so that the reader will be interested in the story and will want to keep reading.

Connect to *Dex: The Heart of a Hero*	
Instead of this …	**… the author wrote this.**
Dexter was a dog.	"Dexter was a little dog. His legs were little, his tail was little, his body was little. He looked like a plump sausage sitting on four little meatballs." (p. 168)

- *Why is the author's beginning better?* It's funny and paints a vivid picture of Dexter that makes you want to learn more about him.

2 Guided Practice/Apply

- Write: *Dexter was a little dog.* Tell children that they will write sentences to tell more about Dexter.

- Have children look at the pictures of Dexter in the beginning of the story. Have them brainstorm interesting details and suggest more sentences about Dexter. Write their suggestions. Possible response: *Dexter was a little dog. He was so little all the other dogs laughed at him. Just to be mean, they sometimes sat on him "by accident."*

- Write: *Dex started training.* Ask children to add interesting details to tell more about Dexter's training. Possible response: *Dex started training. He got up before the sun and raced around the block until he was exhausted. He climbed the garbage pile over and over again and dragged heavy socks filled with sand.*

- Distribute Reader's Notebook Volume 2 page 66 to children to complete independently.

Drafting Have children continue to draft their stories. Remind them to make their beginnings interesting so their readers will want to keep reading. Encourage children to continue using digital media to draft their fictional narratives.

ELA W.2.3, W.2.4, W.2.6, W.2.10 **ELD** ELD.PI.2.10, ELD.PII.2.1

Daily Proofreading Practice

Mouse eats corn, cheese, and crackers. She is full after the party.

ENGLISH LANGUAGE SUPPORT

Peer-Supported Learning

All Proficiencies Model how to write a beginning that is interesting and makes the reader want to read more. Say, *Let's create our own superheroes. My superhero can fly, soar, and land like a bird.* Ask, *Do you want to know more about my superhero?* Organize children into mixed-proficiency small groups and ask them to create their own superheroes. Ask groups to share three things their superhero can do. Write the sentence on the board.

myWriteSmart Children may prewrite, draft, revise, and publish their narrative writing task through *my*WriteSmart beginning on Day 3.

DAY 3

Today's Goals

Vocabulary & Oral Language
- Apply Vocabulary Knowledge

☑ **TARGET VOCABULARY**

depended	gazing
sore	hero
sprang	exercise
studied	overlooked

Phonemic Awareness
- Substitute Phonemes

Phonics & Fluency
- Words with *ar*
- Words with *or, ore*
- Read Decodable Reader: *My Story*
- Fluency: Intonation
- High-Frequency Words

Text-Based Comprehension
- Independent Reading
- Reader's Guide
- Self-Selected Reading

Grammar & Writing
- Commas in a Series
- Narrative Writing: Fictional Story

Spelling
- Words with *or, ore*

Opening Routines

Warm Up with Wordplay

The Never-Ending Story

Children have been reading a story about a dog and a cat who end up as friends. Tell them that today, they will be writing about a different pair of unlikely friends. Each child will make up a small part of the story.

Display and read aloud the following opening for the story:

> ## Elephant and Flea were best friends. No one could understand it. And then . . .

Pick one child to continue the story. When the child has finished the part, he or she says "and then . . ." The next child then adds to the story. **ELA** SL.2.1b **ELD** ELD.PI.2.1

Daily Phonemic Awareness

Substitute Phonemes

- *We can change just one sound in a word to make a new word. Listen: park. What sounds do you hear? /p/ /är/ /k/ Let's change the /är/ to /ôr/. What word does it make? pork*

Change the...	Result
/ō/ in tone to /ôr/	torn
/är/ in car to /ôr/	core
/ŏ/ in pot to /ôr/	port
/är/ in farm to /ôr/	form

- Have children repeat with you, and then by themselves. Have them continue with the words from the chart.

Corrective Feedback

- If a child is unable to make a substitution, say the word, give correction, and model the task. Example: *The word is park. I can change the /är/ in park to /ôr/ and make a new word,* pork.

- Have children make a substitution with you before doing it on their own. Continue with the other words.

Daily High-Frequency Words

- Point to **High-Frequency Word Card 192**, *ready*.

- *Say the word. ready Spell the word. r-e-a-d-y Write the word. Check the word.*

- Repeat the procedure with the words *begins, being, flower, ground, I've, laugh, stood, tall,* and *very.* **ELA** RF.2.3f

Letter Cards

- Provide children with **Letter Cards** for the word *ready*.

- Invite them to take turns using the cards to spell the word correctly.

- Repeat the activity for the words *being* and *I've*.

Corrective Feedback

- If a child does not recognize the word *begins*, say the correct word and have children repeat it. Begins. *What is the word? begins*

- Have children spell the word. *b-e-g-i-n-s How do we say this word? begins*

- Have children reread all of the cards in random order.

Daily Vocabulary Boost

- Guide children to interact with Target Vocabulary by asking the following questions. Remind them to speak clearly when participating in discussion.

  Why is it important to get exercise every day?

  Have you ever had a sore throat? What did it feel like?

  Have you ever studied for something? What might happen if you overlooked doing your homework?

- Have children work together to explain *exercise, sore, studied,* and *overlooked* in their own words. Make sure children follow appropriate rules for discussion, such as listening to speakers, taking turns, and staying on topic. **ELA** SL.2.1a, L.2.6 **ELD** ELD.PI.2.1

exercise
A dog needs exercise every day. This dog wants to run fast.

Vocabulary in Context Cards 153–160

☑ **Target Vocabulary**

depended

sore

sprang

studied

gazing

hero

exercise

overlooked

Phonics

▶ SHARE OBJECTIVES

- Substitute vowel sounds in words.
- Read and sort words with *ar, or, ore* (*r*-controlled vowel syllable).
- Read on-level text with words with *or* and *ore* and High-Frequency Words.

Phonemic Awareness Warm-Up *Let's change vowel sounds in words to make new words. I'll do it first. Listen: car. Listen as I change /är/ in car to /ôr/: core. Try it with me. Say: car. What vowel sound do you hear in car?* /är/ *Change the /är/ in car to /ôr/. What is the new word?* core

Let's try some more. Change the /är/ in farm to /ôr/. form *Change the /ī/ in kite to /är/.* cart *Change the /ôr/ in store to /är/.* star *Change the /ŭ/ in chum to /är/.* charm *Change the /är/ in barn to /ē/.* bean *Change the /ī/ in sky to /är/.* scar

FORMATIVE ASSESSMENT  **RtI**

Corrective Feedback When a child mispronounces a letter-sound, highlight that letter, restate its sound, have children repeat the sound, and then guide them to blend the word. See the example below.

Decoding Error:
A child reads *horse* as *house.*

Correct the error. Say the word. *That word is horse. The letters or stand for the /ôr/ sound.*

Guide Have children repeat the word. *What is the word?* horse

Check *You read the word.* horse

Reinforce Have children continue reading the word list. Record the errors and review those words during the next lesson.

 Go to p. T494 for additional phonics support.

Read and Sort Words Display the **Picture Card** and **Word Card** for *jar.* Have children read the word aloud and identify the vowel sound /är/. Point to *ar* in the word *jar.* Review that the letters *ar* stand for the /är/ sound. Display **Picture Cards** *horse, yard, car, store, yarn, thorn, scarf,* and *fork.* Display the corresponding **Word Cards** one at a time. Ask children to name each picture and identify the matching **Word Card.** Have them read the word together and identify its vowel sound and the letters that stand for it. Then have children write the words in two lists, sorting them according to vowel sounds /är/ and /ôr/.

Next, have children work in pairs to write additional words with *ar, or,* and *ore* spellings. If children have difficulty thinking of words, suggest some or all of the following: *barnyard, anymore, shortly, forget, starfish, forty, ignore, darling, restore.* Have pairs trade lists with another set of partners and read the words aloud. **ELA** RF.2.3b, RF.2.3e

Practice Fluency

Use Instructional Routine 13 to have partners read **Decodable Reader** *My Story* with correct intonation.

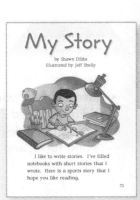

Decodable Reader

Fluency

Intonation

1 Teach/Model

Remind children that when good readers read aloud, the sound of their voice changes. A good reader's voice rises and falls in order to add interest and emphasis to the reading. End punctuation can give clues about whether a reader's voice should go up or down at the end of a sentence. A reader's voice drops slightly at the end of a telling sentence and rises at the end of a question.

Display Projectable 20.6 ⎘. As you read each sentence, model how to use intonation to add interest and emphasis to the reading. Write the first word of the sentence on the line to show the tone of your voice as you start reading. Then write each word of the sentence on or above the line to show how your voice rises and falls.

2 Guided Practice

Have children return to pp. 188–189 of *Dex: The Heart of a Hero* in the **Student Book**. Read aloud part of the text using proper intonation. Have children repeat after you.

3 Apply

Have pairs take turns reading the page to each other two or three times. Remind them to look at end punctuation to help them decide if their voices should go up or down. **ELA** RF.2.4b

Have partners use a signal—such as pointing up or down—to alert one another of places where the voice should rise or fall. Point out changes in a reader's voice help listeners to stay interested and focus on the meaning of a text.

Distribute Reader's Notebook Volume 2 page 67 ⎘ or leveled practice ⎘ in Grab-and-Go™ Resources to children to complete independently.

▶ **SHARE OBJECTIVE**

• Read fluently, changing intonation (prosody).

SMALL GROUP Options

Go to p. T495 for additional fluency support.

ENGLISH LANGUAGE SUPPORT

Intonation

Speakers of Chinese and Vietnamese may need extensive modeling and practice to adjust to the patterns of stress and intonation of English. Cantonese, Mandarin, and Vietnamese are "tonal" languages, and tonal variation is used for each individual syllable, as part of expressing its meaning. In English, syllables within a word, and words within a sentence, get different amounts of stress. In addition to explicitly teaching and modeling patterns of oral language in English, you may wish to engage students in frequent choral readings, repeated readings, and partner reading activities.

Cold Reads: Support for fluent reading and comprehension

Independent Reading

- Read and comprehend literature.
- Ask and answer questions about what you read.
- Use evidence from the text to answer questions and support opinions. LANGUAGE
- Read independently from a "just right" book.

ENGLISH LANGUAGE SUPPORT

Review Key Ideas

Emerging Ask children *yes/no* questions about the selection. **ELD** ELD.PI.2.6

Expanding Ask children some details about the story, such as, *What did Dex do to become a hero?* and *How did Dex get Cleevis out of the tree?* **ELD** ELD.PI.2.6

Bridging Have children summarize the selection, discussing what they learn at the end of the story. **ELD** ELD.PI.2.6

Reader's Guide

Revisit the Anchor Text Lead children in a brief discussion about *Dex: The Heart of a Hero*. Have them retell important events in order and describe Dex. Ask children to summarize what the story is about. Remind children to be respectful when they are waiting for their turn to speak, to listen with care when others are speaking, and to speak one at a time. **ELA** RL.2.2, SL.2.1a **ELD** ELD.PI.2.1, ELD.PI.2.6, ELD.PI.2.12a

Have children read *Dex: The Heart of a Hero* on their own. Then distribute 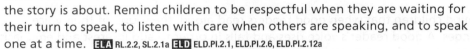 Reader's Notebook Volume 2 pages 68–69 ⬀ and have children complete them independently. **ELA** RL.2.1, RL.2.7 **ELD** ELD.PI.2.6

Model Questioning Demonstrate generating a question about *Dex: The Heart of a Hero*. For example: *How does Dex feel about his hero suit?* Reread **Student Book** p. 175 with children, and look at the illustrations together to respond to the question. **ELA** RL.2.1 **ELD** ELD.PI.2.6

Generate Questions Have children generate questions about *Dex: The Heart of a Hero*. Ask children to share their questions. Begin a class discussion of questions that children have in common or that are most significant to their understanding of the story. Remind students to build on others' talk in conversations by linking comments, and to use complete sentences when providing detail or clarification. **ELA** RL.2.1, SL.2.1a, SL.2.1b, SL.2.1c, SL.2.6 **ELD** ELD.PI.2.1, ELD.PI.2.6

Self-Selected Reading

Genres of Interest Tell children that one way to choose a book is to think about a kind of book, or a genre, that they enjoy. Discuss the following points:

- Ask yourself whether you want to read a book with information and facts about a topic, or whether you want to read something made up.

- *Dex: The Heart of a Hero* is a fantasy story. If you enjoyed this story, think about selecting a book from the fantasy genre.

- There are many genres; there are biographies, histories, graphic novels, plays, and picture books. Can you think of any others?

- Find information about the genre on the jacket of the book.

Tell children that once they have selected a book, they should open the book and read one or two pages to be sure it is "just right." If not, they can choose another book within their genre of interest. **ELA** RL.2.10, RI.2.10

Self-Correction Strategies

Read for Fluency and Intonation Tell children that as they read their self-selected books, they should pay attention to reading in the same way they speak, with intonation. Model intonation by reading aloud the first page of *Dex: The Heart of a Hero*. Call attention to how your voice rises and falls, and how this intonation makes your reading sound like speaking. Have children echo-read with you, echoing your intonation. Then do a choral reading of the same page.

As a class, discuss how punctuation helps us know whether our voice should go up or down at the end of a sentence. Make sure they know that our voices go up at the end when we are asking a question, and go down at the end when we are making a statement.

Have partners practice reading aloud to each other from their self-selected books. Have them practice reading the way they speak, with intonation. Remind them to reread to improve their accuracy, rate, and expression, as well as their understanding. **ELA** RF.2.4a, RF.2.4b

Apply Vocabulary Knowledge

- Use words and phrases acquired through conversations, reading and being read to, and responding to texts. LANGUAGE
- Identify real-life connections between words and their use. LANGUAGE
- Use example sentences in a dictionary. LANGUAGE

ENGLISH LANGUAGE SUPPORT

Access Prior Knowledge

Emerging Have children tell about a time they overlooked something and what they did to solve the situation. They can use the sentence frame *Once, I overlooked my _____. I had to _____.*

Expanding Have partners talk about a person they consider a hero or heroine. Have them explain why they admire that person so much. **ELD** ELD.PI.2.1

Bridging Have children talk about different times they have studied hard for something. What did they do to study? **ELD** ELD.PI.2.1, ELD.PI.2.12a

☑ Review Target Vocabulary

Review with children the Vocabulary in Context Cards on **Student Book** pp. 162–163. Call on children to read the context sentences and explain how the photograph demonstrates the meaning of the word.

Enrich Vocabulary Write the following Related Words on the board. Read each word aloud, and have children repeat after you. Then read the child-friendly explanation for each word. Connect each word's meaning to the story *Dex: The Heart of a Hero* by writing the context sentences on the board and reading them aloud. **ELA** L.2.5a

antics: Antics are playful acts. *Cleevis's antics did not distract Dex from his goal.*

heroics: Things a character does that are like things a superhero would do. *Dex's heroics saved Cleevis from the tree.*

purpose: A big goal to carry out. *Dex exercised to help himself achieve his purpose of becoming a hero.*

fantastic: Something fantastic seems like it must have been made up by someone's imagination. *Dex's superhero moves were fantastic!*

Make Connections Discuss all of the words using the items below to help children make connections between vocabulary words and their use. **ELA** L.2.5a **ELD** ELD.PI.2.1, ELD.PI.2.12a, ELD.PI.2.12b

- Tell about a time you **depended** on someone else for help.
- What types of **antics** make you laugh?
- What is the **purpose** of education?
- If you **overlooked** your lunch when you left for school today, what could you do?
- What subjects have you **studied** in school?
- Show me **gazing**, then show me staring.
- Why is it important to **exercise**?
- Tell about a time your muscles felt **sore**.
- Describe a time you **sprang** into action.
- What **heroics** have you seen or heard about?
- What could make you feel **fantastic**?
- Tell about a person you think is a **hero**.

Cumulative Review Randomly distribute Vocabulary in Context Cards 121–160 evenly to partners or small groups. Have one child in each group choose a card and read aloud the Target Vocabulary word. Then have the other children explain or describe its meaning. As time allows, have groups exchange sets of cards and repeat the process. **ELA** L.2.5a

Dictionary Skills

Discuss Example Sentences Use a beginning dictionary to discuss example sentences.

Ask children to show the location of example sentences as part of a definition. Ask children to tell about the punctuation and style that makes an example sentence stand out, such as italic print.

Have partners work together and take turns looking up the new words *heroics*, *antics*, *purpose*, and *fantastic*. Ask children to read the example sentences. Discuss how the example sentences add to your understanding of the meaning of the word. If children use more than one source, compare the example sentences and phrases they discover. **ELA** SL.2.1a, L.2.4e **ELD** ELD.PI.2.1

QUICKWRITE Read aloud each question below. Pause a few minutes between each item to allow children to write a response. **ELA** L.2.6

1. What are some examples of everyday **heroics**?

2. What are some **antics** that are better done outside than inside?

3. What is a **purpose** that gets you out of bed each morning?

4. How might a **fantastic** day begin?

ENGLISH LANGUAGE SUPPORT Write the following sentence frames on the board to support children in writing: *Two examples of everyday heroics are _____ and _____. Some antics that are better done outside than inside are _____ and _____. One purpose I have for getting out of bed each morning is _____. A fantastic day would begin by _____.* Read the sentence frames aloud with children. Ask them to write to complete the sentences. **ELD** ELD.PI.2.10

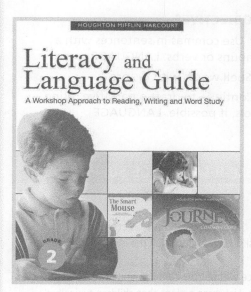

HOUGHTON MIFFLIN HARCOURT

Literacy and Language Guide

A Workshop Approach to Reading, Writing and Word Study

The Smart Mouse

JOURNEYS COMMON CORE

GRADE 2

For additional practice with the lesson's Target Vocabulary words, use the activities on pages 154–155 of the **Literacy and Language Guide.**

- Introduce Target Vocabulary; Prefix *over-*
- Word Sort
- Homophones
- Write About a Hero
- Vocabulary Web

Grammar Commas in a Series

▶ SHARE OBJECTIVES

- **Grammar** Use commas in sentences with a series of nouns or verbs. LANGUAGE
- **Spelling** Spell words with *or, ore*.
- **Writing** Continue to draft a narrative, using digital tools, if possible. LANGUAGE

ENGLISH LANGUAGE SUPPORT
Comprehensible Input

All Proficiencies List three objects children have in their desks. Have children lay the objects on their desks. Say, *You have _____, _____, and _____.* Write the sentence without the commas and have children insert them. List three actions that children typically do at recess. Say, *You (action 1), (action 2), and (action 3) at recess.* Write the sentence without the commas and have children insert them. Repeat with other series of objects and actions.

Linguistic Transfer Articles may be used in the primary language in places where they are not used in English. Children may repeat unnecessary articles when listing items in a series. For example, children may write *I like the dogs, the cats, and the rabbits* instead of *I like dogs, cats, and rabbits.* Offer practice with commas in a series of nouns. **ELD** ELD.PIII.2

1 Teach/Model

Commas in a Series Remind children that sentences can list a series of nouns or a series of verbs.

ENGLISH LANGUAGE SUPPORT Point out to children that when three or more words are listed together in a sentence, this list is called a series. Tell children that the Spanish cognate for *list* is *lista*.

- Review the placement of commas in a sentence that lists a series of nouns or verbs. Review the examples and the Thinking Questions from Day 1 and Day 2.

2 Guided Practice/Apply

- Write: *Pigs, horses, and chickens live in the barn. They eat, drink, and sleep there.*

- Point to the first sentence. *Which nouns are listed in a series?* Pigs, horses, *and* chickens *are the nouns listed in a series.*

- Point to the second sentence. *Which verbs are listed in a series?* Eat, drink, *and* sleep *are the verbs listed in a series.*

- Write the following sentences without commas and have children insert them: *The farm also has cows, goats, and ducks. Children visit to watch, feed, and pet the animals.*

- Distribute Reader's Notebook Volume 2 page 71 ⬀ to children to complete independently.

- To reinforce the concepts as needed, play the GrammarSnap Video ⬀ that supports this lesson.

Spelling Words with *or, ore*

SPELLING WORDS

BASIC

horn	born
story	tore
fork	forget
score	REVIEW
store	for
corn	more
morning*	CHALLENGE
shore	report
short	force

*A form of this word appears in the literature.

Segment Sounds

- Model segmenting sounds. *I'll say the word* store *slowly. Listen for the /ôr/ sound:* stooorrre. *Now you say it with me:* stooorrre.

- Repeat with *shore* and *more*. Tell children that saying sounds slowly will help them spell words.

Build Words with *or* and *ore*

- Use **Letter Cards** to model building *shore*. Have children read the word with you and begin to list the Spelling Words.

sh **ore**

- Have partners use **Letter Cards** to build words with *or/ore* and add each word to their lists.

- Have partners read and spell words they built using **Letter Cards**.

- Distribute Reader's Notebook Volume 2 page 70 ⬀ to children to complete independently. **ELA** L.2.2d

Word Hunt

For additional practice with the Spelling Words, have children complete the Word Hunt activity on page 95 of the **Literacy and Language Guide.**

Narrative Writing Draft

1 Teach/Model

Fictional Story: Strong Endings Discuss the importance of writing a good ending to a story. Remind children that the characters in a story try to solve a problem. Explain that a good ending tells how the problem is solved and ties together all the story events in a satisfying way.

- Reread and discuss the ending in *Dex: The Heart of a Hero* on **Student Book** pp. 186–189.

- *What does the ending say about how Dexter's problem is solved?* The other dogs and animals see that Dexter is a hero. Even Cleevis, who used to make fun of him, sees that Dexter is a hero.

2 Guided Practice/Apply

- Remind children that the problem in the story is that Dexter wants to be a hero.

- Ask children to write a different ending to *Dex: The Heart of a Hero*. Possible response: *Dexter heard yelling outside. He hurried out and saw a huge bulldog was growling at Cleevis. Cleevis was so scared he stood frozen. Dexter stepped between them. Now the bulldog was growling at Dexter! Dexter growled back and showed his teeth. The bulldog spun around and ran off, with Dexter chasing him away. After that day, Cleevis never teased Dexter again.*

Drafting Have children continue to draft their stories. Remind children to make sure their stories have endings that tell how the problems are solved and that let readers know how everything worked out. Have children write two endings for their stories and decide which one is stronger. Encourage children to continue using digital media to draft their fictional narratives.

ELA W.2.3, W.2.4, W.2.6, W.2.10 **ELD** ELD.PI.2.10

Daily Proofreading Practice

story
The storey is about horses, dogs∧
                    are   store
and pigs. They is in a stoe.

my WriteSmart Have children prewrite their narrative writing task through *my*WriteSmart.

Today's Goals

Vocabulary & Oral Language
- **Vocabulary Strategies:** Prefix *over-*

☑ **TARGET VOCABULARY**

depended	gazing
sore	hero
sprang	exercise
studied	overlooked

Phonemic Awareness
- **Substitute Phonemes**

Phonics & Fluency
- **Words with** *or, ore*
- **Words with** *ar*
- **Fluency:** Intonation
- **Read Decodable Reader:** *My Story*
- **High-Frequency Words**

Text-Based Comprehension
- **Connect to the Topic**
- **Read Informational Text:** *Heroes Then and Now*
- **Compare Texts**

Grammar & Writing
- **Spiral Review:** Writing Book Titles
- **Narrative Writing:** Fictional Story

Spelling
- **Words with** *or, ore*

Opening Routines

Warm Up with Wordplay

Using New Vocabulary

Write the following Related Words from p. T456 on the board: *antics, heroics, purpose, fantastic*. Have children read them with you and explain the definitions.

Display the sentence frames below and underline the vocabulary words. Have children read them with you.

> **One of my cat's <u>antics</u> is _____.**
> **The firefighter's <u>heroics</u> helped _____.**
> **My <u>purpose</u> for bringing a bag of apples is _____.**
> **The class painted a <u>fantastic</u> _____.**

Have partners work together to complete each sentence frame. Then have them write a second sentence to elaborate on the event. Have children share and compare their responses with the class. **ELA** L.2.5a, L.2.6

Daily Phonemic Awareness

Substitute Phonemes

- *We are going to change a sound in a word to make a new word, and then we are going to change it again. For example, we can change the /ă/ in pat to an /är/ to make the word* part. *What word do you get when you change the /är/ in* part *to /ôr/?* port

- Model how to change the word *port* back to *part*. Then model changing the word *part* back to *pat*.

- Have children substitute vowel sounds to make changes in other words such as *shut/shirt/short* and *code/card/cord*.

Corrective Feedback

- If a child is unable to make a substitution, provide correction and model the task. Example: *Listen to this word: pat. Change the /ă/ to /är/. What is the new word? part Now change the /är/ to /ôr/. What is the new word? port*

- Have children repeat once with you before doing the activity on their own.

Daily High-Frequency Words

- Point to **High-Frequency Word Card 195**, *stood*.

- *Say the word. stood Spell the word. s-t-o-o-d Write the word. Check the word.*

- Repeat the procedure with the words *begins, being, flower, ground, I've, laugh, ready, tall,* and *very.* **ELA** RF.2.3f

Let's Cheer!

- Have children find the word card for *stood*. Tell them they are going to say a cheer by spelling the word.

- Ask children to repeat each letter after you say it. *Give me an S! S!* and so on. *What does it spell? stood!*

Corrective Feedback

- If a child does not recognize the word *flower*, say the correct word and have children repeat it. *Flower. What is the word? flower*

- Have children spell the word. *f-l-o-w-e-r How do we say this word? flower*

- Have children reread all of the cards in random order.

Daily Vocabulary Boost

- Guide children to interact with Target Vocabulary using the following questions.

  Jacob sprang from his chair. Name some things that might have caused Jacob to do this.

  What are some words that describe a hero?

  How is gazing different from peeking?

- Have children work together to explain *sprang, hero,* and *gazing* in their own words. Make sure children follow appropriate rules for discussion, such as listening to speakers, taking turns, and staying on topic. **ELA** SL.2.1a, L.2.6 **ELD** ELD.PI.2.1

sprang
The cat saw the food. She sprang toward her dish.

Vocabulary in Context Cards 153–160

☑ **Target Vocabulary**

depended

sore

sprang

studied

gazing

hero

exercise

overlooked

Phonics

▶ **SHARE OBJECTIVES**

- Blend, build, and decode regularly spelled words with *or, ore* (r-controlled vowel syllable).
- Review and sort words with *ar, or,* and *ore*.

▶ **SKILLS TRACE**

Words with *or, ore*	
Introduce	pp. T416–T417, T442–T443
Differentiate	pp. T488–T489, T494
Reteach	p. T502
▶ Review	pp. T452, T462–T463; Unit 5 T63
Assess	Weekly Tests, Lesson 20

ENGLISH LANGUAGE SUPPORT

Use Visuals and Gestures

All Proficiencies Preteach the meanings of words in the Make and Read Words activity. Display **Picture Cards** *(fork, horse, store)* and photographs or illustrations *(corn, sport, shore)*. For *north,* show a map with a compass rose as you point toward the north. Say each word and have children echo you. Then ask children to demonstrate understanding by using the words to complete sentences such as the following: *Something good to eat is _____. A cowboy rides a _____. I can buy many things at the _____.*

Review Words with *or, ore*

Phonemic Awareness Warm-Up Have children listen for the sound /ôr/ as you say pairs of words. Tell them to hold up one finger if they hear /ôr/ in the first word of each pair or two fingers if they hear /ôr/ in the second word. *I'll do it first. Listen: porch/peach. I hear /ôr/ in the first word, porch, so I'll hold up one finger.*

Now you do it. Listen to each pair of words and hold up one or two fingers to show which word has the /ôr/ sound: form/fame, *one finger;* snow/snore, *two fingers;* hose/horse, *two fingers;* born/bean, *one finger;* then/thorn, *two fingers.*

Make and Read Words On the board, write the incomplete words as shown below. Then read each clue aloud. After each clue is read, call on individuals to answer the riddle by adding *or* or *ore* to the incomplete word on the board.

The Clues to Read Are:

1. This is a yellow food.

2. Baseball is this kind of activity.

3. This is the opposite of *less*.

4. You can eat with this.

5. You can shop here.

6. This animal may live on a farm.

7. This is where the sea and land meet.

8. This is the opposite of *south*.

Have children read aloud the words they made. Use the **Corrective Feedback** steps if children need additional help. **ELA** RF.2.3e, L.2.2d

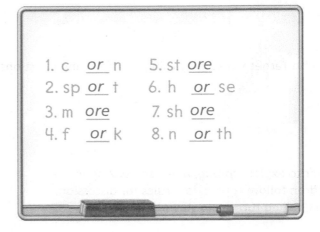

1. c _or_ n   5. st _ore_
2. sp _or_ t   6. h _or_ se
3. m _ore_   7. sh _ore_
4. f _or_ k   8. n _or_ th

Cumulative Review

Phonemic Awareness Warm-Up *Let's change the vowel sounds in words to make new words. I'll do it first. Listen: stay. Now listen as I change /ā/ in stay to /ôr/:* store. *Now you do it. Change /är/ in car to /ôr/.* core *Change /ŭ/ in bun to /är/.* barn *Change /ē/ in steam to /ôr/.* storm *Change /ā/ in make to /är/.* mark

Group Words by Sound

Display **Sound/Spelling Cards** *artist* and *orange*. Name each picture and its vowel sound. Review the *ar* spelling for /är/ and the *or* and *ore* spellings for /ôr/.

Make a two-column chart on the board, using the two **Sound/Spelling Cards** as headings for the columns. Read aloud a series of words. Have children tell you in which column to write each word, depending on its *r*-controlled vowel sound. Use these words: *farm, garden, orbit, artist, anymore, short, score, large, corncob, target, chore, star, hornet, thorn, market, chart.*

Have children copy the completed columns and read the words aloud with partners. Tell them to underline the /är/ and /ôr/ vowel spelling as they read each word.

Corrective Feedback When a child mispronounces a word, point to the word and say it. Call attention to the element that was mispronounced, say the sound, and then guide children to read the word. See the example below.

Decoding Error:
A child reads *shore* as *share*.

Correct the error. *The letters* ore *spell the vowel sound /ôr/ at the end of* shore.

Model the correct sound/spelling as you write the word. *What's the vowel sound in* shore? */ôr/ The letters* ore *usually spell the sound /ôr/ at the end of a word. The letters* ore *spell the sound /ôr/ in* shore.

Guide *What's the vowel sound in* shore? *Say it with me: /ôr/. Say the word with me:* shore.

Check *Say the vowel sound in* shore. */ôr/ Now say the word.* shore

Reinforce Go back to the beginning of the list on the board and reread the words. Make note of errors and review those words in future lessons.

Practice Fluency

Use <u>Instructional Routine 15</u> ⬈ to have partners read **Decodable Reader** *My Story*. Remind children to use proper intonation as they read.

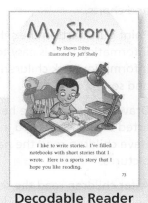

Decodable Reader

Lesson 20

INFORMATIONAL TEXT

☑ **GENRE**

Informational text gives facts about a topic.

☑ **TEXT FOCUS**

A **chart** is a drawing that lists information in a clear way.

HEROES Then and Now

What makes a hero? A hero does something brave or works hard to help others. A hero doesn't give up when things are hard.

Heroes come from different backgrounds and different places. They can be young or old. All heroes are important people, whether they lived in the past or do good deeds today.

Then → Now

These heroes reached for the stars.

Amelia Earhart	Ellen Ochoa
Amelia Earhart became the first woman pilot to fly across the Atlantic Ocean.	Ellen Ochoa became the first Hispanic woman to travel in space.
Amelia studied hard before flying. She spent time with other pilots, gazing at maps and weather charts.	Exercise is important to prepare for space flights. Ellen exercises until her muscles are sore.

194 **ELA** RI.2.7, RI.2.10 **ELD** ELD.PI.2.6

195

🔵 **DOMAIN: Civics**

LESSON TOPIC: What Heroes Do

Cross-Curricular Connection Have children discuss and evaluate the contributions of the four people highlighted in *Heroes Then and Now*. Help them recognize the different ways in which all the contributions are important.

FOR STANDARD ENGLISH LEARNERS

Some children may need help mastering Standard English pronunciations when speaking in a more formal register. Children may have trouble voicing the final /s/ in plurals such as *cents* or *tests*. They may omit the /s/ sound completely. Write this sentence on the board: *She spent time with other pilots, gazing at maps and weather charts.* Read the sentence aloud, emphasizing the /s/ sound in *pilots, maps,* and *charts*. Have children echo your reading several times.

Connect to the Topic: Informational Text

Introduce Genre and Text Focus

- Read with children the genre and text focus information on **Student Book** p. 194. Tell children that they will read an informational text that includes photographs and charts.

- Point out charts in the selection. Explain that a chart is a way to organize and show information so it is easy to understand. A chart is also helpful when comparing information. Ask children to identify the features of these charts (pictures, headings, and so on).

- Draw attention to the headings *Then* and *Now* in the charts. Explain that the heroes listed under *Then* lived in the past. The heroes listed under *Now* are living heroes. Have children read the names of the heroes and point to the corresponding pictures.

- After children read the selection, have them explain how the chart and photos helped them understand what they were reading. **ELA** RI.2.5, RI.2.7, RI.2.10

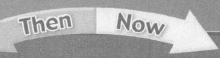

The heroes in this chart helped others.

Sacagawea	Earl Morse
Sacagawea was a Native American woman who lived over 200 years ago. She helped a group of early American explorers.	Earl Morse had an idea to honor veterans. Veterans are men and women who have been in the military. Some veterans were in the military during times of war.
Sacagawea helped the explorers find food and learn about the land. She helped them talk to Native Americans that they met.	Morse helped to start a group that helps pay for veterans to travel to Washington, D.C. There the veterans can see memorials and monuments that honor them.

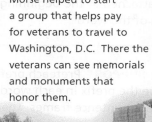

196

Compare Texts

TEXT TO TEXT

Discuss Heroes Think about Dex and the heroes in *Heroes Then and Now*. What makes them heroes? In a small group, make a poster to show your ideas. Include words and pictures. Present the poster to the class.

What Makes a Hero?

TEXT TO SELF

Share a Story Think of a time when you felt the way Dex does at the beginning of *Dex: The Heart of a Hero*. What did you do? Tell a partner.

TEXT TO WORLD

Talk About Dog Heroes What does Dex do to help the other animals? What are some ways dogs can help in your community? Share your ideas with the class.

ELA RL.2.1, RI.2.9, W.2.8 **ELD** ELD.PI.2.1, ELD.PI.2.6, ELD.PI.2.10

197

Compare Texts

TEXT TO TEXT

Discuss Heroes Have children recount the heroic things done by Dex and also the four people featured in *Heroes Then and Now*. Ask, *How are all these heroes alike?* In groups, have children make their own lists of heroic qualities shown by Dex and the people.

ELA RL.2.7, RI.2.9 **ELD** ELD.PI.2.1, ELD.PI.2.3, ELD.PI.2.11

ENGLISH LANGUAGE SUPPORT Work with children to create a chart showing each hero mentioned, what they did that was heroic, and how they became a hero. Have children pick Dex and another hero to display on their poster.

ELD ELD.PI.2.1, ELD.PI.2.3, ELD.PI.2.11

TEXT TO SELF

Share a Story Remind children that at the beginning of the story, Dex lacked confidence. Have children tell partners about the times when they had similar feelings. Suggest that they think about times when they did not know the rules of a game or were not as good at a sport as other children. After talking to their partner, have them write a paragraph about their experience. **ELA** W.2.8, SL.2.4 **ELD** ELD.PI.2.1, ELD.PI.2.12a

TEXT TO WORLD

Dog Heroes Have children name ways Dex helped other animals. Then ask, *Can real dogs do what Dex does in the story? No, because real dogs cannot speak or act like humans.* Ask children what they know about dogs that help blind people, dogs that help people with hearing problems, dogs that protect property, and dogs that provide companionship. Remind children to take turns sharing their ideas. **ELA** SL.2.1a

DAY 4

Vocabulary Strategies

▶ **SHARE OBJECTIVE**

▶ **SHARE OBJECTIVE**

- Determine the meaning of a new word with a known prefix. LANGUAGE

▶ **SKILLS TRACE**

Prefix *over-*	
Introduce	pp. T466–T467
Differentiate	pp. T500–T501
Reteach	p. T503
Assess	Weekly Tests, Lesson 20

ENGLISH LANGUAGE SUPPORT

Access Prior Knowledge

Emerging Remind children that they can make new words by adding prefixes to base words. Put together and pull apart cards saying *over-* and *sleep.*

Expanding Write additional examples of base words and words with the prefix *over-.* Use the words in context sentences. Have children repeat.

Bridging Have partners write sentences using the words *sleep, oversleep, look,* and *overlook.*
ELD ELD.PI.2.2

Prefix *over-*

1 Teach/Model

Terms About Language

prefix a word part attached at the beginning of a base word (or root word) that adds to the meaning of the word

ENGLISH LANGUAGE SUPPORT Preteach prefix *over-.* Write *overhead, overdue,* and *overcoat.* Underline the prefix in each word. Have partners work together to try to complete the following sentence frames. Then, as a class, discuss context clues in each sentence:

1. *When it's cold, I need to wear an _____. overcoat*

2. *These books are _____ at the library. overdue*

3. *I like to look at the clouds _____. overhead* **ELD** ELD.PI.2.1

- Remind children that when they see a word they don't know, they can break the word into smaller parts to try to figure out its meaning.

- Explain that a prefix is a word part that is added to the beginning of a base word (or root word). The prefix adds meaning to the base word.

- Explain that the prefix *over-* means "above" or "beyond."

- Write the following sentence on the board:

> I <u>overlooked</u> the hat that was on the shelf.

- Underline *overlooked.* Display Projectable S8. Model applying Step 2 of the strategy to understand the meaning of *overlooked.*

Think Aloud *To figure out what the word means, I can look for parts of the word that I already know. I see that* looked *is the base word (or root word). I also see that the word has the prefix* over-. *I know that* over *means "above" or "beyond." Overlooked* must mean looked above or beyond something. If I overlooked *the hat, then I looked past it and did not see it on the shelf.*

2 Guided Practice

- Display the top half of Projectable 20.7 and read the first sentence aloud.

- Have children identify words with the prefix *over-* in each sentence. Circle the words.

- Then display the chart on the bottom half of **Projectable 20.7**.

- Help children identify the base word (or root word) and prefix in each word, and use their answers to fill in the chart.

3 Apply

- Have children apply Steps 1 and 2 of the **Vocabulary Strategy** to determine the meaning of each circled word on the Projectable. Have them explain how they used the meanings of the prefixes and the base words to figure out the meanings of the circled words. **ELA** L.2.4b

ENGLISH LANGUAGE SUPPORT Write these frames on the board, and help children use them to participate: *The prefix ___ means ___. I think the word ___ means ___ because ___.*

- Have children use a dictionary to confirm the definitions of any words that are still confusing.

- Distribute Reader's Notebook Volume 2 page 72 or leveled practice in Grab-and-Go™ Resources to children to complete independently.

Interactive Whiteboard Lesson Use **Vocabulary Strategies: Prefix over-** to use knowledge of word parts and the prefix *over-* to determine the meanings of unfamiliar words. **ELA** L.2.4b

FOR STUDENTS WITH DISABILITIES To help children who have difficulty transitioning, signal the transitions ahead of time, while reminding children of expected behaviors. For example, "It's time to stop and get ready for lunch. Please finish working, put away materials, and line up."

FORMATIVE ASSESSMENT △ RtI

Are children able to read and understand words with the prefix over-?

IF...	THEN...
children struggle,	▲ use **Differentiate Vocabulary Strategies** for Struggling Readers, p. T500.
children are on track,	▲ use **Differentiate Vocabulary Strategies** for On-Level Readers, p. T500.
children excel,	▲ use **Differentiate Vocabulary Strategies** for Advanced Readers, p. T501.

 Differentiate Vocabulary Strategies: pp. T500–T501
Scaffold instruction to the English learner's proficiency level.

Grammar Spiral Review: Writing Book Titles

▶ SHARE OBJECTIVES

- **Grammar** Review how to capitalize and underline book titles correctly. LANGUAGE
- **Spelling** Spell words with *or, ore*.
- **Handwriting** Write Spelling Words.
- **Writing** Use digital tools to finish drafting and begin to revise a narrative. LANGUAGE

ENGLISH LANGUAGE SUPPORT

Access Prior Knowledge

All Proficiencies Have children find books in the classroom and read the titles aloud. Write the titles on the board using lowercase letters. Have children compare the titles you wrote with the titles on their books. Ask, *What is different about the way I wrote the title?* Model how to capitalize the words in one book title. Then underline the title. Have children repeat with other titles.

1 Teach/Model

Writing Book Titles Ask children to name some favorite books. Write the titles on the board. Then review these rules for writing book titles.

- The first word, the last word, and each important word in a title begin with a capital letter.

- The title is underlined.

- Short words like *a, an, and, the, in, of, for,* and *at* do not begin with a capital letter unless one of these words is the first word or the last word in the title.

ENGLISH LANGUAGE SUPPORT Hold up several books. Have children point out the titles and say which words have capital letters.

2 Guided Practice/Apply

Write these sentences on the board. Work with children to write the titles correctly.

1. **My teacher read aloud green eggs and ham.** *Green Eggs and Ham*

2. **Then she read from a book called silly jokes.** *Silly Jokes*

3. **My favorite book is firefighter heroes.** *Firefighter Heroes*

4. **My brother likes to read frog and toad.** *Frog and Toad*

- Distribute Reader's Notebook Volume 2 page 74 [and have children complete it independently.

Spelling Words with *or, ore*

SPELLING WORDS

BASIC

horn	born
story	tore
fork	forget
score	**REVIEW**
store	for
corn	more
morning*	**CHALLENGE**
shore	report
short	force

*A form of this word appears in the literature.

Connect to Writing

- Ask children to use the Spelling Words to write a few sentences about a hero.

- Have them proofread their sentences. Then invite volunteers to read their sentences aloud.

- Finally, have the class practice the Spelling Words. Say each word and spell it aloud together.

- Distribute Reader's Notebook Volume 2 p. 73 [to children to complete independently. **ELA** L.2.2d

Handwriting

Model how to form the Basic Words *morning, shore, short, born, tore,* and *forget*. Handwriting models are available on pp. R24–R29 and on the Handwriting Models Blackline Masters [. Remind children to write legibly and stay within the margins. **ELA** L.2.1g

Blind Writing Sort

For additional practice with the Spelling Words, have children complete the Blind Writing Sort activity on page 95 of the **Literacy and Language Guide. ELA** L.2.2d

Narrative Writing Draft and Revise

1 Teach/Model

Fictional Story: Time-Order Words Remind children that stories have a beginning, middle, and end. Explain that good writers use time-order words that tell the order in which story events happen. Time-order words, such as *early, late, next,* and *morning*, make a story easier to understand.

Connect to Dex: *The Heart of a Hero*	
Without Time-Order Words	**With Time-Order Words**
Cleevis asked Dexter if they could be partners.	The next day, Cleevis asked Dexter if they could be partners.

- *What time-order words did the writer add?* The next day
- *How do the time-order words help you understand the events?* The words make it clear when Cleevis asked Dexter if they could be partners.

2 Guided Practice/Apply

- Write: *Curly the dog set out on his journey. He arrived at a little cabin.*

- Ask children to suggest time-order words to show when the events happen. Possible response: *Early in the morning, Curly the dog set out on his journey. In the afternoon, he arrived at a little cabin.*

Drafting Have children finish drafting their stories. Remind them to go back into their word processing document to be sure they've added time-order words in their stories that make the order of events clear to readers. Have children check and correct any spelling mistakes using either a print or digital dictionary.

Writing Conference Distribute **Writing Conference Form**. Have partners hold writing conferences using this page as a guide. Then have them begin revising their word processed document to include the changes made during the conference. Guide children to find, copy, and paste artwork, such as clip art, borders, or photos, to enhance their writing.

ELA W.2.3, W.2.4, W.2.5, W.2.6, W.2.10, L.2.2e **ELD** ELD.PI.2.10, ELD.PII.2.1

Daily Proofreading Practice

This ~~morening~~ morning I danced, played∧and

read. The ~~storey~~ story was about a lion,∧

tiger, and elephant.

ENGLISH LANGUAGE SUPPORT

Peer-Supported Learning

All Proficiencies Have children work with partners to make sure they have used time-order transition words. Have partners circle words that show time-order and suggest places where they could be added to guide understanding for the reader.
ELD ELD.PII.2.2

---

myWriteSmart Have children draft their narrative writing task through *my*WriteSmart.

DAY 5

Today's Goals

Vocabulary & Oral Language
- Domain-Specific Vocabulary
- Speaking & Listening

✓ TARGET VOCABULARY

depended	gazing
sore	hero
sprang	exercise
studied	overlooked

Phonemic Awareness
- Substitute Phonemes

Phonics & Fluency
- Interactive Whiteboard Lesson
- High-Frequency Words

Text-Based Comprehension
- Extend the Topic
- Speaking and Listening: Compare and Contrast

Assess & Reteach
- Assess Skills
- Respond to Assessment

Grammar & Writing
- Commas in a Series
- Narrative Writing: Fictional Story

Spelling
- Words with *or, ore*

Warm Up with Wordplay

Who Am I?

Tell children that Dexter the dog wore a superhero outfit with a *D* on it. Have children answer each of the following riddles with a word that rhymes with *D*.

Display and read aloud the following sentences:

> I cost nothing.
> I'm fun to climb.
> I'm something you can't do in the dark.
> I'm a kind of shirt.
> I live in a hive.
> I'm somewhere between your hip and your foot.

Have partners come up with other words in the *-ee* word family. Then have them list words that rhyme with the letter *D*.

Interactive Whiteboard Lesson

For cumulative review, use **Phonics: Words with *or, ore*** to reinforce blending, reading, and building decodable words with *or* and *ore*. Emphasize in writing. **ELA** L.2.2d

Daily Phonemic Awareness

Substitute Phonemes

- *We are going to change one sound in a word to make a new word.*

- *Say* shot. *We can change the /ŏ/ sound in shot to /ôr/ to make a new word,* short.

- Have children continue with the words from the chart.

Change the...	Result
/ō/ in coat to /ôr/	court
/ûr/ in burn to /ôr/	born
/ŏ/ in spot to /ôr/	*sport*
/är/ in far to /ôr/	*for*
/âr/ in wear to /ôr/	*wore*

Corrective Feedback

- If a child is unable to make a substitution, say the word, give correction, and model the task. Example: *The word is* coat. *I can change the /ō/ sound in* coat *to /ôr/ and make a new word,* court.

- Have children repeat the first few words with you. Then have them continue on their own.

Daily High-Frequency Words

- Point to **High-Frequency Word Card 196**, *very*.

- *Say the word.* very *Spell the word.* v-e-r-y *Write the word. Check the word.*

- Repeat the procedure with the words from this week: *being, flower, laugh*, ready, *tall* and last week *baby, didn't, good, I'll, please.* **ELA** RF.2.3f

Word Box

- Write this week's and last week's High-Frequency Words on multiple slips of paper. Place the papers in a box.

- Have children take turns choosing a paper from the box and reading the word.

- Continue until all the papers have been read.

Corrective Feedback

- If a child does not recognize the word *laugh*, say the correct word and have children repeat it. *Laugh. What is the word?* laugh

- Have children spell the word. *l-a-u-g-h How do we say this word?* laugh

- Have children reread all of the cards in random order.

Daily Vocabulary Boost

- Reread "Ordinary Heroes" aloud to children (pp. T414–T415).

- As you read each Target Vocabulary word in the selection, pause to have a child explain or describe its meaning.

- After reading, review the Target Vocabulary and their definitions. (See p. T414.) Challenge children to use the words in their everyday speech. **ELA** L.2.6 **ELD** ELD.PI.2.5

overlooked
They overlooked, or didn't see, where the dog was hiding.

Vocabulary in Context Cards 153–160

☑ **Target Vocabulary**

depended
sore
sprang
studied
gazing
hero
exercise
overlooked

DAY 5

DOMAIN: **Civics**

LESSON TOPIC: **What Heroes Do**

Extend the Topic

▶ SHARE OBJECTIVES

- Acquire and use domain-specific vocabulary. LANGUAGE
- Participate in conversations about a topic. LANGUAGE
- Describe how characters respond to events and challenges.
- Recount or describe key ideas or details from texts or other media.

Words About the Topic: What Heroes Do

- **charity** an organization that helps people in need
- **grant** to give or to allow
- **improve** to get better
- **figure** to work something out

Domain-Specific Vocabulary

Introduce Words About the Topic. Remind children that this week's topic is What Heroes Do. Display the words shown at left. Tell children that these are words that can help them learn more about the topic. Read aloud the meaning of each word, and have children respond to the following prompts. **ELA** L.2.5a, L.2.6

- *Can you name any charities? What do they do?* Children may know charities such as the Red Cross, which helps sick and injured people around the world.

- *When you do something for someone that they want you to do, you _____ them a favor.* grant

- *If someone helps your life improve, what do they do?* They make it better.

- *What do you do when you add numbers?* You figure out the sum.

ENGLISH LANGUAGE SUPPORT Guide children to interact with the words by discussing as a class questions such as these: *If you were in charge of a charity, what service would you provide? If you were granted one wish, what would it be? What subject area have you improved in, and how did you improve? Who would be more likely to figure out a solution: a newborn baby or a second-grader?*
ELD ELD.PI.2.1, ELD.PI.2.12a

Interact with the Words Have children work in small groups to create a Four-Square Map for each of the domain-specific words. For each of the domain-specific words, children should fold a blank sheet of paper into four equal sections. Work with them to follow the steps below for each word. As needed, display the meanings of the words on the board. Ask individual children to use the words in a sentence orally. Then write the sentence on the board for other children to copy.

1 In the first corner, draw a picture for the word.

2 In the second corner, write the meaning of the word.

3 In the third corner, write a sentence using the word.

4 In the fourth corner, write the word.

When groups have finished, have them share their Four-Square Maps with the class.
ELA L.2.5a, L.2.6 **ELD** ELD.PI.2.1

Speaking and Listening:
Compare and Contrast

Find Similar Characters Ask children about the main character in the selection *Dex: The Heart of a Hero*. *What is special about Dex? What is his dream? How does he make his dream come true?*

Ask children if they can think of any movies in which the main character is or becomes a hero. Remind children to only discuss movies and characters that are age-appropriate. Put the names of the characters on the board. Add other names of movie heroes. Note that they can be superheroes or regular people who act in a heroic way. The movies can be animated or not. **ELD** ELD.PI.2.12a

FOR STUDENTS WITH DISABILITIES To help children listen effectively to instruction or to a discussion, create a graphic organizer that is pertinent to the instruction. Focus on key traits from *Dex: The Heart of a Hero* that would be ideal for comparing and contrasting. Distribute the graphic organizer and go over it before the activity begins. Stop the activity frequently to allow children time to fill in the organizer with additional traits based on the classroom discussion.

Compare and Contrast Characters Divide the class into groups based on movie characters that each child has seen or heard about. Explain that each group is going to compare and contrast how their movie character and Dex each reacted to an emergency.

Remind children how to use a Venn diagram. Display the Tips for Comparing and Contrasting and read them with children. Tell children to be sure they are comparing how the two characters reacted to an emergency, not how they look or dress. It will be necessary to review and recount some details of what happens in the movie and in *Dex: The Heart of a Hero* with children.

After the groups have completed their Venn diagrams, revisit the Tips for Comparing and Contrasting. Tell children that they will use their Venn diagrams and the example words from the tips chart to write a few sentences that compare and contrast the characters. **ELA** RL.2.3

Share with the Class Have each group share its comparison sentences with the class. Remind them to speak loudly and clearly and to answer any questions that classmates have in complete sentences. **ELA** SL.2.1c, SL.2.2, SL.2.3, SL.2.6 **ELD** ELD.PI.2.1

TIPS FOR COMPARING AND CONTRASTING

1. **Compare: Show how the two are alike. Words for comparing:** *like, alike, the same as, similar, equal,* and.

2. **Contrast: Show how the two are different. Words for contrasting:** *different, unlike, more (less) than, on the other hand, but.*

ENGLISH LANGUAGE SUPPORT

Use Sentence Frames

All Proficiencies Encourage children to think more about traits that are viewed as heroic. Have them fill out the following sentence frames.

I think Dex's most heroic trait is _____.

I also like that Dex _____.

A person I admire in real life is _____, because he/she _____.

I think one of my best character traits is _____.

ELD ELD.PI.2.3, ELD.PI.2.11, ELD.PI.2.12a

Grammar Weekly Review: Commas in a Series

▶ SHARE OBJECTIVES

- **Grammar** Use commas in sentences with a series of nouns or verbs. LANGUAGE
- **Spelling** Assess words with *or, ore*.

ENGLISH LANGUAGE SUPPORT

How English Works: Productive

Commas in a Series Write an assortment of verbs on slips of paper, such as *walk, jump, run, sing, read, dance, play, fly, spin,* and *hop*. Place the slips in different bags. Organize children into mixed-proficiency small groups and give one bag to each group. Have children draw verbs from the bags and work together to write sentences using three of the verbs in a series. Call on groups to share their sentences. **ELD** ELD.PII.2.3a

1 Review/Practice

Commas in a Series Read together the text on **Student Book** p. 198. Review with children where to put commas in sentences that list nouns or verbs in a series.

- *When you list three or more nouns, use a comma after each noun. Also use commas with three or more verbs.*
- *The word and goes before the last noun or verb in a series. The last noun or verb does not need a comma after it.*
- Read and discuss the examples in the chart.
- Direct children's attention to the Try This! activity at the bottom of the page. Support children as they insert commas.

2 Connect to Writing

- Read and discuss **Student Book** p. 199. Remind children that they can combine short, choppy sentences to make their writing smoother.
- Read and discuss the examples and the illustrations.
- Together, read the directions for Connect Grammar to Writing ⬀ at the bottom of the page. Support children as they combine sentences. Remind them to use commas correctly.
- Distribute Reader's Notebook Volume 2 page 75 ⬀ to children to complete independently. **ELA** W.2.5 **ELD** ELD.PII.2.6

Spelling Words with *or, ore*

SPELLING WORDS AND SENTENCES

BASIC

1. **horn** The car *horn* is loud.
2. **story** We read a *story* every night.
3. **fork** You use a *fork* to eat.
4. **score** What is the game's *score*?
5. **store** Dad buys food at the *store*.
6. **corn** I like to eat *corn* on the cob.
7. **morning*** We eat breakfast every *morning*.
8. **shore** Waves roll onto the *shore*.
9. **short** *Short* is the opposite of tall.

10. **born** I was *born* on July 26.
11. **tore** I *tore* my pants when I fell down.
12. **forget** Don't *forget* to walk the dog.

REVIEW

13. **for** I bought gifts *for* my friends.
14. **more** We have *more* than we need.

CHALLENGE

15. **report** I wrote a book *report*.
16. **force** The *force* of the storm was strong.

*A form of this word appears in the literature.

Assess

Say each Spelling Word, read aloud its sentence, and then repeat the word. Have children write the word. **ELA** L.2.2d

Corrective Feedback

Review any words that children misspell. If children misspell two or more words, then revisit the Day 2 Open Sort activity on page 94 of the **Literacy and Language Guide.**

Grammar

Commas in a Series When there are three or more **nouns** in a sentence, separate them with **commas** and the word *and*. Also use commas and the word *and* when there are three or more **verbs** in a sentence.

Series of Nouns	Series of Verbs
The dogs, cats, and birds saw Dex.	He jumped, hopped, and climbed.
My sister, my brother, and I want to be heroes.	We stretch, flex, and train our muscles.

Try This! Read the sentences aloud with a partner. Tell where to add commas to make the sentences correct. Then write the sentences correctly.

❶ The cat scratched howled and hissed.

❷ Dex helped boys girls and animals.

❸ He studied ran and practiced.

198   ELA L.2.1f   ELD ELD.PII.2.6

Short, choppy sentences can be combined. This will make your writing smoother.

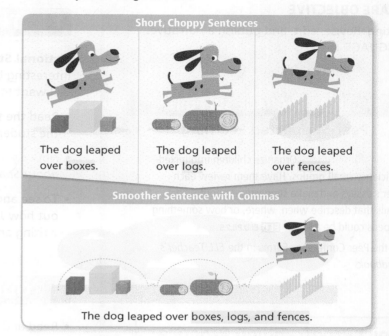

Short, Choppy Sentences

The dog leaped over boxes.

The dog leaped over logs.

The dog leaped over fences.

Smoother Sentence with Commas

The dog leaped over boxes, logs, and fences.

Connect Grammar to Writing

When you revise your story, try combining some short sentences.

199

Try This!

1. The cat scratched,
   howled, and hissed.

2. Dex helped boys, girls,
   and animals.

3. He studied, ran, and
   practiced.

Narrative Writing Revise, Edit, Publish

▶ **SHARE OBJECTIVE**

- **Writing** Revise, edit, and publish a narrative. LANGUAGE

ENGLISH LANGUAGE SUPPORT
Peer-Supported Learning

All Proficiencies Organize children into mixed-proficiency small groups. Have them review each other's essays and make suggestions about where details that describe when, where, or how something happens could be added. **ELD** ELD.PII.2.5

See the Peer Conference Forms in the *ELL Teacher's Handbook*.

Daily Proofreading Practice

A squirrel was ~~bourn~~ born last spring. He rests on branchs, fences, decks, and roofs.

✓my WriteSmart Have children revise, proofread, and publish their narrative writing task through *my*WriteSmart.

1 Teach/Model

Fictional Story: Organization Remind children that a good story starts with an interesting beginning. They should start by telling something interesting so readers will want to keep reading.

- Read the top of **Student Book** p. 200 with the class. Discuss the revisions made by the student writer, Julie.

- *How do Julie's revisions make the beginning more interesting? She tells more about Sparky. She tells us about something only Sparky knows.*

- To see and discuss more revisions made by Julie, display Projectable 20.8 ⌐. Point out how Julie applied these revising skills: making the beginning more interesting, writing an ending that tells how the problem was solved, and adding details.

2 Guided Practice/Apply

- Read and discuss Julie's Final Copy on **Student Book** p. 201.

- Discuss the Reading as a Writer questions.

Revising Have children use the Writing Rubric Blackline Master ⌐ to evaluate their stories.

Proofreading For proofreading support, have the children use the Proofreading Checklist Blackline Master ⌐. Remind children to use a print or digital dictionary to check and correct spelling.

Handwriting If you have children write their final pieces rather than use digital tools, tell them to focus on using their best handwriting. *See also pp. R24–R29 for handwriting support.*

Publishing Have children make a neat final copy either in print or electronically and share their writing.

Present Have children read their stories to the class. Remind listeners to follow discussion rules.

- See Giving Presentations Rubric on p. R22.

ENGLISH LANGUAGE SUPPORT Before children present their stories, provide practice with correct English pronunciation. Hold one-on-one conferences with children to help them with pronunciation and reading fluency. Once children master the pronunciation of the words and are ready to present, tell them to

- look at the audience

- speak slowly, clearly, and loudly

ELA W.2.3, W.2.4, W.2.5, W.2.6, W.2.10, SL.2.1a, SL.2.4a, L.2.2e **ELD** ELD.PI.2.9, ELD.PI.2.10, ELD.PII.2.1, ELD.PII.2.2

Reading-Writing Workshop: Revise

Narrative Writing *my WriteSmart*

☑ **Organization** A good **story** starts with a strong beginning. If the beginning of your story is interesting, it makes your readers want to read more.

Julie wrote a draft of a story about a girl and her special pet. Later, she revised the story's beginning.

Writing Process Checklist

Prewrite

Draft

▶ Revise

☑ Does my story have a beginning, middle, and end?

☑ Does the beginning make the reader want to read more?

☑ Did I include interesting details?

☑ Did I tell how the problem is solved?

Edit

Publish and Share

Revised Draft

Layla had a pet hamster named

Sparky. Sparky was not like any

He could do something no other

other hamster. ∧ hamster could do.

Sparky was small and brown.

Layla thought he was amazing.

He knew when things were wrong.

∧

Final Copy

Sparky and the Giant

by Julie Martine

Layla had a pet hamster named Sparky. Sparky was not like any other hamster. He could do something no other hamster could do.

Sparky was small and brown. Layla thought he was amazing. He knew when things were wrong.

One day Layla and Sparky were walking in the park. Sparky started making noise and running around in Layla's pocket.

"What's up, Sparky?" Layla said as she gently patted her pocket.

Reading as a Writer

How does Julie make her beginning more interesting? How can your beginning be more interesting?

I made the beginning more interesting.

200

ELA W.2.3, W.2.4, W.2.5, W.2.10 ELD ELD.PI.2.10, ELD.PI.2.12b, ELD.PII.2.1

201

NARRATIVE WRITING RUBRIC

See also the Multipurpose Writing Rubric on p. R18.

Score	4	3	2	1	NS
Purpose/Organization	The narrative is clear and well organized. It is appropriately sequenced and has closure. • Plot contains a well-elaborated event or a short sequence of events • Setting and characters are included and well-maintained • Plot events follow a logical sequence • Includes an effective conclusion	The narrative is generally clear and organized. The sequence is adequately maintained, and the plot has closure. • Plot contains a well-elaborated event or a short sequence of events • Characters and setting are included and adequately maintained • Plot events follow an understandable sequence • Includes an adequate conclusion	The narrative is somewhat organized but may be unclear in parts. The sequence is weak. The plot lacks closure. • Minimal development of plot • Characters and setting are included but are minimally maintained • Sequence of events is poorly organized • Conclusion is inadequate or missing	The narrative's focus is unclear, and it is poorly organized. The narrative lacks sequence and has no closure. • Little or no plot • No attempt to maintain characters or setting • Sequence of events is not organized • Conclusion is missing	• not intelligible • not written in English • not on topic • contains text copied from another source • does not address the purpose for writing
Development/ Elaboration	The narrative includes effective elaboration, and details describing actions, thoughts, and feelings. • Clear effort to develop experiences, characters, setting, and events • Contains strong use of details • Writer uses temporal words to signal the order of events	The narrative includes adequate elaboration, and details describing actions, thoughts, and feelings. • Some attempt to develop experiences, characters, setting, and events • Contains adequate use of details • Contains adequate use of temporal words to signal the order of events	The narrative includes only partial or ineffective elaboration. The narrative includes some details. • Little attempt to develop experiences, characters, setting, and events • Contains weak use of details • Contains little use of temporal words. • Order of events is not clear	The narrative provides little or no elaboration and few details. • No attempt to develop experiences, characters, setting, and events • Few or no details • No use of temporal words • Order of events is confusing	• not intelligible • not written in English • not on topic • contains text copied from another source • does not develop the writing

Score	2	1	0	NS
Conventions	The narrative demonstrates adequate command of conventions. • Consistent use of complete sentences, correct sentence structures, punctuation, capitalization, grammar, spelling	The narrative demonstrates partial command of conventions. • Limited use of complete sentences, correct sentence structures, punctuation, capitalization, grammar, spelling	The narrative demonstrates little or no command of conventions. • Does not use complete sentences, correct sentence structures, punctuation, capitalization, grammar, spelling	• not intelligible • not written in English • not on topic • contains text copied from another source

Formative Assessment

Weekly Tests

At the end of the lesson, administer the Weekly Test. This will give you a **snapshot of how children are progressing** with the Reading and Language Arts skills in this lesson and can give you **guidance on grouping, reteaching, and intervention.** Suggestions for adjusting instruction based on these results can be found on the next page.

Access Through Accommodations

When you administer the Weekly Test, some children may have problems accessing all or parts of the assessment. The purpose of the Weekly Test is to determine children's ability to complete the Reading and Language Arts tasks they learned in this lesson. Any barriers to them accessing the tasks demanded of them should be lowered so they can focus on skill demonstration.

When choosing accommodations, you will want to avoid invalidating the test results if you are measuring a child's reading skill. For example, you will not want to read aloud the passage. The following accommodations, if needed, will not interfere with the Weekly Test's validity:

- Read aloud the assessment directions and item prompts. If children are English learners, read aloud the assessment directions and item prompts in the child's native language, if possible.

- Define any unknown words in the directions or item prompts that do not give away the answers to the items.

- Allow for a break during the assessment.

- Simplify the language of assessment directions and item prompts.

- Administer the assessment in a smaller group setting.

- Administer the assessment on a computer or other electronic device.

- Provide audio amplification equipment, colored overlays, or visual magnifying equipment to maintain visual/audio attention and access.

- Allow children to complete the assessment items orally or by having another person transcribe their responses.

Using Data to Adjust Instruction

Use children's scores on the Weekly Test to determine Small Group placement, reteaching, and potential for intervention.

☑ VOCABULARY AND COMPREHENSION

Compare and Contrast; Figurative Language; Anchor Text
Target Vocabulary; Prefix over-

IF STUDENT SCORES...	
...at acceptable,	...below acceptable,
THEN continue core instruction.	THEN use Reteach Comprehension Skill and Vocabulary Strategies lessons. For struggling students, administer the *Intervention Assessments* to determine if students would benefit from intervention.

☑ PHONICS

Words with *or, ore*

IF STUDENT SCORES...	
...at acceptable,	...below acceptable,
THEN continue core instruction.	THEN use Reteach Phonics lesson. Administer the *Intervention Assessments* to determine if students would benefit from intervention.

☑ LANGUAGE ARTS

Commas in a Series

IF STUDENT SCORES...	
...at acceptable,	...below acceptable,
THEN continue core instruction.	THEN use Reteach Language Arts lesson. For struggling students, administer the *Intervention Assessments* to determine if students would benefit from intervention.

☑ FLUENCY

Fluency Plan

Assess one group per week using the Fluency Tests in the *Grab-and-Go™* Resources. Use the suggested plan at the right.

Struggling Readers	Weeks 1, 2, 3
▲ On Level	Week 2
■ Advanced	Week 5

IF...	
...students are reading on-level text fluently,	...students are reading below level,
THEN continue core instruction.	THEN provide additional fluency practice using the **Student Book,** the **Cold Reads,** and the Leveled Readers. For struggling students, administer the *Intervention Assessments* to determine if students would benefit from intervention.

JOURNEYS
Cold Reads
2

The **Cold Reads** passages increase gradually in Lexile® measures throughout the year, from below grade level to above grade level.

- Each passage is accompanied by several selected-response questions and one constructed-response prompt, requiring children to read closely, answer questions at substantial DOK levels, and cite text evidence.

- The **Cold Reads** may be used to provide practice in reading increasingly complex texts and to informally monitor children's progress.

- The **Cold Reads** may be used to estimate children's Lexile® levels in order to recommend appropriately challenging books for small-group instruction or independent reading.

Turn the page for more information about using FORMATIVE ASSESSMENT for ELD AND INTERVENTION.

Assess It Online!

► Language Workshop
  Assessment Handbook

► Intervention
  Assessments

Formative Assessment for ELD and Intervention

Formative Assessment for English Learners

English learners should engage in the same rigorous curriculum and formative assessment as other students. However, it is important to remember that English learners face a dual challenge: they are strengthening their abilities *to use* English at the same time that they are learning challenging content *through* English. Use the following strategies and resources for ongoing assessment of English language development, in addition to the assessments you use with all children:

- A combination of **observational measures,** such as listening in as children read aloud or participate in collaborative conversations. Be prepared to provide **"just-in-time" scaffolding** to support students. For example, if children are retelling a story, you could help them use sentence structures with past-tense verbs and time-order transition words.

- **Constructive feedback** that focuses on communication and meaning-making. Avoid overcorrecting in a way that makes English learners reluctant to speak up. You might try recasting a child's statement more correctly, making a note to address the target form more directly during Designated ELD time.

- **Student self-assessment,** through children's own notes in their vocabulary notebooks or other learning journals. If possible, meet with each child to review his or her self-assessments and provide encouragement and feedback.

- **Formative assessment** notes that are integrated into the Language Workshop Teacher's Guide for use during Designated ELD.

- **Language Workshop Assessment Handbook** for longer-cycle assessment to make sure students are progressing in their English development.

Response to Intervention  RtI

Use the Weekly Tests and Benchmark and Unit Tests, along with your own observations, to determine if individual students are not responding to primary instruction and need additional testing to identify specific needs for targeted intervention.

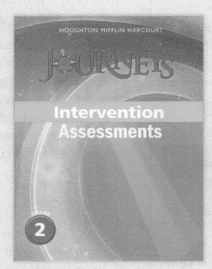

Intervention Assessments

Assessment for Intervention

Administer these assessments to

- children who are receiving supplemental intervention to gauge progress towards exit from the intervention program.

- children who demonstrate lack of success with Weekly Tests, Benchmark and Unit Tests, and core instruction to determine if they might benefit from additional practice or intervention.

Performance Task

Discuss Writing to a Prompt

Point out the Task label on **Student Book** p. 202. Tell children that often they will be given a writing task that begins with a prompt. Explain that a prompt is like directions. It tells exactly what they have to do, and it is important to understand all the parts of the prompt. Tell children that they can follow the steps below to help them respond to writing prompts.

1 Read the prompt carefully.

2 Ask yourself, "What is the prompt asking me to do? What am I supposed to write?" Tell children to figure out if they are supposed to write a story, an opinion piece, or an informational piece.

3 Explain the prompt in your own words to make sure you understand it.

4 Decide which text(s) you may need to look back at to use in your writing.

5 Complete the parts of the writing process: plan, draft, revise, and present.

ENGLISH LANGUAGE SUPPORT Copy onto the board the prompt on **Student Book** p. 202, or project it from the eBook. Model how to break apart the prompt and highlight the key words to help children figure out the task. Underline key words as you think aloud. Vertical slash marks indicate individual parts to focus on and discuss one at a time.

> Look back at _My Name Is Gabriela_ and _Heroes Then and Now_. / _Gabriela Mistral and Amelia Earhart_ took adventures around the same time in history. / _Imagine you_ lived at that time and _went on an adventure together_. / _Write a story_ telling about your adventure to share with your classmates. / _Use information from both texts_ to help you.

Think Aloud _The first sentence of the prompt tells me to look at two selections:_ My Name Is Gabriela _and_ Heroes Then and Now, _which feature information about two real people, Gabriela Mistral and Amelia Earhart. The next part tells me that I need to imagine going on an adventure with these two women. The next part tells me to write a story. I know that a story is made up and not real. The last part says that I should use information from the two selections in my story. I will use this information to include interesting details about the characters in my story._

▶ SHARE OBJECTIVES

- Learn and apply strategies for writing to a prompt.

- Write a narrative that includes events in sequential order, details about the characters, a problem that is solved, pronouns, and a strong ending.

- Gather information from sources to use in writing.

- Follow the steps of the writing process: plan, draft, revise, and publish.

Unit Performance Tasks
Unit 1: Write a Story
Unit 2: Write an Informational Paragraph
Unit 3: Write an Opinion Essay
▶ Unit 4: Write a Story
Unit 5: Write a Response to Literature
Unit 6: Write an Opinion Essay

Digital Resources

To support children before they start this task, use the following **Interactive Whiteboard Lessons.**

▶ Text Analysis

▶ Narrative Writing

Write a Story

- Introduce the Performance Task on **Student Book** p. 202 by reading the task with children. Help them identify the key parts of the prompt. Use steps 1–4 on p. T481 to guide children in analyzing the prompt.

Plan

- Page through *My Name Is Gabriela* and *Heroes Then and Now* with children. Ask them to find and share details about Gabriela Mistral and Amelia Earhart as you write them on the board. *(Gabriela: lived in Chile, saw mountains, loved words, told stories, teacher, writer, visited many countries; Amelia: first woman pilot to cross Atlantic Ocean, studied hard, looked at maps and weather charts)* Tell them that Gabriela and Amelia will be two of the characters in their story.

- Have children think about what they might do if they went on an adventure with these two women. Explain that they will make up the events of the story and choose where their adventure takes place.

Think Aloud *I've looked through the two selections to find details about Gabriela Mistral and Amelia Earhart and the adventures they had. Now I need to fill out the story map. Gabriela wondered what was beyond the mountains near her home. I am going to make that place the setting of my story. Gabriela and Amelia will be characters in my story. I will also be a character. Next I need to figure out what problem my characters have to solve. In my story, we will have to cross tall mountains. My story will tell how we found a way to get to the other side of the mountains.*

- Distribute Graphic Organizer 10 to children. Guide them to complete a story map with details about characters, setting, and events. Remind children that their stories should include a problem the characters must solve. Point out that their stories also need a beginning, a middle, and an ending. Have children complete their story maps. **ELA** W.2.3, W.2.5, W.2.8 **ELD** ELD.PI.2.1, ELD.PI.2.10, ELD.PII.2.2

Write a Story

TASK Look back at *My Name Is Gabriela* and *Heroes Then and Now*. Gabriela Mistral and Amelia Earhart took adventures around the same time in history. Imagine you lived at that time and went on an adventure together. Write a story telling about your adventure to share with your classmates. Use information from both texts to help you.

PLAN

myNotebook

Gather Information Talk with a partner about *My Name Is Gabriela* and *Heroes Then and Now*. What things about each woman can you put into your story?

Then write ideas for your story in a story map.

- Who are the other characters in your story?

- What adventure will you take and where?

- What is the problem?

- How will your story end?

Use the tools in your eBook to remember details about Gabriela Mistral and Amelia Earhart.

Characters	Setting
Plot	

ENGLISH LANGUAGE SUPPORT

Use Sentence Frames

Emerging To help children fill out the story map, have them work with a partner to complete these sentence frames:

My characters are _____.

_____ is the place I chose for my setting.

*The **first** thing that happens is _____.*

*The **next** thing that happens is _____.*

*The **last** thing that happens is _____.* **ELD** ELD.PII.2.2

Expanding In mixed-ability groups, have children use the words *first, next, then,* and *last* to tell what happens in their story. Then have them exchange suggestions before completing their story maps. **ELD** ELD.PII.2.2

Bridging Have children discuss with a partner which characters, settings, problems, and events they want to include in a narrative and why. Then have children discuss what happens at the beginning, middle, and ending of their stories. **ELD** ELD.PII.2.2

Write your
draft in
*my*WriteSmart.

Write Your Story Use the information below to help you organize your story.

Beginning

Write an interesting beginning. Use your story map for ideas. Describe how you meet Gabriela and Amelia, and introduce the problem. Use pronouns correctly.

Middle

Tell about the important events in order. Leave out any events that don't help tell the story.

Ending

Give the story a strong ending. The ending should answer these questions for the reader:

- How do the characters solve the problem?
- How do the characters feel when the story ends?

203

Draft

Write Your Story Read aloud the information on **Student Book** p. 203 with children one step at a time. Remind them to use the information in their completed story maps to help them follow the steps for drafting their stories.

- Explain to children that they should start their stories by describing how they meet Gabriela and Amelia and then telling about the problem the characters must solve. Remind them to use pronouns correctly, such as using *she* to refer to Gabriela or Amelia and *I* to refer to themselves.

- Then they should describe the important events in the story. Help children distinguish between events that move the plot forward and events that are not an essential part of the story. Remind children to use the correct form of each past-tense verb and include details that tell about the two women.

- Tell children to finish their stories with an ending sentence or sentences that describe how the characters solve the problem and how they feel at the end of the adventure.

Circulate as children write their drafts and help them as needed. **ELA** W.2.3, W.2.5, L.2.1c, L.2.1d, L.2.1f
ELD ELD.PI.2.10, ELD.PI.2.12b, ELD.PII.2.1, ELD.PII.2.2, ELD.PII.2.3b, ELD.PII.2.4

ENGLISH LANGUAGE SUPPORT As a class, work together to generate a word bank of frequently used verbs. Include both regular and irregular verbs. Model how to form the past tense of each word. Explain that in most cases the ending *-ed* is added to the end of the present tense verb to form the past tense verb. Point out examples of irregular verbs, such as *go/went* and *see/saw*. Display the list of verbs as children draft their stories. **ELD** ELD.PII.2.3a, ELD.PII.2.3b

Revise

Review Your Draft Read the top of **Student Book** p. 204 with children.

- Have partners think about the Checklist questions as they take turns reading each other's story aloud. Both children should pay special attention to whether the events are told in the correct order and are interesting to the reader.

- Remind partners to ask questions to clear up any confusion in the story. Encourage partners to brainstorm ways to revise, including suggestions for places where text can be added or deleted.

ENGLISH LANGUAGE SUPPORT Model a conversation to help children with the peer review.

Think Aloud *I like that you included details that tell me about Gabriela and Amelia. I would like to know more about how the characters felt at the end of their adventure.*

Provide sentence frames as needed, such as: *I like that you used details such as _____ to tell about the setting. I like how you described _____. I understand what happened in this part, but I think you should _____ in this part. When you refer to _____, you need to use the pronoun _____.*

- As children revise, remind them to tell about the events in the order they happen as well as provide details that help their readers picture what happened. Encourage them to look for places where they can add details that help readers imagine what the characters saw, heard, smelled, touched, and tasted during their adventure.

- Remind all children to proofread their drafts for correct spelling, capitalization, and punctuation.
  ELA W.2.3, W.2.5, SL.2.1c, SL.2.3, L.2.1c, L.2.1d, L.2.1f
  ELD ELD.PI.2.1, ELD.PI.2.5, ELD.PI.2.10, ELD.PII.2.1, ELD.PII.2.5

Present

Create a Finished Copy If children choose to read their stories to a group, remind them to read with expression so that listeners can feel the excitement of the adventure. Point out that good readers read slowly and clearly so their audience can understand what happens during the story.

If students choose to act out the story with their classmates, encourage them to rehearse what they will say and do before they present the story to the group. **ELA** W.2.6, SL.2.4a **ELD** ELD.PI.2.9

Writing Rubric To evaluate student writing, see **Performance Task: Narrative Writing Rubric**, on p. R19.

T484 • Unit 4 (SB p. 204)

REVISE

Review Your Draft Read your writing and make it better. Use the Checklist.

Have a partner read your draft. Talk about how you can make it better.

- Does my story have a beginning that will get the reader's attention?

- Did I include details from the texts to show what Gabriela and Amelia are like?

- Do the characters face a problem and solve it?

- Did I use pronouns correctly?

PRESENT

Share Write or type a copy of your story. Add pictures. Pick a way to share.

- Read your story to classmates.

- Ask classmates to help you act out your story.

204

SMALL GROUP

Differentiate Phonics
- Words with *or, ore*

Vocabulary Reader
- *Everyday Hero*

Differentiate Comprehension
- Compare and Contrast
- Monitor/Clarify

Differentiate
Phonics & Fluency
- Cumulative Review
- Intonation

Leveled Readers
- *Two Heroes*
- *Superheroes to the Rescue*
- *The Mysterious Superhero*
- *Superheroes Save the Day*

Differentiate
Vocabulary Strategies
- Prefix *over-*

Options for Reteaching
- Phonics
- Language Arts
- Vocabulary Strategies
- Comprehension

Literacy Centers

Independent Practice
- Word Study, T406
- Think and Write, T407
- Comprehension and Fluency, T406

Teacher-Led

	DAY 1	DAY 2	DAY 3
Struggling Readers	**Vocabulary Reader,** *Everyday Hero,* Differentiated Instruction, p. T490 **Differentiate Phonics:** Words with *or, ore,* p. T488 **English Language Support,** pp. T489, T491	**Differentiate Comprehension:** Compare and Contrast; Monitor/Clarify, p. T492 **Reread** *A Sporty Game* **English Language Support,** p. T493	**Leveled Reader** *Two Heroes,* p. T496 **Differentiate Phonics:** Cumulative Review, p. T494 **English Language Support,** Leveled Reader Teacher's Guide, p. 5
On Level	**Vocabulary Reader,** *Everyday Hero,* Differentiated Instruction, p. T490 **English Language Support,** pp. T489, T491	**Differentiate Comprehension:** Compare and Contrast; Monitor/Clarify, p. T492 **Reread** *A Sporty Game* **English Language Support,** p. T493	**Leveled Reader** *Superheroes to the Rescue,* p. T497 *Superheroes Save the Day,* p. T499 **Differentiate Fluency:** Intonation, p. T495 **English Language Support,** Leveled Reader Teacher's Guide, p. 5
Advanced	**Vocabulary Reader,** *Everyday Hero,* Differentiated Instruction, p. T491 **English Language Support,** pp. T489, T491	**Differentiate Comprehension:** Compare and Contrast; Monitor/Clarify, p. T493 **Reread** *A Sporty Game* **English Language Support,** p. T493	**Leveled Reader** *The Mysterious Superhero,* p. T498 **Differentiate Fluency:** Intonation, p. T495 **English Language Support,** Leveled Reader Teacher's Guide, p. 5

What are my other children doing?

	DAY 1	DAY 2	DAY 3
Struggling Readers	**Word Building:** Build and read Spelling Words • Leveled Practice, SR20.1	**Partners:** Vocabulary in Context Cards 153–160 **Partners:** Reread *A Sporty Game* • Leveled Practice, SR20.2	**Partners:** Reread Leveled Reader *Two Heroes* • Leveled Practice, SR20.3
On Level	**Word Building:** Build and read words with *or* and *ore* using Letter Cards **Complete** Reader's Notebook, pp. 61–62 or Leveled Practice, EL20.1	**Target Vocabulary:** Practice reading using Vocabulary in Context Cards 153–160 **Reread** *A Sporty Game* **Complete** Reader's Notebook, pp. 63–66 or Leveled Practice, EL20.2	**Partners:** Reread Leveled Reader *Superheroes to the Rescue* or *Superheroes Save the Day* **Complete** Reader's Notebook, pp. 67–71 or Leveled Practice, EL20.3
Advanced	**Vocabulary in Context Cards** 153–160 *Talk It Over* activities • Leveled Practice, A20.1	**Reread** *Dex: The Heart of a Hero,* **Student Book,** pp. 166–189 • Leveled Practice, A20.2	**Partners:** Reread Leveled Reader *The Mysterious Superhero* • Leveled Practice, A20.3

For strategic intervention for this lesson, see pp. S42–S51.

Differentiate Vocabulary Strategies: Prefix over-, p. T500
Reread *My Story*
English Language Support, p. T501

Differentiate Vocabulary Strategies: Prefix over-, p. T500
Reread *My Story*
English Language Support, p. T501

Differentiate Vocabulary Strategies: Prefix over-, p. T501
English Language Support, p. T501

Options for Reteaching, pp. T502–T503
Reread *A Sporty Game* or *My Story* or one of this week's Blend-It Books.

Options for Reteaching, pp. T502–T503
Reread *A Sporty Game* or *My Story* or one of this week's Blend-It Books.

Options for Reteaching, pp. T502–T503
Reread *A Sporty Game* or *My Story* or one of this week's Blend-It Books.

Use the Leveled Reader Teacher's Guide to support ELs during differentiated instruction.

- **Characteristics of the Text** (p. 1)

  Identify challenging language features, such as text structure, literary features, complex sentences, and vocabulary.

- **Cultural Support/Cognates/Vocabulary** (p. 5)

  Explain unfamiliar features of English and help ELs transfer first-language knowledge.

- **Oral Language Development** (p. 5)

  Check comprehension using dialogues that match children's proficiency levels.

Book Share

Use this routine at the end of the week to show children that they have become experts on their Leveled Readers.

Step 1:

Help each group write a presentation of their Leveled Reader **Responding** page. Use the following routine:

- Briefly tell what your book is about.

- Show your graphic organizer and explain what you added to complete it.

- Tell about your favorite part of the book.

Every child should have his or her own presentation to share with a new group.

Step 2:

Have children number off. Assign places in the classroom for 1s to gather, 2s, and so on. Help children find their new groups.

Step 3:

Have children take turns sharing their book presentations in the new groups. Continue until all children have finished sharing. Encourage children to ask questions. Give the following frames for support.

Can you tell me more about _____?

I wonder why _____?

What do you think about _____?

Partners: Reread *My Story*
• Leveled Practice, SR20.4

Partners: Choose among the stories for this week to reread
• Complete and share Literacy Center activities

Reread *My Story*
Complete Reader's Notebook, pp. 72–74 or Leveled Practice, EL20.4

Partners: Reread Leveled Reader *Superheroes to the Rescue* or *Superheroes Save the Day*
• Complete and share Literacy Center activities
• Self-Selected Reading
Complete Reader's Notebook, p. 75

Partners: Reread *Heroes Then and Now,* Student Book, pp. 194–197
• Leveled Practice, A20.4

Partners: Reread Leveled Reader *The Mysterious Superhero*
• Complete and share Literacy Center activities
• Self-Selected Reading

Differentiate Phonics
Words with *or, ore*

ELA RF.2.3b
ELD ELD.PI.2.1

Struggling Readers

I DO IT

- Display the title page of **Decodable Reader** *A Sporty Game*. Read aloud the title, emphasizing the sound /ôr/ as you say the word *Sporty*.

- Write *Sporty* on the board and underline *or*. *The letters* or *spell the sound* /ôr/ *in the word* Sporty.

- Use Instructional Routine 3 to model how to blend *Sporty*.

- Repeat the procedure using the word *more*. Point out the *ore* spelling.

- Review *or* and *ore* words in the **Decodable Reader** *A Sporty Game*.

WE DO IT

- Use **Sound/Spelling Card** *orange* to review the *or* and *ore* spellings for /ôr/.

- Have children name the /ôr/ word in each of these word pairs: *house/horse, form/foam, stare/store*.

- Help children blend the sounds to read the words below. Use the **Corrective Feedback** steps if children need additional help.

or
ore

sore	forget	cord	inform
pork	story	chore	hornet

YOU DO IT

- Have partners take turns using **Letter Cards** to build words with *or* and *ore*. Provide **Corrective Feedback** as necessary.

- Have children record the words they make and read the list to the group.

- Have children reread the **Decodable Reader** *A Sporty Game*.

FORMATIVE ASSESSMENT   RtI

Corrective Feedback
When a child mispronounces a word, point to the word and say it. Call attention to the element that was mispronounced, say the sound, and then guide children to read the word. See the example below.

Phonics Error:
A child reads *chore* as *chair*.

Correct the error. Say the word and the vowel sound. *The word is* chore; *the letters* ore *stand for the sound* /ôr/.

Model as you touch the letters. *I'll blend: /ch/ /ôr/. What's the word?* chore

Guide *Let's blend together:/ch/ /ôr/. What is the word?* chore

Check *You blend. /ch/ /ôr/ What is the word?* chore

Reinforce Go back three or four words in the list and have children continue reading. Make note of errors and review those words during the next lesson.

English Language Support

ELD ELD.PI.2.1

If appropriate, use Letter Cards to provide Struggling Readers, On Level, and Advanced ELs with proficiency-level support during differentiated instruction.

- Display **Letter Cards** *f*, *or*, and *k*. Review the *or* spelling of the vowel sound /ôr/.

- Blend and read the word *fork*. *Listen: /f/ /ôr/ /k/, fork.* Have children blend and read the word with you. *Now you blend the sounds: /f/ /ôr/ /k/. What is the word?* fork

- Repeat the procedure with the word *sore* to review the *ore* spelling of /ôr/.

Emerging

- Contrast the vowel sound /är/ with /ôr/ to help children hear the difference. Use these word pairs: *far/for*, *part/port*, *farm/form*.

Expanding

- Write these words: *horn, store, corn, fork, storm*. Have children read the words and choose one to write and illustrate.

Bridging

- Write these words: *chore, horse, corn, store, short*. Have children read them. Call on volunteers to choose a word and explain its meaning.

On Level

See Literacy Centers—Unit 4 Lesson 20 Word Study

If children have time after completing the purple activity, have them try moving on to the blue activity.

Advanced

See Literacy Centers—Unit 4 Lesson 20 Word Study

If children have time after completing the blue activity, have them reread **Decodable Reader** *A Sporty Game* or another book independently.

Vocabulary Reader
Everyday Hero

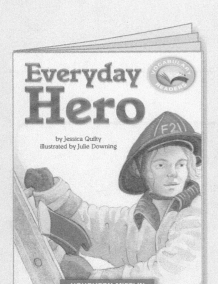

Everyday Hero
by Jessica Quilty
illustrated by Julie Downing

HOUGHTON MIFFLIN

Summary

This selection explains how community helpers keep us healthy and safe.

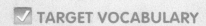

☑ **TARGET VOCABULARY**

depended	gazing
sore	hero
sprang	exercise
studied	overlooked

Struggling Readers

ELA RF.2.4a, L.2.4a
ELD ELD.PI.2.1, ELD.PI.2.5

- Explain to children that there are many kinds of heroes. Some are famous, and some are people you may see in your own city or town.

- Guide children to preview the selection by looking at each illustration. Have them identify the person's job in each picture.

- Have children alternate reading pages of the selection aloud. Guide them to use context to determine the meanings of unfamiliar words (or phrases). As necessary, use the **Vocabulary In Context Cards** to review how the Target Vocabulary is used.

- Have partners work together to complete the Responding page. Then review the directions on Blackline Master 20.4 and guide children to complete it.

On Level

ELA RF.2.4a, L.2.4a
ELD ELD.PI.2.1, ELD.PI.2.5

- Explain to children that heroes can be people of any age or gender. A hero is a person who leads by example. Guide children to preview the selection and talk about how they think the people in the illustrations might lead by example.

- Remind children that they can use context clues to determine the meanings of unfamiliar words (or phrases). Explain that illustrations, in addition to words (or phrases) nearby, can provide clues about the meaning of the unfamiliar word (or phrase).

- Have children alternate reading pages of the selection aloud. Monitor as they use context clues to figure out the meanings of unfamiliar words (or phrases).

- Assign the Responding page and Blackline Master 20.4. Review the directions with children, and have children discuss their responses with a partner.

Advanced

ELA RF.2.4a, L.2.4a
ELD ELD.PI.2.1, ELD.PI.2.5

- Have children preview the selection and make predictions about what they will read, using the illustrations and prior knowledge.

- Remind children to use context clues to determine the meanings of unfamiliar words (or phrases).

- Tell children to read the selection with a partner. Ask them to stop and discuss the meanings of unfamiliar words (or phrases) as necessary.

- Assign the Responding page and Blackline Master 20.4 [. For the Write About It activity, remind children to include facts and details to support their ideas.

English Language Support

ELD ELD.PI.2.1

Provide Struggling Readers, On Level, and Advanced ELs proficiency-level support during differentiated instruction.

Emerging

- Support children's understanding of the selection by conducting a picture walk through *Everyday Hero.* Use gestures and simplified language to review how each example of a hero helps people. Check children's understanding by asking questions such as: *How do police officers help people? What do doctors do to help people?*

Expanding

- Give children sentence frames they can use to describe the illustrations in the selection to their peers. Examples: *The picture on this page shows _____. This person helps _____. I see another example of a hero on page _____.*

Bridging

- Help children complete the Responding page activities by reviewing their completed word webs and guiding them to use the words in sentences that describe heroes. Then have them use those sentences as a model for writing a response to the Write About It activity.

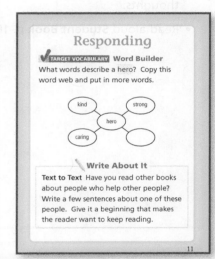

Everyday Hero, p. 11

Differentiate Comprehension
Compare and Contrast; Monitor/Clarify

Struggling Readers

ELA RL.2.4
ELD ELD.PI.2.1, ELD.PI.2.6

I DO IT

- Remind children that stopping to think about how story elements are alike and different can help them better understand what they read. A Venn diagram can help them record their thoughts.

- Read aloud **Student Book** p. 168.

WE DO IT

- Tell children that you will learn about Dex by comparing him to the other animals. Begin to fill in the details you learn on p. 168.

- Have children recall other things they know about the characters.

- Add children's ideas to the Venn diagram, and use the completed graphic organizer to discuss Dex's challenge.

YOU DO IT

- Point out that Cleevis feels differently about Dex at the end of the story. Have children create a Venn diagram that lists details about Cleevis's feelings before and after he gets stuck in the tree.

- Have children clarify their understanding of the story by using the Venn diagram to answer the following question: *Why does Cleevis want to be Dex's partner at the end of the story? Cleevis admires Dex. He wants to be a hero, too.*

On Level

ELA RL.2.4
ELD ELD.PI.2.1, ELD.PI.2.6

I DO IT

- Read aloud **Student Book** pp. 168 and 170 and display the illustrations.

- Use a Venn diagram to compare Dex in real life to Dex in his daydreams.

WE DO IT

- Discuss with children how the Venn diagram helped to clarify that Dex wants to be a hero, but isn't one yet.

- Work with children to make a Venn diagram comparing and contrasting the way Dex looks at the beginning and end of the story.

- Discuss the strategies children used to monitor Dex's appearance as they read.

YOU DO IT

- Remind children how Dex looks at the beginning and at the end of the story. Explain that by the end of the story, his character changed as well as his body.

- Have children use a Venn diagram to compare and contrast Dex's feelings at the beginning and at the end of the story.

- Have children share their graphic organizers and discuss how the details they selected tell about Dex's feelings.

Advanced

ELA RL.2.4
ELD ELD.PI.2.1, ELD.PI.2.6

I DO IT

- Remind children that good readers pause during reading to check their understanding. Read **Student Book** p. 181 and then model pausing to clarify what is happening.

Think Aloud *Cleevis is in danger because he is stuck in a tree. The animals have asked Dex for help. He can't find anything to get him up the tree, but he looks at the crowd. Maybe the crowd has given him an idea. I will keep reading to see what he does.*

WE DO IT

- Remind children that using a Venn diagram to compare and contrast characters, ideas, or events can help them to clarify what they read.

- Have children work in pairs to create a Venn diagram that compares and contrasts how characters treat Dex at the beginning and at the end of the story.

- Ask pairs to share their diagrams with the class. Record their ideas on the board.

YOU DO IT

- Have children use the Venn diagram from the previous activity to think about Dex's feelings. Then have them talk about how he acts because of those feelings.

- Have children work independently to create a Venn diagram that compares and contrasts Dex's feelings and actions at the beginning and at the end of the story.

- Have children share their Venn diagrams with the group.

English Language Support

ELD ELD.PI.2.1

Provide Struggling Readers, On Level, and Advanced ELs proficiency-level support during differentiated instruction.

Emerging

- Model how to look for and record details as they read or listen to a passage.

- Read aloud the first paragraph on **Student Book** p. 168. Have children listen to the description and draw what they see in their minds as they listen. Prompt children to share their drawings, and point out key words such as *little, legs, tail,* and *body.*

- Encourage children to keep recording details in the form of pictures or words as they read the selection and have them refer to the details when they fill in their Venn diagrams.

Expanding

- Model for children how to note details as they read or listen to a passage.

- Display the illustration on **Student Book** p. 169 and use simplified language to explain what is happening. Encourage students to retell your explanation or add details to it.

Bridging

- Give children sentence frames they can complete with details from their Venn diagrams to talk about Dex and Cleevis.

- For example: *At the beginning of the story, Dex is/feels _____. Then, Dex _____. At the end of the story, Dex _____.*

Differentiate Phonics and Fluency

Struggling Readers

ELA L.2.2d
ELD ELD.PIII.2

Phonics

Cumulative Review

I DO IT

- Display **Picture Card** *farm*. Name the picture, emphasizing the vowel sound, /är/.

- Use **Letter Cards** *f, ar, m* to build *farm*.

f	ar	m

- Use Instructional Routine 3 to model how to blend *farm*. Listen: /f/ /är/ /m/, *farm*. Then have children blend the sounds with you.

- Repeat the procedure with *fork* and *store*, pointing out the *or* and *ore* spellings for /ôr/.

WE DO IT

- Display **Sound/Spelling Cards** *artist* and *orange*. Review the *r*-controlled vowel spellings *ar, or, ore*.

- Have children listen and name the /är/ word in each of these word pairs: *dark/dorm, score/scar, form/farm, card/cord*.

- Write the following words on the board: *arch, organ, storage, ignore, arctic, market, seashore*. Help children blend the sounds and read each word.

- Call on an individual to circle the *r*-controlled vowel spelling in each word and say what sound these letters stand for, /är/ or /ôr/.

YOU DO IT

- Have children use **Letter Cards** to build *orbit, sharp, party,* and *restore*. Provide **Corrective Feedback** as necessary.

- Have them read each word aloud.

FORMATIVE ASSESSMENT

Corrective Feedback

When a child mispronounces a word, point to the word and say it. Call attention to the element that was mispronounced, say the sound, and then guide children to read the word. See the example below.

Phonics Error:

A child builds *sharp* as *shap*.

Correct the error. Say the word and isolate the vowel sound. *The word is sharp; the letters ar stand for the vowel sound /är/.*

Model using **Letter Cards** to make *sharp*. I'll *build* sharp: */sh/* sh; */är/* ar; */p/* p: sharp.

Guide *Let's build sharp together: /sh/ sh; /är/ ar; /p/ p. What is the word?* sharp

Check *You build sharp. /sh/ sh; /är/ ar; /p/ p What is the word?* sharp

Reinforce Have children go back two or three words in the activity and practice building the words again. Note any errors and review those words during later lessons.

All Levels

ELA RF.2.4b

Fluency

Intonation

I DO IT

- Write: *Didn't he understand that the suit was just a way to let people know he was there to help?*

- Use a Think Aloud to model reading the sentence with appropriate intonation.

Think Aloud *As I look at this sentence, I think about how I can make my reading sound natural. I want my voice to rise and fall, just as it does when I am telling a story or talking to someone. I'll write each word to show whether my voice will rise or fall as I read. I notice that the sentence ends with a question mark, so I'll be sure to show that my voice will rise at the end of the question.*

- Rewrite the sentence, writing each word on, above, or below a line to show how your voice rises and falls as you read.

WE DO IT

- Choose two sentences from *Two Heroes, Superheroes to the Rescue, The Mysterious Superhero,* and *Superheroes Save the Day* and write them on the board.

- Call on individuals to write the words in each sentence on, above, or below a line to show how their voices rise and fall as they read. Provide **Corrective Feedback.**

- Work with children to place the words correctly.

- Have children take turns reading the sentences. Remind them to make their voices rise and fall naturally, as if they are talking to someone or telling a story.

YOU DO IT

- Have partners choose a page from a **Leveled Reader** and take turns reading aloud.

- Monitor and provide **Corrective Feedback** as needed.

FORMATIVE ASSESSMENT

Corrective Feedback Work with children to correct errors, following the model below.

Fluency Error:
A child has difficulty with intonation.

Correct the error. Remind children to make the sound of their voices rise and fall as they read.

Model reading a sentence with appropriate intonation. *I make the sound of my voice rise and fall to make my reading sound natural and easy to understand.*

Guide children to look for a telling sentence and a question in the text. Read each sentence aloud and have them repeat.

Check Have children read a sentence on their own.

Reinforce Have children go back a sentence or two and begin reading on their own again.

Leveled Readers

 TARGET SKILL
Compare and Contrast

 TARGET STRATEGY
Monitor/Clarify

 TARGET VOCABULARY

depended	overlooked
exercise	sore
gazing	sprang
hero	studied

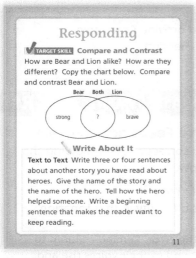

Two Heroes, p. 11

Struggling Readers

ELA RL.2.1, RL.2.3, RF.2.4b
ELD ELD.PI.2.1, ELD.PI.2.6

Two Heroes

Summary *Two Heroes* is a fantasy story about Lion, Fox, and Bear, who combine their strengths in order to help each other out of a jam.

Genre: Fantasy

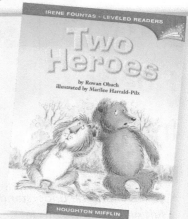

Introducing the Text

- Explain that the animals in *Two Heroes* talk and behave like humans. They argue about who is better and who should save Fox.

- Remind children that using a Venn diagram can help them organize information about how characters are alike and different.

Supporting the Reading

- **p. 7** *How can you figure out that Lion and Bear are not sure how to save Fox? I can look at the picture. I see that Lion looks scared, and Bear looks confused. I also see the word afraid in the text.*

- **p. 10** *How are Bear and Lion alike? They are both heroes. How are Bear and Lion different? Bear is strong. Lion is brave.*

Discussing and Revisiting the Text

Critical Thinking After they discuss the book, have children read the instructions on the top half of Responding p. 11 in *Two Heroes.*

- Have partners identify how Bear and Lion are alike and different on p. 10.

- Help children complete Blackline Master 20.5.

FLUENCY: INTONATION Model using the correct intonation for a variety of sentences. Then have children echo-read p. 2 and focus on varying the sound of their voices and using correct intonation.

On Level

ELA RL.2.1, RL.2.3, RF.2.4b
ELD ELD.PI.2.1, ELD.PI.2.6

 ## Superheroes to the Rescue

Summary In this fantasy, three friends discover their own and their friends' new superhero powers. After helping people all day, their powers disappear. The friends are left to wonder if their superhero powers will ever return.

Genre: Fantasy

Introducing the Text

- Ask children what superhero power they would like to have. Explain that the characters in this story all wake up with superhero powers and use their powers to help other people.

- Remind children that authors do not always describe all the ways characters are alike and different. Good readers use their own knowledge and clues from the text and the pictures to help them compare and contrast characters.

Supporting the Reading

- **pp. 8–9** *What are some ways you can figure out that Raj and Diana didn't know that Mekea had a superpower? I can look at the pictures. I see that Raj and Diana look surprised. The text says they're too surprised to say anything.*

- **p. 11** *On p. 11, how is Diana different from Raj and Mekea? Raj and Mekea have shown off their superpowers. Diana has not shown that she has one yet.*

Discussing and Revisiting the Text

Critical Thinking After they discuss the book, have children read the instructions on the top half of Responding p. 15 in *Superheroes to the Rescue.*

- Have partners choose characters from pp. 3–5 to compare and contrast.

- Have children use these characters to complete Blackline Master 20.6.

FLUENCY: INTONATION After modeling the correct intonation for a variety of sentences on p. 2, have children read p. 2 to a partner using the correct intonation.

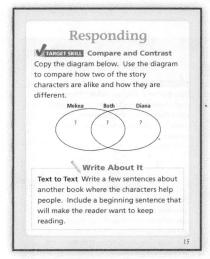

Superheroes to the Rescue, p. 15

Leveled Readers

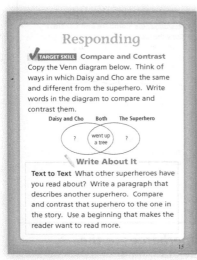

The Mysterious Superhero, p. 15

Advanced

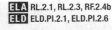

ELA RL.2.1, RL.2.3, RF.2.4b
ELD ELD.PI.2.1, ELD.PI.2.6

 ### *The Mysterious Superhero*

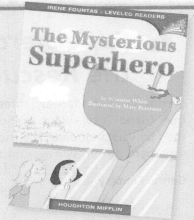

Summary Cho and Daisy look for clues when a mysterious superhero strikes, but they can't discover who it is. When they pretend to get stuck in a tree, the superhero rescues them. Now they know who she is!

Genre: Fantasy

Introducing the Text

• Explain that this selection is about a superhero whom people cannot identify.

• Remind children that authors do not include every detail about characters and events. Sometimes readers must infer or use their imaginations to figure out details about story characters and events.

Supporting the Reading

• **pp. 2–3** *How are the good deeds at the zoo and in town on pp. 2 and 3 alike and different?* They are alike because they show that the superhero will always help and that the superhero is very strong. They are different because at the zoo, the superhero saves an animal. In the town, the superhero saves people.

• **p. 14** *How can you be sure that the girls really know who the mysterious superhero is?* I can look for picture clues and text evidence.

Discussing and Revisiting the Text

Critical Thinking After they discuss the book, have children read the instructions on the top half of Responding p. 15 in *The Mysterious Superhero.*

• Have children work individually or in pairs to compare and contrast Daisy and Cho with the superhero.

• Then have them complete Blackline Master 20.7 .

FLUENCY: INTONATION Have children practice reading sentences with the correct intonation on p. 2: for questions, children's voices go up; for exclamation marks, voices show excitement; for periods, voices drop.

English Language Support

ELD ELD.PI.2.1, ELD.PI.2.6

 Superheroes Save the Day

Summary One morning, three friends find out they each have superhero powers. They are strong in different ways. After helping people all day, their powers go away. Will their powers come back tomorrow?

Genre: Fantasy

Introducing the Text

• Explain that the characters in this story all wake up with superhero powers.

• Remind children that they can look at the pictures or use information in the story to find details about characters to compare and contrast.

Supporting the Reading

• **pp. 4–5** *How are Raj and Diana alike?* Raj and Diana are alike because they have superpowers and are surprised by them.

• **p. 8** *What do the clues on p. 8 tell you about Mekea's superhero power?* When I look at the picture, Mekea's arm is longer than it used to be. Mekea is stretching her arm very far. Now I know her superhero power is stretching.

Discussing and Revisiting the Text

Critical Thinking After they discuss the book, have children read the instructions on the top half of Responding p. 15 in *Superheroes Save the Day*.

• Explain that the outside parts of the Venn diagram show how things are different. The inside part of a Venn diagram shows how things are alike.

• Have partners compare and contrast Mekea and Diana to complete Blackline Master 20.8 [↗].

FLUENCY: INTONATION Point to the different end marks and explain how readers use them to read with correct intonation. Model correct intonation and have children echo-read p. 3.

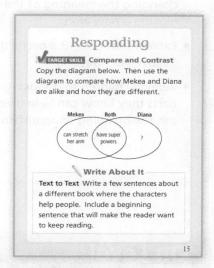

Superheroes Save the Day, p. 15

Differentiate Vocabulary Strategies
Prefix *over-*

Struggling Readers

ELA L.2.4a
ELD ELD.PI.2.1

I DO IT

- Display the word *overlooked*. Then display an example sentence: *The beach house overlooked the ocean.*

- Explain that a prefix is a word part that is added to the beginning of a word, changing the meaning of the word by making a new word.

- Explain that *over-* is a prefix that means "above" or "beyond."

- Remind children that looking for word parts they know can help them figure out the meaning of an unfamiliar word.

WE DO IT

- Read aloud the example sentence you displayed earlier.

- Ask children to identify the base word (or root word) in *overlooked*. Explain that the prefix *over-* adds meaning to the word *looked*. *Overlooked* means "looked above or beyond" or "didn't see."

- Have children use a print or digital dictionary to verify the meaning of *overlooked*.

YOU DO IT

- Write *sleep* and *heat* on the board.

- Have children add the prefix *over-* to each base word (or root word) to form a new word.

- Have children write a sentence for one of the new words and then illustrate their sentence.

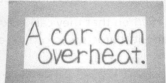

A car can overheat.

On Level

ELA L.2.4a
ELD ELD.PI.2.1

I DO IT

- Explain that a prefix is a word part that is added to the beginning of a base word (or root word) and adds meaning.

- Remind children that the prefix *over-* means "above" or "beyond."

- Tell children that looking for word parts they know can help them figure out the meaning of an unfamiliar word.

WE DO IT

- Write *overlooked* on the board.

- Have a child underline the prefix and base word. Have children use their knowledge of word parts to tell what the word *overlooked* means.

- Have children name other words with the prefix *over-* and give definitions for them. List the words they suggest with their definitions on the board. Have children confirm the meaning of each word in a print or digital dictionary.

YOU DO IT

- Have children select a word from the list on the board. Ask them to write two sentences that demonstrate their understanding of the word they chose.

I overlooked my ball
in the grass.

Advanced

ELA L.2.4a
ELD ELD.PI.2.1

I DO IT

- Write the following words on the board: *dress, achieve, pay.*

- Remind children that a prefix is a word part that is added to the beginning of a base word (or root word).

- Explain that adding a prefix adds meaning to the base word (or root word) and forms a new word.

- Tell children that the prefix *over-* means "above" or "beyond."

WE DO IT

- Have children make new words by writing the prefix *over-* in front of each word on the board.

- Have children use their knowledge of word parts to explain the meaning of each word. Offer feedback, as needed.

- Have children use print or digital dictionaries to confirm the meaning of each word they make.

YOU DO IT

- Have children name and define additional words with the prefix *over-*. List these words on the board.

- Have children choose one word from the list and write a sentence that demonstrates their understanding of it. Have children share their sentences with the class.

English Language Support

ELD ELD.PI.2.1

Provide Struggling Readers, On Level, and Advanced ELs proficiency-level support during differentiated instruction.

Emerging

- As children take part in the We Do It activity for their group, have them define the base word (or root word) first. Ask: *What does* looked *mean?* Then say: *The prefix* over- *means "above" or "beyond." What does* overlooked *mean?* Provide examples of using *overlooked* in context to strengthen children's understanding of how the prefix changes the meaning of the base word (or root word).

Expanding

- Ask children to think of words they know that begin with *over-*.

- Make a list that you can display for children. Define each word on the list together.

- Then ask: *What do all the words on the list have in common?* Guide children to make the connection between the meanings of the words that have the prefix *over-* and how the prefix changes the meaning of the base word (or root word).

Bridging

- If children are having trouble completing the You Do It activity for their group, allow them to make a drawing to accompany their sentences and have them label the drawing with the word they chose to use in the sentence.

- Have children share their drawing with their group and explain how their drawing connects to the sentence they wrote.

Options for Reteaching

ELA L.2.2d **ELD** ELD.PI.2.1

Reteach Phonics

Words with *or, ore*

I DO IT

- Display **Sound/Spelling Card** *orange*. Name the picture and say the sound /ôr/. Have children repeat after you.

- Write *sport* and underline *or*. Use Instructional Routine 3 [→] to blend and read the word. *Listen: /s/ /p/ /ôr/ /t/, sport.* Have children repeat after you.

- Repeat with *chore*, pointing out the *ore* spelling for /ôr/.

WE DO IT

- Write *short* on the board and underline *or*. Blend and read *short* with children.

- Have children find the word *short* on the first page of **Decodable Reader** *My Story*.

- Work with children to find words with the *or* and *ore* spellings for /ôr/ in the **Decodable Reader** *My Story*.

- Call on individuals to write the words they find on the board. Have them read the words aloud.

YOU DO IT

- Have partners work together to read **Decodable Reader** *My Story*.

Decodable Reader

ELD ELD.PI.2.1

Reteach Language Arts

Commas in a Series

I DO IT

- Remind children that a series is three or more nouns or three or more verbs. A comma should follow all words in a series except the last one.

- Write: *June July and August are my favorite months.* Model adding commas to the sentence.

  Think Aloud *Is there a series? Yes. Where do the commas go? A comma goes after each word except the last one. I must add a comma after both June and July.*

WE DO IT

- Have partners work together to write three or four sentences about a hero. Encourage children to include nouns or verbs in a series.

- Guide children to identify which words in a series need commas.

- Have children write commas correctly to separate the nouns or verbs in a series.

YOU DO IT

- Ask children to write three or four sentences that tell about something heroic they wish they could do. Have them include nouns or verbs in a series.

- Have children share their sentences that use nouns or verbs in a series. Have them tell where they put commas and explain why.

Reteach Vocabulary Strategies

ELA L.2.4b ELD ELD.PI.2.1

Prefix *over-*

I DO IT

- Remind children that many words contain smaller, familiar word parts, such as prefixes.

- Explain that identifying prefixes can help children understand the meanings of words they are reading.

- Remind children that the prefix *over-* means "above" or "beyond."

WE DO IT

- Display Projectable 20.7 [↗].

- Help children identify words containing the prefix *over-*.

- Model how to apply the **Vocabulary Strategy** to figure out the meaning of the word *overcook*.

  > **Think Aloud** *I know that the word part over- means "beyond." I also recognize the base word (or root word) cook, which means "to heat food." I think the meaning of this word might be "to heat beyond" or "to heat too much."*

- Have a child look up *overcook* in a print or digital dictionary and read the definition to the class. Discuss whether the meaning you figured out was correct.

YOU DO IT

- Have partners choose and write several *over-* words.

- Have them exchange words and apply the **Vocabulary Strategy** to determine each word's meaning.

- Tell children to use print or digital dictionaries to verify their definitions.

- Provide corrective feedback if children need additional support.

Reteach Comprehension Skill

ELA RL.2.4 ELD ELD.PI.2.1, ELD.PI.2.6

Compare and Contrast

I DO IT

- Remind children that to compare is to think about how two things are the same, and to contrast is to think about how two things are different.

- Model comparing and contrasting a familiar pet, such as your own pet or a class pet, with Dex.

WE DO IT

- Have children read the second paragraph on **Student Book** p. 168. Then have them identify a few of their own feelings or experiences that were like or unlike Dex's.

- Model how to compare and contrast Dex's feelings and experiences with their own.

  > **Think Aloud** *The author writes that nobody pays attention to Dex except when he's being teased. The other dogs don't play with Dex because he is too slow. My life is very different from Dex's because I don't usually get teased. But sometimes, when I'm not good at something, I get left out, just like Dex.*

YOU DO IT

- Distribute Graphic Organizer 14 [↗]: **Venn Diagram**.

- Have children list details about Dex's feelings and experiences on **Student Book** pp. 186–188. *Dex feels happy after he saves Cleevis and everyone cheers; Cleevis asks to be his friend; Dex decides to be friends; Dex feels even happier.* Then have children list their own feelings and experiences that are similar to or different from those of Dex.

- Have partners work together to complete the Venn Diagram and share it with the class.

Teacher Notes

Extended Reading

INFORMATIONAL TEXT

EXEMPLAR

Children will read *Where Do Polar Bears Live?* to

- determine the meaning of words and phrases in a text relevant to a Grade 2 topic or subject area

- identify the main purpose of a text, including what the author wants to answer, explain, or describe

Summary

A polar bear cub emerges from a cave with his mother and begins to learn how to live in its arctic environment. This introduction to polar bears includes details about their physical characteristics, what they eat, how they get their food, and how they raise their young. Woven into the book is information about the Arctic and the other animals that make this icy cold habitat their home.

About the Author

Share the following information with children.

Sarah L. Thomson started reading when she was about seven years old, and she has been reading almost nonstop ever since. She remembers being so engrossed in a book that she often wouldn't notice what was happening around her. Sarah Thomson shares her love of reading by writing books for children. She writes fiction, biographies, and science books, such as *Where Do Polar Bears Live?*

Prepare for Complex Texts

Where Do Polar Bears Live?
by Sarah L. Thomson

GENRE: Informational Text

Why This Text?

Children learn valuable information from nonfiction texts and benefit from exposure to many different styles of nonfiction. This author combines factual information about the geographical conditions in the Arctic, scientific facts about animal adaptations, and sensory details to help readers understand how polar bears are able to survive in the harsh conditions of the Arctic tundra. Maps and supplementary information are provided at the end of the text.

Key Learning Objectives

- Identify the main topic of the text.
- Describe the connection between a series of scientific ideas or concepts.
- Identify the main purpose of the text.
- Understand how polar bears are able to survive in a harsh climate.

⚠ TEXT COMPLEXITY RUBRIC

		Where Do Polar Bears Live?
Quantitative Measures	Lexile	690L
	Guided Reading Level	L
Qualitative Measures	Meaning and Purpose	**Density and Complexity:** The text has a single topic.
	Text Structure	**Organization:** The text features somewhat complex science concepts.
		Use of Graphics: The text includes simple illustrations and maps to supplement key concepts.
	Language Features	**Conventionality and Register:** The text includes some unfamiliar or academic words that may be difficult for some children, but the language is not particularly formal, which provides a good balance.
	Knowledge Demands	**Sentence Structure:** The text uses mostly compound and complex sentences.
		Subject Matter: The text requires some specialized knowledge and presents cause-and-effect relationships.
Reader/Task Considerations		Determine using the professional judgment of the teacher. This varies by individual reader, type of text, and the purpose and complexity of particular tasks.

ENGLISH LANGUAGE SUPPORT Use the Text X-Ray below to prepare for teaching the trade book *Where Do Polar Bears Live?* Use it to plan, support, and scaffold instruction to help children understand the text's **key ideas** and **academic language features**.

Meaning Making

Language Development

Effective Expression

Content Knowledge

Foundational Skills

Zoom In on Key Ideas

Children should understand these **key ideas** after reading *Where Do Polar Bears Live?*

Key Idea | Segment 1, pp. 8–19

Polar bears live in extreme conditions on an island covered in snow where no trees grow. During winter, they survive below-freezing temperatures by hibernating underground. Polar bear cubs are born inside the den and survive on their mother's milk. Bears emerge from the den in the spring. Thick fur, black skin, and a layer of fat help polar bears survive in the cold climate. The black skin soaks up heat from the Sun, and the layer of fat keeps in the bear's body heat. If polar bears get too hot, they cool off by lying on the ice. Mothers take care of their cubs for the first two years of their lives.

Key Idea | Segment 2, pp. 20–28

Polar bears live in the Arctic, which is the area around the North Pole. Large areas are covered by ice. Polar bears hunt the seals that swim in the water under the ice. They must catch seals to survive. They need ice to be able to hunt the seals.

Key Idea | Segment 3, pp. 29–35

In summer, some of the Arctic ice melts. In winter, some of the ice freezes again. If temperatures get warmer, more ice melts, and it takes longer for it to freeze again. The result is that bears have less time to hunt, so they eat less seals. Not as many polar bear cubs are living long enough to become adults. If all the ice in the Arctic were to melt, polar bears would become extinct because they need ice to survive.

Content and Language Instruction

Make note of additional content knowledge and language features children may find challenging in this text. List them here and use them to plan instruction.

Zoom In on Academic Language

Guide children at different proficiencies and skill levels to understand the structure and language of this text.

Focus: Text Level | pp. 8–17

Children should recognize that this is an informational text about a science topic. It begins with descriptive details that appeal to the senses to help readers picture what life is like in the Arctic. It also features facts about the polar bear's adaptations that allow it to survive in such a harsh climate. Have children take note of the factual information and sensory details on pp. 8, 10, 12, 13, 16, and 17.

Focus: Word Level | p. 20

Support English learners and others in understanding domain-specific vocabulary, such as *Arctic, North Pole,* and *tundra* (p. 20). Use the map to explain that the North Pole is the area at the very top of Earth and that the Arctic is the area in white that surrounds the North Pole. Explain that the tundra is a huge area of land that is flat, has no trees, and is always frozen. Have children use these sentence frames to tell about each word:

- *The North Pole is located _____.*
- *The Arctic is a place with _____.*
- *The tundra is an area of land that is _____.*

Focus: Sentence Level | p. 29

On p. 29, the text uses maps to allow readers to compare and contrast the size of the Arctic ice over time. Explain that the white area on each map represents the amount of summer ice in the Arctic in 1980 and in 2007. Guide children to observe the differences between the maps. Help children respond to these sentence frames:

- *If there is less ice, the polar bears _____.*
- *If the polar bears can't hunt and catch seals, _____.*

Weekly Planner

Daily Integrated ENGLISH LANGUAGE SUPPORT	DAY 1	DAY 2
	Materials • Trade Book: *Where Do Polar Bears Live?* • Reader's Notebook Volume 2 pp. 76–81 • GrammarSnap Videos • Multimedia Grammar Glossary	**Materials** • Trade Book: *Where Do Polar Bears Live?* • Reader's Notebook Volume 2 pp. 76–81 • GrammarSnap Videos • Multimedia Grammar Glossary

First Week

	DAY 1	DAY 2
Project Development **Speaking and Listening** **Research and Media Literacy**	**Launch,** T514 Polar Bear Photo Gallery **Teacher Read Aloud** "Dakota's Polar Adventure," T510–T511 **Preview the Topic,** T512	**Discuss,** T517 Focus on Collaboration
Vocabulary **Close Reading**	**Preview Content Vocabulary,** T510 **Introduce the Trade Book,** T513	**Content Vocabulary,** T516 **Segment 1:** First Read, T516
Integrated Language Arts *Review* • Writing • Grammar • Spelling	**Writing / Grammar / Spelling,** T515 **Write About Media** Elaboration Nouns Spelling Review	**Respond to Segment 1,** T516

Second Week

	DAY 1	DAY 2
Project Development **Speaking and Listening** **Research and Media Literacy**	**Prepare,** T527 Create Materials	**Prepare,** T529 Develop the Display
Vocabulary **Close Reading**	**Segment 2:** Second Read, T526	**Content Vocabulary,** T528 **Segment 3:** First Read, T528
Integrated Language Arts *Review* • Writing • Grammar • Spelling	**Write About Reading,** T526	**Respond to Segment 3,** T528

DAY 3

Materials
- Trade Book: *Where Do Polar Bears Live?*
- Reader's Notebook Volume 2 pp. 76–81
- GrammarSnap Videos
- Multimedia Grammar Glossary

Prepare, T519
Plan Roles and Tasks
Manage Time and Resources

Segment 1: Second Read, T518

Write About Reading, T518

Present, T531
Present the Display

Segment 3: Second Read, T530

Write About Reading, T530

DAY 4

Materials
- Trade Book: *Where Do Polar Bears Live?*
- Reader's Notebook Volume 2 pp. 76–81
- GrammarSnap Videos
- Multimedia Grammar Glossary

Prepare, T521
Initiate Research

Content Vocabulary, T520
Segment 2: First Read, T520

Respond to Segment 2, T520

Assess, T533
Score the Project

Your Turn, T532

Write About Reading, T532
Performance Task

DAY 5

Materials
- Trade Book: *Where Do Polar Bears Live?*
- Reader's Notebook Volume 2 pp. 76–81
- GrammarSnap Videos
- Multimedia Grammar Glossary

Prepare, T524
Discuss Peer Critiques
Evaluate Progress

Independent Reading, T522
Extend the Topic, T523
Domain-Specific Vocabulary

Writing / Grammar / Spelling, T525
Write About Reading
Descriptive Paragraph
Subject-Verb Agreement
Spelling Review

Reflect, T536
Reflect on the Project

Independent Reading, T534
Compare Texts

Writing / Grammar / Spelling, T535
Write About Reading
Opinion Writing, Persuasive Essay
The Verb *be*
Spelling Review

Teacher Read Aloud

▶ **SHARE OBJECTIVES**

- Listen to fluent reading.
- Ask and answer questions about details in a text read aloud. LANGUAGE
- Participate in a collaborative conversation. LANGUAGE

ENGLISH LANGUAGE SUPPORT

Use Visuals and Gestures

All Proficiencies Introduce each word to children. Use visuals, gestures, or yes/no questions to help them understand the meaning of each word. Have children listen to the Read Aloud again and signal when they hear a Content Vocabulary word.

☑ PREVIEW

Content Vocabulary

Children will encounter these content vocabulary words in the trade book.

Arctic the region surrounding the North Pole

cub a young bear, wolf, or lion

den the shelter or home of a wild animal

survive to stay alive

tundra an area in the Arctic that has no trees and very few plants

Model Fluency

Expression Explain that when good readers read aloud, they read with expression by varying their voice to reflect the content in the text and the type of sentence. If they read an exclamation, they should read with emotion and excitement. If they read a question, their voice should go up at the end of the sentence. Explain that when they read dialogue, they should try to sound like the characters are speaking.

- Project the first two paragraphs of the Read Aloud. Read aloud the first paragraph, emphasizing the exclamations.

- Point out the exclamation points. Tell children that this punctuation mark indicates that the text should be read with added emotion and excitement. Point out the quotation marks. Tell children that these marks show where the character's words begin and end.

- Reread the passage together with children, reminding them to read with expression to try to make it sound as if the characters are speaking.

Listening Comprehension

Read aloud the passage. Pause at the numbered stopping points to ask children the questions below. Discuss the meanings of the highlighted words, as needed, to support the discussion.

1. *Where does this story take place, and what is it about? Use details from the text in your answer.* Sample answer: *The story takes place in the Arctic; it is about how a polar bear cub and his mother survive in the ice and snow. Details—icy, snow, cub, den* **SETTING**

2. *Why is Dakota so excited about the trip?* Sample answer: *He is looking forward to seeing a seal for the first time.* **UNDERSTANDING CHARACTERS**

3. *Why is it important for the polar bears to be quiet when they are hunting?* Sample answer: *If the seals hear the bears, they will get scared and swim away. Then the bears won't have a chance to catch them.* **CONCLUSIONS**

ELA RL.2.1, RL.2.3, RL.2.5, RL.2.7 **ELD** ELD.PI.2.5, ELD.PI.2.6

Classroom Collaboration

Tell children to paraphrase the story and retell it to a partner.

ELA SL.2.2 **ELD** ELD.PI.2.1, ELD.PI.2.5

ENGLISH LANGUAGE SUPPORT Provide sentence frames like these to support children as they paraphrase and retell the passage: *The text is mostly about _____. It tells about how the bears _____ and _____. At the end, the bears _____.*

ELA SL.2.2 **ELD** ELD.PI.2.1, ELD.PI.2.5

Dakota's Polar Adventure

"Wheeee!" yelled Dakota as he slid down the icy slope. "Let's do that again!" His mother smiled and nodded as her young **cub** scampered back up the hill of snow.

It had only been one month since Dakota and his mother had emerged from the warm, cozy **den** under the ground. It had been their home for the first few months of his life. Now the Sun was out, and it was warm enough for the bears to live above the ground.

Dakota's eyes scanned the vast landscape. All he saw was the bright sun glinting off the smooth ice and endless mounds of white snow. Dakota had never seen a tree or green grass growing in the **tundra**.

"Let's get going, Dakota," said his mother. "We've got a long trip ahead of us."

"Where are we going?" asked the excited cub.

"It's time for you to learn how to hunt and catch seals," she replied. "I know my stomach has been growling a lot."

"Grrrr!" said Dakota. "Mine, too! I can't wait to see my first seal."

Life in the **Arctic** was difficult. A freezing wind swept the snow across the empty land, but Dakota and his mother hardly noticed the cold. Their thick fur kept them warm as they walked across miles and miles of ice. Dakota wondered whether seals had white fur and sharp claws like he had.

When his mother finally stopped, Dakota looked around excitedly, wondering where the seals were. All he could see was ice.

"Why are we stopping here, Mother? I don't see anything but ice. Where are the seals?"

"Shhhh! Just wait. We have to be very quiet. There are holes under the ice. If the seals hear us, they will get scared and swim away."

Dakota nodded and waited, wide eyed, for something to happen. Suddenly, his mother's black nose twitched, and she thrust her huge paws through the ice and into the water below. She pulled back her paws, but they were empty.

The cub peeked nervously into the hole. He caught a glimpse of a gray figure darting away under the water. "I saw it! I saw it!" he squealed excitedly. "It doesn't look anything like me," he said.

"No, it doesn't. But you and the seals both know how to **survive** in the icy Arctic. And one day you will both be excellent swimmers."

Dakota's eyes lit up at the thought of swimming with the seals. "Let's try again, Mother. I know you will catch a seal this time. And then you can teach me how to swim."

The young bear waited silently next to his mother, eagerly awaiting his first meal—and his first swimming lesson.

Preview the Topic

▶ **SHARE OBJECTIVES**

- Gain background knowledge related to the lesson topic and project.
- Develop listening comprehension skills. LANGUAGE
- Respond to multimedia. LANGUAGE
- Participate in a collaborative group discussion. LANGUAGE

ENGLISH LANGUAGE SUPPORT

Use Visuals

All Proficiencies Use photographs related to the Arctic and polar bears to preview the trade book topic and the artwork with children. Enhance understanding by working with children to say short sentences about the topic and to produce answers to the Classroom Collaboration questions. Provide discussion frames, as necessary. **ELD** ELD.PI.2.1, ELD.PI.2.6

Life in the Arctic

Discuss the Topic Explain to children that they will be reading a trade book, called *Where Do Polar Bears Live?*, about how animals survive in the freezing cold of the Arctic. Tell children that they will have the opportunity to use the trade book, as well as other sources, to create a project on this topic.

Point out that the Arctic is a place where no trees grow, the Sun never rises for several months of the year, and the temperatures are often well below freezing. Tell children that although these conditions seem harsh, some plants and animals can survive in the Arctic. Explain that polar bears have special features that help them survive in the cold.

Access Prior Knowledge

Ask children what they know about polar bears from watching television shows or movies or from visiting a zoo. Have volunteers explain what makes polar bears unique and different from other kinds of bears.

Start a word web by writing *Polar Bears* in the center and listing related words in the surrounding ovals. Encourage children to think about what a polar bear looks like, where it lives, and what it eats. **ELA** W.2.8, SL.2.2 **ELD** ELD.PI.2.1, ELD.PI.2.5

▶ View Multimedia

Tell children that they are going to look at artwork that shows a scene in the Arctic and then discuss it in small groups.

Locate online and display for children some realistic paintings of the Arctic by William Bradford, such as *Icebergs in the Arctic*. Have children take turns describing what they see, using sensory words.

💬 Classroom Collaboration

Place children in small groups and have them discuss the following questions. Circulate to encourage collaboration and productive feedback.

- What is the most interesting part of the artwork? What is something new that you learned about the Arctic from the artwork?

- What does the artwork tell you about the place where polar bears make their home?

- What questions do you have about polar bears and where they live?

Tell children that they should look for answers to their questions as they read *Where Do Polar Bears Live?* **ELA** SL.2.1a, SL.2.1b, SL.2.1c, SL.2.2 **ELD** ELD.PI.2.1, ELD.PI.2.5, ELD.PI.2.6

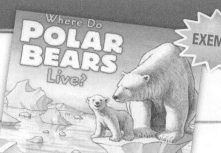

Introduce the Trade Book

Where Do Polar Bears Live?

Discuss Genre Display the book and read the title together. Tell children that this is an informational text about polar bears and how they live in a very cold environment called the Arctic. Review with children that informational text gives facts and information about a topic.

Have children page through the book to examine the text and illustrations, including the maps. Use the following prompts to engage children in discussion: **ELA** RI.2.1, RI.2.5, RI.2.6 **ELD** ELD.PI.2.1, ELD.PI.2.6

- What is the topic of the book?

- How can you tell that this book is an informational text?

- What do you expect to learn from this book?

Predictive Writing

Tell children they will write a paragraph to explain what facts they expect to learn in *Where Do Polar Bears Live?* Guide children to think about the genre and their preview of the book to help them write. **ELA** W.2.2 **ELD** ELD.PI.2.10

Set Purpose

Model setting a reading purpose. Then have children share their personal reading purposes and record them in their journals. **ELA** W.2.2 **ELD** ELD.PI.2.10

> **Think Aloud**
>
> *I know that polar bears are wild animals, which are animals that live in nature and are not tamed by people. But I don't know many other facts about them. I'll read this book to learn more about them.*

ESSENTIAL QUESTION

Read aloud the Essential Question: *What do wild animals need to survive?* Tell children to think about this question as they read *Where Do Polar Bears Live?*

***Where Do Polar Bears Live?* is** presented in three instructional segments.

- Complete the First Read and Second Read instruction for each segment before moving to the next one.

- Then have children read independently and complete the Reader's Notebook pages.

SEGMENT 1	**SEGMENT 2**
pp. 8–19	pp. 20–28

SEGMENT 3
pp. 29–35

Options for Reading

- **Independent/Partner** Children read and complete the Reader's Notebook pages independently or with a partner.

- **Supported** Children read a segment and complete the Reader's Notebook pages with teacher support and then reread the segment with a partner. Encourage children to read at least a portion of each segment on their own. Use children's responses to prompts to determine whether they need additional support.

Scaffold Close Reading

Think Through the Text FIRST READ	**Analyze the Text** SECOND READ	**Independent Reading**
Develop comprehension through - Guided Questioning - Comprehension Strategies - Vocabulary in Context	Children apply what they have learned about analyzing text through collaboration and by generating their own discussion questions. Use directed note-taking by working with children to complete a graphic organizer during reading. Distribute copies of Graphic Organier 7 ☐.	As you reread sections of the book aloud again, children respond to the text on Reader's Notebook Volume 2 pp. 76–81 ☐.

Launch

▶ **SHARE OBJECTIVES**

- Gather relevant information from print and digital sources.
- Build knowledge through topic investigation.
- Collaborate with a group to initiate a project plan.
LANGUAGE

Polar Bear Photo Gallery

✔	Set the Stage
✔	Introduce the Task
✔	Clarify Project Requirements
✔	Form Teams

Set the Stage

You may wish to use ideas such as the ones listed below to immerse children in the topic during the course of the project.

- Display informational books, posters, and maps related to polar bears and the Arctic in a designated area of the classroom.
- Invite a zoologist to talk with children about polar bears.
- Use a zoo's online webcam to observe and listen to polar bears.

Introduce the Task

As children read *Where Do Polar Bears Live?* over the next two weeks, they will gather important facts and details about polar bears and life in the Arctic. They will also research the answer to the Essential Question: *What do wild animals need to survive?*

Display the following project prompt: *You and your teammates are going to become experts in all things related to polar bears. You will create and present a photo gallery that shows how polar bears are able to survive in such a very cold environment. To create your photo display, you will need to gather information about the physical features that help a polar bear stay warm in the cold, stay safe on the ice, and find food. You will need to find a photo that represents each key idea about polar bears and how they survive in the Arctic. Then you will write a caption for each picture that will include facts and details you gathered during your project research.*

Tell children they will use the trade book, as well as other informational books, websites, videos, and online photo galleries, to develop a display that explains what helps polar bears survive in the cold climate of the Artic. **ELA** SL.2.1a, SL.2.1b, SL.2.1c **ELD** ELD.PI.2.1

Have children explore the resources cited on p. T519. These media resources not only build background for accessing the text, but they also build content knowledge for developing the project.

Clarify Project Requirements

Tell children that they will work in small teams over the next two weeks to manage the development of their project and then present it to an audience. Explain to children that, as a team, they will choose their own visuals and write their own captions for their photo gallery.

Tell children that the purpose of the project should answer the Essential Question in a way that teaches their audience about their topic. Work with children to brainstorm qualities of an effective photo gallery. Discuss with children the ideas listed below and encourage children to add their own ideas. **ELA** SL.2.1a, SL.2.1b, SL.2.1c **ELD** ELD.PI.2.1

An Effective Photo Gallery . . .	A Photo Gallery Might Include . . .
<ul><li>clearly conveys the topic</li><li>uses photos to highlight key ideas/points</li><li>features captions that include facts and details that support understanding of what the photos show</li><li>serves to both inform and entertain the audience through the use of important facts and interesting information</li></ul>	<ul><li>a title at the top that describes the topic</li><li>a variety of photos that are large enough to be seen from a short distance away</li><li>captions or short descriptions that are neatly typed or written in complete sentences</li></ul>

Form Teams

Divide the class into teams of three to five children and assign each team member a role for the project. If children are familiar with project work, you may want to allow them to choose their own roles after they have had a chance to discuss the project.

ENGLISH LANGUAGE SUPPORT Ensure that all children are included in teams in which they can be supported as well as challenged. Children at Emerging and Expanding levels may feel more comfortable working with an English-proficient team member to write the photo captions. **ELD** ELD.PI.2.1, ELD.PI.2.10

Point out that children will need to complete several tasks over the course of the two weeks to create their photo gallery. As a group, discuss the steps teams might need to follow to gather information, find their photos, write captions, and organize their display. Tell children that you will work with them this week to help them determine the tasks and help manage time. Then give children time to discuss the project components and how they might approach each one. **ELA** SL.2.1a, SL.2.1b, SL.2.1c **ELD** ELD.PI.2.1

INTEGRATED LANGUAGE ARTS REVIEW

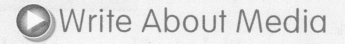 Write About Media

Digital Resources ▶

To support children before they start this task, use the following digital resources.

▶ GrammarSnap Videos: Nouns, Pronouns

▶ Multimedia Grammar Glossary

INTRODUCE THE TASK After children have viewed the artwork, tell them that they will respond to William Bradford's painting by writing sentences that describe something in the artwork. Explain the task:

- Children should choose a detail or an idea from the artwork to write about.
- Children will write sentences that describe that detail or idea.
- The sentences should include details from the artwork that tell about some of the five senses.
- The sentences should be a variety of lengths and include sense words.

Review the Model Display the model sentences that describe from **Student Book** Volume 5, p. 121, and review the proper use of sense words and other adjectives in writing. Point out that the writer has used descriptions that help readers imagine what the beach is like.

PLAN AND DRAFT Display the following list to guide children in writing and organizing their sentences:

- Name the artwork you are writing about.
- What part of the artwork are you going to describe?
- What interesting sense words will you use to describe what you saw?
- Use a capital letter at the beginning of each sentence. Use an end mark at the end of each sentence.

REVISE AND EDIT Guide the class to generate a checklist that children can use as they revise their sentences. For example:

- What adjectives about size and shape can I use?
- What adjectives about color and number can I use?
- How can I include sense words in my writing?
- Did I use complete sentences?
- Did I use end marks correctly?
- Have I corrected any spelling errors?

See Analytic Writing Rubric, p. R17.

SHARE Have children share their sentences with the class.

ELA W.2.3, W.2.5, SL.2.2, L.2.1e, L.2.1f, L.2.3a **ELD** ELD.PI.2.6, ELD.PI.2.10, ELD.PII.2.4

▶ SHARE OBJECTIVES

- Write a response to William Bradford's artwork using sense words. LANGUAGE
- Cite evidence from a media source.
- Use correct punctuation and spelling.

▶ SKILLS REVIEW

Review the following skills, as needed, before children begin to write their response.

- **Writing:** Elaboration (Lessons 16 and 18)
- **Grammar:** Nouns (Lesson 14)
- **Spelling:** Long Vowel Sounds (Lessons 14, 17–19)

ENGLISH LANGUAGE SUPPORT

Sentence Frames

Emerging Help children choose an aspect of the artwork to write about by reading the following sentence frames to them and having them respond:

The artwork shows _____.
The part of the artwork I want to write about is _____.
I can use the words _____ and _____ to describe that part.

Expanding Provide these sentence frames and guide children to complete them:

The part of the artwork I want to describe is _____ because _____.
I will use sense words about _____, _____, and _____ in my sentences.

Bridging Have children share their sentences with a partner. Partners should give each other feedback on how well they used interesting sense words and other adjectives. **ELD** ELD.PI.2.1, ELD.PI.2.2

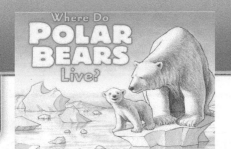

SEGMENT 1
PP. 8–19

▶ **SHARE OBJECTIVES**

- Describe the connection between scientific ideas.
- Monitor understanding while reading and clarify any confusing parts.

Content Vocabulary

Display the words listed below from the trade book. Read each word with children and discuss its meaning.

den (p. 10) the shelter or home of a wild animal

cub (p. 11) a young bear, wolf, or lion

Arctic (p. 12) the region surrounding the North Pole (• *Artic*)

survive (p. 16) to stay alive

• = Spanish cognate

COMPREHENSION STRATEGIES

Use the following strategies flexibly as you read with children by modeling how they can be used to improve comprehension. See scaffolded support for the strategy shown in boldface during this segment's reading.

- **Monitor/Clarify**
- Summarize
- Infer/Predict
- Visualize
- Analyze/Evaluate
- Question

Monitor/Clarify **IF** children have difficulty applying the Monitor/Clarify strategy, **THEN** revisit the strategy by reviewing what happened when the cub was just born in the den. Say:

> **Think Aloud**
>
> *The illustration and the text on p. 12 tell me that when the cub was just born, he was very small, blind, and helpless. He snuggled in his mother's fur, drank her milk, and grew.*

Have children use the strategy to explain that the cub was safe and warm with his mother in the den.

Think Through the Text
Cite Text Evidence

Read Segment 1, Pages 8–19

- Periodically pause to check children's understanding. Examples of key concepts and vocabulary for selected pages follow. Base any additional discussion on children's needs.

Page 10

- *Where do you think the bear's den is? How can you tell?* It must be under the snow, since the bear is peeking out of a hole. **ELA** RI.2.1, RI.2.7 **ELD** ELD.PI.2.6

ENGLISH LANGUAGE SUPPORT Guide children to use details in the illustrations to help them draw conclusions about the bear's den. Ask: *What is poking out of the snow? How do you know? Where did the bear come from? How do you know?* **ELD** ELD.PI.2.6

Page 13

- *What have you learned about arctic winters so far?* The temperatures can drop to fifty degrees below zero. The Sun never rises from October to February.
ELA RI.2.1 **ELD** ELD.PI.2.1

Page 14

- *How is the Arctic spring different from the winter?* The bright Sun is out. The cub is ready to leave the den. **ELA** RI.2.1, RI.2.3 **ELD** ELD.PI.2.6

Page 16

- *How does the polar bear's skin help to keep the bear warm?* The polar bear's skin soaks up the heat of the Sun. **ELA** RI.2.1, RI.2.3 **ELD** ELD.PI.2.6

☑ TARGET STRATEGY

Monitor/Clarify

Tell children to practice the Monitor/Clarify strategy as they read pp. 8–19 silently. Model using the strategy if they need help. When they have finished, ask several children to point out where they used the strategy to help them clarify information.

RESPOND TO SEGMENT 1

Have children summarize details they've learned so far about polar bears. Tell them to ask questions about anything they don't understand about the bears' arctic environment. Review the questions above if children have difficulty.
ELA RI.2.1 **ELD** ELD.PI.2.6

Discuss

▶ SHARE OBJECTIVES

- Gather relevant information from print and digital sources.
- Build knowledge through topic investigation.
- Collaborate with a group to initiate a project plan. LANGUAGE

Focus on Collaboration

✔	Discuss Collaboration
✔	Review Discussion Rules
✔	Discuss Project Roles
✔	Have a Discussion
✔	Reflect on the Discussion

Discuss Collaboration Talk with children as a whole class about working in teams. Explain that when children work together, it is important for them to all participate in the discussions and the work for the project. Remind children that they will each be assigned a role during the project. Since each team will create and present one photo gallery, it is important for each member to contribute something to the project.

Review Discussion Rules Explain that it is important to have rules for a discussion so that everyone won't be speaking at the same time. Present and read aloud the following discussion rules:

- One team member may speak at a time.
- When someone is speaking, the other team members should be quiet and listen.
- If you have a question, raise your hand and wait for your turn to speak.
- Give each team member a chance to share ideas, build on others' comments, and ask questions.

Remind children that there may be several different opinions about what pictures to use or what information to include. Ask: *What is a fair way to make a decision when there is more than one opinion about how to do something? take a vote*

Post the following list of discussion rules. Refer to it and review the rules each time children prepare to work in their teams.

	Discussion Rules
1	Speak one at a time.
2	Listen quietly when someone is speaking.
3	Give each member a turn to share ideas, respond to comments, and ask questions.

Discuss Project Roles Remind children that when team members have specific roles, or jobs, the group discussions run more smoothly:

- **leader:** starts and guides the discussion; keeps it on track
- **recorder:** takes notes about key ideas to share with group members
- **timekeeper:** makes sure the discussion starts and ends on time
- **team members:** participate in the discussion

Have a Discussion Have children work in their teams to discuss the focus on their photo gallery by using the following prompts:

- *What are the key ideas we want to show about how polar bears survive in the Arctic?*
- *What kinds of things will we need to show in the photos?*
- *What questions might our audience have about our topic?*
- *How can we make sure our photo gallery both informs and entertains our audience?*

Before teams begin their discussions, assign roles. Remind children to apply the discussion rules during their discussion. See Collaborative Conversations Rubric, p. R17.

ENGLISH LANGUAGE SUPPORT Use these sentence frames to support participation: *One important idea about polar bears that we should include is _____ because _____. We should find a photo that shows _____. One question people might have is _____. We could make our display more interesting by _____.*
ELD ELD.PI.2.1, ELD.PI.2.3

Reflect on the Discussion Have children reflect on the content and process of the discussion, using the following prompts:

- *Did you come up with a list of key points?*
- *Did everyone get a chance to share ideas and ask questions about the display?*
- *What might you do differently the next time you meet with your team?*
ELA SL.2.1a, S.2.1b, SL.2.1c **ELD** ELD.PI.2.1, ELD.PI.2.3

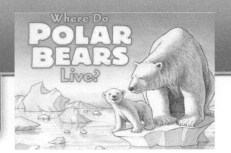

SEGMENT 1
PP. 8–19

Expand Language Production

Emerging For each question in Dig Deeper, accept one-word responses and expand them. For example, if a child's response to the question about what the author wants us to understand about polar bear mothers is "good," expand it by saying: *Yes, polar bears are good mothers because they take care of their cubs and feed them.*

Expanding Provide a sentence frame in response to each question and have children complete it. Then have children repeat the complete response.

Bridging Use these sentence frames to guide children to support their inferences to Write About Reading:

The first part of the book tells how polar bears survive in the Arctic. *During winter,* polar bears escape the cold by staying underground in a den. *They have* thick fur, black skin, and blubber *to keep them warm.* **ELD** ELD.PI.2.1, ELD.PI.2.6

INDEPENDENT READING

Have children read pp. 8–19 independently and complete their Reader's Notebooks Volume 2 pp. 76–77 . Have children share their responses with the class.

Analyze the Text

Analyze the Text

Dig Deeper

- Model deeper thinking. Ask: *Why didn't the cub leave the den before it was four months old?* Explain that you know the answer to your question has something to do with what the cub was like when it was younger. Point out that p. 12 tells about the newborn cub and that p. 13 tells what it was like outside the den.

- Read pp. 12–13 aloud and ask children to listen for details that can help them figure out the answer. *The text says that the cub was small, blind, and helpless when he was younger. This information tells me that the cub would not have been safe in the cold weather outside the den.*

- Ask the question below. Guide children to look back through the text and illustrations on pp. 8–19 to find the answer. Have them reread the appropriate pages and ask volunteers to share their answers. *What does the author want the reader to know about polar bear mothers? Page 12: Mothers keep their cubs safe and feed them. Page 19: Cubs stay with their mothers for their first two years. When a cub gets tired, the mother lets it ride on her back. This information and the illustrations show that the mother takes care of her cubs and keeps them safe.* **ELA** RI.2.1, RI.2.3 **ELD** ELD.PI.2.1, ELD.PI.2.6

Classroom Collaboration

Divide the class into small groups. Ask the question below and have children discuss it. You might also choose to have children generate a question for their own discussion. *How does the polar bear's body help it survive in the Arctic? Use details from the text to support your answer.* Sample answer: *Page 16: The polar bear's body is built to survive in the Arctic because it has long fur, black skin, and a layer of blubber. Page 19: It has fur between the pads on its paws to keep it from slipping on the ice.* **ELA** RI.2.1, RI.2.3 **ELD** ELD.PI.2.1, ELD.PI.2.6

- Reconvene as a whole group and have groups share their answers.

ENGLISH LANGUAGE SUPPORT Have children work with a partner to orally summarize the text. Provide sentence frames such as: *The polar bear can survive in the Arctic because it* has long fur, black skin, *and* a layer of blubber. *Polar bears also have* fur on their paws *so they don't* slip on the ice. **ELD** ELD.PI.2.6

Write About Reading

After children have reread Segment 1, tell them that they will respond to the text by writing a summary paragraph of the information they read.

- Prompt children to explain how polar bears are able to survive in the cold Arctic environment.

- Remind children to include facts and details from the text in their summaries.

Children's summaries should include a topic sentence based on the main idea of the segment, two or three sentences that support the main idea, and a concluding sentence to restate the main idea. Have children share their summaries of Segment 1 with a small group, comparing and explaining their choice of topic sentence and details. **ELA** W.2.2 **ELD** ELD.PI.2.10

Prepare

▶ SHARE OBJECTIVES

• Understand project roles.
• Develop a list of realistic tasks.
• Understand how to manage time and resources.

Plan Roles and Tasks

✔ Assign Roles
✔ Develop a Task Checklist

Assign Roles Assign each team member a role for the project. If children are familiar with project work, you might want to allow them to choose their own roles once they have had a chance to discuss the project. Roles for the project may include the following:

• **fact finder:** finds facts about how polar bears survive and records them

• **photo finder:** finds and prints pictures that support the facts about polar bear survival

• **caption writer:** uses the facts to write one or two sentences about each photo

Discuss the tasks and responsibilities of each role with children and ensure that they are comfortable with their assignments. Allow them time to ask questions and clarify anything they do not understand about their roles.

Develop a Task Checklist As a group, talk about the steps involved in gathering the facts and photos children will need to create their photo galleries. Prompt children to describe what they will need to do first, next, and last. If necessary, ask them to explain how they will find facts about polar bears, find photos to illustrate those facts, write captions for the photos, and organize the photos and captions in an interesting and informative display. Once children have identified all the tasks they must complete, work together to record them in a checklist, such as the one below. Display the task checklist so children can refer to it as they work on their projects. **ELA** SL.2.1a, SL.2.1b, SL.2.1c **ELD** ELD.PI.2.1

	Project Task Checklist
1	Read books and websites for facts about polar bears.
2	Find and record facts and details that show how polar bears survive in the Arctic.
3	Choose which facts to include in the display.
4	Look at pictures in books and online photo galleries.
5	Print photos that support facts about polar bear survival.
6	Use the facts and details to write a caption for each photo.
7	Arrange the photos and captions in a display. Include a title for the display at the top.
8	Get feedback from classmates and the teacher. Make any changes, as needed.
9	Present the photo gallery to the class.

ENGLISH LANGUAGE SUPPORT Take additional time, as needed, to ensure that children understand their role. Model finding and recording a fact in the trade book, choosing a picture and writing a caption about it. Then ask children to describe what they will do for their role in their own words. **ELD** ELD.PI.2.1, ELD.PI.2.5

Manage Time and Resources

✔ Define Schedule and Milestones
✔ Develop a Realistic Schedule
✔ Determine Resource Needs

Define Schedule and Milestones Use a calendar to map out the two weeks of the project. Point out that children are already on Day 3 of the project. You may want to provide children with a blank calendar so they can fill in the tasks and milestones with you.

Guide children to begin by writing the tasks from their checklist on Days 4–7. Tasks should include finding facts and photos, writing captions, organizing the display, receiving peer and teacher feedback, and creating the display. Point out that on Days 8 and 9 they will be presenting their displays and being assessed and that Day 10 will be a time for reflection and celebration.

Develop a Realistic Schedule Work together to estimate the time it will take children to complete each of the tasks they listed. If they are suggesting unrealistic timeframes for any tasks, work with them to more clearly define the task and what they need to do to accomplish it. **ELA** SL.2.1a, SL.2.1b, SL.2.1c **ELD** ELD.PI.2.1

Determine Resource Needs As a group, discuss what resources and materials children will need to gather their information and create their displays. For example, they might use websites for zoos and educational or conservation organizations as well as online videos. Display the material children will use for their displays. Prompt children to think about how many pictures and captions will fit on the display. Remind them that everything should be clear and readable from a short distance. Ask children what they need to print their photos, trim them, and write their captions. As a group, make a list of all the resources and materials children might need and post it for reference.
ELA SL.2.1a, SL.2.1b, SL.2.1c **ELD** ELD.PI.2.1

▶ SHARE OBJECTIVES

- Identify main ideas and the details that support them. LANGUAGE
- Describe the connections between scientific ideas or concepts. LANGUAGE
- Determine the meaning of words and phrases.

Content Vocabulary

Display the words from the trade book listed below. Read each word with children and discuss its meaning.

tundra (p. 20) an area in the Arctic that has no trees and very few plants (• *tundra*)

lemming (p. 28) a small rodent that lives in the Arctic tundra

seaweed (p. 28) a kind of algae that lives in the sea and that can look like a plant

• = Spanish cognate

COMPREHENSION STRATEGIES

Use the following strategies flexibly as you read with children by modeling how they can be used to improve comprehension. See scaffolded support for the strategy shown in boldface during this segment's reading.

- Monitor/Clarify
- Visualize
- Summarize
- Analyze/Evaluate
- Infer/Predict
- **Question**

RtI FORMATIVE ASSESSMENT

Question IF children have difficulty applying the Question strategy, THEN use this model:

> **Think Aloud**
> *Of all the fish and animals under the ice, I ask myself why polar bears don't eat the fish in the sea. I'll reread. The text on page 23 says that seals come to the surface to breathe. It must be easier to catch animals that come to the surface than those that stay underwater.*

Have children explain how the text and illustrations help them use the strategy.

FIRST READ

Think Through the Text
Cite Text Evidence

Read Segment 2, Pages 20–28

- Periodically pause to check children's understanding. Examples of key concepts and vocabulary for selected pages follow. Base any additional discussion on children's needs.

Pages 20–21

- *What does the author want you to know about the Arctic on these pages?* The Arctic is a mix of land and ice. The land is made of cold, rocky islands and tundra, where no trees grow. **ELA** RI.2.1, RI.2.8 **ELD** ELD.PI.2.6

Pages 24–27

- *Why does the mother polar bear need to hunt?* She did not eat over the winter and lost hundreds of pounds. She must eat again. **ELA** RI.2.1 **ELD** ELD.PI.2.6

Page 25

- *What do you know about a polar bear's sense of smell?* The author says the polar bear can smell the seal's breathing hole through three feet of snow. Her sense of smell must be very strong to help her hunt this way. **ELA** RI.2.1 **ELD** ELD.PI.2.6

  ENGLISH LANGUAGE SUPPORT Use these sentence frames to support participation: *The polar bear can smell <u>the seal's breathing hole through the snow</u>. This tells me that <u>her sense of smell is very strong</u>.* **ELD** ELD.PI.2.1

☑ TARGET STRATEGY

Question

Tell children to practice the Question strategy as they read pp. 20–28 silently. When they have finished, ask several children to point out where they used the strategy and what question they asked themselves. Have them explain how they answered the question.

Respond To Segment 2

Help children summarize what they have learned about the Arctic and animals that live there. Ask them to explain how the illustrations help them understand what the ice and sea are like in the Arctic. **ELA** RI.2.1, RI.2.7 **ELD** ELD.PI.2.6

Prepare

▶ SHARE OBJECTIVES

- Choose a research focus. LANGUAGE
- Identify reliable sources.
- Understand how to take notes.

Initiate Research

✔	Focus the Topic
✔	Begin the Research Process
✔	Find Credible Sources
✔	Gather Facts and Photos

Focus the Topic Remind children that the purpose of their display is to show the different things that help polar bears survive in the Arctic. As a group, discuss what children have learned about polar bears so far from the trade book. Model identifying information that relates to the display topic and information that does not. Then have teams brainstorm other information they might need to research to learn more about. **ELA** SL.2.1a, SL.2.1b, SL.2.1c **ELD** ELD.PI.2.1

Begin the Research Process Have teams start listing information from the trade book that they would like to include in their display. Explain that as they continue to read the book, they may come across additional information they want to add. As a group, talk about other sources of information children could use for the research process, such as websites and online videos. Point out that children will also need to find photos online and print them. Discuss proper use of classroom or library computers and printers. You may want to limit the number of photos each group may print. Remind children that even though they each have an assigned role, it is important to share what they find and work together to make the best possible product. **ELA** SL.2.1a, SL.2.1b, SL.2.1c **ELD** ELD.PI.2.1

Find Credible Sources Remind children that the Internet can be a good source of information, but that some websites are more reliable than others. Tell children that websites ending in .edu, .org, and .gov are official sites run by schools, experts, and government officials and are trustworthy sources of information. You may want to suggest or bookmark one or two useful websites to get teams started. As teams work, you may want to create a list of websites that children used during the research process and post it for reference. **ELA** SL.2.1a, SL.2.1b, SL.2.1c **ELD** ELD.PI.2.1

Gather Facts and Photos Remind children to take notes about the key facts and details they find. Explain that they need to record the information, being careful to accurately copy the facts and key points. Point out that key information may be accompanied by helpful photos, illustrations, maps, or graphs. Remind children to print out the visuals that will most effectively illustrate their display topic. Discuss these note-taking tips:

- Record each important point.
- Include facts and details that tell about each important point.
- Write down the source of the information.

Explain that it is important to record each source in case children need to go back to it to check any of the information they listed. Tell children to keep these notes because they will use them to write the captions for their photo gallery. **ELA** W.2.7, W.2.8 **ELD** ELD.PI.2.10

ENGLISH LANGUAGE SUPPORT Have children use Graphic Organizer 7 (Idea Support Map) ⬚ to record their research notes. Using the trade book as a model, show how you write the topic at the top and facts and examples that support it in the boxes. **ELD** ELD.PI.2.10

Independent Reading

- Read and comprehend informational text.
- Refer to details and examples to analyze a text independently.
- Read independently from a "just right" book.
- Read aloud with expression.

ENGLISH LANGUAGE SUPPORT

"Just Right" Books for English Learners

All Proficiencies It may take longer for English learners to read a "just right" book than it will for their English-speaking peers. You may wish to suggest chunking the book into segments of appropriate lengths for children to read in each sitting.

Read to Connect

Share and Compare Texts If children have already demonstrated comprehension and analysis of the first two segments of *Where Do Polar Bears Live?*, have them read a text in print or online on the topic of life in the Arctic. Ask children to use their Reading Logs ⬚ to record their progress and thoughts about their reading. Have partners ask and answer questions such as: *What did you learn from this selection? What more do you want to learn about the Arctic?* **ELA** RI.2.1, RI.2.9, RI.2.10 **ELD** ELD.PI.2.1, ELD.PI.2.6

Self-Selected Reading

Topics of Interest Have children select an independent reading book. To help children select a book, suggest related topics such as polar animals, the North Pole, or life in the Arctic. Ask children to use their Reading Logs ⬚ to record their progress and thoughts about their reading.

Fluency

Partner Read Have children practice reading aloud with expression, using their self-selected reading books. Tell them to select a passage or page and read it to their partner. Have them listen to the partner's feedback about expression. Then have them reread aloud with the comments in mind. **ELA** RF.2.4b **ELD** ELD.PIII.2

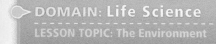

DOMAIN: Life Science
LESSON TOPIC: The Environment

Extend the Topic

Domain-Specific Vocabulary

Discuss Words About the Topic Have children review in their journals the list of content vocabulary words and meanings they have encountered so far in *Where Do Polar Bears Live?* Then display the words shown to the right. Tell children that these words can help them learn more about polar bears and the Arctic. Read aloud the meaning of each word. Then have children respond to the following prompts: **ELA** SL.2.1, L.2.6 **ELD** ELD.PI.2.1, ELD.PI.2.6, ELD.PI.2.7

- The polar bear's thick fur and black skin help it _____ to the cold Arctic conditions. *adapt*

- The polar bear's layer of blubber helps _____ it and keep the bear warm. *insulate*

- The Arctic is a gigantic _____ that covers more than 18 million square miles. *region*

ENGLISH LANGUAGE SUPPORT Support meanings of the content vocabulary words using the illustrations and maps in the trade book. For example, point to the map on p. 20 and say: *This map shows the Arctic region. It is the area on the map that is shown in white.* **ELD** ELD.PI.2.6

Interact with the Words Have children work in small groups, using Graphic Organizer 6 (Four-Square Map) to extend their understanding of each word related to the Arctic and polar bears. Assign one word to each group and have them follow these steps for completing the Four-Square Map with information about the word:

1 In the first corner, draw a picture that represents the word.

2 In the second corner, write the meaning of the word.

3 In the third corner, write a sentence using the word.

4 In the fourth corner, write the word.

When groups have finished, have them share their completed Four-Square Maps with the class. **ELA** W.2.4, L.2.6 **ELD** ELD.PI.2.1, ELD.PI.2.6, ELD.PI.2.10

▶ **SHARE OBJECTIVES**
- Acquire and use domain-specific vocabulary.
- Participate in conversations about a topic. LANGUAGE

> **Words About the Topic:**
> **The Arctic**
>
> - **adapt** to adjust to the surrounding conditions or environment
> - **insulate** to keep warm
> - **region** a large area

Prepare

SHARE OBJECTIVES

- Choose samples to share.
- Give and receive peer feedback. LANGUAGE
- Assess progress.

Discuss Peer Critiques

✔	Discuss Rules for Peer Critiques
✔	Present Samples
✔	Discuss Peer Feedback

Discuss Rules for Peer Critiques Explain that it is often helpful to receive feedback about your work before you reach the presentation stage. Tell children that they will take turns giving feedback about their projects to their peers and receiving feedback about their projects from their peers. Review with children your rules about evaluating the work of others. You may wish to display a list of rules such as these:

- Always start by telling about something the team did well.

- Think about how the team can make its materials clearer or more interesting.

- Give helpful suggestions or ways the team can revise its materials.

- When you are receiving feedback, listen quietly and do not interrupt.

- Ask questions to clarify any comments or suggestions your team received.

Once children fully understand the rules for peer critiques, assign each team another team to work with.

ELA SL.2.1a, SL.2.1b, SL.2.1c, SL.2.3 **ELD** ELD.PI.2.1, ELD.PI.2.3, ELD.PI.2.5, ELD.PI.2.11

ENGLISH LANGUAGE SUPPORT Provide sentence frames to help children share their feedback: *One thing I think you did well is _____. One thing I like about your project is _____ because _____. One thing you could change is _____ because _____. One question I have is _____.* **ELD** ELD.PI.2.1, ELD.PI.2.3

Present Samples Have teams choose two or three facts and related pictures to share with another group. Tell children to present each fact-picture pair and explain how the fact and picture are connected and why they chose them for their display. As children evaluate the samples and offer feedback, have them consider these questions:

- Does each fact relate to the topic of the project?

- Does each picture help you understand a written fact?

- Is each picture large enough? Is it clear?

Allow time for children to give and receive feedback in their teams and ask any questions they may have.

ELA SL.2.1a, SL.2.1b, SL.2.1c **ELD** ELD.PI.2.1, ELD.PI.2.3, ELD.PI.2.11

Discuss Peer Feedback Have teams summarize the feedback they received. Ask them to discuss the key points of the peer critique and decide what changes, if any, they will make in their facts or photos. Remind children that the goal of the critique is to help them improve their project.

ELA SL.2.1a, SL.2.1b, SL.2.1c **ELD** ELD.PI.2.1, ELD.PI.2.3, ELD.PI.2.5

Evaluate Progress

✔	Check Children's Progress
✔	Clarify Expectations
✔	Look Ahead

Check Children's Progress Spend some time with each team to evaluate their progress. Have teams show the facts and photos they have gathered so far and briefly describe how they plan to organize or arrange them for their display. Ask them to tell about the peer feedback they received and describe any changes they plan to make based on these comments. Work with teams to identify additional tasks they need to complete based on your review of their materials and their comments.

ELA SL.2.1a, SL.2.1b, SL.2.1c **ELD** ELD.PI.2.1

Clarify Expectations Bring children back together as a class and remind them of the project components: a photo gallery that includes a topic title and photos or other visuals with informative captions based on their research. Remind children that they need to work cooperatively to complete the project. Explain that they will be evaluated as a team on their photo gallery.

Look Ahead Have children return to their project teams and discuss what they still need to do to complete their project. For most teams, the next step will involve writing the captions for their photos. Tell children to think about whether they will write or type their captions and what materials they will need. Circulate among the teams to offer guidance and feedback, as needed.

ELA SL.2.1a, SL.2.1b, SL.2.1c **ELD** ELD.PI.2.1

INTEGRATED LANGUAGE ARTS REVIEW

Write About Reading

Digital Resources ▶

To support children before they start this task, use the following digital resources.

▶ GrammarSnap Videos: Complete Sentences, Subject-Verb Agreement

▶ Multimedia Grammar Glossary

INTRODUCE THE TASK

After children have finished their independent reading, tell them that they will respond to the text by comparing it with *Where Do Polar Bears Live?* Explain the task:

- Children will draw a picture to represent the topic or content of the two texts.
- Children will identify two ways in which the texts are the same.
- Children will write sentences that describe these similarities below their picture.
- The sentences should include comparison words, such as *both* and *also*.

Review the Model Display the model descriptive paragraph from **Student Book** Volume 4, p. 121, and review the proper use of sense words and other adjectives in writing. Point out that the writer has used descriptions that help readers imagine what the beach is like.

PLAN AND DRAFT

Display the following list to guide children in writing and organizing their sentences:

- Name the two texts you are writing about.
- What did you learn about in both books?
- How can you use comparing words in your sentences?
- Use a capital letter at the beginning of each sentence. Use an end mark at the end of each sentence.

REVISE AND EDIT

Guide the class to generate a checklist that children can use as they revise their sentences. For example:

- Did I include the title of each book?
- Did I explain how the two texts are the same?
- Is there a place where I can add a comparing word in my writing?
- Did I use complete sentences?
- Did I use end marks correctly?
- Have I corrected any spelling errors?

See Analytic Writing Rubric, p. R17.

SHARE

Have children share their pictures and sentences with the class. **ELA** W.2.2, W.2.5 **ELD** ELD.PI.2.1, ELD.PI.2.10

▶ SHARE OBJECTIVES

- Write a response to the independent reading text. LANGUAGE
- Cite evidence from the text.
- Use correct punctuation and spelling.

▶ SKILLS REVIEW

Review the following skills, as needed, before children begin to write their response.

- **Writing:** Descriptive Paragraph (Lesson 18)
- **Grammar:** Subject-Verb Agreement (Lesson 17)
- **Spelling:** Compound Words (Lesson 15)

ENGLISH LANGUAGE SUPPORT

Sentence Frames

Emerging Provide these sentence frames to support participation:

I read _____ and _____. Both texts are about _____.
I learned _____ from the first text. I learned _____ from the second text.

Expanding Provide these sentence frames and guide children to complete them:

I read _____. I learned about _____. Both texts _____.

Bridging Have children share their sentences with a partner. Partners should give each other feedback on how well they used comparing words and details from the two texts. **ELD** ELD.PI.2.1, ELD.PI.2.3

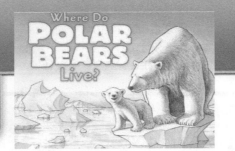

SECOND READ

Analyze the Text

Analyze the Text

Dig Deeper

- Model deeper thinking. Ask: *How does a seal's body help it survive in the Arctic?* Explain that the text and the illustrations give the information to answer that question. Point out that on p. 22, the illustration shows the seal using its tail and flippers to swim. On p. 23, the text describes how the seal creates breathing holes.

- Read p. 23 aloud and ask children to listen for details that can help you figure out the answer. *The text says that seals must come to the surface to breathe. They use the claws on their flippers to scrape away ice, making holes so they can reach the air.*

- Ask the question below. Guide children to look back through the text and illustrations on pp. 20–28 to find the answer. Have them reread the appropriate pages and ask volunteers to share their answers.
  What does the mother polar bear teach her cub about finding food? Pages 24–25: The illustration and text show the mother and cub using their sense of smell to find the seal's breathing hole. Page 26: The illustration and text explain how the mother bear uses her sharp claws and her jaws to catch the seal. The illustration shows that the cub watches his mother hunt.
  ELA RI.2.7 **ELD** ELD.PI.2.1, ELD.PI.2.6

Classroom Collaboration

Divide the class into small groups. Ask the question below and have children discuss it. You might also choose to have children generate a question for their own discussion.

What are the sources of food for polar bears? Which source is the best and why? Sample answer: Polar bears can eat tiny lemmings and nibble grass and seaweed on land. The best source of food is the seal because it is bigger and gives them more meat. **ELA** RI.2.10 **ELD** ELD.PI.2.1, ELD.PI.2.6

- Reconvene as a whole group and have groups share their answers.

Write About Reading

After children have reread Segment 2, tell them that they will respond to the text by writing a summary paragraph of the information they read.

- Prompt children to explain what polar bears eat and how they hunt and catch seals.

- Remind children to include facts and details from the text in their summaries.

Children's summaries should include a topic sentence based on the main idea of the segment, two or three sentences that support the main idea, and a concluding sentence to restate the main idea. Have children share their summaries of Segment 2 with a small group, comparing and explaining their choices of topic sentence and details. **ELA** W.2.2 **ELD** ELD.PI.2.10

Prepare

Create Materials

- ✔ Discuss Tools and Materials
- ✔ Write Captions
- ✔ Edit and Revise
- ✔ Plan Display

Discuss Tools and Materials Now that teams have had a chance to find their facts and photos, explain that it is time to write their captions and then plan and organize their display. As a group, brainstorm options for creating and displaying the captions. For example, explain that if children type their captions on a computer, they can experiment with making the type size bigger so the captions are easier to read and try out a variety of fonts and styles. Point out that they can fix any mistakes before they print their captions. Explain that if children handwrite their captions, they can write them on different colors and sizes of paper. Point out that regardless of which option a team chooses, there are many different ways to add interest to the display. Have teams discuss which tools and materials they would like to use and make a list. **ELA** SL.2.1a, SL.2.1b, SL.2.1c **ELD** ELD.PI.2.1

Write Captions Tell children that they should choose three to six photos for their display (depending on the size of the photos and the size of the display paper). Have them use the facts and details they gathered to write a caption for each photo. Explain that a caption briefly explains a key idea or describes something important in the photo. Point out that a caption does not tell every possible piece of information about what is shown in the photo. Remind children to use sense words to help their audience picture what is shown in each photo. Whether children are typing or writing their captions, remind them that the text needs to be readable from a short distance away from the display.
ELA W.2.2, W.2.7 **ELD** ELD.PI.2.2, ELD.PI.2.10

ENGLISH LANGUAGE SUPPORT Display an informational text and point out examples of captions. Explain that a caption appears below a picture and provides a short description of what is shown in the picture. Point out and discuss the features of a caption. For example, note that a caption should be a complete sentence that begins with a capital letter and ends with the correct end mark. **ELD** ELD.PI.2.5

Edit and Revise Have teams read each caption and proofread it for correct spelling, grammar, and punctuation. You may want to provide an editing and revision checklist such as the one that follows. Once children have finalized their captions, have them print or write the final draft. **ELA** W.2.2, W.2.5, W.2.8 **ELD** ELD.PI.2.2

Editing and Revision Checklist

- Is each caption a complete sentence?
- Does each caption begin with a capital letter and end with the correct end mark?
- Are all the words spelled correctly?
- Does each caption clearly explain or describe the key information in the photo?
- Did we include facts and details from our research?
- Did we include sense words?
- Do we need to add or change any words?

Plan Display Have teams gather their photos and captions and place them on top of their display paper. Explain that children should experiment with different arrangements of their materials to find the one that makes the clearest and most interesting display. Remind them that each visual needs an accompanying caption. Suggest that teams write their display topic or title on a piece of scratch paper and add it to their arrangement to ensure that they leave room for it. **ELA** SL.2.1a, SL.2.1b, SL.2.1c **ELD** ELD.PI.2.1

SEGMENT 3
PP. 29–35

▶ SHARE OBJECTIVES

- Describe how reasons support points the author makes. LANGUAGE
- Analyze and evaluate how well the author achieved her purpose. LANGUAGE

Content Vocabulary

Display the words from the trade book listed below. Read each word with children and discuss its meaning.

fierce (p. 35) wild; powerful

extinct (p. 35) no longer living (• *extincto*)

• = Spanish cognate

COMPREHENSION STRATEGIES

Use the following strategies flexibly as you read with children by modeling how they can be used to improve comprehension. See scaffolded support for the strategy shown in **boldface** during this segment's reading.

- Monitor/Clarify
- Visualize
- Summarize
- **Analyze/Evaluate**
- Infer/Predict
- Question

RtI FORMATIVE ASSESSMENT

Analyze/Evaluate IF children have difficulty applying the Analyze/Evaluate strategy, THEN use this model:

Think Aloud

On p. 29, the text says that a little more ice melts each summer in the Arctic. I'm going to use the illustrations to help me understand this. They are labeled Summer Ice 1980 and 2007.

Have children use the illustrations on p. 29 and the strategy to explain what the illustrations show and how they help readers draw a conclusion about ice.

Think Through the Text

Cite Text Evidence

Read Segment 3, Pages 29–35

- Periodically pause to check children's understanding. Examples of key concepts and vocabulary for selected pages follow. Base any additional discussion on children's needs.

Page 29

- *What can you tell about the Arctic ice from the two maps? The summer Arctic ice has changed over time. The white section on the map from 2007 is much smaller than the white section on the map from 1980.* **ELA** RI.2.1, RI.2.5, RI.2.7 **ELD** ELD.PI.2.1, ELD.PI.2.6

ENGLISH LANGUAGE SUPPORT Point to the white area on the map and explain that this represents the area of the Arctic that is covered by ice. Guide children to compare the size of this area in the two maps.

Page 30

- *What are some problems that thinner polar bears have? Thinner bears do not have as many cubs, and more of their cubs die before they grow up to have their own babies.* **ELA** RI.2.1, RI.2.3 **ELD** ELD.PI.2.1, ELD.PI.2.6

Pages 32–33

- *The author states that the polar bear is the biggest hunter on land. What details from the book tell how big the bear is? If a grown bear stood on its hind legs in a house, its head would brush the ceiling. A grown polar bear weighs as much as three tigers and has footprints wider than a dinner plate.*
ELA RI.2.1, RI.2.8 **ELD** ELD.PI.2.1, ELD.PI.2.6

ENGLISH LANGUAGE SUPPORT Use these sentence frames to support participation: *I can tell a polar bear is big because the text says <u>a grown polar bear would reach the ceiling if it stood up in a house</u>. Another detail that tells about a polar bear's size is <u>it weighs the same as three tigers</u>.* **ELD** ELD.PI.2.1

✓ TARGET STRATEGY

Analyze/Evaluate

Tell children to practice the Analyze/Evaluate strategy as they read pp. 29–35 silently. Remind them that analyzing and evaluating events in a book help readers draw good conclusions. When they have finished, ask several children to point out where they used the strategy to help them make conclusions about the polar bear and its environment.

Respond To Segment 3

Help children summarize what they have learned about how the Arctic is changing and how that affects polar bears. Ask them whether there are any facts or details that they don't understand. Have children describe whether the author gives the reader enough information to form an opinion about whether the changes in the Arctic could be a problem for polar bears. **ELA** RI.2.8 **ELD** ELD.PI.2.7

Prepare

Develop the Display

☑ Making an Effective Display
☑ Conveying Key Points
☑ Audience Responsibilities
☑ Planning, Rehearsal, and Presentation

Making an Effective Display Discuss the features that make a display both informative and interesting. Refer to the two-column chart you presented on Day 1 of the first week. Explain that there should be a good balance between text and visuals. Remind teams to include a title that clearly expresses the topic of their display. Suggest that teams view their display from a few feet away and check to make sure that all the text is readable. Point out that each photo needs a caption that includes facts or other interesting information that supports what is shown in the picture. Allow time for children to ask questions and clarify any of their expectations. **ELA** SL.2.3 **ELD** ELD.PI.2.1, ELD.PI.2.5

Conveying Key Points Explain that each team will display their photo gallery for the rest of the class to see. One team member will remain with the display to summarize the key points. Point out that the team's speaker should summarize the most important information, not merely read the captions. Suggest that teams identify the three or four key points they want to highlight in their presentation. Tell children that some of their classmates may have questions about the display. Explain that answering questions shows that a speaker is knowledgeable about and confident in his or her work. Suggest that teams identify possible questions that might come up and discuss how they could be answered using information in the display. **ELA** SL.2.1a, SL.2.1b, SL.2.1c **ELD** ELD.PI.2.1, ELD.PI.2.5

Audience Responsibilities Remind children that when a team's speaker is discussing the key points of the display, they should give the speaker their full attention. Tell children to listen carefully and think about any ideas or information they might ask a question about. Remind them to wait until the speaker is done before raising their hand and to wait to be called on. Encourage children to share comments about the display, including what the team did well or something they found interesting. Point out that children should not touch or tamper with the display in any way. **ELA** SL.2.1a, SL.2.1b, SL.2.1c **ELD** ELD.PI.2.1, ELD.PI.2.5

ENGLISH LANGUAGE SUPPORT Provide sentence frames children can use to share comments and ask questions as they review the photo galleries: *I like the way your team _____. One question I have is _____.* **ELD** ELD.PI.2.3

Planning, Rehearsal, and Presentation Tell children that this is their last chance to meet as a team to discuss and finalize their display. Explain that they can make any changes to their components to make them clearer, more effective, or more interesting and then attach them to the display paper. Once the team has chosen the key points to highlight, have the team's speaker practice presenting the display to the rest of the team. Remind the speaker to give the audience time to ask questions and make comments. Children should offer constructive feedback about the information and how the speaker presented it. **ELA** SL.2.1a, SL.2.1b, SL.2.1c **ELD** ELD.PI.2.1, ELD.PI.2.5, ELD.PI.2.9

SHARE OBJECTIVES

* Participate in group discussions. LANGUAGE
* Finalize the display.

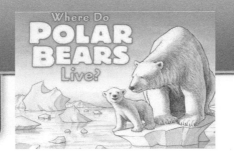

ENGLISH LANGUAGE SUPPORT

Comprehensible Input

Emerging For each question in Dig Deeper, accept one-word responses and expand them. For example, if a child's response to the question about the illustration on p. 33 is "no," expand it by saying: *No, this picture does not show something that could happen in real life.*

Expanding Provide a sentence frame in response to each question and have children complete it. Then have children repeat the complete response.

Bridging Use these sentence frames to guide children to support their responses to Write About Reading: *Polar bears need ice to* <u>catch the seals they eat for food.</u> *If the ice melts,* <u>the polar bears could become extinct one day.</u> **ELD** ELD.PI.2.1

INDEPENDENT READING

Have students read pp. 29–35 independently and complete their Reader's Notebooks Volume 2 pp. 80–81 ⬚. Have children share their responses with the class.

Analyze the Text

Dig Deeper

- Model deeper thinking. Ask: *Why did the author show a polar bear in a human setting?* Explain that this book is an informational text, and most of the illustrations show polar bears in their real environment, the Arctic. It's a surprise to see an illustration of a polar bear in a house. Describe the illustration on p. 32.

- Read aloud p. 32. Ask children to listen for details that can help them answer the question. *The text says that if the polar bear stood on its hind legs, its head would brush the ceiling of your living room.* Point out that you know a polar bear would never be in a living room, so the author must have shown this so that the reader can understand the text better. By showing the polar bear's head touching the ceiling, you can better picture how big it is.

- Ask the question below. Guide children to look back through the text and study the illustration on p. 33 to figure out the answer. Ask volunteers to share their answers.
  Do you think the illustration shows something that happened in real life? No, it is just an illustration to help the reader understand how big the polar bear is compared with three tigers. **ELA** RI.2.1, RI.2.3, RI.2.6 **ELD** ELD.PI.2.3, ELD.PI.2.11

💬 Classroom Collaboration

Divide the class into small groups. Ask the question below and have children discuss it. You might also choose to have children generate a question for their own discussion. **ELA** RI.2.6, RI.2.8 **ELD** ELD.PI.2.6, ELD.PI.2.7

Does the author think that polar bears might become extinct? Why or why not? Sample answer: *Yes, the author believes that polar bears are in danger of becoming extinct. If polar bears are not able to hunt for food, they will not survive.*

- Reconvene as a whole group and have groups share their answers. Tell children that now that they have read what the author thinks may happen to polar bears, they can discuss the author's purpose for writing this book.
  ELA RI.2.6, RI.2.8 **ELD** ELD.PI.2.6, ELD.PI.2.7

Write About Reading

After children have reread Segment 3, tell them that they will respond to the text by writing a summary paragraph of the information they read.

- Prompt children to explain why polar bears are in danger of becoming extinct.

- Remind children to include facts and details from the text in their summaries.

Have children share their summaries of Segment 3 with a small group, comparing and explaining their choices of topic sentence and details. **ELA** W.2.2 **ELD** ELD.PI.2.2, ELD.PI.2.10

Present

▶ SHARE OBJECTIVES

- Present and share information. LANGUAGE
- Ask and answer questions about textual and visual information. LANGUAGE

Present the Display

✔	Set Up Expectations
✔	Record the Event
✔	Discuss Presentation Tips
✔	Provide Feedback

Set Up Expectations Arrange the photo galleries so they are spread out throughout the classroom. Point out that someone will be speaking from each team, so several children will be talking at the same time. Remind them to speak loud enough for their immediate audience but not so loud that they intrude on the other speakers. Remind children that they will be moving in small groups and will have a chance to view, learn about, and comment on each display. Use the assessment strategies and rubric on p. T533 to assess teams and individuals as they present their displays. Determine how much time teams will have to view and learn about each photo gallery before moving on to the next one. You may want to use a timer and have children move in five-minute intervals. Remind children that before they move on to the next display, they should offer a positive comment about the photo gallery or presentation they just saw and heard about. **ELA** SL.2.1a, SL.2.1b, SL.2.1c **ELD** ELD.PI.2.5

Record the Event Tell children that you will make a video recording of each team's speaker presenting the display to a group of classmates. Explain that recording the presentations gives you another way to assess each team's work and how effectively they shared it with their peers. Share the recording with children at a later time and use it to praise the products they created, to comment on the way they worked collaboratively, and to offer constructive feedback for future group or project work. **ELA** W.2.7, W.2.8, SL.2.1a, SL.2.1b, SL.2.1c, SL.2.3 **ELD** ELD.PI.2.1, ELD.PI.2.3, ELD.PI.2.5, ELD.PI.2.6, ELD.PI.2.9

Discuss Presentation Tips Remind children that when a team's speaker is discussing the key points of the display, they should give the speaker their full attention. Remind them to wait until the speaker is done before raising their hand and to wait to be called on. Discuss the characteristics of an effective presentation and model each strategy for the class. You may want to display the list that follows. **ELA** SL.2.1a, SL.2.1b, SL.2.1c **ELD** ELD.PI.2.1, ELD.PI.2.5, ELD.PI.2.9

Presentation Tips
Speak in a loud, clear voice.
Don't rush. Take your time.
Make eye contact with your audience.
Point to the display as you discuss key points.
At the end, ask whether anyone has a comment or question.

ENGLISH LANGUAGE SUPPORT Provide sentence frames children can use to highlight key points in their team's display: *One thing that helps polar bears survive is _____ because _____. This picture shows _____. Another key point is _____.* **ELD** ELD.PI.2.1, ELD.PI.2.9

Provide Feedback Before teams begin their presentations, tell children how proud you are of the photo galleries they have created and how excited you are to hear them share their work with their peers. After the presentations, congratulate children on their work. Make a specific comment about each team's display or presentation.

Your Turn

Cite Text Evidence

▶ SHARE OBJECTIVES

- Follow the rules of a discussion.
- Use words and phrases acquired through reading. LANGUAGE
- Write an opinion paragraph.

ENGLISH LANGUAGE SUPPORT

Use Sentence Frames

Emerging Provide sentence frames such as the following to help children write their opinion and reasons that support it: *I think it is/is not important to care about polar bears. One reason I think this is _____. Another reason that supports my opinion is _____. That is why I think _____.* Have partners work together to complete the sentence frames.

Expanding Guide children to complete a web by writing their opinion in the center and reasons and facts that support their opinion in the surrounding circles. Have children use their completed web to write their opinion paragraph.

Bridging Remind children to use words that link their opinion with their reasons and examples. Model writing a sample sentence, such as: *I think it is important to care about polar bears because they are in danger.* Explain that the linking word *because* connects your opinion and a reason that supports it.

ELD ELD.PI.2.1, ELD.PI.2.3, ELD.PI.2.10, ELD.PI.2.11

RETURN TO THE ESSENTIAL QUESTION

Remind children of the Essential Question: *What do wild animals need to survive?* After initial discussion, guide children to focus on *Where Do Polar Bears Live?* Prompt them to explain that a polar bear is a wild animal and that it lives in the Arctic. Ask partners to work together to answer the Essential Question as it pertains to polar bears. Have them find text evidence in the book that supports their answers. Have partners present their responses to the class. Remind them to speak in complete sentences and to use words and phrases they learned in the book. **ELA** RI.2.1, SL.2.6, L.2.6 **ELD** ELD.PI.2.1, ELD.PI.2.6

 **Classroom Collaboration** Have children discuss any questions they might have about *Where Do Polar Bears Live?* Encourage them to help each other clarify information and to provide further explanations that help answer their questions, referring to the book when necessary. Guide children to follow the agreed-upon rules for discussions. **ELA** SL.2.1a, SL.2.1b, SL.2.1c, SL.2.3 **ELD** ELD.PI.2.1, ELD.PI.2.5

WRITE ABOUT READING

Performance Task

Tell children that they will write an opinion paragraph based on information they learned in *Where Do Polar Bears Live?* Write the following question on the board: *Is it important to care about polar bears?* Remind children that their opinion tells what they think about the question. Tell them to state their opinion, to supply reasons that support the opinion, to use linking words, and to write a closing sentence that sums up their opinion.

Writing Tip Tell children to refer to *Where Do Polar Bears Live?* for information that supports their opinion, if needed. Remind them to use linking words (e.g., *because, and, also*) to connect their opinion and reasons for their opinion. **ELA** RI.2.10, W.2.1, W.2.8 **ELD** ELD.PI.2.11, ELD.PII.2.6

Assess

Score the Project

Scoring the Project Work with children to review the project requirements they were given during the launch and preparation stages. Share the rubric below and tell children that you will work with them to score their project. As you assess and meet with each team, draw attention to project strengths and talk with individual children about areas in which they could have done a better job.

For a child-friendly version of this rubric, see p. R23.

	Collaboration	Research and Text Evidence	Content	Presentation
4	• Children made valuable contributions to each task within the project. • Children provided constructive feedback and input during preparation steps and check-ins. • Discussions were polite and productive. • Group members demonstrated clear understanding of the role of collaboration in project success.	• Information is organized in a clear and logical way. • Children chose a variety of reliable print and digital resources. • Research is carefully documented. • Text evidence is used successfully throughout the project.	• Content maintains a clear focus throughout. • Written portions of the project are well thought out and answer the project question thoroughly. • Visuals are useful and enhance the product. • All parts of the project are free of errors.	• The presentation is dynamic and engages the audience. • Information is shared in an effective way. • The presentation is well organized. • Children are able to give thoughtful answers to questions from the audience.
3	• Children somewhat contributed to each task within the project. • Children provided some useful feedback and input during preparation steps and check-ins. • Discussions were polite but sometimes got off-track. • Group members demonstrated a basic understanding of the role of collaboration in project success.	• Information is mostly organized in a clear and logical way. • Children chose a few reliable print and digital resources. • Research is documented but disorganized or unclear. • Text evidence is used successfully in some parts of the project.	• Content is focused but may stray at times. • Written portions of the project are well thought out and address the project question. • Visuals are useful. • All parts of the project contain minimal errors.	• The presentation is engaging. • Information is shared in an effective way. • The display has parts that could be better organized. • Children are able to answer questions from the audience.
2	• Children made partial contributions to tasks within the project. • Children had trouble providing useful feedback and input during preparation steps and check-ins. • Discussions led to disagreements or were frequently off-topic. • Group members made little effort to collaborate.	• Information is somewhat organized. • Children chose only print or only digital resources. • Research is not documented. • Text evidence is weak or used in a limited way.	• Content is unfocused in some areas. • Written portions of the project provide some information but lack purpose. • Visuals are not useful. • The project contains some errors throughout.	• The presentation is helpful but could be more engaging. • Information is shared but confusing at times. • The display lacks clear organization. • Children struggle to answer questions about their display.
1	• Children made few or no contributions to tasks within the project. • Children were unable to provide useful feedback and input during display steps and check-ins. • Discussions did not take place, or children had trouble interacting with each other. • Group members did not work as a team.	• Information has little to no organization. • There is no evidence of the use of reliable sources. • Research was limited or not conducted. • Text evidence has not been used.	• Content is haphazard throughout. • Written portions of the project are unclear and do not address the project question. • Visuals or multimedia are not present. • The project contains major errors.	• The presentation is off-topic or not taken seriously. • The information shared is irrelevant or confusing. • The display is disorganized. • Children are unable to answer questions about their display.

Independent Reading

▶ SHARE OBJECTIVES

- Research additional texts on a topic.
- Read independently.
- Compare and contrast texts on a topic.

ENGLISH LANGUAGE SUPPORT

Use Sentence Frames

Emerging Guide children to choose a text that has a high level of photographic support. Have children work in pairs. Guide them to complete their charts.

Expanding Review the meaning of the words *similar* and *different* before children complete their charts. Discuss ways in which two texts might be the same or different, such as whether they use illustrations or photos, how the text is organized, the kind of text features they have, and the kind of information they provide.

Bridging Have partners share and discuss the information in their charts before writing their paragraphs. Encourage them to add other information to their charts based on their discussion.

ELD ELD.PI.2.1, ELD.PI.2.2, ELD.PI.2.6, ELD.PI.2.10

Compare Texts

Research Texts on a Topic After children have completed reading *Where Do Polar Bears Live?*, have them research additional texts on the topic of polar bears or the Arctic. Encourage children to research the topic or locate books such as the following:

- *National Geographic Readers: Polar Bears* by Laura Marsh
- *Polar Bear (A Day in the Life: Polar Animals)* by Katie Marsico
- *Polar Bears* by Gail Gibbons
- *Polar Bears (Polar Animals)* by Emily Rose Townsend

Have children select two texts to compare. They should make notes using a chart such as the following. Encourage children to cite at least two ways each text or other source is similar to and different from *Where Do Polar Bears Live?*

Title Source:	Title Source:
How is it similar to *Where Do Polar Bears Live?*	How is it similar to *Where Do Polar Bears Live?*
How is it different from *Where Do Polar Bears Live?*	How is it different from *Where Do Polar Bears Live?*
Facts I learned from this text are _____.	Facts I learned from this text are _____.

ELA RI.2.9, W.2.8 **ELD** ELD.PI.2.1, ELD.PI.2.2, ELD.PI.2.10

INTEGRATED LANGUAGE ARTS REVIEW

Write About Reading

Digital Resources ▸

To support children before they start this task, use the following digital resources.

▸ GrammarSnap Videos: Verb Tenses, Pronouns

▸ Multimedia Grammar Glossary

INTRODUCE THE TASK

After children have finished researching two texts on the topic of polar bears and writing notes about the texts, tell them that they will write a book review based on their findings. Explain the task:

- Children should choose which text they liked better or found more interesting.
- Children should rate the book using a star system (5 stars = excellent, 1 star = poor).
- Children will write sentences that explain their rating.
- The sentences should include details that tell how the book is the same as and different from the trade book.
- The sentences should include reasons and details that support the opinion.

Review the Model Display the Idea Web for opinion writing from **Student Book** Vol. 3, p. 501, and review the steps to adding details and facts to writing. Point out that the writer has added supporting details to make her reasons more convincing.

PLAN AND DRAFT

Display the following list to guide children in writing and organizing their sentences:

- Name the text you are writing about.
- How many stars would you give this book?
- Why did you rate the book this way? List reasons and examples that support your opinion.
- What helpful information or interesting facts did you find?
- How is this text the same as the trade book? How is it different?
- End with a sentence that restates your opinion.
- Use a capital letter at the beginning of each sentence. Use an end mark at the end of each sentence.

REVISE AND EDIT

Guide the class to generate a checklist that children can use as they revise their sentences. For example:

- Did I clearly state my opinion?
- Did I include reasons that support my opinion?
- Did I cite specific facts and examples from the text?
- Did I use complete sentences?
- Did I use end marks correctly?
- Have I corrected any spelling errors?

See Analytic Writing Rubric, p. R17.

SHARE

Have children share their book reviews with the class.

ELA W.2.2, W.2.5, SL.2.1a, SL.2.1b, SL.2.1c, L.2.1f, L.2.2 **ELD** ELD.PI.2.10, ELD.PI.2.11

▸ SHARE OBJECTIVES

- Write a response to the independent reading text. LANGUAGE
- Cite evidence from the text.
- Use correct punctuation and spelling.

▸ SKILLS REVIEW

Review the following skills, as needed, before children begin to write their response.

- **Writing:** Opinion Writing, Persuasive Essay (Lessons 14–15)
- **Grammar:** The Verb *be* (Lesson 18)
- **Spelling:** Vowel Diagraphs (Lessons 12–13)

ENGLISH LANGUAGE SUPPORT

Use Sentence Frames

Emerging Provide sentence frames for children to use: *I read the book _____. I would give this book _____ stars because _____. One interesting fact I learned is _____. I enjoyed reading _____.*

Expanding Before children write their sentences, guide them to complete a web that lists their opinion in the center and reasons and examples that support it in the surrounding circles. Have children use their completed web to write their book review.

Bridging Have children share their sentences with a partner. Partners should give each other feedback on how well they stated their opinion and used reasons and details to support it. **ELD** ELD.PI.2.10, ELD.PI.2.11

Reflect

▶ SHARE OBJECTIVES

- Share feedback about the presentation. LANGUAGE
- Offer comments about the project process. LANGUAGE

Reflect on the Project

✔ Discuss the Presentation
✔ Discuss the Project Process
✔ Celebrate!

Discuss the Presentation Play the video recording of the project presentations for the class. Pause to point out evidence of effective speaking techniques and examples of constructive audience comments. As a class, talk about what children did well or what the class liked about the presentation portion of the project. Prompt children to identify anything they would change or do differently for the next presentation.
ELA SL.2.1a, SL.2.1b, SL.2.1c ELD ELD.PI.2.1

Discuss the Project Process Review the steps and tasks children completed as they worked together on their projects. Make note of situations where teams collaborated to make decisions, complete tasks, and solve problems. Make connections between teams who collaborated and were productive and the effectiveness of the displays they created. Encourage children to identify any challenges or difficulties they faced as they worked in their teams. Work together to suggest ways children can deal with challenges when they work on future projects in small groups.
ELA SL.2.1a, SL.2.1b, SL.2.1c ELD ELD.PI.2.1

Celebrate! Display the photo galleries around the classroom. Take a picture of each team with its display. Acknowledge children's collaborative efforts and the displays they created. Point out that they have become "polar bear experts" and have used that knowledge to create informative and engaging displays. Tell them they should feel proud of what they have accomplished over the two-week period. Have children draw a picture to show one thing they learned about polar bears during the project. Have them take turns sharing their picture and fact as well as one thing they enjoyed about working on the project.
ELA W.2.2, SL.2.1a, SL.2.5 ELD ELD.PI.2.1, ELD.PI.2.2

Allow children to spend some time revisiting the displays and looking more closely at the pictures and captions. You may want to serve light snacks or have children complete a simple craft activity, such as making a polar bear mask using cotton balls, black construction paper, and paper plates.

INTERVENTION

Unit 4 Strategic Intervention

INTRODUCE THE WRITE-IN READER

"Be a Reading Detective!"

Write-In Reader pages ii–iii

- Have children open their **Write-In Readers** to pages ii–iii.

- Point out that a police detective looks for clues to solve a crime. A reading detective looks for clues to understand a story or a nonfiction selection.

- Explain that looking for clues can make reading easier and more fun.

- Read page ii with children. Say, *What questions will you think about when you read?* (Who? Where? When? What? Why?) *Remember to look for clues to answer the questions.*

TRY IT!

- Read the first part of page iii with children. Say, *What clues are you going to look for as you read?* (clues that answer the questions *Who? Where?* and *When?*)

- Then read the passage as children listen for clues.

- Discuss the answers to the questions. If children have difficulty, reread the passage, and have volunteers point to the places where clues can be found.

Classroom Collaboration

- Use the question at the bottom of page iii to discuss the clues children found and how they helped them answer the questions.

- Explain that children will be reading detectives as they read each selection in the **Write-In Reader.**

RETURN TO THE ANCHOR TEXT

At the end of each lesson, children will return to the Anchor Text and look for clues to deepen their understanding. (See the "A" and "B" pages at the end of each lesson in the **Write-In Reader.**)

DAY 1

SHARE OBJECTIVES

- Learn to count syllables.
- Read base words and endings *-ed* and *-ing* after doubling the final consonant.
- Talk about helping people.
- Read to build meaning for Target Vocabulary words.

MATERIALS

Context Cards: *chuckled, disappointed, received, staring*

Write-In Reader pages 152–153

TERMS ABOUT READING/ LANGUAGE ARTS

syllables	vowel
consonant	base word

ENGLISH LANGUAGE SUPPORT

Day 1

Vocabulary Preteach the meanings of the Target Vocabulary words *chuckled, disappointed, received,* and *staring*. Use examples and EL-friendly explanations to support children's understanding. Then ask questions about the words for children to discuss. **ELD** ELD.PI.2.1

Sentence Frames Teach terms and give sentence frames to help children participate in the Talk About It activity. Talk about the term *community service*. Explain what a *community* is, and that *service* is about people helping each other. Guide children to use this frame as they respond. *We do community service when we _____.* **ELD** ELD.PI.2.5

Oral Language Write cloze sentences on the board so that children can fill in the Target Vocabulary. Sample: *A person who is looking a long time at something is _____.* (staring) Have children complete the sentences and read them chorally. Then have partners read the sentences to each other. **ELD** ELD.PI.2.1

Warm Up

Phonemic Awareness
Syllables in Spoken Words

- Say, *I'll say the word:* hopped. *I'll say the syllables:* hopped. Hold up one finger for each syllable. *I hear one syllable.*
- Now have the children say the word, say the syllables, and say how many syllables.
- Continue, using the following words:

waited	wait / ed	2
planned	planned	1
skipped	skipped	1

- Correct errors by repeating the process.

RETEACH

Phonics: *-ed, -ing* with Doubling Final Consonant

- Write the following words on the board or on a pad:

mop	mopped	mopping	sitting
blotted	scrubbing	stopped	begged

- Point to *mop, mopped,* and *mopping*. Explain that when we add *-ed* or *-ing* to words that end in one vowel and one consonant, we double the consonant before we add the ending.

- Point to *mopped*. Say, *I see two consonants after the first vowel. The vowel stands for its short sound, /ŏ/. The base word is* mop; *the whole word is* mopped. Have children do each step on their own.

- Follow the procedure for the remaining words.

- Correct errors by modeling the process. **ELA** RF.2.3d **ELD** ELD.PIII.2

Talk About It

- Ask, *What is a community?* (a group of people who live in one place or a group of people with a common interest) *What does the word* service *mean?* (helping) *Do you know what community service is?* Explain that community service is people helping each other improve their community. Have children name ways people in a community help each other. Record children's answers in a chart.

Kinds of Community Service
Help a friend or family member with chores.
Raise money for a local pet shelter.
Rake a neighbor's lawn.
Help with a food drive for a local food bank.
Visit an elderly neighbor.

- Ask, *What kinds of community service have you done, or what would you like to do?* **ELA** SL.2.1a **ELD** ELD.PI.2.1

RETEACH

Target Vocabulary

Write-In Reader pages 152–153

- Read and discuss each paragraph. Then discuss the meaning of each Target Vocabulary word. Suggest that children underline words or phrases that provide clues to meaning. Also point out the following:

   The base word *chuckle* came from the Middle English word *chukken*, meaning "making a clucking noise."

   The word *disappointed* begins with the prefix *dis-*, which means "not," as in *disagree* and *disapprove*.

- Allow time for children to write their responses. Ask children to choose an answer they would like to read aloud.

Responses: **1.** Responses will vary. **2.** Possible responses include *laughed*, *giggled*, and *snickered*. **3.** Responses will vary. **4.** Responses will vary. **ELA** RF.2.3d, L.2.4a **ELD** ELD.PIII.2

Quick Check Target

Ask each child to use one of the Target Vocabulary words in a sentence.

☑ TARGET VOCABULARY

If you **chuckled** about something, you laughed quietly.

When you are **disappointed,** you feel unhappy because something you hoped for did not happen.

When you have **received** something, someone has given it or sent it to you.

If you were **staring** at something, you were looking at it for a long time.

DAILY FLUENCY

Build automaticity by using **Context Cards** or word lists on display. Point to the words in any order and have children read them aloud. Continue until children can read all words fluently.

SHARE OBJECTIVES

- Read and use high-frequency words.
- Learn about story structure.
- Read to apply skills and strategies.

MATERIALS

Write-In Reader pages 154–157

TERMS ABOUT READING/ LANGUAGE ARTS

story structure	characters
setting	plot
infer	predict

ENGLISH LANGUAGE SUPPORT

Day 2

Vocabulary Preteach the meanings of the high-frequency words *also, fly, gone, said,* and *something*. Sample: *Name something you like to do.* Ask questions for children to discuss. Use visuals, gestures, sounds, or words to support their understanding. **ELD** ELD.PI.2.1

Sentence Frames Give sentence frames to help children participate in the Quick Check activity. Guide them to use these frames as they extend the story. *Omar wakes up and _____. Then Uncle Chaz _____. They _____.* **ELD** ELD.PI.2.9

Oral Language Guide children to write a summary of *Kate's Helping Day* as a class. Use this summary frame and write their responses on the board. *This story is about _____. First, _____. Then _____. Next, _____. At the end, _____.* Have children choral-read the summary when they are finished. **ELD** ELD.PI.2.2

Warm Up

High-Frequency Words

also, fly, gone, said, something

Write the high-frequency words on the board or on a pad. Have partners practice reading the words. Then ask each child to use one word in a sentence. For a challenge, ask if anyone can use two words in just one sentence. **ELA** RF.2.3f **ELD** ELD.PIII.2

RETEACH

Story Structure

- Review the terms **characters** and **setting**. Remind children that a **plot** tells the order of story events. Sometimes the plot is like a timeline. Events follow one another over the course of a day, a week, a month, a year, or longer.

- Write this story on the board and then read it aloud: *The name of this story is* Omar's Day. *Omar woke up early. He had a plan for his day. He was going camping with friends. He packed his things. His Uncle Chaz picked him up. They told stories as they drove to the camp. When they got there, they put up their tents and then they hiked. That evening, they built a campfire and cooked dinner. They told scary stories. Then they crawled into their tents and fell asleep.*

- Ask, *What is the structure of this story?* Draw a story chart on the board, and model how to use it by recording children's responses to each category.

The Story Structure of *Omar's Day*

Characters: Omar and Uncle Chaz **Setting:** A camp

Plot Beginning (Morning)	Plot Middle (Middle of day)	Plot End (Evening)
Omar wakes up. He packs his things for a camping trip.	Uncle Chaz picks Omar up and they drive to the camp. They put up their tents before they hike.	Toward the end of the day, they build a fire, cook their food, tell stories, and finally fall asleep in their tents.

Quick Check **Comprehension**

Invite children to extend the story. Ask, *What do you think might happen during the night?* **ELA** RL.2.5 **ELD** ELD.PI.2.1

READ

Kate's Helping Day

Write-In Reader pages 154–157

- Preview the selection with children using the **Think Aloud** to predict story events. Guide children to use the title, text, and illustrations to make their predictions. Record their ideas.

Think Aloud *I see a title that says* Kate's Helping Day. *I see pictures that show Kate working in a garden and then helping to paint a room. What other clues help you predict events in the story?*

- Together, review the steps to the Infer/Predict Strategy, **Write-In Reader** page 304. As needed, guide children in applying the strategy as they read.

READ

Ask children to read to confirm their predictions. Have children take turns reading the selection with partners. Discuss, confirm, and revise children's predictions based upon story details.

REREAD

Call on individuals to read aloud while others follow along. Point out verbs with *-ed* or *-ing* that have the final consonant doubled, such as *planned*. Stop to discuss each question. Allow time for children to write their responses before proceeding. Sample answers are provided.

Page 154: A word that has the same meaning as <u>staring</u> is _____. (looking, gazing)

Help unpack meaning, if needed, by asking, *When do you stare into space?* (Possible responses include when you're daydreaming, thinking about the future, or thinking about a day that's about to start.) *What is Kate doing in the illustration on page 154?* (Her eyes are wide open, and she is looking up.)

Unpack Meaning: For questions on pages 155–157, you may want to use the notes in the right-hand column.

Page 155: Kate wants to wear a hat and _____. (gloves)

Turn and Talk **Page 156:** Kate helps her mom. She learns about _____. (plants and gardening)

Page 157: Kate puts on old clothes. What does she do next? (She walks to Carol's house.) **ELA** RL.2.1, RL.2.7 **ELD** ELD.PI.2.1

UNPACK MEANING

Use prompts such as these if children have difficulty with a **Stop•Think•Write** question:

Page 155 *What is Kate's mom wearing in the illustration on page 155?* (a hat and gloves) *Why do you think Kate wants to wear a hat?* (She wants to dress like her mom.)

Page 156 *How long does Kate work?* (a long time) *Where does she work?* (in the garden)

Page 157 *Who is Carol?* (She is Kate's friend.) *Where do you think Carol lives?* (She must live in the neighborhood.)

DAILY FLUENCY

Build automaticity by using **Context Cards** or word lists on display. Point to the words in any order and have children read them aloud. Continue until children can read all words fluently.

SHARE OBJECTIVES

- Learn to count syllables.
- Read base words and endings *-ed* and *-ing*, after doubling the final consonant.
- Read to apply skills and strategies.

MATERIALS

Write-In Reader pages 158–160

ENGLISH LANGUAGE SUPPORT

Day 3

Vocabulary Before the Phonemic Awareness lesson, teach the meanings of *printed, saved, hitting,* and *shredded.* Ask questions about the words for children to discuss. Use visuals, gestures, or classroom objects to support understanding if needed. **ELD** ELD.PI.2.1

Sentence Frames Give sentence frames to help children participate in the Quick Check activity. Guide them to use frames such as these as they retell the end of the story. *At Carol's house, _____. That night, Kate feels ____ because _____.* **ELD** ELD.PI.2.12a

Oral Language Have children offer their opinions about the story ending. Did they like the ending? Did they think it was surprising? Why? Guide children to use frames such as these as they share their opinions. *I did/did not like the ending because _____. I did/did not think it was surprising because _____.* **ELD** ELD.PI.2.3

Phonemic Awareness
Syllables in Spoken Words

- Say, *I'll say the word:* printed. *I'll say the syllables:* print / ed. Hold up one finger for each syllable. *I hear two syllables.*

- Now have the children say the word, say the syllables, and say how many syllables.

- Continue, using the following words:

saved	saved	1
hitting	hitt / ing	2
shredded	shredd / ed	2

- Correct errors by repeating the process.

RETEACH

Phonics: *-ed, -ing* with Doubling Final Consonant

- Write the following words on the board or on a pad:

peg	pegged	kidded	eating
grinned	stubbed	driving	striking

- Point to *peg* and *pegged.* Teach that when we add *-ed* or *-ing* to words that end in one vowel and one consonant, we double the consonant before we add the ending.

- Point to *pegged.* Say, *I see two consonants after the first vowel. The vowel stands for its short sound, /e/. The base word is* peg, *the whole word is* pegged. Have children do each step on their own.

- Follow the procedure for the remaining words.

- Correct errors by modeling the process. **ELA** RF.2.3d **ELD** ELD.PIII.2

READ

Kate's Helping Day
Write-In Reader pages 158–160

Review the first part of the story with children. Ask, *What have we learned so far about Kate and the day she has planned?* Then preview today's reading. Have children look for clues to help them predict how this story will end.

READ

Ask children to read to confirm their predictions. Have children take turns reading the selection with partners. Discuss, confirm, and revise predictions based upon story details. Ask if there was anything about the way the story ended that surprised them.

REREAD

Call on individuals to read aloud while others follow along. Stop to discuss each question. Allow time for children to write their responses before proceeding. Sample answers are provided.

Page 158: Kate and Carol _____ about the paint on their clothes. (chuckled)

Help unpack meaning, if needed, by asking, *What happens to Kate and Carol as they paint?* (Their clothes get splashed with paint.) *How do Kate and Carol find out what they look like?* (They look into a mirror.)

Unpack Meaning: For questions on pages 159–160, you may want to use the notes in the right-hand column.

Page 159: Kate is at _____ house. (Ramón's)

Turn and Talk **Page 160:** At the end of the story, Kate feels tired and _____.
(happy) Have children discuss the statement and then share with the group. **ELA** RL.2.1, RL.2.10 **ELD** ELD.PI.2.1

Quick Check | **Retelling**

Have children retell the end of the story. Support the retelling by asking, *What happens at Carol's house? What happens at Ramón's house? How does Kate feel that night?*

UNPACK MEANING

Use prompts such as these if children have difficulty with a **Stop•Think•Write** question:

Page 159 *Whose car are Kate and Ramón washing?* (Ramón's dad) *Where do you think Ramón's dad keeps his car?* (in his driveway or garage)

Page 160 *What does Kate think about before she goes to bed?* (all the things she did during the day) *How do you feel after a long day of work or play?* (Responses will vary.)

DAILY FLUENCY

Build automaticity by using **Context Cards** or word lists on display. Point to the words in any order and have children read them aloud. Continue until children can read all words fluently.

SHARE OBJECTIVES

- Read and use high-frequency words.
- Learn about pronouns.
- Answer questions using evidence from the story.
- Read words fluently at a conversational rate.

MATERIALS

Write-In Reader pages 154–161

TERMS ABOUT READING/ LANGUAGE ARTS

subject pronouns

object pronouns

rate

ENGLISH LANGUAGE SUPPORT

Day 4

Vocabulary Preteach the meanings of the high-frequency words *have, horse, look, river,* and *saw*. Ask questions for children to discuss. Sample: *What is something you would like to have?* Use visuals, gestures, sounds, or words to support their understanding. **ELD** ELD.PI.2.1

Sentence Frames Give sentence frames to help children participate in the Look Back and Respond Turn and Talk activity. Guide them to use frames such as these as they discuss their answers. *Kate helps _____. She helps the people at _____.* **ELD** ELD.PI.2.5

Oral Language Help children write a description of a day of helping. Use this paragraph frame for support. *I will help _____ to _____. I like to _____. We will _____.* Have children practice reading their paragraphs quietly to themselves. Then have partners take turns reading their paragraphs to each other. **ELD** ELD.PI.2.10

High-Frequency Words

have, horse, look, river, saw

Write the high-frequency words on the board or on a pad. Have partners practice reading the words. Then challenge children to use as many of these words as possible in one sentence.

Quick Check High-Frequency Words

Ask each child to use one of the week's words in a sentence.
ELA RF.2.3f **ELD** ELD.PIII.2

RETEACH

Pronouns

- Review that pronouns are words that can take the place of nouns. Personal pronouns—*I, you, he, she, it, we,* and *they*—are used as subjects of verbs and are called subject pronouns.

    I solved the mystery.

- Review that object pronouns—*me, him, her, it, us,* and *them*—can replace nouns that come after a verb.

    I saw *her.*

- Review that reflexive pronouns—such as *myself, yourself, himself, themselves,* and *ourselves*—are also used after a verb.

    We enjoyed *ourselves.*

- Have children find the subject and object pronouns on pages 154–155. (*It, She, you, me, I*)

Turn and Talk Write these sentences on the board or on a pad. Underline the nouns. Have children replace the underlined words with a pronoun.

Mom gave *Lena and Jo* a book.
Carol can really sing.
The party is for *Roger and me.*
Carlos made *Carlos* a snack.

Answers: them, She, us, himself

Quick Check Grammar

Have children write three sentences about helping others, using pronouns as subjects. **ELA** L.2.1c **ELD** ELD.PI.2.5

Look Back and Respond

Write-In Reader pages 154–161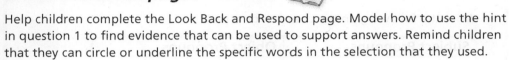

Help children complete the Look Back and Respond page. Model how to use the hint in question 1 to find evidence that can be used to support answers. Remind children that they can circle or underline the specific words in the selection that they used.

1. What is Kate thinking about when the story begins? (She is thinking about all the plans she has made for a day of helping.)

Help unpack meaning, if needed, by asking, *What do you think about when you wake up on a weekend day?* (Possible responses: plans for play, breakfast, places to go) *Look at the illustration of Kate on page 154. How do you think Kate is feeling?* (happy)

Turn and Talk Have children work independently on questions 2 and 3. When children have completed the page, have partners discuss their responses and then share them with the group. Sample responses are provided. Accept reasonable responses.

Unpack Meaning: For questions 2 and 3, you may want to use the notes in the right-hand column to guide the discussion.

2. Whom does Kate help in the story? (She helps her mother, her friend Carol, and Ramón and Ramón's dad.)

3. Where does Kate go to help those people? (She goes to the garden, to Carol's house, and to Ramón's house.) **ELA** SL.2.1a **ELD** ELD.PI.2.1

RETEACH

Fluency: Rate

Write-In Reader page 158

• Explain that you are going to read a page in two different ways. First, read page 158. Change your rate as you read so that you read too slowly at times and too quickly at others. Afterward, ask, *What do you think about my first reading?* Encourage feedback. Be sure children understand that the rate of your reading made understanding difficult.

• Point out that the sentences should be read at a conversational pace. Explain that hesitating or rushing over words can make the meaning of a story hard to understand. Then read page 158 at an appropriate rate. Encourage children to critique your second reading. Then ask, *How would you read page 158?* Invite children to take turns reading page 158 aloud at a conversational rate. **ELA** RF.2.4b **ELD** ELD.PIII.2

UNPACK MEANING

Use prompts such as these if children have difficulty with a question:

2. *Where does Kate go with her mother?* (to the garden) *Where does Kate go next?* (to Carol's house) *Where does she go last?* (to Ramón's house)

3. *Where is the garden?* (at Kate's house) *What did Kate help Carol do?* (paint Carol's room) *Why did Ramón's dad give Kate and Ramón money?* (They washed his car.)

DAILY FLUENCY

Build automaticity by using **Context Cards** or word lists on display. Point to the words in any order and have children read them aloud. Continue until children can read all words fluently.

SHARE OBJECTIVES

- Use and identify pronouns.
- Demonstrate understanding of Target Vocabulary words.
- Preview Sequence of Events and the Visualize Strategy.

MATERIALS

Context Cards: *account, budget, chuckled, disappointed, fund, received, repeated, staring*

Write-In Reader pages 154–160

Leveled Reader: *Our Library*

TERMS ABOUT READING/ LANGUAGE ARTS

sequence of events   visualize

☑ TARGET VOCABULARY

If you have an **account** at a bank, you leave your money with the bank and take money out when you need it.

A **budget** is a plan of how to spend the money that you have.

A **fund** is a collection of money that is raised from an activity or an event and set aside for a special purpose.

If you **repeated** something, you did it or said it again.

ENGLISH LANGUAGE SUPPORT

Day 5

Sentence Frames Give sentence frames to help children participate in the Visualize activity. Guide them to use frames such as these as they describe the pictures in their minds of story events. *The picture I think of shows _____. It helps me _____.* **ELD** ELD.PI.2.5

Oral Grammar
Pronouns

- Write the following on the board or on a pad:

Subject Pronouns		Object Pronouns	
Singular	**Plural**	**Singular**	**Plural**
I	we	me	us
you	you	you	you
he, she, it	they	him, her, it	them

- Explain that pronouns are used as both subjects and objects.

- Tell children that you are going to read a sentence. You will tell them to replace either the subject or object with a pronoun.

1. *Many people like baseball. Subject pronoun?* (They)

2. *Jan hugged the baby girl. Object pronoun?* (her)

3. *My friends and I play handball. Subject pronoun?* (We)

4. *You and your parents will eat with us. Subject pronoun?* (You)

5. *That chair is not comfortable. Subject pronoun?* (It)

6. *My favorite uncle is a lot of fun. Subject pronoun?* (He)

RETEACH

Target Vocabulary
Context Cards

- Display the **Context Cards** for *chuckled, disappointed, received,* and *staring.* Review the meanings of these words. Then have children use the words in oral sentences to describe a time when they helped someone.

- Add the **Context Cards** for *account, budget, fund,* and *repeated.* Deal one card to each of the children. Have each child make up a riddle for his or her word. Have the rest of the group guess the word.

WRITE ABOUT IT

- Ask children to write an e-mail to a friend about something they did to help someone else. Have children use the word *repeated* in their writing. **ELA** L.2.6 **ELD** ELD.PI.2.12b

PRETEACH
Sequence of Events
Visualize

Write-In Reader pages 154–160

- Introduce skill and strategy. Say, *In the next lesson, we are going to focus on the sequence of events in a story. We'll also work on ways to use the Visualize Strategy.*

- Explain, *Writers build stories around an interesting plot, or sequence of important events. When you summarize a story, you should retell these important events in order.*

- Ask, *Can you retell the important events in* Kate's Helping Day? Draw a chart on the board and record children's responses.

Sequence of Events in Kate's Helping Day

Kate wakes up and thinks about her plans for a helping day.

First, Kate helps her mother in the garden.

Then Kate walks to her friend Carol's house and helps her paint her room.

Next, Kate goes to Ramón's house and helps him wash his father's car.

Finally, Kate is tired but happy, as she thinks back over her satisfying day.

- Turn to and review the Visualize Strategy found on page 305 in the **Write-In Reader**. Tell children that when they visualize, they make pictures in their minds of events in a story. Ask children to describe the pictures they made in their minds of Kate gardening. **ELA** RL.2.5 **ELD** ELD.PI.2.12b

APPLY READING SKILLS

Introduce *Our Library*. Choral-read the first few pages with children. Depending on their abilities, have children continue reading with partners or as a group.

Quick Check | **Fluency**

Listen to individual children as they read the **Write-In Reader** selection. Make specific notes about words that presented difficulty.

● **Leveled Reader**

"Be a Reading Detective!"
Student Book pages 15–35
Write-In Reader pages 161A–161B

- Page through "Mr. Tanen's Tie Trouble" with children and review the main characters and events. Encourage volunteers to talk about what is happening on each page.

- Read page 161A of the **Write-In Reader** with children. Remind children that reading detectives find clues in the words and pictures of a story.

- Discuss the questions with children. Guide them to find clues in the words and pictures that help them answer the questions.

- Have children complete item 1 on page 161B on their own. Remind them to include details and examples from the story in their answer. Then have them share their work with a partner. Encourage them to discuss how they knew the answer to the question.

- Read item 2 on page 161B. Have children talk with a partner about why the people in the town return Mr. Tanen's ties. Have them discuss clues that help them understand what happens.

DAILY FLUENCY

Read Around the Room Have one child point to words that are on display in the room. Have the group read the words. Give each child a chance to be the pointer.

SHARE OBJECTIVES

- Segment words and identify vowel sounds.
- Recognize that *igh, ie,* and *y* stand for long *i.*
- Discuss superheroes.
- Read to build meaning for Target Vocabulary Words.

MATERIALS

Sound/Spelling Card: *ice cream*

Word Cards: *pie, sigh, sight, thigh, tie, try*

Write-In Reader pages 162–163

Context Cards: *cheered, extra, final, hurried*

**TERMS ABOUT READING/
LANGUAGE ARTS**

long *i*

ENGLISH LANGUAGE SUPPORT

Day 1

Vocabulary Preteach the meanings of the Target Vocabulary words *cheered, extra, final,* and *hurried.* Use examples and EL-friendly explanations to support children's understanding. Then ask questions about the words for children to discuss. **ELD** ELD.PI.2.1

Sentence Frames Teach terms and give sentence frames to help children participate in the Talk About It activity. Review the term *superhero.* Explain that when you visualize something, you make a picture in your mind about what it is and does and how it looks. Guide children to use this frame as they respond. *A superhero is someone who _____.* **ELD** ELD.PI.2.5

Oral Language Have volunteers take turns generating oral sentences that include one or more Target Vocabulary words. Write the sentences on the board and have children read them chorally. **ELD** ELD.PI.2.1

Phonemic Awareness

Segment Phonemes

- Say, *I'll say a word:* tight. *Now I'll say the sounds in* tight: /t/ /ī/ /t/. *I hear the vowel sound:* /ī/.
- Have children say the word, the sounds, and the vowel sound.
- Continue with the following words.

trip	/t/ /r/ /ĭ/ /p/	/ĭ/
light	/l/ /ī/ /t/	/ī/
lit	/l/ /ĭ/ /t/	/ĭ/

- Correct errors by repeating the process.

RETEACH

Phonics: Long *i*

Sound/Spelling Card, Word Cards

- Write *igh, ie,* and *y* on the board or on a pad. Display the **Sound/Spelling Card** for *ice cream.* Say the word and ask, *What sound do you hear at the beginning of* ice cream? (/ī/) Point to *igh, ie,* and *y.* Teach that *igh* stands for /ī/ and that *ie* and *y* at the end of one-syllable words stand for /ī/.
- Show the **Word Card** for *tie.* Point under *ie* and say /ī/, and then say *tie.* Have children say the sound and read the word with you. Then have children say the sound and read the word on their own.
- Follow the same procedure using the **Word Cards** for *pie, sigh, sight, thigh,* and *try.*
- Correct errors by repeating the procedure. **ELA** RF.2.3a, RF.2.3.e **ELD** ELD.PIII.2

Talk About It

- Ask children to describe their favorite superhero. Encourage children to visualize, or make a picture in their mind, of a superhero. Ask, *What does the superhero wear? What does she or he do? What makes her or him a superhero?* Make a web to record children's responses.

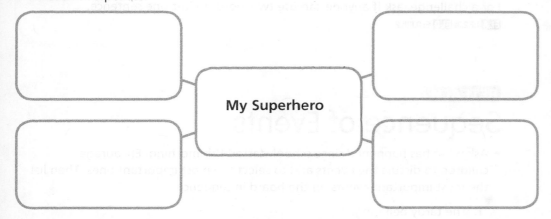

My Superhero

- Ask, *Are all heroes superheroes? Explain.* **ELA** SL.2.1a **ELD** ELD.PI.2.1

RETEACH

Target Vocabulary

Write-In Reader pages 162–163

- Read the directions. Discuss each item. Then discuss the meaning of each Target Vocabulary word. Suggest that children underline words or phrases that provide clues to meaning. Also point out the following:

    Contrast the meaning of *cheered* in this instance with the other familiar meaning of "to make someone happy."

    Extra is an adjective, or describing word, that means "more than what is usual or needed," such as "I brought extra money to the movies." But the noun, or naming word, *extra* means "a person who has a small part in a movie."

- Allow time for children to write their responses. Ask children to choose an answer they would like to read aloud.

Responses: **1.** final **2.** extra **3.** cheered **4.** Possible responses include read, brush teeth, or give Mom a kiss. **5.** Responses will vary.

Quick Check | **Target Vocabulary**

Ask each child to use one of the Target Vocabulary words in a sentence.
ELA L.2.4a **ELD** ELD.PI.2.12b

☑ TARGET VOCABULARY

If you **cheered**, you shouted in happiness or excitement.

Something that is **extra** is more than what is usual or needed.

If something is last or at the end, it is **final**.

If you **hurried** to do something or go somewhere, you tried to finish it or get there quickly.

DAILY FLUENCY

Build automaticity by using **Context Cards** or word lists on display. Point to the words in any order and have children read them aloud. Continue until children can read all words fluently.

SHARE OBJECTIVES

- Read and use high-frequency words.
- Determine a sequence of events.
- Read to apply skills and strategies.

MATERIALS

Write-In Reader pages 164–167

TERMS ABOUT READING/ LANGUAGE ARTS

event   sequence of events

visualize

ENGLISH LANGUAGE SUPPORT

Day 2

Vocabulary Preteach the meanings of the high-frequency words *blue, doing, else, sure,* and *turned.* Ask questions for children to discuss. Sample: *What else are you doing today?* Use visuals, gestures, sounds, or words to support their understanding. **ELD** ELD.PI.2.1

Sentence Frames Give sentence frames to help children participate in the Quick Check activity. Guide them to use these frames as they tell about a sequence of events. *First, _____. Then _____. Next, _____. At the end, _____.* **ELD** ELD.PI.2.5

Oral Language Guide children to write a summary of *True Heroes* as a class. Use this summary frame and write their responses on the board. *This story is about _____. First, _____. Then _____. Next, _____. At the end, _____.* Have children choral-read the summary when they are finished. **ELD** ELD.PI.2.2

Warm Up

High-Frequency Words

blue, doing, else, sure, turned

Write the high-frequency words on the board or on a pad. Have partners practice reading the words. Then ask each child to use one word in a sentence. For a challenge, ask if anyone can use two words in just one sentence.
ELA RF.2.3f **ELD** ELD.PIII.2

RETEACH

Sequence of Events

- Ask what has happened since school started this morning. Encourage children to discuss the events and to select the most important ones. Then list the most important events on the board in sequence.

  1. The tardy bell rang.

  2. We said the Pledge of Allegiance.

  3. We turned in our homework.

  4. We started reading.

- Say, *Things that happen are called* events. *When we put these events in the order they happened, we are putting them in* sequence.

- Point out that many writers organize their stories by sequence. Sometimes they use sequence words, such as *first, next, then,* and *finally,* to indicate the order in which events occurred.

- Have children restate the events on the board or on a pad, using sequence words.

- Emphasize how knowing the sequence of major events can help children summarize a selection.

Quick Check   Comprehension

Have children share the main events of a real-life experience. Encourage children to use sequence words.

READ

True Heroes

Write-In Reader pages 164–167

- Preview the selection with children using the **Think Aloud** to predict the plot. Guide children to use the title and illustrations to make predictions. Record their ideas.

> **Think Aloud** *I see that the title of the story is True Heroes. I think this story will tell about someone who did something truly special. What other clues help you predict the plot?*

- Together, review the steps to the Visualize Strategy, **Write-In Reader** page 305. As needed, guide children in applying the strategy as they read.

READ

Ask children to read to confirm their predictions. Have children take turns reading the selection with partners. Discuss, confirm, and revise children's predictions based upon story details.

REREAD

Call on individuals to read aloud while others follow along. Point out words that have long *i*, such as *like* and *sign*. Stop to discuss each question. Allow time for children to write their responses before proceeding. Sample answers are provided.

Page 164: Josh's favorite baseball team is _____. (the Stars)

Help unpack meaning, if needed, by asking, *What does Josh love?* (baseball) *Where does he watch baseball games?* (at home on TV)

Unpack Meaning: For questions on pages 165–167, you may want to use the notes in the right-hand column.

Page 165: Josh's dad shows Josh tickets to the game. Then Josh is _____. (happy)

Turn and Talk **Page 166:** The score at the end of the game is the _____ score. (final) Have partners discuss the statement and then share with the group.

Page 167: Josh _____ over to Rick Callan because he did not want to miss him. (hurried) **ELA** RL.2.1, RL.2.3 **ELD** ELD.PI.2.1

UNPACK MEANING

Use prompts such as these if children have difficulty with a **Stop•Think•Write** question:

Page 165 *What did Josh do when his dad told him what he had?* (shouted)

Page 166 *What does the word* final *mean?* (last or ending) *When do you know the winner of a game?* (at the end of the game) *What was the score at the end of this game?* (7 to 4)

Page 167 *What does the word* hurried *mean?* (moved quickly) *Why did Josh go toward Rick Callan?* (He admired him and wanted an autograph.) *How would you move if you saw someone you admired walking nearby?* (Possible responses may include *fast* and *speedily*.)

DAILY FLUENCY

Build automaticity by using **Context Cards** or word lists on display. Point to the words in any order and have children read them aloud. Continue until children can read all words fluently.

SHARE OBJECTIVES

- Segment words and identify vowel sounds.
- Read words that end in *-ild* and *-ind*.
- Read to apply skills and strategies.

MATERIALS

Sound/Spelling Card: *ice cream*

Write-In Reader pages 168–170

ENGLISH LANGUAGE SUPPORT

Day 3

Vocabulary Before the Phonemic Awareness lesson, teach the meanings of *child, chilled, kind,* and *kid*. Ask questions about the words for children to discuss. Use visuals, gestures, or classroom objects to support understanding if needed. **ELD** ELD.PI.2.1

Sentence Frames Give sentence frames to help children participate in the Quick Check activity. Guide them to use frames such as these as they retell the end of the story. *At the end, _____. Josh learns _____.* **ELD** ELD.PI.2.12a

Oral Language Have children offer their opinions about heroes. Who is a real hero? Why? Guide children to use frames such as this as they share their opinions. *I think a real hero _____ because _____.* **ELD** ELD.PI.2.3

Warm Up

Phonemic Awareness

Segment Phonemes

- Say, *I'll say a word:* child. *Now I'll say the sounds in* child: /ch/ /ī/ /l/ /d/. *I hear the vowel sound* /ī/.
- Have children say the word, the sounds, and the vowel sound.
- Continue with the following words.

chilled	/ch/ /ĭ/ /l/ /d/	/ĭ/
kind	/k/ /ī/ /n/ /d/	/ī/
kid	/k/ /ĭ/ /d/	/ĭ/

- Correct errors by repeating the process.

RETEACH

Phonics: Long *i*

Sound/Spelling Card

- Display the **Sound/Spelling Card** for *ice cream*. Say the word and ask, *What sound do you hear at the beginning of* ice cream? (/ī/)
- Write the following on a board or on a pad:

| -ild | -ind | wild | kind | mind | child |

- Point under *-ild* and teach that *-ild* stands for /ī/ /l/ /d/. Repeat for *-ind*.
- Point under *-ild* in *wild* and say /ī/ /l/ /d/. Then say the word. Have children say the sounds and the word.
- Follow the procedure for the remaining words. **ELA** RF.2.3a **ELD** ELD.PIII.2

READ

True Heroes

Write-In Reader pages 168–170

Review the first part of the story with children. Ask, *What have we learned about Josh so far?* Then preview today's reading. Have children look for clues to help them predict how this story will end.

READ

Ask children to read to confirm their predictions. Have children take turns reading the selection with partners. Discuss, confirm, and revise predictions based upon story details. Ask if there was anything about the way the story ended that surprised them.

REREAD

Call on individuals to read aloud while others follow along. Stop to discuss each question. Allow time for children to write their responses before proceeding. Sample answers are provided.

Page 168: After meeting Rick Callan, Josh is _____. (upset)

Help unpack meaning, if needed, by asking, *How did Rick Callan act when Josh talked to him?* (Rick said that he was in a rush and kept walking.) *How would you feel if someone you admired treated you like that?* (Possible responses may include upset, disappointed, and angry.)

Unpack Meaning: For questions on pages 169 and 170, you may want to use the notes in the right-hand column.

Page 169: Josh meets Mrs. Evans _____ the game. (after)

Turn and Talk **Page 170:** Josh's dad thinks Mrs. Evans is a _____. (hero) Have partners discuss this statement and then share with the group.

Quick Check **Retelling**

Have children retell the end of the story. Support the retelling by asking, *What did Josh learn about heroes? Does he have new heroes?* **ELA** RL.2.1, RL.2.5 **ELD** ELD.PI.2.1

UNPACK MEANING

Use prompts such as these if children have difficulty with a **Stop•Think•Write** question:

Page 169 *Where was the first place Josh and his dad went?* (to the baseball game) *What hero did Josh meet after the game?* (Rick Callan) *What did Josh's dad decide to do after Josh learned that Rick Callan wasn't a hero?* (He took Josh to Mrs. Evans's house.)

Page 170 *How does Dad know Mrs. Evans?* (She taught him to read.) *What does Dad think about people who teach you something?* (They are heroes.)

DAILY FLUENCY

Build automaticity by using **Context Cards** or word lists on display. Point to the words in any order and have children read them aloud. Continue until children can read all words fluently.

DAY 4

SHARE OBJECTIVES

- Read and use high-frequency words.
- Identify subject-verb agreement with pronouns as the subject.
- Answer questions using evidence from the story.
- Read aloud fluently to improve stress.

MATERIALS

Write-In Reader pages 164–171

TERMS ABOUT READING/ LANGUAGE ARTS

pronouns   subject   verb

ENGLISH LANGUAGE SUPPORT

Day 4

Vocabulary Preteach the meanings of the high-frequency words *any, carry, room, studied,* and *teacher.* Ask questions for children to discuss. Sample: *Who is your teacher this year?* Use visuals, gestures, sounds, or words to support their understanding. **ELD** ELD.PI.2.1

Sentence Frames Give sentence frames to help children participate in the Look Back and Respond Turn and Talk activity. Guide them to use frames such as these. *At the beginning of the story, Josh's hero _____. Josh meets Rick Callan _____. At the end of the story, Josh _____.* **ELD** ELD.PI.2.5

Oral Language Help children write a description of a personal hero. Use this paragraph frame for support. *My hero is _____ because _____. He/She does _____. It makes _____.* Have children practice reading their paragraphs quietly to themselves. Then have partners take turns reading their paragraphs to each other. **ELD** ELD.PI.2.10

High-Frequency Words

any, carry, room, studied, teacher

Write the high-frequency words on the board or on a pad. Have partners practice reading the words. Then challenge children to use as many of these words as possible in one sentence.

Quick Check | High-Frequency Words

Ask each child to use one of the week's words in a sentence. **ELA** RF.2.3f **ELD** ELD.PIII.2

RETEACH

Subject-Verb Agreement

- Review that sentences have two main parts: the subject and the verb. The subject tells who or what a sentence is about while the verb tells what the subject is doing, has done, or will do. Have children turn to page 166 and read the second paragraph aloud.

- Ask, *What is the subject of the first sentence?* (He) *What is the verb?* (loved) Remind children that pronouns such as *he* and *they* may be the subject of a sentence.

Turn and Talk Have children reread the remaining sentences in the paragraph. Ask them to identify the subject and verb in each sentence. Have them underline the sentences that have a pronoun as the subject.

Answers: <u>He played</u>; <u>He hit</u>; score was; Stars won

Quick Check | Grammar

Have children rewrite the last sentence, substituting a pronoun for "The Stars."

Look Back and Respond

Write-In Reader pages 164–171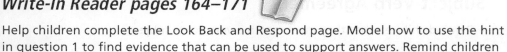

Help children complete the Look Back and Respond page. Model how to use the hint in question 1 to find evidence that can be used to support answers. Remind children that they can circle or underline the specific words in the selection that they used as evidence for their answers.

1. Who is Josh's hero at the beginning of the story? (Rick Callan)

Help unpack meaning, if needed, by asking, *What details about Josh can you find on page 164?* (He loves the Stars baseball team. Rick Callan was his hero.)

Turn and Talk Have children work independently on questions 2 and 3. When children have completed the page, have partners discuss their responses and then share them with the group. Sample responses are provided. Accept reasonable responses.

Unpack Meaning: For questions 2 and 3, you may want to use the notes in the right-hand column to guide the discussion about children's responses.

2. When does Josh meet Rick Callan? (after the game on the way to the car)

3. Who are Josh's heroes at the end of the story? (his dad and Mrs. Evans) **ELA** SL.2.1a **ELD** ELD.PI.2.1

RETEACH

Fluency: Stress

Write-In Reader page 164

Explain that you are going to read from page 164 in two different ways, and you want children to evaluate your reading.

- Read the second sentence, emphasizing "were." Then read the sentence again, emphasizing "favorite."

- Ask, *What did you think of my first reading? Explain. Was my second reading different? Explain. Which makes more sense for this selection? Explain.* Be sure children recognize that the meaning can become clearer when someone stresses an appropriate word.

- Discuss with children their advice to you. Then read the rest of the paragraph, following children's advice. Have children practice reading page 164 aloud stressing appropriate words. **ELA** RF.2.4a **ELD** ELD.PIII.2

UNPACK MEANING

Use prompts such as these if children have difficulty with a question:

2. *Reread page 166. Who could Josh see at the game?* (all the players) *Look at page 167. Where do you think Josh and his dad are?* (the parking lot) *Where are they going?* (to their car) *Why?* (They are leaving the game.)

3. *Who is Josh's dad's hero?* (Mrs. Evans) *Who is Mrs. Evans's hero?* (Josh's dad)

DAILY FLUENCY

Build automaticity by using **Context Cards** or word lists on display. Point to the words in any order and have children read them aloud. Continue until children can read all words fluently.

SHARE OBJECTIVES

- Use subject-verb agreement.
- Demonstrate understanding of Target Vocabulary words.
- Preview Understanding Characters and the Analyze/Evaluate strategy.

MATERIALS

Context Cards: *cheered, curb, extra, final, hurried, position, practice, roared*

Write-In Reader pages 164–170

Leveled Reader: *The Winning Hit*

TERMS ABOUT READING/ LANGUAGE ARTS

characters   traits   analyze/evaluate

TARGET VOCABULARY

The **curb** is where the sidewalk meets the edge of the road.

When someone or something is in a certain **position**, they are sitting, lying, or arranged in that way.

If you **practice** an activity, you do it many times so you get better at it.

When an animal or person **roared**, they made a loud, deep noise.

ENGLISH LANGUAGE SUPPORT

Day 5

Vocabulary Preteach the meanings of the Target Vocabulary words *curb, position, practice,* and *roared.* Use examples and EL-friendly explanations to support children's understanding. Then ask questions about the words for children to discuss. **ELD** ELD.PI.2.1

Warm Up

Oral Grammar

Subject-Verb Agreement

- Remind children that they must match a verb to its subject.

- For most verbs, add -*s* to the verb when the subject is singular and the action is happening now. Add -*es* to verbs ending in *s, sh, ch, tch,* or *x.*

- Plural subjects take a verb that does not end in -*s.*

- The singular pronouns *he, she,* and *it* need a verb that ends in -*s.* The pronouns *I, you, we,* and *they* take a verb without -*s.*

- Read each of the following sentences twice, once with each verb option, and work with children to choose the correct answer for each. For singular verbs, ask children to say whether the word ends in -*s* or -*es.*

  1. *We (play, plays) baseball after school.*

  2. *The baseball player (walk, walks) past the fan.*

  3. *Our players (run, runs) fast.*

  4. *You (catch, catches) really well.*

  5. *I (wish, wishes) I could hit a home run.*

  6. *My father (fix, fixes) supper after a game.*

RETEACH

Target Vocabulary

Context Cards

- Display the **Context Cards** for *cheered, extra, final,* and *hurried.* Review the meanings of these words. Then have children use the words in oral sentences about baseball.

- Add the **Context Cards** for *curb, position, practice,* and *roared.* Deal one card to each child. Have them work in pairs to write headlines for a major sports story, using their words. Have them share their headlines with the rest of the group.

WRITE ABOUT IT

- Ask children to write about a real or imaginary event that happens during sports practice. Have children describe the event using the word *practice.*
ELA L.2.5a **ELD** ELD.PI.2.12b

Understanding Characters
Analyze/Evaluate

Write-In Reader pages 164–170

- Introduce skill and strategy. Say, *In the next lesson, we are going to focus on understanding characters in a story. We'll also work on ways to analyze and evaluate events.*

- Explain, *Writers create interesting characters in their stories. They describe what characters do and say, how they act, problems they have, and how they solve them. Explain that readers can use the information an author provides, along with what they know about real people, to understand characters in a story.*

- Ask, *What did the writer of this week's story tell us about Josh?* (He loves baseball. He gets to meet his hero. Josh has two new heroes at the end of the story.)

- List on the board with children clues that help us understand Josh.

Words	Actions	Feelings
Wow! Can you sign my program? I have two new heroes.	cheered at the game hurried to talk to Rick Callan smiled at Dad and Mrs. Evans	excited about the game upset at Rick Callan happy to learn about his dad and Mrs. Evans
Josh learned that real heroes care about other people.		

- Turn to and review the Analyze/Evaluate strategy found on page 303 in the **Write-In Reader**. Tell children that when they analyze, they should think about the story, the author, and what they already know. Then they can evaluate by deciding what is important. Have them analyze and evaluate character traits to demonstrate an understanding of the characters in the selection. **ELA** RL.2.3 **ELD** ELD.PI.2.1

APPLY READING SKILLS

Introduce *The Winning Hit*. Choral-read the first few pages with children. Depending on their abilities, have children continue reading with partners or as a group.

Leveled Reader

Listen to individual children as they read the **Write-In Reader** selection. Make specific notes about words that presented difficulty.

"Be a Reading Detective!"

Student Book pages 53–73
Write-In Reader pages 171A–171B

- Page through "Luke Goes to Bat" with children and review the main characters and events. Encourage volunteers to talk about what is happening on each page.

- Read page 171A of the **Write-In Reader** with children. Remind children that reading detectives find clues in the words and pictures of a story.

- Discuss the questions with children. Guide them to find clues in the words and pictures that help them answer the questions.

- Have children complete item 1 on page 171B on their own. Remind them to include details and examples from the story in their answer. Then have them share their work with a partner. Encourage them to discuss how they knew the answer to the question.

- Read item 2 on page 171B. Have children talk with a partner about the different people who help Luke learn a lesson. Have them discuss clues from the story that help them answer the question.

Read Around the Room Have one child point to words that are on display in the room. Have the group read the words. Give each child a chance to be the pointer.

DAY 1

SHARE OBJECTIVES

- Identify a sound's position in a word.
- Read words with long e spelled *y*.
- Talk about writers.
- Read to build meaning for Target Vocabulary words.

MATERIALS

Sound/Spelling Card: *eagle*

Write-In Reader pages 172–173

Context Cards: *express, pretend, prize, taught*

TERMS ABOUT READING/ LANGUAGE ARTS

syllable

ENGLISH LANGUAGE SUPPORT

Day 1

Vocabulary Preteach the meanings of the Target Vocabulary words *express, pretend, prize,* and *taught.* Use examples and EL-friendly explanations to support children's understanding. Then ask questions about the words for children to discuss. **ELD** ELD.PI.2.1

Sentence Frames Teach terms and give sentence frames to help children participate in the Talk About It activity. Explain that their favorite books are written by authors who write for a living. Guide children to use these frames as they respond. *My favorite book is _____. I read it _____. I like books about _____. Authors write books by _____.* **ELD** ELD.PI.2.5

Oral Language Have volunteers take turns generating oral sentences that include one or more Target Vocabulary words. Write the sentences on the board and have children read them chorally. **ELD** ELD.PI.2.1

Phonemic Awareness
Identify Sound Placement

- Say, *I'll say a word:* penny. *I hear /ē/ at the end of the word.*
- Say, *Say* penny. (penny) Ask, Where do you hear /ē/? (at the end)
- Continue, using the following words.

deed	in the middle
Eve	at the beginning
baby	at the end

- Correct errors by repeating the process.

RETEACH

Phonics: Long *e*
Sound/Spelling Card

- Display the **Sound/Spelling Card** for *eagle.* Say the word, and ask, *What sound do you hear at the beginning of* eagle? (/ē/) Point to *-y.* Teach that when *y* is at the end of a word with two or more syllables, *y* stands for /ē/.

- Write the following words on the board or on a pad:

penny	bunny	puppy	happy	funny

- For all words, model dividing the word between the two consonants, identifying the sound for the first vowel, identifying the sound for *y,* saying the first part, saying the second part, and saying the whole word. After you model a word, have children perform the steps with you and then on their own. **ELA** RF.2.3e **ELD** ELD.PIII.2

Talk About It

- Explain that a working writer writes books and stories for a living. Ask children to think about their favorite books. Then ask them to imagine the authors who wrote those books. Ask, *What kinds of things does a writer do to get ready to write a book?* List children's ideas.

Writers...
get ideas from their own lives.
get ideas from other people's lives.
watch or observe real people to get ideas for characters.
take notes or keep a journal.
read a lot to learn how other writers write.

- Ask, *If you wrote a book, what would it be about?* **ELA** SL.2.1a **ELD** ELD.PI.2.1

RETEACH

Target Vocabulary

Write-In Reader pages 172–173

- Read and discuss each paragraph. Then discuss the meaning of each Target Vocabulary word. Suggest that children underline words or phrases that provide clues to meaning. Also point out the following:

  In this instance, the word *express* means "to tell or show what a writer is thinking or feeling." Contrast this meaning with the meaning "fast, direct," as in "The express train zoomed away."

  The word *prize*, as it's used in this instance, means "an award," as in "The writer won the Nobel Prize for Literature." But the word *prize* can also mean "to value," as in "They prize the giant pumpkins that grow each year."

- Allow time for children to write their responses. Ask children to choose an answer they would like to read aloud.

Responses: **1.** Possible responses include happiness, anger, and sadness. **2.** Responses will vary. **3.** Responses will vary. **4.** Responses will vary. **ELA** RF.2.3f, L.2.4a **ELD** ELD.PIII.2

Quick Check | **Target Vocabulary**

Ask each child to use one of the Target Vocabulary words in a sentence.

☑ **TARGET VOCABULARY**

When you **express** yourself, you tell or show what you are feeling or thinking.

Something that is **pretend** is imagined, or make-believe.

A **prize** is an award for winning a contest or doing something well.

If you **taught** someone how to do something, you told or showed them what to do.

DAILY FLUENCY

Build automaticity by using **Context Cards** or word lists on display. Point to the words in any order and have children read them aloud. Continue until children can read all words fluently.

DAY 2

SHARE OBJECTIVES

- Read and use high-frequency words.
- Learn about understanding characters.
- Read to apply skills and strategies.

MATERIALS

Write-In Reader pages 174–177

TERMS ABOUT READING/ LANGUAGE ARTS

character   analyze   evaluate

ENGLISH LANGUAGE SUPPORT

Day 2

Vocabulary Preteach the meanings of the high-frequency words *draw, friends, mothers, under,* and *words*. Ask questions for children to discuss. Sample: *What do you like to draw?* Use visuals, gestures, sounds, or words to support their understanding. **ELD** ELD.PI.2.1

Sentence Frames Give sentence frames to help children participate in the Reread discussion. Guide them to use frames such as these as they answer the questions. *Pat Mora grew up _____. Pat's aunt spoke Spanish because _____.* **ELD** ELD.PI.2.5

Oral Language Guide children to write a summary of *Pat Mora* as a class. Use this summary frame and write their responses on the board. *This selection is about _____. First, _____. Then _____. Next, _____. At the end, _____.* Have children choral-read the summary when they are finished. **ELD** ELD.PI.2.2

Warm Up

High-Frequency Words
draw, friends, mothers, under, words

Write the high-frequency words on the board or on a pad. Have partners practice reading the words. Then ask each child to use one word in a sentence. For a challenge, ask if anyone can use two words in just one sentence.
ELA RF.2.3f **ELD** ELD.PIII.2

RETEACH

Understanding Characters

- Explain to children that in order to understand a story, they must understand and think about the main characters. Point out that considering what characters do and say can help children understand the characters in a story and predict what they might do or say next.

- Write this story on the board or read it aloud: *Jemma and Gina are friends. Jemma wants to be an artist when she grows up. Gina wants to be a writer. Jemma doodles in a sketchbook, while Gina scribbles in a journal. Jemma says art speaks for itself. Gina says the characters she writes about speak for her. Jemma wants to go to the art museum, but Gina wants to go see a play.*

- Ask, *Can you help me think about the characters?* Invite children to volunteer things the characters say and do that are important. Record their responses in a chart.

Jemma	Gina
wants to be an artist	wants to be a writer
doodles in a sketchbook	scribbles in a journal
says, "Art speaks for itself."	says, "My characters speak for me."
wants to go to the museum	wants to go to a play

- Then ask, *What will Jemma and Gina decide to do?* (Possible responses include that they will go to the museum first and a play second or will go to a play that has art and costumes.) **ELA** SL.2.1a **ELD** ELD.PI.2.5

Quick Check | **Comprehension**

Have children think about their own positive qualities. Have children draw a chart and list their own positive traits on it. Then invite volunteers to share their charts.

S24 • Lesson 18

READ

Pat Mora

Write-In Reader pages 174–177

- Preview the selection with children using the **Think Aloud** to predict the setting (both time and place). Guide children to scan the text and illustrations to make predictions. Record their ideas.

Think Aloud *I see a little girl with her grandmother. I see the words* Texas, Mexico, English, *and* Spanish *in the text. I see a kitchen, a bedroom, and a schoolroom in the illustrations. This will probably take place at home and at school. What other clues help you make predictions?*

- Together, review the steps to Analyze/Evaluate Strategy, **Write-In Reader** page 303. As needed, guide children in applying the strategy as they read.

READ

Ask children to read to confirm their predictions. Have children take turns reading the selection with partners. Discuss, confirm, and revise children's predictions based upon selection details.

REREAD

Call on individuals to read aloud while others follow along. Point out words that end in long e spelled -y, such as *library*. Stop to discuss each question. Allow time for children to write their responses before proceeding. Sample answers are provided.

Page 174: Pat spoke English and _____. (Spanish)

Help unpack meaning, if needed, by asking, *Where did Pat Mora grow up?* (in Texas) *Where is Texas?* (It is a state in the southwest part of the United States. It is above Mexico.)

Unpack Meaning: For questions on pages 175–177, you may want to use the notes in the right-hand column.

Page 175: Why did Pat's aunt speak Spanish? (She grew up in Mexico.)

Turn and Talk **Page 176:** Pat liked to _____ she was in a faraway place. (pretend) Have children discuss the sentence and then share with the group.

Page 177: Name the things Pat <u>taught</u> her students. (She taught them to read and write.) **ELA** RI.2.1, RI.2.10 **ELD** ELD.PI.2.1

UNPACK MEANING

Use prompts such as these if children have difficulty with a **Stop•Think•Write** question:

Page 175 *What did Pat's aunt do?* (She told stories to Pat.) *Where did Pat's aunt grow up?* (Mexico)

Page 176 *How do you know that reading is important in Pat's family?* (There are always books in the house, and her mother takes Pat to the library.) *When you use your imagination, what faraway places do you think about going to?* (Responses will vary.)

Page 177 *What language did Pat speak at home and at school?* (English) *What did Pat become when she grew up?* (a teacher)

DAILY FLUENCY

Build automaticity by using **Context Cards** or word lists on display. Point to the words in any order and have children read them aloud. Continue until children can read all words fluently.

SHARE OBJECTIVES

- Learn to add sounds to words.
- Read base words and the endings -s and -es, changing y to i.
- Read to apply skills and strategies.

MATERIALS

Write-In Reader pages 178–180

ENGLISH LANGUAGE SUPPORT

Day 3

Vocabulary Before the Phonics lesson, teach the meanings of *penny, bunny, puppy, cry,* and *try.* Ask questions about the words for children to discuss. Use visuals, gestures, or classroom objects to support understanding if needed. **ELD** ELD.PI.2.1

Sentence Frames Give sentence frames to help children participate in the Quick Check activity. Guide them to use frames such as these as they retell the end of the selection. *Besides teaching, Pat wants to _____. I know people like Pat's books because _____.* **ELD** ELD.PI.2.12a

Oral Language Have children offer their opinions about the selection. Did they like it? What part do they like the best? Why? Guide children to use frames such as these as they share their opinions. *I like the selection because _____. I think it is a good selection because _____.* **ELD** ELD.PI.2.3

Warm Up

Phonemic Awareness

Blend Phonemes

- Say, *I'll say a word:* puppy. *I'll make the word plural by adding /z/. The new word is* puppies.
- Have children say *puppy,* add /z/, and say the new word.
- Continue, using the following words.

city	/z/	cities
baby	/z/	babies
penny	/z/	pennies

- Correct errors by repeating the process.

RETEACH

Phonics: -s, -es, Changing y to i

- Write the following words on the board or on a pad:

penny	bunny	puppy	cry	try
pennies	bunnies	puppies	cries	tries

- Explain that when a word ends in *y*, before we can add *-es*, we change the *y* to *i*.
- Tell children that when a word ends in *-ies*, the base word ends in *y*. We read the base word with the correct pronunciation for *y* and then the whole word.
- Point to *pennies.* Ask, *What is the ending?* (-ies) *What letter is at the end of the base word?* (y) *What is the base word?* (penny) *What is the word?* (pennies) If students have difficulty reading *penny*, remind children to divide between the two consonants, read each word part, and read the whole word.
- Follow the procedure for the remaining words.

READ

Pat Mora

Write-In Reader pages 178–180

Review the first part of the story with children. Ask, *What have we learned so far about Pat?* Then preview today's reading. Have children look for clues to help them predict how this selection will end.

READ

Ask children to read to confirm their predictions. Have children take turns reading the selection with partners. Discuss, confirm, and revise predictions based upon selection details. Ask if there was anything about the way the selection ended that surprised them.

REREAD

Call on individuals to read aloud while others follow along. Stop to discuss each question. Allow time for children to write their responses before proceeding. Sample answers are provided.

Page 178: Why did Pat want to write books? (She wanted to express her ideas in words. She also wanted to tell about growing up in Texas and about speaking two languages.)

Help unpack meaning, if needed, by asking, *What does the word* express *mean?* (to tell what you are feeling or thinking) *Why do writers write books?* (Possible responses include to express personal ideas and describe personal experiences.)

Unpack Meaning: For questions on pages 179–180, you may want to use the notes in the right-hand column.

Page 179: Why was Pat's aunt important to her? (Her aunt taught her about storytelling.)

Turn and Talk **Page 180:** What is unusual about some of Pat's books? (Some of her books have both Spanish and English words.) Have children discuss the question and then share with the group. **ELA** RI.2.1, RI.2.10 **ELD** ELD.PI.2.1

Quick Check **Retelling**

Have children retell the end of the story. Support the retelling by asking, *What does Pat want to do besides teaching? How do you know some people think Pat's books are very good? How are Pat's books special?*

UNPACK MEANING

Use prompts such as these if children have difficulty with a **Stop•Think•Write** question:

Page 179 *What stories did Pat's aunt tell her?* (She told Pat about her own childhood in Mexico.) *What does Pat write about?* (families like hers)

Page 180 *Why does Pat write in both English and Spanish?* (Pat grew up speaking both these languages.) *How do you think knowing more than one language could help a writer?* (Possible responses include that it gives you more words to use to express ideas.)

DAILY FLUENCY

Build automaticity by using **Context Cards** or word lists on display. Point to the words in any order and have children read them aloud. Continue until children can read all words fluently.

SHARE OBJECTIVES

- Read and use high-frequency words.
- Use the verb *be*.
- Answer questions using evidence from the selection.
- Read aloud fluently to improve expression.

MATERIALS

Write-In Reader pages 174–181

TERMS ABOUT READING/ LANGUAGE ARTS

being verbs   expression

ENGLISH LANGUAGE SUPPORT

Day 4

Vocabulary Preteach the meanings of the high-frequency words *always, anything, been, soon,* and *watch*. Ask questions for children to discuss. Sample: *Is anything happening today?* Use visuals, gestures, sounds, or words to support their understanding. **ELD** ELD.PI.2.1

Sentence Frames Give sentence frames to help children participate in the Look Back and Respond Turn and Talk activity. Guide them to use frames such as these. *Pat wanted to tell about _____. Pat and her aunt were alike because _____.* **ELD** ELD.PI.2.5

Oral Language Help children write a description of Pat Mora. Use a paragraph frame such as this for support. *Pat Mora grew up in _____. Her grandparents came from _____. She loved to _____. She wanted to _____.* Have children practice reading their paragraphs quietly to themselves. Then have partners take turns reading their paragraphs to each other. **ELD** ELD.PI.2.10

Warm Up

High-Frequency Words

always, anything, been, soon, watch

Write the high-frequency words on the board or on a pad. Have partners practice reading the words. Then challenge children to use as many of these words as possible in one sentence.

Quick Check | **High-Frequency Words**

Ask each child to use one of the week's words in a sentence.

RETEACH

The Verb *be*

- Review that the verb *be* expresses a state of being. Record the following chart on the board or on a pad.

Forms of *Be*			
am	be	being	was
are	been	is	were

- Have children reread the second paragraph on page 176. Ask them to find the sentence with the verb *be*. (There were always books in the house.) Ask, *What is the subject in this sentence?* (There)

- Then say, *Use the chart of forms of* be *to write sentences in both the present and past tense.* Then ask for volunteers to write their sentences on the board. Have the class review the subject and the verb *be* in each sentence. Have them check that the sentences make sense and are complete thoughts.

Turn and Talk Have children reread page 180 and find the sentences that use forms of the verb *be*.

Answers: Some of Pat's books *are* in English; some of her books *are* in Spanish. **ELA** L.2.1d **ELD** ELD.PII.2.3b

Quick Check | **Grammar**

Have children write three sentences with the verb *be*.

Look Back and Respond

Write-In Reader pages 174–181

Help children complete the Look Back and Respond page. Model how to use the hint in question 1 to find evidence that can be used to support answers.

- Explain that evidence is proof, clues, or information.

- Remind children that they can circle or underline the specific words in the selection that they used as evidence for their answers.

1. Where did Pat's family live? (in Texas)

Help unpack meaning, if needed, by asking, *What country did Pat grow up in?* (the United States) *What country did her grandparents and aunt grow up in?* (Mexico)

Turn and Talk Have children work independently on questions 2 and 3. When children have completed the page, have partners discuss their responses and then share them with the group. Sample responses are provided. Accept reasonable responses.

Unpack Meaning: For questions 2 and 3, you may want to use the notes in the right-hand column to guide the discussion about children's responses.

2. Why did Pat want to write books? (She wanted to express her ideas about growing up in Texas and about speaking two languages.)

3. How was Pat like her aunt? (Like her aunt, Pat always loved family stories and storytelling.) **ELA** SL.2.1a **ELD** ELD.PI.2.1

RETEACH

Fluency: Expression

Write-In Reader page 175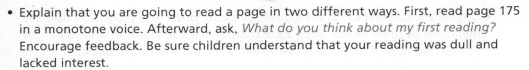

- Explain that you are going to read a page in two different ways. First, read page 175 in a monotone voice. Afterward, ask, *What do you think about my first reading?* Encourage feedback. Be sure children understand that your reading was dull and lacked interest.

- Point out that the sentences should be read in a conversational tone. Explain that a flat tone can make a text dull and uninteresting. It can also make a story harder to understand. Then read page 175 again, this time with expression. Afterward, ask, *How would you read page 175?* Invite children to take turns reading page 175 aloud with expression. **ELA** RF.2.4b **ELD** ELD.PIII.2

DAY 5

SHARE OBJECTIVES

- Use the verb *be*.
- Demonstrate understanding of Target Vocabulary words.
- Preview Text and Graphic Features and the Question Strategy.

MATERIALS

Context Cards: *accepted, express, fluttering, grand, pretend, prize, taught, wonder*

Write-In Reader pages 174–180

Leveled Reader: *Beatrix Potter*

TERMS ABOUT READING/ LANGUAGE ARTS

text   graphics   question

 TARGET VOCABULARY

If you accepted something that was offered to you, you agreed to take it.

Something that is fluttering moves with small, quick movements.

Something grand is large, special, or important.

When you wonder about something, you think and try to guess or understand more about it.

ENGLISH LANGUAGE SUPPORT

Day 5

Vocabulary Preteach the meanings of the Target Vocabulary words *accepted, fluttering, grand,* and *wonder*. Use examples and EL-friendly explanations to support children's understanding. Then ask questions about the words for children to discuss. **ELD** ELD.PI.2.1

S30 • Lesson 18

Oral Grammar
The Verb *be*

- List the following on the board or on a pad:

Present Tense		Past Tense	
Singular	**Plural**	**Singular**	**Plural**
I am	we are	I was	we were
you are	you are	you were	you were
he, she, it is	they are	he, she, it was	they were

- Explain the forms of the verb *be*. Have children read the pronouns and appropriate form of the verb *be*.

- Say each sentence below in the present tense. Have children say the sentence, using the past tense of the verb *be*. **ELA** L.2.1d **ELD** ELD.PII.2.3b

Teacher Prompts	Children Respond
I am going to the store. Yesterday …	I was going to the store.
You are playing soccer. Last summer …	you were playing soccer.
They are going home. Last month …	they were going home.
He is talking. Last night …	he was talking.

RETEACH

Target Vocabulary
Context Cards

- Display the **Context Cards** for *express, pretend, prize,* and *taught*. Review the meanings of these words. Then have children use the words in oral sentences to describe what it might feel like to win a prize for writing a book.

- Add the **Context Cards** for *accepted, fluttering, grand,* and *wonder*. Give one card to each child. Have them take turns acting out their words. Have the rest of the group guess the words. **ELA** L.2.5a **ELD** ELD.PI.2.12b

WRITE ABOUT IT

- Ask children to write a family story they have heard about from their parents or grandparents when they were children. Have children use the word *wonder* in their stories.

PRETEACH

Text and Graphic Features Question

Write-In Reader pages 174–180

- Introduce skill and strategy. Say, *In the next lesson, we are going to focus on text and graphic features in a story. We'll also work on ways to use the Question Strategy.*

- Explain, *Artists illustrate a story or text to extend the meaning in the text and give supporting details that help readers understand what and why they are reading.*

- Ask, *How do the illustrations in the biography* Pat Mora *help you better understand the story?* List children's ideas.

  1. On page 175 the illustration shows how close Pat is to her aunt and how closely she listens to her aunt's stories.

  2. The illustration on page 176 supports the text "Pat loved to read."

  3. The illustrations on pages 178–179 support the text "Pat had a lot of ideas. She wanted to express her ideas in words."

- Turn to and review the Question Strategy found on page 305 in the **Write-In Reader**. Tell students that when they question, they stop to ask questions about what they are reading. Have children use the Question Strategy to consider the illustration on page 175. Ask, *What does this illustration show us about Pat's childhood?*
  ELA RI.2.5, RI.2.7 **ELD** ELD.PI.2.1

APPLY READING SKILLS

Introduce *Beatrix Potter*. Choral-read the first few pages with children. Depending on their abilities, have children continue reading with partners or as a group.

Quick Check | Fluency

Listen to individual children as they read the **Write-In Reader** selection. Make specific notes about words that presented difficulty to them.

● **Leveled Reader**

RETURN TO THE ANCHOR TEXT

"Be a Reading Detective!"
Student Book pages 91–109
Write-In Reader pages 181A–181B

- Page through "My Name is Gabriela" with children and review important ideas and information. Encourage volunteers to talk about each page.

- Read page 181A of the **Write-In Reader** with children. Remind children that reading detectives find clues in the words and pictures to help them understand what they read.

- Discuss the questions with children. Guide them to find clues in the words and pictures that help them answer the questions.

- Have children complete item 1 on page 181B on their own. Remind them to include details and examples from the selection in their answer. Then have them share their work with a partner. Encourage them to discuss how they knew the answer to the question.

- Read item 2 on page 181B. Have children talk with a partner about the different places Gabriela went in her life. Have them discuss clues that help them answer the question.

DAILY FLUENCY

Read Around the Room Have one child point to words that are on display in the room. Have the group read the words. Give each child a chance to be the pointer.

SHARE OBJECTIVES

- Change sounds in words to make new words.
- Read words with *ar*.
- Discuss moving to a new town.
- Read to build meaning for Target Vocabulary words.

MATERIALS

Sound/Spelling Card: *artist*

Write-In Reader pages 182–183

Context Cards: *agreed, failed, polite, trouble*

ENGLISH LANGUAGE SUPPORT

Day 1

Vocabulary Preteach the meanings of the Target Vocabulary words *agreed, failed, polite,* and *trouble.* Use examples and EL-friendly explanations to support children's understanding. Then ask questions about the words for children to discuss. **ELD** ELD.PI.2.1

Sentence Frames Give sentence frames to help children participate in the Talk About It activity. Say that they should imagine moving and what would be different. Guide them to use these frames as they respond. *If I moved, I would miss _____. After moving, the first thing I would do would be to _____.* **ELD** ELD.PI.2.5

Oral Language Have volunteers take turns generating oral sentences that include one or more Target Vocabulary words. Write the sentences on the board and have children read them chorally. **ELD** ELD.PI.2.1

Warm Up

Phonemic Awareness

Substitute Phonemes

- Say, *I'll say a word:* ban. *I'll change* /ă/ *to* /är/, *and say the new word:* barn.
- Have children say *ban.* Tell children to change /ă/ to /är/, and have them say the new word.
- Continue, using the following words:

am	/ă/ to /är/	arm
chat	/ă/ to /är/	chart
cave	/ā/ to /är/	carve

- Correct errors by repeating the process.

RETEACH

Words with: *ar*

Sound/Spelling Card

- Display the **Sound/Spelling Card** for *artist.* Say the word, and ask, *What sound do you hear at the beginning of* artist? (/är/ /r/) Point to *ar.* Explain that *ar* stands for /är/.
- Write the following words on the board or on a pad:

| smart | large | park | yard | spark | hard |

- Point under *ar* and say /är/, and then say the word. Then point under *ar*, and have children say the sound and then the word on their own.
- Repeat for the remaining words.
- Correct errors by modeling the process.

Talk About It

- Ask children to imagine moving. Ask, *Where would you go? What would you miss? What would you look forward to doing?* Have children discuss their ideas. Make a chart to record children's responses.

Things We Would Miss	Things We Would Do
friends	make new friends
a neighborhood playground	visit a park

- Ask, *What's the first thing you would do in your new home?*
  ELA SL.2.1a **ELD** ELD.PI.2.1

RETEACH

Target Vocabulary

Write-In Reader pages 182–183

- Read aloud each item with children. Ask what the highlighted word in each sentence means. Suggest that children underline words or phrases that provide clues to meaning. Also point out the following:

In this instance, the word *trouble* is a noun meaning "a problem that makes something difficult." Contrast this meaning with the verb *trouble*, meaning "to bother," as in "I'm sorry to trouble you, but may I ask you a question?"

- Allow time for children to write their responses. Ask children to choose an answer they would like to read aloud.

Responses: **1.** Responses will vary. **2.** Responses will vary. **3.** Responses will vary. **4.** Possible responses include saying please and thank you, or not interrupting others. **ELA** L.2.4a **ELD** ELD.PI.2.12b

Quick Check | **Target Vocabulary**

Ask each child to use one of the Target Vocabulary words in a sentence.

✓ TARGET VOCABULARY

If you **agreed** with someone, you had the same opinion or idea as that person.

If you **failed** to do something, you did not succeed in doing it.

Someone who has good manners is **polite**.

Trouble is a problem that makes something difficult.

DAILY FLUENCY

Build automaticity by using **Context Cards** or word lists on display. Point to the words in any order and have children read them aloud. Continue until children can read all words fluently.

SHARE OBJECTIVES

- Read and use high-frequency words.
- Identify text and graphic features.
- Read to apply skills and strategies.

MATERIALS

Write-In Reader pages 124–130, 184–187

TERMS ABOUT READING/ LANGUAGE ARTS

title   **author**   **text features**

graphic features

ENGLISH LANGUAGE SUPPORT

Day 2

Vocabulary Preteach the meanings of the high-frequency words *didn't, good, I'll, please,* and *talk.* Ask questions for children to discuss. Sample: *What good will that do?* Use visuals, gestures, sounds, or words to support their understanding. **ELD** ELD.PI.2.1

Sentence Frames Give sentence frames to help children participate in the Quick Check activity. Guide them to use frames such as these as they tell how they used text or graphic features to locate information. *I used headings in a book to _____. I used a photograph in a newspaper to _____.* **ELD** ELD.PI.2.12a

Oral Language Guide children to write a summary of *The Big City* as a class. Use this summary frame and write their responses on the board. *This story is about _____. First, _____. Then _____. Next, _____. At the end, _____.* Have children choral-read the summary when they are finished. **ELD** ELD.PI.2.2

High-Frequency Words
didn't, good, I'll, please, talk

Write the high-frequency words on the board or on a pad. Have partners practice reading the words. Then ask each child to use one word in a sentence. For a challenge, ask if anyone can use two words in one sentence. **ELA** RF.2.3f **ELD** ELD.PIII.2

RETEACH

Text and Graphic Features

- Have children look at page 125 in the **Write-In Reader.** Ask, *What kind of graphics are used in this selection?* (photos) Ask, *Are photos more likely to be used with informational text or stories?* (informational text)

- Have children look at pages 184–190. Ask, *Are photos used in this selection?* (Yes, but illustrations are also used.) Ask, *Why do you think the author chose to use both photos and illustrations?* (Possible responses include a recognition that the story is about a fictional family living in a real place.)

- Point out that the informational text on pages 124–130 has headings. Have children contrast that with this week's story.

- Emphasize that authors use text and graphic features to make their writing clearer. **ELA** SL.2.1a **ELD** ELD.PI.2.1

Quick Check Comprehension

Have children share a real-life experience when text or graphic features have helped them locate information or understand a selection better. List a few of the children's examples.

READ

The Big City

Write-In Reader pages 184–187

- Preview the selection with children using the **Think Aloud** to predict the plot. Guide children to use the title and illustrations to make predictions. Record their ideas.

Think Aloud   *I see an illustration on page 184: The drawing shows people on an airplane. This, along with the title, makes me think that the people are traveling to a city. What other clues help you predict what will happen in this story?*

- Together, review the steps to the Question Strategy, **Write-In Reader** page 305. As needed, guide children in applying the strategy as they read.

READ

Ask children to read to confirm their predictions. Have children choral-read the selection. Discuss, confirm, and revise children's predictions based upon story details.

REREAD

Call on individuals to read aloud while others follow along. Stop to discuss each question. Allow time for children to write their responses before proceeding. Sample answers are provided.

Page 184: Who is the author of this story? (John Berry)

Help unpack meaning, if needed, by asking, *What is an author?* (the person who wrote a story or selection) *Where can you look to find the author's name?* (below the title)

Unpack Meaning: For questions on pages 185–187, you may want to use the notes in the right-hand column.

Page 185: Sam doesn't know the city. He doesn't have any _____ in New York. (friends)

Turn and Talk   **Page 186:** Sam and his dad look at the map to _____ their day. (plan) Have partners discuss the sentence and then share their answers with the group.

Page 187: The family took the wrong subway. They _____ to get to the store. (failed) **ELA** RL.2.1, RL.2.10 **ELD** ELD.PI.2.1

UNPACK MEANING

Use prompts such as these if children have difficulty with a **Stop•Think•Write** question:

Page 185 *How did Sam look at New York?* (He stared.) *How did the city look to Sam?* (tall) *What do Sam's behaviors tell you?* (Possible responses include that Sam had never been to New York before.)

Page 186 *What does Sam's mom say they should do?* (plan) *Look at the illustration. What are Sam and his dad doing?* (looking at a map) *When do you use a map?* (when you need to find your way somewhere)

Page 187 *What does the word* failed *mean?* (to not succeed at something) *Where was Sam's family trying to go?* (the hardware store)

DAILY FLUENCY

Build automaticity by using **Context Cards** or word lists on display. Point to the words in any order and have children read them aloud. Continue until children can read all words fluently.

SHARE OBJECTIVES

- Change sounds in words to make new words.
- Read words with *ar*.
- Read to apply skills and strategies.

MATERIALS

Sound/Spelling Card: *artist*

Write-In Reader pages 188–190

ENGLISH LANGUAGE SUPPORT

Day 3

Vocabulary Before the Phonics lesson, teach the meanings of *party, harvest, artist, charcoal,* and *harness*. Ask questions about the words for children to discuss. Use visuals, gestures, or classroom objects to support understanding if needed. **ELD** ELD.PI.2.1

Sentence Frames Give sentence frames to help children participate in the Quick Check activity. Guide them to use frames such as these as they retell the end of the story. *When Sam's family took the subway, they _____. Sam thinks that New York _____.* **ELD** ELD.PI.2.12a

Oral Language Have children offer their opinions about the story. Did they like it? What do they think of *The Big City*? Why? Guide children to use frames such as these as they share their opinions. *I do/do not like the story because _____. I think* The Big City *is _____ because _____.* **ELD** ELD.PI.2.3

Warm Up

Phonemic Awareness
Substitute Phonemes

- Say, *I'll say a word:* pot. *I'll change* /ŏ/ *to* /är/ *and say the new word:* part.
- Have children say *pot*. Tell children to change /ŏ/ to /är/, and have children say the new word.
- Continue, using the following words:

badge	/ă/ to /är/	barge
shack	/ă/ to /är/	shark
make	/ā/ to /är/	mark

- Correct errors by repeating the process.

RETEACH

Phonics: Words with *ar*
Sound/Spelling Card

- Display the **Sound/Spelling Card** for *artist*. Say the word, and ask, *What sound do you hear at the beginning of* artist? (/är/) Point to *ar*. Explain that *ar* stands for /är/.
- Write the following words on the board or on a pad:

| party | harvest | artist | charcoal | harness |

- Point to *party*. Tell children that we divide the word between the two consonants. Then we read the first word part, the second word part, and the whole word. For the first part, point under *ar* and have children say the sound, the first word part, the second word part, and the whole word.
- Repeat for the remaining words, having children say the sound and word on their own.
- Correct errors by modeling the process.

READ

The Big City

Write-In Reader pages 188–190

Review the first part of the story with children. Ask, *What have we learned about Sam so far?* Then preview today's reading. Have children look for clues to help them predict what else they will learn from this selection.

READ

Ask children to read to confirm their predictions. Have children choral-read the selection. Discuss, confirm, and revise predictions based upon story details. Ask if they learned anything that surprised them.

REREAD

Call on individuals to read aloud while others follow along. Stop to discuss each question. Allow time for children to write their responses before proceeding. Sample answers are provided.

Page 188: Sam and his parents <u>agreed</u>. They would go to the _____. (game)

Help unpack meaning, if needed, by asking, *What does the word* agreed *mean?* (had the same opinion) *Where are Sam and his parents?* (at Yankee Stadium) *What happens at Yankee Stadium?* (Teams play baseball.)

Unpack Meaning: For questions on pages 189–190, you may want to use the notes in the right-hand column.

Page 189: The family is near a _____. (museum)

Turn and Talk **Page 190:** What is the family looking at? (a dinosaur) Have partners discuss this question and then share with the group. **ELA** RL.2.1, RL.2.10 **ELD** ELD.PI.2.1

Quick Check **Retelling**

Have children retell the end of the story. Support the retelling by asking, *What happened each time Sam's family took the wrong subway? How do Sam's feelings about New York change?*

UNPACK MEANING

Use prompts such as these if children have difficulty with a **Stop•Think•Write** question:

Page 189 *Where were Sam and his parents going?* (to shop for curtains) *Why did the family look at a map?* (They got on the wrong subway again and were lost.)

Page 190 *Where are Sam and his family?* (at a museum) *Look at the illustration. What is in the exhibit?* (a dinosaur)

DAILY FLUENCY

Build automaticity by using **Context Cards** or word lists on display. Point to the words in any order and have children read them aloud. Continue until children can read all words fluently.

SHARE OBJECTIVES

- Read and use high-frequency words.
- Use commas in dates and place names.
- Answer questions using evidence from the text.
- Read aloud fluently to improve phrasing.

MATERIALS

Write-In Reader pages 184–191

TERMS ABOUT READING/
LANGUAGE ARTS

commas

ENGLISH LANGUAGE SUPPORT

Day 4

Vocabulary Preteach the meanings of the high-frequency words *are, baby, is, sound,* and *too*. Ask questions for children to discuss. Sample: *What sound does a baby make?* Use visuals, gestures, sounds, or words to support their understanding. **ELD** ELD.PI.2.1

Sentence Frames Give sentence frames to help children participate in the Look Back and Respond Turn and Talk activity. Guide them to use frames such as these. *Sam changed his mind about New York because _____. The story title tells us about _____.* **ELD** ELD.PI.2.5

Oral Language Help children write a description of something that educates and entertains lots of people. *A _____ entertains people. It educates people who _____. It helps them _____.* Then have partners take turns reading their paragraphs to each other. **ELD** ELD.PI.2.10

High-Frequency Words

are, baby, is, sound, too

Write the high-frequency words on the board or on a pad. Have partners practice reading the words. Then challenge children to use as many of these words as possible in one sentence.

Quick Check High-Frequency Words

Ask each child to use one of the week's words in a sentence.

ELA RF.2.3f **ELD** ELD.PIII.2

RETEACH

Commas in Dates and Places

- Review that commas are used in dates and place names. Remind children that the order of a date is month, day, year. Say, *We add just one comma to a date: after the day of the month. We don't use one after the name of the month.*

- Write *November 13 2009* on the board or on a pad and ask children where to insert the comma. (after *13*) Now slowly give several dates and have children raise their hands when they think a comma should be added. Write each date with the comma in the proper location.

- Now have children turn to page 184 and read the first two sentences aloud.

- Ask, *Was a comma used in the second sentence?* (no) Tell children that we don't use a comma if the state is named by itself. Ask, *How would we rewrite the second sentence if we wanted to let the reader know that Sam was leaving Alpine, Texas?* (Alpine, Texas, was fading away.) Point out that a comma separates the city and the state. A comma also separates *Texas* from the rest of the sentence.

Turn and Talk Have children read the last sentence on page 184 and rewrite the sentence using *Alpine, Texas*. (He missed Alpine, Texas, already.)

Quick Check Grammar

Have children write today's date and another date of their own choosing—perhaps a holiday or a birthday.

Look Back and Respond

Write-In Reader pages 184–191

Help children complete the Look Back and Respond page. Model how to use the hint in question 1 to find evidence that can be used to support answers. Remind children that they can circle or underline words in the selection that they used as evidence.

1. Why can't Sam sleep during his first night in New York? (He hears sirens and horns.)

Help unpack meaning, if needed, by asking, *What details about Sam's first night can you find on page 186?* (He heard horns and sirens. His parents couldn't sleep either.)

Turn and Talk Have children work independently on questions 2 and 3. When children have completed the questions, have partners discuss their responses and then share them with the group. Sample responses are provided. Accept reasonable responses.

Unpack Meaning: For questions 2 and 3, you may want to use the notes in the right-hand column to guide the discussion.

2. How does Sam's opinion of New York change? (He doesn't like New York at first. After discovering Yankee Stadium and the museum, he thinks the city is cool.)

3. Is *The Big City* a good title for the story? Explain. (Possible responses include yes, because New York is a very big city.) **ELA** SL.2.1a **ELD** ELD.PI.2.1

RETEACH

Fluency: Phrasing

Write-In Reader page 189

- Explain that you are going to read from page 189 in two different ways, and you want children to evaluate your reading. First, read the second paragraph at a normal rate, ignoring all punctuation marks and pausing wherever you'd like. Then read the passage again, using punctuation appropriately.

- Ask, *What did you think of my first reading? Explain. Was my second reading better? Explain.* Be sure children recognize how hard it is to get the meaning when someone ignores punctuation marks and doesn't group words in meaningful ways.

- Reread with appropriate phrasing, following children's advice. Have children practice reading page 189 aloud using proper phrasing. **ELA** RF.2.4b **ELD** ELD.PIII.2

Use prompts such as these if children have difficulty with a question:

2. *Reread the last paragraph on page 184. How did Sam feel?* (sad) *What trouble did Sam describe on page 185?* (He had no friends.) *What did Sam think about the game at Yankee Stadium?* (It was great.)

3. *Where did Sam's family move?* (to New York) *What do the photos and illustrations in this story tell you about New York?* (It is a very big city.)

DAILY FLUENCY

Build automaticity by using **Context Cards** or word lists on display. Point to the words in any order and have children read them aloud. Continue until children can read all words fluently.

DAY 5

SHARE OBJECTIVES

- Learn to place commas.
- Demonstrate understanding of Target Vocabulary words.
- Preview Compare and Contrast and the Monitor/Clarify Strategy.

MATERIALS

Context Cards: *agreed, assistant, cleared, failed, polite, tearing, trouble, wisdom*

Write-In Reader pages 184–190

Leveled Reader: *Aldo and Abby*

TERMS ABOUT READING/ LANGUAGE ARTS

compare	contrast
monitor	clarify

 **TARGET VOCABULARY**

An **assistant** is a person who helps someone else.

If you **cleared** a place, you made it neat or empty by taking things away.

Tearing something down is pulling or ripping it apart.

Wisdom is knowledge or understanding that comes from experience.

ENGLISH LANGUAGE SUPPORT

Day 5

Vocabulary Preteach the meanings of the Target Vocabulary words *assistant, cleared, tearing,* and *wisdom.* Use examples and EL-friendly explanations to support children's understanding. Then ask questions about the words for children to discuss. **ELD** ELD.PI.2.1

Oral Grammar

Commas in Place Names

- Explain that we separate addresses, cities, and states with commas. Write this example on the board or on a pad:

  The history museum is at 1800 North Congress Avenue, Austin, Texas.

- Say the following sentences without expression. Have children give a thumbs-up signal when they hear where a comma belongs.

  1. *My grandmother lives in Los Angeles, California.*

  2. *You can see Spanish art at 5900 Bishop Drive, Dallas, Texas.*

  3. *When we go to Portland, Oregon, we go fishing and swimming.*

  4. *The Pioneer Village is at 2122 Saint Joseph Street, Gonzalez, Texas.*

  5. *Sometimes we visit New Orleans, Louisiana.*

RETEACH

Target Vocabulary

Context Cards

- Display the **Context Cards** for *agreed, failed, polite,* and *trouble.* Review the meanings of these words. Then have children use the words in oral sentences about moving to a new city.

- Add the **Context Cards** for *assistant, cleared, tearing,* and *wisdom.* Deal one card to each child. Have each child draw a picture of himself or herself guiding someone who is lost. Have children write a caption for their drawings using their assigned words. **ELA** SL.2.6 **ELD** ELD.PI.2.12b

WRITE ABOUT IT

- Ask children to imagine being a tour guide at the museum Sam and his family visited in New York. Ask them to write what they like best about their job, using the word *wisdom* in their descriptions.

PRETEACH

Compare and Contrast
Monitor/Clarify

Write-In Reader pages 184–190

- Introduce skill and strategy. Say, *In the next lesson, we are going to focus on comparing and contrasting. We'll also work on monitoring our reading and clarifying where necessary.*

- Explain, *We can compare and contrast stories and story elements to see how they are alike or how they are different. To* compare *means to find ways in which two or more things are alike. To* contrast *means to find ways in which they are different.*

- Say, *Let's compare and contrast Texas and New York using clues the author provides.* (Note that some details about Texas will have to be inferred.)

- Record the children's ideas in a Venn diagram.

Texas and New York City

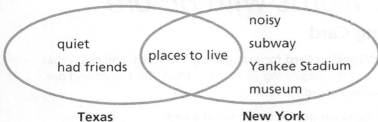

quiet
had friends

places to live

noisy
subway
Yankee Stadium
museum

Texas

New York

- Turn to and review the Monitor/Clarify Strategy found on page 304 in the **Write-In Reader**. Tell children that when they monitor their reading, they should make sure things make sense as they read. Have them compare and contrast story elements to clarify their understanding of the story. **ELA** SL.2.1a **ELD** ELD.PI.2.1

APPLY READING SKILLS

Introduce *Aldo and Abby*. Choral-read the first few pages with children. Depending on their abilities, have children continue reading with partners or as a group.

Quick Check Fluency

Listen to individual children as they read the **Write-In Reader** selection. Make specific notes about words that presented difficulty to them.

● **Leveled Reader**

RETURN TO THE ANCHOR TEXT

"Be a Reading Detective!"

Student Book pages 127–149
Write-In Reader pages 191A–191B

- Page through "The Signmaker's Assistant" with children and review the main characters and events. Encourage volunteers to talk about what is happening on each page.

- Read page 191A of the **Write-In Reader** with children. Remind children that reading detectives find clues in the words and pictures of a story.

- Discuss the questions with children. Guide them to find clues in the words and pictures that help them answer the questions.

- Have children complete item 1 on page 191B on their own. Remind them to include details and examples from the story in their answer. Then have them share their work with a partner. Encourage them to discuss how they knew the answer to the question.

- Read item 2 on page 191B. Have children talk with a partner about how Norman's signs cause trouble. Have them discuss clues that help them answer the question.

DAILY FLUENCY

Read Around the Room Have one child point to words that are on display in the room. Have the group read the words. Give each child a chance to be the pointer.

SHARE OBJECTIVES

- Learn to substitute vowel sounds.
- Read words with vowel-*r* syllables *or* and *ore*.
- Talk about what children know about trees.
- Read to build meaning for Target Vocabulary words.

MATERIALS

Sound/Spelling Card: *orange*

Write-In Reader pages 192–193

Context Cards: *gazing, sore, sprang, studied*

TERMS ABOUT READING/ LANGUAGE ARTS

vowels

ENGLISH LANGUAGE SUPPORT

Day 1

Vocabulary Preteach the meanings of the Target Vocabulary words *gazing, sore, sprang,* and *studied*. Use examples and EL-friendly explanations to support children's understanding. Then ask questions about the words for children to discuss. **ELD** ELD.PI.2.1

Sentence Frames Teach terms and give sentence frames to help children participate in the Talk About It activity. Explain that a forest contains many different kinds of trees. Guide children to use these frames as they share what they know about trees. *I know that some trees _____. In fall, some trees _____. Some trees don't _____.* **ELD** ELD.PI.2.5

Oral Language Have volunteers take turns generating oral sentences that include one or more Target Vocabulary words. Write the sentences on the board and have children read them chorally. **ELD** ELD.PI.2.1

Warm Up

Phonemic Awareness
Substitute Phonemes

- Say, *I'll say the word:* card. *I'll change* /är/ *to* /ôr/ *and say the new word:* cord.
- Have children say *card*. Tell children the sound to change, and have children say the new word on their own.
- Continue, using the following words:

patch	/ă/ to /ôr/	porch
fake	/ā/ to /ôr/	fork
barn	/ä/ /r/ to /ôr/	born

- Correct errors by repeating the process.

RETEACH

Phonics: Words with *or, ore*
Sound/Spelling Card

- Display the **Sound/Spelling Card** for *orange*. Say the word, and ask, *What sound do you hear at the beginning of* orange? (/ôr/) Point to *or* and *ore*. Explain that *or* and *ore* stand for /ôr/.
- Write the following words on the board or on a pad:

shore	score	torn	store	fort	thorn

- Point under *ore* and say /ôr/, and then say the word. Point under *ore*. Have the children say the sound and then blend the sounds to read the word on their own.
- Repeat for the remaining words, having children say the sound and word on their own.
- Correct errors by modeling the process.

Talk About It

- Ask children to share what they know about trees. Lead the discussion with questions like those in the chart below. Draw the chart on the board or on a pad. Record children's answers in the chart.

What do trees have on their branches?	leaves
What do we call a tree's "skin"?	bark
How do some trees change throughout the year?	Their leaves change color in autumn and fall off. New leaves grow in spring.
What animals live in trees?	squirrels, birds
What do people use trees for?	shade, wood, fruits, seeds, and nuts

- Ask, *What do you think you would like most about being a tree? Explain.* **ELA** SL.2.1a **ELD** ELD.PI.2.1

RETEACH

Target Vocabulary

Write-In Reader pages 192–193

- Read and discuss each paragraph. Then discuss the meaning of each Target Vocabulary word. Suggest that children underline words or phrases that provide clues to meaning. Also point out the following:

    Explain that the word *sore* in this example is a describing word. It means "painful or tender." Then explain that the word *sore* can also be a naming word. It means "a blister."

    Tell children that the word *sprang* is the past form of the action word *spring*. Then explain that the word *spring* comes from the Old English word *springan*, which means "to leap or fly up."

- Allow time for children to write their responses. Ask children to choose an answer they would like to read aloud.

Responses: **1.** gazing **2.** studied **3.** sprang **4.** sore **5.** gazing

Quick Check Target Vocabulary

Ask each child to use one of the Target Vocabulary words in a sentence. **ELA** L.2.4a **ELD** ELD.PI.2.12b

✓ TARGET VOCABULARY

When you are **gazing** at something, you are looking at it for a long time.

Your body is **sore** if it feels painful or tender.

If a person or animal **sprang,** they suddenly moved upwards or forwards.

If you **studied** a subject, you spent time learning about it.

DAILY FLUENCY

Build automaticity by using **Context Cards** or word lists on display. Point to the words in any order and have children read them aloud. Continue until children can read all words fluently.

SHARE OBJECTIVES

- Read and use high-frequency words.
- Learn how to compare and contrast.
- Read to apply skills and strategies.

MATERIALS

Write-In Reader pages 194–197

TERMS ABOUT READING/ LANGUAGE ARTS

compare	contrast
monitor	clarify

ENGLISH LANGUAGE SUPPORT

Day 2

Vocabulary Preteach the meanings of the high-frequency words *being, I've, ready, stood,* and *tall.* Ask questions for children to discuss. Sample: *How tall are you?* Use visuals, gestures, sounds, or words to support their understanding. **ELD** ELD.PI.2.1

Sentence Frames Give sentence frames to help children participate in the Compare and Contrast activity. Guide them to use frames such as these. *A forest during the day and a forest at night are alike in that _____. They are different in that _____.*

ELD ELD.PI.2.5

Oral Language Guide children to write a summary of *Sue and the Tired Wolf* as a class. Use this summary frame and write their responses on the board. *This story is about _____. First, _____. Then _____. Next, _____. At the end, _____.* Have children choral-read the summary when they are finished. **ELD** ELD.PI.2.2

High-Frequency Words

being, I've, ready, stood, tall

Write the high-frequency words on the board or on a pad. Have partners practice reading the words. Then ask each child to use one word in a sentence. For a challenge, ask if anyone can use two words in just one sentence. **ELA** RF.2.3f **ELD** ELD.PIII.2

RETEACH

Compare and Contrast

- Hold up two leaves, each one from a different kind of tree. Then ask children, *How are the leaves alike? How are they different?* Draw a Venn diagram on the board to record children's responses.

Oak Leaf Both Maple Leaf

long

notched

lined or veined

green

broad

- Review that when children **compare** two things, they find ways in which the two things are alike. When children **contrast** two things, they find ways in which the things are different.

- Explain that when readers **compare and contrast**, they think about how parts of the story are alike and different.

- Point out that it is helpful to think about how two characters in a story are alike and different. Also explain that considering how a main character changes over the course of the story is important. Thinking about how a character is different from how they were at the beginning of the story is helpful in understanding the purpose of the story.

- Point out that children can also think about how settings in a story may be alike and different.

Quick Check Comprehension

Have children compare two settings, such as a forest during the day and a forest at night or a forest and a desert. Create a new chart and add children's responses to the chart. **ELA** SL.2.1a **ELD** ELD.PI.2.1

READ

Sue and the Tired Wolf

Write-In Reader pages 194–197

- Preview the selection with children using the **Think Aloud** to predict the setting (both time and place). Guide children to use illustrations to make predictions. Record their ideas.

> **Think Aloud** *I see an illustration of a house surrounded by woods. Another illustration shows a girl playing a flute in the woods. Falling leaves around her are red and orange. I think this story takes place in a forest during the fall. What other clues help you predict the setting?*

- Together, review the steps to Monitor/Clarify Strategy, **Write-In Reader** page 304. As needed, guide children in applying the strategy as they read.

READ

Ask children to read to confirm their predictions. Have children take turns reading the selection with partners. Discuss, confirm, and revise children's predictions based upon story details.

REREAD

Call on individuals to read aloud while others follow along. Point out words that have vowel-*r* syllables, such as *bored*, *explore*, and *forest*. Stop to discuss each question. Allow time for children to write their responses before proceeding. Sample answers are provided.

Page 194: Sue's house is next to a _____. (forest)

Help unpack meaning, if needed, by asking, *Look at the illustration. What do you see in front of the house?* (the yard) *What do you see behind it?* (lots of yellow trees)

Unpack Meaning: For questions on pages 195–197, you may want to use the notes in the right-hand column.

Page 195: Sue's mom and dad want less _____. (noise)

> **Turn and Talk** **Page 196:** Why does Sue walk into the forest? (She is bored and wants to explore the woods.)

Page 197: The wolf likes Sue's music. He thinks the forest is too _____. (quiet) Have children discuss this question and then share their answers with the group.

ELA RL.2.3, RL.2.7 **ELD** ELD.PI.2.1

Use prompts such as these if children have difficulty with a **Stop•Think•Write** question:

Page 195 *Why does Sue go outside?* (She wants to make her parents happy.) *How does Sue play her flute outside?* (She plays loudly.)

Page 196 *How does Sue feel?* (She feels bored.) *Why does Sue like playing in the forest?* (She likes the sound of the flute in the forest.)

Page 197 *What do you imagine a forest sounds like?* (Possible responses may include that a forest can be filled with bird songs and the chatter of small animals like squirrels.) *How do you think a forest would sound if a wolf were near?* (Possible responses include that the presence of a wolf would silence the birds and small animals.)

DAILY FLUENCY

Build automaticity by using **Context Cards** or word lists on display. Point to the words in any order and have children read them aloud. Continue until children can read all words fluently.

SHARE OBJECTIVES

- Learn to substitute vowel sounds.
- Read words with vowel-*r* syllables *or* and *ore*.
- Read to apply skills and strategies.

MATERIALS

Sound/Spelling Card: *orange*

Write-In Reader pages 198–200

TERMS ABOUT READING/ LANGUAGE ARTS

vowels

ENGLISH LANGUAGE SUPPORT

Day 3

Vocabulary Before the Phonemic Awareness lesson, teach the meanings of *car, core, farm, form, moan,* and *morn*. Ask questions about the words for children to discuss. Use visuals, gestures, or classroom objects to support understanding if needed. **ELA** ELD.PI.2.1

Sentence Frames Give sentence frames to help children participate in the Quick Check activity. Guide them to use frames such as these as they retell the end of the story. *At the end, _____. Sue _____ because _____.* **ELA** ELD.PI.2.12a

Oral Language Have children offer their opinions about the story. Did they like it? What do they think of how Sue escapes from the wolf? Why? Guide children to use frames such as these as they share their opinions. *I do/do not like the story because _____. I think the story is _____ because _____.* **ELA** ELD.PI.2.3

Warm Up

Phonemic Awareness
Substitute Phonemes

- Say, *I'll say the word: card. I'll change /är/ to /ôr/ and say the new word: cord.*
- Have children say *card*. Tell children the sound to change, and have children say the new word on their own.
- Continue, using the following words:

car	/är/ to /ôr/	core
farm	/är/ to /ôr/	form
moan	/ō/ to /ôr/	morn

- Correct errors by repeating the process.

RETEACH

Phonics: Words with *or, ore*
Sound/Spelling Card

- Display the **Sound/Spelling Card** for *orange*. Say the word and ask, *What sound do you hear at the beginning of* orange? (/ôr/) Point to *or* and *ore*. Explain that *or* and *ore* stand for /ôr/.
- Write the following words on the board or on a pad:

ignore	forget	barnstorm	popcorn	forty

- Say that we divide words between the two consonants. Then we read the first word part, the second word part, and the whole word. Ask children where to divide *ignore*. Point under *ore* and have children say the sound. Have children read the first part, the second part, and the whole word.
- Repeat for the remaining words, having children say the sound and word on their own.
- Correct errors by modeling the process.

READ

Sue and the Tired Wolf

Write-In Reader pages 198–200

Review the first part of the story with children. Ask, *What have we learned so far about Sue?* Then preview today's reading. Have children look for clues to help them predict how this story will end.

READ

Ask children to read to confirm their predictions. Have children take turns reading the selection with partners. Discuss, confirm, and revise predictions based upon story details. Ask if there was anything about the way the story ended that surprised them.

REREAD

Call on individuals to read aloud while others follow along. Stop to discuss each question. Allow time for children to write their responses before proceeding. Sample answers are provided.

Page 198: The wolf has been hunting all day. His muscles hurt. He is _____. (sore)

Help unpack meaning, if needed, by asking, *When you play hard at sports, how do your muscles feel?* (Possible responses may include sore.) *What does the word* sore *mean?* (painful or tender)

Unpack Meaning: For questions on pages 199 and 200, you may want to use the notes in the right-hand column.

Turn and Talk **Page 199:** The wolf woke up. Then he _____ off the rock. (sprang)
Have partners discuss this question and then share with the group.

Page 200: How does Sue get away from the wolf? (She plays her flute so that he falls asleep. Then she takes a few steps and plays again so that he stays asleep. She keeps doing this trick until she gets home.)

Quick Check Retelling

Have children retell the end of the story. Support the retelling by asking, *Why does Sue go into the forest? What does Sue do in the forest? Who is listening to Sue play? How does Sue get away from the wolf and back home?* **ELA** RL.2.1, RL.2.10 **ELD** ELD.PI.2.1

UNPACK MEANING

Use prompts such as these if children have difficulty with a **Stop•Think•Write** question:

Page 199 *Why does the wolf wake up?* (Sue stops playing.) *What does the word* sprang *mean?* (to move upward or forward)

Page 200 *What happens to the wolf when Sue plays?* (The wolf goes to sleep.) *How does Sue get out of the forest?* (She plays her flute as she walks out of the woods.)

DAILY FLUENCY

Build automaticity by using **Context Cards** or word lists on display. Point to the words in any order and have children read them aloud. Continue until children can read all words fluently.

SHARE OBJECTIVES

- Read and use high-frequency words.
- Use commas in a series.
- Answer questions using evidence from the text.
- Read aloud fluently to improve intonation and expression.

MATERIALS

Write-In Reader pages 194–201

TERMS ABOUT READING/ LANGUAGE ARTS

commas   intonation

expression

ENGLISH LANGUAGE SUPPORT

Day 4

Vocabulary Preteach the meanings of the high-frequency words *begins, flower, ground, laugh,* and *very.* Ask questions for children to discuss. Sample: *What new flower have you planted?* Use visuals, gestures, sounds, or words to support their understanding. **ELD** ELD.PI.2.1

Sentence Frames Give sentence frames to help children participate in the Look Back and Respond Turn and Talk activity. Guide them to use frames such as these. *Sue learned that _____. Now Sue _____.* **ELD** ELD.PI.2.5

Oral Language Help children write a description of a playground they have been to. Use this paragraph frame for support. *The playground had _____. Children could _____. I liked to _____.* Have children practice reading their paragraphs quietly to themselves. Then have partners take turns reading their paragraphs to each other. **ELD** ELD.PI.2.10

High-Frequency Words

begins, flower, ground, laugh, very

Write the high-frequency words on the board or on a pad. Have partners practice reading the words. Then challenge children to use as many of these words as possible in one sentence.

Quick Check High-Frequency Words

Ask each child to use one of the week's words in a sentence.

ELA RF.2.3f **ELD** ELD.PIII.2

RETEACH

Using Commas in a Series

- Review that commas should be used to separate items in a series. The items may be nouns or verbs.

Nouns	Verbs
The coach handed out baseballs, bats, gloves, and hats.	The pitcher wound up, threw, and caught the ball.
Joe, Sue, and Lee went fishing.	He ran, walked, and slid to the finish line.
We want sandwiches, soup, and tacos for lunch.	We dove, swam, and floated in the lake.
The art teacher shared her paints, pens, and colored pencils.	The girl laughed, giggled, and smiled.

- Point out that words usually used in pairs, like macaroni and cheese, are set off as one item in a series.

- If all the items in a series are joined by *and, or,* or *nor,* do not use commas to separate them. Example: We ran and walked and even crawled to the drinking fountain.

Turn and Talk Have children write a sentence about the wolf or about Sue using a series of three verbs.

Possible responses: The wolf grew sleepy, closed his eyes, and snored loudly; Sue blew a new tune, walked a few steps, and played again.

Quick Check Grammar

Have children write a sentence with two or three adjectives separated by commas in a series.

Look Back and Respond

Write-In Reader pages 194–201

Help children complete the Look Back and Respond page. Model how to use the hint in question 1 to find evidence that can be used to support answers. Remind children that they can circle or underline the specific words that they used as evidence for their answers.

1. Sue's yard is safe to play in. What is the forest like? (The forest is not safe because a wolf lives there.)

Help unpack meaning, if needed, by asking, *What kinds of things do you do in your yard or on a playground?* (play games, read quietly, talk to friends) *Look at the illustrations on pages 196 and 197. What kinds of things could you find in a forest that you couldn't find in a yard?* (wild animals, huge trees blocking the sun)

Turn and Talk   Have children work independently on questions 2 and 3. When children have completed the page, have partners discuss their responses and then share them with the group. Sample responses are provided.

Unpack Meaning: For questions 2 and 3, you may want to use the notes in the right-hand column to guide the discussion about children's responses.

2. What does the wolf think of Sue's music? (The wolf loves her music. It helps him rest.)

3. Do you think Sue will go back to the forest? (No, Sue has learned her lesson and will stay in the yard.) **ELA** SL.2.1a **ELD** ELD.PI.2.1

RETEACH

Fluency: Intonation

Write-In Reader page 200

- Explain that you are going to read a page in two different ways. First, read page 200 in a flat tone. Ask, *What do you think about my first reading?* Encourage feedback. Be sure children understand that your reading was flat and without expression.

- Explain that readers should pay attention to punctuation for clues about how to read. Reading with intonation and expression helps readers and listeners understand the meaning of a story. Then read page 200 with expression and intonation. Ask, *How would you read page 200?* Invite children to take turns reading the sentences with expression and intonation. **ELA** RF.2.4b **ELD** ELD.PIII.2

UNPACK MEANING

Use prompts such as these if children have difficulty with a question:

2. *When do you think music is too noisy?* (Possible responses include when the music is so loud you have to cover your ears.) *Reread page 196. Why do you think Sue likes the sound of her playing in the forest?* (Possible responses include that the forest is quiet and the sound echoes through the trees.)

3. *How does Sue feel when she sees the wolf?* (scared) *What does she do after she sees the wolf?* (She tries to get away.)

DAILY FLUENCY

Build automaticity by using **Context Cards** or word lists on display. Point to the words in any order and have children read them aloud. Continue until children can read all words fluently.

DAY 5

SHARE OBJECTIVES

- Identify commas in a series.
- Demonstrate understanding of Target Vocabulary words.
- Preview the Main Ideas and Details and the Infer/Predict Strategy.

MATERIALS

Context Cards: *depended, exercise, gazing, hero, overlooked, sore, sprang, studied*

Write-In Reader pages 194–200

Leveled Reader: *Two Heroes*

TERMS ABOUT READING/ LANGUAGE ARTS

main idea	details
infer	predict

☑ TARGET VOCABULARY

If you **depended** on someone, you needed that person's help.

Exercise is physical activity that helps you become strong and healthy.

A **hero** is someone who is admired for doing something brave or good.

If you **overlooked** something, you didn't notice it or didn't see it.

ENGLISH LANGUAGE SUPPORT

Day 5

Vocabulary Preteach the meanings of the Target Vocabulary words *depended, exercise, hero,* and *overlooked*. Use examples and EL-friendly explanations to support children's understanding. Then ask questions about the words for children to discuss. **ELD** ELD.PI.2.1

Oral Grammar

Commas in a Series

- Tell children that you are going to read several sentences. First, you will read each sentence quickly, and then you will reread it. Tell children they will give the thumbs-up signal when a comma is needed.

- Read each of the following sentences two times without pausing for where commas should be. Model, using the first sentence. (Commas are needed after the words in boldface.)

1. *I like to eat **apples carrots cheese** and plums.*

2. *When you play soccer, you **run kick pass** and throw.*

3. *I like most pets, including **dogs cats hamsters horses lizards** and birds.*

4. *My dog **eats sleeps plays** and barks.*

5. *We **swim splash** and dive at the pool.*

RETEACH

Target Vocabulary

Context Cards

- Display the **Context Cards** for *gazing, sore, sprang,* and *studied*. Review the meanings of these words. Then have children use the words in oral sentences to describe a walk in a dark forest.

- Add the **Context Cards** for *depended, exercise, hero,* and *overlooked*. Deal one card to each child. Have children write a sentence for their word, leaving out the context card word. Have the rest of the group guess which word completes the sentence.

WRITE ABOUT IT

- Ask children to pretend they are the wolf from the story. Have them write what they think about Sue's music, using the word *depended*.
  ELA SL.2.6 **ELD** ELD.PI.2.12b

PRETEACH

Main Idea and Details
Infer/Predict

Write-In Reader pages 194–200

- Introduce skill and strategy. Say, *In the next lesson, we are going to focus on the main ideas and details of a story. We'll also work on ways to infer and predict events or character actions.*

- Explain, *Writers organize their stories in paragraphs, chapters, or sections that are built around a theme. The main idea is the most important idea or message in a paragraph, chapter, or section. Important details are clues to what the main idea is.*

- Ask, *What clues or details did the writer of* Sue and the Tired Wolf *use to make the main idea clear?*

- List on the board with children the main ideas and important details in the selection.

  Main Idea: Sue plays her flute to escape danger.

  Details:

  1. Sue grows bored playing her flute in the yard.

  2. Sue enters the woods.

  3. Sue meets a tired wolf.

  4. The sound of Sue's flute puts the wolf to sleep.

  5. Sue escapes from the wolf by playing her flute.

  Turn to and review the Infer/Predict Strategy found on page 304 in the **Write-In Reader**. Tell children that when they infer/predict, they tell what will happen based on what they have observed in the characters and events so far. Have children use the infer/predict strategy to tell what Sue will do after she gets back to her house.
  ELA RL.2.2, RL.2.3 **ELD** ELD.PI.2.1

APPLY READING SKILLS

Introduce *Two Heroes*. Choral-read the first few pages with children. Depending on their abilities, have children continue reading with partners or as a group.

Quick Check Fluency

Listen to individual children as they read the **Write-In Reader** selection. Make specific notes about words that presented difficulty to them.

● **Leveled Reader**

RETURN TO THE ANCHOR TEXT

"Be a Reading Detective!"

Student Book pages 167–189
Write-In Reader pages 201A–201B

- Page through "Dex: The Heart of a Hero" with children and review the main characters and events. Encourage volunteers to talk about what is happening on each page.

- Read page 201A of the **Write-In Reader** with children. Remind children that reading detectives find clues in the words and pictures of a story.

- Discuss the questions with children. Guide them to find clues in the words and pictures that help them answer the questions.

- Have children complete item 1 on page 201B on their own. Remind them to include details and examples from the story in their answer. Then have them share their work with a partner. Encourage them to discuss how they knew the answer to the question.

- Read item 2 on page 201B. Have children talk with a partner about what makes Dex a hero. Have them discuss what clues help them understand what happens in the story.

DAILY FLUENCY

Read Around the Room Have one child point to words that are on display in the room. Have the group read the words. Give each child a chance to be the pointer.

RESOURCES

Resources

Contents

- Alphabetize a list of spelling or vocabulary words.

MATERIALS

- paper
- pencils
- print or digital dictionary

ELA W.2.7

Alphabetical Order

1 Teach/Model

Explain that it is important to be able to alphabetize words. Remind children that dictionaries and encyclopedias list words and topics in alphabetical order and that as they complete their research, they will need to look up topics quickly and easily using materials such as these.

- Write the following words on the board:

forest	deep	fish	trunk
branch	trees	dens	bears

- Tell children that when alphabetizing words, they should start by looking at the first letter of each word. Words that begin with *A* will come first, words that begin with *B* will come next, and so on.

- Explain that often two or more words in a list begin with the same letter. Tell children that to alphabetize words that begin with the same letter, they must look at the second letter of each word. If the first two letters are the same, they must look at the third letter.

- Have individuals help you alphabetize the list of words.

2 Guided Practice/Apply

- Have children write their weekly spelling or vocabulary words in alphabetical order. Have them use a print or digital dictionary to check that they've placed the words in the correct order.

- Learn to choose an appropriate reference source.

MATERIALS

- dictionary
- encyclopedia
- thesaurus

ELA W.2.7, L.2.4e

Choose Appropriate Sources

1 Teach/Model

Explain that different reference sources are used for different purposes.

- A **dictionary** is used to find the correct spelling, meaning, or pronunciation of a word.

- An **encyclopedia** is used to find more information on a topic.

- A **thesaurus** is used to find a word's synonyms and antonyms.

Show children an entry in each source.

- Explain how the information is different in each one.

- Ask children to point out different text features they notice, such as guide words, headings, and captions.

- Explain that knowing what type of reference source to use will make their research easier.

2 Guided Practice/Apply

- Have children work in groups.

- Provide each group with a dictionary, an encyclopedia, and a thesaurus.

- Ask questions such as, *What does the word* fortitude *mean? When was Benjamin Franklin born? What is a synonym for* sick*?*

- Have groups hold up the source they would use to find the answer to each question. Ask children to explain why they chose each reference. Challenge them to find the answers.

- Have each group ask similar questions for the other groups to answer.

SHARE OBJECTIVE
• Learn how to use an encyclopedia.

MATERIALS
• encyclopedia (printed and electronic)
• index cards

ELA W.2.7

Use an Encyclopedia

1 Teach/Model

Explain that an encyclopedia is a type of reference that has information on a wide variety of topics. They will use encyclopedias often as they do research. There are both printed and electronic versions of encyclopedias.

• A printed version of an encyclopedia has several volumes. Within each volume, the topics are organized alphabetically.

• An electronic encyclopedia has information arranged by general categories, such as history, geography, science, and art. You can browse through the topic you are interested in, looking through several entries at once. You can also enter, or type in, key words in the search box to help you find information more quickly.

• Demonstrate how to find information on weather, using both a print and an electronic encyclopedia.

2 Guided Practice/Apply

• Ask partners to write questions about the weather on index cards.

• Have children use an encyclopedia to find answers to their questions.

SHARE OBJECTIVE
• Use an atlas to find information.

MATERIALS
• atlas(es) of the United States
• index cards

ELA W.2.7

Use an Atlas

1 Teach/Model

Explain that an atlas is a collection of maps and information about different places. Tell them that they can use an atlas when doing research about a place. Tell children that there are different types of atlases.

• A road atlas shows highways and city streets.

• A world atlas shows maps of different countries around the world and their capital cities.

• An atlas of the United States has maps of all fifty states and includes information about each one.

Demonstrate how to use an atlas.

• Point out the table of contents, index, and page headings. Discuss with children what each feature tells them and how they would use it to find information.

• Discuss the different types of information found in the atlas.

• Open the atlas to a map of one of the states. Have individuals find the bordering states and the state capital. Ask what other information they see.

2 Guided Practice/Apply

• Have partners choose a state and find its map in the atlas.

• Ask partners to write on index cards three questions about the state they chose, using the atlas to find the answers.

• Have two sets of partners trade their questions and use the atlas to locate the answers.

Research and Media Literacy

▶ SHARE OBJECTIVE
• Read and make a chart.

MATERIALS
• paper
• pencil

ELA RI.2.5, RI.2.7, W.2.7

Read a Chart

1 Teach/Model

Explain that a chart is a picture that presents information in a way that is easy to understand. Tell them that they may have to read or make charts as part of their research. A chart's title tells what information is in the chart.

• Draw the following chart on the board.

Maria's Weekly Activities

Monday	soccer
Tuesday	piano
Wednesday	soccer
Thursday	swimming
Friday	chess club

• Explain that the chart shows Maria's activities for the week.

• Ask questions such as, *What does Maria do on Friday? How many days a week does she have soccer? When does Maria swim?*

2 Guided Practice/Apply

• Have children work in groups to make a chart.

• Give children two or three choices for their charts, such as class jobs, daily school activities, or favorite summer sports. Guide them to create a chart using these topics, helping them brainstorm and layout the information.

• Ask groups to trade charts. Have them take turns asking each other questions that can be answered using the charts.

• Have children discuss how using a chart makes the information easier to find and use.

▶ SHARE OBJECTIVE
• Identify factual information and elements of fantasy in selections.

MATERIALS
• **Student Book** Vol. 2

ELA RL.2.10, RI.2.10

Distinguish Fact from Fantasy

1 Teach/Model

Explain that a fact is something that is proven to be true and that fantasy is something that is imagined or unrealistic.

• Tell children that some books are factual and contain information about real things or people.

• Have children open to the selection *Jackie Robinson*, **Student Book** pp. 78–80. Help children identify facts in this selection.

• Point out that some books contain events that could not really happen. These are called fantasies.

• Have children open to the selection *Luke Goes to Bat*, **Student Book** pp. 68–71. Work with children to identify what makes this section of the story fantasy.

2 Guided Practice/Apply

• Have children turn to **Student Book** pp. 166–189, *Dex the Heart of a Hero*. Ask, *Is this selection based on fact or is it a fantasy? How do you know?*

• Have children write some examples of the elements of fantasy from the story.

• Have children turn to **Student Book** pp. 368–370, *Super Soil*. Ask, *Is this selection based on fact or is it a fantasy? How do you know?*

• Have children list some facts found in the selection.

SHARE OBJECTIVE
- Gather information through an interview.

ELA W.2.7, SL.2.2, SL.2.4, SL.2.6

Interview

1 Teach/Model

Explain that reading books and other informational texts is one way to get information when doing research. Another way to get information is by talking with, or interviewing, people.

- Discuss different reasons for interviewing someone. Ask children if they have ever seen or read about an interview. Ask, *Why was the person being interviewed?*

- Point out that before a person begins an interview, they must think about the purpose of the interview. The purpose affects the type of questions that the person asks. Having a purpose before starting will help them plan the questions to make sure they get useful information.

Tell children that they will be interviewing different teachers and staff members at school.

- Explain that the purpose of the interviews will be to learn more about each person's job to know all of the jobs and duties it takes to run a school.

- Brainstorm with children a list of questions they can ask in the interview for each type of staff member.

2 Guided Practice/Apply

- Have children work in groups. Provide each group with a name of a teacher or staff member that they will interview.

- Children should work together to choose and list questions to ask in the interview.

- Have children conduct the interview and then share the information they learned with the class. Remind them to share details from the interview and their experience by speaking clearly in complete sentences.

SHARE OBJECTIVE
- Decide which sources of information provide relevant information.

MATERIALS
- encyclopedia
- informational books on astronauts
- newspaper
- science magazine
- computer

ELA W.2.7

Use Multiple Sources

1 Teach/Model

Explain that when doing research, it is often a good idea to use several different resources. This allows you to compare the sources and the information in each one.

- Create with children a list of informational sources that could be used for a research project. Include encyclopedias, informational books, newspapers, magazines, interviews, and the Internet.

- Explain the importance of evaluating the sources by thinking about where the information is coming from. Remind children that information from the Internet should be used only from reliable websites. Point out that they should also be aware of the date the information was collected because information changes over time.

- Help children think about the value of each resource by asking these questions: *Which source gives you news about daily events? Which source would you use to find information about many different topics? What information can you get from an interview that you might not get from an informational book?*

- Guide children to see that some sources are better for finding facts, while others are best for finding special information about people and their opinions.

2 Guided Practice/Apply

- Have children work in groups.

- Tell children to think about researching astronauts. Have each group choose a source that they could use from the ones you provide.

- Ask each group to evaluate how useful the source they chose would be in finding information about astronauts. Have children discuss their ideas.

Keyboarding Skills

Use these lessons to introduce children to good keyboarding technique when they are ready. Becoming fluent keyboarders will help children become more effective writers, enabling them to devote more of their mental energy to *what* they are keyboarding—their ideas, supporting details, sentence structures, and writing conventions.

Lesson 1: Posture

Help children develop good keyboarding habits by modeling good posture, adjusting as needed for children with specific physical requirements:

- Place both feet flat on the floor, aligned with your shoulders.
- Relax your shoulders and hold your head and spine straight.
- Place your hands on the home row—[ASDF] and [JKL;]—with your wrists straight and fingers curved.
- If using a mouse, it should be positioned next to the keyboard.

Explain to children that proper posture will help them keep from getting tired and can even prevent overuse injuries. Encourage children to stand and gently stretch at regular intervals for good health, and model doing the same.

Tell children that anyone using a computer should take their eyes off the screen once every 15 minutes or so and look at an object across the room. In addition, you can encourage children to pause periodically and close their eyes to rest them. Explain that resting their eyes and stretching their bodies will help children avoid problems that can result from too much uninterrupted screen time.

Lesson 2: Home Row

Tell children to begin keyboarding by placing their hands on the home row: [ASDF] and [JKL;]. Explain that when practicing keyboarding, they will match each finger to a key on the home row. Have children position the fingers of their left hand over the keys [A] [S] [D] [F] and their right hand over the keys [J] [K] [L] [;]. Then have children practice correct technique for the home row keys as well as [Enter/Return] and [Space Bar]:

- Start from the home row.
- Use your thumb to tap the Space Bar.
- Use your [;] finger to tap the Enter/Return key.

Have children find each key and practice tapping it and then returning to the home row. Remind them to keep their eyes on the monitor, not on the keys. Then have children practice typing the keys in the home row:

- Tap each key quickly as I say it: aa SPACE, ss SPACE, dd SPACE, ff SPACE, jj SPACE, kk SPACE, ll SPACE, ;; ENTER/RETURN

Lesson 3: Home Row (Review) and Backspacing

Review that children should always start from "Home Row" when keyboarding. Explain that they should try to keep their eyes on the screen, not on the keyboard, as they type, and that using "Home Row" will help them do that. Then have children practice correct technique for the Home Row keys plus ENTER/RETURN and the SPACE bar:

- Start from Home Row.
- Display these words and combinations (without the commas between them), or read them aloud by spelling out the words letter by letter, and have children practice typing them: ask SPACE, add SPACE, dad SPACE, fall SPACE, lad SPACE, sad SPACE, salad ENTER/RETURN.

If necessary, teach children how to use the BACKSPACE or DELETE key to back up and fix errors. Practice by having them type each word above and then delete it to type the next.

Lesson 4: Home Row and Keys E, H

Remind children to start from Home Row. Practice proper technique for keyboarding e and h:

- Start from Home Row. Use your "d finger" to type e. Use your "j finger" to type h. Have children find each key and practice typing it and then returning to Home Row.
- Display these words and combinations (without the commas between them), or read them aloud by spelling out the words letter by letter, and have children practice typing them: she, sells, sheds, he, fleas, held, a, ask, he, leaf. Have children retype the phrases with three spaces after each one and then with a return after each one, to reinforce use of ENTER/RETURN and the SPACE bar.

Lesson 5: Keys G, I

Remind children to start from Home Row. Practice proper technique for keyboarding g and i:

- Start from Home Row. Use your "f finger" to type g. Use your "k finger" to type i. Have children find each key and practice typing it and then returning to Home Row.

- Display these words and combinations (without the commas between them), or read them aloud by spelling out the words letter by letter, and have children practice typing them: kid, lid, gas, gill, hike, hid, kiss, hill, sail.

Lesson 6: Keys R, O

Remind children to start from Home Row. Practice proper technique for keyboarding r and o:

- Start from Home Row. Use your "f finger" to type r. Use your "l finger" to type o. Have children find each key and practice typing it and then returning to Home Row.

- Display these words and combinations (without the commas between them), or read them aloud by spelling out the words letter by letter, and have children practice typing them: rid, rod, free, grill, rag, ear, old, fold, ride, roll, log.

Lesson 7: SHIFT, PERIOD Keys

Remind children to start from Home Row. Practice proper technique for the shift and period keys:

- Start from Home Row. Use your "a finger" to type the left-hand SHIFT. Use your "; finger" to type the right-hand SHIFT. Use your "l finger" to type a period. Have children find each key and practice typing it and then returning to Home Row.

- Read aloud each set of capital letters, and have children key them. Remind them to use the right-hand shift key for these capitals: AA, SS, DD, FF, GG, EE, RR. Remind children to use the left-hand shift key for these capitals: JJ, KK, LL, HH, II, OO.

- Have children practice the period key with these abbreviations and names: Dr., Jr., Sr.

Lesson 8: Keys T, U

Remind children to start from Home Row. Practice proper technique for keyboarding t and u:

- Start from Home Row. Use your "f finger" to type t. Use your "j finger" to type u. Have children find each key and practice typing it and then returning to Home Row.

- Display these words and combinations (without the commas between them), or read them aloud by spelling out the words letter by letter, and have children practice typing them: tile, toe, tug, at, use, rug, hug.

Keyboarding Skills

Lesson 9: Keys W, ?

Remind children to start from Home Row. Practice proper technique for keyboarding w and ?:

- Start from Home Row. Use your "s finger" to type w. Have children find the key and practice typing it and then returning to Home Row.

- Say: *Notice that the ? symbol is on the upper part of the key. That means you have to hold down the SHIFT key when you type a question mark.* Have children practice using the "a finger" to hold SHIFT while typing the ?.

- Display these words and combinations (without the commas between them), or read them aloud by spelling out the words letter by letter, and have children practice typing them: was, wash, wad, with, wig, What? Where? How?

Lesson 10: Keys C, N

Remind children to start from Home Row. Practice proper technique for keyboarding c and n:

- Start from Home Row. Use your "d finger" to type c. Use your "j finger" to type n. Have children find each key and practice typing it and then returning to Home Row.

- Display these words and combinations (without the commas between them), or read them aloud by spelling out the words letter by letter, and have children practice typing them: cat, car, cart, code, noon, not, can.

Lesson 11: Keys P, B

Remind children to start from Home Row. Practice proper technique for keyboarding p and b:

- Start from Home Row. Use your "; finger" to type p. Use your "f finger" to type b. Have children find each key and practice typing it and then returning to Home Row.

- Display these words and combinations (without the commas between them), or read them aloud by spelling out the words letter by letter, and have children practice typing them: pad, pill, pal, pot, bad, ball, bid.

Lesson 12: Keys M, !

Remind children to start from Home Row. Practice proper technique for keyboarding m and !:

- Start from Home Row. Use your "j finger" to type m. Have children find the key and practice typing it and then returning to Home Row.

- Say: *Notice that the ! symbol is on the upper part of the key. That means you have to hold down the SHIFT key when you type an exclamation point.* Have children practice using the "; finger" to hold SHIFT while typing the ! with the "a finger."

- Display these words and combinations (without the commas between them), or read them aloud by spelling out the words letter by letter, and have children practice typing them: mad, men, ham, come. Jump! Won! Run!

Lesson 13: Keys Q, Y

Remind children to start from Home Row. Practice proper technique for keyboarding q and y:

- Start from Home Row. Use your "a finger" to type q. Use your "j finger" to type y. Have children find each key and practice typing it and then returning to Home Row.

- Display these words and combinations (without the commas between them), or read them aloud by spelling out the words letter by letter, and have children practice typing them: yam, day, say, your, quit, quick.

Lesson 14: Keys V, Z

Remind children to start from Home Row. Practice proper technique for keyboarding v and z:

- Start from Home Row. Use your "f finger" to type v. Use your "a finger" to type z. Have children find each key and practice typing it and then returning to Home Row.

- Display these words and combinations (without the commas between them), or read them aloud by spelling out the words letter by letter, and have children practice typing them: vote, dive, van, zoo, zip, have, zap.

Lesson 15: Keys X, COMMA

Remind children to start from Home Row, to keep their feet flat on the floor, and to try to watch the monitor as they type. Practice proper technique for keyboarding x and the comma:

- Start from Home Row. Use your "s finger" to type x. Use your "k finger" to type a comma. Have children find each key and practice typing it and then returning to Home Row.

- Display these words and combinations (with the commas between them), or read them aloud by spelling out the words letter by letter, and have children practice typing them: mix, tax, exit, fox, box, six. Check that children have kept a space after each comma.

Lesson 16: Keys ' and :

Explain to children that the apostrophe (') is used in contractions to show where a letter or letters are missing and in possessives to show ownership. The colon (:) is used in many ways, including to introduce a list and to separate the hour from the minutes when showing the time. Practice proper technique for keyboarding these symbols.

- Start from Home Row. The apostrophe is to the right of the semicolon, so you will use your "; finger" to type '. The colon is on the same key as the semicolon, so you will use the same finger, but you will need to press SHIFT with your left hand at the same time. Have children find each key and practice typing it and then returning to Home Row.

- Display these words and combinations (with the punctuation), or read them aloud by spelling out the words letter by letter, and have children practice typing them: Tom's pen, Jan's car, Juan's box. When: [ENTER/RETURN] Where: [ENTER/RETURN].

Word Lists

	HIGH-FREQUENCY WORDS		☑ TARGET VOCABULARY		DOMAIN-SPECIFIC VOCABULARY	SPELLING WORDS			TERMS ABOUT READING/ LANGUAGE ARTS
Lesson 1	around be five help next	or pull take until walked	curly straight floppy collars	drooled weighed stood row	trait offspring inherit	sad dig jam glad list win	flat if fix rip kit mask	**Review** as his **Challenge** sandwich picnic	sequence of events infer predict
Lesson 2	bring children comes do family	like make those use with	remembered porch crown cousin	spend stuck visit piano	conflict related siblings unity interact	wet job hug rest spot mud	left help plum nut net hot	**Review** get not **Challenge** lunch spend	characters connect compare contrast
Lesson 3	city full no other places	put school sing think this	hairy mammals litter stayed	canned chews clipped coat	reproduce characteristic canine adapt	cake mine plate size ate grape	prize wipe race line pile rake	**Review** gave bike **Challenge** mistake while	author's purpose infer analyze evaluate
Lesson 4	by cheer could hello hundred	mind play read see today	insects dangerous scare sticky	rotten screaming breeze judge	appreciate compliment cooperate peer	doze nose use rose pole close	cute woke mule rode role tune	**Review** home joke **Challenge** wrote ice cube	cause effect context
Lesson 5	both cold eat find green	little long says table we	wonderful noises quiet sprinkled	share noticed bursting suddenly	community diagram suburb	spin clap grade swim place last	test skin drag glide just stage	**Review** slip drive **Challenge** climb price	plot retell characters setting

Word Lists

	HIGH-FREQUENCY WORDS		☑ TARGET VOCABULARY		DOMAIN-SPECIFIC VOCABULARY	SPELLING WORDS			TERMS ABOUT READING/ LANGUAGE ARTS
Lesson 6	animals bear know most myself	second she sleep three work	shaped branches pond beaks	deepest break hang winding	habitat shelter pasture	next end camp sank sing drink	hunt stand long stamp pond bring	**Review** jump left **Challenge** young friend	boldface print graphic features text features base word prefix
Lesson 7	air car cried funny he	pictures pretty told try window	blooming shovels scent tough	wrinkled plain muscles nodded	nutrients seedling solar energy	dress spell class full add neck	stuck kick rock black trick doll	**Review** will off **Challenge** across pocket	conclusion analyze homophones
Lesson 8	before eye few happy high	my open people starts yellow	beware damage bend flash	pounding prevent reach equal	lightning precipitation water vapor	dish than chest such thin push	shine chase white while these flash	**Review** which then **Challenge** catch thumb	main idea supporting detail topic visualize
Lesson 9	afraid dark for kept many	might own show why would	tunnel curled height direction	toward healed brag tease	tradition culture literature	liked using riding chased spilled making	closed hoping baked hiding standing asked	**Review** mixed sleeping **Challenge** teasing knocking	character traits infer summarize
Lesson 10	because better go me old	really right they was you	millions choices drift simple	weaker wrapped disgusting decide	oceanography gulf current	I'm don't isn't can't we'll it's	I've didn't you're that's wasn't you've	**Review** us them **Challenge** they're wouldn't	fact monitor opinion clarify
Extended Reading	See pp. T503–T534 for the Content Vocabulary that appears in *Poppleton in Winter*.								

Word Lists

	HIGH-FREQUENCY WORDS	☑ TARGET VOCABULARY	DOMAIN-SPECIFIC VOCABULARY	SPELLING WORDS	TERMS ABOUT READING/ LANGUAGE ARTS
Lesson 11	another far grow hard heard / kind light more some to	understand gathered impatient impossible / believe problem demand furious	notify announce companion	hens eggs ducks bikes boxes wishes / dresses names bells stamps dishes grapes / **Review** jets frogs **Challenge** stitches fences	conclusion infer signal words base word prefix
Lesson 12	against along bird different girl / hold morning night part someone	vibration tune volume expression / creative performance concentrate relieved	pitch percussion creativity	pay wait paint train pail clay / tray plain stain hay gray away / **Review** stay day **Challenge** raisin birthday	characters plot setting solution idiom
Lesson 13	about everything first her of / slowly store story two world	culture community languages wear / subjects lessons special transportation	education public schedule tutor	free teach teeth please beach wheel / team speak sneeze sheep meaning weave / **Review** eat read **Challenge** between reason	main idea supporting detail analyze dictionary entry
Lesson 14	all food front hair never / party sky started stories warm	knowledge curious motion silence / illness imitated darkness behavior	nonverbal visual communicate	own most soap float both know / loan goat flow loaf throw coach / **Review** so grow **Challenge** swallow ocean	author's purpose author's message infer suffix
Lesson 15	after book care ever live / new off over small thought	obeys safety attention buddy / station speech shocked enormous	risk protection hazard inform	cannot pancake maybe baseball playground someone / myself classroom sunshine outside upon nothing / **Review** into inside **Challenge** nobody everywhere	cause effect infer dictionary entry guide words

Word Lists

	HIGH-FREQUENCY WORDS		☑ TARGET VOCABULARY		DOMAIN-SPECIFIC VOCABULARY	SPELLING WORDS			TERMS ABOUT READING/ LANGUAGE ARTS
Lesson 16	also fly gone have horse	look river said saw something	received account budget fund	chuckled staring repeated disappointed	duties citizen responsibility	running clapped stopped hopping batted selling	pinned cutting sitting rubbed missed grabbed	**Review** mixed going **Challenge** wrapped swelling	infer predict story elements characters
Lesson 17	any blue carry doing else	room studied sure teacher turned	practice hurried position roared	extra curb cheered final	determined morals respect	night kind spy child light find	right high wild July fry sigh	**Review** by why **Challenge** behind lightning	sequence of events infer visualize antonyms
Lesson 18	always anything been draw friends	mother soon under watch words	accepted express taught grand	pretend prize wonder fluttering	print journalist exchange publish	happy pretty baby very puppy funny	carry lucky only sunny penny city	**Review** tiny many **Challenge** sorry noisy	infer trait analyze evaluate
Lesson 19	are baby didn't good I'll	is please sound talk too	assistant agreed polite failed	tearing wisdom cleared trouble	advertise announcement post beacon	car dark arm star park yard	party hard farm start part spark	**Review** art jar **Challenge** carpet apartment	graphic features text features synonyms
Lesson 20	I've begins being flower ground	laugh ready stood tall very	depended sore sprang studied	gazing hero exercise overlooked	charity grant improve figure	horn story fork score store corn	morning shore short born tore forget	**Review** for more **Challenge** report force	connect similar compare contrast
Extended Reading	See pp. T505–T536 for the Content Vocabulary that appears in *Where Do Polar Bears Live?*								

Word Lists

	HIGH-FREQUENCY WORDS		☑ TARGET VOCABULARY		DOMAIN-SPECIFIC VOCABULARY	SPELLING WORDS			TERMS ABOUT READING/ LANGUAGE ARTS
Lesson 21	across behind house how move	nothing one out took voice	webbed waterproof steer whistle	otherwise junior slippery finally	development life cycle climate	father over under herd water verb	paper cracker offer cover germ master	**Review** fern ever **Challenge** remember feather	infer main idea supporting detail topic dictionary entry
Lesson 22	boy does everyone field floor	found into their toward what's	knot copy planning lonely	heavily seriously answered guessed	force flight pressure	meet meat week weak mane main	tail tale be bee too two	**Review** sea see **Challenge** threw through	characters traits infer relationships idiom
Lesson 23	coming down four give great	idea knew large though write	yarn strands spinning dye	weave sharpening duplicated delicious	craft fiber loom textile	helpful sadly hopeful thankful slowly wishful	kindly useful safely painful mouthful weakly	**Review** jumped saying **Challenge** quickly wonderful	conclusion summarize context multiple-meaning words
Lesson 24	away began brothers brown earth	here learning surprised there without	tumbling flung tangled empty	swift peacefully stream blazed	customs classic honor	unhappy retell untangle unkind repaint refill	unlike remake unpack reread unlock replay	**Review** read happy **Challenge** rewrite overheard	cause effect infer visualize antonyms
Lesson 25	ball done hear learn leaves	only our through were young	pod soak shoot root	nutrition tasty soften grain	process bud sprout	tall saw dog draw call fall	soft paw ball yawn log small	**Review** all walk **Challenge** awful wallpaper	graphic features text features infer clarify context

Word Lists

	HIGH-FREQUENCY WORDS	TARGET VOCABULARY	DOMAIN-SPECIFIC VOCABULARY	SPELLING WORDS	TERMS ABOUT READING/ LANGUAGE ARTS
Lesson 26	again follow ago goes alone head don't now every won't	ordinary sensible control confused cage training upset suspiciously	larva biology organism	root room **Review** crew you zoo spoon stew noon few boost **Challenge** bloom scoop shampoo grew flew balloon	infer predict generate dictionary entry
Lesson 27	buy outside called tomorrow even town father water maybe where	exact amazed discovered explained remove guard growled souvenirs	impression remains organic material	took hood **Review** books wood look foot stood good hoof shook **Challenge** cook crook crooked nook cookbook bookcase	distinguish fact opinion synonyms
Lesson 28	above loved enough should falling sorry happened want lived while	served concealed overjoyed glimmering valuable content worn task	oral tradition multicultural generation	cow found **Review** house loud out town brown now shout ground **Challenge** down pound towel mouse flower pounce	sequence of events classify categorize
Lesson 29	eight upon near wash once who paper woman seven your	search leaned contained tossed startled grateful odd village	tales values beliefs	aim gain **Review** snail sly tray bay chain try braid shy **Challenge** ray bright contain always fright thigh	characters traits visualize relationships antonyms
Lesson 30	almost pushed dear remember door sometimes from together money years	inventions achieve remarkable composed designed result amounts accomplishments	patriot pioneer symbol historical	seated groan **Review** keeps roast green speed bowls snow seen crow **Challenge** means owe peace clean grown below	compare contrast visualize connect dictionary entry
Extended Reading	See pp. T501–T532 for the Content Vocabulary that appears in *Exploring Space Travel*.				

Using Rubrics

A rubric is a tool a teacher can use to score a student's work. A rubric lists the criteria for evaluating the work, and it describes different levels of success in meeting those criteria.

Rubrics are useful assessment tools for teachers, but they can be just as useful for children. In fact, rubrics can be powerful teaching tools.

Rubrics for Collaborative Conversations

- Before children engage in a discussion, walk them through the criteria listed on the rubric, making sure they understand the discussion rules and their individual roles in the discussion.

- Have children focus on the criteria for excellence listed on the rubric so that they can aim for specific goals.

Rubrics for Presentations

- Before children make a presentation, discuss the criteria listed on the rubric. Have children focus on the criteria for excellence listed on the rubric so that they can aim for specific goals.

- Discuss the criteria for listening with children who will be in the audience. Point out the criteria for excellence listed on the rubric so that they can target specific goals.

- As children develop their projects in the Extended Reading lessons, they can measure and evaluate their progress against a student-friendly version of the rubric that appears on the Teacher's Edition page.

- Be sure that children understand the criteria by which their project work, both individually and as part of a team, will be assessed. Point out that these criteria include measures for collaboration, research, and presentation skills.

Rubrics for Performance Tasks and Writing

- As children face the prospect of high-stakes writing assessments, multiple practice opportunities with clear success criteria are vital to success.

- When you introduce children to analytical writing and performance tasks in a variety of writing modes, discuss the criteria listed on the rubric, and discuss with children how their own writing can meet each criterion.

- Before children attempt a writing task of any kind, have them focus on the criteria for excellence listed on the specific rubrics so that they can set and keep clear goals.

- During both the drafting and revising stages, remind children to check their writing against the rubric to keep their focus and to determine if there are any aspects of their writing that they can improve.

- Children can use the rubrics to score their own writing. They can keep the marked rubric in their portfolios with the corresponding piece of writing. The marked rubrics will help children see their progress through the school year. In conferences with children and family members, you can refer to the rubrics to point out both strengths and weaknesses in children's writing.

- *See Grab-and-Go™ Resources for a student rubric.*

Collaborative Conversations RUBRIC

Score of 2

- The child participates in collaborative conversations with peers and adults in small and larger groups.
- The child follows agreed-upon rules for discussions.
- The child builds on others' talk in conversations by linking their comments to the remarks of others.
- The child asks for clarification and further explanation as needed about the topics and texts under discussion.

Score of 1

- The child somewhat participates in collaborative conversations with peers and adults in small and larger groups, but may lose focus.
- The child mostly follows agreed-upon rules for discussions.
- The child is sometimes able to build on others' talk in conversations by linking their comments to the remarks of others.
- The child sometimes asks for clarification and further explanation as needed about the topics and texts under discussion.

Score of 0

- The child does not participate in collaborative conversations.
- The child does not follow agreed-upon rules for discussions.
- The child rarely builds on others' talk in conversations.
- The child asks few, if any, questions to clear up confusion.

Analytic Writing RUBRIC

Score of 2

- The response makes sense and is organized.
- The response shows that the child was able to understand the text.
- The response includes clear evidence from the text that supports child's response.
- The response includes specific details that relate to the text.

Score of 1

- The response makes sense, but may not be organized.
- The response shows that the child may not have clearly understood the text.
- The response includes little evidence from the text that supports child's response.
- The response includes some details that relate to the text.

Score of 0

- The response does not make sense and is not organized.
- The response shows that the child did not understand the text.
- The response includes no evidence or details from the text.

	Score of 6	Score of 5	Score of 4	Score of 3	Score of 2	Score of 1
FOCUS / SUPPORT	The writer adheres to the topic, is interesting, has a sense of completeness. Develops topic or events with relevant facts or details.	The writer adheres to the topic, is usually interesting, has sense of completeness. Mostly develops topic or events with relevant facts or details.	The writer mostly adheres to the topic, is somewhat interesting, has some sense of completeness. Adequately develops topic or events with relevant facts or details.	The writer adheres to the topic somewhat, and has adequate sense of completeness. Develops topic or events with some relevant facts or details.	The writer does not always adhere to the topic, and has limited sense of completeness. Develops topic or events with few relevant facts or details.	The writer does not adhere to the topic, and has no sense of completeness. May not develop topic or events with relevant facts or details.
ORGANIZATION	The writer introduces topic or situation clearly; organizes ideas clearly to support purpose; provides a strong sense of closure.	The writer introduces topic or situation; organizes ideas to support purpose; provides some sense of closure.	The writer introduces topic or situation; organizes ideas somewhat to support purpose; provides adequate sense of closure.	The writer partially introduces topic or situation; organizes some ideas to support purpose; provides minimal sense of closure.	The writer may introduce topic or situation; organizes few ideas to support purpose; provides little sense of closure.	The writer may attempt to introduce topic or situation; may not organize ideas to support purpose; may not provide sense of closure.
WORD CHOICE / VOICE	The writer uses vivid verbs, strong adjectives, and specific nouns. Effectively uses words to link ideas. Connects with reader in a unique, personal way.	The writer uses some vivid verbs, strong adjectives, and specific nouns. Uses words to link ideas. Connects with reader in a way that is personal and often unique.	The writer uses some specific and descriptive verbs, adjectives, and nouns. Sometimes uses words to link ideas. Generally connects with reader in a way that is somewhat personal and sometimes unique.	The writer uses some specific verbs, adjectives, and nouns. Sometimes uses words to link ideas. Connects with reader in a way that is somewhat personal but rarely unique.	The writer uses mostly simple nouns and verbs, and may have a few adjectives. Attempts to use words to link ideas. Connects with reader in a way that is somewhat personal but not unique.	The writer uses only simple nouns and verbs, some inaccurate. May not use words to link ideas. Writing is not descriptive. Does not connect with reader. Does not sound personal or unique.
CONVENTIONS / SENTENCE FLUENCY	The writer demonstrates exemplary command of grammar, spelling, capitalization, and punctuation. Includes a variety of complete sentences that flow smoothly, naturally.	The writer demonstrates good command of conventions of grammar, spelling, capitalization, and punctuation. Includes some variety of mostly complete sentences. Some parts flow smoothly, naturally.	The writer demonstrates adequate command of grammar, spelling, capitalization, and punctuation. Includes little variety of complete sentences. Few flow smoothly, naturally.	The writer demonstrates some command of grammar, spelling, capitalization, and punctuation. Includes mostly simple sentences, some of which are incomplete.	The writer demonstrates growing command of grammar, spelling, capitalization, and punctuation, with errors. Includes mostly simple sentences; some do not vary. Incomplete sentences hinder meaning.	The writer demonstrates little or no command of grammar, spelling, capitalization, and punctuation. Sentences do not vary; Incomplete sentences hinder meaning.

Performance Task: Narrative Writing — RUBRIC

	PURPOSE/ORGANIZATION	DEVELOPMENT/ELABORATION	CONVENTIONS
Score of 4 (Conventions: **Score of 2**)	The narrative is clear and well organized. It is appropriately sequenced and has closure. • Plot contains a well-elaborated event or a short sequence of events • Setting and characters are included and well-maintained • Plot events follow a logical sequence • Includes an effective conclusion	The narrative includes effective elaboration and details describing actions, thoughts, and feelings. • Links to sources may enrich the narrative • Clear effort to develop experiences, characters, setting, and events • Contains strong use of details • Writer uses temporal words to signal the order of events	The narrative demonstrates adequate command of conventions. • Consistent use of correct sentence structures, punctuation, capitalization, grammar, and spelling
Score of 3 (Conventions: **Score of 1**)	The narrative is generally clear and organized. The sequence is adequately maintained, and the plot has closure. • Plot contains a well-elaborated event or a short sequence of events • Characters and setting are included and adequately maintained • Plot events follow an understandable sequence • Includes an adequate conclusion	The narrative includes adequate elaboration and details describing actions, thoughts, and feelings. • Links to sources may contribute to the narrative • Some attempt to develop experiences, characters, setting, and events • Contains adequate use of details • Contains adequate use of temporal words to signal the order of events	The narrative demonstrates partial command of conventions. • Limited use of correct sentence structures, punctuation, capitalization, grammar, and spelling
Score of 2 (Conventions: **Score of 0**)	The narrative is somewhat organized but may be unclear in parts. The sequence is weak. The plot lacks closure. • Minimal development of plot • Characters and setting are included but are minimally maintained • Sequence of events is poorly organized • Conclusion is inadequate or missing	The narrative includes only partial or ineffective elaboration. The narrative includes some details. • Links to sources may be unsuccessful but do not detract from the narrative • Little attempt to develop experiences, characters, setting, and events • Contains weak use of details • Contains little use of temporal words • The order of events is not clear	The narrative demonstrates little or no command of conventions. • Rare use of correct sentence structures, punctuation, capitalization, grammar, and spelling
Score of 1	The narrative's focus is unclear, and it is poorly organized. The narrative lacks sequence and has no closure. • Little or no plot • No attempt to maintain characters or setting • Sequence of events is not organized • Conclusion is missing	The narrative provides little or no elaboration and few details. • Links to sources, if present, may interfere with the narrative • No attempt to develop experiences, characters, setting, and events • Few or no details • No use of temporal words • The order of events is confusing	
NS	• not intelligible • not written in English • not on topic • contains text copied from another source • does not address the purpose for writing	• not intelligible • not written in English • not on topic • contains text copied from another source • does not develop the writing	• not intelligible • not written in English • not on topic • contains text copied from source

Performance Task: Informative/Explanatory Writing — RUBRIC

PURPOSE/ORGANIZATION

Score of 4
- The response is clear and well organized throughout.
- Main or central idea is clear, focused, and effective for task, audience, and purpose
- Ideas follow a logical sequence
- Includes an effective introduction and conclusion

Score of 3
- The response is generally clear and organized.
- Main or central idea is clear, mostly focused, and mostly effective for task, audience, and purpose
- Ideas follow an adequate sequence
- Includes an adequate introduction and conclusion

Score of 2
- The response is somewhat organized but may be unclear in parts.
- Main or central idea may be somewhat unclear, lack focus, or be ineffective for task, audience, and purpose
- Sequence of ideas may be weak or unclear
- Introduction and conclusion need improvement

Score of 1
- The response's focus is unclear and it is poorly organized.
- Main or central idea may be confusing; response may be inappropriate for task, audience, and purpose
- Sequence of ideas is unorganized
- Introduction and/or conclusion may be missing

NS
- not intelligible
- not written in English
- not on topic
- contains text copied from source
- does not address the purpose for writing

EVIDENCE/ ELABORATION

Score of 4
- The response presents strong support for the main and supporting ideas with effective elaboration.
- Evidence from sources is integrated, relevant, and supports key ideas
- Details are clear and appropriate for task, audience, and purpose

Score of 3
- The response presents adequate support for the main and supporting ideas with adequate elaboration.
- Evidence from sources is integrated, relevant, and adequately supports key ideas
- Details are mostly appropriate for task, audience, and purpose

Score of 2
- The response presents inconsistent support for the main and supporting ideas with limited elaboration.
- Evidence from sources may be poorly integrated or irrelevant, or only loosely supports key ideas
- Details are somewhat inappropriate for task, audience, and purpose

Score of 1
- The response presents little support for the main and supporting ideas with little or no elaboration.
- Evidence from sources, if present, may be irrelevant with little support for key ideas
- Details are inappropriate for task, audience, and purpose

NS
- not intelligible
- not written in English
- not on topic
- contains text copied from source
- does not address the purpose for writing

CONVENTIONS

Score of 2
- The response demonstrates adequate command of conventions.
- Consistent use of correct sentence structures, punctuation, capitalization, grammar, and spelling

Score of 1
- The response demonstrates partial command of conventions.
- Limited use of correct sentence structures, punctuation, capitalization, grammar, and spelling

Score of 0
- The response demonstrates little or no command of conventions.
- Rare use of correct sentence structures, punctuation, capitalization, grammar, and spelling

NS
- not intelligible
- not written in English
- not on topic
- contains text copied from source

Performance Task: Opinion Writing — RUBRIC

PURPOSE/ORGANIZATION

Score of 4
- The response is clear and well organized throughout.
- Opinion is presented, clear, focused, and effective for task, audience, and purpose.
- Ideas follow a logical sequence
- Includes an effective introduction and conclusion

Score of 3
- The response is generally clear and organized.
- Opinion is clear, mostly focused, and mostly effective for task, audience, and purpose
- Ideas follow an adequate sequence
- Includes an adequate introduction and conclusion

Score of 2
- The response is somewhat organized but may be unclear in parts.
- Opinion may be somewhat unclear, lack focus, or be ineffective for task, audience, and purpose
- Sequence of ideas may be weak or unclear
- Introduction and conclusion need improvement

Score of 1
- The response's focus is unclear and it is poorly organized.
- Opinion may be confusing; response may be inappropriate for task, audience, and purpose
- Sequence of ideas is unorganized
- Introduction and/or conclusion may be missing

NS
- not intelligible
- not written in English
- not on topic
- does not address the purpose for writing

EVIDENCE/ELABORATION

Score of 4
- The response presents strong support for the opinion with effective elaboration.
- Evidence from sources is integrated, relevant, and supports key ideas
- Details are clear and appropriate for task, audience, and purpose

Score of 3
- The response presents adequate support for the opinion with adequate elaboration.
- Evidence from sources is integrated, relevant, and adequately supports key ideas
- Details are mostly appropriate for task, audience, and purpose

Score of 2
- The response presents inconsistent support for the opinion with limited elaboration.
- Evidence from sources may be poorly integrated or irrelevant, or only loosely supports key ideas
- Details are somewhat inappropriate for task, audience, and purpose

Score of 1
- The response presents little support for the opinion with little or no elaboration.
- Evidence from sources, if present, may be irrelevant, with little support for key ideas
- Details are inappropriate for task, audience, and purpose

NS
- not intelligible
- not written in English
- not on topic
- contains text copied from source
- does not address the purpose for writing

CONVENTIONS

Score of 2
- The response demonstrates adequate command of conventions.
- Consistent use of correct sentence structures, punctuation, capitalization, grammar, and spelling

Score of 1
- The response demonstrates partial command of conventions.
- Limited use of correct sentence structures, punctuation, capitalization, grammar, and spelling

Score of 0
- The response demonstrates little or no command of conventions.
- Rare use of correct sentence structures, punctuation, capitalization, grammar, and spelling

NS
- not intelligible
- not written in English
- not on topic
- contains text copied from source

RUBRIC for Giving Presentations

	Score of 4	Score of 3	Score of 2	Score of 1
HANDWRITING	The slant of the letters is the same throughout the whole paper. The letters are clearly formed and the spacing between words is equal, which makes the text very easy to read.	The slant of the letters is usually the same. The letters are clearly formed most of the time. The spacing between words is usually equal.	The handwriting is readable. There are some differences in letter shape and form, slant, and spacing that make some words easier to read than others.	The letters are not formed correctly. The slant spacing is not the same throughout the paper, or there is no regular space between words. The paper is very difficult to read.
TECHNOLOGY	Fonts and sizes are used very well, which helps the reader enjoy reading the text. Multimedia components are very effective.	Fonts and sizes are used fairly well, but could be improved upon. Multimedia components are effective.	Fonts and sizes are used well in some places, but make the paper look cluttered in others. Multimedia components are somewhat effective.	The writer has used too many different fonts and sizes. It is very distracting to the reader. Multimedia components are not effective.
MARKERS	The title, subheads, page numbers, and bullets are used very well. They make it easy for the reader to find information in the text. These markers clearly show organized information.	The title, subheads, page numbers, and bullets are used fairly well. They usually help the reader find information.	The writer uses some markers such as a title, page numbers, or bullets. However, the use of markers could be improved upon to help the reader get more meaning from the text.	There are no markers such as title, page numbers, bullets, or subheads.
VISUALS	The writer uses visuals such as illustrations, charts, graphs, maps, and tables very well. The text and visuals clearly relate to each other.	The writer uses visuals fairly well.	The writer uses visuals with the text, but the reader may not understand how they are related.	The visuals do not make sense with the text.
SPEAKING	The speaker uses very effective pace, volume, intonation, and expression.	The speaker uses effective pace, volume, intonation, and expression.	The speaker uses somewhat effective pace, volume, intonation, and expression.	The speaker's techniques are unclear or distracting to the listener.

Student Project RUBRIC

	Score of 4	Score of 3	Score of 2	Score of 1
COLLABORATION	• I helped my group complete the project. • I offered my help and ideas. • I was polite when I talked to my group. • I did the role I was given and finished all of my work.	• I helped my group complete the project. • I usually offered my help and ideas. • I was polite when I talked to my group, but sometimes I got off-topic. • I did the role I was given and finished most of my work.	• I sometimes helped my group complete the project. • I offered some help and ideas, but I could do better. • I wasn't always polite when I talked to my group. I got off-topic. • I mostly did the role I was given, but I didn't finish my work.	• I could have done more to help my group complete the project. • I did not offer my help or ideas. • I was not polite when I talked to my group. I got off-topic. • I did not do my role in the group or finish my work.
RESEARCH AND TEXT EVIDENCE	• Ideas are organized and make sense. • My group used a mix of sources for our research. • My group kept a record of where we found our information. • My group used text evidence in our project.	• Ideas are mostly organized and make sense. • My group used some different sources for our research. • My group kept some record of where we found our information. • My group used text evidence in parts of our project.	• Ideas are organized but could make more sense. • My group used just a few sources for our research. • My group did not keep a good record of where we found our information. • My group used little text evidence in our project.	• Ideas are not organized. • My group did very little research. • My group used no text evidence in our project.
CONTENT	• The project stays on-topic. • Our writing answers the project question. • Pictures, sounds, or movies make the project better. • The project has no errors.	• The project mostly stays on-topic. • Our writing answers the project question. • Pictures make the project better. • The project has a few errors.	• The project mostly stays on-topic, but might go off-topic a little. • Our writing mostly answers the project question. • Pictures do not make the project better, or we did not include pictures. • The project has some errors.	• The project goes off-topic. • Our writing does not answer the project question. • There are no pictures. • The project has major errors.
PRESENTATION	• Our presentation is exciting. People listened to it. • Our presentation is in an order that makes sense. • My group is able to give answers to audience questions.	• Our presentation is exciting. People listened to it. • Our presentation is mostly in an order that makes sense. • My group is able to give answers to most audience questions.	• Our presentation is helpful but it could be more interesting. • Our presentation does not make sense in some parts. • My group could only give answers to a few audience questions.	• Our presentation is not interesting. • Our presentation does not make sense. • My group could not answer any audience questions.

Handwriting

Individual children have various levels of handwriting skills, but they all have the desire to communicate effectively. To write correctly, they must be familiar with concepts of

- size (tall, short)
- open and closed
- capital and lowercase letters
- manuscript vs. cursive letters
- letter and word spacing
- punctuation

Explain Stroke and Letter Formation

Tell children that most manuscript letters are formed with a continuous stroke, so children will not often pick up their pencils when writing a single letter. Explain that when they begin to use cursive handwriting, children will have to lift their pencils from the paper less frequently and will be able to write more fluently. Choose one of the handwriting models on the pages that follow, and distribute it to children for reference. Handwriting blackline masters for letter formation practice appear in the *Grab-and-Go™ Additional Resources* booklet, pp. 41–48. **ELA** L.2.1g

Teach Writing Position

Establishing the correct posture, pen or pencil grip, and paper position for writing will help prevent handwriting problems.

Posture Tell children to sit with both feet on the floor and with hips to the back of the chair. They can lean forward slightly but should not slouch. Ask them to make sure their writing surface is smooth and flat. It should be at a height that allows their upper arms to be perpendicular to the surface and the elbows to be under the shoulders.

Writing Instrument Have children use an adult-sized number-two lead pencil for their writing assignments. Explain that as they become proficient in the use of cursive handwriting, they can use pens to write final drafts.

Paper Position and Pencil Grip Explain to children that as they write, the position of the paper plays an important role. The paper should be slanted along the line of the child's writing arm, and the child should use his or her nonwriting hand to hold the paper in place. Tell children to hold their pencils or pens slightly above the paint line—about one inch from the lead tip.

Then ask children to assume their writing position. Check each student's position, providing adjustments as necessary. **ELA** L.2.1g

Develop Handwriting

The best instruction builds on what children already know and can do. Given the wide range in children's handwriting abilities, a variety of approaches and types of activities may be needed. Use the following activities as you choose to provide regular handwriting practice to children of all proficiency levels.

Practice Letter Formation Have children practice forming letters, using the handwriting blackline masters in the *Grab-and-Go™ Additional Resources* booklet, pp. 41–48. Children may practice a particular letter or letters they have difficulty writing or work through the entire alphabet as you assign the letters.

Write Short Sentences Identify letters that children have difficulty forming. Pair partners who need practice forming the same letters, and have them practice writing that letter on a dry erase board. After sufficient time for practice, have partners brainstorm a list of words that contain that letter. Then ask partners to work together to write a short sentence for three of the words on their list. Remind them to use their best handwriting. Demonstrate how children can use their pencil or a finger to check for appropriate spacing between words. **ELA** L.2.1g

Trade Questions Have children each write a question they would like to ask a partner, such as *What is your favorite color?* or *What kind of weather do you like?* Remind them to print neatly and to leave plenty of room for the question to be answered. Then have children trade papers with a partner and answer one another's question using complete sentences, using their best handwriting. **ELA** L.2.1g

Make a Sign Have partners work together to create a sign for the classroom. Tell children to choose a familiar safety or behavior rule and to create a short phrase or sentence to remind their classmates of what to do. Tell children to write their words carefully, using legible print that will be easy to read. Children may illustrate their signs if they wish. **ELA** L.2.1g

Copy a Quote Write a meaningful quote or saying on the board and briefly discuss its meaning with children. Then have them copy the quote in their best handwriting to display in the classroom or in their home. **ELA** L.2.1g

See and Write Choose or write a paragraph of 3–5 sentences. Use a projector or large paper tablet to show the individual sentences to children. Have children copy the sentences they see onto a clean sheet of paper, forming legible letters and using appropriate spacing between words. Point out that they can use their pencil or a finger to check the spacing. **ELA** L.2.1g

Label a School Map Tell children to pretend a new visitor is coming to the school and will need help finding the right classroom, as well as key areas such as the cafeteria or multipurpose room, library, and principal's office. Have children draw a basic map of the school and label each important area, using their best handwriting to create a helpful document. **ELA** L.2.1g

Write About the School Day Work with children to brainstorm a list of activities they complete each day while in school. Then have children use the list to write a short paragraph to describe the events of a typical school day. Tell them to print legibly and to use their pencils or a finger to check for appropriate spacing between words and sentences. **ELA** L.2.1g

Assess Handwriting

To assess children's handwriting skills, review samples of their written work. Note whether they use correct letter formation and appropriate size and spacing. Note whether children follow the conventions of print, such as correct capitalization and punctuation. When writing messages, notes, and letters, or when publishing their writing, children should leave adequate spacing between letters and words to make the work readable for their audience. **ELA** L.2.1g

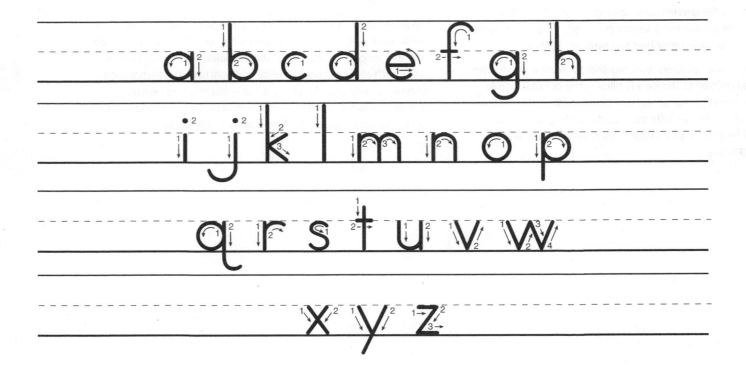

A B C D E F G H

I J K L M N O P

Q R S T U V W

X Y Z

a b c d e f g h

i j k l m n o p

q r s t u v w

x y z

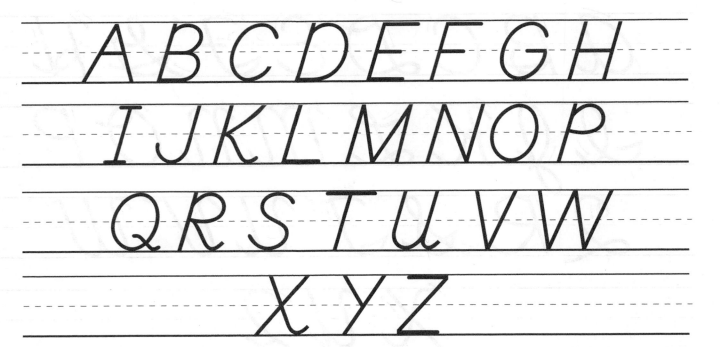

ABCDEFGH
IJKLMNOP
QRSTUVW
XYZ

abcdefgh
ijklmnop
qrstuvw
xyz

A B C D E F G H
I J K L M N O P
Q R S T U V W
X Y Z

a b c d e f g h
i j k l m n o p
q r s t u v w
x y z

Glossary

Glossary

This glossary can help you find the meanings of some of the words in this book. The meanings given are the meanings of the words as they are used in the book. Sometimes a second meaning is also given.

A

accept
To take what is given: *I accept your gift and would like to give you something too.*

accepted
A form of **accept**: *He accepted the package and waited until he was alone to open it.*

accomplish
To do completely, or carry out: *They accomplish the job by working together.*

accomplishments
A form of **accomplish**: *The concert showed the accomplishments of each musician.*

account
A record of money received or spent: *A savings account helps you keep track of money you put in the bank.*

achieve
To succeed in doing: *Some people achieve a lot by studying on the Internet.*

agree
To have the same idea or opinion: *I agree with you that it is a good day to go swimming.*

agreed
A form of **agree**: *The two friends agreed to meet at the bridge after school.*

G1

amaze
To surprise or to fill with wonder: *The huge redwood trees amaze many visitors.*

amazed
A form of **amaze**: *We were amazed when we saw the first whale.*

amounts
Quantity or sum of quantities: *Always measure the amounts of juice before you add them to the batter.*

amount

answer
To say, write, or do something in reply: *When you answer the questions, write the numbers to go with them.*

answered
A form of **answer**: *Nobody answered my call at first, but then I heard a tiny voice.*

assistant
A helper, or one who assists: *He needed an assistant to work with the animals.*

B

blaze
To burn: *The sun may blaze too strongly for us to stay at the beach.*

blazed
A form of **blaze**: *Our campfire blazed in the darkness and kept us warm all evening.*

budget
A plan for how money will be spent: *Our family budget includes amounts for food, clothing, and heat.*

G2

C

cage
A space closed around with wire or bars: *Sometimes they shut all their windows and let the bird out of her cage.*

cheer
To shout in happiness or in praise: *Everybody will cheer and clap when the musicians take their bows.*

cheered
A form of **cheer**: *The crowd cheered when the mayor gave her the award.*

chuckle
To laugh quietly: *I sometimes chuckle when I think about the silly things we did.*

chuckled
A form of **chuckle**: *They chuckled at the comic strip in the newspaper.*

clear
To get rid of or remove: *After the storm, we will clear away the branches from the path.*

cleared
A form of **clear**: *When they cleared the table after the meal, they planned what to do next.*

compose
To create or make up: *He likes to compose songs for the musical each year.*

composed
A form of **compose**: *She composed a duet for flute and piano.*

conceal
To hide something so that it cannot be seen: *I tried to conceal the gift I bought for my aunt because I wanted to surprise her.*

G3

concealed
A form of **conceal**: *I concealed my diary in my closet so that my sister couldn't find it.*

confuse
To mix up: *Sometimes people confuse twins who look very much alike.*

confused
A form of **confuse**: *The cookies taste salty because he confused the sugar with the salt.*

contain
To keep inside or hold: *Oranges contain vitamins and other things that are good for your health.*

contained
A form of **contain**: *The box contained a new set of pencils.*

contained

content
To be happy or satisfied: *The lazy cat is content to lie in the sun all morning.*

control
To direct or be in charge of: *The children learned to control the hand puppets.*

copy
To make something exactly like an original: *I will copy this picture in color so you can see the details.*

curb
A stone rim along the edge of a sidewalk or road: *Workers are fixing the curb along this street.*

D

delicious
Tasting or smelling very good: *He made some vegetable soup that was delicious.*

G4

depend
To rely on or need for support: *Dogs **depend** on their owners to feed them.*

depended
A form of **depend**: *The group **depended** on her to lead the way out of the forest.*

design
To make a plan for: *We always **design** furniture before we build it.*

designed
A form of **design**: *She **designed** this desk to hold a computer and a printer.*

disappoint
To let down hopes or wishes: *I don't want to **disappoint** my parents, so I try to do my best in school.*

disappointed
A form of **disappoint**: *They were **disappointed** that their team did not make the final round.*

discover
To find out, or to find: *It is exciting to **discover** a hidden treasure.*

discovered
A form of **discover**: *When she **discovered** the shiny stones, she showed them to her teacher.*

duplicate
To make an exact copy of: *It is hard to **duplicate** a painting with many details.*

duplicated
A form of **duplicate**: *We **duplicated** these pictures on a copier.*

dye
Something that gives or adds color to cloth, paper, or other material: *We colored shirts by dipping them in **dye**.*

G5

E

empty
Containing nothing: *The bottle is almost **empty**, but you can have the last few sips of water.*

exact
Accurate in every detail: *He hoped to make an **exact** copy of the statue.*

exercise
Activity that helps the body: *People and animals need **exercise** every day.*

explain
To make clear or give reasons for: *If you **explain** what to do, I will try to do it.*

explained
A form of **explain**: *After my father **explained** how the camera worked, I began to use it.*

express
To make known: *Her stories **express** the feelings of the characters very well.*

extra
More than what is usual or needed: *She made an **extra** loaf of bread to give to me.*

F

fail
To be unsuccessful: *We don't want to **fail** to reach the top of the mountain.*

failed
A form of **fail**: *They **failed** to find the missing gloves, but at least they found the scarf.*

final
Coming at the end: *We took a **final** spelling test at the end of the school year.*

finally
At last, after a long while: ***Finally** the long car ride was over.*

G6

fling
Throw hard: *If I **fling** this rock into the water, it might skip over the waves.*

flung
A form of **fling**: *She **flung** the ball so hard it went way past home plate and into the bleachers.*

flutter
To flap, beat, or wave rapidly: *Moths **flutter** around the porch light in the evening.*

fluttering
A form of **flutter**: *A hummingbird was **fluttering** around the bright garden flowers.*

fluttering

fortune
The luck that comes to a person: *I had the good **fortune** to win a ticket to the big game.*

fund
A sum of money raised or kept for a certain purpose: *The family has a vacation **fund** that helps them save for summer travel.*

G

gaze
To look for a long time: *We **gaze** in wonder at the snowy mountains.*

gazing
A form of **gaze**: *They were **gazing** at the pink and purple clouds in the sunset sky.*

glimmering
Shiny or sparkling: *The **glimmering** jewels are very beautiful.*

G7

grain
A very small part of something: *A **grain** of sand is so small that you can barely see it.*

grand
Wonderful or important: *He felt **grand** when he marched in the parade.*

grateful
Feeling thankful or showing thanks: *They were so **grateful** for her help that they gave her a gift.*

growl
To make a low, deep, angry sound: *We don't want the bear to **growl** at us.*

growled
A form of **growl**: *When the wolf **growled**, she jumped back.*

guard
Someone who protects or watches over: *The **guard** kept watch all night long.*

guess
To have or offer an idea without all the needed information: *I'll **guess** that there are about three hundred pennies in the jar.*

guessed
A form of **guess**: *She **guessed** that the skates would still fit, but she would soon find out.*

H

heavily
A form of **heavy**: *The snow was falling so **heavily** that we had to shovel the path again.*

heavy
Weighing a lot, thick, or hard to bear: *This is a **heavy** box for one person to carry.*

hero
A person who is admired for brave, kind, or important actions: *She is a **hero** because she helped so many people find safety.*

G8

Glossary

hurried
A form of **hurry:** *We all* ***hurried*** *inside because the rain got very heavy.*

hurry
To act or move quickly: *Sometimes I* ***hurry*** *to get to the bus on time.*

I

inventions
Original machines, systems, or processes: *Radios, telephones, and cameras were important* ***inventions*** *in the past.*

invention

J

junior
Younger in a family or group: *The* ***junior*** *players learned from the senior players.*

K

knot
Tied-together piece of rope or string: *The* ***knot*** *was so tight that I had to cut the string.*

L

lean
To slant to one side or to rest on: *You can* ***lean*** *your head on my shoulder if you are sleepy.*

leaned
A form of **lean:** *Some people* ***leaned*** *against the wall because there were no chairs left.*

lonely
Sad about being alone or far from friends: *He felt* ***lonely*** *after his brother left for summer camp.*

N

nutrition
What our body gets from food in order to grow and stay healthy: *An orange is a food that has a lot of* ***nutrition.***

O

odd
Unusual or strange: *The car was making an* ***odd*** *noise, so we stopped to check.*

ordinary
Common, usual: *This bread you baked tastes better than* ***ordinary*** *bread.*

otherwise
If not or if things were different: *I ran fast, because* ***otherwise*** *I would have missed the train.*

overjoyed
A feeling of being very happy: *I was* ***overjoyed*** *to find out that my poem won first place.*

overlook
To miss seeing, or not notice: *Please don't* ***overlook*** *the people who helped make costumes for the play.*

overlooked
A form of **overlook:** *The smallest kitten was* ***overlooked*** *at first, but then we found him.*

P

peace
Calm: *If you want* ***peace*** *and quiet, try camping in the wilderness.*

peacefully
A form of **peace:** *The cat dozed* ***peacefully*** *on the sofa.*

plan
To decide on what to do: *We* ***plan*** *to travel all day.*

planning
A form of **plan:** *If you are* ***planning*** *for the party, be sure to get balloons.*

pod
A shell that covers some seeds: *You can eat some peas while they are still in their* ***pod.***

polite
Having or showing good manners: *Their parents showed them how to be* ***polite.***

position
Location, or area that a team player is assigned: *Some players wanted to change their* ***position*** *on the soccer team.*

practice
To do over and over to gain skill: *I* ***practice*** *playing the drums twice a week.*

pretend
To make believe or act as though something is true: *We are riding* ***pretend*** *horses when we ride our bikes.*

prize
Something won in a contest: *The* ***prize*** *for the best dancers was a blue ribbon.*

prize

R

receive
To take or get something that is sent or given: *We* ***receive*** *many cards for the holiday every year.*

received
A form of **receive:** *They* ***received*** *a notice about what to recycle and where to put it.*

remarkable
Deserving notice, or outstanding: *The landing on the moon was a* ***remarkable*** *event.*

remove
To take out, take away: *You can* ***remove*** *the seeds of the apple after you slice it.*

repeat
To do or say again: *Please* ***repeat*** *the directions and I will try to follow them.*

repeated
A form of **repeat:** *The game was so much fun that they* ***repeated*** *it the next day.*

result
Something that happens because of something else: *The class mural was a* ***result*** *of days of planning and painting.*

roar
To make a loud, deep sound or noise: *Engines* ***roar*** *and wheels roll before the planes take off.*

roared
A form of **roar:** *When the lion* ***roared,*** *the smaller animals turned and ran.*

root
The part of a plant that grows down into the ground: *You cannot see the* ***root*** *of a plant because it is underground.*

S

search
To look over or go through carefully: *We will search along the path for the missing gloves.*

sense
Clear reason or good judgment: *It makes sense to wear boots in deep snow.*

sensible
A form of **sense**: *Be sensible enough to take an extra swimsuit on vacation.*

serious
Thoughtful, important, not joking: *This is a serious topic, so please listen carefully.*

seriously
A form of **serious**: *If you take it seriously, you should practice the piano every day.*

serve
To prepare and offer something: *We used trays to help us carry and serve the tea at the party.*

serve

served
A form of **serve**: *The waitress served the desserts last.*

sharp
Having a fine point or cutting edge: *The knives are sharp, so please be careful.*

sharpening
A form of **sharp**: *By sharpening the pencil, he could draw very fine lines.*

shoot
A plant that has just begun to grow up through the soil: *I was happy to see the shoot of my plant poke through the dirt.*

slippery
Slick or likely to cause slipping: *The rain froze overnight so the streets were slippery.*

soak
To make something completely wet by placing it in liquid or by pouring liquid on it: *The heavy rain will soak the soil.*

soften
To make something softer or less hard: *The ice cream began to soften because I left it on the counter.*

sore
Painful or feeling hurt: *The shoes were so tight that she had a sore toe.*

souvenir
Something kept to recall a special time or place: *I wish that I had a souvenir from the trip.*

souvenir

spin
To twist cotton or wool to make yarn or thread: *We learned to spin thread when we studied how families lived long ago.*

spinning
A form of **spin**: *While spinning the yarn, she hummed a tune.*

sprang
A form of **spring**: *The fox sprang out of the tall grass and chased the chipmunk.*

spring
To leap, or move up in a quick motion: *The squirrels spring from the tree to the porch roof.*

stare
To look with a steady, often wide-eyed gaze: *Many people don't like to have someone stare at them.*

staring
A form of **stare**: *Everybody was staring at the huge box and guessing what was inside.*

startle
To cause a sudden movement, as of surprise: *Talking might startle the deer, so be very quiet.*

startled
A form of **startle**: *The ducks were startled by the truck and flew away.*

steer
To guide or direct the course of: *I'm glad that we learned to steer the boat.*

strand
One of the long pieces that are twisted together to make rope or yarn: *The strong rope was made from many strands.*

stream
A body of water that flows in a bed or channel: *A few miles from here, that small trickle of water turns into a flowing stream.*

studied
A form of **study**: *Long ago sailors studied the stars by watching the sky at night.*

study
To try to learn from, or to look closely at: *They study the ant farm to find out how ants work together.*

suspicious
Not trusting, or having doubts: *We were suspicious because last time she tried to fool us.*

suspiciously
A form of **suspicious**: *The mouse watched the snake suspiciously from far off.*

swift
Fast: *A swift rabbit can run away from a hungry fox.*

T

tangle
Snarl or twist: *We tangle the string every time we try to fly our kite.*

tangled
A form of **tangle**: *The kittens played with the tangled ball of yarn.*

task
A job or chore: *Cleaning my messy room is a difficult task!*

tasty
Having a lot of good flavor: *I asked for more of my grandmother's tasty soup.*

taught
A form of **teach**: *My grandma taught me how to build a birdhouse.*

teach
To give knowledge or lessons: *I can teach you how to do that kind of puzzle.*

tear
To pull apart or rip: *I like to tear colored paper and make designs.*

tearing
A form of **tear**: *After tearing down the old barn, they built a newer, stronger one.*

Glossary/Acknowledgments

toss
To throw or pitch: *In this game, you toss balls into a basket.*

toss

tossed
A form of **toss**: *The two children tossed the beanbag back and forth.*

train
To teach skills or ways to act: *You can train your dog to wait quietly.*

training
A form of **train**: *After many weeks of training, the team won every game.*

trouble
Something that is difficult, dangerous, or upsetting: *He didn't want to cause trouble, so he worked very carefully.*

tumble
To roll or do somersaults: *Mikael likes to tumble all the way down that steep hill!*

tumbling
A form of **tumble**: *After tumbling across the mat, the gymnast did a split and a cartwheel.*

U

upset
To be disturbed or turned over: *The birds were upset when the cat climbed toward their nest.*

V

valuable
Important, or worth a lot of money: *Be careful to not break the antique plate. It is very valuable.*

G17

village
A group of houses that make up a community smaller than a town: *There were about fifty people in the whole village.*

W

waterproof
Able to keep water off or out: *For hiking in the rain, you need a raincoat and a waterproof hat.*

weave
To pass something such as yarn or twigs over and under one another: *The children learned how to weave a small basket.*

web
Material that connects or ties together: *The spider spun a web between two branches of the tree.*

webbed
A form of **web**: *Ducks, geese, and penguins have webbed feet.*

webbed

whistle
Something that makes a high, clear sound when air is blown through it: *The coach blew a whistle when he wanted the team to stop and listen.*

wisdom
Being able to judge what is best and right: *People say that you gain wisdom after many years of living and making mistakes.*

G18

wonder
To be curious about: *I wonder how birds feel when they are flying.*

worn
Damaged by being used too much: *My little brother's blanket looks very worn because he takes it with him wherever he goes.*

Y

yarn
Spun wool or nylon for weaving or knitting: *She loved the colors and feel of the yarn in the knitting store.*

yarn

G19

R34 • Unit 4

Acknowledgments

Main Literature Selections

Dex: The Heart of a Hero by Caralyn Buehner, illustrated by Mark Buehner. Text copyright ©2004 by Caralyn Buehner. Illustrations copyright ©2004 by Mark Buehner. All rights reserved. Reprinted by permission of HarperCollins Publishers.

The Dog that Dug for Dinosaurs by Shirley Raye Redmond, illustrated by Simon Sullivan. Text copyright ©2004 by Shirley Raye Redmond. Illustrations copyright ©2004 by Simon Sullivan. Reprinted by permission of Aladdin Paperbacks, an imprint of Simon & Schuster's Children's Publishing Division. All rights reserved.

Excerpt from *Exploring Space Travel* by Laura Hamilton Waxman. Copyright ©2012 by Lerner Publishing Group, Inc. Reprinted by permission of Lerner Publishing Group, Inc.

From Seed to Plant by Gail Gibbons. Copyright ©1991 by Gail Gibbons. All rights reserved. Reprinted by permission of Holiday House, Inc.

"Gloria Who Might Be My Best Friend" from *The Stories Julian Tells* by Ann Cameron. Text copyright ©1981 by Ann Cameron. All rights reserved. Reprinted by permission of Random House Children's Books, a division of Random House, Inc., and Ann Cameron.

The Goat in the Rug by Charles L. Blood and Martin Link, illustrated by Nancy Winslow Parker. Text copyright ©1976 by Charles L. Blood and Martin A. Link. Illustrations copyright ©1976 by Nancy Winslow Parker. Reprinted by permission of Simon & Schuster Books for Young Readers, an Imprint of Simon & Schuster Children's Publishing Division. All rights reserved.

Half-Chicken/Mediopollito by Ala Flor Ada, illustrated by Kim Howard. Text copyright ©1995 by Ala Flor Ada. Illustrations copyright ©1995 by Kim Howard. Reprinted by permission of BookStop Literary Agency, LLC.

"Keep a Poem in Your Pocket" from *Something Special* by Beatrice Schenk de Reginers. Text copyright ©1958, 1986 by Beatrice Schenk de Reginers. Reprinted by permission of Marian Reiner, Literary Agent.

Luke Goes to Bat by Rachel Isadora. Copyright ©2005 by Rachel Isadora. Reprinted by permission of G. P. Putnam's Sons, a division of Penguin Young Readers Group, a member of Penguin Group (USA) Inc. All rights reserved.

Mr. Tanen's Tie Trouble written and illustrated by Maryann Cocca-Lefler. Text and illustrations copyright ©2003 by Maryann Cocca-Lefler. Adapted by permission of Albert Whitman & Company.

My Name is Gabriela/Me llamo Gabriela by Monica Brown, illustrated by John Parra. Text copyright ©by Monica Brown. Illustrations copyright ©by John Para, Vicki Prentice Associates, Inc. NYC. Translations ©2005 by Luna Rising, a division of Cooper Square Publishing. Reprinted by permission of Rowman & Littlefield Publishing Group.

The Mysterious Tadpole written and illustrated by Steven Kellogg. Copyright ©2002 by Steven Kellogg. All rights reserved including the right of reproduction in whole or in part in any form. Reprinted by permission of Dial Books for Young Readers, a member of Penguin's Young Readers Group, a division of Penguin Group (USA) Inc.

Now & Ben: The Modern Inventions of Benjamin Franklin by Gene Barretta. Copyright ©2006 by Gene Barretta. All rights reserved. Reprinted by permission of Henry Holt and Company LLC.

Penguin Chick by Betty Tatham, illustrated by Helen K. Davie. Text copyright ©2002 by Betty Tatham. Illustrations copyright ©2002 by Helen K. Davie. All rights reserved. Reprinted by permission of HarperCollins Children's Books, a division of HarperCollins Publishers.

"The Period" from *On Your Marks: A Package of Punctuation* by Richard Armour. Text copyright ©1969 by Richard Armour. Reprinted by permission of Geoffrey Armour, who controls all rights.

"Share the Adventure" by Patricia and Frederick McKissack. Text copyright ©1993 by Patricia and Frederick McKissack. First appeared as a National Children's Book Week Poem by The Children's Book Council. Reprinted by permission of Curtis Brown, Ltd.

The Signmaker's Assistant written and illustrated by Tedd Arnold. Text copyright ©1992 by Tedd Arnold. All rights reserved. Reprinted by permission of Dial Books for Young Readers, a member of Penguin Young Readers Group, a division of Penguin Group (USA), Inc.

Two of Everything by Lily Toy Hong. Copyright ©1993 by Lily Toy Hong. Adapted by permission of Albert Whitman & Company.

Cover illustration from *Where Do Polar Bears Live?* by Sarah L. Thomson. Illustration copyright ©2010 by Jason Chin. Reprinted by permission of HarperCollins Publishers.

Research Bibliography

Achieve, Inc. (2007). *Closing the expectations gap 2007: An annual 50-state progress report on the alignment of high school policies with the demands of college and work.* Washington, DC: Author. http://www.achieve.org/files/50-state-07-Final.pdf.

Achugar, M., Schleppegrell, M., & Oteíza, T. (2007). Engaging teachers in language analysis: A functional linguistics approach to reflective literacy. *English Teaching: Practice and Critique,* 6 (2), 8–24.

ACT, Inc. (2006). *Reading between the lines: What the ACT reveals about college readiness in reading.* Iowa City, IA: Author.

ACT, Inc. (2009). *ACT National Curriculum Survey 2009.* Iowa City, IA: Author.

ACT, Inc. (2009). *The condition of college readiness 2009.* Iowa City, IA: Author.

Adams, M. J. (2009). The challenge of advanced texts: The interdependence of reading and learning. In E. H. Hiebert (Ed.), *Reading more, reading better: Are American students reading enough of the right stuff?* (pp. 163–189). New York, NY: Guilford.

Adams, M. J. (2000). *Beginning to Read: Thinking and Learning About Print.* Cambridge: MIT Press.

Afflerbach, P., Pearson, P. D., & Paris, S. G. (2008). Clarifying differences between reading skills and reading strategies. *The Reading Teacher,* 61, 364–373.

Anderson, Jeff. (2005). *Mechanically Inclined: Building Grammar, Usage, and Style into Writer's Workshop.* Portsmouth, NH: Heinemann.

Angelillo, Janet. (2002). *A Fresh Approach to Teaching Punctuation.* New York: Scholastic.

Armbruster, B., Anderson, T. H., & Ostertag, J. (1987). Does text structure/summarization instruction facilitate learning from expository text? *Reading Research Quarterly,* 22 (3), 331–346.

Armbruster, B., Lehr, F., & Osborn, J. (2001). *Put Reading First: The Research Building Blocks for Teaching Children to Read* (pp. 21–31). Washington, DC: National Institute for Literacy.

Askew, B. J. & Fountas, I. C. (1998). Building an early reading process: Active from the start! *The Reading Teacher,* 52 (2), 126–134.

August, D., Carlo, M., Dressler, C., & Snow, C. (2005). The Critical Role of Vocabulary Development for English Language Learners. Learning Disabilities Research and Practice, 20 (1), 50–57.

August, D., & Shanahan, T. (2006). Developing literacy in second-language learners; Report of the National Literacy Panel on Language-Minority Children and Youth. Mahwah, NJ: Lawrence Erlbaum.

Baker, S. K., Chard, D. J., Ketterlin-Geller, L. R., Apichatabutra, C., & Doabler, C. (2009). The basis of evidence for Self-Regulated Strategy Development for students with or at risk for learning disabilities. *Exceptional Children.*

Ball, E., & Blachman, B. (1991). Does phoneme awareness training in kindergarten make a difference in early word recognition and developmental spelling? *Reading Research Quarterly,* 26 (1), 49–66.

Balmuth, M. (1992). *The roots of phonics: A historical introduction.* Baltimore, MD: York Press.

Bardovi-Harlig, K. (2000). *Tense and aspect in second language acquisition: Form, meaning, and use.* Language Learning Monograph Series. Malden, MA: Blackwell.

Bartholomae, D. (1980). The study of error. *College Composition and Communication,* 31 (3), 253–269.

Baumann, J. F. & Bergeron, B. S. (1993). Story map instruction using children's literature: Effects on first graders' comprehension of central narrative elements. *Journal of Reading Behavior,* 25 (4), 407–437.

Baumann, J. F., & Kame'enui, E. J. (1991). Research on vocabulary instruction: Ode to Voltaire. In J. Flood, J. M. Jensen, D. Lapp, & J. R. Squire (Eds.), *Handbook of research on teaching the English language arts* (pp. 604–632). New York, NY: Macmillan.

Baumann, J. F. & Kame'enui, E. J. (Eds.). (2004). *Vocabulary Instruction: Research to Practice.* New York: Guilford Press.

Baumann, J. F., Seifert-Kessell, N., & Jones, L. A. (1992). Effect of think-aloud instruction on elementary students' comprehension monitoring abilities. *Journal of Reading Behavior,* 24 (2), 143–172.

Bear, D. R. & Templeton, S. (1998). Explorations in developmental spelling: Foundations for learning and teaching phonics, spelling, and vocabulary. *The Reading Teacher,* 52 (3), 222–242.

Beck, I. L. (2006). *Making Sense of Phonics: The Hows and Whys.* New York: Guilford Press.

Beck, I. L. & McKeown, M. (2006). *Improving Comprehension with Questioning the Author: A Fresh and Expanded View of a Powerful Approach (Theory and Practice).* New York, NY: Scholastic.

Beck, I. L., & McKeown, M. G., (2001). Text talk: Capturing the benefits of read-aloud experiences for young children. *The Reading Teacher,* 55 (1), 10–20.

Beck, I. L., McKeown, M., Hamilton, R., & Kucan, L. (1997). *Questioning the Author: An Approach for Enhancing Student Engagement with Text.* Newark, DE: International Reading Association.

Beck, I. L., McKeown, M., Hamilton, R., & Kucan, L. (1998). Getting at the meaning. *American Educator,* Summer, 66–71.

Beck, I. L., McKeown, M. G., & Kucan, L. (2002). *Bringing Words to Life: Robust Vocabulary Instruction.* New York: Guilford Press.

Beck, I. L., McKeown, M. G., & Kucan, L. (2008). *Creating robust vocabulary: Frequently asked questions and extended examples.* New York, NY: Guilford.

Beck, I. L., Perfetti, C. A., & McKeown, M. G. (1982). Effects of long-term vocabulary instruction on lexical access and reading comprehension. *Journal of Educational Psychology,* 74 (4), 506–521.

Becker, W. C. (1977). Teaching reading and language to the disadvantaged—What we have learned from field research. *Harvard Educational Review,* 47, 518–543.

Bereiter, C. & Bird, M. (1985). Use of thinking aloud in identification and teaching of reading comprehension strategies. *Cognition and Instruction,* 2, 131–156.

Bettinger, E., & Long, B. T. (2009). Addressing the needs of underprepared students in higher education: Does college remediation work? *Journal of Human Resources,* 44, 736–771.

Betts, E. A. (1946). *Foundations of reading instruction, with emphasis on differentiated guidance.* New York, NY: American Book Company.

Biber, D. (1991). *Variation across speech and writing.* Cambridge, England: Cambridge University Press.

Biemiller, A. (2001). Teaching vocabulary: Early, direct, and sequential. *American Educator,* 25 (1), 24–28, 47.

Biemiller, A. (2001). Vocabulary development and instruction: A prerequisite for school learning. In D. Dickinson & S. Neuman (Eds.), *Handbook of Early Literacy Research,* (Vol. 2), New York: Guilford Press.

Biemiller, A. (2005). Size and sequence in vocabulary development: Implications for choosing words for primary grade vocabulary. In E. H. Hiebert & M. L. Kamil (Eds.), *Teaching and Learning Vocabulary* (pp. 223–242). Mahwah, NJ: Lawrence Erlbaum.

Biemiller, A. & Slonim, N. (2001). Estimating root word vocabulary growth in normative and advantaged populations: Evidence for a common sequence of vocabulary acquisition. *Journal of Educational Psychology,* 93 (3), 498–520.

Blachman, B. (2000). Phonological awareness. In M. Kamil, P. Mosenthal, P. D. Pearson, & R. Barr (Eds.), *Handbook of Reading Research,* (Vol. 3). Mahwah, NJ: Lawrence Erlbaum.

Blachman, B., Ball, E. W., Black, R. S., & Tangel, D. M. (1994). Kindergarten teachers develop phoneme awareness in low-income, inner-city classrooms: Does it make a difference? *Reading and Writing: An Interdisciplinary Journal,* 6 (1), 1–18.

Bowen, G. M., & Roth, W.-M. (1999, March). "Do-able" questions, covariation, and graphical representation: Do we adequately prepare preservice science teachers to teach inquiry? Paper presented at the annual conference of the National Association for Research in Science Teaching, Boston, MA.

Bowen, G. M., Roth, W.-M., & McGinn, M. K. (1999). Interpretations of graphs by university biology students and practicing scientists: Towards a social practice view of scientific representation practices. *Journal of Research in Science Teaching,* 36, 1020–1043.

Bowen, G. M., Roth, W.-M., & McGinn, M. K. (2002). Why students may not learn to interpret scientific inscriptions. *Research in Science Education,* 32, 303–327.

Brown, I. S. & Felton, R. H. (1990). Effects of instruction on beginning reading skills in children at risk for reading disability. *Reading and Writing: An Interdisciplinary Journal,* 2 (3), 223–241.

Bryson, B. (1990). *The mother tongue: English and how it got that way.* New York, NY: Avon Books.

Buck Institute for Education (2011). *PBL in the Elementary Grades.* Novato, CA: Buck Institute for Education.

Bus, A. G., Van Ijzendoorn, M. H., & Pellegrini, A. D. (1995). *Joint book reading makes for success in reading: A meta-analysis on intergenerational transmission of literacy.* Review of Educational Research, 65 (5), 1–21.

Calderón, M., August, D., Slavin, R., Duran, D., Madden, N., & Cheung, A. (2005). Bring Words to Life in Classrooms with English Language Learners. In E. H. Hiebert & M. L. Kamil (Eds.), Teaching and Learning Vocabulary: Bringing Research to Practice. Mahwah, NJ: Lawrence Erlbaum.

Carlo, M. (2004). Closing the gap: Addressing the vocabulary needs of English-language learners in bilingual and mainstream classrooms. *Reading Research Quarterly,* 39 (2), 188–215.

Carver, R. P. (1994). Percentage of unknown vocabulary words in text as a function of the relative difficulty of the text: Implications for instruction. *Journal of Reading Behavior,* 26, 413–437.

Catts, H., Adolf, S. M., & Weismer, S. E. (2006). Language deficits in poor comprehenders: A case for the simple view of reading. *Journal of Speech, Language, and Hearing Research,* 49, 278–293.

Chall, J. (1996). *Learning to Read: The Great Debate (revised, with a new foreword).* New York: McGraw-Hill.

Chall, J. S., Conard, S., & Harris, S. (1977). *An analysis of textbooks in relation to declining SAT scores.* Princeton, NJ: College Entrance Examination Board.

Chard, D. J., Ketterlin-Geller, L. R., Baker, S. K., Doabler, C., & Apichatabutra, C. (2009). Repeated reading interventions for students with learning disabilities: Status of the evidence. *Exceptional Children,* 75 (3), 263–281.

Chard, D. J., Stoolmiller, M., Harn, B., Vaughn, S., Wanzek, J., Linan-Thompson, S., & Kame'enui, E. J. (2008). Predicting reading success in a multi-level school-wide reading model: A retrospective analysis. *Journal of Learning Disabilities,* 41 (2), 174–188.

Charity, A. H., Scarborough, H. E., & Griffin, D. M. (2004). Familiarity with school English in African American children and its relation to early reading achievement. *Child Development,* 75 (5), 1340–1356.

Chiappe, P. & Siegel, L. S. (2006). A longitudinal study of reading development of Canadian children from diverse linguistic backgrounds. *Elementary School Journal,* 107 (2), 135–152.

Coyne, M. D., Kame'enui, E. J., & Simmons, D. C. (2004). Improving beginning reading instruction and intervention for students with LD: Reconciling "all" with "each." *Journal of Learning Disabilities,* 37 (3), 231–239.

Coyne, M. D., Kame'enui, E. J., Simmons, D. C., & Harn, B. A. (2004). Beginning reading intervention as inoculation or insulin: First-grade reading performance of strong responders to kindergarten intervention. *Journal of Learning Disabilities,* 37 (2), 90–104.

Coyne, M. D., Zipoli Jr., R. P., Chard, D. J., Faggella-Luby, M., Ruby, M., Santoro, L. E., & Baker, S. (2009). Direct instruction of comprehension: Instructional examples from intervention research on listening and reading comprehension. *Reading & Writing Quarterly,* 25 (2), 221–245.

Coyne, M. D., Zipoli Jr., R. P., & Ruby, M. (2006). Beginning reading instruction for students at risk for reading disabilities: What, how, and when. *Intervention in School and Clinic,* 41 (3), 161–168.

Craig, H. K. & Washington, J. A. (2001). Recent research on the language and literacy skills of African American students in early years. In D. Dickinson & S. Neuman (Eds.), *Handbook of Early Literacy Research,* (Vol. 2), New York: Guilford Press.

Craig, H. K. & Washington, J. A. (2006). *Malik Goes to School: Examining the Language Skills of African American Students From Preschool-5th Grade.* Mahwah, NJ: Lawrence Erlbaum Associates.

Daneman, M, & Green, I. (1986). Individual differences in comprehending and producing words in context. *Journal of Memory and Language,* 25 (1), 1–18.

DeVilliers, J., & DeVilliers, P. (1973). A cross-sectional study of the acquisition of grammatical morphemes in child speech. *Journal of Psycholinguistic Research,* 2, 267–278.

Dickinson, D. K., & Smith, M. W. (1994). Long-term effects of preschool teachers' book readings on low-income children's vocabulary and story comprehension. *Reading Research Quarterly,* 29, 104–123.

Dixon, R. C., Isaacson, S., & Stein, M. (2002). Effective strategies for teaching writing. In E. J. Kame'enui, D. W. Carnine, R. C. Dixon, D. C. Simmons, & M. D. Coyne (Eds.), *Effective Teaching Strategies That Accommodate Diverse Learners* (2nd ed., pp. 93–119). Upper Saddle River, NJ: Merrill Prentice Hall.

Dowhower, S. L. (1987). Effects of repeated reading on second-grade transitional readers' fluency and comprehension. *Reading Research Quarterly,* 22 (4), 389–406.

Duke, N. K. (2000). 3.6 minutes a day: The scarcity of informational text in first grade. *Reading Research Quarterly,* 35 (2), 202–224.

Research Bibliography

Duke, N. K. & Pearson, P. D. (2002). Effective practices for developing reading comprehension. In A. E. Farstrup & S. J. Samuels (Eds.), *What Research Has to Say About Reading Instruction* (3rd ed., pp. 205–242). Newark, DE: International Reading Association.

Durán, E., Shefelbine, J., Carnine, L., Maldonado-Colón, E., & Gunn, B. (2003). *Systematic Instruction in Reading for Spanish-Speaking Students.* Springfield, IL: Charles C. Thomas.

Durkin, D. (1978). What classroom observations reveal about comprehension instruction. *Reading Research Quarterly,* 14, 481–533.

Edwards Santoro, L., Chard, D. J., Howard, L., & Baker, S. K. (2008). Making the VERY most of classroom read alouds: How to promote comprehension and vocabulary in K-2 classrooms. *The Reading Teacher,* 61 (5), 396–408.

Ehri, L. C. (1998). Grapheme-phoneme knowledge is essential for learning to read words in English. In J. Metsala & L. Ehri (Eds.), *Word Recognition in Beginning Literacy* (pp. 3–40). Hillsdale, NJ: Lawrence Erlbaum Associates.

Ehri, L. & Nunes, S. R. (2002). The role of phonemic awareness in learning to read. In A. E. Farstrup & S. J. Samuels (Eds.), *What Research Has to Say About Reading Instruction* (3rd ed., pp. 110–139). Newark, DE: International Reading Association.

Ehri, L. & Wilce, L. (1987). Does learning to spell help beginners learn to read words? *Reading Research Quarterly,* 22 (1), 48–65.

Erickson, B. L., & Strommer, D. W. (1991). *Teaching college freshmen.* San Francisco, CA: Jossey-Bass.

Farr, R. (1990). Reading. *Educational Leadership,* 47 (5), 82–83.

Farr, R., Lewis, M., Faszholz, J., Pinsky, E., Towle, S., Lipschutz, J. & Faulds, B. P. (1990). Writing in response to reading. *Educational Leadership,* 47 (6), 66–69.

Feitelson, D., Goldstein, Z., Iraqui, J., & Share, D. I. (1993). Effects of listening to story reading on aspects of literacy acquisition in a diglossic situation. *Reading Research Quarterly,* 28, 70–79.

Feitelson, D., Kita, B., & Goldstein, Z. (1986). Effects of listening to series stories on first graders' comprehension and use of language. *Research in the Teaching of English,* 20, 339–356.

Fletcher, J. M. & Lyon, G. R. (1998). Reading: A research-based approach. In Evers, W. M. (Ed.), *What's Gone Wrong in America's Classroom?* Palo Alto, CA: Hoover Institution Press, Stanford University.

Fogel, H., & Ehri, L. C. (2000). Teaching elementary students who speak Black English Vernacular to write in Standard English: Effects of dialect transformation practice. *Contemporary Educational Psychology,* 25, 212–235.

Foorman, B. (Ed.). (2003). *Preventing and Remediating Reading Difficulties.* Baltimore, MD: York Press.

Foorman, B. R., Francis, D. J., Fletcher, J., Schatschneider, C., & Mehta, P. (1998). The role of instruction in learning to read: Preventing reading failure in at-risk children. *Journal of Educational Psychology,* 90 (1), 37–55.

Fountas, Irene & Pinnell, Gay Su. (2001). *Guiding Readers and Writers: Grades 3-6.* Portsmouth, NH: Heinemann.

Francis D. J., Rivera, M., Lesaux, N., Kieffer, M., & Rivera, H. (2006). Practical Guidelines for the Education of English Language Learners: Research-based recommendations for instruction and academic interventions (Book 1). Texas Institute for Measurement, Evaluation, and Statistics. University of Houston for the Center on Instruction.

Francis D. J., Rivera, M., Lesaux, N., Kieffer, M., & Rivera, H. (2006). Practical Guidelines for the Education of English Language Learners: Research-based recommendations for serving adolescent newcomers (Book 2). Texas Institute for Measurement, Evaluation, and Statistics. University of Houston for the Center on Instruction.

Fromkin, V., Rodman, R., & Hyams, N. (2006). *An introduction to language* (8th ed.). Florence, KY: Wadsworth.

Fuchs, L., Fuchs, D., & Hosp, M. (2001). Oral reading fluency as an indicator of reading competence: A theoretical, empirical, and historical analysis. *Scientific Studies of Reading,* 5 (3), 239–256.

Fukkink, R. G. & de Glopper, K. (1998). Effects of instruction in deriving word meaning from context: A meta-analysis. *Review of Educational Research,* 68 (4), 450–469.

Fulkerson, R. (1996). *Teaching the argument in writing.* Urbana, IL: National Council of Teachers of English.

Gambrell, L. B., Morrow, L. M., & Pennington, C. (2002). Early childhood and elementary literature-based instruction: Current perspectives… *Reading Online,* 5 (6), 26–39.

Ganske, K. (2000). *Word journeys.* New York, NY: Guilford.

García, G. G., & Beltrám, D. (2003). Revisioning the blueprint: Building for the academic success of English learners. In G. G. García (Ed.), *English Learners* (pp. 197–226). Newark, DE: International Reading Association.

Gargani, J. (2006). *UC Davis/SCUSD Teaching American History Grant technical memo: Years 1 & 2 essay and CST analysis results.* Unpublished report.

Gebhard, M., Willett, J., Jiménez, J., & Piedra, A. (2011). Systemic Functional Linguistics, Teachers' Professional Development, and ELLs' Academic Literacy Practices. In T. Lucas (Ed.), Teacher Preparation for Linguistically Diverse Classrooms: A Resource for Teacher Educators (pp. 91–110). New York: Routledge/Taylor and Francis.

Genesee, F., Lindholm-Leary, K., Saunders, B., & Christian, D. (2006). Educating English Language Learners: A Synthesis of Research Evidence. New York: Cambridge University Press.

Gersten, R. (2005). Behind the scenes of an intervention research study. *Learning Disabilities Research & Practice,* 20 (4), 200–212.

Gersten, R. & Baker, S. (2000). What we know about effective instructional practices for English learners. *Exceptional Children,* 66 (4), 454–470.

Gersten, R., Baker, S. K., Haager, D., & Graves, A. W. (2005). Exploring the role of teacher quality in predicting reading outcomes for first-grade English learners: An observational study. *Remedial and Special Education,* 26 (4), 197–206.

Gersten, R. & Geva, E. (2003). Teaching reading to early language learners. *Educational Leadership,* 60 (7), 44–49.

Gersten, R. & Jiménez, R. (2002). Modulating instruction for English-language learners. In E. J. Kame'enui, D. W. Carnine, R. C. Dixon, D. C. Simmons, & M. D. Coyne (Eds.), *Effective Teaching Strategies That Accommodate Diverse Learners.* Upper Saddle River, NJ: Merrill Prentice Hall.

Gibbons, P. (2009). English Learners, Academic Literacy, and Thinking: Learning in the Challenge Zone. Portsmouth, NH: Heinemann.

Gipe, J. P. & Arnold, R. D. (1979). Teaching vocabulary through familiar associations and contexts. *Journal of Reading Behavior,* 11 (3), 281–285.

Goldenberg, C. (2008). Teaching English language learners: What the research does—and does not—say. **American Educator,** 32 (2), 8–23, 42–44.

Graff, G. (2003). *Clueless in academe.* New Haven, CT: Yale University Press.

Graham, Steve & Hebert, Michael. (2010). *Writing to Read: Evidence for How Writing Can Improve Reading. A Carnegie Corporation Time to Act Report.* Washington, DC: Alliance for Excellent Education.

Graves, M. F. (2009). Teaching individual words: One size does not fit all. New York, NY: Teachers College Press and International Reading Association.

Griffith, P. L., Klesius, J. P., & Kromrey, J. D. (1992). The effect of phonemic awareness on the literacy development of first grade children in a traditional or a whole language classroom. *Journal of Research in Childhood Education,* 6 (2), 85–92.

Guthrie, J. & Wigfield, A. (2000). Engagement and motivation in reading. In M. Kamil, P. Mosenthal, P. Pearson, & R. Barr, (Eds.), *Handbook of Reading Research, Vol. III,* 403–422.

Guthrie, J. T., Wigfield, A., Barbosa, P., Perencevich, K. C., Taboada, A., Davis, M. H., et al. (2004). Increasing reading comprehension and engagement through concept-oriented reading instruction. *Journal of Educational Psychology,* 96 (3), 403–423.

Hale, Elizabeth. (2008). *Crafting Writers: K-6.* Portsmouth, NH: Heinemann.

Hall, S. L. & Moats, L. C. (1999). *Straight Talk About Reading.* Chicago, IL: Contemporary Books.

Halliday, M. (1993). Toward a Language-Based Theory of Education. Linguistics and Education 5, 93–116.

Hammond, J., & Gibbons, P. (2005). Putting Scaffolding to Work: The Contribution of Scaffolding in Articulating ESL Education. Prospect Special Issue 20 (1), 6–30.

Hanna, P. R., Hanna, S., Hodges, R. E., & Rudorf, E. H. (1966). *Phoneme-grapheme correspondences as cues to spelling improvement.* Washington, DC: Department of Health, Education, and Welfare.

Harm, M. W., McCandliss, B. D. & Seidenberg, M. S. (2003). Modeling the successes and failures of interventions for disabled readers. *Scientific Studies of Reading,* 7 (2), 155–182.

Harn, B. A., Stoolmiller, M., & Chard, D. (2008). Identifying the dimensions of alphabetic principle on the reading development of first graders: The role of automaticity and unitization. *Journal of Learning Disabilities,* 41 (2), 143–157.

Hart, B., & Risley, T. R. (1995). *Meaningful differences in the everyday experience of young American children.* Baltimore, MD: Brookes.

Hasbrouck, J. & Tindal, G. A. (2006). Oral reading fluency norms: A valuable assessment tool for reading teachers. *The Reading Teacher,* 59 (7), 636–644.

Hayes, D., & Ahrens, M. (1988). Vocabulary simplification for children: A special case of "motherese"? *Journal of Child Language,* 15, 395–410.

Hayes, D. P., & Ward, M. (1992, December). *Learning from texts: Effects of similar and dissimilar features of analogies in study guides.* Paper presented at the 42nd Annual Meeting of the National Reading Conference, San Antonio, TX.

Hayes, D. P., Wolfer, L. T., & Wolfe, M. F. (1996). Sourcebook simplification and its relation to the decline in SAT-Verbal scores. *American Educational Research Journal,* 33, 489–508.

Heller, R., & Greenleaf, C. (2007). *Literacy instruction in the content areas: Getting to the core of middle and high school improvement.* Washington, DC: Alliance for Excellent Education.

Henry, M. (2003). *Unlocking literacy: Effective decoding and spelling instruction.* Baltimore, MD: Brookes.

Herman, P. A., Anderson, R. C., Pearson, P. D., & Nagy, W. E. (1987). Incidental acquisition of word meaning from expositions with varied text features. *Reading Research Quarterly,* 22, 263–284.

Hiebert, E. H. & Kamil, M. L. (Eds.). (2005). *Teaching and Learning Vocabulary: Bringing Research to Practice.* Mahwah, NJ: Lawrence Erlbaum Associates.

Hoffman, J., Sabo, D., Bliss, J., & Hoy, W. (1994). Building a culture of trust. *Journal of School Leadership,* 4, 484–501.

Hoover, W. A., & Gough, P. B. (1990). The simple view of reading. *Reading and Writing,* 2, 127–160.

Horn, Martha, & Giacobbe, Mary Ellen. (2007). *Talking, Drawing, Writing: Lessons for Our Youngest Writers.* Portland, ME: Stenhouse.

Hseuh-chao, M. H., & Nation, P. (2000). Unknown vocabulary density and reading comprehension. *Reading in a Foreign Language,* 13 (1), 403–430.

Hudson, R., (2006). Using Repeated Reading and Readers Theater to Increase Fluency. Reading First National Conference. http://www3.ksde.org/sfp/rdgfirst/natl_rdgfirst_conf_2006/hudson_using_repeated_reading_to_increase_fluency.pdf.

Hudson, R., Lane, H., & Pullen, P. (2005). Reading fluency assessment and instruction: What, why, and how? *The Reading Teacher,* 58 (8), 702–714.

Hulit, L. M., Howard, M. R., & Fahey, K. R. (2010). Born to talk: An introduction to speech and language development. Boston, MA: Allyn & Bacon.

Intersegmental Committee of the Academic Senates of the California Community Colleges, the California State University, and the University of California (ICAS). (2002). *Academic literacy: A statement of competencies expected of students entering California's public colleges and universities.* Sacramento, CA: Author.

Juel, C. (1988). Learning to read and write: A longitudinal study of fifty-four children from first through fourth grades. *Journal of Educational Psychology,* 80 (4), 437–447.

Juel, C., & Minden-Cupp, C. (2000). Learning to read words: Linguistic units and instructional strategies. *Reading Research Quarterly,* 35 (4), 458–492.

Kamil, M. L., Mosenthal, P. B., Pearson, P. D., & Barr, R. (2000). *Handbook of Reading Research.* Vol. III. Mahway, NJ: Lawrence Erlbaum Associates.

Kieffer, M., & Lesaux, N. (2008). The Role of Derivational Morphology in the Reading Comprehension of Spanish Speaking English Language Learners. Reading and Writing: An Interdisciplinary Journal, 21 (8), 783–804.

Kintsch, W. (1998). *Comprehension: A paradigm for cognition.* New York, NY: Cambridge University Press.

Kintsch, W. (2009). Learning and constructivism. In S. Tobias & M. Duffy (Eds.), *Constructivist instruction: Success or failure?* (pp. 223–241). New York, NY: Routledge.

Krauthamer, H. S. (1999). *Spoken language interference patterns in written English.* New York, NY: Peter Lang.

Kutner, M., Greenberg, E., Jin, Y., Boyle, B., Hsu, Y., & Dunleavy, E. (2007). *Literacy in everyday life: Results from the 2003 National Assessment of Adult Literacy* (NCES 2007–480). U.S. Department of Education. Washington, DC: National Center for Education Statistics.

Landauer, T. K., & Dumais, S. T. (1997). A solution to Plato's problem: The latent semantic analysis theory of acquisition, induction, and representation of knowledge. *Psychological Review,* 104, 211–240.

Landauer, T. K., McNamara, D. S., Dennis, S., & Kintsch, W. (Eds.) (2007). *Handbook of latent semantic analysis.* London, England: Psychology Press.

Research Bibliography

Laufer, B. (1988). What percentage of text-lexis is essential for comprehension? In C. Laurén & M. Nordman (Eds.), *Special language: From humans to thinking machines* (pp. 316–323). Clevedon, England: Multilingual Matters.

Lefstein, A. (2009). Rhetorical grammar and the grammar of schooling: Teaching "powerful verbs" in the English National Literacy Strategy. *Linguistics and Education,* 20, 378–400.

Lehr, F. & Osborn, J. (2005). A Focus on Comprehension. Pacific Resources for Education and Learning (PREL) Monograph. U.S. Department of Education. www.prel.org/programs/rel/rel.asp.

Lehr, F., Osborn, J., & Hiebert, E. H. (2004). A Focus on Vocabulary. Pacific Resources for Education and Learning (PREL) Monograph. U.S. Department of Education. www.prel.org/programs/rel/rel.asp.

Lesaux, N. K., Kieffer, M. J., Faller, S. E., & Kelley, J. G. (2010). The effectiveness and ease of implementation of an academic English vocabulary intervention for linguistically diverse students in urban middle schools. *Reading Research Quarterly,* 45, 196–228.

Lesaux, N. K. & Siegel, L. S. (2003). The development of reading in children who speak English as a second language. *Developmental Psychology,* 39 (6), 1005–1019.

Lipson, M. Y., Mosenthal, J. H., Mekkelsen, J., & Russ, B. (2004). Building knowledge and fashioning success one school at a time. *The Reading Teacher,* 57 (6), 534–542.

Lipson, M. Y. & Wixson, K. K. (2008). New IRA commission will address RTI issues. *Reading Today,* 26 (1), 1, 5.

Lonigan, C. J., Burgess, S. R., & Anthony, J. L. (2000). Development of emergent literacy and early reading skills in preschool children: Evidence from a latent-variable longitudinal study. *Developmental Psychology,* 36 (5), 596–613.

Lundberg, I., Frost, J., & Petersen O. (1988). Effects of an extensive program for stimulating phonological awareness in preschool children. *Reading Research Quarterly,* 23 (3), 263–284.

McCardle, P. & Chhabra, V. (Eds.). (2004). *The Voice of Evidence in Reading Research.* Baltimore: Brooks.

McIntosh, A. S., Graves, A., & Gersten, R. (2007). The effects of response to intervention on literacy development in multiple-language settings. *Learning Disability Quarterly,* 30 (3), 197–212.

McIntosh, K., Chard, D. J., Boland, J. B., & Horner, R. H. (2006). Demonstration of combined efforts in school-wide academic and behavioral systems and incidence of reading and behavior challenges in early elementary grades. *Journal of Positive Behavior Interventions,* 8 (3), 146–154.

McIntosh, K., Horner, R. H., Chard, D. J., Boland, J. B., Good, R. H. (2006). The use of reading and behavior screening measures to predict non-response to school-wide positive behavior support: A longitudinal analysis. *School Psychology Review,* 35 (2), 275–291.

McIntosh, K., Horner, R. H., Chard, D. J., Dickey, C. R., & Braun, D. H. (2008). Reading skills and function of problem behavior in typical school settings. *The Journal of Special Education,* 42 (3), 131–147.

McKenna, M. C. & Stahl, S. A. (2003). *Assessment for Reading Instruction,* New York: Guilford Press.

McKeown, M. G. & Beck, I. L. (2001). Encouraging young children's language interactions with stories. In D. Dickinson & S. Neuman (Eds.), *Handbook of Early Literacy Research* (Vol. 2). New York: Guilford Press.

McKeown, M. G., Beck, I. L., Omanson, R. C., & Pople, M. T. (1985). Some effects of the nature and frequency of vocabulary instruction on the knowledge and use of words. *Reading Research Quarterly,* 20 (5), 522–535.

McNamara, D. S., Graesser, A. C., & Louwerse, M. M. (in press). Sources of text difficulty: Across the ages and genres. In J. P. Sabatini & E. Albro (Eds.), *Assessing reading in the 21st century: Aligning and applying advances in the reading and measurement sciences.* Lanham, MD: R&L Education.

Merino, B. & Scarcella, R. (2005). Teaching science to English learners. *University of California Linguistic Minority Research Institute Newsletter,* 14 (4).

Mesmer, H. A. E. (2008). *Tools for matching readers to texts: Research-based practices.* New York, NY: Guilford.

Milewski, G. B., Johnson, D., Glazer, N., & Kubota, M. (2005). *A survey to evaluate the alignment of the new SAT Writing and Critical Reading sections to curricula and instructional practices* (College Board Research Report No. 2005-1 / ETS RR-05-07). New York, NY: College Entrance Examination Board.

Miller, G. A. (1999). On knowing a word. *Annual Review of Psychology,* 50, 1–19.

Moats, L. (2001). When older students can't read. *Educational Leadership,* 58 (6), 36–46.

Moats, L. (2004). Efficacy of a structured, systematic language curriculum for adolescent poor readers. *Reading & Writing Quarterly,* 20, (2), 145–159.

Moats, L. C. (1998). Teaching decoding. *American Educator,* 22 (1 & 2), 42–49, 95–96.

Moats, L. C. (1999). *Teaching Reading Is Rocket Science.* Washington, DC: American Federation of Teachers.

Moats, L. C. (2000). *Speech to Print: Language Essentials for Teachers.* Baltimore, MD: Paul H. Brookes Publishing Co., Inc.

Moats, L. C. (2008). *Spellography for teachers: How English spelling works.* (LETRS Module 3). Longmont, CO: Sopris West.

Morrow, L. M. (2004). Developmentally appropriate practice in early literacy instruction. *The Reading Teacher,* 58 (1), 88–89.

Morrow, L. M., Kuhn, M. R., & Schwanenflugel, P. J. (2006/2007). The family fluency program. *The Reading Teacher,* 60 (4), 322–333.

Morrow, L. M. & Tracey, D. H. (1997). Strategies used for phonics instruction in early childhood classrooms. *The Reading Teacher,* 50 (8), 644–651.

Morrow, L. M., Tracey, D. H., Woo, D. G., & Pressley, M. (1999). Characteristics of exemplary first-grade literacy instruction. *The Reading Teacher,* 52 (5), 462–476.

Mosenthal, J. H., Lipson, M. Y., Torncello, S., Russ, B., & Mekkelsen, J. (2004). Contexts and practices of six schools successful in obtaining reading achievement. *Elementary School Journal,* 104 (5), 343–367. ABSTRACT ONLY.

Moss, B., & Newton, E. (2002). An examination of the informational text genre in basal readers. *Reading Psychology,* 23 (1), 1–13.

Nagy, W. E., Anderson, R. C., & Herman, P. A. (1987). Learning word meanings from context during normal reading. *American Educational Research Journal,* 24, 237–270.

Nagy, W. E., Herman, P., & Anderson, R. C. (1985). Learning words from context. *Reading Research Quarterly,* 20, 233–253.

Nagy, W. E. & Scott, J. A. (2000). Vocabulary processes. In M. L. Kamil, P. B. Mosenthal, P. D. Pearson, & R. Barr (Eds.), *Handbook of Reading Research,* (Vol. 3, 269–284). Mahwah, NJ: Erlbaum.

Nagy, W., & Townsend, D. (2012). Words as tools: Learning academic vocabulary as language acquisition. *eading Research Quarterly,* 47 (1), 91–108.

National Assessment Governing Board. (2006). *Writing framework and specifications for the 2007 National Assessment of Educational Progress.* Washington, DC: U.S. Government Printing Office.

National Assessment Governing Board. (2007). *Writing framework for the 2011 National Assessment of Educational Progress,* pre-publication edition. Iowa City, IA: ACT, Inc.

National Center to Improve Tools of Educators. NCITE: http://idea.uoregon.edu/~ncite/.

National Commission on Writing. (2004). *Writing: A Ticket to Work…or a Ticket Out.* New York: The College Board.

National Endowment for the Arts. (2004). *Reading at risk: A survey of literary reading in America.* Washington, DC: Author.

National Institute of Child Health and Human Development. (2000). *Report of the National Reading Panel. Teaching children to read: An evidence-based assessment of the scientific research literature on reading and its implications for reading instruction* (NIH Publication No. 00-4769). Washington, DC: U.S. Government Printing Office.

National Reading Panel. (2000). *Teaching children to read: An evidence-based assessment of the scientific research literature on reading and its implications for reading instruction.* (NIH Publication No. 00-4754). Washington, DC: National Institute of Child Health and Human Development.

Neuman, S. B., & Dickinson, D. K., (Eds.). (2002). *Handbook of Early Literacy Research.* New York: Guilford Press.

O'Connor, R., Jenkins, J. R., & Slocum, T. A. (1995). Transfer among phonological tasks in kindergarten: Essential instructional content. *Journal of Educational Psychology,* 87 (2), 202–217.

Orkwis, R. & McLane, K. (1998, Fall). *A Curriculum Every Student Can Use: Design Principles for Student Access.* ERIC/OSEP Special Project, ERIC Clearinghouse on Disabilities and Gifted Education, Council for Exceptional Children.

Osborn, J. & Lehr, F. (2003). *A Focus on Fluency: Research-Based Practices in Early Reading Series.* Honolulu, HI: Pacific Resources for Education and Learning.

O'Shea, L. J., Sindelar, P. T., & O'Shea, D. J. (1985). The effects of repeated readings and attentional cues on reading fluency and comprehension. *Journal of Reading Behavior,* 17 (2), 129–142.

Paris, S. G., Cross, D. R., & Lipson, M. Y. (1984). Informed strategies for learning: A program to improve children's reading awareness and comprehension. *Journal of Educational Psychology,* 76 (6), 1239–1252.

The Partnership for Reading. (2003). *Put Reading First: The Research Building Blocks for Teaching Children to Read.* (2nd ed.). MD: National Institute for Literacy.

Patton, Alec (2012). Work that matters: The teacher's guide to project-based learning. Paul Hamlyn Foundation.

Payne, B. D., & Manning, B. H. (1992). Basal reader instruction: Effects of comprehension monitoring training on reading comprehension, strategy use and attitude. *Reading Research and Instruction,* 32 (1), 29–38.

Pence, K. L., & Justice, L. M. (2007). *Language development from theory to practice.* Upper Saddle River, NJ: Prentice-Hall.

Perfetti, C. A., Landi, N., & Oakhill, J. (2005). The acquisition of reading comprehension skill. In M. J. Snowling & C. Hulme (Eds.), *The science of reading: A handbook* (pp. 227–247). Oxford, England: Blackwell.

Phillips, B. M. & Torgesen, J. K. (2001). Phonemic awareness and reading: Beyond growth of initial reading accuracy. In D. Dickinson & S. Neuman (Eds.), *Handbook of Early Literacy Research* (Vol. 2). New York: Guilford Press.

Pikulski, J. J., (1998). Business we should finish. *Reading Today,* 15 (5), 30.

Pikulski, J. J., & Chard, D. J. (2005). Fluency: Bridge between decoding and reading comprehension. *The Reading Teacher,* 58 (6), 510–519.

Postman, N. (1997). *The end of education.* New York, NY: Knopf.

Pressley, M. (1998). *Reading Instruction That Works: The Case for Balanced Teaching.* New York: The Guilford Press.

Pritchard, M. E., Wilson, G. S., & Yamnitz, B. (2007). What predicts adjustment among college students? A longitudinal panel study. *Journal of American College Health,* 56 (1), 15–22.

Quinn, H., Lee, O., & Valdés, G. (2012). Language demands and opportunities in relation to next generation science standards for English language learners: What teachers need to know. Paper for the Understanding Language Initiative, Stanford University. Retrieved from http://ell.stanford.edu/publication/language-demands-and-opportunities-relation-next-generation-science-standards-ells.

RAND Reading Study Group. (2002). *Reading for understanding: Toward an R & D program in reading comprehension.* Santa Monica, CA: RAND.

Rasinski, T. (2003). *The Fluent Reader: Oral Reading Strategies for Building Word Recognition, Fluency and Comprehension.* New York: Scholastic.

Rasinski, T. V., Padak, N., Linek, W., & Sturtevant, E. (1994). Effects of fluency development on urban second-grade readers. *Journal of Educational Research,* 87 (3), 158–165.

Rayner, K., Foorman, B. R., Perfetti, C. A., Pesetsky, D., & Seidenberg, M. S. (2001). How psychological science informs the teaching of reading. *Psychological Science in the Public Interest,* 2 (2), 31–74.

Rayner, K., Foorman, B. R., Perfetti, C. A., Pesetsky, D., & Seidenberg, M. S. (2002) How should reading be taught? *Scientific American,* pp. 85–91.

Report from the National Reading Panel. (2000). *Teaching Children to Read: An Evidence-Based Assessment of the Scientific Research Literature on Reading and its Implications for Reading Instruction.* Bethesda, MD: National Institute of Child Health and Human Development. http://www.nationalreadingpanel.org/Publications/summary.htm.

Rinehart, S. D., Stahl, S. A., & Erickson, L. G. (1986). Some effects of summarization training on reading and studying. *Reading Research Quarterly,* 21 (4), 422–438.

Robbins, C. & Ehri, L. C. (1994). Reading storybooks to kindergartners helps them learn new vocabulary words. *Journal of Educational Psychology,* 86 (1), 54–64.

Rosenshine, B., & Meister, C. (1994). Reciprocal teaching: A review of research. *Review of Educational Research,* 64 (4), 479–530.

Rosenshine, B., Meister, C., & Chapman, S. (1996). Teaching students to generate questions: A review of the intervention studies. *Review of Educational Research,* 66 (2), 181–221.

Routman, R. (2000). *Conversations: Strategies for Teaching, Learning, and Evaluating.* Portsmouth, NH: Heinemann.

Samuels, S., Schermer, N., & Reinking, D. (1992). Reading fluency: Techniques for making decoding automatic. In S. J. Samuels & A. E. Farstrup (Eds.), *What Research Has to Say About Reading Instruction* (pp. 124–143). Newark, DE: International Reading Association.

Research Bibliography

Samuels, S. J. & Farstrup, A. E. (2006). *What Research Has to Say About Fluency Instruction.* Newark, DE: International Reading Association.

Saunders, W., & O'Brien, G. (2006). Oral Language. In F. Genesee, K. Lindholm-Leary, W. Saunders & D. Christian (Eds.) Educating English Language Learners: A Synthesis of Research Evidence. New York: Cambridge University Press.

Scarcella, R. (2003) Academic English: A conceptual framework. *The University of California Linguistic Minority Research Institute, Technical Report* 2003-1.

Scarcella, R. English learners and writing: Responding to linguistic diversity. http://wps. ablongman.com/wps/media/objects/133/136243/ english.pdf.

Scarcella, R. (1990). *Teaching Language Minority Students in the Multicultural Classroom.* Englewood Cliffs, NJ: Prentice Hall Regents.

Scharer, P. L., Pinnell, G. S., Lyons, C., & Fountas, I. (2005). Becoming an engaged reader. *Educational Leadership,* 63 (2), 24–29.

Schleppegrell, M. (2001). Linguistic features of the language of schooling. *Linguistics and Education,* 12, 431–459.

Schleppegrell, M. (2004). *Teaching Academic Writing to English Learners,* 13 (2). Grant Report: University of California Linguistic Minority Research Institute.

Scott, J., & Nagy, W. E. (1997). Understanding the definitions of unfamiliar verbs. *Reading Research Quarterly,* 32, 184–200.

Sénéchal, M. (1997). The differential effect of storybook reading on preschoolers' acquisition of expressive and receptive vocabulary. *Journal of Child Language,* 24 (1), 123–138.

Shanahan, T. (2005). FAQs about Fluency. http:// www.springfield.k12.il.us/resources/languagearts/ readingwriting/readfluency.html.

Shanahan, T., & Shanahan, C. (2008). Teaching disciplinary literacy to adolescents: Rethinking content-area literacy. *Harvard Educational Review,* 78 (1), 40–59.

Shany, M. T. & Biemiller, A. (1995). Assisted reading practice: Effects on performance for poor readers in grades 3 and 4. *Reading Research Quarterly,* 30 (3), 382–395.

Shaughnessy, M. P. (1979). *Errors and expectations: A guide for the teacher of basic writing.* New York, NY: Oxford University Press.

Shaywitz, S. (2003). *Overcoming Dyslexia.* New York: Alfred A Knopf.

Short, D. J., & Fitzsimmons, S. (2007). *Double the work: Challenges and solutions to acquiring language and academic literacy for adolescent English language learners.* New York, NY: Alliance for Excellent Education.

Simmons, D. C., Kame'enui, E. J, Coyne, M. D. & Chard, D. J. (2002). Effective strategies for teaching beginning reading. In E. J. Kame'enui, D. W. Carnine, R. C. Dixon, D. C. Simmons, & M. D. Coyne (Eds.), *Effective Teaching Strategies That Accommodate Diverse Learners.* Upper Saddle River, NJ: Merrill Prentice Hall.

Sindelar, P. T., Monda, L. E., & O'Shea, L. J. (1990). Effects of repeated readings on instructional- and mastery-level readers. *Journal of Educational Research,* 83 (4), 220–226.

Snow, C., Burns, M., & Griffin, P. (Eds.). (1998). *Preventing Reading Difficulties in Young Children.* Washington, DC: National Academy Press.

Stahl, S. A. & Fairbanks, M. M. (1986). The effects of vocabulary instruction: A model-based meta-analysis. *Review of Educational Research,* 56 (1), 72–110.

Stanovich, K. E. (1986). Matthew effects in reading: Some consequences of individual differences in the acquisition of literacy. *Reading Research Quarterly,* 21, 360–407.

Stanovich, K. E. & Stanovich, P. J. (2003). Using research and reason in education: How teachers can use scientifically based research to make curricular & instructional decisions. Jessup, MD: National Institute for Literacy. Retrieved January, 26, 2006, http:// www.nifl.gov/partnershipforreading/publications/pdf/ Stanovich_Color.pdf.

Stenner, A. J., Koons, H., & Swartz, C. W. (2010). *Text complexity and developing expertise in reading.* Chapel Hill, NC: MetaMetrics, Inc.

Sternberg, R. J., & Powell, J. S. (1983). Comprehending verbal comprehension. *American Psychologist,* 38, 878–893.

Sticht, T. G., & James, J. H. (1984). Listening and reading. In P. D. Pearson, R. Barr, M. L. Kamil, & P. Mosenthal (Eds.), *Handbook of reading research* (Vol. 1) (pp. 293–317). White Plains, NY: Longman.

Strickland, D. S. (2002). The importance of effective early intervention. In A. E. Farstrup & S. J. Samuels (Eds.), *What Research Has to Say About Reading Instruction* (3rd ed., pp. 69–86). Newark, DE: International Reading Association.

Strickland, D. S. & Morrow, L. M. (2000). *Beginning Reading and Writing.* Newark, DE: International Reading Association.

Strickland, D. S., Snow, C., Griffin, P., Burns, S. M. & McNamara, P. (2002). *Preparing Our Teachers: Opportunities for Better Reading Instruction.* Washington, DC: Joseph Henry Press.

Stuart, L., Wright, F., Grigor, S., & Howey, A. (2002). *Spoken language difficulties: Practical strategies and activities for teachers and other professionals.* London, England: Fulton.

Tabors, P. O. & Snow, C. E. (2002). Young bilingual children and early literacy development. In S. Neuman & D. K. Dickinson (Eds.), *Handbook of Early Literacy Research* (pp. 159–178). New York: Guilford Press.

Templeton, S. (1986). Synthesis of research on the learning and teaching of spelling. *Educational Leadership,* 43 (6), 73–78.

Templeton, S., Cain, C. T., & Miller, J. O. (1981). Reconceptualizing readability: The relationship between surface and underlying structure analyses in predicting the difficulty of basal reader stories. *Journal of Educational Research,* 74 (6), 382–387.

Torgesen, J., Morgan, S., & Davis, C. (1992). Effects of two types of phonological awareness training on word learning in kindergarten children. *Journal of Educational Psychology,* 84 (3), 364–370.

Torgesen, J., Wagner, R., Rashotte, C., Rose, E., Lindamood, P., Conway, T., & Garvan, C. (1999). Preventing reading failure in young children with phonological processing disabilities: Group and individual responses to instruction. *Journal of Educational Psychology,* 91 (4), 579–593.

Torgesen, J. K. & Hudson, R. (2006). Reading fluency: Critical issues for struggling readers. In S. J. Samuels & A. Farstrup (Eds.), *What Research Has to Say About Fluency Instruction.* Newark, DE: International Reading Association.

Torgesen, J. K., & Mathes, P. (2000). *A Basic Guide to Understanding, Assessing, and Teaching Phonological Awareness.* Austin, TX: PRO-ED.

Torgesen, J. K., Rashotte, C. A., & Alexander, A. (2001). Principles of fluency instruction in reading: Relationships with established empirical outcomes. In M. Wolf (Ed.), *Dyslexia, Fluency, and the Brain.* Parkton, MD: York Press.

Valdés, G. (2014). Second language acquisition, learner differences and teacher knowledge in an age of mass migration. Paper presented at the Workshop on Immigration, Cultural Sustainability and Social Cohesion, National Academy of Education, Washington, DC.

Valencia, S. W., Au, K. H., Scheu, J. A., & Kawakami, A. J. (1990). Assessment of students' ownership of literacy. *The Reading Teacher,* 44 (2), 154–156.

Valencia, S. W. & Buly, M. R. (2004). Behind test scores: What struggling readers *really* need. *The Reading Teacher,* 57 (6), 520–531.

Valencia, S. W. & Sulzby, E. (1991). Assessment of emergent literacy: Storybook reading. *The Reading Teacher,* 44 (7), 498–500.

van den Broek, P., Lorch, Jr., R. F., Linderholm, T., & Gustafson, M. (2001). The effects of readers' goals on inference generation and memory for texts. *Memory and Cognition,* 29, 1081–1087.

van den Broek, P., Risden, K., & Husebye-Hartmann, E. (1995). The role of readers' standards for coherence in the generation of inferences during reading. In R. F. Lorch & E. J. O'Brien (Eds.), *Sources of coherence in reading* (pp. 353–373). Hillsdale, NJ: Erlbaum.

Vaughn, S. & Linan-Thompson, S. (2004). *Research-Based Methods of Reading Instruction: Grades K-3.* Alexandria, VA: ASCD.

Vaughn, S., Linan-Thompson, S., Pollard-Durodola, S. D., Mathes, P. G. & Hagan, E. C. (2001). Effective interventions for English language learners (Spanish-English) at risk for reading difficulties. In D. Dickinson & S. Neuman (Eds.), *Handbook of Early Literacy Research* (Vol. 2, pp. 185–197). New York: Guilford Press.

Vaughn, S., Moody, S. W., & Shuman, J. S. (1998). Broken promises: Reading instruction in the resource room. *Exceptional Children,* 64 (2), 211–225.

Vellutino, F. R., & Scanlon, D. M. (1987). Phonological coding, phonological awareness, and reading ability: Evidence from a longitudinal and experimental study. *Merrill-Palmer Quarterly,* 33 (3), 321–363.

Venezky, R. (2001). *The American way of spelling.* New York, NY: Guilford.

Vogt, M. (2004/2005). Fitful nights. *Reading Today,* 22 (3), 6.

Vogt, M. & Nagano, P. (2003). Turn it on with light bulb reading!: Sound-switching strategies for struggling readers. *The Reading Teacher,* 57 (3), 214–221.

Vygotsky, L. S. (1978). Mind In Society: The Development of Higher Psychological Processes. Cambridge: Cambridge University Press.

Walqui, A., & van Lier, L. (2010). Scaffolding the Academic Success of Adolescent English Language Learners: A Pedagogy of Promise. San Francisco: WestEd.

Washington, J. A. (2001). Early literacy skills in African-American children: Research considerations. *Learning Disabilities Research and Practice,* 16 (4), 213–221.

Weaver, Constance. (2007). *The Grammar Plan Book: A Guide to Smart Teaching.* Portsmouth, NH: Heinemann.

Wheeler, R., & Swords, R. (2004). Code-switching: Tools of language and culture transform the dialectally diverse classroom. *Language Arts,* 81, 470–480.

Whipple, G. (Ed.) (1925). The Twenty-fourth Yearbook of the National Society for the Study of Education: Report of the National Committee on Reading. Bloomington, IL: Public School Publishing Company.

White, T. G., Graves, M. F., & Slater, W. H. (1990). Growth of reading vocabulary in diverse elementary schools: Decoding and word meaning. *Journal of Educational Psychology,* 82 (2), 281–290.

Whitehurst G. J., Falco, F. L., Lonigan, C. J., Fischel, J. E., DeBaryshe, B. D., Valdez-Menchaca, M. C., & Caufield, M. (1988). Accelerating language development through picture book reading. *Developmental Psychology,* 24, 552–558.

Williams, G. (2000). Children's literature, children and uses of language description. In L. Unsworth (Ed.), *Researching Language in Schools and Communities: Functional Linguistic Perspectives* (pp. 111–129). London, England: Cassell.

Williams, G. (2005). Grammatics in schools. In R. Hasan, C. M. I. M. Matthiessen, & J. Webster (Eds.), *Continuing discourse on language* (pp. 281–310). London, England: Equinox.

Williams, J. M., & McEnerney, L. (n.d.). *Writing in college: A short guide to college writing.* http://writing-program.uchicago.edu/resources/collegewriting/index.htm.

Williamson, G. L. (2006). *Aligning the journey with a destination: A model for K–16 reading standards.* Durham, NC: MetaMetrics, Inc.

Wirt, J., Choy, S., Rooney, P., Provasnik, S., Sen, A., & Tobin, R. (2004). The condition of education 2004 (NCES 2004-077). U.S. Department of Education, National Center for Education Statistics. Washington, DC: U.S. Government Printing Office. http://nces.ed.gov/pubs2004/2004077.pdf.

Wixson, K. K. (1986). Vocabulary instruction and children's comprehension of basal stories. *Reading Research Quarterly,* 21 (3), 317–329.

Wong Fillmore, L., & Fillmore, C. (2012). What Does Text Complexity Mean for English Learners and Language Minority Students? Paper for the Understanding Language Initiative, Stanford University. Retrieved from http://ell.stanford.edu/publication/what-does-text-complexity-mean-english-learners-and-language-minority-students.

Yopp, H. K., & Yopp, R. H. (2006). Primary students and informational texts. *Science and Children,* 44 (3), 22–25.

Index

Index

Index

Index

Index

stress, **2-2:** T414, T419, T493, T494–T497, S49; **2-4:** T114, T119, T153, T191, T192–T195, S19

word recognition, **2-1:** T14, T19, T49, T87, T88–T91, T247, T449; **2-2:** T355; **2-3:** T245; **2-4:** T155; **2-5:** T155; **2-6:** T55, T249

words connected in text, **2-1:** T110, T185, T186–T189; **2-3:** T443

Fluency Plan, 2-1: T75, T173, T271, T373, T473; **2-2:** T77, T179, T277, T379, T477; **2-3:** T77, T171, T269, T367, T469; **2-4:** T79, T179, T379, T479; **2-5:** T79, T179, T279, T379, T475; **2-6:** T79, T179, T275, T375, T475

fluency tests. *See* assessment, fluency tests; Cold Reads

Focus Wall, 2-1: T1, T97, T195, T293, T395; **2-2:** T1, T99, T201, T299, T401; **2-3:** T1, T99, T193, T291, T389; **2-4:** T1, T101, T201, T301, T401; **2-5:** T1, T101, T201, T301, T401; **2-6:** T1, T101, T201, T297, T397

folktale. *See* genre, folktale

formal and informal language. *See* vocabulary strategies, formal and informal language

Formative Assessment

access through accommodations, **2-1:** T74, T172, T372, T472; **2-2:** T76, T178, T276, T378, T476; **2-3:** T76, T170, T268, T366, T468; **2-4:** T78, T178, T278, T378, T478; **2-5:** T78, T178, T278, T378, T474; **2-6:** T78, T178, T274, T374, T474

Anchor Text, **2-1:** T128, T224, T323, T426; **2-2:** T30, T130, T229, T330, T432; **2-3:** T32, T126, T222, T318, T418; **2-4:** T32, T132, T230, T332, T432; **2-5:** T30, T130, T232, T332, T430; **2-6:** T30, T131, T228, T328, T426

Decodable Readers, **2-1:** T19, T48, T115, T146, T213, T244, T311, T346, T413; **2-2:** T19, T117, T129, T152, T250, T317, T352, T419; **2-3:** T19, T117, T211, T309, T407, T442; **2-4:** T19, T119, T219, T252, T319, T419; **2-5:** T19, T52, T119, T152, T219, T252, T319, T352, T419; **2-6:** T19, T54, T119, T152, T219, T248, T315, T348, T415, T448

Dig Deeper, **2-1:** T39, T137, T235, T337, T439; **2-2:** T41, T143, T241, T343, T443; **2-3:** T43, T137, T235, T333, T433; **2-4:** T45, T145, T243, T345, T445; **2-5:** T43, T143, T243, T343, T441; **2-6:** T45, T143, T239, T339, T439

extended reading, **2-2:** T514, T524; **2-4:** T516, T520, T526, T528; **2-6:** T512, T516, T522, T524

fluency, **2-1:** T75, T87, T173, T185, T271, T283, T373, T385, T473, T489; **2-2:** T77, T89, T179, T191, T277, T289, T379, T391, T477, T493; **2-3:** T77, T89, T171, T183, T269, T281, T367, T379, T469, T485; **2-4:** T79, T91, T179, T191, T279, T291, T379, T391, T479, T495; **2-5:** T79, T91, T179, T191, T279, T291, T379, T391, T475,

T491; **2-6:** T79, T91, T179, T191, T275, T287, T375, T387, T475, T491

for English Learners, **2-1:** T76, T174, T272, T374, T474; **2-2:** T78, T180, T278, T380, T478; **2-3:** T78, T172, T270, T368, T470; **2-4:** T80, T180, T280, T380, T480; **2-5:** T80, T180, T280, T380, T476; **2-6:** T80, T180, T276, T376, T476

Intervention Assessment, **2-1:** T76, T174, T272, T374, T474; **2-2:** T78, T180, T277, T380, T478; **2-3:** T78, T172, T270, T368, T470; **2-4:** T80, T180, T280, T380, T480; **2-5:** T80, T180, T280, T380, T476; **2-6:** T80, T180, T276, T376, T476

introduce vocabulary, **2-1:** T21, T117, T313, T415; **2-2:** T21, T119, T221, T319, T421; **2-3:** T21, T119, T213, T311, T409; **2-4:** T21, T121, T221, T321, T421; **2-5:** T21, T121, T221, T321, T421; **2-6:** T21, T121, T221, T317, T417

phonemic awareness, **2-1:** T13, T35, T45, T57, T67, T109, T133, T143, T155, T165, T207, T231, T241, T253, T263, T305, T333, T343, T355, T365, T407, T435, T445, T465; **2-2:** T13, T37, T47, T57, T69, T111, T139, T149, T161, T171, T213, T237, T247, T259, T269, T311, T339, T349, T361, T371, T413, T439, T449, T459, T469; **2-3:** T13, T39, T49, T59, T69, T111, T133, T143, T153, T163, T205, T231, T241, T251, T261, T303, T329, T339, T349, T359, T401, T429, T439, T451, T461; **2-4:** T13, T41, T51, T61, T71, T113, T141, T151, T161, T171, T213, T239, T249, T261, T271, T313, T341, T361, T371, T413, T441, T451, T461, T471; **2-5:** T13, T39, T49, T61, T71, T113, T139, T149, T161, T171, T213, T239, T249, T261, T271, T313, T339, T349, T361, T371, T413, T437, T447, T457, T467; **2-6:** T13, T41, T51, T61, T71, T113, T139, T149, T161, T171, T213, T235, T245, T255, T267, T309, T335, T345, T357, T367, T409, T435, T445, T457, T467

phonics, **2-1:** T17, T37, T47, T59, T81, T86, T113, T135, T145, T157, T178, T184, T211, T233, T243, T255, T276, T282, T309, T335, T345, T357, T378, T384, T411, T437, T446, T457, T482, T488; **2-2:** T17, T39, T48, T59, T82, T88, T115, T141, T151, T163, T184, T190, T217, T239, T249, T261, T282, T288, T315, T341, T351, T361, T363, T384, T390, T417, T441, T450, T461, T492; **2-3:** T17, T41, T50, T82, T88, T115, T135, T144, T155, T176, T182, T209, T233, T242, T253, T274, T280, T307, T331, T340, T351, T372, T378, T405, T431, T441, T453, T478, T484; **2-4:** T17, T43, T52, T63, T84, T90, T117, T143, T152, T163, T184, T190, T217, T241, T251, T263, T284, T290, T317, T343, T344–T345, T352, T363, T384, T390, T417, T441, T443, T452, T463, T488, T494; **2-5:** T17, T41, T51, T63, T84, T90, T117, T141, T151, T163,

T184, T190, T217, T241, T251, T263, T284, T290, T317, T341, T351, T363, T384, T390, T417, T439, T448, T459, T484, T490; **2-6:** T17, T43, T52, T63, T84, T90, T117, T141, T151, T163, T184, T190, T217, T237, T246, T257, T280, T286, T313, T337, T347, T359, T380, T386, T413, T437, T447, T459, T484, T490

scaffold instruction, **2-1:** T39, T137, T235, T337, T439; **2-2:** T41, T143, T241, T343, T443; **2-3:** T43, T137, T235, T333, T433; **2-4:** T45, T145, T243, T345, T445; **2-5:** T43, T143, T243, T343, T441; **2-6:** T45, T143, T239, T339, T439

using data to adjust instruction, **2-1:** T75, T173, T271, T373, T473; **2-2:** T77, T179, T277, T379, T477; **2-3:** T77, T171, T269, T367, T469; **2-4:** T79, T179, T279, T379, T479; **2-5:** T79, T179, T279, T379, T475; **2-6:** T79, T179, T275, T375, T475

vocabulary strategies, **2-1:** T63, T161, T259, T361, T461; **2-2:** T65, T167, T265, T367, T465; **2-3:** T65, T159, T257, T355, T457; **2-4:** T67, T167, T267, T367, T467; **2-5:** T67, T167, T267, T367, T463; **2-6:** T67, T167, T263, T363, T463

Weekly Tests, **2-1:** T74, T172, T372, T472; **2-2:** T76, T178, T276, T378, T476; **2-3:** T76, T170, T268, T366, T468; **2-4:** T78, T178, T278, T378, T478; **2-5:** T78, T178, T278, T378, T474; **2-6:** T78, T178, T274, T374, T474

Whole Group Resources, **2-1:** T3, T99, T197, T295, T397; **2-2:** T3, T101, T203, T301, T403; **2-3:** T3, T101, T195, T293, T391; **2-4:** T3, T103, T203, T303, T403; **2-5:** T3, T103, T203, T303, T403; **2-6:** T3, T103, T203, T299, T399

Index

Index

Index

Index

Index

Index

T

Teacher Read Aloud
Adventures at Scout Camp, **2-3**: T403
Bats: Beastly or Beautiful?, **2-1**: T307
A Better Way to Save, **2-4**: T15
Cinderella Stories, **2-6**: T215
City Life Is for the Birds, **2-2**: T15
The Crowd Roared!, **2-4**: T115
Diego's Double Surprise, **2-6**: T15
Doctor Salk's Treasure, **2-4**: T215
Don't Play Cards with a Dog in the Room!, **2-3**: T15
Eperson's Icicle, **2-6**: T115
Exploring Space Travel, **2-6**: T506–T511
Floods: Dangerous Water, **2-2**: T215
From Duckling to Duck, **2-5**: T15
Johnny Appleseed and His Apples, **2-5**: T415
A Lesson in Happiness, **2-6**: T311
Lester, **2-1**: T409
The Middle Seat, **2-5**: T115
More Than a Best Friend, **2-1**: T111
Music in the Snow, **2-3**: T113
Nothing But a Quilt, **2-5**: T215
On Thin Ice, **2-2**: T313
One-Room Schoolhouse, **2-3**: T207
Ordinary Heroes, **2-4**: T415
The Perfect Pet, **2-1**: T15
Poppleton in Winter, **2-2**: T508–T509
Sharks on the Run!, **2-2**: T415
Steve Jobs: Inventor, **2-6**: T411
Tiger in the Water, **2-5**: T315
Trouble in the Lily Garden, **2-2**: T113
Whale of a Lesson, **2-3**: T305
Where Do Polar Bears Live?, **2-4**: T510–T511
Wild Friends, Wow!, **2-4**: T315

tenses. *See* grammar, verb tense

text and graphic features. *See* comprehension skills, text and graphic features

text-based comprehension. *See* Analyze the Text; comprehension skills; comprehension strategies; Dig Deeper; Read and Comprehend; Think Through the Text; Your Turn

text complexity. *See* Prepare for Complex Texts; rubrics, text complexity

text evidence. *See* comprehension skills, text evidence; Dig Deeper; Think Through the Text; writing traits, evidence; Your Turn

Text X-Ray, 2-1: T2, T9, T98, T105, T196, T203, T294, T301, T396, T403; **2-2:** T2, T9, T100, T107, T202, T209, T300, T307, T402, T409, T505; **2-3:** T2, T9, T100, T107, T194, T201, T292, T299, T390, T397; **2-4:** T2, T9, T102, T109, T202, T209, T302, T309,

T402, T409, T507; **2-5:** T2, T9, T102, T109, T202, T209, T302, T309, T402, T409; **2-6:** T2, T9, T102, T109, T202, T209, T298, T305, T398, T405, T503

theme. *See* comprehension skills, theme; 21st Century Themes

Thesaurus Skills, 2-2: T455; **2-5:** T57

Think Aloud, 2-1: T24, T25, T29, T32, T38, T42, T54, T55, T62, T64, T65, T84, T87, T94–T95, T120, T121, T123, T130, T136, T138, T152, T153, T160, T162, T163, T182, T185, T192–T193, T218, T219, T221, T228, T234, T250, T251, T258, T260, T261, T280, T283, T290–T291, T316, T317, T319, T323, T330, T336, T352, T353, T360, T362, T363, T382, T385, T392–T393, T418, T419, T421, T426, T432, T433, T438, T452, T460, T462, T475, T476, T478, T486, T489, T496–T497, S5, S15, S25, S35, S45; **2-2:** T24, T25, T27, T30, T34, T40, T44, T54, T55, T64, T67, T86, T89, T96–T97, T122, T123, T127, T136, T142, T146, T158, T159, T166, T169, T188, T191, T198–T199, T224, T225, T227, T229, T234, T240, T244, T256, T257, T264, T267, T286, T289, T296–T297, T322, T323, T325, T330, T336, T342, T346, T358, T359, T366, T369, T388, T391, T398–T399, T424, T425, T429, T432, T436, T442, T446, T456, T464, T479, T480, T482, T490, T493, T500–T501, T511, T514, T524, S5, S15, S25, S35, S45; **2-3:** T24, T25, T34, T36, T42, T46, T56, T57, T64, T67, T86, T89, T96–T97, T122, T123, T125, T126, T130, T136, T140, T150, T151, T158, T161, T180, T183, T190–T191, T216, T217, T219, T222, T228, T234, T238, T248, T249, T256, T259, T278, T281, T288–T289, T314, T315, T317, T318, T326, T332, T336, T346, T347, T354, T357, T376, T379, T386–T387, T412, T413, T416, T418, T426, T427, T432, T436, T456, T471, T472, T474, T482, T485, T492–T493, S5, S15, S25, S35, S45; **2-4:** T24, T25, T27, T32, T38, T44, T48, T59, T66, T69, T88, T91, T98–T99, T124, T125, T127, T132, T138, T144, T148, T159, T166, T169, T188, T191, T198–T199, T224, T225, T227, T230, T236, T242, T246, T259, T266, T269, T288, T291, T298–T299, T324, T325, T327, T332, T338, T344, T348, T359, T366, T369, T388, T391, T398–T399, T424, T425, T427, T432, T438, T439, T444, T448, T466, T469, T481, T482, T484, T492, T495, T502–T503, T513, T516, T520, T528, S5, S15, S25, S35, S45; **2-5:** T24, T25, T27, T30, T36, T42, T46, T58, T59, T66, T69, T88, T91, T98–T99, T124, T125, T130, T136, T142, T146, T158, T159, T166, T169, T188, T191, T198–T199, T224, T225, T227, T232, T236, T242, T246, T258, T259, T266, T269, T288, T291, T298–T299, T324, T325, T327, T332, T336, T342, T346, T358, T359, T366, T369, T388, T391, T398–T399, T424, T425, T427, T430, T434, T435, T440, T444, T454, T462, T465, T477, T478, T480, T488, T491, T498–T499,

S5, S15, S25, S35, S45; **2-6:** T24, T25, T29, T30, T44, T48, T58, T59, T66, T69, T88, T91, T98–T99, T124, T125, T131, T136, T142, T146, T158, T159, T166, T169, T188, T191, T198–T199, T224, T225, T227, T232, T238, T242, T252, T253, T262, T265, T284, T287, T294–T295, T320, T321, T323, T328, T332, T338, T342, T354, T355, T362, T365, T384, T387, T394–T395, T420, T421, T423, T426, T432, T433, T438, T442, T454, T462, T464, T477, T478, T480, T488, T491, T498–T499, T509, T512, T516, T524, S5, S15, S25, S45

Think and Write, 2-1: T7, T103, T201, T299, T401; **2-2:** T7, T105, T207, T305, T407; **2-3:** T7, T105, T199, T297, T395; **2-4:** T7, T107, T207, T307, T407; **2-5:** T7, T107, T207, T307, T407; **2-6:** T7, T107, T207, T303, T403

think critically. *See* Analyze the Text; Compare Texts; Dig Deeper; Think Through the Text; Your Turn

Think Through the Text, 2-1: T26–T30, T122–T128, T220–T226, T318–T328, T420–T430; **2-2:** T26–T32, T124–T134, T226–T232, T324–T333, T426–T433, T511, T514, T524; **2-3:** T26–T34, T124–T128, T218–T225, T316–T323, T414–T424; **2-4:** T26–T35, T126–T135, T226–T234, T326–T336, T426–T436, T513, T516, T520, T528; **2-5:** T26–T33, T126–T133, T226–T234, T326–T333, T426–T432; **2-6:** T26–T35, T126–T133, T226–T229, T259–T260, T322–T329, T422–T430, T509, T512, T516, T524

Third Read. *See* reading, independent (Third Read)

topic. *See* lesson topics

Trade Books
Exploring Space Travel, **2-6**: T501–T532
Poppleton in Water, **2-2**: T495–T534
Where Do Polar Bears Live?, **2-4**: T505–T536

traditional tale. *See* genre, traditional tale; lesson topics, traditional tales

21st Century Themes
civic literacy, **2-1**: T2, T294; **2-2**: T300; **2-4**: T402; **2-6**: T398
environmental literacy, **2-2**: T2, T202, T402; **2-3**: T2; **2-5**: T2, T402; **2-6**: T2, T102
financial, business, and entrepreneurial literacy, **2-4**: T2; **2-5**: T202
global awareness, **2-1**: T98, T196, T396; **2-3**: T100, T194, T292; **2-4**: T102, T202, T302; **2-5**: T102, T302; **2-6**: T202, T298, T398
health literacy, **2-2**: T100; **2-3**: T390

U

Unit Assessments. *See* assessments, Unit Assessments

Index

Pat Mora, **2-4:** S1, S23, S25, S27, S29, S31

The Play Date, **2-3:** S1, S3, S5, S7, S9, S11

Rosa's Garden, **2-2:** S1, S13, S15, S17, S19, S21

Sue and the Tired Wolf, **2-4:** S1, S43, S45, S47, S49, S51

Tortoise Gets a Home, **2-2:** S1, S33, S35, S37, S39, S41

True Heroes, **2-4:** S1, S13, S15, S17, S19, S21

The Twelve Months, **2-6:** S1, S23, S25, S27, S29, S31

Who Made These?, **2-2:** S1, S3, S5, S7, S9, S11

writer's craft. *See* author's craft; writing traits

writing. *See also* handwriting; Performance Tasks; rubrics, writing

audience, **2-3:** T249

beginning, middle, end, **2-4:** T349

closing, **2-3:** T459; **2-6:** T465

compare and contrast, **2-5:** T137, T159, T169, T176

Connect Sounds to Writing, **2-1:** T18, T114, T210, T212, T310, T412; **2-2:** T18, T116, T118, T128, T316, T418; **2-3:** T18, T116, T210, T308, T406; **2-4:** T18, T118, T218, T319, T418; **2-5:** T18, T118, T218, T318, T418; **2-6:** T18, T118, T218, T314, T414

Connect to Anchor Text, **2-1:** T43, T55, T141, T339, T341, T443, T453; **2-2:** T45, T55, T147, T159, T245, T257, T447; **2-3:** T47, T337, T437; **2-4:** T49, T149, T159, T169, T247, T269, T369, T449, T469; **2-5:** T47, T59, T247, T259, T347; **2-6:** T49, T147, T159, T243, T253, T265, T343, T355, T365, T443, T455, T465

Connect to Writing, **2-1:** T64, T66, T70, T168, T260, T266, T362, T368, T462, T468; **2-2:** T66, T72, T168, T266, T272, T368, T374, T466, T472; **2-3:** T66, T72, T160, T166, T258, T264, T356, T362, T458, T464; **2-4:** T68, T74, T168, T174, T268, T274, T368, T374, T474; **2-5:** T68, T74, T168, T174, T268, T274, T368, T374, T470; **2-6:** T68, T74, T168, T174, T264, T270, T370, T464, T470

details, **2-1:** T43, T261, T363; **2-2:** T45, T55; **2-4:** T49; **2-5:** T147, T347; **2-6:** T243

dialogue, **2-4:** T69, T149

examples, **2-6:** T253, T265, T343, T365

facts and supporting details, **2-2:** T55, T257; **2-3:** T357

feelings, **2-1:** T141; **2-3:** T141

goal setting, **2-3:** T47

introduction, **2-2:** T457

main idea, **2-1:** T341; **2-2:** T159, T257

main idea and supporting details, **2-2:** T45

models, **2-1:** T33, T131, T229, T331; **2-2:** T35, T137, T235, T337; **2-3:** T37, T131, T229, T327; **2-4:** T39, T139, T237, T339; **2-5:** T37, T137, T237, T337; **2-6:** T39, T137, T233, T333

order

steps in order, **2-2:** T369

steps in process, **2-2:** T347

time-order words, **2-1:** T443; **2-4:** T369, T469

predictive writing, **2-1:** T25, T121, T219, T317, T419; **2-2:** T25, T123, T225, T323, T425, T511; **2-3:** T25, T123, T217, T315, T413; **2-4:** T25, T125, T225, T325, T425, T513; **2-5:** T25, T125, T225, T325, T425; **2-6:** T25, T125, T225, T321, T421, T509

problems and solutions, **2-4:** T359; **2-5:** T59, T69, T76

Quickwrite, **2-1:** T53, T151, T249, T349, T451; **2-2:** T53, T157, T255, T357, T455; **2-3:** T55, T149, T247, T345, T447; **2-4:** T57, T157, T257, T357, T457; **2-5:** T57, T157, T257, T357, T453; **2-6:** T57, T157, T251, T353, T453

quotations, **2-6:** T365

reasons, **2-3:** T57, T151; **2-6:** T159, T355

response paragraph, **2-6:** T233, T253, T265, T272

rhyme, **2-6:** T59, T69

rhythm, **2-6:** T69

sentences, **2-2:** T67, T169, T267, T467; **2-3:** T259, T437; **2-4:** T169; **2-5:** T269, T455; **2-6:** T147

sequence of events, **2-1:** T55; **2-4:** T159; **2-5:** T259; **2-6:** T455

setting, **2-4:** T59

shared writing, **2-2:** T513, T523, T533; **2-4:** T515, T525, T535; **2-6:** T511, T513, T521, T531

showing and telling, **2-4:** T259

summary paragraph, **2-2:** T137, T159, T169

taking notes, **2-5:** T369

Think and Write, Literacy Centers, **2-1:** T7, T103, T201, T299, T401; **2-2:** T7, T105, T207, T305, T407; **2-3:** T7, T105, T199, T297, T395; **2-4:** T7, T107, T207, T307, T407; **2-5:** T7, T107, T207, T307, T407; **2-6:** T7, T107, T207, T303, T403

using definitions, **2-2:** T245; **2-5:** T465

Write About It, **2-1:** S10, S20, S30, S40, S50; **2-2:** S10, S20, S30, S50; **2-3:** S10, S20, S30, S40, S50; **2-4:** S10, S20, S30, S40, S50; **2-5:** S10, S20, S30, S40, S50; **2-6:** S10, S20, S30, S40, S50

Writing Conference, 2-1: T463; **2-2:** T467; **2-3:** T459; **2-4:** T469; **2-5:** T465; **2-6:** T465

writing forms. *See also* rubrics, writing

book report, **2-6:** T137, T159, T169

descriptive writing, **2-1:** T229, T251, T261, T268; **2-4:** T237, T259, T269, T276

informative writing, **2-1:** T251; **2-2:** T35, T45, T55, T67, T74, T137, T147, T159, T169, T176, T235, T245, T257, T267, T274, T337, T347, T359, T369, T376, T437, T447, T457, T467, T474, T480; **2-5:** T37, T47, T59, T69, T76, T137, T147, T159, T169, T176, T237, T247, T259, T269, T276, T337, T347, T359, T369, T376, T435,

T445, T455, T465, T472

instructions, **2-2:** T337, T359, T369, T376, T437, T467, T474

letters

friendly letter, **2-1:** T131, T153, T163, T170

persuasive letter, **2-3:** T37, T57, T67, T74

narrative writing, **2-1:** T33, T43, T55, T65, T72, T131, T141, T153, T163, T170, T229, T239, T251, T261, T268, T331, T341, T353, T363, T370, T433, T443, T453, T463, T470; **2-4:** T39, T49, T59, T69, T76, T139, T149, T159, T169, T176, T237, T247, T259, T269, T276, T339, T349, T359, T369, T376, T439, T449, T459, T469, T476

opinion writing, **2-3:** T37, T47, T57, T67, T74, T131, T141, T151, T161, T168, T229, T239, T249, T259, T266, T327, T337, T347, T357, T364, T427, T437, T449, T459, T466; **2-6:** T39, T49, T59, T69, T76, T137, T147, T159, T169, T176, T233, T243, T253, T265, T272, T333, T343, T355, T365, T372, T433, T443, T455, T465, T472

order

steps in order, **2-2:** T369

steps in process, **2-2:** T347

time-order words, **2-1:** T443; **2-4:** T369, T469

persuasive writing, **2-3:** T229, T249, T259, T327, T347, T357, T364, T427, T449, T459, T466

poetry, **2-6:** T39, T59, T69, T76

research report, **2-5:** T337, T359, T369, T376, T435, T455, T465, T472

response to literature, **2-5:** T478; **2-6:** T333, T355, T365, T372, T433, T455, T465, T472

stories, **2-1:** T33, T55, T65, T72, T331, T353, T363, T370, T433, T453, T463, T470, T476; **2-4:** T39, T59, T69, T76, T139, T159, T169, T176, T339, T359, T369, T376, T439, T449, T459, T469, T476, T482

writing handbook. *See* Common Core Writing Handbook

writing process

brainstorm, **2-1:** T367; **2-3:** T347; **2-4:** T359; **2-5:** T359

draft, **2-1:** T65, T163, T261, T433, T453, T463; **2-2:** T67, T169, T267, T437, T457, T467, T513, T523, T533; **2-3:** T67, T161, T259, T427, T449, T459; **2-4:** T69, T169, T269, T369, T439, T459, T469, T515, T525, T535; **2-5:** T69, T169, T269, T435, T455, T465; **2-6:** T69, T169, T265, T433, T455, T465, T511, T513, T521, T531

edit, **2-1:** T72, T170, T268, T470; **2-2:** T74, T176, T274, T474; **2-3:** T74, T266, T466; **2-4:** T76, T176, T276, T476; **2-5:** T76, T176, T276, T472; **2-6:** T76, T176, T272, T472

Index

Credits